# SOC

(SŌSH)

## What makes *SOC* special?

*SOC* offers instructors **scholarly content** and *unmatched currency* in a succinct magazine format that engages students. *SOC* consistently encourages students to **foster their sociological imagination** and encourages them to get involved and MAKE A DIFFERENCE in the world around them.

### What's Inside

Engaging pedagogy designed to be eye-catching and visually appealing can be found throughout the text. *SOC* shows students how they can apply sociological concepts to their everyday lives.

>

< **"At the Movies"** lists movies that relate to sociology.

< **"From Me to You"** provides down-to-earth explanations of sociological concepts using the author's experiences as examples.

< **"Hot or Not?"** boxes ask students to consider their opinion on a "hot" issue of current interest.

< **"Get Involved"** sections push students to actively participate in sociological issues that are relevant to them.

< **"Pop Soc"** teaches sociological concepts through popular culture.

# SOC 2009

VICE PRESIDENT & EDITOR IN CHIEF **Michael Ryan**

PUBLISHER **Frank Mortimer**

AUTHOR **Jon Witt**

EDITOR AT LARGE **Gina Boedeker**

FIELD CORRESPONDENT **Richard T. Schaefer**

MANAGING EDITOR **Lisa Pinto**

DEVELOPMENT **O'Donnell & Associates, LLC**

CREATIVE DIRECTOR **Meredith Grant**

STYLE DIRECTOR **Jordan Killam**

FILM ADVISOR **Drew Henry**

EXECUTIVE MARKETING MANAGER **Leslie Oberhuber**

MARKETING MANAGER **Joyce Chiu**

SENIOR PRODUCTION EDITOR **Carey Eisner**

SENIOR PRODUCTION SUPERVISOR **Tandra Jorgensen**

COMPOSITOR **TBH Typecast, Inc.**

PRINTER **Quebecor World, Inc.**

ART MANAGER **Robin Mouat**

DESIGN MANAGER **Cassandra Chu**

INTERIOR DESIGNER **Maureen McCutcheon**

COVER DESIGNER **Linda Beaupré**

PHOTO WRANGLERS **Brian J. Pecko, Nora Agbayani, Sonia Brown**

ILLUSTRATION **Ayelet Arbel, Lineworks, John and Judy Waller, and Argosy Publishing, Inc.**

AUTHOR PORTRAIT **Arthur Mount**

To our esteemed author, Dr. Richard Schaefer: We thank you for your invaluable contributions to *SOC*.

---

**SOC 2009**

Published by McGraw-Hill, an imprint of The McGraw-Hill Companies, Inc., 1221 Avenue of the Americas, New York, NY 10020.

This book is printed on acid-free paper.

4 5 6 7 8 9 0 WCK/WCK 0 9

ISBN 978-0-07-352824-3

ISBN 0-07-352824-2

Cover: Three friends on car foreground, © Burke/Triolo Productions/Brand X/Corbis; Sky background, © Paul Edmondson/Corbis.

---

**Library of Congress Cataloging-in-Publication Data**

Witt, Jon

Soc / Jon Witt. -- 1st ed.
       p. cm.
Includes bibliographical references and index.
ISBN-13: 978-0-07-352824-3 (alk. paper)
ISBN-10: 0-07-352824-2 (alk. paper)
1. Sociology. I. Title.

HM586.W58 2009
301—dc22

2008041213

www.mhhe.com

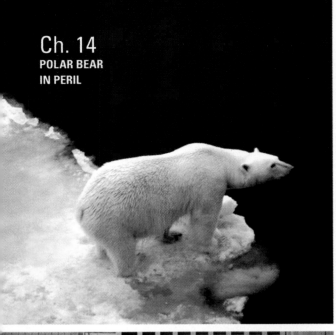

**Ch. 14**
POLAR BEAR
IN PERIL

**^**
**Ch. 10**
THE CLASS
DIVIDE

**Ch. 12 >**
"DOING"
GENDER

< **Ch. 6**
WHO IS DEVIANT?

# SOC
## 2009 Edition

## BRIEF CONTENTS

**Name:** Jon Witt (though my mom calls me Jonathan)

**Occupations:** Sociologist, father, and dog-walker

**Hobbies:** I like reading, writing, and messing around on computers—and I'm addicted to my iPhone

**Childhood ambition:** To be a printer like my dad—or, as I learned when I was old enough to say it, an offset lithographer

**Family:** Lori and I have been married for over 20 years, and we have two daughters—Emily, 14, and Eleanor, 12

**Last book read:** David Wroblewski's *The Story of Edgar Sawtelle*

**Favorite film:** Right now it's WALL·E

**Favorite soundtrack:** "Live in Dublin" from Bruce Springsteen with the Seeger Sessions Band

**Latest accomplishment:** This book!

**Quote:** There may be fields of sociological science quite beyond the average mind, and rightly left to the learned specialist; but that is no reason why we should not learn enough of the nature and habits of society to insure a more profitable and pleasant life.
—Charlotte Perkins Gilman, *Human Work*, 1904

**My blog:** www.soc101.com

Table of Contents

# 4 > Socialization 65

# 5 > Social Structure and Interaction 89

1

THE SOCIOLO

# THE INDIVIDUAL AND SOCIETY

George Bailey never got the chance to live the kind of life he wanted to live. He desperately wanted to escape small-town life, go to college, travel the world, design bridges, and achieve even more, but obligations and a sense of duty conspired against him. Now, feeling like a failure, he stands on a snowy bridge ready to commit suicide. So begins the holiday film classic *It's a Wonderful Life*.

Just as George prepares to jump, an angel named Clarence shows up and gives him a chance to see what the world would have been like had George never existed. It is not a pretty sight. People die whom George helped save, homes are lost that his family building-and-loan business helped finance, and life in the local community is grim largely due to the underhanded dealings of the evil tycoon Mr. Potter. George learns that he has had a major impact on family, friends, and community. In the words of Clarence, "One [person's] life touches so many others, when he [or she]'s not there, it leaves an awfully big hole." George changes his mind about suicide and rushes home to waiting family and friends, who unite to save his business from financial ruin.

The film's focus on the relationship between the individual and society is fundamentally sociological. On the one hand, the film presents a story about one of the lessons learned from sociology: that our individual actions matter and that it is through our actions that "society" is made. On the other hand, the film is also about the power of community, of family, and of social context. It is about the ways in which the options available to us are limited by position and circumstance.

Perhaps there is a bit of George Bailey in all of us. We create society by the choices we make and the things we do. At the same time, we are products of society, shaped by the people around us. For each of us, just as for George Bailey, many endings are possible—that is the nature of individual choice—but not all endings are equally probable—that is the nature of social position and the unequal distribution of resources. Throughout its history, sociology has sought to describe and explain this relationship between the individual and society.

# GICAL
# IMAGINATION

# As You READ >>

- What is sociology?
- How do sociologists look at the world?
- How might someone practice sociology?

## >> What Is Sociology?

We need each other. We may like to think that we can make it on our own, but our individualism is made possible by our interdependence. We praise the Olympic gold medalist for her impressive skill, dedicated training, and single-minded determination. Yet, if it weren't for her mom driving her to the pool every day, for the building manager waking up at 4:00 A.M. to make sure the pool is open, for the women working overnight to make sure the locker room is clean and safe, and so many others who fade into the background in such moments of glory, she would never have had that chance to stand on the podium.

Sociology as a discipline is committed to investigating and understanding the full scope of our interdependence. **Sociology** is the systematic study of the relationship between the individual and society and of the consequences of difference. It focuses on social relationships, looking at how others influence our behavior; how major social institutions like the government, religion, and the economy affect us; and how we ourselves affect other individuals, groups, and even organizations. In doing this analysis, sociologists focus less on what one individual does or does not do than on what people do as members of a group or in interaction with one another, and on what that means for individuals and for society as a whole.

Sociology at its heart seeks to understand and explain our interdependence. With whom do we connect? How do we organize those connections? What gets in the way? Who benefits? Whether sitting in a classroom, working in an office or a factory, or exercising in a health club, we rely on others who shape how we think and act. As individuals, we do choose, but we cannot divorce our individual preferences from the influence of parents, teachers, friends, enemies, the media, and more, or from our access to resources such as money, social networks, and knowledge. We influence and are influenced by the world around us. Sociology studies those influences.

**sociology** The systematic study of the relationship between the individual and society and of the consequences of difference.

**sociological imagination** An awareness of the relationship between an individual and the wider society.

**private troubles** Obstacles that individuals face as individuals rather than as a consequence of their social position.

### THE SOCIOLOGICAL IMAGINATION

Sociology is a way of seeing the world. A leading sociologist, C. Wright Mills, described this perspective as the **sociological imagination**—an awareness of the relationship between an individual and the wider society. This awareness allows us to look at how we as individuals connect with the larger social and historical forces that shape our lives, to comprehend the links between our immediate, personal social settings and the remote, impersonal social world that surrounds and helps to shape us. Mills wrote that "neither the life of an individual nor the history of society can be understood without understanding both" (1959:3). Practicing the sociological imagination involves grasping the intersection between biography and history, between self and society.

A key element in the sociological imagination is the ability to view our society as an outsider might, rather than relying only on our individual perspective, which is shaped by our cultural biases. Consider something as simple as sporting events. On college campuses across the United States, thousands of students cheer for well-trained football players. In Bali, Indonesia, dozens of spectators gather around a ring to cheer on well-trained roosters engaged in cockfights. In both instances, the spectators root for their favorites and might bet on the outcome. Yet what is considered a normal sporting event in one part of the world is considered unusual in another part.

In applying the sociological imagination, Mills (1959) suggested that we distinguish between obstacles that individuals face as individuals, which he called **private troubles,** and obstacles that individuals in similar positions face, which he called **public issues**—or what sociologists often call "social problems." Consider unemployment. An individual might lose his or her job because of some inappropriate action or personal incompetence. In such

# 5 Movies on THE SOCIOLOGICAL IMAGINATION

### Castaway
*A man is isolated from society on a remote, deserted island.*

### Mockingbird Don't Sing
*Inspired by the story of Genie; a girl is introduced to society for the first time after being held captive for the first 12 years of her life.*

### Harry Potter and the Sorcerer's Stone
*A young boy is introduced to an entirely new society of wizards for the first time at age 11.*

### Babel
*How individual cultures and societies view and interact with each other.*

### One Flew over the Cuckoo's Nest
*Normalization of individuals in society; taking oneself out of mainstream society and finding a niche (in this case, a mental institution).*

an instance, it might be enough to explain what happened only on an individual level—we might say that the person got what he or she deserved. In applying the sociological imagination, however, we know that unemployment rates vary based on shifts in the larger economy. At such times, to blame unemployment only on individuals is an insufficient diagnosis of the problem. For example, a rise in gas prices leads to an increase in transporta-

tion prices, which leads to a rise in product costs, which leads to a decrease in demand, which leads to fewer production workers, which leads to layoffs and unemployment. Even in the above instance, the individual's inappropriate action or personal incompetence may be tied to social position, which shaped his or her access to resources, knowledge, and training.

> **public issues** Obstacles that individuals in similar positions face; also referred to by sociologists as "social problems."

The sociological imagination is an empowering tool. It allows us to go beyond a limited understanding of human behavior, to see the world and its people in a new way and through a broader lens than we might otherwise use. It may be as simple as understanding why a roommate prefers country music to hip-hop, or it may open up a whole new way of understanding other populations in the world. For example, in the aftermath of the terrorist attacks of September 11, 2001, many Americans wanted to understand how Muslims throughout the world perceived their country, and why. It was Mills' hope that we would use the sociological imagination to understand the impact that society has on our lives.

## THE HAMBURGER AS MIRACLE

Many people take for granted that it would be easy to provide for their needs if they had to, and they are eager to strike out on their own and prove themselves. As an example of using the sociological imagination, however, suppose you had to do something as seemingly simple as making a hamburger but had to do so without relying on any knowledge, skills, tools, or resources obtained from someone else. Without an interdependent network of people performing myriad small tasks that we take for granted, we would be hard-pressed to provide for ourselves. As we will see, like anything we might produce, a hamburger is a miracle because it is a symbol of our society's shared knowledge and skills.

How hard can it be to make a hamburger from scratch? Considering the

## SOCthink

> > > Imagine spending the afternoon people watching at the mall. What differences might you observe in how people present themselves? What factors might shape how they dress and talk, whether they are alone or in a group, and how much they buy? How might C. Wright Mills have explained such differences?

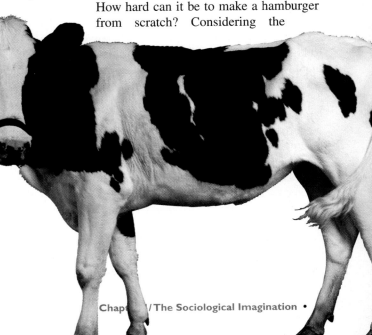

ingredients, which seem fairly simple, there are any number of ways to proceed. Let's begin with the burger itself. First, you need to find a cow. How hard can that be? Well, you can't buy one from a farmer, as doing so means relying on resources from others. For the same reason, you can't go out to the country (getting there itself might present something of a challenge) and steal one from a farm

apply the sociological imagination—the hamburger seems a miracle. It's miraculous not in a supernatural sense, but as a symbol pointing to the astonishing complexity and taken-for-grantedness of our human interdependence and to the knowledge we share collectively without even realizing it. Of course, this is true not just for hamburgers but for virtually any product we use. It could be a veggieburger, a book,

> The function of sociology, as of every science, is to reveal that which is hidden.
>
> Pierre Bourdieu

(which implies a farmer, which means dependence on another person). So you need to find a wild cow.

Assuming you do find a wild cow, you then have to kill it. Perhaps you might bash it with a large rock or stampede it off a cliff. Next, you need to butcher it, but cow hide is tough. Imagine what it takes to produce a metal knife (finding ore, smelting, forging, tempering, and so on). Perhaps a sharp rock will do. Assuming you came up with a cutting tool, you now have a chunk of raw cow meat. Given that it's hamburger we're after (though you might want to settle for steak at this point), next you need to grind the meat. You might use a couple of those rocks to pulverize the meat into something of a meat mash, although a meat grinder would work better if it weren't so hard to make one. In any event, at last you have a raw hamburger patty.

Now you need to cook it. How will you do that? Where will you get the fire? Perhaps you could strike two rocks together in hopes of creating a spark, or maybe rub two sticks together. If you were allowed to get help from an outside source, you might check how Tom Hanks' character did it in the film *Cast Away*—but you aren't. Perhaps it would be easiest to wait around for lightning to strike a nearby tree. In any case, after you get fire, you still have to cook the meat. No frying pans are available, so either you make one or perhaps cook it on that handy rock you used to kill the cow. Or you could just put the meat on a stick that you cut down and whittled with the knife you made (or was that a "sharp" stone?) and roast it over the fire.

Assuming you are successful, you now have a cooked hamburger patty. But that's not enough. There are still many other steps that need to be completed. You need a bun, which involves figuring out how to come up with flour, water, salt, oil, sugar, and yeast. What about condiments such as ketchup, mustard, pickles, and onions? What if at the end of all that you decide to make it a cheeseburger?

Making something that seems so simple, that we take for granted, that we can get for a dollar at McDonald's, turns out to be quite complicated. The knowledge and skill to acquire all the ingredients in a hamburger is beyond the capacity of most individuals. Yet when we eat a burger, we think nothing of it. When you think about it—when you

a desk, a shirt, a car, a house, or a computer. Look around you and try to imagine making, by yourself, all the things that we as humans have produced. The knowledge and skill that these things represent is overwhelming. Thankfully, our interdependence means that we do not have to rely on our own knowledge and skill alone for our survival.

## KEY COMPONENTS OF SOCIOLOGY

To better understand what sociology involves, we will look at each of the four key components of the definition in turn.

**Systematic Study** Sociologists are engaged with the world, gathering empirical data through systematic research. Relying on empirical data means that sociologists draw their conclusions about society based on experiences or observations rather than beliefs or the authority of others. If they want to understand the impact of television on community or the phenomenon of binge drinking on college campuses, they must gather data from those involved in these activities and base their conclusions upon that information.

Sociological research historically has been divided between quantitative and qualitative approaches to data collection. Quantitative approaches emphasize counting things and analyzing them mathematically or statistically. The most common way to collect this type of data is through surveys. In contrast, qualitative approaches focus on listening to and observing people and allowing them to interpret what is happening in their own lives. The most common way to collect this type of data is through participant observation, in which the researcher interacts with those she or he studies. In practice, sociologists often draw on both techniques in conducting their research. We will investigate these research techniques, along with others, in more detail in Chapter 2.

**The Individual** Although sociology is most commonly associated with the study of groups, there is no such thing as a group apart from the individuals who compose it. As individuals we are constantly choosing what do to next.

Most of the time, we follow guidelines for behavior we have learned from others, but we have the ability to reject those guidelines at any time. A term sociologists sometimes use to describe this capacity is **agency,** meaning the freedom individuals have to choose and to act. In professional sports, for example, we use the term "free agent" to describe a player who has the power to negotiate with whatever team he or she wishes. We, too, have such freedom. We could choose not to go to class, not to go to work, not to get out of bed in the morning, not to obey traffic

"*Actually, Lou, I think it was more than just my being in the right place at the right time. I think it was my being the right race, the right religion, the right sex, the right socioeconomic group, having the right accent, the right clothes, going to the right schools . . .*"

signals, not to respond when spoken to, not to read the next sentence in this book, and on and on.

Our self exists in an interactive relationship with its environment, and we act within the context of our relationships. The same is true for that sports free agent. While he or she can choose any team, in order to get a big payday, he or she is limited to choosing within the confines of the league. Our choices, too, are constrained by our positions. Having access to varieties of resources, we choose among an array of options with knowledge of various possible outcomes. We usually follow "paths of least resistance"—the accepted and expected actions and beliefs—but the choice of whether to continue to follow them is ours each and every second of our lives (Johnson 1997).

**Society** The study of society is at the core of sociology. While we will spend most of this book describing various aspects of society, we can begin by thinking of it as our social environment. Society consists of persistent patterns of relationships and social networks within which we operate. The social structure it provides is analogous to a building: the structure of a building both encourages and discourages different activities in different rooms (such as kitchens, bedrooms, and bathrooms), and many of the most essential operations of a building (such as heating and air conditioning) are mostly invisible to us. In the same way, the structure of our *institutions*—a term sociologists use to describe some of the key components of social structure, including economy, family, education, government, and religion—shapes what is expected of us. For example, the choices that are available to us in the context of the modern family, such as to go off and pursue our own education and career, are much different than the obligations we would face in more traditional family contexts. Nested within institutions are the groups, subgroups, and statuses that we occupy. Within the context of society, we construct culture and engage in social interaction. We will address the topics of structure, culture, and interaction in detail in coming chapters.

> **agency** The freedom individuals have to choose and to act.

**The Consequences of Difference** The final part of the definition of sociology involves the consequences of difference. Sociology does more than just describe our structure, culture, and interaction; it also looks at how economic, social, and cultural resources are distributed and at the consequences of these patterns in terms of the opportunities and obstacles they create for individuals and groups.

Since the founding of sociology, sociologists have been concerned with the impact our social positions have on our opportunities or lack thereof.

Sociologists have noted, for example, that the 2004 Indian Ocean tsunami affected Indonesian men and women differently. When the waves hit, following traditional cultural patterns, mothers and grandmothers were at home with the children; men were outside working, where they were more likely to become aware of the impending disaster. Moreover, most of the men knew how to swim, a survival skill that women in these traditional societies usually do not learn. As a result, many more men than women survived the catastrophe—about 10 men for every 1 woman. In one typical Indonesian village, 97 of 1300 people survived; only 4 were women. The impact of this gender imbalance will be felt for some time, given women's primary role as caregivers for children and the elderly (BBC 2005a).

The analysis of social power deserves particular attention because it shapes how and why we think and act as we do. The simple fact

is that those who have access to and control over valued material, social, and cultural resources have different options available to them than do those without such access. One of the main tasks of sociology is to reveal and report the degree of **social inequality**—a condition in which members of society have differing amounts of wealth, prestige, or power. That is why the definition of sociology draws particular attention to the consequences of difference.

In combination, these four aspects of sociology help us to understand the things that influence our beliefs and actions and, in so doing, can help us to make choices that are more free. Failure to appreciate the relationship between the individual and society, for example, leads us to misdiagnose our individual and social problems, and so to develop inadequate cures for those things that ail us. French sociologist Pierre Bourdieu (1998a) put it this way: "Sociology teaches how groups function and how to make use of the laws governing the way they function so as to try to circumvent them" (p. 57). Only by appreciating the degree

# Poverty Rates in Hurricane Katrina Disaster Area

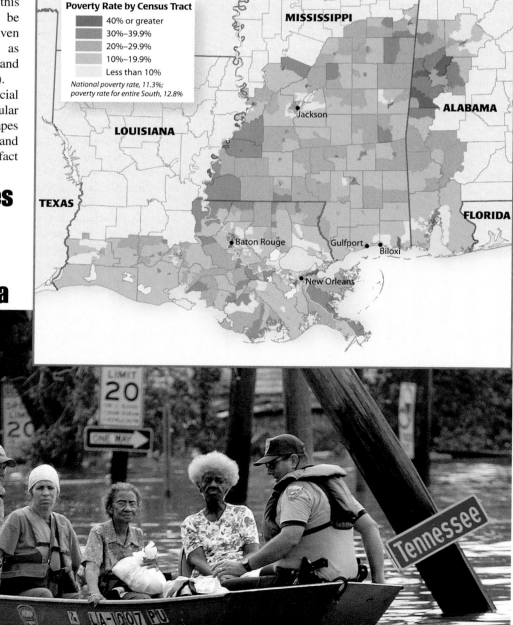

**Poverty Rate by Census Tract**
- 40% or greater
- 30%–39.9%
- 20%–29.9%
- 10%–19.9%
- Less than 10%

*National poverty rate, 11.3%; poverty rate for entire South, 12.8%*

to which our thoughts and actions are determined by our social position and our lack of freedom are we able to make more realistic choices to change ourselves and our worlds.

## SOCIOLOGY AND THE SOCIAL SCIENCES

Is sociology a science? The term **science** refers to the body of knowledge obtained by methods based on systematic observation. Just like other scientific disciplines, sociology involves the organized, systematic study of phenomena (in this case, human behavior) in order to enhance understanding. All scientists, whether studying mushrooms or murderers, attempt to collect precise information through methods of study that are as objective as possible. They rely on the careful recording of observations and the accumulation of data.

Of course, there is a great difference between, say, sociology and physics, or between psychology and astronomy. For this reason, the sciences are commonly divided into natural and social sciences. **Natural science** is the study of the physical features of nature and the ways in which they interact and change. Astronomy, biology, chemistry, geology, and physics are all natural sciences. **Social science** is the study of the social features of humans and the ways in which they interact and change. The social sciences include sociology, anthropology, economics, history, psychology, and political science.

These social science disciplines have a common focus on the social behavior of people, yet each has a particular orientation. Anthropologists usually study past cultures and preindustrial societies that continue today, as well as the origins of humans. Economists explore the ways in which people produce and exchange goods and services, along with money and other resources. Historians are concerned with the peoples and events of the past and their significance for us today. Psychologists investigate personality and individual behavior. Political scientists study international relations, the workings of government, and the exercise of power and authority. Sociologists, as we have already seen, study the influence that society has on people's attitudes and behavior and the ways in which people interact and shape society.

Let's consider how different social sciences would study the impact of Hurricane Katrina, which ravaged the Gulf Coast of the United States in 2005. Historians would compare the damage done by natural disasters in the 20th century to that caused by Katrina. Economists would conduct research on the economic impact of the damage, not just in the Southeast but throughout the nation and the world. Psychologists would study individual cases to assess the emotional trauma of the event. And political scientists would study the stances taken by different elected officials, along with their implications for the government's response to the disaster.

What approach would sociologists take? They might look at Katrina's impact on different communities and on different social classes. Some sociologists have undertaken neighborhood and community studies to determine how to maintain the integrity of storm-struck neighborhoods during the rebuilding phase. Researchers have focused in particular on Katrina's impact on marginalized groups; they found that issues of race, class, and disability were key. The disaster area was among the poorest in the United States. In terms of family income, for example, New Orleans ranked 63rd (7th lowest) among the nation's 70 largest cities. With Katrina bearing down on the Gulf Coast, thousands of poor inner-city residents had no automobiles or other available means by which to escape the storm. Added to that difficulty was the high incidence of disability in the area. New Orleans ranked second among the nation's 70 largest cities in the proportion of people over age 65 who are disabled—56 percent. Moving wheelchair-bound residents to safety requires specially equipped vehicles, to say nothing of handicap-accessible accommodations in public shelters. Clearly, officials must consider such factors in developing evacuation plans (Bureau of the Census 2005f).

**natural science** The study of the physical features of nature and the ways in which they interact and change.

**social science** The study of the social features of humans and the ways in which they interact and change.

Sociologists would take a similar approach in studying episodes of extreme violence. In March 2007, just as students at Virginia Tech were beginning to focus on the impending end of the semester, tragedy struck. In a two-hour shooting spree, a mentally disturbed senior armed with automatic weapons killed a total of 32 students and faculty at Virginia's largest university. Observers struggled to describe the events and place them in some social context. For sociologists in particular, the event raised numerous issues and topics for study, including the role of the media in reporting breaking news events, the presence of violence in schools, the politics of gun control, concerns about gender, the inadequacy of the nation's mental health care system, and the stereotyping and stigmatizing of people who suffer from mental illness.

## SOCIOLOGY AND COMMON SENSE

At times all of us practice some form of the sociological imagination, weighing the balance between individual and society. So what's the difference between sociology and common sense—the knowledge we get from our experiences and conversations, from what we read, from what we see on television, and so forth? Commonsense knowledge, while sometimes accurate, is not always reliable, because it rests on

*Sociological research shows that the choice of a marriage partner is heavily influenced by societal expectations.*

commonly held beliefs rather than on systematic analysis of facts.

Contrary to the common notion that women tend to be chatty compared to men, for instance, researchers have found little difference between the sexes in terms of their talkativeness. Over a five-year period, they placed unobtrusive microphones on 396 college students in various settings, on campuses in Mexico as well as the United States. They found that both men and women spoke about 16,000 words per day (Mehl et al. 2007).

**theory** In sociology a set of statements that seeks to explain problems, actions, or behavior.

Similarly, "common sense" tells us that in the United States today, military marriages are more likely to end in separation or divorce than in the past due to the strain of long deployments in Iraq and Afghanistan. Yet a study released in 2007 shows no significant increase in the divorce rate among U.S. soldiers over the past decade. In fact, the rate of marital dissolution among members of the military is comparable to that of nonmilitary families. Interestingly, this is not the first study to disprove the widely held notion that military service strains the marital bond. Two generations earlier, during the Vietnam era, researchers came to the same conclusion (Call and Teachman 1991; Karney and Crown 2007).

Like other social scientists, sociologists do not accept something as fact just because "everyone knows it." At times, the findings of sociologists may seem like common sense because they deal with familiar facets of everyday life. The difference is that such findings have been tested by researchers, analyzed in relation to other data, and evaluated in light of what is known by sociologists in the form of sociological theory.

## >> What Is Sociological Theory?

Sociology, like all sciences, involves a conversation between theory and research. We gather data through systematic research, and we seek to describe and explain what we find using theories. Theories represent our attempts to tell the stories of our lives but they do so in a particular way. Initially, theories might be general and vague. However, over time, as they become more fully informed by research, they are modified and refined into fuller, more accurate accounts of why we think and act as we do. Émile Durkheim's research on suicide provides a classic example.

### FORMULATING SOCIOLOGICAL THEORIES

Why do people commit suicide? Durkheim's answer to this question over a hundred years ago helped to establish sociology as a discipline. Among the traditional common-sense answers that Durkheim rejected were the notions that people inherit the desire to kill themselves or that sunspots drive people to take their own lives. He even suspected that psychological or biological explanations that pointed toward depression or chemical imbalance as causal factors were insufficient. He sought to prove that social forces existed that influenced an individual's likelihood of committing suicide.

In order to undertake this research, Durkheim developed a theory that offered a general explanation of suicidal behavior. We can think of theories as attempts to explain events, forces, materials, ideas, or behavior in a comprehensive manner. In sociology a **theory** is a set of statements that seeks to explain problems, actions, or behavior. An effective theory may have both explanatory and predictive power. That is, it can help us to see the relationships among seemingly isolated phenomena, as well as to understand how one type of change in an environment leads to other changes.

Durkheim theorized that people commit suicide because they lack the social integration to prevent them from taking this most final and individualistic of all acts. His hypothesis was this: "Suicide varies inversely with the degree of integration of the social groups of which the individual forms a part" ([1897] 1951:209). He chose religious affiliation as an indicator of social integration, arguing that Protestants are less socially integrated than are Roman Catholics. He claimed that Catholicism is a traditional faith with a hierarchical system of authority in which variation in belief (on such topics as birth control, abortion, married priests, and women priests) is not up to the individual. Protestantism, in contrast, puts the Bible into the believers' hands to interpret. The many schisms found among Protestants occurred as a consequence of individuals choosing to interpret matters of faith based on their own understanding of God's word. Whereas there is only one Roman Catholic Church, Protestantism includes Baptist, Methodist, Reformed, Episcopalian, Presbyterian, and many other denominational and nondenominational

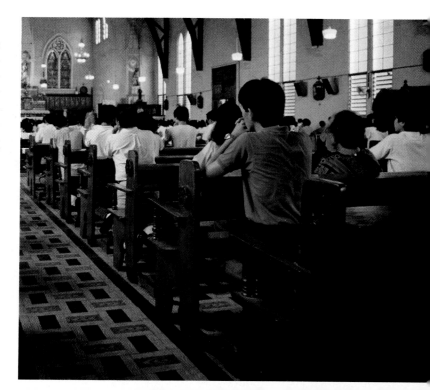

churches. These contrasting contexts shaped the degree to which individuals felt integrated into the religious community, leading Durkheim to predict that Protestants would be more likely to commit suicide than Catholics.

## TESTING SOCIOLOGICAL THEORIES

In order to test his theory, Durkhiem gathered data from different countries to see if suicide rates varied. Looking at France, England, and Denmark, he found that whereas England had only 67 reported suicides per million inhabitants, France had 135 per million and Denmark had 277 per million. The question then became: "Why did Denmark have a comparatively high rate of reported suicide?" Durkheim concluded that it was due to the fact that Denmark was a more Protestant nation than either France or England. In other words, it was the social makeup of these nations that shaped their suicide rates. More recent research focusing on individuals rather than national rates continues to find this same relationship.

In extending his analysis to look at other indicators of social integration, Durkheim continued to obtain results that confirmed his underlying theory: the unmarried had much higher rates of suicide than married people; and soldiers were more likely to take their lives than civilians. In addition, there seemed to be higher rates of suicide in times of peace than in times of war and revolution, as well as higher rates in times of economic instability and recession rather than in times of prosperity. Durkheim concluded that the suicide rates of a society reflects the extent to which people are or are not integrated into the group life of the society. Durkheim presented his results in his landmark work *Suicide,* published in 1897.

## APPLYING SOCIOLOGICAL THEORIES

Built into Durkheim's theory is the presupposition that we find meaning in life through our interconnections with others. The more interconnected and interdependent we feel, the less likely we are to kill ourselves. Attempting to summarize the significance of our attachment to society, Durkheim put it this way: "The individual alone is not a sufficient end for his activity. He is too little. . . . When, therefore, we have no other object than ourselves we cannot avoid the thought that our efforts will finally end in nothingness. . . . Under these conditions one would lose the courage to live, that is, to act and struggle" ([1897]

### SOCthink

> > > If Durkheim is correct and level of social integration influences the likelihood of suicide, why do rates vary for the groups listed in the Suicide Rates figure? Why is the rate for men four times higher than that for women? Why is the rate for non-Hispanic Whites higher than that for any other racial/ethnic groups? Why do White, non-Hispanic males have the highest suicide rate of all? Why is the rate for the elderly highest of all age groups? Why is there a midlife suicide peak? What might the top-five or bottom-five states have in common? What might these patterns suggest about the social integration of people in these categories?

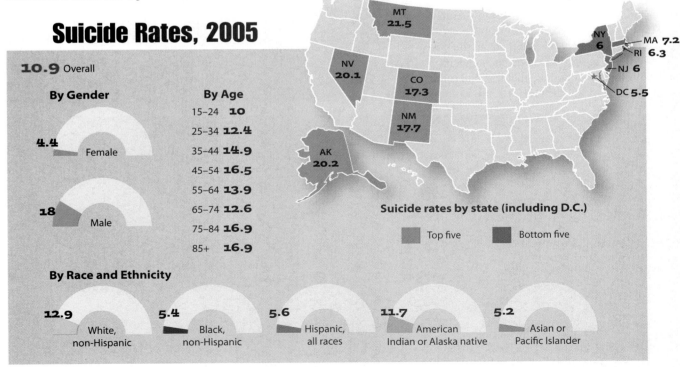

## Suicide Rates, 2005

**10.9** Overall

**By Gender**

4.4 Female

18 Male

**By Age**

| | |
|---|---|
| 15–24 | **10** |
| 25–34 | **12.4** |
| 35–44 | **14.9** |
| 45–54 | **16.5** |
| 55–64 | **13.9** |
| 65–74 | **12.6** |
| 75–84 | **16.9** |
| 85+ | **16.9** |

**By Race and Ethnicity**

12.9 White, non-Hispanic

5.4 Black, non-Hispanic

5.6 Hispanic, all races

11.7 American Indian or Alaska native

5.2 Asian or Pacific Islander

MT **21.5**
NV **20.1**
CO **17.3**
NM **17.7**
NY **6**
MA **7.2**
RI **6.3**
NJ **6**
DC **5.5**
AK **20.2**

**Suicide rates by state (including D.C.)**

Top five     Bottom five

*Note:* Rates are per 100,000, not percentage.

*Source:* National Center for Health Statistics 2007; Kung, Hoyert, Xu, and Murphy 2008.

### What Makes a Country Happy?

Looking on the bright side of life, happiness rates also vary from country to country. The five nations that score highest on the Happiness Index are Denmark, Switzerland, Austria, Iceland, and Finland. The bottom five are Tanzania, Zimbabwe, Moldova, Ukraine, and Armenia. The United States ranks 17th out of 95 nations. Researcher Stefan Klein (2006) suggests that societies that are characterized by a strong sense of social solidarity, active civic engagement, a commitment to social equality, and sufficient individual autonomy tend to be happier.

1951:210). Human beings are, at their very foundation, social beings. According to Durkheim, we cannot consider what it means to be an individual apart from our position in society. This social dimension of individual behavior is what Durkheim wants sociology to explore, elaborate, and explain.

Durkheim's work on suicide provides a classic case of sociological theory at work. He theorized that social forces shape individual actions. He tested this theory by investigating suicide as one such individual choice—perhaps the most individual of all choices—and demonstrated that the likelihood of committing suicide varied based on group membership. Analysis of more recent data (see figure on page 9) shows that suicide rates continue to vary based on social position. Durkheim maintained that if social forces are at work in such an extreme example

of individual choice, probably most of our choices are similarly shaped. He argued that if social forces have such power in our lives, there must be a discipline dedicated to their study. As a result, Durkheim established Europe's first department of sociology at the University of Bordeaux in 1895.

## >> The Development of Sociology

Given the complexity of human life, not surprisingly, sociologists have developed a wide range of theories in which they describe and explain the diversity of social behavior. Sometimes their theories can be grand in scope, seeking to encompass the "big picture"; other times they can be more personal, intimate, and immediate. While we will spend most of the rest of this book investigating the insights sociological theories provide, here we will briefly address just five questions sociologists have asked because they represent significant doors sociologists have opened as they have enlarged on what is meant by the sociological perspective. The questions are these: How is social

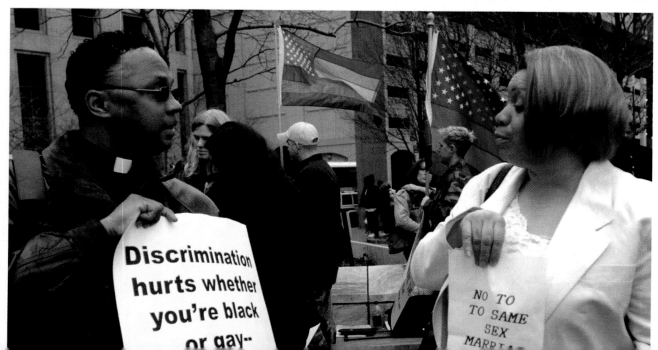

order maintained? How do power and inequality shape outcomes? How do we construct our worlds and ourselves through everyday interaction? How does group membership (especially class, race, and gender) shape opportunity? What responsibility do sociologists bear to bring about positive social change?

## SOCIAL ORDER

The discipline of sociology grew up in the midst of significant social upheaval. The advent of the Industrial Revolution and urbanization in the early 19th century led to changes in patterns of government, thought, work, and everyday life. Aristocracy was on the decline while democracy was spreading; people were moving from a primary reliance on religious explanations to more scientific ones; and the world of the village and farm was rapidly giving way to the world of the city and factory. It was in this context that Auguste Comte (1798–1857), in hopes of emulating what natural scientists did for nature, sought to establish a science of society that would reveal the basic "laws of society." Comte believed that knowing these laws would help us to understand what he referred to as "social statics"—the principles by which societies hold together and order is maintained—and social dynamics—the factors that bring about change and that shape the nature and direction of that change. Sociologists would then use their knowledge of these laws to help lead us toward the good society, balancing the needs for social order and positive social change. Comte coined the term *sociology*—which literally means "the study of the processes of companionship"—to describe this new science (Abercrombie, Hill, and Turner 2000:333).

Scholars learned of Comte's works largely through translations by the English sociologist Harriet Martineau (1802–1876). Seeking to systematize the research essential to conducting a science of society, Martineau ([1838] 1989) wrote the first book on sociological methods. But she was a pathbreaking theorist in her own right, introducing the significance of inequality and power into the discipline. Martineau's book *Society in America* ([1837] 1962) examined religion, politics, child rearing, and immigration in the young nation. It gave special attention to social class distinctions and to such factors as gender and race. In Martineau's ([1837] 1962) view, intellectuals and scholars should not simply offer observations of social conditions; they should act on their convictions in a manner that will benefit society. She spoke out in favor of the rights of women, the emancipation of slaves, and religious tolerance.

These two themes—analysis of social order and analysis of social inequality—have shaped the theoretical paths sociologists have pursued since this beginning. In early sociological theory, they find their fullest development in the works of Émile Durkheim and Karl Marx, respectively. As we will see throughout this book, they continue to be primary concerns for sociologists.

Émile Durkheim (1858–1917) emphasized the significance of social order. As we saw in his analysis of suicide, he saw society as a real, external force existing above the level of the individual and exerting its influence on individual behavior. Durkheim was particularly concerned about what happens when the power of society declines, resulting in weakened social integration. He theorized that an increase in the division of labor, a defining characteristic of modern societies, meant that individuals shared

**POPSOC**

Harriet Martineau ([1838] 1989) argued that we could learn a lot about a culture by analyzing the ideas, images, and themes reflected in their popular songs. She wrote, "The Songs of every nation must always be the most familiar and truly popular part of its poetry.... They present also the most prevalent feelings on subjects of the highest popular interest. If it were not so, they would not have been popular songs." What might we learn about American culture based on analysis of the lyrics of the current top-10 songs? (Lists are available at "The Billboard Hot 100" or www.top10songs.com.)

fewer common experiences, ideas, and values. As workers became much more specialized in their tasks, they were at greater risk of what Durkheim called **anomie**—the loss of direction felt in a society when social control of individual behavior has become ineffective. Anomie increases the likelihood of alienation, loneliness, and isolation. Inspired by Comte's vision, Durkheim sought to establish sociology as a science to study these processes.

## POWER AND INEQUALITY

While Karl Marx (1818–1883), like all sociologists, was concerned about social order and integration, his work emphasized the significance of power and control over resources. Marx viewed our creative capacity to transform raw materials into products—for example, to take clay and make a pot, or a tree and make a desk—as the key factor distinguishing humans from other animals (whose behavior is ruled by their instincts). For Marx, human history is the progressive unfolding of human creativity in the form of new technology through which we establish our relationship to the natural world and with each other. Unfortunately, for most of human history, we lacked sufficient technology to provide enough material goods (such as food, clothes, and shelter) to meet everyone's needs, so not all people had enough.

Social inequality for Marx, then, is determined by ownership, or lack thereof, of key material resources. Those who own and control the means of production—the tools and resources necessary for that transformation to happen—rule the world. Members of the working class, in contrast, own only their capacity to transform raw materi-

Karl Marx

als into products, something they cannot do absent access to the means of production, which is controlled by the ruling class. While Durkheim was concerned with anomie, Marx was concerned with alienation, by which he meant loss of control over our creative human capacity to produce, separation from the products we make, and isolation from our fellow workers. We will consider Marx's work as it relates to capitalism in more detail in a later chapter. His influence on sociological theory, however, extends beyond social class to an analysis of group identification and association, such as how class, gender, race, ethnicity, nationality, and age influence individual opportunity.

Seeking to expand sociological theory further, Max Weber (1864–1920; pronounced "VAY-ber") offered a more general theory of power that was less wedded to capitalism and ownership of the means of production. Weber argued that, although social class and its associated control over material resources may determine who has power in most instances, these are not the only possible foundations for power. Others he identified include social status, in which people defer to others out of respect for their social position or prestige, and organizational resources, in which members of a group gain power through their ability to organize to accomplish some specific goal by maximizing their available resources. Weber argued that these social resources draw their power from people's willingness to obey the authority of another person, which in turn is based on their perception of the legitimacy of that person's right to rule.

## INTERACTION

Much of the work of Durkheim, Marx, and Weber involves **macrosociology,** which concentrates on large-scale phenomena or entire civilizations. A later school of sociologists turned away from this approach in fa-

Max Weber

*Émile Durkheim*

vor of **microsociology,** which stresses the study of small groups and the analysis of our everyday experiences and interactions. Microsociology emphasizes the significance of perception, of how we see others and how they see us. Sociologist Erving Goffman (1922–1982) popularized a method known as the *dramaturgical approach* (see Chapter 4), which compares everyday life to the setting of the theater and stage and sees people as theatrical performers. Just as actors project certain images to an audience, all of us seek to present particular features of our personalities to others even as we hide certain qualities. Thus, in a class, we may feel the need to project a serious image; at a party, we want to look relaxed and friendly. In this approach, sociologists must analyze our lived experience at the everyday level where our actions create, sustain, and modify our understanding of reality itself.

## GROUPS AND OPPORTUNITY

Over time, sociologists came to more fully understand and appreciate the consequences that group membership, especially class, race, and gender, has for opportunity. Black sociologist W. E. B. Du Bois (1868–1963; pronounced "dew BOYS") combined an emphasis on the analysis of the everyday lived experience with a commitment to investigating power and inequality based on race. He was critical of those who relied on common sense or on all-too-brief investigations, arguing that a researcher has to be more than just a "car-window sociologist" because true understanding demands more than "the few leisure hours of a holiday trip to unravel the snarl of centuries" (Du Bois [1903] 1994:94). Through engaged and sustained research on the lives of African Americans, he documented their relatively low status in Philadelphia and Atlanta. Through this research he revealed the social processes that contributed to the maintenance of racial separation, which extended beyond material differences to include social separation, which he referred to as the "color line."

Similarly, feminist scholarship has broadened our understanding of social behavior by extending the analysis beyond the male point of view that dominated classic sociology. An early example of this perspective can be seen in the life and writings of Ida Wells-Barnett (1862–1931). Carrying on a tradition begun with Martineau, Wells-Barnett argued that societies can be judged based on whether the

... According to the Thomas theorem, established by sociologists W. I. Thomas and Dorothy Swaine Thomas, "If men define situations as real, they are real in their consequences" (Thomas and Thomas 1928:571–572). In other words, our perceptions of what is real determine how we act more so than does reality itself.

## Did You Know?

principles they claim to believe in match their actions. Wells-Barnett found that when it came to the principles of equality and opportunity for women and African Americans, America came up short. Part of the task for the sociologist, then, is to bring to light such inconsistencies that may otherwise go largely unnoticed. This is something Wells-Barnett sought to do in her groundbreaking publications in the 1890s on the practice of lynching African Americans, as well as with her advocacy of women's rights, especially the struggle to win the vote for women. Like feminist theorists who succeeded her, Wells-Barnett used her analysis of society as a means of resisting oppression. In her case, she researched what it meant to be African American, a woman in the United States, and a Black woman in the United States (Wells-Barnett 1970).

Sociologists categorize and describe the above sociological insights by dividing them into three approaches: functionalist, conflict, and interactionist. Durkheim's work is considered an example of the **functionalist perspective,** which views society as akin to a living organism in which each part of the organism contributes to its survival. The various parts of a society, including institutions such as the family and government, are structured to maintain its stability. Where the functionalist approach focuses

**anomie** The loss of direction felt in a society when social control of individual behavior has become ineffective.

**macrosociology** Sociological investigation that concentrates on large-scale phenomena or entire civilizations.

**microsociology** Sociological investigation that stresses the study of small groups and the analysis of our everyday experiences and interactions.

**functionalist perspective** A sociological approach that emphasizes the way in which the parts of a society are structured to maintain its stability.

## Did You Know?

... **Martin Luther King, Jr., graduated with a B.A. in sociology from Morehouse College in Atlanta, Georgia, in 1948.**

more on stability and consensus, the **conflict perspective** emphasizes the distribution of power and the allocation of resources in society. According to the conflict perspective, social order cannot be fully understood apart from a consideration of how the status quo is established and maintained and who benefits and who suffers from the existing system. Marx's work fits best within the conflict perspective. Finally, whereas functionalist and conflict theorists both analyze large-scale, society-wide patterns of behavior, theorists such as Goffman who take the **interactionist perspective** generalize about everyday forms of social interaction in order to explain society as a whole.

# Three Perspectives on Sports

**Functionalist: Social Order**

- Sports socialize young people into such values as competition and patriotism.

- Sports bring together members of a community (supporting local athletes and teams) or even a nation (as seen during World Cup soccer matches and the Olympics) and promote an overall feeling of unity and social solidarity.

**Conflict: Inequality & Power**

- Sports are a form of big business in which profits are more important than the health and safety of the workers (athletes).

- Sports serve as an "opiate" that encourages people to seek a "fix" or temporary "high" rather than focus on personal problems and social issues.

**Interactionist: Perception & Interaction**

- Despite class, racial, and religious differences, teammates may work together harmoniously and may even abandon previous stereotypes and prejudices.

- Relationships in the sports world are defined by people's social positions as players, coaches, and referees—as well as by the high or low status that individuals hold as a result of their performances and reputations.

## SOCthink

> > > Sometimes it seems like we are experiencing "credential inflation," with more and more education needed to get decent entry-level jobs. Why do you think this has happened? How might looking at the issue from the functionalist, conflict, and interactionist perspectives shape how we frame an answer?

The three-perspectives model has the advantage of providing us with conceptual hooks that allow us to recall some of the key concerns and issues sociologists have raised. A key disadvantage, however, is that it gives the illusion that these three are discrete categories with fundamentally different and incompatible ways of looking at the world. In practice, research rooted in one perspective almost inevitably should draw on or address insights from the other two.

## PURSUING SOCIAL CHANGE

Throughout sociology's history, a recurring theme common to all perspectives has been the idea that sociological theory and research should contribute to positive social change. In the early 1900s, many leading sociologists in the United States saw themselves as social reformers dedicated to systematically studying and then improving a corrupt society. They were genuinely concerned about the lives of immigrants in the nation's growing cities, whether those immigrants came from Europe or from the rural American South. Early female sociologists, in particular, often took active roles in poor urban areas as leaders of community centers known as settlement houses. For example, Jane Addams (1860–1935), an early member of the American Sociological Society, cofounded the famous Chicago settlement, Hull House. Addams and other pioneering female sociologists commonly combined intellectual inquiry, social service work, and political activism—all with the goal of assisting the underprivileged and creating a more egalitarian society. Working with Ida Wells-Barnett, Addams successfully prevented racial segregation in the Chicago public schools, and her efforts to establish a juvenile court system and a women's trade union reflect the practical focus of her work (Addams 1910, 1930; Deegan 1991; Lengermann and Niebrugge-Brantley 1998).

*Sources:* Acosta and Carpenter 2001; H. Edwards 1973; Eitzen 2003; Fine 1987.

# From Me to You

*Taking an introductory sociology course can be a bit overwhelming. There are so many terms, concepts, facts, and figures that it can be difficult to make sense of it all. After I finished taking "Intro Soc" I felt a bit bewildered, but by then I knew there was something really interesting in the midst of it all. I took another course and was hooked. I encourage you to watch for and make note of things in the text that pique your interest and to recognize that any particular topic is but the tip of the iceberg built upon much more in-depth coverage and analysis to which sociologists have dedicated their lives. Consider following up on those interests later by tracking down some of those sources or taking a follow-up course.*

This commitment to positive social change was not unique to Addams and her colleagues. From the very beginning and on down to the present, sociologists have recognized an obligation to go beyond explaining how the world works and become actively engaged in making the world a better place. In the words of French sociologist Pierre Bourdieu, "I have come to believe that those who have the good fortune to be able to devote their lives to the study of the social world cannot stand aside, neutral and indifferent, from the struggles in which the future of that world is at stake" (1998a:11). For some this has meant releasing the results of their re-

*Jane Addams*

search to the public so that we might make more informed decisions; for others it has meant active engagement in establishing social policy or assisting in the lives of others. For example, Durkheim, who considered an educated citizenry essential to democratic success, used his appointment to the Department of Science of Education and Sociology at the Sorbonne in Paris, along with his political connections and appointments, to shape French educational policy and practice. Du Bois cofounded the National Association for the Advancement of Colored People, better known as the NAACP. In fact, one of the dominant reasons students choose to major in sociology is because they want to make a difference, and sociology provides a pathway to do just that.

**conflict perspective** A sociological approach that assumes that social behavior is best understood in terms of tension between groups over power or the allocation of resources, including housing, money, access to services, and political representation.

**interactionist perspective** A sociological approach that generalizes about everyday forms of social interaction in order to explain society as a whole.

**applied sociology** The use of the discipline of sociology with the specific intent of yielding practical applications for human behavior and organizations.

## >> Practicing Sociology

For those who would like to pursue a career in sociology, a variety of paths are available. In recent decades, the number of U.S. college students who have graduated with a degree in sociology has risen steadily (see figure on page 16). While few occupations specifically require an undergraduate degree in sociology, sociological skills such as the ability to observe, interpret, and report on both macro- and micro-patterns; to analyze and interpret data; and to work to bring about positive change are important assets in a wide range of occupations. Employment options for sociology majors include entry-level positions in business, social services, community organizations, not-for-profit groups, law enforcement, and more. The figure on page 16 summarizes the sources of employment for those with B.A. or B.S. degrees in sociology. One way to investigate a possible future in sociology is through an internship. Studies show that students who choose an internship have less trouble finding jobs, obtain better jobs, and enjoy greater job satisfaction than students without internship placements (American Sociological Association 2006a; Salem and Grabarek 1986).

### APPLIED SOCIOLOGY

**Applied sociology** is the use of the discipline of sociology with the specific intent of yielding practical

**Hot or Not?**

Is it your responsibility to get involved to make things better for society?

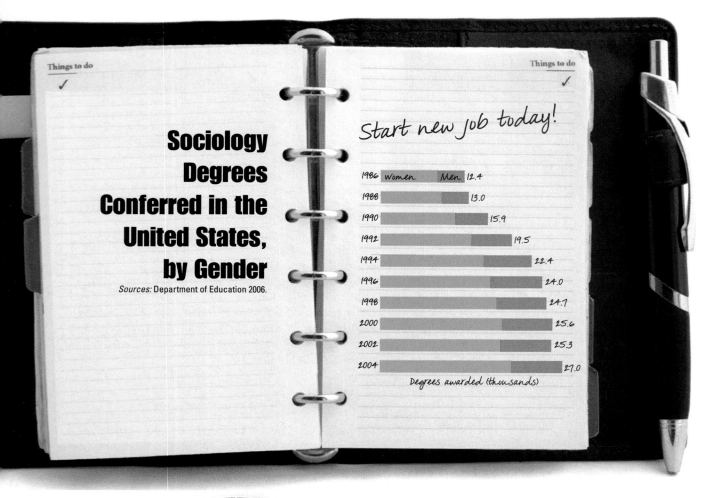

## Sociology Degrees Conferred in the United States, by Gender

*Sources:* Department of Education 2006.

*Start new job today!*

| Year | | Degrees awarded (thousands) |
|---|---|---|
| 1986 | Women / Men | 12.4 |
| 1988 | | 13.0 |
| 1990 | | 15.9 |
| 1992 | | 19.5 |
| 1994 | | 22.4 |
| 1996 | | 24.0 |
| 1998 | | 24.7 |
| 2000 | | 25.6 |
| 2002 | | 25.3 |
| 2004 | | 27.0 |

*Degrees awarded (thousands)*

Education **14.3%**
Government **27.1%**
Not sure **27.4%**
Private (nonprofit) **20.1%**
Private (for-profit) **11.1%**

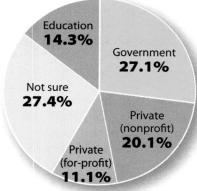

applications for human behavior and organizations. Often, the goal of such work is to assist in resolving a social problem. For example, in the past 40 years, eight presidents of the United States have established commissions to delve into major societal concerns facing our nation. Sociologists are often asked to apply their expertise to studying such issues as violence, pornography, crime, immigration, and population. In Europe both academic and governmental research departments are offering increasing financial support for applied studies.

One example of applied sociology involves the growing interest in the ways in which nationally recognized social problems manifest themselves locally. Since 2003, sociologist Greg Scott and his colleagues have been seeking to better understand the connection between illicit drug use and the spread of HIV/AIDS. The study, which will run through 2009, has so far employed 14 researchers from colleges and public health agencies, assisted by 15 graduate and 16 undergraduate students. By combining a variety of methods, including interviews and observation, with photo

## Preferred Employment Sector of Graduating Sociology Majors

*Note:* Based on spring 2005 national survey of 1248 college seniors majoring in sociology.
*Source:* Adapted from American Sociological Association 2006:29.

and video documentation, these researchers have found that across all drug users, HIV/AIDS transmission is highest among users of crystal methamphetamine. Meth users are also most likely to engage in risky sexual behavior and to have partners who do so. Fortunately, of all drug users, meth users are the ones most closely connected to treatment programs, which allows them to receive substance abuse education and treatment from their health care providers. However, their cases, brought to the forefront by Scott and his team, highlight the need for public health officials to identify other individuals who engage in high-risk sexual behavior and to get them into appropriate treatment programs (G. Scott 2005).

Growing interest in applied sociology has led to such specializations as medical sociology and environmental sociology. The former includes research on how health care professionals and patients deal with disease. For example, medical sociologists have studied the social impact of the AIDS crisis on families, friends, and communities. Environmental sociologists examine the relationship between human societies and the physical environment. One focus of their work is the issue of "environmental justice," raised when researchers and community activists found that hazardous waste dumps are especially likely to be situated in poor and minority neighborhoods (M. Martin 1996).

## CLINICAL SOCIOLOGY

The growing popularity of applied sociology has led to the rise of the specialty of clinical sociology. While applied sociology may involve simply evaluating social issues, **clinical sociology** is dedicated to facilitating change by altering social relationships (as in family therapy) or restructuring social institutions (as in the reorganization of a medical center). Louis Wirth (1931) wrote about clinical sociology more than 75 years ago, but the term itself has become popular only in recent years. The Association for Applied Clinical Sociology was founded in 1978 to promote the application of sociological knowledge in interventions for individual and social change. This professional group has developed a procedure for certifying clinical sociologists—much as physical therapists or psychologists are certified.

Applied sociologists generally leave it to others to act on their evaluations. By contrast, clinical sociologists take direct responsibility for implementation and view those with whom they work as their clients. This specialty has become increasingly attractive to graduate students in sociology because it offers an opportunity to apply intellectual learning in practical ways. A shrinking job market in the academic world has made such alternative career routes appealing.

For sociology graduates interested in academic careers, the road to a Ph.D. (or doctorate) can be long and difficult. This degree symbolizes competence in original research; each candidate must prepare a book-length study known as a dissertation. Typically, a doctoral student in sociology will engage in four to seven years of intensive work, including the time required to complete the dissertation. Yet even this effort is no guarantee of a job as a sociology professor.

Most people who take an introductory course in sociology will never take another sociology course, so what does sociology have to offer

them? Practicing sociology is about so much more than a career; it is a way of looking at the world around us and understanding its complexity and interconnections in a new way. It is about understanding others from their perspective and even understanding ourselves through their eyes. It is a way of assessing the accuracy of claims and refining our knowledge about why we think the way we think and act the way we act. Sociology is something you do; it's a way of life. Sociology is a verb.

> **clinical sociology** The use of the discipline of sociology with the specific intent of altering social relationships or restructuring social institutions.
>
> **globalization** The worldwide integration of government policies, cultures, social movements, and financial markets through trade and the exchange of ideas.

# >> Developing a Sociological Imagination

Learning to apply the sociological imagination may be more important now than ever. Through **globalization**—the worldwide integration of government policies, cultures, social movements, and financial markets through trade and the exchange of ideas—our lives are more connected with and dependent upon diverse groups of people around the world whose beliefs and practices may be quite different from our own. University campuses often provide a microcosm of this trend, drawing together people from around the world with radically different values, political views, customs, and more into a relatively confined social space and providing opportunities for them to interact. If such interactions are to be meaningful, positive, and respectful, we must learn to use the sociological imagination to better understand ourselves and our culture.

## SOCthink

> > > Consider the obstacles to cross-cultural interaction on college campuses. What function might such group homogeneity serve? How might it perpetuate inequality? Why might people be unwilling to interact with others who have different cultural practices?

Sociologists expect the next quarter century to be perhaps the most exciting and critical period in the history of the discipline. That is because of a growing recognition—both in the United States and around the world—that current social problems must be addressed before their magnitude overwhelms human societies. Sociologists plan to play an increasing role through theory, research, and action.

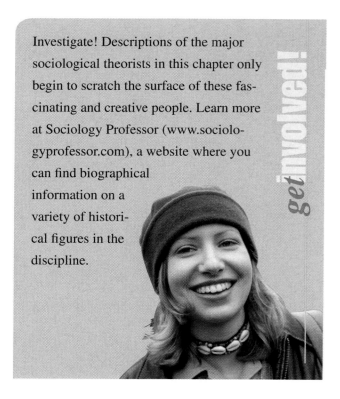

Investigate! Descriptions of the major sociological theorists in this chapter only begin to scratch the surface of these fascinating and creative people. Learn more at Sociology Professor (www.sociologyprofessor.com), a website where you can find biographical information on a variety of historical figures in the discipline.

*get involved!*

# For REVIEW

I. **What is sociology?**
- Sociology is a way of seeing that joins theory and research to investigate the relationship between the individual and society and the impact unequal distribution of resources has on opportunity.

II. **How do sociologists look at the world?**
- Sociologists develop theories that provide windows into our lives, allowing us to better understand social order, inequality, and interaction.

III. **How might someone practice sociology?**
- Sociology can provide a pathway to a career in a related applied, clinical, or academic context. But more than that, we can practice sociology in our everyday lives by utilizing the sociological imagination to better understand ourselves and others.

# Pop Quiz

1. Sociology is
   a. the analysis of individual motivations and internal struggles.
   b. concerned with predicting what particular individuals do or do not do.
   c. the systematic study of the relationship between the individual and society and of the consequences of difference.
   d. the integration of government policies, cultures, social movements, and financial markets through trade and the exchange of ideas.

2. Which of the following thinkers introduced the concept of the sociological imagination?
   a. Émile Durkheim
   b. Max Weber
   c. Karl Marx
   d. C. Wright Mills

3. Émile Durkheim's research on suicide found that
   a. Catholics had much higher suicide rates than Protestants.
   b. there seemed to be higher rates of suicide in times of peace than in times of war and revolution.
   c. civilians were more likely to take their lives than soldiers.
   d. suicide is a solitary act, unrelated to group life.

4. Karl Marx argued that in order to understand social order we must include analysis of
   a. anomie.
   b. ownership of the means of production.
   c. the sociological imagination.
   d. microsociology.

5. According to Erving Goffman's dramaturgical theory
   a. analysis of inequality and power must be front and center.
   b. social order is a critical problem for sociologists to investigate due to the threats to social order presented by the Industrial Revolution.

   c. early sociological research failed to see the significant impact that group membership (especially gender, race, and social class) played in shaping individual action and opportunity.
   d. we can analyze social interaction as if we were actors in a play.

6. Which sociologist made a major contribution to society through his in-depth studies of urban life, including both Blacks and Whites?
   a. W. E. B. Du Bois
   b. Robert Merton
   c. Auguste Comte
   d. Charles Horton Cooley

7. In the late 19th century the ideas behind the feminist perspective appeared in the writings of
   a. Karl Marx.
   b. Ida Wells-Barnett.
   c. Betty Friedan.
   d. Pierre Bourdieu.

8. Thinking of society as a living organism in which each part of the organism contributes to its survival is a reflection of which theoretical perspective?
   a. the functionalist perspective
   b. the conflict perspective
   c. the feminist perspective
   d. the interactionist perspective

9. Karl Marx's view of the struggle between social classes inspired the contemporary
   a. functionalist perspective.
   b. conflict perspective.
   c. interactionist perspective.
   d. dramaturgical approach.

10. The career path with the specific intent of altering social relationships or restructuring social institutions is known as
    a. dramaturgical sociology.
    b. applied sociology.
    c. academic sociology.
    d. clinical sociology.

1 (c); 2 (d); 3 (b); 4 (b); 5 (d); 6 (a); 7 (b); 8 (a); 9 (b); 10 (d)

2

# SOCIOLOG

## ASKING QUESTIONS AND FINDING ANSWERS

Part of the fun of sociology is asking questions and finding answers, and sociologists Patricia and Peter Adler seem to have had more fun than most. Their search to understand our social lives has lead them to spend extended periods of time with college athletes, drug dealers, school kids, Hawaiian resort workers, graduate students, self-injurers, and others. In each such study their underlying sociological commitment has remained the same: to answer the questions "Why do we think the way we think?" and "Why do we act the way we act?"

To better understand the tourism industry, for example, the Adlers spent eight years gathering information at five Hawaiian hotels, studying the staff and operations in minute detail (Adler and Adler 2004). This allowed them to better understand how tourist experiences are scripted (including the ceremonial lei provided upon arrival) and the significance of race, ethnicity, and social class when it comes to access to resources (including the kinds of jobs available to new immigrants such as Filipinos, Samoans, and Vietnamese).

Similarly, in their effort to better understand self-injury—including self-cutting, burning, branding, biting, and bone-breaking—the Adlers conducted lengthy, emotionally intense interviews with self-injurers over a six-year period, becoming friends with many. "Rather than remaining strictly detached from our subjects," they write, "we became involved in their lives, helping them and giving voice to their experiences and beliefs" (2007:542).

In other studies they found that college athletes go to big-time college sports schools with the best of intentions to be good students but get worn down by the obligations of being an athlete, and resign themselves to inferior academic performance (Adler and Adler 1985).

As is the case with all good sociological research, such studies seek to tell our stories and help us to understand ourselves in light of our interdependence. Sociologists such as the Adlers systematically gather our stories together through research and make sense of them with theory.

# ICAL RESEARCH

- What steps do sociologists take when seeking to answer why people think and act the way they do?
- What techniques do sociologists use to collect data?
- What ethical concerns must sociologists consider while conducting research?

## >> Steps in the Research Process

Sociology at its core represents a conversation between theory and research. Sociologists seek to describe and explain the patterns and practices of our lives through systematic investigation of what we do and why. If we want to know why people think and act the way they do, we need to know more about what they actually think and do. We need to observe them, ask them questions, participate in their lives, or in other ways come to understand their experiences from their perspective. We cannot sit back and guess.

Sociology inherits this commitment in part from early attempts by some sociologists to emulate the scientific method. The **scientific method** is a systematic, organized series of steps that ensures maximum objectivity and consistency in researching a problem. While not all sociologists today would tie the task of sociology as strongly to the natural science model, the commitment to making sense of the world through engagement with the world remains.

Conducting sociological research in the spirit of the scientific method requires adherence to a series of steps designed to ensure the accuracy of the results. Sociologists and other researchers follow five basic steps in the scientific method: (1) defining the problem, (2) reviewing the literature, (3) formulating the hypothesis, (4) selecting the research design and then collecting and analyzing data, and (5) developing the conclusion (see the figure at left). To better understand the process, we will follow an example about the relationship between education and income from start to finish.

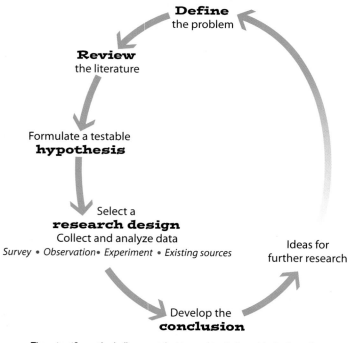

**The Scientific Method**

Define the problem

Review the literature

Formulate a testable **hypothesis**

Select a **research design**
Collect and analyze data
*Survey • Observation • Experiment • Existing sources*

Ideas for further research

Develop the **conclusion**

*The scientific method allows sociologists to objectively and logically evaluate the data they collect. Their findings can suggest ideas for further sociological research.*

### DEFINING THE PROBLEM

Does it "pay" to go to college? Many people make great sacrifices and work hard to get a college degree. Parents borrow money for their children's tuition. Students work part-time or even take full-time jobs while attending evening or weekend classes. Does it pay off? Are there sufficient monetary returns for getting that degree?

The first step in any research project is to state as clearly as possible what you hope to investigate—that is, to define the problem. Typically, this means explicitly identifying both the concepts we are interested in learning more about and the nature of the relationship we suspect might exist between those concepts. In our example, we are interested in knowing if increased education influences economic position.

In defining the problem, we draw on theories about why people think and act the way they do. These theories might be fairly simple and tentative guesses about the relationships, or they might be more elaborate and fully formed, such as we saw in the works of Karl Marx, Max Weber, and Émile Durkheim. For example, Durkheim developed a prediction regarding suicide based on his theory that social integration influences individual action, and he set about to test this theory using social research. Through research we seek to assess and refine our theories so that the explanations and descriptions of the world we get through sociology are fuller and more complete, more accurately reflecting both the simplicity and the complexity of human behavior.

Several competing theories exist concerning the relationship between education and income. One theory states that society needs people to develop their skills in order for society to realize its full potential, so it rewards those who make the sacrifices necessary to develop those skills through education. Another theory states that education does not so much provide opportunity as reinforce the existing system of inequality by providing the illusion of opportunity. In this theory, people more or less end up in the same economic position in which they began their educational journey. Which theory we start with will shape the kind of data we collect. We will look into both of these theories about education in a later chapter, but for the purpose of our example, we will focus on the first.

Often the concepts in our theories are too general or abstract to study in a systematic fashion. In order to investigate those concepts, we need to move from the abstract to the concrete. To do so, social science researchers develop an operational definition of each concept being studied. An **operational definition** transforms an abstract concept into indicators that are observable and measurable, allowing researchers to assess the concept. For example, a sociologist interested in status might use membership in exclusive social clubs as an operational definition of status. Someone studying religiosity might consider the frequency of a person's participation in religious services or the amount of time spent in prayer or meditation as an operational definition of how religious the person is. In our example, we need operational definitions for both education and earnings. Although we could argue that education involves more than just years of schooling completed, it is conventional to operationalize it that way. Similarly, income is conventionally operationalized as the total income an individual reports having received in the last year.

> **scientific method** A systematic, organized series of steps that ensures maximum objectivity and consistency in researching a problem.
> **operational definition** Transformation of an abstract concept into indicators that are observable and measurable.

## REVIEWING THE LITERATURE

The next phase of research involves a review of the literature: investigating previous research conducted by sociologists and others regarding the concepts we wish to study. Analyzing how others have studied these concepts allows researchers to refine the problem under study, clarify possible techniques for collecting data, and eliminate or reduce avoidable mistakes. An excellent place to start such research is the many sociological journals that regularly publish articles in which sociologists carefully document their findings. (See the "Finding Information" table on page 24 for more useful tips.)

In our example, we would need to seek out existing research about the relationship between education and income. In that literature we would find significant evidence that the two are linked. We would also learn that other factors besides years of schooling influence earning potential. For example, a person's occupational category (such as plumber, tool-and-die worker, secretary, or pro-

## Finding Information

**Begin** with material you already have, including this text and others.

**Check out** Wikipedia, which can be a good place to start since it points toward other materials, but don't stop there.

**Search** using computerized periodical indexes to find related academic journal articles.

**Use** the library catalog.

**Examine** government documents (including the U.S. Census).

**Contact** people, organizations, and agencies related to your topic.

**Use** newspapers.

**When using the Internet,** consider the source; always double-check claims with a reputable source or organization.

**Consult** with your instructor, teaching assistant, or reference librarian.

fessor) might shape her or his income in a way different than just educational level alone. We would also find that background factors such as class, gender, and race affect income. For example, the children of rich parents are more likely to go to college than those from modest backgrounds, so we might consider the possibility that the same parents may later help their children secure better-paying jobs. This might lead us to consider adding additional concepts to our definition of the problem.

**hypothesis** A testable statement about the relationship between two or more variables.

### FORMULATING THE HYPOTHESIS

After reviewing earlier studies and drawing on the contributions of sociological theorists, we would next formulate our hypothesis. A **hypothesis** is more than just an educated guess; it is a testable statement about the relationship between two or more factors known as variables. Income, religion, occupation, and gender can all serve as variables in a study. We can define a **variable** as a measurable trait or characteristic that is subject to change under different conditions.

Hypotheses are built on a presupposition of cause-and-effect relationships, and researchers who formulate a hypothesis generally must suggest how one variable influences or affects another. The variable hypothesized to cause or influence another is called the **independent variable.** The variable that is affected is known as the **dependent variable** because change in it depends on the influence of the in-

### Did You Know?

... U.S. government agencies regularly release reports with information on income, education, poverty, and health care. According to the Census Bureau, median household income in 2006 was $48,201. According to the U.S. Department of Education, of people ages 25–29, 86 percent had received their high school diploma or equivalent, and 28.4 percent had earned a bachelor's degree or more.

dependent variable. In other words, the researcher believes that the independent variable predicts or causes change in the dependent variable. For example, a researcher in sociology might anticipate that the availability of affordable housing (the independent variable; often referred to in equations as *x*) affects the level of homelessness in a community (the dependent variable; typically represented in equations as *y*).

We can put these pieces together to generate a generic hypothesis statement: knowledge of the independent variable (*x*) allows us to better explain or predict the value or position of the dependent variable (*y*). We could then place variables we are interested in studying, such as those in the figure to the right, into this statement in order to clearly present the nature of the relationships we expect to find between variables we wish to study.

In our example, our hypothesis suggests that knowing how many years of schooling a person has completed will allow us to better predict how much money he or she will earn. Further, we expect that this relationship will be positive, meaning the higher a person's educational attainment, the more money she or he will make. The independent variable we are measuring is the level of education, and income is the dependent variable.

# Causal Logic

| Independent variable | Dependent variable |
| --- | --- |
| $x$ | $y$ |
| Level of educational degree | Level of income |
| Degree of lack of integration into society | Likelihood of suicide |
| Availability of affordable housing | Level of homelessness |
| Parents' church attendance | Children's church attendance |
| Time spent preparing for quiz | Performance on quiz |
| Parents' income | Likelihood of children's enrolling in college |

## SOCthink

> > > What independent variables do you think would best explain college grade point average (GPA)? To what extent do you think each of the independent variables listed in the figure "Causal Logic" would contribute to explaining GPA performance?

Identifying independent and dependent variables is a critical step in clarifying cause-and-effect relationships. **Causal logic** involves the relationship between a condition or variable and a particular consequence, with one event leading to the other. For instance, as Durkheim hypothesized, being less integrated into society produces a greater likelihood of suicide. Similarly, the time students spend reviewing material for a quiz may bring about a greater likelihood of getting a high score on the quiz. In our example, we are suggesting that increased education results in higher income.

Sometimes a change in one variable coincides with a change in the other but is not necessarily caused by it. Such a relationship between two variables is called a **correlation.** For example, data indicate that people who prefer to watch televised news programs are less knowledgeable than those who read newspapers and newsmagazines. This correlation between people's relative knowledge and their choice of news media seems to make sense because it agrees with the common belief that television "dumbs

down" information. But the correlation between the two variables is actually caused by a third variable, people's training in processing large amounts of information. People with poor reading skills are much more likely than others to get their news from television, while those who are more educated or skilled turn more often to the print media. Thus, although television viewing is correlated with lower news comprehension, it does not *cause* it. Correlation does not equal causation. Sociologists seek to identify the *causal* link between variables; the suspected causal link is generally described in the hypothesis (Neuman 2000:139).

## COLLECTING AND ANALYZING DATA

How do you test a hypothesis in order to support or refute it? You must collect data. There are a variety of ways, known as research designs, that sociologists go about doing this, including surveys, observation, experiments, and use of existing data. Because the design selected is so critical to the research process, we will go into greater depth about each of those research designs later in this chapter.

**variable** A measurable trait or characteristic that is subject to change under different conditions.

**independent variable** The variable in a causal relationship that causes or influences a change in a second variable.

**dependent variable** The variable in a causal relationship that is subject to the influence of another variable.

**causal logic** The relationship between a condition or variable and a particular consequence, with one event leading to the other.

**correlation** A relationship between two variables in which a change in one coincides with a change in the other.

For now we will focus on some key issues that you must address regardless of which research design you select.

**Selecting the Sample** Sociologists cannot study everybody, so they seek ways to select individuals and groups that are representative of the population that is the subject of the research. In most large-scale studies, social scientists carefully choose what is known as a **sample**—a selection from a larger population that is statistically representative of that population. There are many kinds of samples, but the one social scientists use most frequently is the random sample. In a **random sample,** every member of the entire population being studied has the same chance of being selected. Thus, if researchers want to examine the opinions of people listed in a city directory (a book that, unlike the telephone directory, lists all households), they might use a computer to randomly select names from the directory. The results would constitute a random sample. The advantage of using specialized sampling techniques is that sociologists can be confident that the results they obtain will be representative of the larger population, freeing them from having to question everyone in the population (Igo 2007).

It is all too easy to confuse the careful scientific techniques used in representative sampling with the many nonscientific polls that receive so much more media attention. For example, television viewers are often encouraged to "visit our website and express your views" in an online poll

sample A selection from a larger population that is statistically representative of that population.

random sample A sample for which every member of an entire population has the same chance of being selected.

about headline news or political contests. Such polls reflect nothing more than the views of those who happened to see the television program and took the time to register their opinions. These data do not necessarily reflect (and indeed may distort) the views of the broader population. Not everyone has access to a television or radio, time to watch or listen to a program, or the means and/or inclination to vote in this way. Even when these techniques include answers from tens of thousands of people, they will be far less accurate than a carefully selected representative sample of 1500 respondents.

For the purposes of our research example of education and income, we will use information collected in the General Social Survey (GSS). Since 1972, the National Opinion Research Center (NORC) has conducted this national survey 26 times, most recently in 2006. In the GSS, administered in both English and Spanish, a representative sample of the adult population is interviewed in depth on a variety of topics. Our investigation of the relationship between education and income is based on analysis of the 4,510 people interviewed in the 2006 GSS (Schaefer 2009).

**Ensuring Validity and Reliability** In order to have confidence in their findings, and in keeping with the scientific method, sociologists pursue research results that are both valid and reliable. **Validity** refers to the degree to which a measure or scale truly reflects the phenomenon under study. In our example, a valid measure of income would accurately represent how much money a person earned in a given year. Although income can be a touchy subject, various studies show that people are reasonably accurate in reporting how much money they earned in the most recent year. If a question is written unclearly, however, the resulting data might not be accurate. For example, respondents to an unclear question about income might report partial-year earnings or total household income (perhaps including their parents' or spouse's income as well as their own).

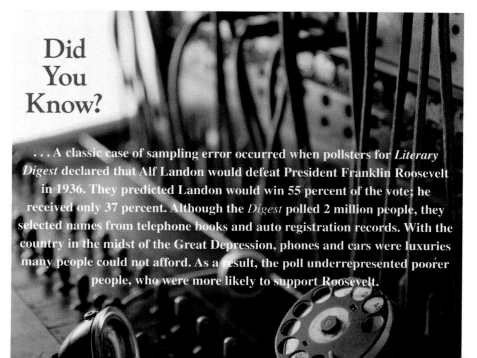

Did You Know?

. . . A classic case of sampling error occurred when pollsters for *Literary Digest* declared that Alf Landon would defeat President Franklin Roosevelt in 1936. They predicted Landon would win 55 percent of the vote; he received only 37 percent. Although the *Digest* polled 2 million people, they selected names from telephone books and auto registration records. With the country in the midst of the Great Depression, phones and cars were luxuries many people could not afford. As a result, the poll underrepresented poorer people, who were more likely to support Roosevelt.

**Reliability** refers to the extent to which a measure produces consistent results. Some people may not disclose accurate information, but most do. In the GSS, only 9 percent of the respondents refused to give their income or indicated they did not know what their income was. That means 91 percent of the respondents gave their income, which we can assume is reasonably accurate (given their responses about occupation and years in the labor force).

## DEVELOPING THE CONCLUSION

Sociological research, like all scientific studies, does not aim to answer all the questions that can be raised about a particular subject. Therefore, the conclusion of a research study represents both an end and a beginning. It terminates one specific phase of the investigation but should also generate ideas for future study.

**Supporting Hypotheses** In our example, we find that the data support our hypothesis: People with more formal schooling do earn more money than those with less schooling. Data consistently show that those with a high school diploma earn more than those who failed to complete high school, that those with some college earn more than do those with just a high school diploma, that those with a college degree earn still more, and on up the line so that those with graduate degrees earn the most. The figure below demonstrates this relationship. Those with a high school diploma or less have a very small portion of the high-income slice of the pie compared to those who have more education.

The relationship is not perfect, however. There are people who have a high school degree or less who end up with high incomes, and there are those with advanced degrees who earn modest incomes. A successful entrepreneur, for example, might not have much formal schooling, while a holder of a doctorate may choose to work for a low-paying, not-for-profit institution. Sociologically speaking, both these findings—that education shapes income and that the relationship is not perfect—are interesting and would likely lead to more questions about how and why such variation occurs.

## SOCthink

> > > While education plays a significant role in explaining income, some people with minimal education earn high incomes, and some with advanced degrees earn relatively little. What additional social factors do you think might help to explain a person's income? What impact might a person's gender, race, ethnicity, religion, age, or social background have on income?

Sociological studies do not always generate data that support the original hypothesis. In many instances, the results refute the hypothesis, and researchers must reformulate their conclusions. This often leads to additional research in which sociologists reexamine their theory and methods, making appropriate changes in their research design.

**validity** The degree to which a measure or scale truly reflects the phenomenon under study.
**reliability** The extent to which a measure produces consistent results.
**control variable** A factor that is held constant to test the relative impact of an independent variable.

**Controlling for Other Factors** Given the complexity of human behavior, it is seldom sufficient to study only the independent and dependent variables. While such analyses can provide us with insight, we also need to consider other causal factors that might influence the dependent variable. One way to do this is to introduce a **control variable,** which is a factor that the researcher holds constant to test the relative impact of an independent variable. For example, if researchers wanted to explain neighborhood crime rates as a dependent variable, they might look at the neighborhood's poverty rate as an independent variable. It is likely, however, that additional factors influence crime rates, so they might introduce familiarity—the degree to which neighbors know and regularly interact with each other—as a control variable. They would find that neighborhoods with a high level of familiarity do have lower crime rates than those with low familiarity rates. The introduction of the control variable allows us to see that some of the variation in neighborhood

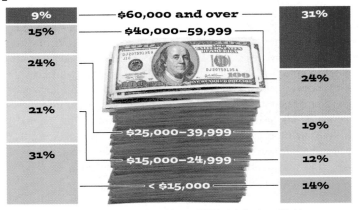

# Impact of a College Education on Income

| High school diploma or less | | Associate's degree or more |
|---|---|---|
| 9% | $60,000 and over | 31% |
| 15% | $40,000–59,999 | |
| 24% | | 24% |
| 21% | $25,000–39,999 | 19% |
| 31% | $15,000–24,999 | 12% |
| | < $15,000 | 14% |

*Source:* Author's analysis of General Social Survey 2006 in J. A. Davis and Smith 2007.

*Fifty-two percent of people with a high school diploma or less (left) earn under $25,000 a year, while only 26 percent earn $40,000 or more. In contrast, 55 percent of those with an associate's degree or higher (right) earn $40,000 or more, while only 26 percent earn less than $25,000.*

crime rates that was initially assumed to be due to poverty is actually due to the influence of the control variable.

In our example, as we have already implied, we might want to control for the effect of additional variables that shape income. Not everyone enjoys equal educational opportunities, a disparity linked to income inequality. What impact does a person's race or gender have? Is a woman with a college degree likely to earn as much as a man with similar schooling? In later chapters, we will consider such additional factors and variables. That is, we will examine the impact that education has on income while controlling for variables such as gender and race.

## SOCthink

> > > What might be the effects, both positive and negative, of a college education on society as a whole? Think of some potential effects on the family, government, and the economy.

## IN SUMMARY:
## THE RESEARCH PROCESS

We began with a general question about the relationship between education and income. By following the steps in the research process—defining the problem, reviewing the literature, formulating a hypothesis, collecting and analyzing data, and developing a conclusion—we were able to show that education does pay. One of the ways we can check the validity of our findings is to share them with sociologists, policy makers, and others in a public forum in the form of a paper at a professional conference or an article in a refereed academic journal. By exposing what we did, how we did it, and what we found, others can serve as a useful check to make sure we did not miss anything and that we proceeded in an appropriate manner.

Research is cyclical in nature. At the end of the process, researchers almost always find that they have more questions they would like to pursue, and most research papers include a specific section addressing how they might define the problem and carry out the research next time. Along the way, researchers may have discovered new concepts they should consider, better ways to ask questions to get the information they need, individuals or groups they should include in the study, or a whole host of other possibilities. In the end, the studies researchers produce become part of the literature review for the next project, whether theirs or someone else's.

research design A detailed plan or method for obtaining data scientifically.
survey A study, generally in the form of an interview or questionnaire, that provides researchers with information about how people think and act.

## >> Major Research Designs

As we have seen, sociologists go about gathering and making sense of the stories of our lives in a variety of ways. Sometimes sociologists want to tell our larger collective story; other times they want to tell the stories of individuals and groups who are often left out of such large-scale accounts. Different research designs are available to tell these different types of stories. For example, large national surveys allow us to get a sense of the national mood about issues such as politics or religion, and statistics can give insight into where we stand in relationship to each other on such issues. To explore the stories of individuals, researchers may employ methods, such as observation, that emphasize more direct and personal interaction with their subjects.

Sociologists draw on a variety of research designs when considering how to collect their data. A **research design** is a detailed plan or method for obtaining data scientifically. Often a research design is based on the theories and hypotheses the researcher starts with (Merton 1948). The choice requires creativity and ingenuity because it directly influences both the cost of the project and the time needed to collect the data. As noted previously, research designs that sociologists regularly use to generate data include surveys, observation, experiments, and existing sources.

## SURVEYS

Almost all of us have responded to surveys of one kind or another. We may have been asked what kind of detergent we use, which presidential candidate we intend to vote for, or what our favorite television program is. A **survey** is a study, generally in the form of an interview or questionnaire, that provides researchers with information about how people think and act. Among the United States' best-known opinion surveys are the Gallup poll and the Harris poll. As anyone who watches the news during presidential campaigns knows, these polls have become a staple of political life.

**Issues in Designing Surveys** As indicated earlier, a survey must be based on precise, representative sampling if it is to genuinely reflect a broad range of the population. We might be skeptical that feedback from just a few hun-

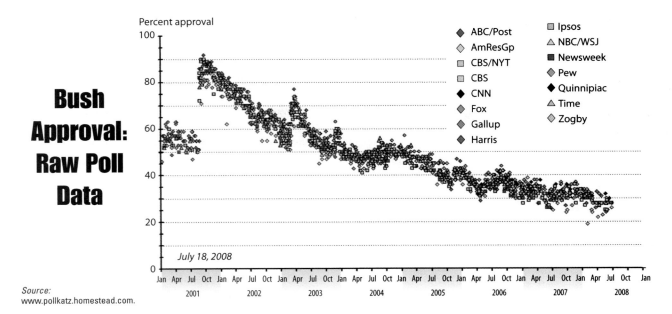

**Bush Approval: Raw Poll Data**

Percent approval

◆ ABC/Post
◇ AmResGp
▢ CBS/NYT
▢ CBS
◆ CNN
◆ Fox
◆ Gallup
◆ Harris
▢ Ipsos
△ NBC/WSJ
▪ Newsweek
◆ Pew
◆ Quinnipiac
△ Time
◇ Zogby

*July 18, 2008*

Jan Apr Jul Oct | Jan Apr Jul Oct | Jan Apr Jul Oct | Jan Apr Jul Oct | Jan Apr Jul Oct | Jan Apr Jul Oct | Jan Apr Jul Oct | Jan
2001 | 2002 | 2003 | 2004 | 2005 | 2006 | 2007 | 2008

Source:
www.pollkatz.homestead.com.

dred people can provide an accurate picture of how 300 million people think, but correctly run surveys can do just that. When it comes to presidential polling, for example, we can compare the results of such polls against actual election results. In a study of the historical accuracy of presidential polls, political scientist Michael W. Traugott (2005) reports that, based on one common measure of assessing results, the polls from 1956 to 2004 were, on average, within 2 percent of accurately predicting the final result. We can also get a sense of the accuracy of polls by looking at "polls of polls" that combine various results into a single report or graph to better see the pattern that the polls collectively demonstrate (see the figure above). Examples of such polls for presidential and congressional approval ratings are available at sites such as www.pollster.com. While the pollsters sometimes fail to "get it right" (for example, predicting that Dewey would defeat Truman in the 1948 presidential election), most often they do, and with amazing precision.

In preparing to conduct a survey, sociologists need not only to develop representative samples but also to exercise great care in the wording of questions. An effective survey question must be simple and clear enough for people to understand. It must also be specific enough that researchers have no

problems interpreting the results. Open-ended questions ("What do you think of the programming on educational television?") must be carefully phrased to solicit the type

*Going* **GLOBAL**

### Why Are We in Iraq?

Researchers can gather information even under difficult circumstances. In a 2006 nationwide survey in Iraq, Iraqis were asked about "the three main reasons for the U.S. invasion of Iraq." A large majority—76 percent—said the United States wanted "to control Iraqi oil." A sizable 41 percent thought the United States' intention was "to build military bases," and almost a third, 32 percent, thought it was "to help Israel." Fewer than 2 percent of the respondents thought the United States went to war "to bring democracy to Iraq."

*Chicago Daily Tribune*
**DEWEY DEFEATS TRUMAN**

of information desired. Surveys can be indispensable sources of information, but only if the sampling is done properly and the questions are worded accurately and without bias.

Studies have also shown that the characteristics of the interviewer have an impact on survey data. For example, female interviewers tend to receive more feminist responses from female subjects than do male researchers, and African American interviewers tend to receive more detailed responses about race-related issues from Black subjects than do White interviewers. The possible impact of gender and race indicates again how much care social research requires (D.W. Davis 1997; Huddy et al. 1997).

**Types of Surveys** There are two main forms of the survey: the **interview,** in which a researcher obtains information through face-to-face or telephone questioning, and the **questionnaire,** in which a researcher uses a printed or written form to obtain information from a respondent. Each of these has its advantages. An interviewer can obtain a higher response rate because people find it more difficult to turn down a personal request for an interview than to throw away a written questionnaire. In addition, a skillful interviewer can go beyond written questions and probe for a subject's underlying feelings and reasons. For their part, questionnaires have the advantage of being cheaper, especially in large samples. Either way, what we can learn from surveys can be amazing.

interview A face-to-face or telephone questioning of a respondent to obtain desired information.
questionnaire A printed or written form used to obtain information from a respondent.
quantitative research Research that collects and reports data primarily in numerical form.
mean A number calculated by adding a series of values and then dividing by the number of values.
median The midpoint, or number that divides a series of values into two groups of equal numbers of values.

Why do people have sex? A straightforward question, but until recently one that rarely was investigated scientifically, despite its significance to public health, marital counseling, and criminology. In an exploratory study published in 2007, researchers surveyed nearly 2000 undergraduates at the University of Texas at Austin. They began phase 1 of the research by asking approximately 400 students in a variety of psychology courses to answer this question: "Please list all the reasons you can think of why you, or someone you have known, has engaged in sexual intercourse in the past." The explanations were highly diverse, ranging from "I was drunk" to "I wanted to feel closer to God."

In phase 2 of the research, the team asked another sample of 1500 students to rate the importance of each of the 287 reasons given by the first group. Nearly every one of the reasons was rated most important by at least some respondents. Although there were some gender differences in the replies, there was significant consensus between men and women on the top 12 reasons (see the table below). Based on their overall results, the researchers identified four major categories of reasons why people have sex: Physical (pleasure, stress reduction), Goal Attainment (social status, revenge), Emotional (love, commitment), and Insecurity (self-esteem boost, duty/pressure) (Meston and Buss 2007). After reviewing the study results, critics argued that the researchers' sample was not sufficiently representative to permit generalizing their findings to the population as a whole. The researchers acknowledged as much from the beginning, having undertaken the project as exploratory research. They have since conducted research using a more representative sample, and their findings were largely the same (Melby 2007).

# Top 12 Reasons Why Men and Women Had Sex

| Men | Reason | Women |
|---|---|---|
| 1 | I was attracted to the person | 1 |
| 2 | It feels good | 3 |
| 3 | I wanted to experience the physical pleasure | 2 |
| 4 | It's fun | 8 |
| 5 | I wanted to show my affection to the person | 4 |
| 6 | I was sexually aroused and wanted the release | 6 |
| 7 | I was "horny" | 7 |
| 8 | I wanted to express my love for the person | 5 |
| 9 | I wanted to achieve an orgasm | 14 |
| 10 | I wanted to please my partner | 11 |
| 17 | I realized I was in love | 9 |
| 13 | I was "in the heat of the moment" | 10 |

Source: Meston and Buss 2007:506.

**Quantitative and Qualitative Research** Surveys most often represent an example of **quantitative research,** which collects and reports data primarily in numerical form. Analysis of these data depends upon statistics, from the simple to the complex, which provide basic summaries describing what variables look like and how they are related. Basic descriptive statistics, such as percentages, are likely familiar. The **mean,** or average, is a number calculated by adding a series of values and then dividing by the number of values. The **median,** or midpoint, is the number that divides a series of values into two groups of equal numbers of values. The median is most often used when there are extreme scores that would distort the mean. The **mode** is the single most common value in a series of scores and is seldom used in sociological research. The mean, median, and mode all seek to provide a single score that is representative of or provides a summary for the whole distribution of scores. When it comes to analyzing relationships between variables, researchers usually rely on computer programs to deal with more complex analysis of quantitative data.

While quantitative research can make use of large samples, it can't offer great depth and detail on a topic. That is why researchers also make use of **qualitative research,** which relies on what they see in field and naturalistic settings, often focusing on small groups and communities rather than on large groups or whole nations. Here, too, sociologists rely on computers to assist their analysis. Numerous software programs allow researchers not only to record observations but to identify common behavioral

**Research is formalized curiosity. It is poking and prying with a purpose.**

Zora Neale Hurston

patterns or concerns expressed in interviews. The most common form of qualitative research is observation.

## OBSERVATION

Investigators who collect information by participating directly and/or by closely watching a group or community are engaged in **observation.** This method allows sociologists to examine certain behaviors and communities that they could not investigate through other research techniques. Though observation may seem a relatively informal method compared to surveys, researchers are careful to take detailed notes while observing their subjects.

An increasingly popular form of qualitative research in sociology today is **ethnography**—the study of an entire social setting through extended systematic observation. Typically, the emphasis is on how the subjects themselves view their social life in some setting. In some cases, the sociologist actually joins the group for a period to get an accurate sense of how it operates. This approach is called *participant observation.*

During the late 1930s, in a classic example of participant observation research, William F. Whyte moved into a low-income Italian neighborhood in Boston. For nearly four years, he was a member of the social circle of "corner boys" whom he described in *Street Corner Society.* Whyte revealed his identity to these men and joined in their conversations, bowling, and other leisure-time activities. His

goal was to gain greater insight into the community that these men had established. As Whyte (1981:303) listened to Doc, the leader of the group, he "learned the answers to questions I would not even have had the sense to ask if I had been getting my information solely on an interviewing basis." Whyte's work was especially valuable since, at the time, the academic world had little direct knowledge of the poor and tended to rely for information on the records of social service agencies, hospitals, and courts (P. Adler et al. 1992).

The initial challenge that Whyte faced—and that every participant observer encounters—was to gain acceptance into an unfamiliar group. It is no simple matter for a college-trained sociologist to win the trust of a religious cult, a youth gang, a poor Appalachian community, or a circle of skid row residents. It requires a great deal of patience and an accepting, nonthreatening type of personality on the part of the observer.

Observation research poses other complex challenges for investigators. Sociologists must be able to fully understand what they are observing. In a sense, then, researchers

**mode** The single most common value in a series of scores.
**qualitative research** Research that relies on what is seen in field or naturalistic settings more than on statistical data.
**observation** A research technique in which an investigator collects information through direct participation and/or by closely watching a group or community.
**ethnography** The study of an entire social setting through extended systematic observation.

must learn to see the world as the group sees it in order to fully comprehend the events taking place around them.

## SOCthink

> > > What social group or context (such as a religious group, political organization, sorority/fraternity, laboratory, or office) might you want to learn more about through in-depth participant observation? How would you go about making contact? How would you gain members' trust?

This raises a delicate issue. If the research is to be successful, the observer cannot allow the close associations or even friendships that inevitably develop to influence the subjects' behavior or the conclusions of the study. Anson Shupe and David Bromley (1980), two sociologists who have used participant observation, have likened this challenge to that of walking a tightrope. Even while working hard to gain acceptance from the group being studied, the participant observer *must* maintain some degree of detachment.

Recently, the issue of detachment became a controversial one for social scientists embedded with the U.S. military in Afghanistan and Iraq. Among other studies, the researchers participated in the creation of the Army's Human Terrain System, a $4-million effort to identify the customs, kinship structures, and internal social conflicts in the two countries. The intention was to provide military leaders with information that would help them make better decisions. Although the idea of scholars cooperating in any way with soldiers struck many social science researchers as inappropriate, others countered that the information they developed would help the military to avoid needless violence and might even facilitate the withdrawal of troops from the region (Glenn 2007).

**experiment** An artificially created situation that allows a researcher to manipulate variables.

**experimental group** The subjects in an experiment who are exposed to an independent variable introduced by a researcher.

**control group** The subjects in an experiment who are not introduced to the independent variable by the researcher.

**Hawthorne effect** The unintended influence that observers of experiments can have on their subjects.

**secondary analysis** A variety of research techniques that make use of previously collected and publicly accessible information and data.

## From Me to You

Students in my sociology of religion course must conduct a semester-long research project on a religious group that is unlike their own. Combining observation and surveys, they must visit the group's religious services numerous times and interview both leaders and followers. At first, students are nervous about making first contact, concerned about what kind of people they might find, and worried that the group will try to convert them. By the end, however, they typically come away with a sense of respect for the believers, glad to have had the opportunity to get to know them. While research can seem scary, give it a try. It provides a pathway to greater knowledge and understanding..

**NEWFOUND RESPECT**

sociologists tend not to use them as frequently as the other research designs, because they are typically more interested in understanding people's natural responses.

The classic experimental design selects two groups of people and matches them on similar characteristics, such as age or education. The researchers then assign the subjects to one of two groups: the experimental or the control group. The **experimental group** is exposed to an independent variable; the **control group** is not. Thus, if scientists were testing a new type of antibiotic, they would administer the drug to an experimental group but not to a control group.

One of the disadvantages of experiments, just as in observation research, is that the presence of a social scientist or other observer may affect the behavior of the people being studied. The recognition of this phenomenon grew out

## EXPERIMENTS

When scientists want to study a possible cause-and-effect relationship, they conduct an **experiment**—an artificially created situation that allows a researcher to manipulate variables. Researchers carefully control the experimental context in order to measure the degree to which the independent variable causes change in the dependent variable

## SOCthink

> > > Imagine you are a researcher interested in the effect TV watching has on schoolchildren's grades. How might you go about setting up an experiment to measure this effect?

of an experiment conducted during the 1920s and 1930s at the Hawthorne plant of the Western Electric Company. A group of researchers set out to determine how to improve the productivity of workers at the plant. The investigators manipulated such variables as lighting and working hours to see what impact the changes would have on productivity. To their surprise, they found that every step they took seemed to increase productivity. Even measures that seemed likely to have the opposite effect, such as reducing the amount of lighting in the plant, led to higher productivity.

Why did the plant's employees work harder even under less favorable conditions? The researchers concluded that the worker's modified their behavior because they knew they were being studied. They responded positively to the novelty of being subjects in an experiment and to the fact that researchers were interested in them. Since that time, sociologists have used the term **Hawthorne effect** to describe the unintended influence that observers of experiments can have on their subjects (S. Jones 1992; Lang 1992; Pelton 1994). It highlights the difficulties experiments present in seeking to understand how people behave in their real-world environments.

Sociologists do sometimes try to approximate experimental conditions in the field. Sociologist Devah Pager (2003) devised an experiment to assess the impact of a criminal background on individuals' employment opportunities. She sent four polite, well-dressed young men out to look for an entry-level job in Milwaukee, Wisconsin. All four were 23-year-old college students, but they presented themselves as high school graduates with similar job histories. Two of the men were Black and two were White. One Black applicant and one White applicant claimed to have served 18 months in jail for a felony

## White Privilege in Job Seeking

Percent chance of getting a call back

White — No criminal record — 34%

17% Criminal record

Black — No criminal record — 14%

5% Criminal record

*Source:* Pager 2003:958.

conviction—possession of cocaine with intent to distribute.

The experiences of the four men with 350 potential employers were vastly different. The White applicant with a purported prison record received only half as many callbacks as the other White applicant—17 percent compared to 34 percent (see the graphic above). But as dramatic as the effect of his criminal record was, the effect of his race was more significant. Despite his prison record, he received slightly more callbacks than the Black applicant with no criminal record (17 percent compared to 14 percent). Race, it seems, was more of a concern to potential employers than a criminal background.

## USE OF EXISTING SOURCES

Sociologists do not necessarily need to collect new data in order to conduct research and test hypotheses. The term **secondary analysis** refers to a variety of research techniques that make use of previously collected and publicly accessible information and data. Generally, in conducting secondary analysis, researchers use data in ways that were unintended by the initial collectors of the informa-

# What's in a Name?

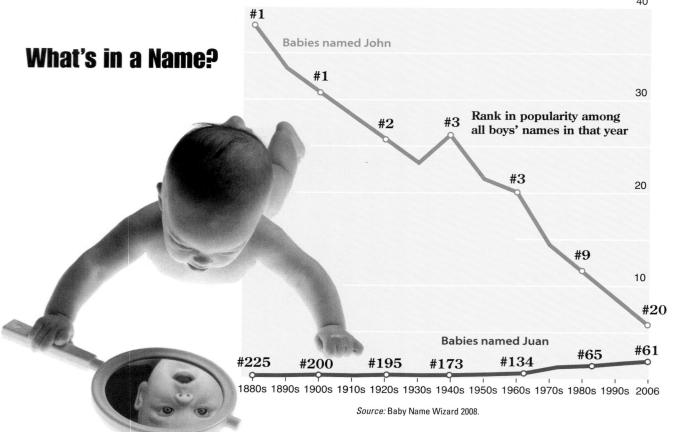

Number of babies (thousands)

Babies named John — #1, #1, #2, #3, #3, #9, #20

Rank in popularity among all boys' names in that year

Babies named Juan — #225, #200, #195, #173, #134, #65, #61

1880s 1890s 1900s 1910s 1920s 1930s 1940s 1950s 1960s 1970s 1980s 1990s 2006

*Source:* Baby Name Wizard 2008.

## SOCthink

> > > "NameVoyager" at www.babynamewizard.com is a very cool application that allows you to type in any name to trace its popularity over time. Go there and enter several names to see how they have changed over time. Considering some of the specific names you tried, what factors might have contributed to their rise and fall? How popular is your first name? How and why has its popularity changed over time?

tion. For example, the federal government compiles census data for its own specific uses, but marketing specialists also find the data valuable for locating everything from bicycle stores to nursing homes.

Sociologists can learn a great deal using available information. For example, every year the Social Security Administration receives thousands of registrations for newborn babies. Using these data, we can recognize shifts in cultural trends in the population. As the figure "What's in a Name?" shows, for example, John has been an extremely popular boy's name for over a century. In 2006, over 5000 babies were named John, making it the 20th most popular name that year. Though only about half as many babies were named Juan in 2006, that name has been gaining in popularity in recent generations, reflect-

## Major Research Designs

| Method | Examples | Advantages | Limitations |
|---|---|---|---|
| Survey | Questionnaires Interviews | Yields information about specific issues | Can be expensive and time-consuming |
| Observation | Ethnography | Yields detailed information about specific groups or organizations | Involves months if not years of labor-intensive data collection |
| Experiment | Deliberate manipulation of people's social behavior | Yields direct measures of people's behavior | Has ethical limitations on the degree to which subjects' behavior can be manipulated |
| Existing sources/ Secondary analysis | Analysis of census or health data Analysis of films or TV commercials | Cost-efficiency | Limited to data collected for some other purpose |

In examining these sources, researchers employ a technique known as **content analysis**—the systematic coding and objective recording of data, guided by a given rationale.

> **content analysis** The systematic coding and objective recording of data, guided by some rationale.

Using content analysis, Erving Goffman (1979) conducted a pioneering exploration of how advertisements portray women. The ads he studied typically showed women as subordinate to or dependent on others, or as taking instruction from men. Women engaged in caressing and touching gestures more than men. Even when presented in leadership roles, women were likely to be shown striking seductive poses or gazing out into space.

## You can observe a lot by just watching.

Yogi Berra

ing the growing impact of the Latino population in the United States.

Existing data from another source confirms this shift. Analysis of data released by the U.S. Census Bureau tracking people's family names in 2007 revealed that although Smith remained the most common surname in the United States, Garcia and Rodriguez had risen into the top 10. The announcement marked the first time in the nation's history that a non-Anglo name had been counted among the most common names. Such name changes reflect an overall shift in the U.S. population from a nation comprised primarily of European descendants to one that is more globally diverse, a trend sociologists expect will continue (Baby Name Wizard 2008; Levitt and Dubner 2005; Lieberson 2000; Word et al. 2007).

Part of the appeal of secondary analysis to sociologists is that it is nonreactive—that is, doing this type of study does not influence what you find. For example, Émile Durkheim's statistical analysis of existing suicide data neither increased nor decreased human self-destruction. Researchers, then, can avoid the Hawthorne effect by using secondary analysis. However, there is one inherent problem: The researcher who relies on data collected by someone else may not find exactly what he or she needs. Social scientists who are studying family violence can use statistics from police and social service agencies on reported cases of spouse abuse and child abuse, but how many cases are not reported? Government bodies have no precise data on all cases of abuse.

Secondary analysis also allows us to study social contexts, both present and past, through careful analysis of cultural, economic, and political documents, including newspapers, periodicals, radio and television tapes, the Internet, scripts, diaries, songs, folklore, and legal papers.

Today researchers who analyze film content are finding an increase in smoking in motion pictures, despite heightened public health concerns. Research studying television programs demonstrates that sexual content on TV continues to rise (see the figure below). Other researchers have

## Percentage of Television Shows That Contain Sexual Content

*Source:* Kaiser Family Foundation 2005:4.

found a growing difference in the way men and women use sexually explicit language. For example, an analysis of the lyrics of *Billboard* magazine's top 100 hits indicates that, since 1958, male artists have increased their use of such language while female artists have decreased theirs (American Lung Association 2003; Dukes et al. 2003). In all such cases, content analysis allows us a better understanding of our cultural practices.

## >> Research Ethics

A biochemist cannot inject a drug into a human being unless the drug has been thoroughly tested and the subject agrees to the shot. To do otherwise would be both unethical and illegal. Sociologists, too, must abide by certain specific standards in conducting research, called a **code of ethics.** The professional society of the discipline, the American Sociological Association (ASA), first published its *Code of Ethics* in 1971 and revised it most recently in 1997. It puts forth the following basic principles:

*Content analysis of popular song lyrics shows that over the last 50 years, top female artists such as Beyoncé Knowles have used fewer sexually explicit words, while male artists like Jay-Z have used more.*

## POPSOC

Sociologists Stephen J. Scanlan and Seth L. Feinberg suggest that we can better understand key sociological concepts by analyzing the *The Simpsons*. One example they provide, among many, is the episode "Lisa vs. Malibu Stacy," in which eight-year-old Lisa is outraged because her talking doll says things like, "Let's buy makeup so the boys will like us." They say this raises sociological issues related to gender socialization, inequality, consumerism, and more. Additional issues raised in other episodes include social class, deviance, education, marriage and family, and religion. What might we learn about society by analyzing popular culture through the lens of sociology?

- Maintain objectivity and integrity in research.
- Respect the subject's right to privacy and dignity.
- Protect subjects from personal harm.
- Preserve confidentiality.
- Seek informed consent when data are collected from research participants or when behavior occurs in a private context.
- Acknowledge research collaboration and assistance.
- Disclose all sources of financial support.

Because most sociological research uses people as sources of information—as respondents to survey questions, subjects of observation, or participants in experiments—these principles are important. In all cases, sociologists need to be certain they are not invading their subjects' privacy. Generally, they do so by assuring subjects of anonymity or by guaranteeing the confidentiality of personal information. In addition, research proposals that involve human subjects are now subject to oversight by a review board, whose members seek to ensure that the research does not place subjects at an unreasonable level of risk. If necessary, the board may ask researchers to revise their research designs to conform to the *Code of Ethics.*

These basic principles and procedures may seem clear-cut in the abstract but can be difficult to adhere to in practice. For example, should a sociologist who is engaged in participant observation research always protect the confidentiality of subjects? What if the subjects are members of a group involved in unethical or illegal activities? What if the sociologist is interviewing political activists and is questioned by government authorities about the research?

## CONFIDENTIALITY

Like journalists, sociologists occasionally find themselves facing the ethical dilemma of whether to reveal their sources to law enforcement authorities. In May 1993, sociologist Rik Scarce was jailed for contempt of court because he declined to tell a federal grand jury what he knew—or even whether he knew anything—about a 1991 raid on a university research laboratory by animal rights activists. At the time, Scarce was doing research for a book about environmental protestors and knew at least one suspect in the break-in. Although he was chastised by a federal judge, Scarce won respect from fellow prison inmates, who regarded him as a man who "wouldn't snitch" (Monaghan 1993:A8).

**Hot or Not?**

Should researchers sometimes deceive subjects, even if it might result in their emotional harm, in order to get more genuine responses?

The ASA, in defense of the principle of confidentiality, supported Scarce's position when he appealed his sentence. Scarce maintained his silence. Ultimately, the judge ruled that nothing would be gained by further incarceration, and Scarce was released after spending 159 days in jail. The U.S. Supreme Court ultimately declined to hear Scarce's case on appeal. The Court's failure to consider his case led Scarce (1994, 1995, 2005) to argue that federal legislation is needed to clarify the right of scholars and members of the press to preserve the confidentiality of those they interview.

## RESEARCH FUNDING

Disclosing all the sources of funding for a study is the final principle of the ASA's *Code of Ethics,* but it is not a sufficient guarantee of ethical conduct. Accepting funds from a private organization or even a government agency that stands to benefit from a study's results can clash with the ASA's first principle of maintaining objectivity and integrity in research. The previously mentioned controversy surrounding the involvement of social scientists in the U.S. Army's Human Terrain System is one example of this conflict of interest.

> **code of ethics** The standards of acceptable behavior developed by and for members of a profession.

Another example is the Exxon Corporation's support for research on jury verdicts. On March 24, 1989, the Exxon oil tanker *Valdez* hit a reef off the coast of Alaska, spilling over 11 million gallons of oil into Prince William Sound. Two decades later, the *Valdez* disaster is still regarded as the world's worst oil spill in terms of its environmental impact. In 1994, a federal court ordered Exxon to pay $5.3 billion in damages for the accident. Exxon appealed the verdict and began approaching legal scholars, sociologists, and psychologists who might be willing to study jury deliberations. The corporation's objective was to develop academic support for its lawyers' contention that the punitive judgments in such cases result from faulty deliberations and do not deter future incidents.

Some scholars have questioned the propriety of accepting funds under these circumstances, even if the source is disclosed. The scholars who accepted Exxon's support deny that it influenced their work or changed their conclusions. To date, Exxon has spent roughly $1 million on the research, and at least one compilation of studies congenial to the corporation's point of view has been published. As ethical considerations require, the academics who conducted the studies disclosed Exxon's role in funding the research. In 2006, drawing on these studies, Exxon's law-

Some sociologists believe that neutrality is impossible. They worry that Weber's insistence on value-free sociology may lead the public to accept sociological conclusions without exploring researchers' biases. Others have suggested that sociologists may use objectivity as a justification for remaining uncritical of existing institutions and centers of power (Gouldner 1970). Despite the early work of W. E. B. Du Bois and Jane Addams, sociologists still need to be reminded that the discipline often fails to adequately consider all people's social behavior.

> ## If we knew what it was we were doing, it would not be called research, would it?
>
> Albert Einstein

yers succeeded in persuading an appeals court to reduce the corporation's legal damages from $5.3 to $2.5 billion (Associated Press 2007; Freudenburg 2005). Then, in 2008, the amount was reduced to a mere $500 million.

## VALUE NEUTRALITY

The ethical considerations of sociologists lie not only in the methods they use and the funding they accept but in the way they interpret their results. Max Weber ([1904] 1949) recognized that personal values would influence the topics that sociologists select for research. In his view, that was perfectly acceptable, but he argued that researchers should not allow their personal feelings to influence the interpretation of data. In Weber's phrase, sociologists must practice **value neutrality** in their research.

**value neutrality** Max Weber's term for objectivity of sociologists in the interpretation of data.

As part of this neutrality, investigators have an ethical obligation to accept research findings even when the data run counter to their own personal views, to theoretically based explanations, or to widely accepted beliefs. For example, Émile Durkheim challenged popular conceptions when he reported that social (rather than supernatural) forces were an important factor in suicide.

Sociologists should not focus only on those in the majority but must also seek out the stories of those who are often invisible due to their relative lack of power and resources. In her book *The Death of White Sociology* (1973), Joyce Ladner called attention to the tendency of mainstream sociologists to investigate the lives of African Americans in the context of social problems. More recently, feminist sociologist Shulamit Reinharz (1992) has argued that sociological research should be not only inclusive but open to drawing on relevant research by nonsociologists who might provide additional depth and understanding of social life. Both Reinharz and Ladner maintain that researchers should always analyze whether women's unequal social status has affected their studies in any way. For example, we might broaden the study of the impact of education on income to consider the implications of the unequal pay status of men and women. The issue of value neutrality does not mean that sociologists can't have opinions, but it does mean that they must work to overcome any biases, however unintentional, that they may bring to their analysis of research.

## FEMINIST METHODOLOGY

Although researchers must be objective, their theoretical orientation necessarily influences the questions they ask—or just as important, the questions they fail to ask. Because their contributions have opened up so many new lines of inquiry, sociologists using the feminist perspective have had perhaps the greatest impact on the current generation of social researchers. Until recently, for example, researchers frequently studied work and family separately, as if they were two discrete institutions. Feminist theorists, however, reject the notion that these are separate spheres. They were the first sociologists to look at housework as real work and to investigate the struggles people face in balancing the demands of work and family (Hochschild 1989; Lopata 1971).

## SOCthink

> > > Is it possible to maintain value neutrality when studying a social group with which you might disagree (such as White supremacists or convicted child molesters)? Why might sociologists choose to study such groups?

Feminist theorists have also drawn attention to researchers' tendency to overlook women in sociological studies. For most of the history of sociology, researchers conducted studies of male subjects or male-led groups and organizations, then generalized their findings to all people. For many decades, for example, ethnographic studies of urban life focused on street corners, neighborhood taverns, and bowling alleys—places where men typically congregated. Although researchers gained some valuable insights in this way, they did not form a true impression of city life, because they overlooked the areas where women were likely to gather, such as playgrounds, grocery stores, and front stoops. These are the arenas that the feminist perspective focuses on.

Feminist scholars have also contributed to a greater global awareness within sociology. To feminist theorists, the traditional distinction between industrial nations and developing countries overlooks the close relationship between these two supposedly separate worlds. Feminist theorists have called for more research on the special role that immigrant women play in maintaining their households, on the use of domestic workers from less developed nations by households in industrial countries, and on the global trafficking of sex workers (Cheng 2003; Cooper et al. 2007; Sprague 2005).

Finally, feminist researchers tend to involve and consult their subjects more than other researchers, contributing to a significant increase in more qualitative and participatory research. They are also more oriented toward seeking change, raising the public consciousness, and influencing policy, which represents a return to sociology's roots (Baker 1999; Lofland 1975; Reinharz 1992).

Sociologists must be engaged with the world. While there are numerous ways in which they accomplish this, first and foremost this involvement comes through research. As we have seen throughout this chapter, it is not enough for sociologists to stand back and theorize or even hypothesize about why we think and act the way we do. We must go out, collect data, and use it to inform our interpretations and explanations of human behavior. Having done so, we bear a responsibility for that knowledge, whether that means simply sharing it with other sociologists through conference presentations and journal articles or actively working for positive social change.

# For REVIEW

I.  **What steps do sociologists take when seeking to answer why people think and act the way they do?**
    - They need to define the problem, review existing literature, formulate a hypothesis, collect and analyze data, and develop a conclusion.

II. **What techniques do they use to collect data?**
    - Research designs used to collect data include surveys, observation, experiments, and use of existing sources.

III. **What ethical concerns must they consider while conducting research?**
    - They have a responsibility to follow the ASA Code of Ethics, particularly respecting confidentiality, revealing research funding, maintaining value neutrality, and overall, treating their subjects with respect.

## Pop Quiz

1.  The first step in any sociological research project is to
    a. collect data.
    b. define the problem.
    c. review previous research.
    d. formulate a hypothesis.

2.  An explanation of an abstract concept that is specific enough to allow a researcher to measure the concept is a(n)
    a. hypothesis.
    b. correlation.
    c. operational definition.
    d. variable.

3.  The variable hypothesized to cause or influence another is called the
    a. dependent variable.
    b. hypothetical variable.
    c. correlation variable.
    d. independent variable.

4.  A correlation exists when
    a. one variable causes something to occur in another variable.
    b. two or more variables are causally related.
    c. a change in one variable coincides with a change in another variable.
    d. a negative relationship exists between two variables.

5.  Through which type of research technique does a sociologist ensure that data are statistically representative of the population being studied?
    a. sampling
    b. experiments
    c. validity
    d. control variables

6.  In order to obtain a random sample, a researcher might
    a. administer a questionnaire to every fifth woman who enters a business office.
    b. examine the attitudes of residents of a city by interviewing every 20th name in the city's telephone book.
    c. study the attitudes of registered Democratic voters by choosing every 10th name found on a city's list of registered Democrats.
    d. do all of the above.

7.  A researcher can obtain a higher response rate by using which type of survey?
    a. an interview
    b. a questionnaire
    c. representative samples
    d. observation techniques

8.  In the 1930s, William F. Whyte moved into a low-income Italian neighborhood in Boston. For nearly four years, he was a member of the social circle of "corner boys" whom he describes in *Street Corner*

1 (b); 2 (c); 3 (d); 4 (c); 5 (a); 6 (c); 7 (a);

*Society.* His goal was to gain greater insight into the community established by these men. What type of research technique did Whyte use?

a. experiment
b. survey
c. secondary analysis
d. participant observation

9. When sociologists want to study a possible cause-and-effect relationship, they may engage in what kind of research design?

a. ethnography
b. survey research
c. secondary analysis
d. experimental research

10. Émile Durkheim's statistical analysis of suicide was an example of what kind of research technique?

a. ethnography
b. observation research
c. secondary analysis
d. experimental research

8 (d); 9 (d); 10 (c)

**3**

# CULTURE

# BREAKING RULES AND LOWERING BARRIERS

**Juan Mann was depressed. His fiancée had left him. His parents had just divorced. He had dropped out of college, and his friends had scattered. He felt all alone in the world.** So on Wednesday, June 30, 2004, he decided to do something different. He took a homemade sign to the Pitt Street Mall in Sydney, Australia, that said "Free Hugs." Someone at a party had given him his first hug in a long time, and it had brightened his day. He figured that if he needed a hug like that more than he even knew, there were probably many other people out there feeling similarly isolated who might want one too. Every Thursday he would head back to the mall to offer more. Before long, with the help of a viral video on the Internet, Juan's "Free Hugs Campaign" went global with over 25 million views on YouTube alone. People were not just watching the video; in many countries and in many languages, they were making their own signs and heading out to a public place to offer hugs. (A YouTube or Google image search on "free hugs" will turn up the original video along with many other videos and images of people from around the world who were inspired by it.)

One of the interesting things about this movement is that it calls for us to go outside our comfort zones and act in ways that are not "normal." As children we are told not to talk to strangers, much less hug them. If we see a stranger offering a hug, we wonder if something suspicious is up. We have rules about such things—laws even. When people do things differently, we get nervous. It disrupts our sense of order. We want and need the actions of others to be predictable, so we create both formal and informal rules to guide our behaviors. Such rules are part of culture.

But culture is not set in stone. We create it, and we therefore have the power to change it. People doing new things, stepping outside the lines of expected behavior, is precisely how change happens. So, when confronted with the offer "Free Hugs," we face a choice: Act like the majority of people who pass free huggers by, thus reaffirming expected behaviors, or seize the opportunity to do the unexpected, thereby creating new pathways for us to follow. It is in such moments that new culture is born.

# As You READ

>>

- Why do humans create culture?
- What does culture consist of?
- How does culture both enable and constrain?

## >> Culture and Society

We need culture. As humans, we lack the complex instincts other species are born with that enable them to survive. Unlike birds, for example, our genes do not provide us with the knowledge of how to build nests (or homes) for ourselves, and we lack the good sense to fly to warmer climates for the winter. In place of such instincts, we construct culture through which we establish relationships both to the natural world and with each other. **Culture** consists of the totality of our shared language, knowledge, material objects, and behavior.

> **culture** The totality of our shared language, knowledge, material objects, and behavior.

Culture shapes our perception, knowledge, and understanding of the external world. While our senses experience the external world in a physical way, we must interpret the meaning and significance of those sensations. We do not perceive nature directly; we perceive the world around us through the lens of culture. Our retinas may send visual images to our brains, but recognition comes only through culture. We see this at work with optical illusions: We can look at the same thing over and over, but it is not until someone says to us, "No, look at it this way" that we recognize it.

### SOCthink

> > > Something as seemingly simple as reading these words relies on taken-for-granted cultural knowledge. What cultural knowledge does reading this chapter take for granted?

Culture thus provides us with a kind of tool kit of habits, skills, and styles (Swidler 1986). It allows us to take for granted that others will understand what we mean, and it helps make it possible for us to get what we want. Shared culture simplifies day-to-day interactions. For example, if we buy a big-ticket item such as an airline ticket, a plasma television, or a computer, we take for granted that we do not have to bring along hundreds or thousands of dollars in cash; we can pay with a credit card. In a similar vein, we assume that theaters will provide seats for the audience, physicians will not disclose confidential information, and parents will be careful when crossing the street with young children. All these assumptions reflect basic values, beliefs, and customs of our culture.

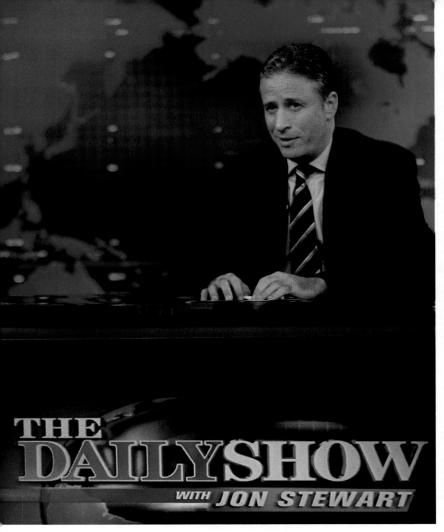

Because our culture represents the core of who we are, including our knowledge, values, beliefs, rules for behavior, and more, we seek both to preserve it and to pass it along to others. We preserve it through literature, art, video recordings, and other means of expression. We pass it along in families, through mass media, among peers, and, more formally, at school, investing substantial amounts of resources to do so. Were it not for the social transmission of culture, each generation would have to start from scratch, reinventing not just the wheel but all other forms of culture as well.

While it is through culture that we establish a relationship to the external world, society provides the context within which those relationships develop. **Society** consists of the structure of relationships within which culture is cre-

ated and shared through regularized patterns of social interaction. How we structure society constrains the kind of culture we construct. Some ways of thinking, acting, and making are more acceptable, while others may not even be recognized as possible. People often confront this reality when they travel abroad and find their taken-for-granted ideas and actions to be out of place and inappropriate.

Cultural preferences vary across societies. Educational methods, marriage ceremonies, religious doctrines, and other aspects of culture are learned and transmitted through human interaction within specific societies. Parents in India are accustomed to arranging marriages for their children; in the United States parents typically leave marital decisions up to their children. Lifelong residents of Cairo consider it natural to speak Arabic; lifelong residents of Buenos Aires feel the same way about Spanish.

## >> The Development of Culture Around the World

Through our creation of culture, we have come a long way from our prehistoric heritage. The human species has managed to produce such achievements as novels by Doris Lessing, paintings by Picasso, poems by Langston Hughes, and films such as *Schindler's List*. We now take for granted what once seemed impossible, from air travel, to the cloning of cells, to organ transplants. We can peer into the outermost reaches of the universe or analyze our innermost feelings. In all these ways, our cultural creativity sets us apart as remarkably different from other species of the animal kingdom.

### CULTURAL UNIVERSALS

Given that we have a certain amount of freedom to construct culture in a multitude of ways, one of the early sociological questions was whether there are any aspects of culture shared by all people. Some sociologists sought to discover whether there are fundamental laws of society, equivalent to long-known laws of nature. Such patterns were referred to as **cultural universals**—common practices and beliefs shared by all societies. What this search revealed was that components of culture can be called universal only if they are expressed in the most general terms. Many cultural universals are, in fact, adaptations to meet essential human needs, such as the need for food, shelter, and clothing. Anthropologist George Murdock's (1945:124) list of cultural universals included sports, cooking, funeral ceremonies, medicine, marriage, and sexual restrictions.

> **society** The structure of relationships within which culture is created and shared through regularized patterns of social interaction.
>
> **cultural universal** A common practice or belief shared by all societies.

**SOC**think

> > > How does social context influence how we relate to others? If you were talking about how school is going, how might you respond differently at home with your parents as compared to in a dorm with friends or at work with colleagues?

The foods people eat, and the customs around eating and preparation of food, reflect their culture as well as their economic circumstances.

The ways in which different groups address these human needs vary significantly. One group may not allow marriage between first cousins while another encourages it. Not only does the expression of cultural universals vary from one society to another, but it can change dramatically over time.

**Sociobiology** is a discipline committed to the systematic study of how biology affects human social behavior; it looks at cultural universals from a biological perspective. Sociobiologists argue that our thoughts and actions as a species can ultimately be explained through our genes and our biological makeup. While most sociologists would agree that our biology can certainly influence our social behavior, the degree of variability within and between societies suggests that sociobiological theories are limited as a means to explain complex human behavior.

**sociobiology** The systematic study of how biology affects human social behavior.

**innovation** The process of introducing a new idea or object to a culture through discovery or invention.

Part of the reason sociologists are suspicious of biological explanations for human behavior is the fact that such claims have been used in the past to justify inequality—claims that were later revealed to be scientifically untrue. For example, it was once thought that women were not capable of success in college because their brains were too small and their uterus made them too emotional. Over time we learned that such presuppositions are false—women now make up almost 60 percent of college graduates—but at one time they were accepted as "natural" and therefore resistant to change. One of the lessons we learn about culture throughout human history is that variety and change are the norm.

## INNOVATION

Humans have the ability to create new things. A robin's nest in the year 2009 looks very much like one in 1999 or 999 because robins act on a nest-building instinct. Human abodes, however, vary widely—we can live in a cave, a castle, a sod house, a pueblo, a high-rise apartment, a McMansion, or a dorm room. Such variation is possible because we are free to innovate. **Innovation**—the process of introducing a new idea or object to a culture—interests sociologists because it can have ripple effects across a society.

## SOCthink

> > > How has the invention of the microscope changed our lives (including our lifespan) and therefore our communities? How has the personal computer changed the way we interact?

There are two main forms of innovation: discovery and invention. **Discovery** involves making known or sharing the existence of an aspect of reality. The finding of the DNA molecule and the identification of a new moon of Saturn are both acts of discovery. A significant factor in the process of discovery is the sharing of newfound knowledge with others. By contrast, an **invention** results when existing cultural items are combined into a form that did not exist before. The bow and arrow, the automobile, and the television are all examples of inventions, as are abstract concepts such as Protestantism and democracy.

# Going GLOBAL

## Communication, Corporations, and Consumerism

Communication, corporations, and consumerism combine to spread particular cultural preferences around the globe. What are the consequences of such diffusion for local cultures around the world?

## GLOBALIZATION AND DIFFUSION

Cultural innovation can be highly globalized in today's world. Imagine walking into Starbucks with its familiar green logo and ordering a decaf latte and a cinnamon ring—only this Starbucks happens to be located in the heart of Beijing's Forbidden City, just outside the Palace of Heavenly Purity, former residence of Chinese emperors. The first Starbucks in mainland China opened in 1999, and by 2008 there were more than 300, with 65 stores in Beijing alone. The success of Starbucks in a country in which coffee drinking is still a novelty (most Chinese are tea drinkers) has been striking (*China Daily* 2004).

The emergence of Starbucks in China demonstrates the cultural impact of globalization. Starbucks' expansion affects not only coffee consumption patterns but also the international trade in coffee beans, which are harvested mainly in developing countries. Our consumption-oriented culture supports a retail price of two to three dollars for a single cup of premium coffee. At the same time, the price of coffee beans on the world market has fallen so low that millions of farmers around the world can barely eke out a living. Worldwide, the growing demand for coffee, tea, chocolate, fruit, and other natural resources is straining the environment, as poor farmers in developing countries clear more and more forestland to enlarge their fields.

> **discovery** The process of making known or sharing the existence of an aspect of reality.
>
> **invention** The combination of existing cultural items into a form that did not exist before.
>
> **diffusion** The process by which a cultural item spreads from group to group or society to society.

Even as people in Asia have begun to drink coffee, people in North America have discovered the Japanese cuisine known as sushi. More and more cultural expressions and practices are crossing national borders and influencing the traditions and customs of the societies exposed to them. Sociologists use the term **diffusion** to refer to the process by which some aspect of culture spreads from group to group or society to society. Historically, diffusion typically occurred through a variety of means, including exploration, war, military conquest, and missionary work. Today, societal boundaries that were once relatively closed due to the constraints of transportation and communication have become more permeable, with cross-cultural exchange occurring more quickly. Through the mass media, the Internet, immigration, and tourism, we regularly confront the people, beliefs, practices, and artifacts of other cultures.

Diffusion often comes at a cost. In practice, globalization has led to the cultural domination of developing nations by more affluent nations. In these encounters, people in developed nations often pick and choose the cultural practices they find intriguing or exotic, while people in developing nations often lose their traditional values and begin to identify with the culture of the dominant nations. They may discard or neglect their native language and dress, attempting to imitate the icons of mass-market entertainment and fashion. In this way Western popular culture represents a threat to native cultures. As Sembene Ousmane, one of Africa's most prominent writers and filmmakers, noted, "[Today] we are more familiar with European fairy tales than with our own traditional stories" (World Development Forum 1990:4). So something is gained and something is lost through diffusion, and often it is the poorer societies that sacrifice more of their culture.

**material culture** The physical or technological aspects of our daily lives.

**nonmaterial culture** Ways of using material objects, as well as customs, ideas, expressions, beliefs, knowledge, philosophies, governments, and patterns of communication.

**technology** "Cultural information about how to use the material resources of the environment to satisfy human needs and desires."

## >> Elements of Culture

To better understand how culture operates, it is helpful to distinguish among its different forms. A simple twofold model of culture was proposed by sociologist William F. Ogburn (1922). He drew a line between material and nonmaterial culture. **Material culture** refers to the physical or technological aspects of our daily lives, including food, houses, factories, and raw materials. **Nonmaterial culture** refers to ways of using material objects and to customs, ideas, expressions, beliefs, knowledge, philosophies, governments, and patterns of communica-

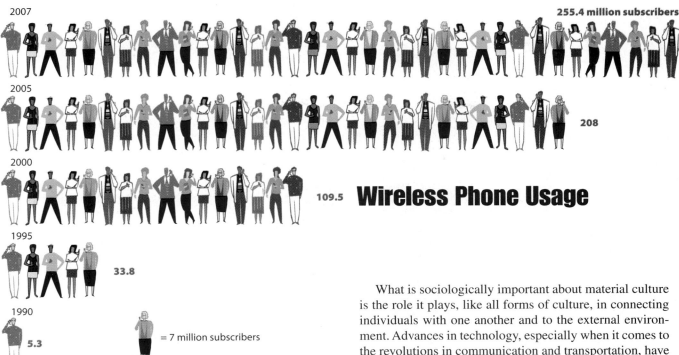

2007                                                    **255.4 million subscribers**

2005                                            **208**

2000                                    **109.5**

1995

**33.8**

1990

**5.3**        = 7 million subscribers

1985
0.3

*Technology makes it possible for us to keep in touch with almost anyone anywhere, as these numbers showing the explosion in the number of wireless phone subscribers since 1985 demonstrates.*

*Source:* http://files.ctia.org/pdf/CTIA_Survey_Year_End_2007_Graphics.pdf.

tion. While this simple division is helpful, the concept of nonmaterial culture is so inclusive that we break it down into four key components: language, values, norms, and sanctions.

## MATERIAL CULTURE AND TECHNOLOGY

It is easy to underestimate the degree to which we live in a humanly constructed world. Even for those of us who live close to nature, material culture is everywhere. It includes the clothes we wear, the books we read, the chairs we sit in, the carpets we walk on, the lights we use, the buildings we live in, the cars we drive, the roads we drive on, and so much more. Even those things that seem natural, like yards or parks, are human constructs.

## SOCthink

> > > We send an average of 1.6 billion text messages per day in the United States—more than 2.5 times as many as in 2006. How does frequent "texting" and less talking affect the nature of our relationships, both positively and negatively?

# Wireless Phone Usage

What is sociologically important about material culture is the role it plays, like all forms of culture, in connecting individuals with one another and to the external environment. Advances in technology, especially when it comes to the revolutions in communication and transportation, have linked more individuals in a global network than was ever possible in the past. Cell phones, for example, enable us to stay in touch with friends and family from almost anywhere, and laptop computers allow us to bring the workplace with us wherever we go.

However, while the objects we create open up new possibilities, they also constrain us. The material objects we construct direct us toward certain ends but have the unintended consequence of limiting our awareness of possible alternatives. The invention of cars, for example, led to changes in the layout of cities—as an overview shot of New York City versus Chicago versus Los Angeles shows—altering the makeup of neighborhoods, possibilities for face-to-face interaction, and the nature of local community.

Technology is a form of material culture. We tend to think of it only as the physical object itself, but sociologist Gerhard Lenski suggests that it represents a way of knowing. He defined **technology** as "cultural information about how to use the material resources of the environment to satisfy human needs and desires" (Nolan and Lenski 2006:37). Technology enhances our human abilities, giving us power, speed, and even flight.

## Culture, Technology, and Superhero Powers

What makes characters such as Ironman, Batman, and even the villain Syndrome so impressive is that, unlike mutants who are born with superhuman powers, they come by their powers the old-fashioned way: they invent them. In the same way, technology, starting at least with the steam engine, gave us the strength and stamina to exert great physical force over and over again.

Sometimes technological change outstrips our capacity to interpret and understand the impact of such changes. Because it goes to the core of our perception of reality, nonmaterial culture is often more resistant to change than is the material culture. Ogburn introduced the term **culture lag** to refer to the period of adjustment when the nonmaterial culture is struggling to adapt to new conditions of the material culture. For example, the ethics of the Internet—particularly issues concerning privacy and censorship—have not yet caught up with the explosion in Internet use and technology.

## LANGUAGE

Turning to nonmaterial culture, we begin with language, its most basic building block. **Language** is a system of shared symbols; it includes speech, written characters, numerals, symbols, and nonverbal gestures and expressions. It provides the foundation of a common culture because it facilitates day-to-day exchanges with others, making collective action possible.

Even as we learn the meanings of existing words through interactions with others, we create new words and modify old meanings—especially in our modern culture, where innovation is never ending. Dictio-

naries are regularly modified to include new words. Not so long ago, words such as *ginormous, spamming, feng shui, crunk, IED, caffe latte, hoodie, frankenfood,* and *longneck* did not appear in English-language dictionaries. Whether something is recognized as a word can be a contested process. McDonald's Corporation, for example is seeking to get the word *McJob,* a term coined by sociologist Amitai Etzioni, removed from the Oxford English Dictionary for fear that people might see their products and jobs as something less than prestigious.

Analysis of language gives us insight into cultures. The English language, for example, makes extensive use of words related to war. We speak of "conquering" space, "fighting the battle" of the budget, "waging war" on drugs, making a "killing" in the stock market, and "bombing" an examination; something monumental or great is "the bomb." An observer from another culture could gauge the importance of warfare and the military in our culture simply by recognizing the prominence of militaristic terms in our language. As another example, in the Old West, words such as *gelding, stallion, mare, piebald,* and *sorrel* were all used to describe one animal—the horse. Even if we knew little about that period in history, we could conclude from the list of terms that horses were important to the culture. Similarly, the Slave Indians of northern Canada, who live in a frigid climate, have 14 terms to describe ice, including 8 for different kinds of "solid ice" and others for "seamed ice," "cracked ice," and "floating ice." Clearly, language reflects the values and priorities of a culture (Basso 1972; Haviland 2002).

Different languages express reality in different ways, and crossing one language with another can lead to embarrassment. To lend authenticity to his 1990 film *Dances with Wolves,* actor-director Kevin Costner hired a Lakota woman to teach the Lakota language to the cast. Lakota is a gendered language in which women and men speak slightly different dialects. The cast members found the language so difficult to learn that the teacher decided to dispense with the complexities of gendered speech. When members of the Lakota Sioux tribe saw the film, they could not help laughing at the men sounding like women (Haviland et al. 2005:109).

Because different groups share different languages, the ability to speak other languages is crucial to intercultural relations. Throughout the Cold War era, beginning in the 1950s and continuing well into the 1970s, the U.S. government

## From Me to You

*During a family hike, my wife Lori and daughter Emily were falling farther and farther behind my daughter Eleanor and me. Eleanor, who was four at the time, turned her head to see what was taking them so long and yelled to them as loud as she could, "Stop chickenjagging!" We loved this new word and have used it in our family ever since to mean "going slowly and holding others back." We all have the power to create words to make sense of our world and to connect with each other; anyone can create words, but they become meaningful only when they are shared with others.*

ages a distinctive interpretation of reality by focusing our attention on certain phenomena.

In a literal sense, language may color how we see the world. Berlin and Kay (1991) noted that humans possess the physical ability to make millions of color distinctions, yet languages differ in the number of colors they recognize. For example, the English language distinguishes between yellow and orange, but some other languages do not. In the Dugum Dani language of New Guinea's West Highlands, there are only two basic color terms— *modla* for "white" and *mili* for "black." By contrast, there are 11 basic terms in English. Russian and Hungarian, though, have 12 color terms. Russians have terms for light blue and dark blue, while Hungarians have terms for two different shades of red (Roberson et al. 2000).

Feminists have noted that gender-related language can reflect—although in itself it does not determine—the traditional acceptance of men and women in certain occupations. Each time we use a term such as *mailman, policeman,* or *fireman,* we are implying (especially to young children) that these occupations can be filled only by males. Yet many women work as *letter carriers, police officers,* and *firefighters*—a fact that is being increasingly recognized and legitimized through the use of such nonsexist language.

> **culture lag** A period of adjustment when the nonmaterial culture is still struggling to adapt to new material conditions.
>
> **language** A system of shared symbols; it includes speech, written characters, numerals, symbols, and nonverbal gestures and expressions.
>
> **Sapir-Whorf hypothesis** The idea that the language a person uses shapes his or her perception of reality and therefore his or her thoughts and actions.

encouraged the study of Russian by developing special language schools for diplomats, intelligence agents, and military advisors. And following the terrorist attacks of September 11, 2001, the nation recognized how few skilled translators it had for Arabic and other languages spoken in Muslim countries. Language quickly became a key not only to tracking potential terrorists but also to building diplomatic bridges with Muslim countries willing to help in the war against terrorism.

**Sapir-Whorf Hypothesis** Language does more than simply describe reality; it also shapes the reality of a culture. For example, most people in the United States cannot easily make the verbal distinctions concerning ice that are possible in the Slave Indian culture. As a result, they are less likely to notice differences in types of ice.

According to the **Sapir-Whorf hypothesis,** named for two linguists, the language a person uses shapes his or her perception of reality and therefore his or her thoughts and actions. Edward Sapir and Benjamin Whorf argued that since people can conceptualize the world only through language, language *precedes* thought. Thus, the word symbols and grammar of our language organize the world for us. The Sapir-Whorf hypothesis also holds that language is not a given. Rather, it is culturally determined and encour-

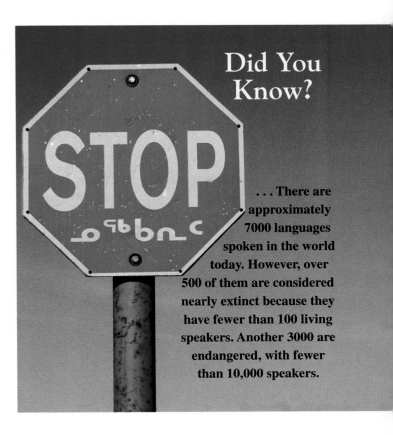

## Did You Know?

. . . There are approximately 7000 languages spoken in the world today. However, over 500 of them are considered nearly extinct because they have fewer than 100 living speakers. Another 3000 are endangered, with fewer than 10,000 speakers.

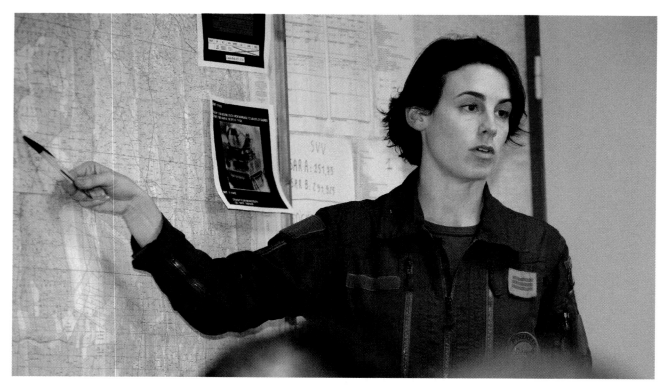

Language can also transmit stereotypes related to race. Look up the meanings of the adjective *black* in dictionaries published in the United States, and you will find "dismal, gloomy or forbidding, destitute of moral light or goodness, atrocious, evil, threatening, clouded with anger." By contrast, dictionaries list "pure" and "innocent" among the meanings of the adjective *white*. Through such patterns of language, our culture reinforces positive associations with the term (and skin color) *white* and negative associations with *black*. Is it surprising, then, that a list meant to prevent people from working in a profession is called a "blacklist," while a fib that we think of as somewhat acceptable is called a "white lie"?

## SOCthink

> > > What are some slang terms we use to refer to men and to women? What images do such terms convey for what it means to be male or female?

As you can see from these examples, language can shape how we see, taste, smell, feel, and hear. It also influences the way we think about the people, ideas, and objects around us.

**Nonverbal Communication** Of course, we communicate using more than just words. If you do not like the way a meeting is going, you might suddenly sit back,

fold your arms, and turn down the corners of your mouth. When you see a friend in tears, you may give her a quick hug. After winning a big game, you may high-five your teammates. These are all examples of **nonverbal communication**—the use of gestures, facial expressions, and other visual images to communicate. We are not born with these expressions. We learn them, just as we learn other forms of language, from people who share our culture. We learn how to show—and to recognize—happiness, sadness, pleasure, shame, distress, and other emotional states (Fridlund et al. 1987).

Like other forms of language, nonverbal communication is not the same in all cultures. For example, people from various cultures differ in the degree to which they touch others during the course of normal social interactions. Even experienced travelers are sometimes caught off guard by these differences. In Saudi Arabia a middle-aged man may want to hold hands with a male partner after closing a business deal. The gesture, which would shock an American, is considered a compliment in that culture. The meaning of hand signals is another form of nonverbal communication that can differ from one culture to the next. For instance, in Australia the thumbs-up sign is considered rude (Passero 2002).

debates and billboards promoting conflicting causes tell us that much.

The values of a culture may change, but most remain relatively stable during any one person's lifetime. Socially shared, intensely felt values are a fundamental part of our lives in the United States. Sociologist Robin Williams (1970) has offered a list of our basic values. These include achievement, efficiency, material comfort, nationalism, equality, and the supremacy of science and reason over faith. Obviously, not all 305 million people in the United States agree on all these values, but such a list serves as a starting point in defining America's national character.

## SOCthink

> > > Look at Williams' list of basic values. How might some of them potentially conflict with one another? For example, what conflict might arise over valuing both achievement and equality?

In recent decades, scholars have made extensive efforts to compare values in different nations, even while recognizing the challenges in interpreting value concepts in a similar manner across cultures. Psychologist Shalom Schwartz has measured values in more than 60 countries. Around the world, certain values are widely shared, including benevolence, which is defined as "forgiveness and loyalty." In contrast, power, defined as "control or dominance over people and resources," is a value that is endorsed much less often (Hitlin and Piliavin 2004; S. Schwartz and Bardi 2001).

**nonverbal communication** The use of gestures, facial expressions, and other visual images to communicate.

**value** A collective conception of what is considered good, desirable, and proper—or bad, undesirable, and improper—in a culture.

Each year more than 289,000 first-year college students at 440 of the nation's four-year colleges fill out a questionnaire asking them which values are most important to them. Because of its coverage, content, and scope, this survey provides a kind of barometer of the nation's values. Over the past four decades, the value of "being very well-off financially" has shown the strongest gain in popularity; the proportion of first-year college students who endorse this value as "essential" or "very important" rose from 44 percent in 1967 to 74.5 percent in 2005. By contrast,

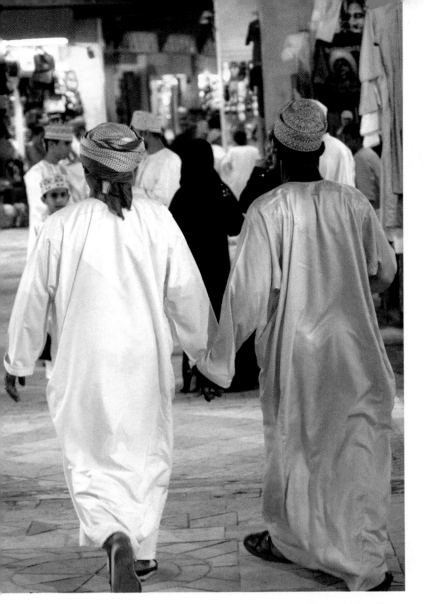

*In Arab cultures, men may hold hands as a sign of affection and friendship.*

## VALUES

Although each of us has our own personal set of standards—which may include caring or fitness or entrepreneurship—we also share a general set of objectives as members of a society. **Values** are these collective conceptions of what is considered good, desirable, and proper—or bad, undesirable, and improper—in a culture. Values may be specific, such as honoring one's parents and owning a home, or they may be more general, such as health, love, and democracy. Even individualism represents a collective value. As Richard Rodriguez points out, "American individualism is a communally derived value, not truly an expression of individuality. The teenager persists in rebelling against her parents, against tradition or custom, because she is shielded . . . by American culture from the knowledge that she inherited her rebellion from dead ancestors and living parents" (2002:130). Of course, all members of a society do not uniformly share its values. Angry political

## Life Goals of First-Year College Students in the United States, 1966–2007

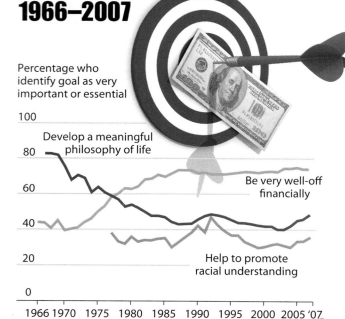

Percentage who identify goal as very important or essential

Develop a meaningful philosophy of life

Be very well-off financially

Help to promote racial understanding

100
80
60
40
20
0

1966 1970  1975   1980   1985   1990   1995   2000   2005 '07

*Source:* UCLA Higher Education Research Institute, as reported in Astin et al. 1994; Pryor et al. 2007b.

the value that has shown the most striking decline in endorsement by students is "developing a meaningful philosophy of life." This value was the most popular in the 1967 survey, endorsed by more than 80 percent of respondents. However, it had fallen to seventh place on the list by 2005, when it was endorsed by only 45 percent of students.

During the 1980s and 1990s, first-year college students expressed increased support for values having to do with money, power, and status. At the same time, their support for values having to do with social awareness and altruism, such as "helping others," declined. According to the 2005 nationwide survey, only 39 percent of students stated that "influencing social values" was an "essential" or "very important" goal. The proportion of students for whom "helping to promote racial understanding" was an essential or very important goal reached a record high of 42 percent in 1992, then fell to 33 percent in 2005. Like other aspects of nonmaterial culture, such as language and norms, a nation's values are not necessarily fixed.

Cheating is a significant concern on college campuses. Professors who take advantage of computerized services that can identify plagiarism, such as the search engine Google or TurnItIn.com, have found that many of the

**norm** An established standard of behavior maintained by a society.

**formal norm** A norm that generally has been written down and that specifies strict punishments for violators.

**laws** Formal norms enforced by the state.

papers their students hand in are plagiarized, in whole or in part. When high school students were asked how many times they had copied an Internet document for a classroom assignment in the past year, 32.9 percent said that they had done so at least once. When asked how many times they had cheated during a test at school in the past year, 60.2 percent said that they had done so at least once (Josephson Institute of Ethics 2006). Perhaps cheating has become a normal part of student culture even if it is at odds with the dominant school values.

Another value that has begun to change recently, not just among students but among the public in general, is the right to privacy. Americans have always valued their privacy and resented government intrusions into their personal lives. In the aftermath of the terrorist attacks of September 11, 2001, however, many citizens called for greater protection against the threat of terrorism. In response, the federal government broadened its surveillance powers and increased its ability to monitor people's behavior without court approval. In 2001, shortly after the attacks, Congress passed the USA Patriot Act, which empowers the FBI to access individuals' medical, library, student, and phone records without informing them or obtaining a search warrant.

## NORMS

While values express our core beliefs, norms provide guidance for how to act: "Wash your hands before dinner." "Thou shalt not kill." "Respect your elders." All societies have ways of encouraging and enforcing what they view as appropriate behavior while discouraging and sanctioning what they consider to be improper behavior. **Norms** are the established standards of behavior maintained by a society. However, they are more than just the rules we think about and know—we come to embody them as part of our everyday actions.

For a norm to become significant, it must be widely shared and understood. For example, in movie theaters in the United States, we typically expect that people will be quiet while the film is shown. Of course, context matters, and the application of this norm can vary, depending on the particular film and type of audience. People who are viewing a serious artistic film will be more likely to insist on the norm of silence than those who are watching a slapstick comedy or a horror movie.

**Hot or Not?**

If you could cheat on your next sociology test and get away with it, would you? Why or why not?

**Types of Norms** Sociologists distinguish between norms in two ways. First, norms are classified as either formal or informal. **Formal norms** generally have been written down and specify strict punishments for violators. In the United States we often formalize norms into laws, which are very precise in defining proper and improper behavior. Sociologist Donald Black (1995) defined *law* as "governmental social control"; that is, **laws** are formal norms enforced by the state. But laws are just one example of formal norms. The requirements for a college major and the rules of a card game are also considered formal norms.

By contrast, **informal norms** are generally understood but not precisely recorded. Standards of proper dress are a common example of informal norms. Our society has no specific punishment or sanction for a person who comes to school wearing, say, a monkey suit. Making fun of the nonconforming student is the most likely response.

## SOCthink

> > > What norms are you abiding by right now, as you read this book?

Norms are also classified by their relative importance to society. When classified in this way, they are known as *mores* and *folkways*. **Mores** (pronounced "MOR-ays") are norms deemed highly necessary to the welfare of a society, often because they embody the most cherished principles of a people. Each society demands obedience to its mores; violation can lead to severe penalties. Thus, the United

### Break-a-Norm Day

- Wearing formal clothes in an informal setting
- Eating with the wrong utensil or none at all
- Responding to friends or family the same as to a boss or teacher
- Having long gaps in speech when talking with someone
- Standing just a little too close to or far from someone when talking with him or her
- Facing the back of an elevator instead of getting in and turning around

*Norms provide us with rules that guide our everyday behavior. All we need to do is step outside the lines even a little bit to see the influence they have over our lives. These are some examples of how people violate norms. How would you feel about violating any of these norms? How might others respond to you?*

States has strong mores against murder, treason, and child abuse, which have been institutionalized into formal norms.

**Folkways** are norms governing everyday behavior. They play an important role in shaping the daily behavior of members of a culture. Society is less likely to formalize folkways than mores, and their violation raises comparatively little concern. For example, fashion is a folkway, and there is wide latitude in what we might wear. But what about not wearing *any* clothes in public? For most of us, most of the time, that would be crossing the line into the territory of mores, and we might expect a strong and swift response. However, this too may be undergoing a change: in April 2008, *The New York Times* reported that the nude vacation business is booming (Higgins 2008).

In many societies around the world, folkways exist to reinforce patterns of male dominance. For example, various folkways reveal men's hierarchical position above women within the traditional Buddhist areas of Southeast Asia. In the sleeping cars of trains, women do not sleep in upper berths, above men. Hospitals that house men on the first floor do not place female patients on the second floor. Even on clotheslines, folkways in Southeast Asia dictate male dominance: women's attire is hung lower than that of men (Bulle 1987).

**informal norm** A norm that is generally understood but not precisely recorded.

**mores** Norms deemed highly necessary to the welfare of a society.

**folkways** Norms governing everyday behavior, whose violation raise comparatively little concern.

## 5 Movies on U.S. CULTURE

**A Raisin in the Sun**
*Trying for a better life in the 1950s.*

**The Stepford Wives**
*A satire of the American Dream.*

**The Pursuit of Happyness**
*Struggling to make ends meet in America.*

**The Namesake**
*A first-generation American.*

**Super Size Me**
*A month of meals at McDonald's, the symbol of America around the world.*

**Acceptance of Norms** People do not follow norms, whether mores or folkways, in all situations. In some cases they can evade a norm because they know it is weakly enforced. For instance, it is illegal for American teenagers to drink alcoholic beverages, yet drinking by minors is common throughout the nation. In fact, teenage alcoholism is a serious social problem.

In some instances behavior that appears to violate society's norms may actually represent adherence to the stances, can cause one to be viewed as either a hero or a villain. For instance, secretly taping telephone conversations is normally considered not just illegal but abhorrent. However, it can be done with a court order to obtain valid evidence for a criminal trial. We would heap praise on a government agent who used such methods to convict an organized crime figure. In our culture we tolerate killing another human being in self-defense, and we actually reward killing in warfare.

> ## Strangers in a new culture see only what they know.
>
> **Anonymous**

norms of a particular group. Teenage drinkers are often conforming to the standards of their peer group when they violate norms that condemn underage drinking. Similarly, business executives who use shady accounting techniques may be responding to a corporate culture that demands the maximization of profits at any cost, including the deception of investors and government regulatory agencies.

Norms are violated in some instances because one norm conflicts with another. For example, suppose you live in an apartment building and one night hear the screams of the woman next door, who is being beaten by her husband. If you decide to intervene by knocking on their door or calling the police, you are violating the norm of minding your own business while at the same time following the norm of assisting a victim of domestic violence.

Even if norms do not conflict, there are exceptions to any norm. The same action, under different circum-

Acceptance of norms is subject to change as the political, economic, and social conditions of a culture are transformed. Until the 1960s, for example, formal norms throughout much of the United States prohibited the marriage of people from different racial groups. Over the past half century, however, such legal prohibitions have been cast aside. The process of change can be seen today in the increasing acceptance of single parents and the growing support for the legalization of marriage for same-sex couples.

When circumstances require the sudden violation of longstanding cultural norms, the change can upset an entire population. In Iraq, where Muslim custom strictly forbids touching by strangers for men and especially for women, the war that began in 2003 has brought numerous daily violations of the norm. Outside mosques, government offices, and other facilities likely to be targeted by terrorists, visitors must now be patted down and have their bags searched by Iraqi security forces. To

A female U.S. soldier searches Iraqi women.

reduce the discomfort caused by the procedure, women are searched by female guards and men by male guards. Despite that concession, and the fact that many Iraqis admit to or even insist on the need for such measures, people still wince at the invasion of their personal privacy. In reaction to the searches, Iraqi women have begun to limit the contents of the bags they carry or simply to leave them at home (Rubin 2003).

ditions. The difficulty, and it is an immense difficulty, is to find a proper equilibrium between stability and variability." In a world of norms, we constantly face this tension: to obey or not to obey.

> **sanction** A penalty or reward for conduct concerning a social norm.
>
> **dominant ideology** A set of cultural beliefs and practices that legitimates existing powerful social, economic, and political interests.

## 5 Movies on CULTURES OUTSIDE THE U.S.

**Rabbit-Proof Fence**
*Aborigines in Australia.*

**Tsotsi**
*A harsh tale from Africa.*

**Eat Drink Man Woman**
*Romance and cooking in Taiwan.*

**Children of Heaven**
*Iranian schoolchildren.*

**Satin Rouge**
*A Tunisian widow studying belly dancing.*

### SANCTIONS

Suppose your basketball coach sends you into the game as the sixth player on your team. Or imagine you have graduated from college and show up in shorts for a job interview at a large bank. Or, on the way to that interview, suppose you park your car on the street but neglect to put any money into the parking meter. In each case you have violated widely shared and understood norms. So what happens? In each of these situations, you would receive some form of negative repercussion if your behavior was detected.

**Sanctions** are penalties and rewards for conduct concerning a social norm. They include both negative and positive responses to behavior; their purpose is to influence future behavior. Adhering to norms can lead to positive sanctions such as a pay raise, a medal, a word of gratitude, or a pat on the back. Negative sanctions might include fines, threats, imprisonment, and stares of contempt. In this way sanctions work to enforce the order that the norms represent. Most of the time we do not even need others to sanction our acts. Having internalized society's norms, we police ourselves, using such internal motivations as guilt or self-satisfaction to regulate our own behavior.

As we saw with the "Free Hugs" campaign, norms provide order, but norms change, and change represents potential chaos. As social scientist Gustave Le Bon said in 1895, "Civilization is impossible without traditions, and progress impossible without the destruction of those tra-

## >> Culture and the Dominant Ideology

Together the elements of culture provide us with social coherence and order. Culture clarifies for us what we think is good and bad, and right and wrong, giving us a sense of direction. That is not to say, however, that there is universal agreement on values and norms or that culture works on behalf of all for the greater good. While culture helps to unify and provide meaning, it also serves the interests of some individuals and groups to the detriment of others. Some people benefit from existing norms and values, while others are denied opportunities or access to resources simply due to the positions they occupy—positions we have culturally defined as inferior.

One of the ways culture can function to maintain the privileges of certain groups is through the establishment of a **dominant ideology**—the set of cultural beliefs and practices that legitimate existing powerful social, economic, and political interests. The dominant ideology helps to explain and justify who gets what and why in a way that supports and maintains the status quo. Dominant ideas can even squelch alternative expressions

*Agricultural strikes in the 1960s and 1970s alerted the nation to the harsh economic plight of migrant workers.*

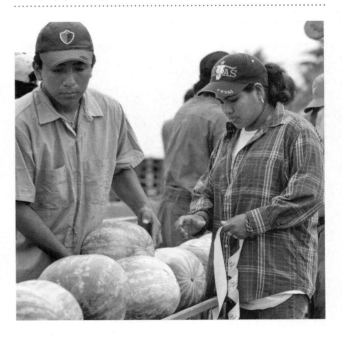

of what might be, casting such alternatives as threats to the existing order. This concept was first proposed by Hungarian Marxist Georg Lukács (1923) and Italian Marxist Antonio Gramsci (1929), but it did not gain an audience in the United States until the early 1970s. In Karl Marx's view, a capitalist society has a dominant ideology that serves the interests of the ruling class.

A society's most powerful groups and institutions control wealth and property. Armed with a dominant ideology, they can also control the means of producing beliefs about reality through religion, education, and the media, and in so doing, they can shape what we come to accept as true. For example, feminists would argue that if all of society's most important institutions send the message that women should be subservient to men, this dominant ideology will help to control and subordinate women.

One of the limitations of the dominant ideology thesis is that, in the United States, it is not easy to identify a singular, all-inclusive "core culture." Studies report a lack of consensus on national values and a wide range of cultural traits from a variety of cultural traditions. In addition, as we saw in the surveys of young people's values, significant shifts in cultural values can occur. Yet there is no denying that certain expressions of values have greater influence than others, even in so complex a society as the United States. For example, the value of competition in the marketplace—a cornerstone of any capitalist economy—remains powerful, and we often look down on those who we suspect might be lazy.

**subculture** A segment of society that shares a distinctive pattern of mores, folkways, and values that differs from the pattern of the larger society.

**argot** Specialized language used by members of a group or subculture.

## >> Cultural Variation

While societies can be defined in part by the culture their inhabitants share, culture varies both among and within so-cieties. Inuit tribes in northern Canada, clad in furs and dieting on whale blubber, have little in common with farmers in Southeast Asia, who dress for the heat and subsist mainly on the rice they grow in their paddies. Cultures adapt to meet specific sets of circumstances, such as climate, level of technology, population, and geography. This adaptation to different conditions shows up in differences in all elements of culture, including language, values, norms, and sanctions. Thus, despite the presence of cultural universals such as courtship and religion, great diversity exists among the world's many cultures. Moreover, even within a single nation, certain segments of the populace develop cultural patterns that differ from the patterns of the dominant society.

## ASPECTS OF CULTURAL VARIATION

**Subcultures** Rodeo riders, residents of a retirement community, workers on an offshore oil rig—all are examples of what sociologists refer to as *subcultures*. A **subculture** is a segment of society that shares a distinctive pattern of mores, folkways, and values that differs from the pattern of the larger society. In a sense, a subculture can be thought of as a culture existing within a larger, dominant culture. The existence of many subcultures is characteristic of complex societies such as the United States.

### SOCthink

> > > Are people who participate in *World of Warcraft* or *Second Life* part of subcultures? What are some characteristics of these groups that typify subcultures?

Members of a subculture participate in the dominant culture while at the same time engaging in unique and dis-

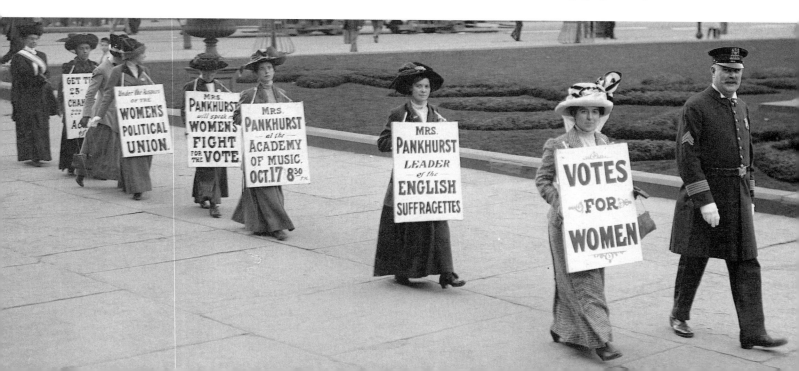

tinctive forms of behavior. Frequently, a subculture will develop its own slang known as **argot**—specialized language that distinguishes it from the wider society. For example, back in the 1940s and 1950s, New York City's sanitation workers developed a humorous argot used to this day to describe the dirty and smelly aspects of their job. They call themselves *g-men* (a term more typically applied to government agents); a garbage scow or barge is known as a *honey boat;* and trash thrown from an upper-story window is called *airmail.* More recent coinages include *disco rice* (maggots) and *urban whitefish* (used condoms). Administrators at the Sanitation Department practice a more reserved humor than those who work on the trucks. When they send a *honey boat* to New Jersey, they are not dumping the city's garbage; they're *exporting* it. Policy makers at the department have also invented some novel acronyms to describe New Yorkers' attitude toward the construction of new sanitation facilities: *banana* (build absolutely nothing anywhere near anyone) and *nope* (not on planet earth) (Urbina 2004).

Such argot allows insiders—the members of the subculture—to understand words with special meanings and establishes patterns of communication that outsiders cannot understand. In so doing, it clarifies the boundary between "us" and "them" and reinforces a shared identity. We see something like this in the taken-for-granted words and acronyms in the instant-messaging and text-messaging world. There, abbreviations come fast and furious, from the well-known, such as *lol* (laughing out loud), *brb* (be right back), and *g2g* (got to go), to the more obscure, such as *1337* (meaning "elite" and referring to symbolic language or "leet-speak") or *pwned* (leet term meaning "defeated").

In India a new subculture has developed among employees at the international call centers established by multinational corporations. To serve customers in the United States and Europe, the young men and women who work there must be fluent speakers of English. But the corporations that employ them demand more than proficiency in a foreign language; they expect their Indian employees to adopt Western values and work habits, including the grueling pace that U.S. workers take for granted. In return, the corporations offer perks such as Western-style dinners and dances and coveted consumer goods. Ironically, they allow employees to take the day off only on American holidays like Labor Day and Thanksgiving—not on Indian holidays like Diwali, the Hindu festival of lights. While most Indian families are home celebrating, call center employees see only each other; when they have the day off, no one else is free to socialize with them. As a result, these employees have formed a tight-knit subculture based on hard work and a taste for Western luxury goods and leisure time pursuits. Increasingly, they are the object of criticism from Indians who live a more conventional Indian lifestyle centered on family and holiday traditions (Kalita 2006).

## Subculture Slang

**Anime and Manga Fans**
Chibi eyes: the characteristic, big childlike eyes used in anime

Majoko: a girl anime character with magical powers who must save the world

**Carnival Workers**
86'ed: banned from carnival grounds

Blade glommer: a sword swallower

Flat store: a carnival game rigged so that it can't be won

**Graffiti Writers**
Bite: to copy another graffiti writer's work

Burner: a stylistically impressive, brilliantly colored piece of graffiti, usually written in a complex pattern of interlocking letters and other visual elements

Toy: an inexperienced or unskilled graffiti writer

Kill: to saturate an area with one's graffiti

**Bikers (Motorcyclists)**
Brain bucket: a helmet

Ink slinger: a tattoo artist

Pucker factor: the degree of panic felt during a near-accident

Yard shark: a dog that races out to attack passing motorcyclists

**Skateboarders**
Deck: a skateboard platform

Face plant: a face-first crash

Sketchy: in reference to a trick, poorly done

*Subcultures often produce their own unique jargon. The words may be appropriate in those subcultures, but they have the effect of drawing a line between insiders and the rest of us.*

Source: Luc Reid. 2006. *Talk the Talk: The Slang of 65 American Subcultures.* Cincinnati, OH: Writer's Digest Books.

**Countercultures** Sometimes a subculture can develop that seeks to set itself up as an alternative to the dominant culture. When a subculture conspicuously and deliberately opposes certain aspects of the larger culture, it is known as a **counterculture.** Countercultures typically thrive among the young, who have the least investment in the existing culture.

The 1960s, now often characterized by the phrase "sex and drugs and rock 'n' roll," provide a classic case of an extensive counterculture. Largely composed of young people, members of this counterculture were turned off by a society they believed was too materialistic and technological. It included many political radicals and "hippies" who had "dropped out" of mainstream social institutions, but its membership was extensive and diverse. The young people expressed

**counterculture** A subculture that deliberately opposes certain aspects of the larger culture.

in their writings, speeches, and songs their visions, hopes, and dreams for a new society. These young women and men rejected the pressure to accumulate more expensive cars, larger homes, and an endless array of material goods. Instead, they expressed a desire to live in a culture based on more humanistic values, such as sharing, love, and co-existence with the environment. As a political force, they worked for peace—opposing U.S. involvement in the war in Vietnam and encouraging draft resistance—as well as racial and gender equality (Flacks 1971; Roszak 1969).

In the wake of the attacks of September 11, 2001, people around the United States learned of the existence of

terrorist groups operating as a counterculture within their own country. In Northern Ireland, Israel, the Palestinian territory, and other parts of the world, many generations have lived in such circumstances. But terrorist cells are not necessarily fueled only by outsiders. Frequently, people become disenchanted with the policies of their own country, and a few take very violent steps (Juergensmeyer 2003).

**Culture Shock** Today we are more and more likely to come into contact with and even immerse ourselves in cultures unlike our own. For example, it has become increasingly common for students to study abroad. Though they may well have predeparture orientation sessions, when they get in-country, they often have a difficult time adjusting because so many of the little things that they took for granted, things they barely noticed before, no longer apply. Anyone who feels disoriented, uncertain, out of place, or even fearful when they encounter unfamiliar cultural practices may be experiencing **culture shock.** For example, a resident of the United States who visits certain areas in China and wants meat for dinner may be stunned to learn that the local specialty is dog meat. Similarly, some-

**culture shock** The feelings of disorientation, uncertainty, and even fear that people experience when they encounter unfamiliar cultural practices.

one from a strict Islamic culture may be shocked upon first seeing the comparatively provocative dress styles and open displays of affection that are common in the United States and other Western cultures.

Interestingly, once students who study abroad return home, they may experience a kind of reverse culture shock. Their time away has changed them, often in ways they were unaware of, and they find that they cannot so easily slip back into the old routines that those who remained at home expect of them. Culture shock reveals to us both the power and the taken-for-granted nature of culture. The rules we follow are so ingrained that we barely notice that we were following them until they are no longer there to provide the structure and order we assume as a given.

All of us, to some extent, take for granted the cultural practices of our society. As a result, it can be surprising and even disturbing to realize that other cultures do not follow our way of life. The fact is, customs that seem strange to us are considered normal and proper in other cultures, which may view our own mores and folkways as odd.

## ATTITUDES TOWARD CULTURAL VARIATION

**Ethnocentrism** Because we are now more likely to encounter people from a whole range of cultural backgrounds than we were in the past, we are also more likely to struggle with what we think about the beliefs, values, and practices of others. When we hear people talking about "our" culture versus "their" culture, we are often confronted with statements that reflect the attitude that "our" culture is best. Terms such as *under-*

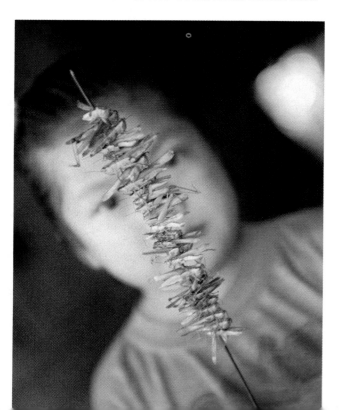

*developed, backward,* and *primitive* may be used to refer to other societies. What "we" believe is a religion; what "they" believe is superstition and mythology.

It is tempting to evaluate the practices of other cultures on the basis of our own perspectives. Sociologist William Graham Sumner (1906) coined the term **ethnocentrism** to refer to the tendency to assume that one's own culture and way of life represent the norm or are superior to all others. The ethnocentric person sees his or her own group as the center or defining point of culture and views all other cultures as deviations from what is "normal." Thus, Westerners who see cattle as a food source might look down on the Hindu religion and culture, which view the cow as sacred. People in one culture may dismiss as unthinkable the mate selection or child-rearing practices of another culture.

Ethnocentric value judgments have complicated U.S. efforts at democratic reform of the Iraqi government. Prior to the 2003 war in Iraq, U.S. planners had assumed that Iraqis would adapt to a new form of government in the same way the Germans and Japanese did following World War II. But in the Iraqi culture, unlike the German and Japanese cultures, loyalty to the family and the extended clan comes before patriotism and the common good. In a country in which almost half of all people, even those in the cities, marry a first or second cousin, citizens are predisposed to favor their own kin in government and business dealings. Why trust a stranger from outside the family? What Westerners would criticize as nepotism, then, is actually an acceptable, even admirable, practice to Iraqis (J. Tierney 2003).

One of the reasons ethnocentrism develops is because it contributes to a sense of solidarity by promoting group pride. Denigrating other nations and cultures can enhance our own patriotic feelings and belief in our way of life. Yet this type of social stability is established at the expense of other peoples. One of the negative consequences of ethnocentric value judgments is that they serve to devalue groups and to deny equal opportunities.

Of course, ethnocentrism is hardly limited to citizens of the United States. Visitors from many African cultures are surprised at the disrespect that children in the United States show their parents. People from India may be repelled by our practice of living in the same household with dogs and cats. Many Islamic fundamentalists in the Arab world and Asia view the United States as corrupt, decadent, and doomed to destruction. All these people may feel comforted by membership in cultures that in their view are superior to ours.

> You don't have to burn books to destroy a culture. Just get people to stop reading them.
>
> Ray Bradbury

**Cultural Relativism** Whereas ethnocentrism means evaluating foreign cultures using the familiar culture of the observer as a standard of correct behavior, **cultural relativism** means viewing people's behavior from the perspective of their own culture. It places a priority on understanding other cultures, rather than dismissing them as "strange" or "exotic." Unlike ethnocentrists, cultural relativists employ the kind of value neutrality in scientific study that Max Weber saw as so important.

Cultural relativism stresses that different social contexts give rise to different norms and values. Thus, we must examine practices such as polygamy, bullfighting, and monarchy within the particular contexts of the cultures in which they are found. Cultural relativism is not the same as moral relativism and thus does not suggest that we must unquestionably accept every cultural variation. But it does require a serious and unbiased effort to evaluate norms, values, and customs in light of their distinctive culture.

**ethnocentrism** The tendency to assume that one's own culture and way of life represent the norm or are superior to all others.

**cultural relativism** The viewing of people's behavior from the perspective of their own culture.

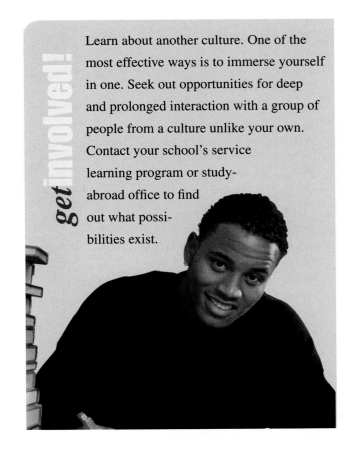

*get involved!*

Learn about another culture. One of the most effective ways is to immerse yourself in one. Seek out opportunities for deep and prolonged interaction with a group of people from a culture unlike your own. Contact your school's service learning program or study-abroad office to find out what possibilities exist.

Practicing the sociological imagination calls for us to be more fully aware of the culture we as humans have created for ourselves and to be better attuned to the varieties of culture other people have established for themselves. Culture shapes our everyday behaviors all the time, and for the most part, we are not aware of the degree to which we are immersed in a world of our own making. Whether that includes the capacity to read a book, make a meal, or hug a stranger on the street, it is through culture that we establish our relationship to the external world and with each other.

# For REVIEW

I. **Why do humans create culture?**
- Humans lack the complex instincts present in other animals, and as such they must construct a relationship to nature and with each other. We do this through the construction of shared culture.

II. **What does culture consist of?**
- Culture can be broken down into two categories. The first is nonmaterial culture, which consists of our modification of the physical environment and includes technology. The second is nonmaterial culture, which consists of a number of components including language, values, norms, and sanctions.

III. **How does culture both enable and constrain?**
- While culture provides us with the knowledge, rules, and artifacts we need to survive, it also limits our options. Words enable us to see, and tools enable us to make things, but both are designed for particular purposes and shield us from alternative possibilities. Further, with ethnocentrism, we cut ourselves off to new possibilities from different cultures.

# Pop Quiz

1. Which of the following is an aspect of culture?
   a. a comic book
   b. the patriotic attachment to the flag of the United States
   c. slang
   d. all of the above

2. People's need for food, shelter, and clothing are examples of what George Murdock referred to as
   a. norms.
   b. folkways.
   c. cultural universals.
   d. cultural practices.

3. The appearance of Starbucks coffeehouses in China is a sign of which aspect of culture?
   a. innovation
   b. globalization
   c. discovery
   d. cultural relativism

4. What term do sociologists use to refer to the process by which a cultural item spreads from group to group or society to society?
   a. diffusion
   b. globalization
   c. innovation
   d. cultural relativism

5. Which of the following statements is true according to the Sapir-Whorf hypothesis?
   a. Language simply describes reality.
   b. Language does not transmit stereotypes related to race.
   c. Language shapes our perception of reality.
   d. Language is not an example of a cultural universal.

6. Which of the following statements about values is correct?
   a. Values never change.
   b. The values of a culture may change, but most remain relatively stable during any one person's lifetime.
   c. Values are constantly changing; sociologists view them as being very unstable.
   d. all of the above

1 (d); 2 (c); 3 (b); 4 (a); 5 (c); 6 (b);

7. Which of the following statements about norms is correct?
   a. People do not follow norms in all situations. In some cases, they evade a norm because they know it is weakly enforced.
   b. In some instances, behavior that appears to violate society's norms may actually reflect adherence to the norms of a particular group.
   c. Norms are violated in some instances because one norm conflicts with another.
   d. all of the above

8. Which of the following terms describes the set of cultural beliefs and practices that help to maintain powerful social, economic, and political interests?
   a. mores
   b. dominant ideology
   c. consensus
   d. values

9. Terrorist groups are examples of
   a. cultural universals.
   b. subcultures.
   c. countercultures.
   d. dominant ideologies.

10. What is the term used when one seeks to understand another culture from its perspective, rather than dismissing it as "strange" or "exotic"?
    a. ethnocentrism
    b. culture shock
    c. cultural relativism
    d. cultural value

# 4

# SOCIALIZA

## ISOLATION AND SOCIALIZATION

For the first six years of her life, Isabelle lived in almost total seclusion in a darkened room. She had little contact with other people, with the exception of her mother, who could neither speak nor hear. Isabelle's grandparents had been so deeply ashamed of Isabelle's illegitimate birth that they kept her hidden away from the world. Ohio authorities finally discovered Isabelle in 1938, when her mother escaped from her parents' home, taking Isabelle with her.

Six years old at the time of her rescue, Isabelle could not speak. While she could make various croaking sounds, her only communication with her mother involved simple gestures. Isabelle had been largely deprived of the typical interactions and socialization experiences of childhood. Since she had seen few people, she initially showed a strong fear of strangers and reacted almost like a wild animal when confronted with an unfamiliar person. As she became accustomed to seeing certain individuals, her reaction changed to one of extreme apathy. At first, observers believed that Isabelle was deaf, but she soon began to react to nearby sounds. On tests of her educational development, she scored at the level of an infant rather than a six-year-old.

Specialists developed a systematic training program to help Isabelle adapt to human relationships and socialization. After a few days of training, she made her first attempt to verbalize. Although she started slowly, Isabelle quickly passed through six years of development. In a little over two months, she was speaking in complete sentences. Nine months later, she could identify both words and sentences. Before Isabelle reached the age of nine, she was ready to attend school with other children. By her 14th year she was in sixth grade, doing well in school, and emotionally well adjusted.

Yet without an opportunity to experience socialization in her first six years, Isabelle initially lacked what we often take for granted as natural human abilities. While we may be born with the propensity toward language and other social skills, Isabelle's inability to communicate at the time of her discovery—despite her physical and cognitive potential to learn—and her remarkable progress over the next few years underscore the importance of socialization in human development (K. Davis 1940, 1947).

# ATION

# As You READ >>

- How do we become ourselves?
- Who shapes our socialization?
- How does our development change over time?

## >> The Role of Socialization

What makes us who we are? Is it the genes we are born with, or the environment in which we grow up? Researchers have traditionally clashed over the relative importance of biological inheritance and environmental factors in human development—a conflict called the nature versus nurture (or heredity versus environment) debate.

**socialization** The lifelong process through which people learn the attitudes, values, and behaviors appropriate for members of a particular culture.

While most social scientists today acknowledge the significance of the interaction between these variables in shaping human development, sociologists tend to come down more strongly on the side of nurture. They argue that the rules we follow, the language we speak, and the values we believe in have less to do with our DNA than with the cultural context into which we emerge. Parents, teachers, friends, co-workers, and even television personalities provide us with the cultural tools we require to survive and thrive. We need to internalize the culture that has been constructed by

### SOCthink

> > > List the skills you had to learn by the age of two. Why do we tend to think of such skills as "natural"?

others who came before us, and we do this through **socialization**—the life-long process through which people learn the attitudes, values, and behaviors appropriate for members of a particular culture.

## SOCIAL ENVIRONMENT: THE IMPACT OF ISOLATION

We can better appreciate how heredity and environment interact and influence the socialization process by examining situations in which one factor operates almost entirely without the other (Homans 1979). As we saw above, Isabelle was able to proceed through the typical stages of socialization with the help of experts. Unfortunately, others raised in even more extreme isolation have not been so fortunate. Similarly, as we will see below, experiments with monkeys point toward our desire for intimacy and interaction. We want and need the influence of others.

**Extreme Childhood Isolation** Children who have been isolated or severely neglected typically have a difficult time recovering from the loss of early childhood socialization. For example, in 1970, California authorities discovered a 14-year-old girl named Genie locked in a room where she had been confined since she was 20 months old. During her years of isolation, no family member had spoken to her, nor could she hear anything other than swearing. Since there was no television or radio in her home, she had never heard the sounds of normal human speech. One year after beginning extensive therapy, Genie's grammar resembled that of a typical 18-month-old. Though she made further advances with continued therapy, she never achieved full language ability. Today Genie, now in her early fifties, lives in a home for developmentally disabled adults (Curtiss 1977, 1985; Rymer 1993).

While researchers know of only a few cases of children reared in near total isolation, they are aware of many cases of children raised in extremely neglectful social circumstances. Infants and young children in orphanages in the formerly communist countries of Eastern Europe often suffer from profound neglect. In many Romanian orphanages, babies once lay in their cribs for 18–20 hours a day, curled against their feeding bottles and receiving little adult care. Such minimal attention continued for the first five years of their lives.

# Ten Modern Cases of Feral Children

| | |
|---|---|
| Shamdeo, the Sultanpur Wolf Boy | He was about 4 years old when discovered playing with wolves in 1974. |
| Memmie LeBlanc, the Wild Girl of Champagne | About 18 to 20 years old when found, she had learned language before having been abandoned. |
| John Ssebunya, the Ugandan Monkey Boy | Found living with a pack of monkeys in 1991 at age 6, he now gives talks about his experience. |
| The Syrian Gazelle Boy | An agile runner, he was found among gazelles at about the age of 10 in 1946. |
| Oxana Malaya, the Ukrainian Dog Girl | She was found living in the dog pen in her family's back yard in 1991 at the age of 8. |
| The Russian Bird Boy | Found in February 2008, he was cared for by his mother but never spoken to and chirps like a bird. |
| The Leopard Boy of Dihungi | He was found among leopards at age 5 in 1915 after having been in the wild three years. |
| Kamala and Amala, the Wolf Girls of Midnapore | These two girls were found living among wolves at about the ages of 8 and 2 in 1920. |
| The Turkish Bear Girl | This 9-year-old girl was found living with bears in 1937. |
| Wild Peter | One of the earliest famous cases, he was found in the wild in Germany at age 12 in 1724. |

Kamala

tance of the earliest socialization experiences for children. We now know that it is not enough to attend to an infant's physical needs; parents must also concern themselves with children's social development. If parents discourage their children from having friends—even as toddlers—those children will miss out on social interactions with peers that are critical for emotional growth.

**Primate Studies** Studies of animals raised in isolation also support the importance of socialization in development. Harry Harlow (1971), a researcher at the primate laboratory of the University of Wisconsin, conducted tests with rhesus monkeys that had been raised away from their mothers and away from contact with other monkeys. As was the case with Isabelle, the rhesus monkeys raised in isolation were fearful and easily frightened. They did not mate, and the females who were artificially inseminated became abusive mothers. Apparently, isolation had a damaging effect on the monkeys.

A creative aspect of Harlow's experimentation was his use of "artificial mothers." In one such experiment, Harlow presented monkeys raised in isolation with two substitute mothers—one a cloth-covered replica and one a wire-covered model that had the capacity to offer milk. Monkey after monkey went to the wire mother for the life-giving milk, yet spent much more time clinging to the more motherlike cloth model. Apparently, the infant monkeys developed greater social attachments based on their need for warmth, comfort, and intimacy than their need for milk.

## THE INFLUENCE OF HEREDITY

Researchers who argue for a stronger role for biological explanations of our behavior point to different research to support their position—studies of twins, especially identical twins raised apart from each other. Oskar Stohr and Jack Yufe, identical twins who were separated soon after their birth, were raised on different continents and in very different cultural settings. Oskar was reared as a strict Catholic by his maternal grandmother in the Sudetenland of Czechoslovakia. As a member of the Hitler Youth movement in Nazi Germany, he learned to hate Jews. By contrast, his brother Jack was reared in Trinidad by the twins' Jewish father. Jack joined an Israeli kibbutz (a collective settlement) at age 17 and later served in the Israeli army. When the twins were reunited in middle age, however, some startling similarities emerged. They both wore wire-rimmed glasses and mustaches. They both liked spicy foods and sweet liqueurs, were absent-

A cloth-covered "artificial mother" of the type used by Harry Harlow.

Many of them were fearful of human contact and prone to unpredictable antisocial behavior.

This situation came to light only when families in North America and Europe began adopting thousands of these children in the 1990s. The adjustment problems were often so dramatic that about 20 percent of the adopting families concluded that they were ill-suited to be adoptive parents. Many of them have asked for assistance in dealing with the children. Since these conditions were brought to light by international aid workers, the Romanian government has made efforts to introduce the deprived youngsters to social interaction and its consequent feelings of attachment, which they have never experienced before (Groza et al. 1999; Craig Smith 2006).

Cases of extreme isolation demonstrate the imporminded, flushed the toilet before using it, stored rubber bands on their wrists, and dipped buttered toast in their coffee (Holden 1980).

It is tempting in such cases to focus almost exclusively on such quirky similarities, but the twins also differed in many important respects. For example, Jack was a workaholic, while Oskar enjoyed leisure-time activities. Whereas Oskar was a traditionalist who was domineering toward

> ## It matters not what someone is born, but what they grow to be.
>
> J. K. Rowling

women, Jack was a political liberal much more accepting of feminism. Finally, Jack was extremely proud of being Jewish, while Oskar never mentioned his Jewish heritage. Oskar and Jack are prime examples of the interplay of heredity and environment (Holden 1987).

For a number of years, the Minnesota Twin Family Study has been following pairs of identical twins reared apart to determine what similarities, if any, they show in personality traits, behavior, and intelligence. Preliminary results from the available twin studies indicate that both genetic factors and socialization experiences are influential in human development. Certain characteristics—such as temperament, voice patterns, nervous habits, and leadership or dominance tendencies—appear to be strikingly similar even in twins reared apart, suggesting that these qualities may be linked to heredity. However, identical twins reared apart differ far more in their attitudes; values; chosen mates; need for intimacy, comfort and assistance; and even drinking habits. These qualities, it would seem, are influenced by environmental factors.

## Did You Know?

... The birth rate for twins has risen 70 percent since 1980, and the birth rate for triplets-plus rose 400 percent from 1980 to 1998 (though it has declined in the years since then). Technological advances in both in vitro fertilization and embryo transfer are the primary cause for these increases, providing more cases for researchers to investigate to better understand the interplay between nature and nurture.

Researchers have also been impressed with the similar scores on intelligence tests of twins reared apart in *roughly similar* social settings. Most of the identical twins register scores even closer than those that would be expected if the same person took a test twice. However, identical twins brought up in *dramatically different* social environments score quite differently on intelligence tests—a finding that supports the importance of socialization in human development (Joseph 2004; McGue and Bouchard 1998; Minnesota Center for Twin and Family Research 2008).

Results from twin studies suggest that the nature–nurture debate is likely to continue. As sociologists we cannot dismiss the significance of biology in shaping human behavior. It does appear, however, that while some general behavioral propensities may be shaped by our genes, their manifestation is dependent upon socialization and cultural context. For example, while we may inherit tendencies toward temperament, the ways we express anger (or other emotions) depends upon our environment.

> **self** A distinct identity that sets us apart from others.

## >> The Self and Socialization

At the heart of this debate about nature versus nurture is the question "Who am I?" In both approaches the implicit assumption is that we are shaped by factors beyond our control. Sociologically speaking, however, we are not simply passive recipients of external forces. As individuals we are engaged in an ongoing dance with the world. We choose what to think and how to act, but we do so within the confines of the cultural resources to which we have access.

### SOCIOLOGICAL APPROACHES TO THE SELF

Our concept of who we are, our self, emerges as we interact with others. The **self** is a distinct identity that sets us apart from others. It is not a static phenomenon but continues to develop and change throughout our lives. Sociologists and psychologists alike have expressed interest in how the individual develops and modifies his or her sense of self as a result of social interaction.

**Cooley: The Looking-Glass Self** In the early 1900s, American sociologist Charles Horton Cooley

(1864–1929) proposed that we learn who we are by interacting with others. Our view of ourselves, then, comes not only from direct contemplation of our personal qualities but also from the use of others as a mirror through which we develop our impressions of our self. Cooley used the phrase **looking-glass self** to emphasize that the self is the product of our social interactions.

The process of developing a self-identity, or self-concept, has three phases. First, we imagine how others see us—relatives, friends, even strangers on the street. Then we imagine how others evaluate what we think they see—as intelligent, attractive, shy, or strange. Finally, we define our self as a result of these impressions—"I am smart" or "I am beautiful" (Cooley 1902; M. Howard 1989). This process is ongoing; it happens during each and every one of our interactions. Our understanding of our self, then, involves a complex calculation in which we come to be who we are based not simply on how others see us or how they will judge us but also on how we think they will see us and how we think they will judge us based on what we think they see.

According to Cooley, then, our self results from our "imagination" of how others view us. As a result, we can develop self-identities based on *incorrect* perceptions of how others see us. We can develop a sense of confidence or a sense of doubt based on how we think others react to our performance, but we might be completely wrong. Imagine you are on a first date. All the cues you receive throughout the evening are positive—your companion smiles, laughs, and seems to be having a genuinely good time. You go home feeling happy, confident that the evening went really well. But your date never returns your calls, and there is no second date. You go from a feeling of elation and confidence to a sense of disappointment and doubt, perhaps even asking, "What's wrong with me?"

**Mead: Stages of the Self** George Herbert Mead (1863–1931), another American sociologist, sought to expand upon Cooley's theory that we become our self through interaction with others. He argued that there are two core components of the self: the "I" and the "Me." The **I** is our acting self. It is the part of us that walks, reads, sings, smiles, speaks, or performs any other action we might undertake. The **Me** is our socialized self. Based on the standards we have learned from others, the Me plans action and then judges our performance afterward.

For Mead the self represents an ongoing interaction between our socialized self and our acting self. The Me plans. The I acts. The Me judges. Take participating in classroom discussions as an example. Our Me may have something to say but fears that the words won't come out quite right, which could lead to embarrassment, so our I stays silent. Our Me then kicks our self afterwards when someone else says exactly what we planned to say and receives praise from the professor for having said it.

It is through our interactions with others that we get the social expectations of the Me into our heads. According to Mead (1964b), when we are young, we see ourselves as the center of the universe and find it difficult to consider the perspectives of others. For example, when shown a mountain scene and asked to describe what an observer on the opposite side of the mountain might see, young children describe only objects visible from their own vantage point. Although we always retain a certain level of self-centeredness, as we mature, the self changes and begins to reflect greater concern with the reactions of others.

Parents, friends, co-workers, coaches, and teachers are often among those who play a major role in shaping a person's self. The term **significant others** refers to individuals who are most important in the development of the self. Many young people, for example, choose the same occupational field

> I wanted to change the world. But I have found that the only thing one can be sure of changing is oneself.
>
> **Aldous Huxley**

**looking-glass self** A concept that emphasizes the self as the product of our social interactions.

**I** The acting self that exists in relation to the Me.

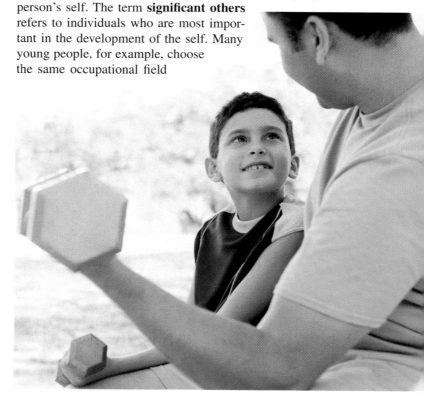

## SOCthink

> > > What cues do you rely on to know if things are going well on a first date? How about on a job interview? To what extent do you think it is possible to fake such cues?

as their parents or adopt the same pop culture preferences as their friends (Sullivan [1953] 1968).

As we grow up, we develop a sense of who people are, how they fit together, and where we might fit into that map. We take the cues we learn from our significant others and learn how to jump through the necessary hoops to get to where and who we want to be. Mead (1934, 1964a) described that transformation as a three-stage process of self-development: the preparatory stage, the play stage, and the game stage.

*The Preparatory Stage* During the *preparatory stage,* which lasts until about age three, children merely imitate the people around them, especially family members with whom they continually interact. Thus, a small child will bang on a piece of wood while a parent is engaged in carpentry work or will try to throw a ball if an older sibling is doing so nearby. This imitation is largely mindless—simple parroting of the actions of others.

As they grow older, children begin to realize that we attach meanings to our actions, and they become more adept at using symbols to communicate with others. **Symbols** are the gestures, objects, and words that form the basis of human communication. By interacting with family and friends, as well as by watching cartoons on television and looking at picture books, children in the preparatory stage begin to develop interaction skills they will use throughout their lives. They learn that they can use symbols to get their way, such as saying please and thank you, or perhaps throwing a tantrum in the candy aisle of the local supermarket.

*The Play Stage* As children develop skill in communicating through symbols, they gradually become more aware of social relationships out of which those symbols grow. During the *play stage*, from about ages three through five, they begin to pretend to be other people: a doctor, parent, superhero, or teacher. Such play need not make a lot of sense or be particularly coherent to adults, and children, especially when they are young, are able to move in and out of various characters with ease. For Mead, playing make-believe is more than just fun; it is a critical part of our self-development.

Mead, in fact, noted that an important aspect of the play stage is role playing. **Role taking** is the process of mentally assuming the perspective of another and responding from that imagined viewpoint. Through this process a young child internalizes the performances of other people and gradually learns, for example, when it is best to ask a parent for favors. If the parent usually comes home from work in a bad mood, the child will wait until after dinner, when the parent is more relaxed and approachable.

*The Game Stage* In Mead's third stage, the *game stage,* the child of about six to nine years of age no longer merely plays roles but now begins to consider several tasks and relationships simultaneously. At this point in development, children grasp not only their own social positions but also those of others around them. The transition from play to game is evident when teaching kids to play team sports such as t-ball or soccer. When they are little, you will often see a clump of kids chasing after a ball or moving up the field together. They have yet to learn that different people play different positions and that they will be more successful as a team if everyone plays the position to which they are assigned. When they do, they can take for granted that someone will be covering a base so they can throw a runner out or that a goalie will be there to make a save if the ball gets behind them. This map of who should be where and who should do what serves as a kind of blueprint for society, and internalizing it represents the final stage of development in Mead's model; the child can now respond to numerous members of the social environment.

**Me** The socialized self that plans actions and judges performances based on the standards we have learned from others.

**significant other** An individual who is most important in the development of the self, such as a parent, friend, or teacher.

**symbol** A gesture, object, or word that forms the basis of human communication.

**role taking** The process of mentally assuming the perspective of another and responding from that imagined viewpoint.

**generalized other** The attitudes, viewpoints, and expectations of society as a whole that a child takes into account in his or her behavior.

Mead uses the term **generalized other** to refer to the attitudes, viewpoints, and expectations of society as a whole that a child takes into account in his or her behavior. Simply put, this concept suggests that when an individual acts, he or she takes into account an entire group of people. For example, a child will not act courteously merely to please a particular parent. Rather, the child comes to understand that courtesy is a widespread social value endorsed by parents, teachers, and religious leaders.

At the game stage, children can take a more sophisticated view of people and the social environment. They now understand what specific occupations and social positions are and no longer equate Mr. Williams only with the role of "librarian" or Ms. Sanchez only with "principal." It has become clear to the child that Mr. Williams can be a librarian, a parent, and a marathon runner at the same time and that Ms. Sanchez is one of many principals in our society. Thus, the child has reached a new level of sophistication in observations of individuals and institutions.

### Goffman: Presentation of the Self

Given that others play such a powerful role in shaping who we are and how we think about ourselves, the way we represent our self to others becomes a major concern for us and a significant interest to sociologists. Erving Goffman, a Canadian sociologist, provided a helpful model for better understanding how we go about constructing and maintaining our self through interactions with others. He suggested that each of us seeks to convey impressions of who we are to others even as those others are doing the same, creating a kind of performance that we can analyze and understand.

To analyze our everyday social interactions, Goffman offers the **dramaturgical approach,** which studies interaction as if we were all actors

POPSOC

### Momsense

From June Cleaver in the 1950s to Marge Simpson today, TV moms have played with the idea that there are common scripts that mothers use as they perform their role. Comedian Anita Renfroe has taken this a step further. She condensed the things a mom would say in a 24-hour period down to 2 minutes and 35 seconds and set it to the William Tell Overture. A YouTube search on "Momsense" will take you there.

on a stage. Our interactions can be better understood, according to Goffman, when viewed as attempts to carry out successful performances, equivalent to putting on a play. We perform front stage, largely following scripts, having already prepared for our performance backstage. We use appropriate props, including costumes, to make our performance believable. While some improvisation is permissible, too much threatens the credibility of the character we are trying to play and may ruin the show. In order to give a successful performance, we also may need other cast members with whom we work as a team. Finally, our performance is carried out before an audience that judges how well we do. Whether in our role as students, restaurant servers, or even lovers, we all know that we have a part to play and that if we don't say the right lines or use the correct props the show will collapse, undermining our sense of self.

Early in life, the individual learns to slant his or her presentation of the self in order to

# SOCthink

> > > Imagine that going to class is like performing in a play. Who are the key players? What are some of their most-used lines? What props do they use to be convincing? How might the performance break down, and what steps might be taken to save the show?

create distinctive appearances and satisfy particular audiences. Goffman (1959) referred to this altering of the presentation of the self as **impression management.** We want others to see us in a positive light, and in order to maximize the possibility of this outcome, we engage in **face-work.** How often do you initiate some kind of face-saving behavior when you feel embarrassed or rejected? In response to a rejection at a singles' bar, a person may engage in face-work by saying, "There really isn't an interesting person in this entire crowd." Or, if we do poorly on an exam, we may say to a friend who did likewise, "This professor is incompetent." We feel the need to maintain a proper image of the self if we are to continue social interaction.

In some cultures, people engage in elaborate deceptions to avoid losing face. In Japan, for example, where lifetime employment has until recently been the norm, "company men" thrown out of work during a severe economic recession may feign employment, rising as usual in the morning, donning suit and tie, and heading for the business district. But instead of going to the office, they congregate at places such as Tokyo's Hibiya Library, where they pass the time by reading before returning home at the usual hour. Many of these men are trying to protect family members, who would be shamed if neighbors discovered that the family

breadwinner was unemployed. Others are deceiving their wives and families as well (French 2000).

Goffman's work on the self represents a logical progression of sociological studies begun by Cooley and Mead on how personality is acquired through socialization and how we manage the presentation of our self to others. Cooley stressed the process by which we create a self; Mead focused on how the self develops as we learn to interact with others; Goffman emphasized the ways in which we consciously create images of ourselves for others.

## PSYCHOLOGICAL APPROACHES TO THE SELF

Psychologists have shared the interest of Cooley, Mead, and other sociologists in the development of the self. Early work in psychology, such as that of Sigmund Freud (1856–1939), stressed the role of inborn drives—among them the drive for sexual gratification—in channeling human behavior. Later psychologists such as Jean Piaget emphasized the stages through which human beings progress as the self develops.

Like Cooley and Mead, Freud believed that the self is a social product and that aspects of one's personality are influenced by other people (especially one's parents). However, unlike Cooley and Mead, Freud suggested that the self has components that work in opposition to each other. According to Freud, we have a natural instinct that seeks limitless pleasure, but this is at odds with our societal needs for order and constraint. By interacting with others, we learn the expectations of society and then select behavior most appropriate to our own culture. (Of course, as Freud was well aware, we sometimes distort reality and behave irrationally.)

**dramaturgical approach** A view of social interaction in which people are seen as theatrical performers.

**impression management** The altering of the presentation of the self in order to create distinctive appearances and satisfy particular audiences.

**face-work** The efforts people make to maintain a proper image and avoid public embarrassment.

Through his research on children, including newborns, the Swiss child psychologist Jean Piaget (1896–1980) underscored the importance of social interactions in developing a sense of self. In his well-known **cognitive theory of development,** Piaget (1954) identified four stages in the development of children's thought processes. In the first, or *sensorimotor,* stage, young children use their senses to make discoveries. For example, through touching they discover that their hands are actually a part of themselves. During the second, or *preoperational,* stage, children begin to use words and symbols to distinguish objects and ideas. The milestone in the third, or *concrete operational,* stage is that children engage in more logical thinking. For example, they learn that even when a formless lump of clay is shaped into a snake, it is still the same clay. Finally, in the fourth, or *formal operational,* stage, adolescents become capable of sophisticated abstract thought and can deal with ideas and values in a logical manner.

Piaget suggested that moral development becomes an important part of socialization as children develop the ability to think more abstractly. When children learn the rules of a game such as checkers or jacks, they are learning to obey societal norms. Those under eight years of age display a rather basic level of morality: rules are rules, and there is no concept of "extenuating circumstances." As they

**cognitive theory of development** The theory that children's thought progresses through four stages of development.

mature, children become capable of greater autonomy, and they begin to experience moral dilemmas and doubts as to what constitutes proper behavior.

According to Piaget, social interaction is the key to development. As children grow older, they pay increasing attention to how other people think and why they act in particular ways. In order to develop a distinct personality, each of us needs opportunities to interact with others. As we saw earlier, Isabelle was deprived of the chance for normal social interactions, and the consequences were severe (Kitchener 1991).

## >> Agents of Socialization

The people with whom we interact influence how we think about ourselves and how we represent ourselves to others, and the positions they occupy determine the kind of influence they have. Family, friends, schools, peers, the mass media, the workplace, religion, and the state are among the agents of socialization that play the most powerful roles in shaping the self.

### FAMILY

The family is the most important agent of socialization, especially for children. We can see the power of family socialization among the Amish. Children in Amish communities are raised in a highly structured and disciplined manner, but they are not immune to the temptations posed by their peers in the non-Amish world. During a period of discovery called *rumspringa,* a term that means "running around," Amish young people attend barn dances where taboos like drinking, smoking, and driving cars are commonly violated. Parents often react by looking the other way, sometimes literally, pretending not to notice. They remain secure in the knowledge that their children almost always return to traditional Amish lifestyle. Research shows that only about 20 percent of Amish youths leave the fold, and most of them join one of the only somewhat more modern Mennonite groups. Rarely does a baptized adult leave (Meyers 1992; Schachtman 2006; Zellner and Schaefer 2006).

While the Amish provide what seems like an extreme case, the truth is that all families play a powerful role in shaping their children. Although peer groups and the media do influence us, almost all available research shows that the role of the family in socializing a child cannot be overestimated (W. Williams 1998; for a different view see J. Harris 1998). The lifelong process of learning begins shortly after birth. Since newborns can hear, see, smell, and taste, and can feel heat, cold, and pain, they are constantly orienting themselves to the surrounding world. Human beings, especially family members, constitute an important part of their social environment. People minister to the baby's needs by feeding, cleaning, carrying, and comforting her or him. It is in the context of families that we learn to talk, walk, feed ourselves, go to the bathroom, and so on—basic skills that we take for granted as natural but that we learned thanks to our families.

**Cultural Influences**   As both Cooley and Mead noted, the development of the self is a critical aspect of the early years of one's life. How children develop this sense of self, however, can vary from one society to another. For example, most parents in the United States do not send six-year-olds to school unsupervised. However, that is the norm in Japan, where parents push their children to commute to school on their own from an early age. In cities like Tokyo, first-graders must learn to negotiate buses, subways, and long walks. To ensure their safety, parents carefully lay out rules: never talk to strangers; check with a station attendant if you get off at the wrong stop; stay on to the end of the line, then call, if you miss your stop; take stairs, not escalators; don't fall asleep. Some parents equip the children with cell phones or pagers. One parent acknowledges that she worries, "but after they are 6, children are supposed to start being independent from the mother. If you're still taking your child to school after the first month, everyone looks at you funny" (Tolbert 2000:17).

Family structures also reproduce themselves through socialization. In the contexts of families, children learn expectations regarding marriage and parenthood. Children observe their parents expressing affection, dealing with finances, quarreling, complaining about in-laws, and so forth. Their learning represents an informal process of an-

ticipatory socialization in which they develop a tentative model of what being married and being a parent are like.

While we consider the family's role in socialization, we need to remember, however, that children are not simply robots that we can program as we wish. They do not play a passive role in their socialization. As Mead's "I" implies, they choose, sometimes to the consternation of their parents, and in so doing are active participants in their self-creation. Through the choices they make, they influence and alter the families, schools, and communities of which they are a part.

**The Impact of Race and Gender**   In the United States, social development includes exposure to cultural assumptions regarding gender and race. African American parents, for example, have learned that children as young as two years old can absorb negative messages about Blacks in children's books, toys, and television shows—the vast majority of which are designed primarily for White consumers. At the same time, African American children are exposed more often than others to the inner-city youth gang culture. Because most Blacks, even those who are middle class, live near very poor neighborhoods, their children are susceptible to these influences, despite their parents' strong family values (Linn and Poussaint 1999; Pattillo-McCoy 1999).

The term **gender roles** refers to expectations regarding the proper behavior, attitudes, and activities of males and females. For example, we traditionally think of "toughness" as masculine—and desirable only in men—while we view "tenderness" as feminine. As we will see in Chapter 12, other cultures do not necessarily assign these qualities to each gender in the way that our culture does. As the primary agents of childhood socialization, parents play a critical role in guiding children into those gender roles deemed appropriate in a society.

Other adults, older siblings, the mass media, and religious and educational institutions also have a noticeable impact on a child's socialization into feminine and masculine norms. A culture or subculture may require that one sex or the other take primary responsibility for the socialization of children, economic support of the family, or religious or intellectual leadership. In some societies girls are socialized mainly by their mothers and boys by their fathers—an arrangement that may prevent girls from learning critical survival skills. In South Asia, for example, fathers teach their sons to swim to prepare them for a life as fishermen; girls typically do not learn to swim. When the deadly tsunami hit the coast of South Asia in 2004, many more men than women survived.

## SCHOOL

In school we typically move beyond the more sheltered confines of our family and learn to become members of the larger social groups to which we belong. Schools teach us the taken-for-granted knowledge of the broader society—not only basic skills such as reading, writing, and 'rithmatic but also shared cultural knowledge such as the national anthem, the heroes of the American Revolution, and the pillars of good character. Like the family, schools have an explicit mandate to socialize people in the United States—and especially children—into the norms and values of U.S. culture.

Schools teach children the values and customs of the larger society because that shared culture provides the glue that holds us together as a society. If we did not transmit our knowledge and skills from one generation to the next, society would collapse. The knowledge we gain there, however, goes beyond just the official curriculum to include the more informal lessons we learn on the playground. We do learn the facts and figures of history, science, reading, math, and more, but we also learn how to stand up for ourselves when our parents or teachers are not there to hover over us or to bail us out.

In addition to providing social order, schools open doors for us as individuals. We are exposed to new ways of thinking and acting that allow us to make new choices about our future. While this can include training for careers that allow us to "get ahead," it also involves exposure to new cultures, ideas, practices, and possibilities. It might even lead us to an unexpected future such as a career in sociology!

While schools provide both social order and individual opportunity, they can also reinforce existing inequality through the ways students are socialized. As economists Samuel Bowles and Herbert Gintis (1976) have observed, schools produce teachable students who become manageable workers. They argue that schools have less to do with transmitting academic content than with socializing students into the proper attitudes and behaviors of the workplace. Schools teach students how to work for rewards, how to work in teams, how to meet deadlines, how to take responsibility for a task or work product, how to comply with instructions, and so on. The students who internalize these skills best are rewarded with opportunities in the workplace while others are left behind.

These differential outcomes are compounded by the fact that your position when you enter school shapes where you end up. For example, higher education in the United States is costly despite the existence of public colleges and universities and financial aid programs. Students from affluent backgrounds therefore have an advantage in gaining access to universities and professional training. At the same time, less affluent young people may never receive the preparation that would qualify them for the best-paying and most prestigious jobs.

## PEER GROUPS

While families and schools do shape us, if you ask any 13-year-old who matters most in his or her life, the likely answer is "friends." As children grow older, the family becomes somewhat less important in social development. Instead, peer groups increasingly assume the role of Mead's significant other. Within the peer group, young people associate with others who are approximately their own age and who often enjoy a similar social status (Giordano 2003).

In the context of peer groups, a hierarchy often develops. Sociologists Patricia and Peter Adler conducted participant observation at elementary schools to investigate how popularity works amongst fourth- through sixth-grade students. They found that, even this early, a pecking order is established ranging from the "popular clique" at the top that includes the "cool kids" on down to what they call the "social isolates" at the bottom, whom other kids sometimes call "dweebs" or "nerds" (Adler and Adler, 1996). Children get the message about where they fit and how they should behave.

> **gender role** Expectations regarding the proper behavior, attitudes, and activities of males and females.

In other research the Adlers also found that popularity reinforces gender stereotypes. To be popular as a boy is to be athletic, tough, and not too academic. To be popular as a girl is to be attractive, to be able to manipulate others using social skills, and to come from a family wealthy enough to permit shopping for the latest cool stuff (Adler, Kless, and Adler 1992). In similar research, college students were asked to reflect back on what made people popular in high school. Researchers found that male and female students named many of the same paths to popularity—such as physical attractiveness, participation in sports, and

# High School Popularity

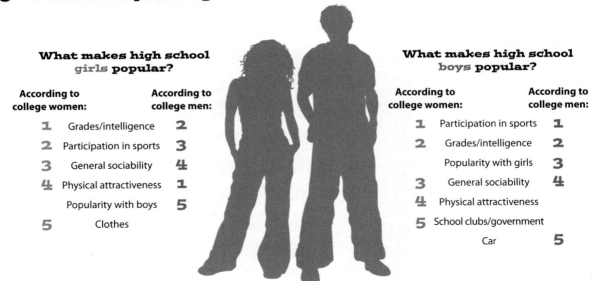

**What makes high school _girls_ popular?**

| According to college women: | | According to college men: |
|---|---|---|
| 1 | Grades/intelligence | 2 |
| 2 | Participation in sports | 3 |
| 3 | General sociability | 4 |
| 4 | Physical attractiveness | 1 |
| | Popularity with boys | 5 |
| 5 | Clothes | |

**What makes high school _boys_ popular?**

| According to college women: | | According to college men: |
|---|---|---|
| 1 | Participation in sports | 1 |
| 2 | Grades/intelligence | 2 |
| | Popularity with girls | 3 |
| 3 | General sociability | 4 |
| 4 | Physical attractiveness | |
| 5 | School clubs/government | |
| | Car | 5 |

*Note:* Students at the following universities were asked in which ways adolescents in their high schools had gained prestige with their peers: Cornell University, Louisiana State University, Southeastern Louisiana University, State University of New York at Albany, State University of New York at Stony Brook, the University of Georgia, and the University of New Hampshire.

*Source:* Suitor et al. 2001:445.

grades/intelligence—but gave them different orders of importance. While neither men nor women named sexual activity, drug use, or alcohol use as one of the top five paths, college men were much more likely than women to mention those behaviors as a means to becoming popular, for both boys and girls (Suitor et al. 2001).

Though we value the importance of kids establishing themselves as individuals, the irony is that peer culture is not very individualistic. Children, and especially adolescents, run in packs and look, talk, and act alike (often in the name of individualism). Of course, although parents often lecture their kids about not giving in to peer pressure, they don't really mean it. What they mean is to not give in to the *wrong kinds* of peer pressure. They love peer pressure if it makes their children more like the "good kids" or, even better, if the form of social pressure they give in to is parental pressure.

## MASS MEDIA AND TECHNOLOGY

In the past 80 or so years, media innovations—radio, motion pictures, recorded music, television, and the Internet—have become important agents of socialization. One national survey indicates that 68 percent of U.S. children have a television in their bedroom, and nearly half of all youths ages 8–18 use the Internet every day (Rideout et al. 2005). We are spending more and more of our time interacting with technology, which has an inevitable impact on our interactions with each other.

Television programs and even commercials can introduce young people to unfamiliar lifestyles and cultures.

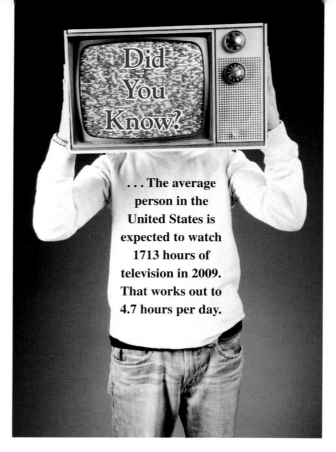

Did You Know?

... The average person in the United States is expected to watch 1713 hours of television in 2009. That works out to 4.7 hours per day.

On PBS alone, children are exposed to life in the city, on the farm, and across the world. The same thing happens in other countries and regions. In the Palestinian-held Gaza Strip, for example, Hamas—a group better known for its

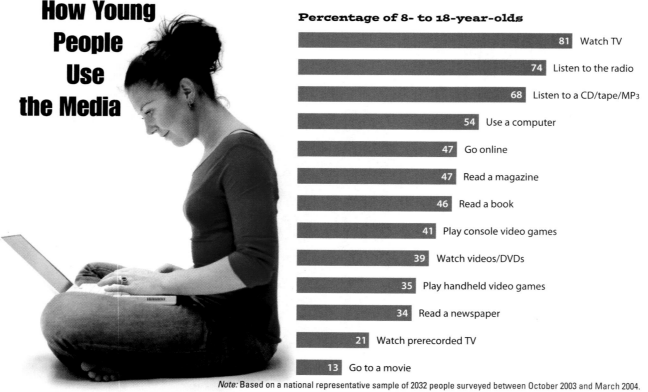

## How Young People Use the Media

**Percentage of 8- to 18-year-olds**

| | |
|---|---|
| 81 | Watch TV |
| 74 | Listen to the radio |
| 68 | Listen to a CD/tape/MP3 |
| 54 | Use a computer |
| 47 | Go online |
| 47 | Read a magazine |
| 46 | Read a book |
| 41 | Play console video games |
| 39 | Watch videos/DVDs |
| 35 | Play handheld video games |
| 34 | Read a newspaper |
| 21 | Watch prerecorded TV |
| 13 | Go to a movie |

*Note:* Based on a national representative sample of 2032 people surveyed between October 2003 and March 2004.
*Source:* Rideout et al. 2005:7.

suicide bombing campaigns—has launched a television program meant to familiarize children with the Palestinian position on the disputed territories. In between lectures on revered sites such as Nablus and Al Aksa Mosque, the show's host, known as Uncle Hazim, takes on-air phone calls from viewers and talks with animal characters reminiscent of those on *Sesame Street*. Designed with a child-age audience in mind, the show omits all mention of violence and armed conflict in pursuit of Hamas's goals (Craig Smith 2006).

New technologies are changing how we interact with family, friends, and even strangers. Through email, cell phones, texting, and instant messaging, we can maintain close, almost constant, connections with family and friends both near and far. Through Facebook and MySpace, we can establish and extend networks with "friends" both known and unknown. But new technologies can also lead to narrowcasting, in which we interact mainly with people who are most like ourselves. This can limit the number of significant relationships we have with people with whom we might share fundamental differences, thus weakening our conflict resolution skills. Other skills, however, may be strengthened. Researchers studying technology use among families in northern California's Silicon Valley (a technology corridor) found that families are socialized into multitasking (doing more than one task at a time) as the social norm; devoting one's full attention to one task—even eating or driving—is less and less common on a typical day (Silicon Valley Cultures Project 2004).

Not just in Silicon Valley but in Africa and other developing areas people have been socialized into relying

## SOCthink

> > > According to a recent commercial, "snurfing" involves surfing the Internet while you are talking to someone on the phone. To what extent does multitasking such as this have a negative impact on our interpersonal skills? How do you feel when people do this to you? Why might you have done it to others?

on new communications technologies. For instance, not long ago, if Zadhe Iyombe wanted to talk to his mother, he had to make an eight-day trip from the capital city of Kinshasa (in the Democratic Republic of the Congo) up the Congo River by boat to the rural town where he was born. Now both he and his mother have access to a cell phone, and they send text messages to each other daily. And Iyombe and his mother are not atypical. Although cell phones aren't cheap, 1.4 billion owners in developing countries have come to consider them a necessity. Today, there are more cell phones in developing countries than in industrial nations—the first time in history that developing countries have outpaced the developed world in the adoption of a telecommunications technology (K. Sullivan 2006).

Access to media can increase social cohesion by presenting a common, more or less standardized view of culture

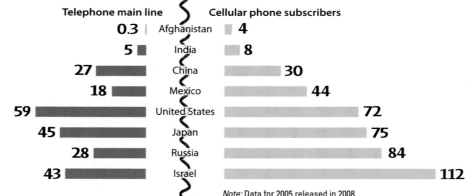

# Telephones and Cell Phones by Country, 2005 (rates per 100 people)

| | Telephone main line | | Cellular phone subscribers |
|---|---|---|---|
| Afghanistan | 0.3 | | 4 |
| India | 5 | | 8 |
| China | 27 | | 30 |
| Mexico | 18 | | 44 |
| United States | 59 | | 72 |
| Japan | 45 | | 75 |
| Russia | 28 | | 84 |
| Israel | 43 | | 112 |

*Note:* Data for 2005 released in 2008.

*Source:* Bureau of the Census. *Statistical Abstract of the United States: 2008.* Table 1354, p. 856.

through mass communication. Sociologist Robert Park (1922) studied how newspapers helped immigrants to the United States adjust to their environment by changing their customary habits and teaching them the values and views of people in their new home country. Unquestionably, the mass media play a significant role in providing a collective experience for members of society. Think about how the mass media bring together members of a community or even a nation by broadcasting important events and ceremonies (such as inaugurations, press conferences, parades, state funerals, and the Olympics) and by covering disasters.

Which media outlets did people turn to in the aftermath of the September 11, 2001, terrorist attacks? Television and telephone were the primary means by which people in the United States bonded. But the Internet also played a prominent role. About half of all Internet users—more than 53 million people—received some kind of news about the attacks online. Nearly three-fourths of Internet users com-

municated via email to show their patriotism, discuss events with their families, or reconnect with old friends. More than a third of Internet users read or posted material in online forums. In the first 30 days alone, the Library of Congress collected from one Internet site more than half a million pages having to do with the terrorist attacks. As a library director noted, "The Internet has become for many the public commons, a place where they can come together and talk" (D. L. Miller and Darlington 2002; Mirapaul 2001:E2; Rainie 2001).

## THE WORKPLACE

Learning to behave appropriately in an occupation is a fundamental aspect of human socialization. In the United States, working full time confirms adult status; it indicates that one has passed out of adolescence. In a sense, socialization into an occupation can represent both a harsh reality ("I have to work in order to buy food and pay the rent") and the realization of an ambition ("I've always wanted to be an airline pilot") (W. Moore 1968:862).

It used to be that our work life began with the end of our formal schooling, but that is no longer necessarily the case, at least not in the United States. More and more young people work today, and not just for a parent or relative. Adolescents generally seek jobs in order to earn spending money; 80 percent of high school seniors say that little or none of what they earn goes to family expenses. These teens rarely look on their employment as a means of exploring vocational interests or getting on-the-job training.

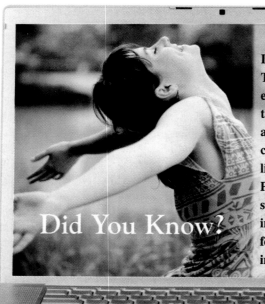

... May 3, 2008, was **International Shutdown Day.** This is an annual event to encourage people to turn off their computer for 24 hours and reflect on the impact computers have on our lives and our communities. Participants are urged to spend the time they save interacting with friends, going for a hike, or volunteering in the community.

Did You Know?

# Child Care Arrangements for Preschoolers

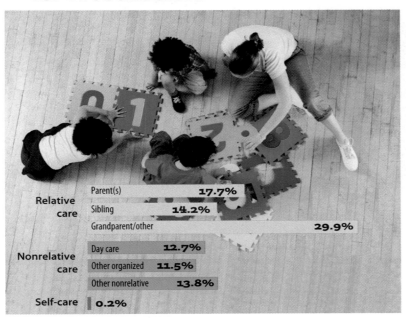

| Relative care | Parent(s) | 17.7% |
| | Sibling | 14.2% |
| | Grandparent/other | 29.9% |
| Nonrelative care | Day care | 12.7% |
| | Other organized | 11.5% |
| | Other nonrelative | 13.8% |
| Self-care | | 0.2% |

*Note:* Data for 2002 reported in 2005.
*Source:* J. Johnson 2005:2.

Some observers feel that the increasing number of teenagers who are working earlier in life and for longer hours are finding the workplace to be almost as important an agent of socialization as school. In fact, a number of educators complain that time spent at work is adversely affecting students' schoolwork. The level of teenage employment in the United States is the highest among industrial countries, which may provide one explanation for why U.S. high school students lag behind those in other countries on international achievement tests.

Socialization in the workplace changes when it involves a more permanent shift from an after-school job to full-time employment. Occupational socialization can be most intense during the transition from school to job, but it continues throughout one's work history. Technological advances and corporate reorganization may alter the requirements of the position and necessitate new training. According to the Bureau of Labor Statistics (2006), between the ages of 18 to 36 alone, the typical person holds 11 different jobs. We can no longer assume that we will have a job-for-life, so whether by choice or by necessity, we must be open to ongoing occupational socialization.

## RELIGION AND THE STATE

Increasingly, social scientists are recognizing the growing importance of government ("the state") and the continued significance of religion as agents of socialization. Traditionally, family members served as the primary caregivers in U.S. culture, but in the 20th century, the family's protective function was steadily transferred to outside agencies such as public schools, hospitals, mental health clinics, and child care centers, many of which are run by the state. Historically, religious groups also provided such care and protection. Despite early sociological predictions that religion would cease to play a substantial role in modern society, these groups continue to provide private schools, hospitals, day care facilities, nursing homes, and more.

Preschool children in particular are often cared for by someone other than a parent. Seventy-three percent of employed mothers depend on others to care for their children, and 30 percent of mothers who aren't employed have regular care arrangements. Over a third of children under age five are cared for by nonrelatives in nursery schools, Head Start programs, day care centers, family day care, and other providers. Children this age are also more likely to be cared for on a daily basis by grandparents than by their parents (J. Johnson 2005).

Both government and organized religion act to provide markers representing significant life course transitions. For example, religious organizations continue to celebrate meaningful ritual events—such as baptism, bismillah, or bar/bat mitzvah—that often bring together all the members of an extended family, even if they never

## Hot or Not?

Should government play a larger role in socializing children by funding public education for all children starting at the age of two?

*Muslim men at prayer.*

Although many 18-year-olds choose not to vote, voter turnout in the 2004 presidential election was the highest it had been in decades, causing long lines at some polling stations.

borns to the world in the Soboa ceremony by stepping over the seven-day-old infant seven times. And Naval Academy seniors celebrate their graduation from college by hurling their hats skyward.

## THE LIFE COURSE

Such specific ceremonies mark stages of development in the life course. They indicate that the process of socialization continues through all stages of the life cycle. In fact, some researchers have chosen to concentrate on socialization as a lifelong process. Sociologists and other social scientists who take such a **life course approach** look closely at the social factors, including gender and income, that influence people throughout their lives, from birth to death. They recognize that biological changes help mold but do not dictate human behavior.

In the transition from childhood to adulthood, we can identify certain markers that signify the passage from one life stage to the next. These milestones vary from one society and even one generation to the next. In the United States, according to one national survey, completion of

meet for any other reason. Government regulations stipulate the ages at which a person may drive a car, drink

**rite of passage** A ritual marking the symbolic transition from one social position to another.

**life course approach** A research orientation in which sociologists and other social scientists look closely at the social factors that influence people throughout their lives, from birth to death.

alcohol, vote in elections, marry without parental permission, work overtime, and retire. While these regulations do not constitute strict rites of passage—most 18-year-olds choose not to vote, and most people choose their age of retirement without reference to government dictates—they do symbolize the fact that we have moved on to a different stage of our life, with different expectations regarding our behavior.

## >> Socialization Throughout the Life Course

Adolescents among the Kota people of the Congo in Africa paint themselves blue. Cuban American girls go on a daylong religious retreat before dancing the night away. These are all **rites of passage**—symbolic representations of significant transitions that serve as a means of dramatizing and validating changes in a person's status.

In the Kota rite the color blue—the color of death—symbolizes the death of childhood and the passage to adulthood. For adolescent girls in Miami's Cuban American community, the *quinceañera* ceremony celebrating the attainment of womanhood at age 15 supports a network of party planners, caterers, dress designers, and the Miss Quinceañera Latina pageant. For thousands of years, Egyptian mothers have welcomed their new-

Body painting is a ritual marking the passage to puberty in some cultures.

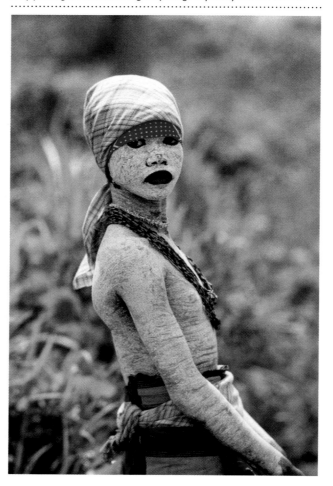

# Milestones in the Transition to Adulthood

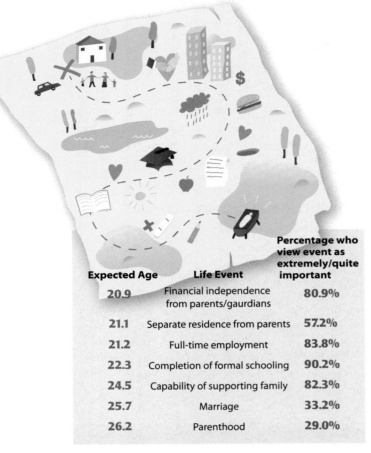

| Expected Age | Life Event | Percentage who view event as extremely/quite important |
|---|---|---|
| 20.9 | Financial independence from parents/gaurdians | 80.9% |
| 21.1 | Separate residence from parents | 57.2% |
| 21.2 | Full-time employment | 83.8% |
| 22.3 | Completion of formal schooling | 90.2% |
| 24.5 | Capability of supporting family | 82.3% |
| 25.7 | Marriage | 33.2% |
| 26.2 | Parenthood | 29.0% |

*Note:* Based on the 2002 General Social Survey of 1398 people.
*Source:* Smith 2003.

formal schooling has risen to the top, with 90 percent of people identifying it as an important rite of passage. On average, Americans expect this milestone to be attained by a person's 23rd birthday. Other major events in the life course, such as getting married or becoming a parent, are expected to follow three or four years later. Interestingly, the significance of these markers has declined, with only about one-third of survey respondents identifying marriage and less than one-third identifying parenthood as important milestones representing adulthood (S. Furstenberg et al. 2004; Smith 2003).

One result of these staggered steps to independence is that in the United States, unlike some other societies, there is no clear dividing line between adolescence and adulthood. Nowadays, the number of years between childhood and adulthood has grown, and few young people finish school, get married, and leave home at about the same age, clearly establishing their transition to adulthood. The term *youthhood* has been coined to describe the prolonged ambiguous status that young people in their twenties experience (Côté 2000).

## ANTICIPATORY SOCIALIZATION AND RESOCIALIZATION

In our journey through our lives, we seek to prepare ourselves for what is coming and to adapt to change as necessary. To prepare, we undergo **anticipatory socialization,** which refers to processes of socialization in which a person "rehearses" for future positions, occupations, and social relationships. A culture can function more efficiently and smoothly if members become acquainted with the norms, values, and behavior associated with a social position before actually assuming that status. Preparation for many aspects of adult life begins with anticipatory socialization during childhood and adolescence and continues throughout our lives as we prepare for new responsibilities.

High school students experience a bit of anticipatory socialization when they prepare for college. They begin to imagine what college life will be like and what kind of person they will be when they get there. They may seek out information from friends and family in order to get a better sense of what to expect, but increasingly, they also rely on campus websites and Facebook entries. To assist in this process and to attract more students, colleges are investing more time and money in websites through which students can take "virtual" campus tours, listen to podcasts, and stream videos of everything from the school song to a sample zoology lecture.

Occasionally, assuming a new social or occupational position requires that we *unlearn* an established orientation. **Resocialization** refers to the process of discarding old behavior patterns and accepting new ones as part of a life transition. Often resocialization results from explicit efforts to transform an individual, as happens in reform schools, therapy groups, prisons, religious conversion settings, and political indoctrination camps. The process of resocialization typically involves considerable stress for the individual— much more so than socialization in general, or even anticipatory socialization (Gecas 1992).

Resocialization is particularly effective when it occurs within a total institution. Erving Goffman (1961) coined the term **total institution** to refer to an institution that reg-

**anticipatory socialization** Processes of socialization in which a person "rehearses" for future positions, occupations, and social relationships.

**resocialization** The process of discarding former behavior patterns and accepting new ones as part of a transition in one's life.

**total institution** An institution that regulates all aspects of a person's life under a single authority, such as a prison, the military, a mental hospital, or a convent.

ulates all aspects of a person's life under a single authority. Examples can be more or less extreme, from summer camp or boarding school to prison, the military, a mental hospital, or a convent. Because the total institution is generally cut off from the rest of society, it provides for all the needs of its members. In its extreme form, so elaborate are its requirements, and so all-encompassing its activities, that the total institution represents a miniature society.

**degradation ceremony** An aspect of the socialization process within some total institutions, in which people are subjected to humiliating rituals.

Goffman (1961) identified several common traits of total institutions:

- All aspects of life are conducted in the same place under the control of a single authority.
- Any activities within the institution are conducted in the company of others in the same circumstances—for example, army recruits or novices in a convent.
- The authorities devise rules and schedule activities without consulting the participants.
- All aspects of life within a total institution are designed to fulfill the purpose of the organization. Thus, all activities in a monastery might be centered on prayer and communion with God (Davies 1989; P. Rose et al. 1979).

People often lose their individuality within total institutions. For example, a person entering prison may experience the humiliation of a **degradation ceremony** as he or she is stripped of clothing, jewelry, and other personal possessions. From that point on, scheduled daily routines allow for little or no personal initiative. The individual becomes secondary and rather invisible in the overbearing social environment (Garfinkel 1956).

## SOCthink

> > > To what extent is summer camp, a cruise, or even life at a residential college similar to a total institution? In what ways is it different?

## ROLE TRANSITIONS DURING THE LIFE COURSE

As we have seen, one of the key transitional stages we pass through occurs as we enter the adult world, perhaps by moving out of the parental home, beginning a career, or entering a marriage. As we age, we move into the midlife transition, which typically begins at about age 40. Men and women often experience a stressful period of self-evaluation, commonly known as the **midlife crisis,** in which they realize that they have not achieved basic goals and ambitions and may feel they have little time left to do so. Psy-

*Life in prison is highly regulated—even recreation time.*

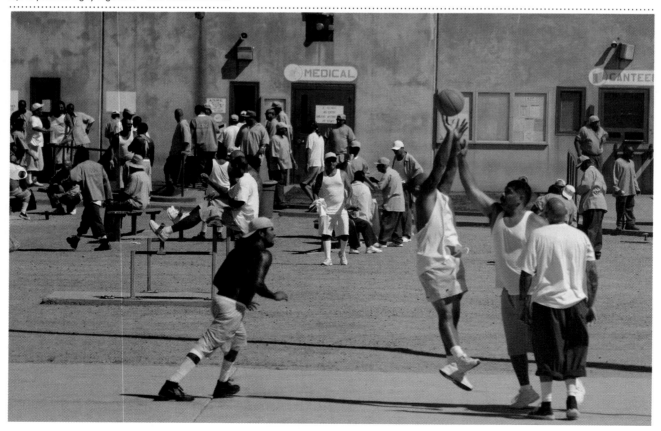

chologist Daniel Levinson (1978, 1996) found that most adults surveyed experienced tumultuous midlife conflicts within the self and with the external world. Compounding such stresses that are often associated with one's career or partner is the growing responsibility for caring for two generations at once.

During the late 1990s, social scientists focused on the **sandwich generation**—adults who simulta-

## 5 Movies on SOCIALIZATION

**Nell**
*A woman who grew up in isolation is brought into civilization by a sociologist.*

**Great Expectations**
*A poor, lower-class boy is introduced to high society.*

**Witness**
*A man is introduced and integrated into Amish culture while trying to protect a young witness to a murder.*

**Hannibal**
*A sociopathic cannibal lacks social skills.*

**The Last King of Scotland**
*A Scottish man is introduced to the horrors of authoritarian-ruled Uganda.*

neously try to meet the competing needs of their parents and their children. Their caregiving goes in two directions: to children, who even as young adults may still require significant support and direction, and to aging parents, whose health and economic problems may demand intervention by their adult children.

Like the role of caring for children, that of caring for aging parents falls disproportionately on women. Overall, women provide 60 percent of the care their parents receive, and even more as the demands of the role grow more intense and time consuming. Increasingly, middle-aged women and younger are finding themselves on the "daughter track," as their time and attention are diverted by the needs of their aging mothers and fathers (Gross 2005).

## ADJUSTING TO RETIREMENT

The last major transition identified by Levinson occurs after age 60—sometimes well after that age, due to advances in health care, greater longevity, and gradual acceptance by society of older people. In fact, yesterday's 60 may be today's 70 or even 75. Nonetheless, at some point, people transition to a different lifestyle.

Retirement is a rite of passage that marks a critical transition from one phase of a person's life to another. Typically,

symbolic events are associated with this rite of passage, such as retirement gifts, a retirement party, and special moments on the last day on the job. The preretirement period itself can be emotionally charged, especially if the retiree is expected to train his or her successor (Atchley 1976).

From 1950 to the mid-1990s, the average age at retirement in the United States declined, but in recent years it has reversed direction. In 2003, 6 percent of women and 12 percent of men over 70 were still working. A variety of factors explains this reversal: changes in Social Security benefits, an economic shift away from hard manual labor, and workers' concern with maintaining their health insurance and pension benefits. At the same time, longevity has increased, and the quality of people's health has improved (He et al. 2005:89).

Gerontologist Robert Atchley (1976) has identified several phases of the retirement experience:

- *Preretirement,* a period of anticipatory socialization as the person prepares for retirement.

- *The near phase,* when the person establishes a specific departure date from his or her job.

- *The honeymoon phase,* an often euphoric period in which the person pursues activities that he or she never had time for before.

- *The disenchantment phase,* in which retirees feel a sense of letdown or even depression as they cope with their new lives, which may include illness or poverty.

- *The reorientation phase,* which involves the development of a more realistic view of retirement alternatives.

- *The stability phase,* in which the person has learned to deal with life after retirement in a reasonable and comfortable fashion.

- *The termination phase,* which begins when the person can no longer engage in basic, day-to-day activities such as self-care and housework.

Retirement is not a single transition, then, but a series of adjustments that varies from one person to another. The length and timing of each phase will differ for each individual, depending on such factors as financial and health status. In fact, a person will not necessarily go through all the phases identified by Atchley. For example, people who are forced to retire or who face financial difficulties may never experience a honeymoon phase. And many retirees continue to be part of the paid labor force of the United States, often taking part-time jobs to supplement their pensions. That is certainly the expectation of baby boomers, as fully 79 percent expect to work in some capacity after they retire (see "Retirement Expectations" on page 86).

**midlife crisis** A stressful period of self-evaluation that begins at about age 40.

**sandwich generation** The generation of adults who simultaneously try to meet the competing needs of their parents and their children.

# Retirement Expectations

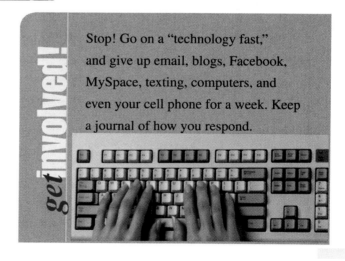

Other/don't know **4%**

Retire from your current job but work full-time doing something else **7%**

Not work at all **20%**

Start your own business/go into business for yourself **15%**

Work part-time mainly for interest or enjoyment **30%**

Work part-time mainly for needed income it provides **25%**

*Note:* Survey of the baby boom generation (people born from 1946 to 1964) conducted in 2003.

*Source: Baby Boomers Envision Retirement II: Survey of Baby Boomers' Expectations for Retirement.* AARP, 2004.

nic minority groups work intermittently after retirement more often than older Whites (National Institute on Aging 1999; Quadagno 2005).

We encounter some of the most difficult socialization challenges (and rites of passage) in these later years of life. Retirement undermines the sense of self we had that was based in our occupation, a particularly significant source of identity in the United States. Similarly, taking stock of our accomplishments and disappointments, coping with declining physical abilities, and recognizing the inevitability of death may lead to painful adjustments. Part of the difficulty is that potential answers to the "Now what?" question that we might have asked in previous life stages are dwindling, and we begin to face the end of our days.

And yet, as we reflect on the story of our lives, we can look back to see all the people who shaped us into becoming who we are. Such relationships play a crucial role in our overall self-concept and self-satisfaction. As we have already seen, we are interdependent. And, though the influences of others on our life can be both a blessing and a curse, we wouldn't be who we are without them.

Like other aspects of life in the United States, the experience of retirement varies according to gender, race, and ethnicity. White males are most likely to benefit from retirement wages, as well as to have participated in a formal retirement preparation program. As a result, anticipatory socialization for retirement is most systematic for White men. In contrast, members of racial and ethnic minority groups—especially African Americans—are more likely to exit the paid labor force through disability than through retirement. Because of their comparatively lower incomes and smaller savings, men and women from racial and eth-

*get involved!*

Stop! Go on a "technology fast," and give up email, blogs, Facebook, MySpace, texting, computers, and even your cell phone for a week. Keep a journal of how you respond.

# For REVIEW

**I.  How do we become our self?**

- While we are born with innate tendencies, we depend upon the socializing influences of others with whom we interact to provide us with the cultural tools necessary for our survival.

**II.  Who shapes our socialization?**

- While almost anyone with whom we interact can have a significant influence on us, particularly important to our development are the family, school, peer group, mass media, religion, and the state.

**III.  How does our development change over time?**

- We learn new things at various stages of our life course, experiencing significant transitions as we pass from childhood to adulthood and again from adulthood into retirement. At each stage, the kinds of things expected of us by others shift significantly.

# Pop Quiz

1. Which of the following social scientists used the phrase *looking-glass self* to emphasize that the self is the product of our social interactions with other people?
   a. George Herbert Mead
   b. Charles Horton Cooley
   c. Erving Goffman
   d. Jean Piaget

2. In what he called the *play stage* of socialization, George Herbert Mead asserted that people mentally assume the perspectives of others, thereby enabling them to respond from that imagined viewpoint. This process is referred to as
   a. role taking.
   b. the generalized other.
   c. the significant other.
   d. impression management.

3. George Herbert Mead is best known for his theory of what?
   a. presentation of the self
   b. cognitive development
   c. the self
   d. impression management

4. Suppose a clerk tries to appear busier than he or she actually is when a supervisor happens to be watching. Erving Goffman would say this is a form of what?
   a. degradation ceremony
   b. impression management
   c. resocialization
   d. looking-glass self

5. According to child psychologist Jean Piaget's cognitive theory of development, children begin to use words and symbols to distinguish objects and ideas during which stage in the development of the thought process?
   a. the sensorimotor stage
   b. the preoperational stage
   c. the concrete operational stage
   d. the formal operational stage

6. On the first day of basic training in the army, a male recruit has his civilian clothes replaced with army "greens," has his hair shaved off, loses his privacy, and finds that he must use a communal bathroom. All of these humiliating activities are part of
   a. becoming a significant other.
   b. impression management.
   c. a degradation ceremony.
   d. face-work.

7. Which social institution is considered to be the most important agent of socialization in the United States, especially for children?
   a. the family
   b. the school
   c. the peer group
   d. the mass media

8. The term *gender role* refers to
   a. the biological fact that we are male or female.
   b. a role that is given to us by a teacher.
   c. a role that is given to us in a play.
   d. expectations regarding the proper behavior, attitudes, and activities of males and females.

9. Which of the following statements about peer groups is *not* true?
   a. Peer groups have become less significant in U.S. culture.
   b. Peers can be the source of harassment as well as support.
   c. Peer groups increasingly assume the role of Mead's generalized other.
   d. Boys and girls are socialized differently.

10. The process of discarding former behavior patterns and taking on new ones is known as what?
    a. resocialization
    b. impression management
    c. anticipatory socialization
    d. the I

1. (b); 2. (a); 3. (c); 4. (b); 5. (b); 6. (c); 7. (a); 8. (d); 9. (a); 10. (a)

5

# SOCIAL

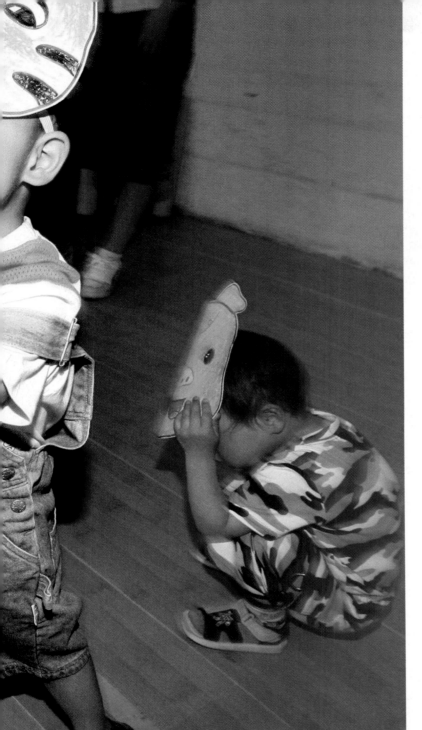

# BECOMING AN INDIVIDUAL IN SOCIETY

"Tattooing had really never entered my awareness very much. When it did, the associations were always with sailors first, ex-convicts second, and various toughs and gangsters last. . . . I had read in some obscure novel about the three signs of 'badness'—socks rolled down to the ankle, long sideburns, and a tattoo showing on the wrist. Robert Mitchum's demented killer had *Love* and *Hate* tattooed on the fingers of each hand." So writes Samuel M. Steward (1990:8) of his perception of tattoos back in the 1950s, a perception widely shared by others at the time. Steward had been a college professor for 20 years, but he decided to walk away from that to become a tattoo artist. You might say he was ahead of his time.

Times change, and so do we. Nowadays almost 40 percent of people 18–40 years old have at least one tattoo. So many people have them—including society's trendsetters and major sports figures—that mainstream culture accepts tattoos. Yet, for those who grew up in an earlier era, perhaps the stigma remains: Only 10 percent of people aged 41–64 have tattoos.

In fact, knowing a person's age allows us to predict a variety of things about how they think and what they do. Research on what has been called "Generation Next," which includes people born between 1981 and 1988, finds them less cynical about government and political leaders, less critical of business, and more tolerant on issues of immigration, race, and homosexuality than those from earlier generations. When it comes to technology, they were actually less likely to have sent or received an email within the past 24 hours than those ages 26–40. However, just over half had sent or received a text message making them twice as likely to have done so (Kohut 2007a).

While we like to think of our preferences as a matter of our own individual choice, the age into which we are born shapes our tastes. Like age, our gender, race, class, ethnicity, nationality, education, religious affiliation, occupation, and income all shape how we think, what we do, and even how we feel. Sociology investigates how those positions combine to form our social structure.

# STRUCTURE &INTERACTION

- What makes up society?
- How does social structure shape individual action?
- How do sociologists describe traditional versus modern societies?

## >> Social Interaction

When we create culture, we establish a relationship with each other and to the external world. The more we share culture with others, the more resistant it becomes to change, because change would involve getting all the people who now share that culture to think and act in new ways. Because shared culture tends to remain stable, over time we come to take certain cultural expectations for granted. In so doing, we construct the context or social environment within which we live. The result is society—the structure of relationships within which culture is created and shared through regularized patterns of social interaction.

**social interaction** The ways in which people respond to one another.

**social structure** The way in which a society is organized into predictable relationships.

Sociologists use the term **social interaction** to refer to the ways in which people respond to one another, whether face-to-face, over the telephone, or on the computer. It is through interaction that society comes alive. To use an analogy, think of society as a board game. The various components of the game—the board, game pieces, dice, rules, and so on—provide the structure of the game, but it is not truly a game until someone plays it. Society, too, must be enacted, embodied, and brought to life by individuals interacting.

How we interact with other people is shaped by our perception of their position relative to our own. According to sociologist Herbert Blumer (1969:79), the distinctive characteristic of social interaction is that "human beings interpret or 'define' each other's actions instead of merely reacting to each other's actions." In other words, we respond to someone's behavior based on the meaning we attach to his or her actions. Our perceptions, evaluations, and definitions shape our reality. The meanings we ascribe to others' actions typically reflect the norms and values of the dominant culture and our socialization experiences within that culture. Our understanding of social reality is liter-

ally constructed from our social interactions (Berger and Luckmann 1966).

The ability to define social reality reflects a group's power within a society. In fact, one of the crucial aspects of the relationship between dominant and subordinate groups is the ability of the former to define a society's values. Sociologist William I. Thomas (1923), an early critic of theories of racial and gender differences, recognized that the "definition of the situation" could mold the thinking and personality of the individual. Thomas observed that people respond not only to the objective features of a person or situation but also to the meaning that person or situation has for them.

Changing the meanings we attach to the positions people occupy often involves a struggle because those who wield power and influence in a society are reluctant to relinquish their positions of control. Since the mid-1900s—starting with the civil rights movement of the 1950s and 1960s and continuing among such groups as women, the elderly, gays and lesbians, and people with disabilities—an important aspect of the process of social change has involved redefining or reconstructing social reality. When members of subordinate groups challenge traditional so-

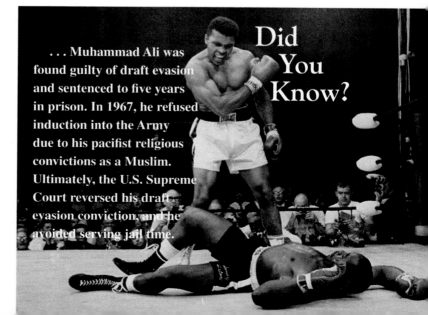

... Muhammad Ali was found guilty of draft evasion and sentenced to five years in prison. In 1967, he refused induction into the Army due to his pacifist religious convictions as a Muslim. Ultimately, the U.S. Supreme Court reversed his draft evasion conviction, and he avoided serving jail time.

Did You Know?

cial assumptions, they can raise our consciousness about the consequences of group membership or social position and help us perceive and experience reality in a new way. For example, when Olympic gold medalist Muhammad Ali began his professional boxing career in the early 1960s, he was much like any other young Black fighter. He was managed and sponsored by a White syndicate and went by his given name, Cassius Clay. Soon, however, the young boxer rebelled against the old stereotypes of the self-effacing Black athlete and began to define his own social role. He converted to Islam, becoming a member of the U.S.-based Nation of Islam, and abandoned his "slave name" to take the name Muhammad Ali. He insisted on expressing his own political views, including refusing to fight in the Vietnam War. Ali not only changed the world of sports but also helped to alter the world of race relations. Viewed from a sociological perspective, then, Ali was redefining social reality by rebelling against the racist thinking and terminology that restricted him and other African Americans.

## >> Elements of Social Structure

All social interaction takes place within a **social structure**—a series of predictable relationships composed of various positions that people occupy. Occupying those positions shapes how we think and act and what resources we have access to. For example, our position as parent, employee, or student exists in relation to other positions, such as child, boss, or professor. Further, each of these positions implies certain expectations and obligations on our part, such as discipline, labor, and studying. In short, how we interact with others is shaped by the positions we occupy.

For purposes of study, we can break down any social structure into six elements: statuses, social roles, groups, social networks, virtual worlds, and social institutions. These elements make up the social structure just as a foundation, walls, and ceilings make up a building's structure. The elements of social structure are developed through the lifelong process of socialization described in Chapter 4.

### STATUSES

We normally think of a person's "status" as having to do with influence, wealth, and fame. However, sociologists use the term **status** to refer to any of the full range of socially defined positions within a large group or society, from the lowest to the highest. Within our society, a person can occupy the status of president of the United States, fruit picker, son or daughter, violinist, teenager, resident of St. Louis, dental technician, or neighbor. A person can hold a number of statuses at the same time.

**Ascribed and Achieved Status** Sociologists categorize statuses as either ascribed or achieved (see the

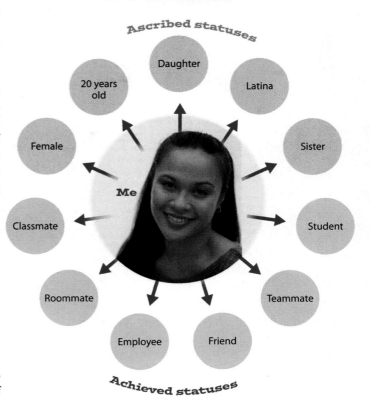

## Social Statuses

Ascribed statuses

Daughter
20 years old
Latina
Female
Sister
Me
Classmate
Student
Roommate
Teammate
Employee
Friend

Achieved statuses

"Social Statuses" figure above). An **ascribed status** is assigned to a person by society without regard for the person's unique talents or characteristics. Generally, the assignment takes place at birth; thus, a person's age, race/ethnicity, and gender are all considered ascribed statuses. Though such characteristics are biological in origin, the key is the social meaning we attach to such categories. Ascribed statuses are often used to justify privileges or reflect a person's membership in a subordinate group. We will analyze the social meanings of race, ethnicity, and gender more fully in Chapters 12 and 13.

In most cases, we can do little to change an ascribed status. We can, however, attempt to change the traditional constraints associated with it. For example, since its founding in 1971, the activist political group Gray Panthers has worked for the rights of older people and tried to modify society's negative and confining stereotypes of the elderly. As a result of their work and that of other groups supporting older citizens, the ascribed status of "senior citizen" is no longer as difficult for millions of older people.

An ascribed status does not necessarily have the same social meaning in every society. In a cross-cultural study, sociologist Gary Huang (1988) confirmed the long-held view that respect for the elderly is an important cultural norm in China. There, in many cases, the prefix "old" is used

> **status** A term used by sociologists to refer to any of the full range of socially defined positions within a large group or society.
> **ascribed status** A social position assigned to a person by society without regard for the person's unique talents or characteristics.

who died of AIDS in 1993, had a remarkable career in tennis, but at the end of his life, his status as a well-known personality with AIDS may have outweighed his statuses as a retired athlete, author, and political activist.

People with disabilities frequently observe that the nondisabled see them only as blind, or only as wheelchair users, and so on, rather than as complex human beings with individual strengths and weaknesses whose disability is merely one aspect of their lives. Often people with disabilities find that their status as "disabled" receives undue weight, overshadowing their actual ability to hold meaningful employment and contributing to widespread prejudice, discrimination, and segregation. For example, most voting places are inaccessible to wheelchair users and fail to provide ballots that can be used by the blind. Activists argue that such unnecessary and discriminatory barriers present in the environment—both physical and attitudinal—restrict people with disabilities more than do any biological limitations.

respectfully: calling someone "old teacher" or "old person" is like calling a judge in the United States "your honor." Huang points out that such positive old-age-related language distinctions are uncommon in the United States; consequently, we view the term "old man" as more of an insult than a celebration of seniority and wisdom.

Unlike ascribed statuses, an **achieved status** is a social position that is within our power to change. Both bank president and prison guard are achieved statuses, as are lawyer, pianist, sorority member, convict, and social worker. We must do something to acquire an achieved status—go to school, learn a skill, establish a friendship, invent a new product, and so on. But as we will see in the next section, our ascribed status heavily influences our achieved status. Being male in the United States, for example, still decreases the likelihood that a person will consider child care as a career.

**achieved status** A social position that is within our power to change.

**master status** A status that dominates others and thereby determines a person's general position in society.

**social role** A set of expectations for people who occupy a given social position or status.

**Master Status** Each of us holds many different and sometimes conflicting statuses; some may connote a higher social position, and others a lower position. How, then, do others view our overall social position? According to sociologist Everett Hughes (1945), societies deal with inconsistencies by agreeing that certain statuses are more important than others. A **master status** is a status that dominates others and thereby determines a person's general position in society. For example, Arthur Ashe,

## SOCthink

> > > Why do you think nondisabled people see disability as the most important characteristic of a disabled person? What can be done to help people see beyond the wheelchair and the seeing-eye dog?

Ascribed statuses frequently influence our achieved status. The African American activist Malcolm X (1925–1965), an eloquent and controversial advocate of Black power and Black pride in the 1960s, recalled that his feelings and perspectives changed dramatically while in eighth grade. When his English teacher, a White man, advised him that his goal of becoming a lawyer was "no realistic goal for a nigger" and encouraged him instead to become a carpenter, Malcolm X (1964:37) found that his position as a Black man (ascribed status) was an obstacle to his dream of becoming a lawyer (achieved status). In the United States, the ascribed statuses of race and gender can function as master statuses that play an important part in one's efforts to achieve a desired professional and social status.

## SOCIAL ROLES

Throughout our lives, we acquire what sociologists call social roles. A **social role** is a set of expectations for people who occupy a given social position or status. While we occupy a status, we play a role. Thus, in the United States, we expect that cab drivers will know how to get around a city, that receptionists will handle phone messages, and that police officers will take action if they see a citizen being threatened. With each distinctive social status—whether ascribed or achieved—come particular role expectations. However, actual performance varies from individual to individual. One secretary may assume extensive administrative responsibilities, while another may focus on clerical duties.

Roles are a significant component of social structure. Roles can contribute to a society's stability by enabling members to anticipate the behavior of others and to pattern their own actions accordingly. Yet social roles can also restrict people's interactions and relationships. If we view a person *only* as a police officer or a supervisor, it will be difficult to relate to him or her as a friend or neighbor.

**Role Conflict** Sometimes the positions we occupy can clash. **Role conflict** occurs when incompatible expectations arise from two or more social positions held by the same person. Fulfillment of the roles associated with one status

### Hot or Not?

Is there is no such thing as our true self? Are we only actors performing roles based on the positions we occupy?

may directly violate the roles linked to a second status.

Imagine the delicate situation of a woman who has worked for a decade on an assembly line in an electrical plant and has recently been named supervisor of her unit. How is this woman expected to relate to her longtime friends and co-workers? Should she still have lunch with them, as she has done almost daily for years? Should she recommend the firing of an old friend who cannot keep up with the demands of the assembly line? She will most likely experience a sharp conflict between her social and occupational roles. Such role conflicts involve difficult ethical choices. The new supervisor will have to make a difficult decision about how much allegiance she owes her friend and how much she owes her employers, who have given her supervisory responsibilities.

Another type of role conflict occurs when individuals move into occupations that are not common among people with their ascribed status. Male pre-school teachers and female police officers experience this type of role conflict. In the latter case, the women must strive to reconcile their workplace role in law enforcement with the societal view of a woman's proper role, which historically has not embraced many skills associated with police work. And even as female police officers encounter sexual harassment, as women do throughout the labor force, they must also deal with the "code of silence," an informal norm that precludes their implicating

> **role conflict** The situation that occurs when incompatible expectations arise from two or more social positions held by the same person.

fellow officers in wrongdoing (Fletcher 1995; S. Martin 1994).

### Role Strain

Role conflict describes the situation of a person dealing with the

## SOCthink

> > > List the social statuses you occupy. Which ones are ascribed, and which are achieved? What roles are you expected to play as a consequence of the positions you occupy? How do you resolve possible role conflicts?

challenge of occupying two social positions simultaneously. However, even a single position can cause problems. Sociologists use the term **role strain** to describe the difficulty that arises when the same social position imposes conflicting demands and expectations.

People who belong to minority cultures may experience role strain while working in the mainstream culture. Criminologist Larry Gould (2002) interviewed officers of the Navajo Nation Police Department about their relations with conventional law enforcement officials, such as sheriffs and FBI agents. Besides enforcing the law, Navajo Nation officers practice an alternative form of justice known as Peacemaking, in which they seek reconciliation between the parties to a crime or grievance. The officers expressed great confidence in Peacemaking but worried that if they did not make arrests, other law enforcement officials would think they were too soft or were "just taking care of their own." Regardless of the strength of their ties to traditional Navajo ways, all felt the strain of being considered "too Navajo" or "not Navajo enough."

> **role strain** The difficulty that arises when the same social position imposes conflicting demands and expectations.

**Role Exit** Often, when we think of assuming a social role, we focus on the preparation and anticipatory socialization a person undergoes for that role. Such is true if a person is about to become an attorney, a chef, a spouse, or a parent. Yet, social scientists have paid less attention to the adjustments involved in leaving social roles.

Sociologist Helen Rose Fuchs Ebaugh (1988) used the term **role exit** to describe the process of disengagement from a role that is central to one's self-identity in order to establish a new role and identity. Drawing on interviews—with, among others, ex-convicts, divorced men and women, recovering alcoholics, ex-nuns, former doctors, retirees, and transsexuals—Ebaugh (herself a former nun) studied the process of voluntarily exiting from significant social roles.

Ebaugh has offered a four-stage model of role exit. The first stage begins with doubt. The person experiences frustration, burnout, or simply unhappiness with an accustomed status and the roles associated with that social position. The second stage involves a search for alternatives. An individual who is unhappy with his or her career may take a leave of absence; an unhappily married couple may begin what they see as a trial separation.

The third stage of role exit is the action stage, or departure. Ebaugh found that the vast majority of her respondents could identify a clear turning point when it became essential to take final action and leave their jobs, end their marriages, or engage in some other type of role exit. Only 20 percent of respondents saw their role exit as a gradual, evolutionary process that had no single turning point.

The last stage of role exit involves the creation of a new identity. Traditionally, students experience a form of role exit when they make the transition from high school to college. They may leave behind the role of a child living at home and take on the role of a somewhat independent college student living with peers in a dorm. Sociologist Ira Silver (1996) has studied the central role that material objects play in this transition. The objects students choose to leave at home (like stuffed animals and dolls) are associated with their prior identities. They may remain deeply attached to those objects but not want them to be seen as part of their new identities at college. The objects they bring with them symbolize how they now see themselves and how they wish to be perceived. iPods and wall posters, for example, are calculated to say, "This is me."

## SOCthink

> > > Whether from a sports team, a religious group, the military, or some other close-knit group, what experience, if any, have you had with role exiting? To what extent does your experience match the four stages Ebaugh describes?

*Sociologist Helen Rose Fuchs Ebaugh interviewed transsexuals (as pictured here) and others exiting from significant social roles in order to develop her four-stage model of role exit.*

## From Me to You

*While I love teaching, I hate grading. When I mention that to students they say I have no one to blame but myself; if I didn't assign things I wouldn't have to grade them. But I don't teach in a vacuum. If I didn't assign papers and tests students would focus their time and energy on their looming chemistry test or their literature paper instead of reading for, participating in, or even attending my course. It is not that students aren't interested or sincere; it's that they are forced to budget their time according to their most pressing demands. Because we exist in social systems, the expectations of those systems limit the amount of innovation we might desire.*

# GROUPS

Statuses combine in various ways to form social groups. In sociological terms, a **group** is any number of people with similar norms, values, and expectations who interact with one another on a regular basis. The members of a women's basketball team, a hospital's business office, a synagogue, or a symphony orchestra constitute a group. However, the residents of a suburb would not be considered a group, since they rarely interact with one another at one time.

Groups play a vital part in a society's social structure. Much of our social interaction takes place within groups and is influenced by their norms and sanctions. Being a teenager or a retired person, for example, takes on special meaning when we interact within groups designed for people with that particular status. The expectations associated with many social roles, including those accompanying the statuses of sibling and student, become more clearly defined in the context of a group.

### Primary and Secondary Groups

Charles Horton Cooley (1902) coined the term **primary group** to refer to a small group characterized by intimate, face-to-face association and cooperation. Such groups often entail long-term commitment and involve more of what we think of as our whole self. The members of a street gang can constitute a primary group; so can members of a family occupying the same household, or a group of "sisters" living in a college sorority.

Primary groups shape who we are and what we think about ourselves, thus playing a pivotal role both in the socialization process and in the development of our statuses and roles. Indeed, whether with family, friends, or teammates, primary groups can be instrumental in our day-to-day existence. When we find ourselves identifying closely with a group, it is probably a primary group.

We also participate in many groups that are not characterized by close bonds of friendship, such as large college classes and business associations. The term **secondary group** refers to a formal, impersonal group in which there is little social intimacy or mutual understanding. Participation in such groups is often more instrumental or goal-directed, often involving only what we think of as one part of our self. Given these characteristics, we are more likely to move into and out of such groups as suits our needs. The distinction between primary and secondary groups is not always clear-cut, however. Some social clubs may become so large and impersonal that they no longer function as primary groups; similarly, some work groups can become so close-knit that they are experienced as primary groups (Hochschild 1989).

**role exit** The process of disengagement from a role that is central to one's self-identity in order to establish a new role and identity.

**group** Any number of people with similar norms, values, and expectations who interact with one another on a regular basis.

**primary group** A small group characterized by intimate, face-to-face association and cooperation.

**secondary group** A formal, impersonal group in which there is little social intimacy or mutual understanding

# Comparison of Primary and Secondary Groups

| Primary group | Secondary group |
|---|---|
| Generally small | Usually large |
| Relatively long period of interaction | Relatively short duration, often temporary |
| Intimate, face-to-face association | Little social intimacy or mutual understanding |
| Some emotional depth to relationships | Relationships generally superficial |
| Cooperative, friendly | More formal and impersonal |

The accompanying table demonstrates some significant differences between primary and secondary groups.

**In-Groups and Out-Groups** In addition to degree of intimacy, groups can hold special meaning for members because of their relationship to other groups. For example, people in one group sometimes feel antagonistic toward or threatened by another group, especially if that group is perceived as being different either culturally or racially. To identify these "we" and "they" feelings, sociologists use two terms first employed by William Graham Sumner (1906): in-group and out-group.

An **in-group** can be defined as any group or category to which people feel they belong. Simply put, it comprises everyone who is regarded as "we" or "us." The in-group may be as narrow as a teenage clique or as broad as an entire society. The very existence of an in-group implies the existence of an out-group that is viewed as "they" or "them." An **out-group** is a group or category to which people feel they do not belong.

In-group members typically feel distinct and superior, seeing themselves as better than people in the out-group. Proper behavior for the in-group is simultaneously viewed as unacceptable behavior for the out-group. This double standard enhances the sense of superiority. Sociologist Robert Merton (1968) described this process as the conversion of "in-group virtues" into "out-group vices." We can see this differential standard operating in the context of terrorism. When a group or a nation takes aggressive actions, it usually justifies them as necessary even if civilians are hurt or killed. Opponents are quick to assign the emotion-laden label of *terrorist* to such actions and to appeal to the world community for condemnation. Yet these same people may themselves retaliate with actions that hurt civilians, which the first group will then condemn.

Conflict between in-groups and out-groups can turn violent on a personal as well as a political level. In 1999 two disaffected students at Columbine High School in Littleton, Colorado, launched an attack in the school that left 15 students and teachers dead, including themselves. The gunmen, members of an out-group that other students referred to as the Trenchcoat Mafia, apparently resented the continual taunting of an in-group known as the Jocks. Similar episodes have occurred in schools across the nation, where rejected adolescents, overwhelmed by personal and family problems, peer group pressure, academic responsibilities, or media images of violence, have lashed out against more popular classmates.

We're getting closer to our nature.

Clifford Geertz

## SOCthink

> > > How do in-groups and out-groups function in a typical U.S. high school? What groups are common? How are boundaries separating insiders and outsiders maintained?

**Reference Groups** Both in-groups and primary groups can dramatically influence the way an individual thinks and behaves. Sociologists call any group that individuals use as a standard for evaluating themselves and their own behavior a **reference group.** For example, a high school student who aspires to join a social circle of hip-hop music devotees will pattern his or her behavior after that of the group. The student will begin dressing like these peers, listening to the same downloads and DVDs, and hanging out at the same stores and clubs.

Reference groups have two basic purposes. They serve a normative function by setting and enforcing standards of conduct and belief. The high school student who wants the approval of the hip-hop crowd will have to follow the group's dictates, at least to some extent. Reference groups also perform a comparison function by serving as a standard against which people can measure themselves and others. An actor will evaluate him- or herself against a reference group composed of others in the acting profession (Merton and Kitt 1950).

Often, two or more reference groups influence us at the same time. Our family members, neighbors, and co-workers all shape different aspects of our self-evaluation. In addition, reference group attachments change during the life cycle. A corporate executive who quits the rat race at age 45 to become a social worker will find new reference groups to use as standards for evaluation. We shift reference groups as we take on different statuses during our lives.

**in-group** Any group or category to which people feel they belong.

**out-group** A group or category to which people feel they do not belong.

**reference group** Any group that individuals use as a standard for evaluating themselves and their own behavior.

**coalition** A temporary or permanent alliance geared toward a common goal.

**Coalitions** As groups grow larger, coalitions begin to develop. A **coalition** is an alliance, whether temporary or permanent, geared toward a common goal. Coalitions can be broad-based or narrow and can take on many different objectives. Sociologist William Julius Wilson (1999) has reported on community-based organizations in Texas that include Whites and Latinos, working-class and affluent, who banded together to work for improved sidewalks, better drainage systems, and comprehensive street paving. Out of this type of coalition building, Wilson hopes, will emerge better interracial understanding.

Some coalitions are intentionally short-lived. Short-term coalition building is a key to success in popular TV programs like *Survivor* and *Big Brother* in which players gain a strategic advantage by banding together to vote others off the island or out of the house. The political world is also the scene of many temporary coalitions. For example, in 1997, big tobacco companies joined with antismoking groups to hammer out terms for reimbursing states for tobacco-related medical costs. Soon after the settlement was announced, the coalition members returned to their decades-long fight against each other (Pear 1997).

## SOCIAL NETWORKS

Groups do not merely serve to define other elements of the social structure, such as roles and statuses; they also link the individual with the larger society. We all belong to a number of groups, and through our acquaintances, we connect with people in different social circles. These connections are known as a **social network**—a series of social relationships that links individuals directly to others, and through them indirectly to still more people. Social networks can center on virtually any activity, from sharing job information to exchanging news and gossip. Some networks may constrain people by limiting the range of their interactions, yet networks can also empower people by making vast resources available to them (Watts 2004).

Sometimes the connections are intentional and public; other times networks can develop that link us together in ways that are not intentional or apparent. Sociologists Peter Bearman, James Moody, and Katherine Stovel (2004) investigated one such network, asking themselves this question: If you drew a chart of the romantic relationship network at a typical American high school, what would it look like? Using careful data collection techniques to enhance the validity of their findings, they found that 573 of the 832 students they surveyed had been either romantically or sexually involved in the past 18 months. Of these, 63 couples connected only with each other as pairs with no other partners. Other students connected directly or indirectly with a handful of partners. One larger group, however, connected 288 students directly or indirectly into a single extended network (see the figure below). Such an example points to the fact that the

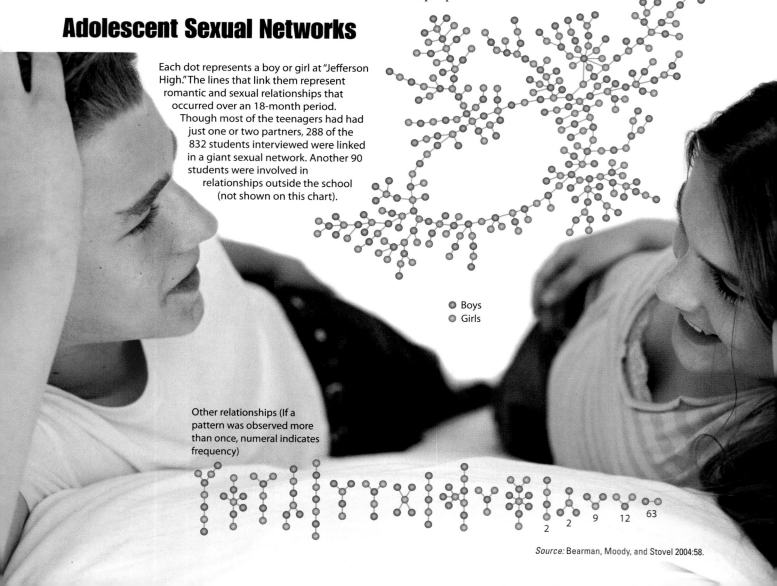

# Adolescent Sexual Networks

Each dot represents a boy or girl at "Jefferson High." The lines that link them represent romantic and sexual relationships that occurred over an 18-month period. Though most of the teenagers had had just one or two partners, 288 of the 832 students interviewed were linked in a giant sexual network. Another 90 students were involved in relationships outside the school (not shown on this chart).

● Boys
● Girls

Other relationships (If a pattern was observed more than once, numeral indicates frequency)

2    2    9    12    63

*Source:* Bearman, Moody, and Stovel 2004:58.

choices we make often link us with others both known and unknown.

Networks can also serve as a social resource that is every bit as valuable to us as economic resources when it comes to shaping our opportunities. Involvement in social networks—commonly known as "networking"—can be especially valuable in finding employment. Albert Einstein was successful in finding a job only when a classmate's father put him in touch with his future employer. These kinds of contacts—even those that are weak and distant—can be crucial in establishing social networks and facilitating the transmission of information.

In the workplace, networking pays off more for men than for women because of the traditional presence of men in leadership positions. One survey of executives found that 63 percent of the men used networking to find new jobs, compared to 41 percent of the women. Thirty-one percent of the women used classified ads to find jobs, compared to only 13 percent of the men. Still, women at all levels of the paid labor force are beginning to make effective use of social networks. A study of women who were leaving the welfare rolls to enter the paid workforce found that networking was an effective tool in their search for employment. Infor-mal networking also helped them to locate child care and better housing—keys to successful employment (Carey and McLean 1997; Henly 1999).

## VIRTUAL WORLDS

Today, with recent advances in technology, people can maintain their social networks electronically; they don't need face-to-face contacts. Whether through text messaging, Blackberry devices, or social networking sites like Facebook, a significant amount of networking occurs online. Adolescents can now interact freely with distant friends, even under close scrutiny by parents or teachers. And employees with a taste for adventure can escape their work environments without leaving their cubicles.

> **social network** A series of social relationships that links individuals directly to others, and through them indirectly to still more people.
> **avatar** A person's online representation as a character, whether in the form of a 2-D or 3-D image or simply through text.

The future of virtual networking and the effects it will have are difficult to imagine. Consider Second Life (SL), a virtual world that included about 14 million networked "players" as of June 2008. Nearly 500,000 of those players were active over a seven-day period. Participants in such virtual worlds typically create an **avatar** that is their online representation as a character, whether in the form of a 2-D or 3-D image or simply through text. The avatar that a player assumes may represent a very different looking-glass self from his or her actual identity. Once equipped with an avatar, the player goes about his or her life in the virtual world, establishing a business and even buying and decorating a home (Bainbridge 2007; Second Life 2008).

Just like real worlds, virtual worlds have become politicized and consumer-oriented. MySpace has been purchased by the global media giant News Corp, which has added targeted advertising to the site. If a My-Space user confesses to liking, say, tacos, a banner ad for Taco Bell may appear at the top the page. And SL is now open to real-world corporations that want to "build" their stores in SL. The commercialization of these spaces has been met with a good deal of antagonism: Reebok has weathered a virtual nuclear bomb attack, and "customers" have been "shot" outside the American Apparel store. Elsewhere in SL, virtual protesters have marched on behalf of a far-right French group in a confrontation with anti-Nazi protesters. In 2007, Sweden became the first real-world country to place an "embassy" in SL (Burkeman 2007; A. Hamilton 2007; Semuels 2007).

Virtual life can and does migrate into real life. In 2007, college housing officials became worried when freshmen and their parents began checking out the Facebook profiles of prospective roommates. Soon, colleges were fielding requests for new roommates before students even arrived on campus. Concerns went far beyond tastes in music; the reservations expressed most often by parents included a potential roommate's race, religion, and sexual orientation (Collura 2007).

Sociologist Manuel Castells (1997, 1998, 2000) views these emerging electronic social networks as fundamental to new organizations and the growth of existing businesses and associations. With other scholars, sociologists are now scrambling to understand these environments and their social processes. Internet consultant and analyst Clay Shirky (2008) suggests that what makes the Internet unique relative to previous media revolutions is that it combines both two-way communication (like the telephone) and group formation (such as newspaper readers or television viewers). He summarizes its significance this way: "group action just got easier." He suggests that we are seeing only the beginnings of the collective action made possible through the social networking potential that the Internet represents (see the accompanying table).

Finally, virtual networks can help to preserve real-world networks interrupted by war and other dislocations. In 2003 the deployment of U.S. troops in the Middle East increased many people's reliance on email. Today, digital photos and sound files accompany email messages between soldiers and their families and friends. GIs can even view siblings' graduations or children's birthday parties live, via webcams. And U.S. soldiers and Iraqi citizens have begun to post their opinions of the war in Iraq in online journals or blogs. Though critics are skeptical of the identity of some of the authors, these postings have become yet another source of news about the war (Faith 2005; O'Connor 2004; Sisson 2007).

As something of a spoof, CNET's online game review site, GameSpot, offered a tongue-in-cheek review of "Real Life." They gave it a 9.6 out of 10, saying that it features "believable characters, plenty of lasting appeal, and a lot of challenge and variety," and they described the game play as "extremely open-ended." They concluded that "if you take a step back and look at the big picture, you'll see that real life is an impressive and exciting experience, despite its occasional and sometimes noticeable problems." Part of what makes such a post amusing is that there is a sense that the boundary between the "real world" and virtual reality continues to blur. What, for example, are the consequences for a real-life marriage when one of the partners marries someone else's virtual-world character (Alter 2007; Kasavin 2003)?

# Shirky's Four Steps Toward Increased Internet Interaction

| Step | Site |
| --- | --- |
| Sharing | Flikr; Bit Torrent; Del.icio.us |
| Conversation | Forums; MAKE; How To |
| Collaboration | Linux; Aegisub |
| Collective action | Flash Mob activism; NetRoots activisism |

*Source:* Based on Shirky, 2008.

## SOCIAL INSTITUTIONS

Combinations of statuses, groups, and networks can coalesce to address the needs of a particular sector of society, forming what sociologists refer to as institutions. A **social institution** is an organized pattern of beliefs and behavior centered on basic social needs. The family, education, government, religion, and the economy are all examples of social institutions found in our society. For example, in the context of families, we reproduce members of the society, and in the context of government, we work to preserve order. Though these institutions frequently overlap and interact, the concept is helpful in thinking about the various aspects of society that we need to take into account as we seek to better understand why we think and act the way we do.

One way to understand social institutions is to see how they fulfill essential functions. This approach emphasizes the importance of social order. It identifies five major needs or tasks that all societies must address, and it connects these tasks to five major institutions (Aberle et al. 1950; Mack and Bradford 1979). First, if they are to continue to exist, all societies must reproduce their membership. The primary means is biological reproduction, which takes place in the context of families. Societies also often gain members through immigration, which tends to be regulated by the government. A second task involves reproducing the culture by teaching it to those new members. This, too, is carried out primarily in the context of families, but education serves to teach people the knowledge and skills they need to be members of the wider society. A third task involves producing and distributing goods and services so that people's needs are fulfilled; the economy is the primary institution for this function. A fourth task is preserving order, a function carried out through the policing and diplomatic responsibilities of government. Finally, societies must provide and maintain a sense of meaning and purpose, a role histori-

cally filled by religion, although patriotism often plays a critical role as well.

This list of functional prerequisites does not specify how a society and its corresponding social institutions will perform each task. For example, one society may protect itself from external attack by amassing a large arsenal of weaponry, while another may make determined efforts to remain neutral in world politics and to promote cooperative relationships with its neighbors. No matter what its particular strategy, any society or relatively permanent group must address all these functional prerequisites for survival.

> **social institution** An organized pattern of beliefs and behavior centered on basic social needs.

While this approach does a good job of laying out some of the issues we must address as we seek to understand and establish social order, it often implies that the way things are is the way things should be. Sociologists who focus more on power, the consequences of difference, and resource distribution suggest that we must also look at the ways our construction of these institutions reinforces inequality. We can meet these needs in a variety of ways, so we must address the interest some groups have in maintaining the status quo.

## SOCthink

> > > How is it possible for education to provide both a path for opportunity and an instrument for maintaining inequality? Where in your experience have you seen both at work?

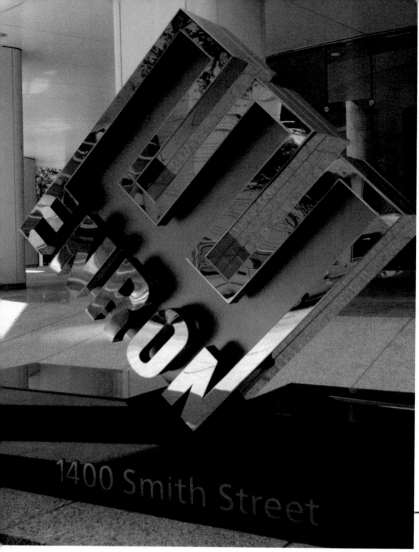

halls or outside the washroom) and shared a critical view of the firm's attorneys and day-shift secretaries. Expressing their frustration about their relative lack of power and respect, the word processors routinely suggested that their assignments represented work that the "lazy" secretaries should have completed during the normal workday. One word processor, seeking to reclaim a sense of personal power, reacted against the lawyers' superior attitude and pointedly refused to recognize or speak with any attorney who would not address her by name (Duneier 1994b). Through such analysis, sociologists can better explain both how social order is attained and how social inequality is produced in the context of the economy.

Such approaches to viewing life in the contexts of social institutions allow us to better understand what it means to live in the world as it is structured today. Looking at society through the lens of social institutions gives us a sense of what is going on with regard to both the "big picture" and the intimate details of our daily interactions. One of the ways that sociologists have characterized the structure of our modern world is in terms of bureaucracy, which not only describes the social structure but also shapes our everyday experiences.

"Frankly, at this point in the flow chart, we don't know what happens to these people..."

Major institutions, such as education, help to maintain the privileges of the most powerful individuals and groups within a society while contributing to the powerlessness of others. To give one example, public schools in the United States are financed largely through property taxes. This arrangement allows more affluent areas to provide their children with better-equipped schools and better-paid teachers than low-income areas can afford. As a result, children from prosperous communities are better prepared to compete academically than children from impoverished communities. The structure of the nation's educational system permits and even promotes such unequal treatment of schoolchildren.

By focusing on everyday interactions within the contexts of these institutions, we can further understand why we think and act the way we do. Focusing on the economy, sociologist Mitchell Duneier (1994a, 1994b) studied the social behavior of the word processors, all women, who worked in the service center of a large Chicago law firm. Duneier was interested in the informal social norms that emerged in this work environment and the rich social network these female employees created.

Duneier learned that, despite working in a large office, these women found private moments to talk (often in the

## >> Bureaucracy

A **bureaucracy** is a component of a formal organization that uses rules and hierarchical ranking to achieve efficiency. Rows of desks staffed by seemingly faceless people, endless lines and forms, impossibly complex language, and frustrating encounters with red tape—all these unpleasant images have combined to make "bureaucracy" a dirty word and an easy target in political campaigns. As a result, few people want to identify their occupation as "bureaucrat," despite the fact that all of us perform various bureaucratic tasks. In an industrial society, elements of bureaucracy enter into almost every occupation.

## CHARACTERISTICS OF A BUREAUCRACY

Max Weber ([1913–1922] 1947) first directed researchers to the significance of bureaucratic structure. In an important sociological advance, Weber emphasized the basic similarity of structure and process found in the otherwise dissimilar enterprises of religion, government, education, and business. Weber saw bureaucracy as a form of organization quite different from the family-run business. For analytical purposes, he developed an ideal type of bureaucracy that would reflect the most characteristic aspects of all human organizations. By **ideal type** Weber meant a construct or model for evaluating specific cases. In actuality, perfect bureaucracies do not exist; no real-world organization corresponds exactly to Weber's ideal type.

Weber proposed that whether the purpose is to run a church, a corporation, or an army, the ideal bureaucracy displays five basic characteristics: division of labor, hierarchy of authority, written rules and regulations, impersonality, and employment based on technical qualifications. Let's look at each in turn; the accompanying table provides a summary.

**Division of Labor** Specialized experts perform specific tasks. In a college bureaucracy, for example, the admissions officer does not do the job of registrar; the academic advisor doesn't see to the maintenance of buildings. By working at a specific task, people are more likely to become highly skilled and carry out a job with maximum efficiency. This emphasis on specialization is so basic a part of our lives that we may not realize it is a fairly recent development in Western culture.

Division of labor has freed people up to specialize, enhancing their knowledge and skill and leading to significant advances and innovation. However, fragmenting work into smaller and smaller tasks can isolate workers from one another and weaken any connection they might feel to the overall objective of the bureaucracy. In *The Communist Manifesto* (1848), Karl Marx and Friedrich Engels charged that capitalism's inherent drive toward increased efficiency and productivity reduces workers to a mere "appendage of the machine" (L. Feuer 1989). Such a work arrangement, they wrote, produces extreme **alienation**—loss of control over our creative human capacity to produce, separation from the products we make, and isolation from our fellow producers. Restricting workers to very small tasks also can lessen their job security, since new employees can easily be trained to replace them.

Another potential downside of the division of labor is that, even though it makes us more interdependent, our relative isolation can result in our failing to recognize our links with others. As we saw with the "hamburger as miracle" example in Chapter 1, we take other people's skills for granted and assume they will do their jobs, even though we are unaware of what most of those jobs are. In some cases this can lead to **trained incapacity**—a situation in which

> **bureaucracy** A component of formal organization that uses rules and hierarchical ranking to achieve efficiency.
> **ideal type** A construct or model for evaluating specific cases.
> **alienation** Loss of control over our creative human capacity to produce, separation from the products we make, and isolation from our fellow producers.
> **trained incapacity** The tendency of workers in a bureaucracy to become so specialized that they develop blind spots and fail to notice potential problems.

# Characteristics of a Bureaucracy

| | Positive consequences | Negative consequences | |
| --- | --- | --- | --- |
| | | **For the individual** | **For the organization** |
| **Division of labor** | Produces efficiency in a large-scale corporation | Produces trained incapacity | Produces a narrow perspective |
| **Hierarchy of authority** | Clarifies who is in command | Deprives employees of a voice in decision making | Permits concealment of mistakes |
| **Written rules and regulations** | Let workers know what is expected of them | Stifle initiative and imagination | Lead to goal displacement |
| **Impersonality** | Reduces bias | Contributes to feelings of alienation | Discourages loyalty to company |
| **Employment based on technical qualifications** | Discourages favoritism and reduces petty rivalries | Discourages ambition to improve oneself elsewhere | Fosters "Peter principle" |

workers become so specialized that they develop blind spots and fail to notice potential problems. Even worse, workers can become so isolated that they may not care about what is happening in the next department. Some observers believe that such developments have caused workers in the United States to become less productive on the job.

In some cases, the bureaucratic division of labor can have tragic results. In the wake of the terrorist attacks on the World Trade Center and the Pentagon on September 11, 2001, many Americans wondered how the FBI and CIA could have failed to detect the terrorists' elaborately planned operation. The problem, in part, turned out to be the division of labor between the FBI, which focuses on domestic matters, and the CIA, which operates overseas. Officials at these intelligence-gathering organizations, both of which are huge bureaucracies, are well known for jealously guarding information from one another. Subsequent investigation revealed that they knew about Osama bin Laden and his al Qaeda terrorist network in the early 1990s. Unfortunately, five federal agencies—the CIA, FBI, National Security Agency, Defense Intelligence Agency, and National Reconnaissance Office—failed to share their information on the network. Although the hijacking of the four commercial airliners used in the massive attacks may not have been preventable, the bureaucratic division of labor definitely hindered efforts to defend against terrorism, undermining U.S. national security.

**goal displacement** Overzealous conformity to official regulations of a bureaucracy.

**Hierarchy of Authority** Bureaucracies follow the principle of hierarchy; that is, each position is under the supervision of a higher authority. A president heads a college bureaucracy; he or she selects members of the administration, who in turn hire their own staff. In the Roman Catholic Church, the pope is the supreme authority; under him are cardinals, bishops, and so forth. In businesses, the most basic relation is between boss and worker, but in large corporations there are various levels of authority. To track relationships, such companies map those connections using organizational charts that identify all the links of who

The organizations of major corporations can be complex but most typically have a single CEO. Debra Lee, pictured here, is president and CEO of Black Entertainment Television.

answers to whom, ultimately leading up to the president or CEO at the top.

**Written Rules and Regulations** Through written rules and regulations, bureaucracies generally offer employees clear standards for an adequate (or exceptional) performance. If situations arise that are not covered by the rules, bureaucracies are self-correcting. They have rules in place to ensure that new rules are established that make work expectations as clear and comprehensive as possible. Because bureaucracies are hierarchical systems of interrelated positions, such procedures provide a valuable sense of continuity for the organization. Individual workers may come and go, but the structure and past records of the organization give it a life of its own that outlives the services of any one particular person.

## SOCthink

> > > Why do we tend to associate bureaucracies with red tape and inefficiency when they are explicitly organized to be the opposite? To what extent is our desire to be treated as an individual at odds with the principles of bureaucracies?

Of course, rules and regulations can overshadow the larger goals of an organization to the point that they become dysfunctional. What if a hospital emergency room physician failed to treat a seriously injured person because he or she had no valid proof of U.S. citizenship? If blindly applied, rules no longer serve as a means to achieving an objective but instead become important (perhaps too important) in their own right. Robert Merton (1968) used the term **goal displacement** to refer to overzealous conformity to official regulations.

**Impersonality** Max Weber wrote that, in a bureaucracy, work is carried out *sine ira et studio*—"without hatred or passion." Bureaucratic norms dictate that officials perform their duties without giving personal consideration to people as individuals. Although this norm is intended to guarantee equal treatment for each person, it also contributes to the cold, uncaring feeling often associated with modern organizations.

> We all know we are unique individuals, but we tend to see others as representatives of groups.
>
> Deborah Tannen

We typically think of big government and big business when we think of impersonal bureaucracies, and bureaucratic impersonality often produces frustration and disaffection. Whether it involves registering for college classes or getting tech support for a malfunctioning computer, most people have had some experience of feeling like a number and longing for some personal attention. The larger the organization or society, however, the less possible such personal care becomes, because attending to individual wants and needs is inefficient.

**Employment Based on Technical Qualifications** Within the ideal bureaucracy, hiring is based on technical qualifications rather than on favoritism, and performance is measured against specific standards. Written personnel policies dictate who gets promoted, and people often have a right to appeal if they believe that particular rules have been violated. In combination with the principle

of impersonality, the driving personnel principle is supposed to be that it is "what you know, not who you know" that counts. Such procedures protect bureaucrats against arbitrary dismissal, provide a measure of security, and encourage loyalty to the organization.

Although any bureaucracy ideally will value technical and professional competence, personnel decisions do not always follow that ideal pattern. Dysfunctions within bureaucracies have become well publicized, particularly because of the work of Laurence J. Peter. According to the **Peter principle,** every employee within a hierarchy tends to rise to his or her level of incompetence (Peter and Hull 1969). This hypothesis, which has not been directly or systematically tested, reflects a possible dysfunctional ultimate outcome of advancement on the basis of merit. Talented people receive promotion after promotion until, sadly, some of them finally achieve positions that they cannot handle with their usual competence (Blau and Meyer 1987).

Weber developed his five indicators of bureaucracy almost 100 years ago, and they describe an ideal type rather than bureaucracy in practice. Not every formal organization will fully realize all of Weber's characteristics. The underlying logic they represent, however, points toward a way of doing things that is typical of life in modern societies.

**Peter principle** A principle of organizational life according to which every employee within a hierarchy tends to rise to his or her level of incompetence.
**bureaucratization** The process by which a group, organization, or social movement increasingly relies on technical-rational decision making in the pursuit of efficiency.
**McDonaldization** The process by which the principles of efficiency, calculability, predictability, and control shape organization and decision making, in the United States and around the world.

## BUREAUCRATIZATION AS A WAY OF LIFE

Bureaucracy for Weber was an indicator of a larger trend in modern society toward rational calculation of all decision making using efficiency and productivity as the primary standards of success. We recognize this pattern first at the level of businesses and organizations. More companies seek greater efficiency through **bureaucratization**—the process by which a group, organization, or social movement increasingly relies on technical-rational decision making in the pursuit of efficiency. Over time, however, the technical-rational approach pervades more and more areas of our lives.

**The Spread of Bureaucratization** One example of the expansion of bureaucratization is found in the spread of what sociologist George Ritzer (2008) calls **McDonaldization**—the process by which the principles

... The U.S. Census Bureau identifies 472 distinct occupational categories, such as Chief Executive and Crossing Guard, each of which contain at least 10,000 workers. They break these down into 14 occupational groups with 9 job categories.

Did You Know?

of efficiency, calculability, predictability, and control shape organization and decision making, in the United States and around the world. Ritzer argues that these principles, which are at the heart of the McDonald's fast-food

Normally, we think of bureaucratization in terms of large organizations, but bureaucratization also takes place within small-group settings. Sociologist Jennifer Bickman Mendez (1998) studied domestic houseworkers employed

## Civilization degrades the many to exalt the few.

Amos Bronson Alcot

chain's success, have been emulated by many organizations, ranging from medical care to wedding planning to education. Even sporting events reflect the influence of McDonaldization. Around the world, stadiums are becoming increasingly similar, both physically and in the way they present the sport to spectators. Swipe cards, "sports city" garages and parking lots, and automated ticket sales maximize efficiency. All seats offer spectators an unrestricted view, and a big screen guarantees them access to instant replays. Scores, player statistics, and attendance figures are updated by computer and displayed on an automated scoreboard. Spectator enthusiasm is manufactured through video displays urging applause or rhythmic chanting. At food counters, refreshments include well-known brands whose customer loyalty has been nourished by advertisers for decades. And, of course, the merchandising of teams' and even players' names and images is highly controlled.

**iron law of oligarchy** A principle of organizational life under which even a democratic organization will eventually develop into a bureaucracy ruled by a few individuals.

in central California by a nationwide franchise. She found that housekeeping tasks were minutely defined, to the point that employees had to follow 22 written steps for cleaning a bathroom. Complaints and special requests went not to the workers but to an office-based manager.

Weber predicted that eventually even the private sphere would become rationalized. That is, we would turn to rational techniques in an effort to manage our self in order to handle the many challenges of modern life. A trip to any bookstore would seem to prove his point: we find countless self-help books, each with its own system of steps to help us solve life's problems and reach our goals.

Weber was concerned about the depersonalizing consequences of such rationalization, but he saw no way out. Because it is guided by the principle of maximum efficiency, the only way to beat bureaucratization, he thought, was to be more bureaucratic. He added that, unfortunately, something human was lost in the process. Culture critic Mike Daisey describes something like this through his experience working at Amazon.com. His job performance was measured based on five factors: time spent on each call, number of phone contacts per hour, time spent on

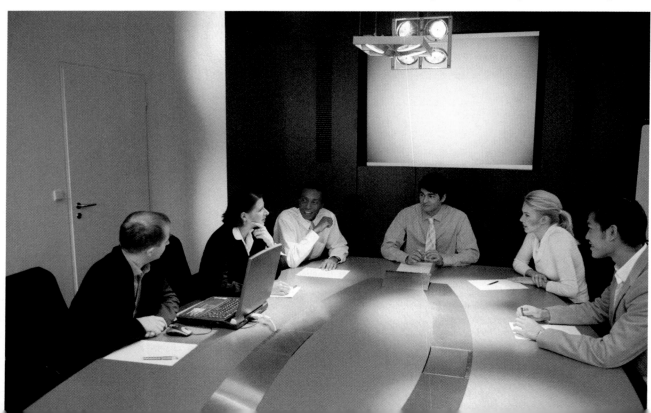

each customer email, number of email contacts per hour, and the sum total of phone and email contacts per hour. Of these calculations, he writes, "Those five numbers are who you are. They are, in fact, all you are. . . . Metrics will do exactly what it claims to do: it will track everything your employees do, say, and breathe, and consequently create a measurable increase in their productivity" (Daisey 2002:114). Metrics do work, but they do so by dehumanizing the worker. "The sad thing," Daisey continues, "is that metrics work so well precisely because it strips away dignity—it's that absence that makes it possible to

see precisely who is pulling his weight and who is not" (p. 114). When workers' performance is measured only in numbers, the only part of the self that counts is that part that produces those numbers. Weber predicted that those parts of the self deemed not necessary to the job, such as emotional needs and family responsibilities, would be dismissed as irrelevant.

**From Bureaucracy to Oligarchy** One of the dangers, then, is that bureaucratization overwhelms other values and principles, that how we organize to accomplish our goals overwhelms and alters the goals themselves. Sociologist Robert Michels (1915) studied socialist parties and labor unions in Europe prior to World War I and found that such organizations were becoming increasingly bureaucratic. The emerging leaders of the organizations—even some of the most radical—had a vested interest in clinging

to power. If they lost their leadership posts, they would have to return to full-time work as manual laborers.

Through his research, Michels originated the idea of the **iron law of oligarchy,** which describes how even a democratic organization will eventually develop into a bureaucracy ruled by a few (called an oligarchy). Why do oligarchies emerge? People who achieve leadership roles usually have the skills, knowledge, or charisma to direct, if not control, others. Michels argued that the rank and file of a movement or organization look to leaders for direction and thereby reinforce the process of rule by a few. In addition, members of an oligarchy are strongly motivated to maintain their leadership roles, privileges, and power.

In such instances, actions that violate the core principles of bureaucracy can seep in. Ascribed statuses such as gender, race, and ethnicity can influence how people are treated in formal organizations. For example, a study of women lawyers in the nation's largest law firms found significant differences in the women's self-images, depending on the relative presence or absence of women in positions of power. In firms in which fewer than 15 percent of partners were women, the female lawyers were likely to believe that "feminine" traits were strongly devalued and that masculinity was equated with success. As one female attorney put it, "Let's face it: this is a man's environment, and it's sort of Jock City, especially at my firm." Women in firms where female lawyers were better represented in positions of power had a stronger desire for and higher expectations of promotion (Ely 1995:619).

## BUREAUCRACY AND ORGANIZATIONAL CULTURE

Weber's model also predicted that organizations would take steps to remedy worker concerns. Faced with sabotage and decreasingly productive workers, for example, early bureaucratic managers realized that they could not totally dismiss workers' emotional needs as irrelevant. Various schools of management arose in an attempt to establish meaningful relationships within the context of the workplace in order to enhance productivity.

According to the **classical theory** of formal organizations, also known as the **scientific management approach,** workers are motivated almost entirely by economic rewards. This theory stresses that only the physical constraints on workers limit their productivity. Therefore, workers may be treated as a resource, much like the machines that began to replace them in the 20th century. Under the scientific management approach, man-

> **classical theory** An approach to the study of formal organizations that views workers as being motivated almost entirely by economic rewards.
> **scientific management approach** Another name for the classical theory of formal organizations.

**5 Movies on SOCIAL STRUCTURE AND INTERACTION**

**Clueless**
*Jane Austen's* Emma *recast in the guise of Beverley Hills high school students.*

**The Breakfast Club**
*Teenagers from five different high school cliques spend time in detention.*

**My Fair Lady**
*A high-society man learns to be a gentleman while teaching a lower-class woman to speak like a lady.*

**Fight Club**
*First rule of fight club: You do not talk about fight club.*

**The Outsiders**
*Teenage boys battle over social divisions.*

agement attempts to achieve maximum work efficiency through scientific planning, established performance standards, and careful supervision of workers and production. Planning involves efficiency studies but not studies of workers' attitudes or job satisfaction.

Not until workers organized unions—and forced management to recognize that they were not objects—did theorists of formal organizations begin to revise the classical approach. Along with management and administrators, social scientists became aware that informal groups of workers have an important impact on organizations (Perrow 1986). An alternative way of considering bureaucratic dynamics, the **human relations approach,** emphasizes the role of people, communication, and participation in a bureaucracy. This type of analysis reflects the significance of interaction and small-group behavior. Unlike planning under the scientific management approach, planning based on the human relations perspective focuses on workers' feelings, frustrations, and emotional need for job satisfaction. Today, many workplaces—primarily for those in higher-status occupations—have been transformed to more family-friendly environments. To the extent that managers are convinced that helping workers meet all their needs increases productivity, care and concern are instituted as a result of rational calculation.

**human relations approach** An approach to the study of formal organizations that emphasizes the role of people, communication, and participation in a bureaucracy and tends to focus on the informal structure of the organization.
**Gemeinschaft** A close-knit community, often found in rural areas, in which strong personal bonds unite members.
**Gesellschaft** A community, often urban, that is large and impersonal, with little commitment to the group or consensus on values.
**mechanical solidarity** Social cohesion based on shared experiences, knowledge, and skills in which things function more or less the way they always have, with minimal change.

## >> Social Structure in Global Perspective

Principles of bureaucratization may influence more and more spheres of our lives today, but it has not always been thus. In fact, sociology arose as a discipline in order to better understand and direct the transition from traditional to modern society. Early sociologists sought to develop models that described the basic differences between the two. They hoped that by better understanding how traditional societies operate, we might more effectively identify the underlying factors that shape core concerns in modern society, such as social order, inequality, and interaction.

### GEMEINSCHAFT AND GESELLSCHAFT

Ferdinand Tönnies (1855–1936) was appalled by the rise of industrial cities in his native Germany during the late 1800s. In his view, the city marked a dramatic change from the ideal of a close-knit community, which Tönnies termed a *Gemeinschaft,* to that of an impersonal mass society, or *Gesellschaft* (Tönnies [1887] 1988).

The *Gemeinschaft* (pronounced "guh-MINE-shoft") is typical of rural life. It is a small community in which people have similar backgrounds and life experiences. Virtually everyone knows one another, and social interactions are intimate and familiar, almost like an extended family. In this community there is a sense of commitment to the larger social group and a sense of togetherness among members. People relate to others in a personal way, not just as, say, clerk or manager. However, with such personal interaction comes little privacy: Community members have few secrets from one another.

Social control in the *Gemeinschaft* is maintained through informal means such as moral persuasion, gossip, and even gestures. These techniques work effectively because people genuinely care how others feel about them. Social change is relatively limited in the *Gemeinschaft;* the lives of members of one generation may be quite similar to those of their parents, grandparents, and so on.

In contrast, the *Gesellschaft* (pronounced "guh-ZELL-shoft") is characteristic of modern urban life. In modern societies most people are strangers who feel little in common with other residents. Relationships are governed by social roles that grow out of immediate tasks, such as purchasing a product or arranging a business meeting. Self-interest dominates, and there is little consensus concerning values or commitment to the group. As a result, social control must rest on more formal techniques, such as laws and legally defined sanctions. Social change is a normal part of life in the *Gesellschaft,* with substantial shifts evident even within a single generation.

Sociologists have used these two terms to compare social structures that stress close relationships with those that feature less personal ties. It is easy to view the *Gemeinschaft* with nostalgia, as a far better way of life than the rat race of contemporary existence. However, the more intimate relationships of the *Gemeinschaft* come at a price. The prejudice and discrimination found there can be quite confining; ascribed statuses such as family background often outweigh a person's unique talents and achievements. In addition, the *Gemeinschaft* tends to distrust individuals who are creative or simply different.

## SOCthink

> > > How would you classify the communities with which you are familiar? Are they more *Gemeinschaft* or *Gesellschaft?*

### MECHANICAL AND ORGANIC SOLIDARITY

While Tönnies looked nostalgically back on the *Gemeinschaft,* Émile Durkheim was more interested in the transition to modern society, which he felt represented the birth of a new form of social order. Durkheim hoped to use sociology as a science to better understand this transition. In his book *The Division of Labor in Society* ([1893] 1933), Durkheim, not unlike Weber, highlighted the significance of the degree to which jobs are specialized in society. For Durkheim, however, the amount of division of labor that exists in a society shapes the degree to which people feel connected with each other.

In societies in which there is minimal division of labor, a shared way of thinking develops that emphasizes group solidarity. Durkheim termed this collective frame of mind **mechanical solidarity.** It involves a sense of social cohesion based on shared experiences, knowledge, and skill, in which things function more or less the way they always have, with minimal change. Most individuals perform the same basic tasks, and they do so together. In this type of society, no one needs to ask, "What do your parents do?" since all are engaged in similar work. Each person hunts, prepares food, makes clothing, builds homes, and so forth. Because people have few options regarding what to do with their lives, there is little concern for individual needs. Instead, the group is the dominant force in society. Both social interaction and negotiation are based on close, intimate, face-to-face social contacts. Since there is little specialization, there are few social roles.

As societies become more advanced technologically, they rely on greater division of labor. The person who cuts down timber is not the same person who puts up your roof. With increasing specialization, many different tasks must be performed by many different individuals—even in manufacturing a single item, such as a radio or stove. In general, social interactions become less personal than in societies characterized by mechanical solidarity. People begin relating to others on the basis of their social positions (butcher, nurse, and so on) rather than their distinctive human qualities. Because the overall social structure of the society continues to change, statuses and social roles are in perpetual flux.

As we saw in the "hamburger as miracle" example in Chapter 1, once society has become more complex and division of labor is greater, no individual can go it alone. Dependence on others becomes essential for group survival. In Durkheim's terms, mechanical solidarity is replaced by **organic solidarity**—a collective consciousness resting on the need a society's members have for one another. Durkheim chose the term organic solidarity because he believed that role specialization forces individuals to become interdependent in much the same way as the various organs of the human body: Each performs a vital function, but none can exist alone. Also, like a living organism, society can grow and adapt to change.

## TECHNOLOGY AND SOCIETY

Some sociologists focus more explicitly on technology than on social organization, expressed as division of labor, to understand distinctions between traditional and modern societies. In sociologist Gerhard Lenski's view, a society's level of technology is critical to the way it is organized. As we saw in Chapter 3, Lenski defines technology as "cultural information about the ways in which the material resources of the environment may be used to satisfy human needs and desires" (Nolan and Lenski 2006:361). As technology changes, new social forms arise, from preindustrial, to industrial, to postindustrial. The available technology does not completely define the form that a particular society and its social structure will take. Nevertheless, a low level of technology may limit the degree to which a society can depend on such things as irrigation or complex machinery.

**Preindustrial Societies** Perhaps the earliest form of preindustrial society to emerge in human history was the **hunting-and-gathering society,** in which people simply rely on whatever foods and fibers are readily available. Such groups are typically small and widely dispersed, and technology in such societies is minimal. Organized into groups, people move constantly in search of food. There is little division of labor into specialized tasks because everyone is engaged in the same basic activities. Since resources are scarce, there is relatively little inequality in terms of material goods.

In **horticultural societies,** people plant seeds and crops rather than merely subsist on available foods. Members of horticultural societies are much less nomadic than hunter-gatherers. They place greater emphasis on the production of tools and household objects. Yet technology remains rather limited in these societies, whose members cultivate crops with the aid of digging sticks or hoes (Wilford 1997).

The third type of preindustrial development is the **agrarian society.** As in horticultural societies, members of agrarian societies are engaged primarily in the production of food, but technological innovations such as the plow allow

> **organic solidarity** A collective consciousness that rests on mutual interdependence, characteristic of societies with a complex division of labor.
> **hunting-and-gathering society** A preindustrial society in which people rely on whatever foods and fibers are readily available in order to survive.
> **horticultural society** A preindustrial society in which people plant seeds and crops rather than merely subsist on available foods.
> **agrarian society** The most technologically advanced form of preindustrial society. Members are engaged primarily in the production of food, but they increase their crop yields through technological innovations such as the plow.

farmers to dramatically increase their crop yields and cultivate the same fields over generations. As a result it becomes possible for larger, more permanent settlements to develop.

Agrarian societies continue to rely on the physical power of humans and animals (as opposed to mechanical power). Division of labor increases because technological advances free some people up from food production to focus on specialized tasks, such as the repair of fishing nets or blacksmithing. As human settlements become stabler and more established, social institutions become more elaborate and property rights more important. The comparative permanence and greater surpluses of an agrarian society allow members to specialize in creating artifacts such as statues, public monuments, and art objects and to pass them on from one generation to the next.

**industrial society** A society that depends on mechanization to produce its goods and services.

**postindustrial society** A society whose economic system is engaged primarily in the processing and control of information.

**Industrial Societies** The Industrial Revolution transformed social life in England during the late 1700s, and within a century its impact had extended around the world. By applying nonanimal (mechanical) sources of power to most labor tasks, industrialization significantly altered the way people lived and worked, and it undercut taken-for-granted norms and values. An **industrial society** is one that depends on mechanization to produce its goods and services. Industrial societies rely on new inventions that facilitate agricultural and industrial production, and on new sources of energy, such as steam.

During the Industrial Revolution, many societies underwent an irrevocable shift from an agrarian-oriented economy to an industrial base. Specialization of tasks and manufacture of goods increasingly replaced the practice of individuals or families making an entire product in a home workshop. Workers, generally men but also women and even children, left their family homesteads to work in central locations such as urban factories.

The process of industrialization had distinctive social consequences. Families and communities could not continue to function as self-sufficient units. Individuals, villages, and regions began to exchange goods and services and to become interdependent. As people came to rely on the labor of members of other communities, the family lost its unique position as the main source of power and authority. The need for specialized knowledge led to more formalized schooling, and education emerged as a social institution distinct from the family.

**Postindustrial Societies** Mechanized production continues to play a substantial role in shaping social order, relationships, and opportunities, but technological innovation once again has reshaped social structure by freeing up some people from the demands of material production. This has led to the rise of the service sector of the economy in many technologically advanced countries. In the 1970s, sociologist Daniel Bell wrote about the technologically advanced **postindustrial society,** whose economic system is engaged primarily in the processing and control of information. The main output of a postindustrial society is services rather than manufactured goods. Large numbers of people become involved in occupations devoted to the teaching, generation, or dissemination of ideas. Jobs in fields such as advertising, public relations, human resources, and computer information systems are typical of a postindustrial society (D. Bell 1999).

Some sociologists, including Bell, view this transition from industrial to postindustrial society as largely a positive development. Others, however, point to the often hidden consequences that result from differential access to resources in postindustrial society. For example, Michael Harrington (1980), who alerted the nation to the problems of the poor in his book *The Other America,* questions the significance that Bell attaches to the growing class of white-collar workers. Harrington concedes that scientists, engineers, and economists are involved in important political and economic decisions, but he disagrees with Bell's claim that they have a free hand in decision making, independent of the interests of the rich. Harrington follows in the tradition of Marx by arguing that conflict between social classes will continue in the postindustrial society.

## POSTMODERN LIFE

Sociologists recently have gone beyond discussion of the postindustrial society to contemplate the emergence of postmodern society. A **postmodern society** is a technologically sophisticated, pluralistic, interconnected, globalized society. While it is difficult to summarize what a whole range of thinkers have said about postmodern life, four elements provide a sense of the key characteristics of such societies today: stories, images, choices, and networks.

Did You Know?

. . . TV talk-show host Regis Philbin was a sociology major. He graduated from the University of Notre Dame with a B.A. in sociology in 1953. Sociology, he says, "gave me a great insight into human nature."

## International U.S. Favorability Ratings

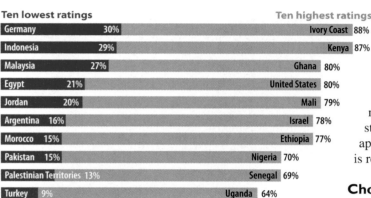

| Ten lowest ratings | | Ten highest ratings | |
|---|---|---|---|
| Germany | 30% | Ivory Coast | 88% |
| Indonesia | 29% | Kenya | 87% |
| Malaysia | 27% | Ghana | 80% |
| Egypt | 21% | United States | 80% |
| Jordan | 20% | Mali | 79% |
| Argentina | 16% | Israel | 78% |
| Morocco | 15% | Ethiopia | 77% |
| Pakistan | 15% | Nigeria | 70% |
| Palestinian Territories | 13% | Senegal | 69% |
| Turkey | 9% | Uganda | 64% |

*Source:* Kohut 2007b.

Because we exist in an interdependent global network, the consequences of our actions, both large and small, reverberate throughout the world. In a global survey of 47 nations conducted in 2007, the Pew Research Center looked at international favorability ratings for the United States. How favorably do other nations view the United States? The average national score was 47.3 percent, but there was significant variation by country.

**Stories** Because postmodern societies are pluralistic and individualistic, people hold many different, often competing, sets of norms and values. Fewer people assume that a single, all-inclusive story—whether a particular religious tradition, or an all-encompassing scientific theory of everything, or even the faith many early sociologists had in the inevitability of modern progress—can unite us all under a common umbrella. Instead, we embrace the various individual and group stories that help us to make sense of the world and our place in it. We do so in the full knowledge that others out there are doing exactly the same thing and often coming to dramatically different conclusions. This multiplicity of stories undercuts the authority that singular accounts of reality have had in the past.

**Images** Postmodern society is also characterized by the explosion of the mass media, which emphasizes the importance of images. As we saw in Chapter 4, the average person in the United States watches almost five hours of television per day (Bureau of the Census 2008a). This works out to the equivalent of over 71 full days per year. We are bombarded by images everywhere we turn, but in postmodern theory, the significance of the image goes much deeper than television and advertisements; it impacts our taken-for-granted notion of material reality itself. Theorists argue that we do not confront or interact with the

material world directly. Just as language shapes our perception of reality according to the Sapir-Whorf hypothesis, our experience of "reality" is always mediated through representations of reality in the form of signs, symbols, and words. According to postmodernists, our images or models of reality come before reality itself. Postmodern theorists use a geography metaphor to illuminate this concept: "the map precedes the territory" (Baudrillard [1981] 1994). In other words, the images we construct draw our attention to certain features that we might not otherwise single out. A road map, for example, highlights different features, and for different purposes, than does a topographical map or political map. In so doing, it shapes what we see. We cannot step around or look through such cultural constructs to approach the thing itself, and so our knowledge of what is real is always constrained by the images we construct.

**Choices** In a postmodern world, reality is not simply given; it is negotiated. We pick and choose our reality from the buffet of images and experiences presented to us. In fact, we *must* choose. In contrast to societies characterized by mechanical solidarity, where one's life path is virtually set at birth, members of postmodern societies must make life choices all the time. Assuming we have access to sufficient resources, we choose what to eat, what to wear, and what to drive. Shopping, which in the past would have been viewed primarily as an instrumental necessity to provide for our basic needs, becomes an act of self-creation. As James B. Twitchell (2000) put it, "We don't buy things, we buy meanings" (p. 47). An iPhone, a Coach purse, and a MINI Cooper are more than just a phone, a handbag, and a car. They are statements about the kind of person we are or want to be. The significance of choice goes much deeper than just consumer products. We also choose our partners, our schools, our jobs, our faith, and even our identities. As individuals, we may choose to affirm traditions, language, diet, and values we inherited from our family through socialization, but we can also choose to pursue our own path.

**Networks** Members of postmodern societies live in a globally interconnected world. The food we eat, the clothes we wear, the books we read, and the products we choose often come to us from the other side of the world. The computer technician we talk to for assistance in the United States may be located in India. McDonald's has even experimented with centralized drive-through attendants—who might even be located in another state—who take your order and transmit it to the restaurant you are ordering from. Increasingly, all corners of the globe are linked into a vast, interrelated social, cultural, political, and economic system. A rural Iowa farmer, for example, must be concerned with more than just the local weather and community concerns; he or she must know about international innovations in farming

> **postmodern society** A technologically sophisticated, pluralistic, interconnected, globalized society.

technology, including biotech, as well as the current and future state of international markets.

Whether in the form of traditional, modern, or postmodern society, social structure provides order, shaping the options that are available to us. It provides the context within which we interact with others. The statuses we occupy shape the roles we perform. What we think and do is influenced by the relationships we have with others in the contexts of groups, networks, and institutions. Sociology as a discipline is committed to making sense of our structural context and the impact it has on our lives.

Still, society and social structure are not singular things—as the turn toward the micro, bottom-up perspective in sociology has helped us to appreciate. Though we are, in many respects, products of society, socialized to think and act in appropriate ways, we always have the option to think and act in new ways and to construct new culture. The possibility for such change may be more apparent in our pluralistic world. Ours is a world not of "the" structure, "the" family, and "the" religion, but of structures, families, and religions. We have the possibility for more contact with more people who have more ways of thinking and acting than at any time in the past. As such, we can become aware of more alternatives for how we might think and act that might lead us to change our worlds.

**get involved!**

Explore! We occupy many statuses over the course of our lives, and they can both open and close doors for us. Ask five people in various positions— whether as parents, professors, child care providers, custodians, managers, religious leaders, or so on—how they came to be in those positions. How have the positions they occupy enabled them to accomplish their personal and collective goals? How have they been constrained by their positions?

# For REVIEW

I. **What makes up society?**
- Society provides a structure that is built up out of the statuses we occupy, the roles we perform, and the groups, networks, and institutions that connect us.

II. **How does social structure shape individual action?**
- The positions we occupy shape our perceptions, the resources to which we have access, and the options that are available. For example, in the context of bureaucracies, our social position, connections, and performance expectations are clearly defined.

III. **How do sociologists describe traditional versus modern societies?**
- Sociologists highlight the impact that division of labor and technological development have on the organization of community, work, and social interaction in traditional and modern societies.

# Pop Quiz

1.  A social position we inherit and about which we can do little to change, such as age, race, or sex, is known as
    a.  an ascribed status.
    b.  role strain.
    c.  goal displacement.
    d.  a master status.

2.  In the United States, we expect that cab drivers will know how to get around a city. This expectation is an example of which of the following?
    a.  role conflict
    b.  role strain
    c.  social role
    d.  master status

3.  What occurs when incompatible expectations arise from two or more social positions held by the same person?
    a.  role conflict
    b.  role strain
    c.  role exit
    d.  both a and b

4.  In sociological terms, what do we call any number of people with similar norms, values, and expectations who interact with one another on a regular basis?
    a.  a category
    b.  a group
    c.  an aggregate
    d.  a society

5.  Primary groups are characterized by
    a.  a series of relationships that link individuals directly to others and through them indirectly to still more people.
    b.  formal, impersonal relationships with minimal social intimacy or mutual understanding.
    c.  a sense of belonging.
    d.  intimate, face-to-face association and cooperation.

6.  The U.S. Postal Service, Def Jam Records, and the college or university in which you are currently enrolled as a student are all examples of
    a.  primary groups.
    b.  reference groups.
    c.  formal organizations.
    d.  triads.

7.  The principle of bureaucracy that establishes that work should be carried out "without hatred or passion" is known as
    a.  impersonality.
    b.  hierarchy of authority.
    c.  written rules and regulations.
    d.  employment based on technical qualifications.

8.  According to the Peter principle,
    a.  all bureaucracies are notoriously inefficient.
    b.  if something *can* go wrong, it *will*.
    c.  every employee within a hierarchy tends to rise to his or her level of incompetence.
    d.  all line workers get burned in the end.

9.  Social control in what Ferdinand Tönnies termed a *Gemeinschaft* community is maintained through all but which of the following means?
    a.  moral persuasion
    b.  gossip
    c.  legally defined punishment
    d.  gestures

10. Sociologist Daniel Bell uses which of the following terms to refer to a society whose economic system is engaged primarily in the processing and control of information?
    a.  postmodern
    b.  horticultural
    c.  industrial
    d.  postindustrial

1. (a); 2. (c); 3. (a); 4. (b); 5. (d); 6. (c); 7. (a); 8. (c); 9. (c); 10. (d)

# 6

# DEVIANC

# LIVING THE GANG LIFE

Sociology student Sudhir Venkatesh (2008), wanting to better understand the lives of poor African Americans, ventured into the housing projects in inner-city Chicago. After a rocky beginning, his naïveté and genuine curiosity helped to open the door to what became a seven-year, in-depth participation research project about gangs, drugs, crime, public housing, and more.

Venkatesh's commitment to going beyond what W. E. B. Du Bois dismissed as "car-window sociology" ultimately provided him access to information about crime and deviance that he could never have found through a survey. Through his research he learned that gangs have a highly organized structure, with those at the top of the gang hierarchy doing well financially, and the foot soldiers at the bottom, who make up 95 percent of the membership, averaging only $3.30 per hour (Levitt and Dubner 2005). They also have an astonishingly high death rate. These two facts together led one of Venkatesh's collaborators to say that selling drugs for a gang is perhaps "the worst job in all of America."

While it may not yield much money, dealing drugs does allow gang members to help support their families. Venkatesh argued that their willingness to work these jobs, even in the face of minimal return and high risk, demonstrated their desire to work, but they found so few viable options that some actually worked at McDonald's to supplement their drug-dealing income.

Venkatesh found that gangs seek to contribute to the local community, giving money to women who work in the buildings looking after children and the elderly. They require their young members to stay in school, and prohibit members from using hard drugs—in part because they cannot be good at business if they are high, and in part because it is bad for the image of the gang.

Through research like Venkatesh's, sociologists can better understand crime and deviance. The gang Venkatesh studied tried to create a level of stability in their neighborhood, but they relied on crime and violence as tools of their trade. What social factors lead to such outcomes, and can those factors or outcomes be changed? In this chapter we will look at these questions and more.

# As You READ >>

- How do groups maintain social control?
- What is the difference between deviance and crime?
- How do sociologists explain deviance and crime?

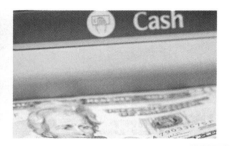

## >> Social Control

The tension between the individual and society, between our freedom to do whatever we want and our need for social order, is at the heart of the definition of sociology. Sociologists study social control, deviance, and crime to more fully understand and explain this balance. In this chapter we will address all three.

We seek to enforce the norms we create whether in the form of laws, dress codes, organizational by-laws, course requirements, or the rules of sports and games. We do so through **social control**—the techniques and strategies for preventing deviant human behavior in any society. Social control occurs on all levels of society. In the family, we are socialized to obey our parents simply because they are our parents. Peer groups introduce us to informal norms, such as dress codes, that govern the behavior of their members. Colleges establish the standards they expect of students. In bureaucratic organizations, workers encounter a formal system of rules and regulations. Finally, the government of every society legislates and enforces social norms.

Most of us respect and accept basic social norms and assume that others will do the same. Even without thinking, we usually obey the instructions of police officers, follow the day-to-day rules at our jobs, and move to the rear of elevators when people enter. Such behavior reflects an effective process of socializa-tion to the dominant standards of a culture. At the same time, we are well aware that individuals, groups, and institutions expect us to act "properly." This expectation is enforced through **sanctions**—penalties and rewards for conduct concerning a social norm. If we fail to live up to the norm, we may face punishment through informal sanctions such as fear and ridicule or formal sanctions such as jail sentences or fines.

Sanctions point to the reality that all societies, institutions, and groups rely on the use of power. On the one hand, we want people to respect social norms so that the group or society can survive. Society is defined in part by people's willingness to accept shared beliefs and practices, even if doing so sometimes constrains their selfish pursuits. On the other hand, society can be oppressive, limiting individual freedom and advancing the interests of some at the expense of others. Entrenched interests seek to maintain the status quo and use their power over sanctions to do so. In fact, positive social change often comes through resistance to the status quo, with individuals and groups rejecting existing norms and following new paths. Such attempts may meet with significant opposition, as was evident in the civil rights movement. Similar struggles were necessary in America to win independence from England, to overturn the institution of slavery, to earn women the vote, and to force an end to the war in Vietnam.

### CONFORMITY AND OBEDIENCE

Techniques for social control operate on both the group and the societal level. People we think of as peers or equals influence us to act in particular ways; the same is true of people who hold authority over us or whose positions we respect. Social psychologist Stanley Milgram (1975) made a useful distinction between these two levels of social control.

Milgram used the term **conformity** to mean going along with peers—individuals of our own status who have no special right to direct our behavior. In contrast, **obedience** is compliance with higher authorities in a hierarchical structure. Thus, a recruit entering military service will typically conform to the habits and language of other recruits and obey the orders of superiors. Students will conform to the drinking behavior of their peers and obey the requests of campus security officers.

In a classic experiment, Milgram (1963, 1975) sought to answer this question: Would you comply with a scientific researcher's instruction to administer increasingly painful electric shocks to a subject? He found that, contrary to what we might believe about ourselves, most of us would obey such orders. In his words (1975:xi), "Behavior that is unthinkable in an individual . . . acting on his own may be executed without hesitation when carried out under orders."

Milgram placed advertisements in New Haven, Connecticut, newspapers to recruit subjects for a learning experiment at Yale University. Participants included postal clerks, engineers, high school teachers, and laborers. They were told that the purpose of the research was to investigate the effects of punishment on learning. The experimenter, dressed in a gray technician's coat, explained that in each test, one subject would be randomly selected as the "learner" and another would function as the "teacher." However, the experiment was rigged so that the "real" subject would always be the teacher while an associate of Milgram's served as the learner.

At this point, the learner's hand was strapped to an electric apparatus. The teacher was taken to an electronic "shock generator" with 30 levered switches labeled from 15 to 450 volts. Before beginning the experiment, all subjects received sample shocks of 45 volts, to convince them of the authenticity of the experiment. The experimenter then instructed the teacher to apply shocks of increasing voltage each time the learner gave an incorrect answer on a memory test. Teachers were told that "although the shocks can be extremely painful, they cause no permanent tissue damage." In reality, the learner did not receive any shocks.

In a prearranged script, the learner deliberately gave incorrect answers and feigned pain when "shocked." For example, at 150 volts, the learner would cry out, "Get me out of here!" At 270 volts, the learner would scream in agony. When the shock reached 350 volts, the

> **social control** The techniques and strategies for preventing deviant human behavior in any society.
> **sanction** A penalty or reward for conduct concerning a social norm.
> **conformity** The act of going along with peers—individuals of our own status who have no special right to direct our behavior.
> **obedience** Compliance with higher authorities in a hierarchical structure.

**Did You Know?**

. . . Some prosecutors have sought to bring charges against college fraternities as gangs. They argued that the fraternity as an organization systematically promotes criminal behavior, including underage drinking and abusive actions toward women. Venkatesh suggests that, if you define a gang as "an established organization whose members come together for solidarity reasons and who engage in delinquent and/or criminal activities," then perhaps those prosecutors might be onto something (Dubner 2007).

learner would fall silent. If the teacher wanted to stop the experiment, the experimenter would insist that the teacher continue, using such statements as "The experiment requires that you continue" and "You have no other choice; you *must* go on" (Milgram 1975:19–23).

The results of this unusual experiment stunned and dismayed Milgram and other social scientists. A sample of psychiatrists had predicted that virtually all subjects would refuse to shock innocent victims. In their view, only a "pathological fringe" of fewer than 2 percent would continue administering shocks up to the maximum level. Yet almost two-thirds of participants fell into the category of "obedient subjects."

Why did these subjects obey? Why were they willing to inflict seemingly painful shocks on innocent victims who had never done them any harm? There is no evidence that these subjects were unusually sadistic; few seemed to enjoy administering the shocks. Instead, in Milgram's view, the key to obedience was the experimenter's social role as "scientist" and "seeker of knowledge."

Milgram pointed out that in the modern industrial world, we are accustomed to submitting to impersonal authority figures whose status is indicated by a title (professor, lieutenant, doctor) or by a uniform (the technician's coat). Because we view the authority as more important than the individual, we shift responsibility for our behavior to the authority figure. Milgram's subjects frequently stated, "If it were up to me, I would not have

administered shocks." They saw themselves as merely doing their duty (Milgram 1975).

Milgram launched his experimental study of obedience in part to better understand the involvement of Germans in the annihilation of 6 million Jews and millions of other people during World War II. In an interview conducted long after the publication of his study, he suggested that "if a system of death camps were set up in the United States of the sort we had seen in Nazi Germany, one would be able to find sufficient personnel for those camps in any medium-sized American town." Though many people questioned this statement, the revealing photos taken at Iraq's Abu Ghraib prison in 2004, showing U.S. military guards humiliating if not torturing Iraqi prisoners, recalled the experiment Milgram had done two generations earlier. Under conducive circumstances, otherwise normal people can and often do treat one another inhumanely (CBS News 1979:7–8; Hayden 2004; Zimbardo 2007).

## INFORMAL AND FORMAL SOCIAL CONTROL

The sanctions that society uses to encourage conformity and obedience—and to discourage violation of social norms—are carried out through both informal and formal social control. As the term

A participant in the Milgram experiment.

implies, people use **informal social control** casually to enforce norms. Examples include smiles, laughter, a raised eyebrow, and ridicule. We seek to read such cues in new situations such as a first date or a job interview so that we might adjust our behavior accordingly.

## SOCthink

> > > All groups must use some form of social control if they are to maintain any sense of order. What mechanisms of formal and informal social control are evident in your college classes and in day-to-day life and social interactions at your school?

**Formal social control** is carried out by authorized agents, such as police officers, judges, school administrators, employers, military officers, and managers. It can serve as a last resort when socialization and informal sanctions do not bring about desired behavior. An increasingly significant means of formal social control in the United States is imprisonment. During the course of a year, 7 million adults undergo some form of correctional supervision—jail, prison, probation, or parole. Put another way, almost 1 out of every 30 adult Americans is subject to this very formal type of social control every year (Glaze and Palla 2005).

In 2007, in the wake of the mass shootings at Virginia Tech, many college officials reviewed security measures on their campuses. Administrators were reluctant to end or even limit the relative freedom of movement students on their campuses enjoyed. Instead, they concentrated on improving emergency communications between campus police and students, faculty, and staff. Reflecting a reliance on technology to maintain social control, college leaders called for replacement of the "old" technology of email with instant alerts that could be sent to people's cell phones via instant messaging.

Six years earlier, in the aftermath of the terrorist attacks of September 11, 2001, new measures of social control became the norm in the United States. Some of them, such as stepped-up security at airports and high-rise buildings, were highly visible to the public. The federal government has also publicly urged citizens to engage in informal social control by watching for and reporting people whose actions seem suspicious. But many other measures taken by the government have increased the covert surveillance of private records and communications.

Just 45 days after September 11, with virtually no debate, Congress passed the USA Patriot Act of 2001. Sections of this sweeping legislation revoked legal checks on the power of law enforcement agencies. Without a warrant or probable cause, the FBI can now secretly access most private records, including medical histories, library accounts, and student registrations. In 2002, for example, the FBI searched the records of hundreds of dive shops and scuba organizations. Agents had been directed to identify every person who had taken diving lessons in the past three years because of speculation that terrorists might try to approach their targets underwater (Moss and Fessenden 2002).

Many people think that this kind of social control goes too far. Civil rights advocates also worry that the government's request for information on suspicious activities may encourage negative stereotyping of Muslims and Arab Americans. Clearly, there is a trade-off between the benefits of surveillance and violation of the right to privacy.

**informal social control** Social control that is carried out casually by ordinary people through such means as laughter, smiles, and ridicule.
**formal social control** Social control that is carried out by authorized agents, such as police officers, judges, school administrators, and employers.

The interplay between formal and informal social control can be complicated because we sometimes have to balance one source of control against another. College students, for example, receive conflicting messages about the acceptability of binge drinking. On the one hand, it represents deviance from the standards of conduct expected of those in an academic context. On the other hand, binge drinking shows conformity to the peer culture, especially in the context of sororities and fraternities (see the figure "Binge Drinking on Campus"). Increasingly, colleges and

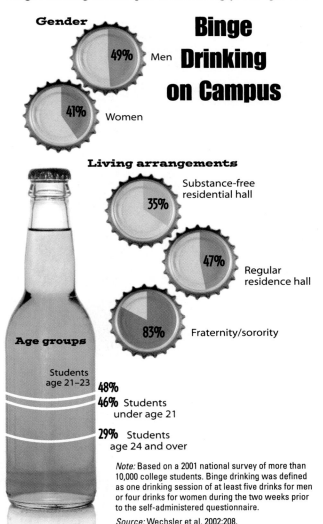

**Binge Drinking on Campus**

**Gender**
49% Men
41% Women

**Living arrangements**
35% Substance-free residential hall
47% Regular residence hall
83% Fraternity/sorority

**Age groups**
Students age 21–23 48%
46% Students under age 21
29% Students age 24 and over

*Note:* Based on a 2001 national survey of more than 10,000 college students. Binge drinking was defined as one drinking session of at least five drinks for men or four drinks for women during the two weeks prior to the self-administered questionnaire.

*Source:* Wechsler et al. 2002:208.

universities are taking steps to exert greater social control by instituting rules banning kegs, closing fraternities and sororities, expelling students after multiple alcohol-related violations, and working with local liquor retailers to discourage high-volume sales to students.

**law** Governmental social control.

**control theory** A view of conformity and deviance that suggests that our connection to members of society leads us to systematically conform to society's norms.

## LAW AND SOCIETY

Some norms are so important to a society that they are formalized into laws limiting people's behavior. **Law** may be defined as governmental social control (Black 1995). Some laws, such as the prohibition against murder, are directed at all members of society. Others, such as fishing and hunting regulations, primarily affect particular categories of people. Still others govern the behavior of social institutions (for instance, corporate law and laws regarding the taxing of nonprofit enterprises).

Sociologists see the creation of laws as a social process. Because laws are passed in response to a perceived need for formal social control, sociologists have sought to explain how and why such a perception arises. In their view, law is not merely a static body of rules handed down from generation to generation. Rather, it reflects continually changing standards of what is right and wrong, of how violations are to be determined, and of what sanctions are to be applied (Schur 1968).

# Formal Procedure: How a Bill Becomes Law

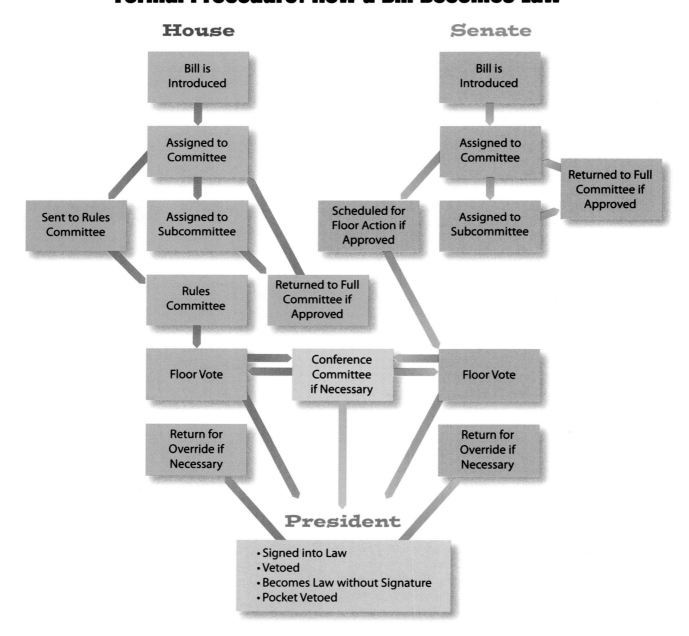

**House**

Bill is Introduced → Assigned to Committee → Sent to Rules Committee / Assigned to Subcommittee → Rules Committee / Returned to Full Committee if Approved → Floor Vote → Conference Committee if Necessary → Return for Override if Necessary

**Senate**

Bill is Introduced → Assigned to Committee → Scheduled for Floor Action if Approved / Assigned to Subcommittee → Returned to Full Committee if Approved → Floor Vote → Return for Override if Necessary

**President**

- Signed into Law
- Vetoed
- Becomes Law without Signature
- Pocket Vetoed

Sociologists representing varying theoretical perspectives agree that the legal order reflects the values of those in a position to exercise authority. Therefore, the creation of civil and criminal law can be a most controversial matter. For example, should it be against the law to employ illegal immigrants? To have an abortion? To allow prayer in public schools? To smoke on an airplane? Such issues have been bitterly debated, because they require a choice among competing values. Not surprisingly, unpopular laws—such as the Eighteenth Amendment, which prohibited the manufacture and sale of alcohol (ratified in 1919), or the nationwide 55-mile-per-hour speed limit that was imposed in 1974—become difficult to enforce when there is no consensus supporting the norms. In both cases, the public commonly violated the stated government policy, and the laws proved unenforceable; the states repealed Prohibition in 1933, and Congress overturned the national speed-limit policy in 1987.

The current debate over whether to allow people to use marijuana legally for medical purposes illustrates the difficulty in crafting laws that govern private behavior. Although the majority of adults polled in national surveys support such use, the federal government continues to regard all uses of marijuana as illegal. In 2005, the U.S. Supreme Court upheld the federal government's position. Nevertheless, 12 states have granted citizens the right to use marijuana for medical purposes (see the figure "Medical Marijuana Laws").

Socialization is the primary vehicle for instilling conforming and obedient behavior, including obedience to law. Generally, it is not external pressure from a peer group or authority figure that makes us go along with social norms. Rather, we have internalized such norms as valid and desirable and are committed to observing them. In a profound sense, we want to see ourselves (and to be seen) as loyal, cooperative, responsible, and respectful of others. In the United States and other societies around the world, people are socialized both to want to belong and to fear being viewed as different or deviant.

■ Maryland protects medical marijuana patients from jail, but not from the threat of arrest.

■ Washington, DC

■ 12 states have laws that allow the cultivation of medical marijuana and that protect patients who possess medical marijuana (with their doctor's recommendations or certifications) from criminal penalties.

■ 17 states and the District of Columbia have laws that recognize marijuana's medical value, but these laws are ineffective because they rely on federal cooperation.

## Medical Marijuana Laws

**Control theory** suggests that our connection to other members of society leads us to conform systematically to society's norms. According to sociologist Travis Hirschi and other control theorists, our bonds to family members, friends, and peers induce us to follow the mores and folkways of our society. We give little conscious thought to whether we will be sanctioned if we fail to conform. Socialization develops our self-control so well that we don't need further pressure to obey social norms. While control theory does not explain the rationale for every conforming act, it nevertheless reminds us that while the media may focus on crime and disorder, most members of most societies conform to and obey basic norms most of the time (Gottfredson and Hirschi 1990; Hirschi 1969).

## >> Deviance

For sociologists, the term *deviance* does not mean perversion or depravity. **Deviance** is behavior that violates the standards of conduct or expectations of a group or society (Wickman 1991:85). In the United States, most people classify those who are alcoholics, compulsive gamblers, or mentally ill as deviant. Being late for class is categorized as a deviant act, as is wearing jeans to a formal wedding. On the basis of the sociological definition, we are all deviant from time to time. Each

**deviance** Behavior that violates the standards of conduct or expectations of a group or society.

of us violates common social norms in certain situations.

## WHAT BEHAVIOR IS DEVIANT?

### Hot or Not?

Do colleges and universities have a responsibility to crack down on file sharing over their networks?

Because deviance involves violation of some group's norms, defining an act as deviant depends on the context. File sharing on the Internet—including MP3s, movies, computer games, books, and almost anything else that can be digitized—provides an example of how deviance can be in the eye of the beholder. Sharing files, whether through Napster, Kazaa, Morpheus, and now BitTorrent, has become widespread. New movies are sometimes available online even before they have been released in the theater. Because the "property" these files represent is not physical, it can be reproduced for virtually no cost. Anyone with a computer and an Internet connection can grab them from people who are willing to share, then pass them along to others. Just how deviant is this? Record and movie companies take it very seriously; they have actively pursued lawsuits against those who share files in part to scare those who might think of doing it. However, the widespread availability of these files suggests that many people do not view this practice as particularly deviant. Some even view it as an act of protest against what they consider unfair prices charged by big corporations.

In most instances, those individuals and groups with the greatest status and power define what is acceptable and what is deviant.

*Present-day fans of bullfighting, which has a long and rich history in Spain and elsewhere, are now often stigmatized for their admiration of a sport that often results in pain and death for the bulls.*

For example, serious medical warnings of the dangers of tobacco appeared as early as 1964, yet cigarette smoking continued to be accepted for decades—in good part because of the power of tobacco farmers and cigarette manufacturers. Only after public health and anticancer activists led a long campaign against cigarette smoking did smoking become more of a deviant activity. Today, many state and local laws limit where people can smoke.

Of course, deviation from norms is not always negative, let alone criminal. A member of an exclusive social club who speaks out against a traditional policy of excluding women, Blacks, and Jews from admittance is deviating from the club's norms. So is a police officer who blows the whistle on corruption or brutality within the department.

## DEVIANCE AND SOCIAL STIGMA

Some people are unwillingly cast in negative social roles because of physical or behavioral characteristics. Whole groups of people—for instance, "short people" or "redheads"—may be labeled in this way. Once individuals have been assigned a deviant role, they can have trouble presenting a positive image to others and may even experience lowered self-esteem. Sociologist Erving Goffman coined the term **stigma** to describe the labels society uses to devalue members of certain social groups (Goffman 1963; Heckert and Best 1997).

We face pressure not to deviate too far from expected norms. To avoid stigma, for example, women can feel pressured to approximate what Naomi Wolf (1992) refers to as the "beauty myth"—an exaggerated ideal of beauty, beyond the reach of all but a few females. As a result, "ex-convict," "recovering alcoholic," and "ex–mental patient" can stick to a person for life. Goffman draws a useful distinction between a prestige symbol that calls attention to a positive aspect of one's identity, such as a wedding band or a badge, and a stigma symbol that discredits or debases one's identity, such as a conviction for child molestation. While stigma symbols may not always be obvious, they can become a matter of public knowledge. Starting in 1994, many states required convicted sex offenders to register with local police departments. Some communities publish the names and addresses, and in some instances even the pictures, of convicted sex offenders on the Web.

> **stigma** A label used to devalue members of certain social groups.
> **crime** A violation of criminal law for which some governmental authority applies formal penalties.

A person need not be guilty of a crime to be stigmatized. Homeless people often have trouble getting a job because employers are wary of applicants who cannot give a home address. Moreover, hiding one's homelessness is difficult, since agencies generally use the telephone to contact applicants about job openings. If a homeless person has access to a telephone at a shelter, the staff generally answers the phone by announcing the name of the institution—a sure way to discourage prospective employers. Even if a homeless person surmounts these obstacles and manages to get a job, she or he is often fired when the employer learns of the situation. Regardless of a person's positive attributes, employers regard the negative connotation of homelessness as sufficient reason to dismiss an employee.

many of the one million cosmetic procedures done every year in the United States are performed on women who would be defined objectively as having a normal appearance. Although feminist sociologists have accurately noted that the beauty myth makes many women feel uncomfortable with themselves, men too lack confidence in their appearance. The number of males who choose to undergo cosmetic procedures has risen sharply in recent years; men now account for 21 percent of such surgeries (American Academy of Cosmetic Surgery 2007).

Often people are stigmatized for deviant behaviors that they may no longer practice. The labels "former gambler,"

## >> Crime

If deviance means breaking group norms, **crime** is a violation of law for which some governmental authority applies formal penalties. It is a type of deviance representing a violation of social norms administered by the state. Laws divide crimes into various categories, depending on the severity of the offense, the age of the offender, the potential punishment, and the court that holds jurisdiction over the case.

## OFFICIAL CRIME REPORTS

When we think of crime, the categories most likely to come to mind are what we might think of as street crimes. The FBI breaks such crimes into two major categories: violent crimes and property crimes. They do not include all types of crime in these reports, focusing only on four major types within each category. Violent crimes include murder, forcible rape, robbery, and aggravated assault; property crimes include burglary, larceny-theft, motor vehicle theft, and arson. The FBI provides an annual account of the number of these crimes in their *Uniform Crime Reports* (UCR), which is available online. Because they are tracked so closely by the FBI and have been for a long time, these crimes have come to be known as **index crimes.**

> **index crimes** The eight types of crime reported annually by the FBI in the *Uniform Crime Reports:* murder, forcible rape, robbery, aggravated assault, burglary, larceny-theft, motor vehicle theft, and arson.

As we can see in the accompanying table, property crimes occur at a much higher rate than do violent crimes. In fact, according to the "crime clock" that the FBI provides as part of its report, a property crime occurs on average every 3.2 seconds. The most frequent property crime is larceny-theft, which includes incidents such as shoplifting and stealing items from cars. By contrast, a violent crime occurs every 22.2 seconds. Robbery, which involves the use or threat of force, is the most frequent violent crime, with one oc-curring every 1.2 minutes. Murder is the least frequent of the index crimes, with one occurring every 30.9 minutes (United States Department of Justice, Federal Bureau of Investigation 2007).

**Trends in Crime** One major trend revealed in these reports is a significant decline in violent crime nationwide following many years of increases. Sociologists have offered a number of explanations for this, including

- A booming economy and falling unemployment rates through most of the 1990s.
- Community-oriented policing and crime prevention programs.
- New gun control laws.
- A massive increase in the prison population, which at least prevents inmates from committing crimes outside prison.

In the past five years rates have held steady, but even with the previous declines, rates of reported crime remain well above both those of other nations and those of the United States just 20 years earlier. Feminist scholars draw our attention to one significant variation: the proportion of major crimes committed by women has increased. In a recent 10-year period (1997–2006), female arrests for major reported crimes increased 4 percent, while comparable male arrests declined 7 percent (Department of Justice 2007a:Table 33).

# National Crime Rates and Percentage Change

| Offenses in 2004 | Number reported | Rate per 100,000 inhabitants | Percentage change in rate Since 1995 | Since 2000 |
|---|---|---|---|---|
| **Murder** | 16,137 | 6 | -33 | -1 |
| **Forcible rape** | 94,635 | 32 | -13 | 1 |
| **Robbery** | 401,326 | 137 | -38 | -6 |
| **Aggravated assault** | 854,911 | 291 | -30 | -10 |
| **Total** (Violent crimes) | 1,367,009 | 466 | -32 | -8 |
| **Burglary** | 2,143,456 | 730 | -26 | 0 |
| **Larceny-theft** | 6,947,685 | 2,366 | -22 | -5 |
| **Motor vehicle theft** | 1,237,114 | 421 | -25 | 2 |
| **Total** (Property crimes) | 10,328,255 | 3,517 | -23 | -3 |

*Notes:* Arson was designated an index offense beginning in 1979; data on arson were still incomplete as of 2004. Because of rounding, the offenses may not add to totals.

*Source:* Department of Justice 2005: Table 1.

## Victimization Rates, 1973–2006

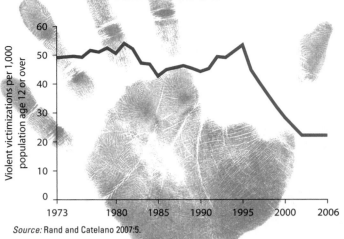

Violent victimizations per 1,000 population age 12 or over

60
50
40
30
20
10
0

1973    1980    1985    1990    1995    2000    2006

Source: Rand and Catelano 2007:5.

**Limitations of Crime Statistics** There are limitations to official crime statistics, the most serious of which is that they include only those crimes reported to law enforcement agencies. Because members of racial and ethnic minority groups often distrust law enforcement agencies, they may not contact the police when they are victimized. Further, feminist sociologists and others have noted that many women do not report rape or spousal abuse out of fear they will be blamed for the crime.

Partly because of such deficiencies in official statistics, the U.S. Department of Justice initiated the National Crime Victimization Survey in 1972. In compiling this annual report, the department's Bureau of Justice Statistics not only gathers information from law enforcement agencies but also interviews members of over 76,000 households to determine if they were victims of a specific set of crimes during the preceding year. In general, those who administer **victimization surveys** question ordinary people, not police officers, to determine whether they have been victims of crime.

Even using such surveys, the threat of underreporting the actual number of crimes remains. Surveys require that victims understand what has happened to them and that

**SOC**think

> > > The Clery Act, passed in 1990, requires timely reports of campus crime. Why do you think such a law was passed in the first place? To what extent do you think such reporting makes a difference? Why might reports of crime on college campuses underestimate actual incidents?

they be willing to disclose such information to interviewers. People are particularly reluctant to report crimes such as fraud, income tax evasion, and blackmail in victimization studies. Nevertheless, 91 percent of all households have been willing to cooperate with investigators for the National Crime Victimization Survey. As shown in the figure at left, data from these surveys reveal a fluctuating victimization rate with significant declines in both the early 1980s and the late 1990s (Catalano 2005).

> **victimization survey** A questionnaire or interview given to a sample of the population to determine whether people have been victims of crime.
> **white-collar crime** Illegal acts committed by affluent, "respectable" individuals in the course of business activities.

Another limitation of the UCR official statistics is that they exclude many offenses that we would count as criminal. In so doing, they minimize the degree to which we see perpetrators of other types of crime as criminal in the same way as violators of the index crimes. We turn next to several such categories, including white-collar crime, victimless crimes, and organized crime.

## WHITE-COLLAR CRIME

Income tax evasion, stock manipulation, consumer fraud, bribery and extraction of kickbacks, embezzlement, and misrepresentation in advertising—these are all examples of **white-collar crime,** or illegal acts committed in the course of business activities, often by affluent, "respectable" people. Historically, we have viewed such crimes differently because they are often perpetrated through respected occupational roles (Sutherland 1949, 1983).

Edwin Sutherland (1940) coined the term *white-collar crime* in 1939 to refer to acts by in-

*"I swear I wasn't looking at smut—I was just stealing music."*

dividuals, but the term has been broadened more recently to include offenses by businesses and corporations as well. Corporate crime, or any act by a corporation that is punishable by the government, takes many forms and includes individuals, organizations, and institutions among its victims. Corporations may engage in anticompetitive behavior, environmental pollution, medical fraud, tax fraud, stock fraud and manipulation, accounting fraud, the production of unsafe goods, bribery and corruption, and health and safety violations (J. Coleman 2006).

Corporate wrongdoers have often used their money and prestige to get off lightly in court. For example, they have documented their long history of charitable contributions and agreed to help law enforcement officials find other white-collar criminals. In 2003, 10 investment firms and two stock analysts collectively paid a $1.4-billion settlement for providing fraudulent information to investors. While the magnitude of the fine grabbed headlines nationwide, it must be balanced against the millions of investors who were lured into buying billions of dollars' worth of shares in companies that the accused knew were either troubled or on the verge of collapse. The bottom line is that no individual served a jail sentence as part of the settlement, and no firm lost its license to do business. Prosecutors in other investigations into corporate scandals have pledged to pursue jail sentences for white-collar criminals, but to date most defendants have only been fined (Labaton 2003; O'Donnell and Willing 2003).

Conviction for corporate crime does not generally harm a person's reputation and career aspirations nearly as much as conviction for street crime would. Apparently, the label "white-collar criminal" does not carry the stigma of the label "felon convicted of a violent crime." Conflict theorists don't find such differential treatment surprising. They argue that the criminal justice system largely disregards the crimes of the affluent, focusing on crimes committed by the poor. Generally, if an offender holds a position of status and influence, his or her crime is treated as less serious than others' crimes, and the sanction is much more lenient.

A new type of white-collar crime has emerged in recent decades: computer crime. The use of high technology allows criminals to carry out embezzlement or electronic fraud, often leaving few traces, or to gain access to a company's inventory without leaving home. According to the FBI and the National White

Collar Crime Center, over one million Internet crimes were reported in less than four years, ranging from scams to identity theft (Internet Crime Complaint Center 2007). According to a 2007 report, each year 3.7 percent of all adults find that their personal information has been misused for criminal purposes. Unfortunately, with our society's growing reliance on electronic financial trans-

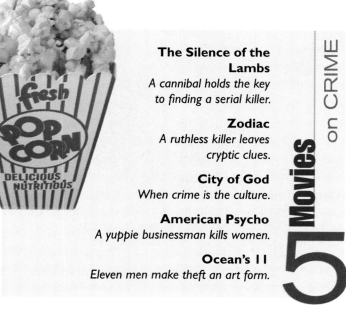

## 5 Movies on CRIME

**The Silence of the Lambs**
*A cannibal holds the key to finding a serial killer.*

**Zodiac**
*A ruthless killer leaves cryptic clues.*

**City of God**
*When crime is the culture.*

**American Psycho**
*A yuppie businessman kills women.*

**Ocean's 11**
*Eleven men make theft an art form.*

actions, assuming someone else's identity has become significantly easier (Baum 2006; Monahan 2007).

## VICTIMLESS CRIMES

Another category of crimes that raises questions about how we define deviance consists of so-called victimless crimes. **Victimless crime** refers to the willing exchange among adults of widely desired, but illegal, goods and services, such as drugs or prostitution (Schur 1965, 1985). The fact that the parties involved are willing has led some people to suggest that such transactions should not constitute crimes.

Some activists are working to decriminalize many of these illegal practices. Supporters of decriminalization are troubled by the attempt to legislate a moral code for adults. In their view, prostitution, drug abuse, gambling, and other victimless crimes are impossible to prevent. The already overburdened criminal justice system should instead devote its resources to "street crimes" and other offenses with obvious victims.

Despite widespread use of the term *victimless crime,* however, many people object to the notion that there is no victim other than the offender in such crimes. Excessive drinking, compulsive gambling, and illegal drug use contribute to an enormous amount of personal and property damage. A person with a drinking problem can become abusive to a spouse or children; a compulsive gambler or drug user may steal to pursue his or her obsession. Feminist sociologists contend that prostitution, as well as the more

**Hot or Not?**

Should gambling, prostitution, and recreational drugs be legalized?

disturbing aspects of pornography, reinforce the misconception that women are "toys" who can be treated as objects rather than people. According to critics of decriminalization, society must not give tacit approval to conduct that has such harmful consequences (Meier and Geis 1997).

## ORGANIZED CRIME

When it comes to organized crime, the name Tony Soprano is the first that comes to mind for many people. He was the fictional boss of the DiMeo crime family on HBO's hit series *The Sopranos*. In real life, examples of organized crime groups go beyond the Mafia to include the Japanese Yakuza, the Russian Organization, Colombian drug cartels, and many other international crime syndicates. For our purposes, we will consider **organized crime** to be the work of a group that regulates relations among criminal enterprises involved in illegal activities, including prostitution, gambling, and the smuggling and sale of illegal drugs.

Organized crime dominates the world of illegal business, just as large corporations dominate the conventional business world. It allocates territory, sets prices for goods and services, and acts as an arbiter in internal disputes. A secret, conspiratorial activity, organized crime generally evades law enforcement. It takes over legitimate businesses, gains influence over labor unions, corrupts public officials, intimidates witnesses in criminal trials, and even "taxes" merchants in exchange for "protection" (National Advisory Commission on Criminal Justice 1976).

Historically, organized crime has provided a means of upward mobility for groups of people struggling to escape poverty. Sociologist Daniel Bell (1953) used the term *ethnic succession* to describe the sequential passage of leadership from Irish Americans in the early 1900s to Jewish Americans in the 1920s and then to Italian Americans in the early 1930s. Recently, ethnic succession has become more complex, reflecting the diversity of the nation's latest immigrants. Colombian, Mexican, Russian, Chinese, Pakistani, and Nigerian immigrants are among those who have begun to play a significant role in organized crime activities (Chin 1996; Kleinknecht 1996).

> **victimless crime** A term used by sociologists to describe the willing exchange among adults of widely desired, but illegal, goods and services.
> **organized crime** The work of a group that regulates relations among criminal enterprises involved in illegal activities, including prostitution, gambling, and the smuggling and sale of illegal drugs.
> **transnational crime** Crime that occurs across multiple national borders.

There has always been a global element in organized crime. However, law enforcement officials and policy makers now acknowledge the emergence of a new form of organized crime that takes advantage of advances in electronic communications. Transnational organized crime includes drug and arms smuggling, money laundering, and trafficking in illegal immigrants and stolen goods (Lumpe 2003; Office of Justice Programs 1999).

## INTERNATIONAL CRIME

In the past, international crime was often limited to the clandestine shipment of goods across the border between

**POPSOC**

**Where there are rules there will always be violations of those rules.**

Joel M. Charon

The success of shows such as *The Sopranos, CSI, NCIS, Criminal Minds,* and *Without a Trace* continue a long tradition of TV crime shows.

two countries. Increasingly, however, crime is no more restricted by such borders than is legal commerce. Rather than concentrating on specific countries, international crime now spans the globe.

**Transnational Crime** More and more, scholars and law enforcement officials are turning their attention to **transnational crime,** or crime that occurs across multiple national borders. Historically, probably the most dreaded example of transnational crime has been slavery. At first, governments did not regard slavery as a crime but merely regulated it as they would trade in any other good. In the 20th century, transnational crime grew to embrace trafficking in endangered species, drugs, and stolen art and antiquities.

Transnational crime is not exclusive of some of the other types of crime we have discussed. For example, organized

**International Incarceration Rates**

**Rank**
(out of 217 nations)

**International incarceration rates**
(prison population rates per 100,000 of the national population)

| Rank | Nation | Rate |
|------|--------|------|
| 1 | United States of America | 751 |
| 2 | Russian Federation | 632 |
| 24 | South Africa | 348 |
| 33 | Israel | 305 |
| 59 | Mexico | 198 |
| 86 | England and Wales | 152 |
| 102 | Kenya | 130 |
| 113 | China | 119 |
| 123 | Canada | 108 |
| 157 | Sweden | 79 |
| 177 | Japan | 63 |
| 203 | India | 32 |

Prison Population Rates per 100,000 of the National Population, Selected Nations, 2008

*Source:* International Centre for Prison Studies 2008.

criminal networks are increasingly global. Technology definitely facilitates their illegal activities, such as trafficking in child pornography. Beginning in the 1990s, the United Nations began to categorize transnational crimes, such as hijacking, illegal drug trade, sea piracy, and terrorism.

One way to fight such crime has been through bilateral cooperation in which countries cooperate to pursue border-crossing crime. The first global effort to control international crime was the International Criminal Police Organization (Interpol), a cooperative network of European police forces founded to stem the movement of political revolutionaries across borders. While such efforts to fight transnational crime may seem lofty—an activity with which any government would want to cooperate—they are complicated by sensitive legal and security issues. Most nations that have signed protocols issued by the United Nations, including the United States, have expressed concern over potential encroachments on their national judicial systems, as well as concern over their national security. Thus, they have been reluctant to share certain types of intelligence data. The terrorist attacks of September 11, 2001, increased both the interest in combating transnational crime and sensitivity to the risks

**anomie** Durkheim's term for the loss of direction felt in a society when social control of individual behavior has become ineffective.

of sharing intelligence data (Deflem 2005; Felson and Kalaitzidis 2005).

**International Crime Rates** Taking an international perspective on crime reinforces one of the key sociological lessons about crime and deviance: Place matters. While cross-national data comparison can be difficult, we can offer preliminary conclusions about how crime rates differ around the world.

During the 1980s and 1990s, violent crimes were much more common in the United States than in the nations of Western Europe. Murders, rapes, and robberies were reported to the police at much higher rates in the United States. Yet the incidence of certain other types of crime appears to be higher elsewhere. For example, England, Italy, Australia, and New Zealand all have higher rates of car theft than the United States. Developing nations have significant rates of reported homicide due to civil unrest and political conflict among civilians (International Crime Victim Survey 2004; World Bank 2003a). But when it comes to putting offenders in jail, the United States tops them all. On a typical day, the United States imprisons 751 of every 100,000 adults, compared to 632 in Russia, fewer than 198 in Mexico, and 108 in Canada.

Why are rates of violent crime so much higher in the United States than in Western Europe? Sociologist Elliot Currie (1985, 1998) has suggested that our society places greater emphasis on individual economic achievement than other societies. At the same time, many observers have noted that the culture of the United States has long tolerated, if not condoned, many forms of violence. Coupled with sharp disparities between poor and affluent citizens, significant unemployment, and substantial alcohol and drug abuse, these factors combine to produce a climate conducive to crime.

However, disturbing increases in violent crime are evident in other Western societies. For example, crime has skyrocketed in Russia since the overthrow of Communist Party rule (with its strict controls on guns and criminals) in 1991. In 1998 there were fewer than 260 homicides in Moscow; now there are more than 1000 homicides a year. Organized crime has filled the power vacuum in Moscow: One result is that gangland shootouts and premeditated "contract hits" have become more common. Some prominent reformist politicians have been targeted as well. Russia incarcerates an extremely high proportion of its citizens—almost as high as the United States.

## >> Sociological Perspectives on Deviance and Crime

Why do people violate social norms? We have seen that deviant acts are subject to both informal and formal social control. The nonconforming or disobedient person may face disapproval, loss of friends, fines, or even imprisonment. Why, then, does deviance occur?

Sociologists have been interested in crime and deviance from the very beginning and have generated numerous theories of deviance and crime. Though we might wish otherwise, there is no one, simple, universal theory that explains all such acts. Here we will look to just a few of the theories that sociologists have offered in order to identify significant factors that we must consider in our attempt to understand deviance and crime more fully.

## 5 Movies on DEVIANCE

**Harold and Maude**
*Not your average couple.*

**American Beauty**
*Various people disregard the norm in their search for happiness.*

**A Clockwork Orange**
*The success and failure of rehabilitating a delinquent.*

**Pulp Fiction**
*Don't be such a "square."*

**To Wong Foo, Thanks for Everything!**
*Three transvestites in Smalltown, USA.*

## SOCIAL ORDER, DEVIANCE, AND CRIME

Émile Durkheim's ([1895] 1964) emphasis on the importance of social order led him to investigate the nature and causes of deviance and crime. Why are such activities, which would seem to undermine order, found in all societies? For Durkheim the answer rested with how such actions were perceived by others.

**Durkheim's Theory of Deviance** Durkheim argued that there is nothing inherently deviant or criminal in any act; the key is how society responds to the act. He put it this way: "We must not say that an action shocks the common consciousness because it is criminal, but rather that it is criminal because it shocks that consciousness" ([1895] 1964:123–24). In other words, nothing is criminal or worthy of condemnation unless we decide it is. For example, we do not regard killing in self-defense or in combat in the same way we view killing in cold blood. At least, that is the case until we change our minds about how we view wartime killing, as has happened at various times in our past. When it comes to war, for example, our attitudes about what is appropriate can shift. In both Vietnam and Iraq, strong public support gave way to serious misgivings about U.S. involvement in these nations. In both cases, this

was driven in part by images from the conflict, including, for example, the treatment of prisoners at Abu Ghraib. In this way, our understanding of what constitutes deviance and crime are tied to issues of social solidarity.

In fact, Durkheim concluded that deviance and crime actually can have a positive impact on society in a variety of ways. For example, identifying acts as deviant clarifies our shared beliefs and values and thus brings us closer together. We say, in effect, "This is who we are, and if you want to be one of us you cannot cross this line. Some things we might let go, but if you push the limits too far you will face sanctions." Punishment, too, can draw a group together, uniting members in their opposition to the offender. Sanctions also discourage others from similar violations, thus increasing conformity. When we see a driver receiving a speeding ticket, a department store cashier being fired for yelling at a customer, or a college student getting a failing grade for plagiarizing a term paper, we are reminded of our collective norms and values and of the consequences of their violation. Finally, Durkheim did recognize that deviant acts might also force us to recognize the limits of our existing beliefs and practices, opening up new doors and leading to cultural innovation.

Based on Durkheim's analysis, it is possible to conclude that societies identify criminals for the sake of social order. No matter how much unity a society might appear to have, there will always be some who push the limits. Regardless of how "good" such people may appear to be to outsiders, they may face sanction within the group for the good of the whole.

## SOCthink

> > > Durkheim argues that increased division of labor results in fewer shared experiences and thus a weakened sense of community. Might this imply that we need ever more shocking violations of our remaining shared values in order to bring us together?

Durkheim did, however, also recognize that some social circumstances increase the likelihood of turning toward deviance and crime. As we have already seen, Durkheim ([1897] 1951) introduced the term **anomie** into the sociological literature to describe the loss of direction felt in a society when social control of individual behavior has become ineffective. Anomie is a state of normlessness that typically occurs during a period of profound social change and disorder, such as a time of economic collapse, political or social revolution, or even sudden prosperity. The power of society to constrain deviant action at such times is limited because there is no clear consensus on shared norms and values. Just as we saw with Durkheim's analysis of suicide, at times when social integration is weak, people are freer to pursue their own deviant paths.

### Merton's Theory of Deviance

Sociologist Robert Merton (1968) took Durkheim's theory a step further. He realized that sometimes members of a society share collective values or goals and other times they do not. He also realized that some people accept the means to attain those goals and others don't. To understand deviance and crime, he felt it was necessary to go beyond the general state of society to look more closely at where people fit in relationship to both goals and means.

Conformity to social norms, the most common adaptation in Merton's typology, is the opposite of deviance. It involves acceptance of both the overall societal goal (for example, to become wealthy) and the approved means (hard work). In Merton's view, there must be some consensus regarding accepted cultural goals and the legitimate means for attaining them. Without such a consensus, societies could exist only as collectives of people rather than as unified cultures, and they might experience continual chaos.

The other four types of behavior all involve some departure from conformity. The "innovator" accepts the goals of society but pursues them with means that are regarded as

## Law and justice are not always the same.

Gloria Steinem

Merton maintained that one important cultural goal in the United States is success, measured largely in terms of money. In addition to providing this goal for people, our society offers specific instructions on how to pursue success—go to school, work hard, do not quit, take advantage of opportunities, and so forth. A mugger and a merchant may share the common goal of economic success, but their means of attaining it are radically different. What happens to individuals in a society with a heavy emphasis on wealth as a basic symbol of success? Merton reasoned that people adapt in certain ways, either by conforming to or by deviating from such cultural expectations. His **anomie theory of deviance** posits five basic forms of adaptation.

improper. For instance, a safecracker may steal money to buy consumer goods and expensive vacations.

In Merton's typology, the "ritualist" has abandoned the goal of material success and become compulsively committed to the institutional means. Work becomes simply a way of life rather than a means to the goal of success. An example would be the bureaucratic official who blindly applies rules and regulations without remembering the larger goals of the organization. Certainly, that would be true of a welfare caseworker who refuses to assist a homeless family because their last apartment was in another district.

The "retreatist," as described by Merton, has basically withdrawn (or retreated) from both the goals and the means of society. In the United States, drug addicts and vagrants are typically portrayed as retreatists. Concern has been growing that adolescents who are addicted to alcohol will become retreatists at an early age.

The final adaptation identified by Merton reflects people's attempts to create a *new* social structure. The "rebel" feels alienated from the dominant means and goals and may seek a dramatically different social order. Members of a revolutionary political organization, such as a militia group, can be categorized as rebels according to Merton's model.

Merton's theory, though popular, does not fully account for patterns of deviance and crime. While it is useful in explaining certain types of behavior, such as illegal gambling by disadvantaged "innovators," it fails to explain key differences in crime rates. Why, for example, do some disadvantaged groups have lower rates of reported crime than others? Why do many people in adverse circumstances reject criminal activity as a viable alternative? Merton's theory does not easily answer such questions (Clinard and Miller 1998). In order to more fully appreciate such nuances, we must add to what we can learn from Merton by turning to theories that seek to better understand deviance and crime at an interpersonal level.

## INTERPERSONAL INTERACTION AND LOCAL CONTEXT

Perhaps the likelihood of committing deviant acts is not solely shaped by social integration or the acceptance of society's larger goals and means to attain them. Maybe moms around the world were right all along that it really does depend on who your friends are. If we are to understand and explain such acts, we must also consider the local context and the importance of social interaction.

### Cultural Transmission

As humans, we learn how to behave in social situations, whether properly or improperly. Sociologist Edwin Sutherland (1883–1950) proposed that, just as individuals are socialized to conform to society's basic norms and values, so also are they socialized to learn deviant acts. It's not that we are born to be wild; we learn to be wild.

Sutherland drew on the **cultural**

**transmission** school, which emphasizes that individuals learn criminal behavior by interacting with others. Such learning includes not only the techniques of lawbreaking (for example, how to break into a car quickly and quietly) but also the motives, drives, and rationalizations of the criminal. The cultural transmission approach can also be used to explain the behavior of those who habitually abuse alcohol or drugs.

Sutherland maintained that through interactions with a primary group and significant others, people acquire definitions of proper and improper behavior. He used the term **differential association** to describe the process through which exposure to attitudes favorable to criminal acts leads to the violation of rules. Research suggests that this view of differential association also applies to noncriminal deviant acts, such as smoking, truancy, and early sexual behavior (E. Jackson et al. 1986).

To what extent will a given person engage in activity that is regarded as proper or improper? For each individual, it will depend on the frequency, duration, and importance of two types of social interaction—those experiences that endorse deviant behavior and those that promote acceptance of social norms. People are more likely to engage in norm-defying behavior if they are part of a group or subculture that stresses deviant values, such as a street gang.

Sutherland offers the example of a boy who is sociable, outgoing, and athletic and who lives in an area with a high rate of delinquency. The youth is very likely to come into contact with peers who commit acts of vandalism, fail to attend school, and so forth, and he may come to adopt such behavior. However, an introverted boy who lives in the same neighborhood may stay away from his peers and avoid delinquency. In another community, an outgoing and athletic boy may join a Little League baseball team or a scout troop because

> **anomie theory of deviance** Merton's theory of deviance as an adaptation of socially prescribed goals or of the means governing their attainment, or both.
>
> **cultural transmission** A school of criminology that argues that criminal behavior is learned through social interactions.
>
> **differential association** A theory of deviance that holds that violation of rules results from exposure to attitudes favorable to criminal acts.

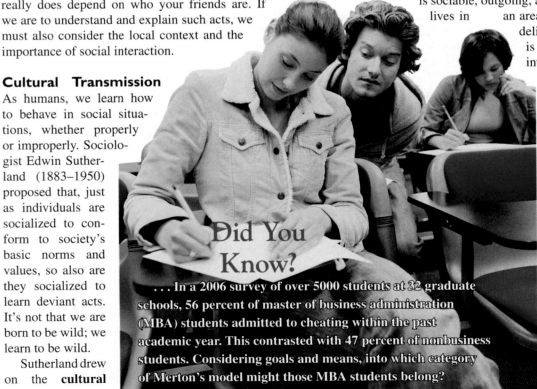

**Did You Know?**

... In a 2006 survey of over 5000 students at 32 graduate schools, 56 percent of master of business administration (MBA) students admitted to cheating within the past academic year. This contrasted with 47 percent of nonbusiness students. Considering goals and means, into which category of Merton's model might those MBA students belong?

of his interactions with peers. Thus, Sutherland views improper behavior as the result of the types of groups to which one belongs and the kinds of friendships one has (Sutherland et al. 1992).

While the cultural transmission approach may not explain the conduct of the first-time, impulsive shoplifter or the impoverished person who steals out of necessity, it does help to explain the deviant behavior of juvenile delinquents or graffiti artists. It directs our attention to the paramount role of social interaction and context in increasing a person's motivation to engage in deviant behavior (Morselli et al. 2006; Sutherland et al. 1992).

**Social Disorganization Theory** The social relationships that exist in a community or neighborhood affect people's behavior. Psychologist Philip Zimbardo (2007:24–25) conducted an experiment that demonstrated the power of communal relationships. He abandoned a car in each of two different neighborhoods, leaving its hood up and removing its hub caps. In one neighborhood, people started to strip the car for parts even before Zimbardo had finished setting up a remote video camera to record their behavior. In the other neighborhood, weeks passed without the car being touched, except for a pedestrian who stopped to close the hood during a rainstorm.

**Social disorganization theory** attributes increases in crime and deviance to the absence or breakdown of communal relationships and social institutions, such as the family, school, church, and local government. The lack of such local community connections, with their associated cross-age relationships, makes it difficult to exert informal control within the community, especially of children. Without community supervision and controls, playing outside becomes an opportunity for deviance, and older violators socialize children into inappropriate paths. Crime becomes a normal response to a local context.

This theory was developed at the University of Chicago in the early 1900s to describe the apparent disorganization that occurred as cities expanded with immigrants from abroad and migrants from rural areas. Using the latest survey techniques, Clifford Shaw and Henry McKay literally mapped the distribution of social problems in Chicago. They found high rates of social problems in neighborhoods where buildings had deteriorated and the population had declined. Interestingly, the patterns persisted over time, despite changes in the neighborhoods' ethnic and racial composition.

**Labeling Theory** Sometimes when it comes to deviance, what you see is what you get. The Saints and Roughnecks were two groups of high school males who were continually engaged in excessive drinking, reckless driving, truancy,

## From Me to You

The cafeteria at the school where I teach has an all-you-can-eat policy, but you cannot take food with you when you leave. Most of my students admit they violate this policy. When I suggest that what they are doing might be criminal, they are offended. They justify their theft in any number of ways: They pay a lot for their meal plan, they sometimes miss meals, it wouldn't make sense to throw the food away, etc. Yet there are people in prison who have taken things costing less than the total value of food taken by the average student. Why is it that those of us, like me, who are guilty of having taken food do not view ourselves as criminal?

petty theft, and vandalism. There the similarity ended. None of the Saints was ever arrested, but every Roughneck was frequently in trouble with police and townspeople. Why the disparity in their treatment? On the basis of observation research in their high school, sociologist William Chambliss (1973) concluded that how they were seen, as rooted in their social class positions, played an important role in the varying fortunes of the two groups.

The Saints hid behind a facade of respectability. They came from "good families," were active in school organizations, planned on attending college, and received good grades. People generally viewed their delinquent acts as a few isolated cases of sowing wild oats. The Roughnecks had no such aura of respectability. They drove around town in beat-up cars, were generally unsuccessful in school, and aroused suspicion no matter what they did.

We can understand such discrepancies by using an approach to deviance known as **labeling theory,** which emphasizes how a person comes to be labeled as deviant or to accept that label. Unlike Sutherland's work, labeling theory does not focus on why some individuals come to commit deviant acts. Instead, it attempts to explain why society views certain people (such as the Roughnecks) as deviants, delinquents, bad kids, losers, and criminals, while it sees others whose behavior is similar (such as the

Saints) in less harsh terms. Sociologist Howard Becker (1963:9; 1964), who popularized this approach, summed up labeling theory with this statement: "Deviant behavior is behavior that people so label."

Labeling theory is also called the **societal-reaction approach,** reminding us that it is the response to an act, not the act itself, that determines deviance. Traditionally, research on deviance has focused on people who violate social norms. In contrast, labeling theory focuses on police, probation officers, psychiatrists, judges, teachers, employers, school officials, and other regulators of social control. These agents, it is argued, play a significant role in creating the deviant identity by designating certain people (and not others) as deviant. An important aspect of labeling theory is the recognition that some individuals or groups have the power to define labels and apply them to others. This view ties into the conflict perspective's emphasis on the social significance of power.

In recent years, the practice of racial profiling, in which people are identified as criminal suspects purely on the basis of their race, has come under public scrutiny. Studies confirm the public's suspicion that in some jurisdictions, police officers are much more likely to stop African American males than White males for routine traffic violations, in the expectation of finding drugs or guns in their cars. Civil rights activists refer to these cases sarcastically as DWB (Driving While Black) violations. Beginning in late 2001, profiling took a new turn as people who appeared to be Arab or Muslim came under special scrutiny.

While the labeling approach does not fully explain why certain people accept a label and others manage to reject it, labeling theorists do suggest that the power an individual has relative to others is important in determining his or her ability to resist an undesirable label. It opens the door to additional emphasis on the undeniably important actions of people with power who can shape what counts as deviance (N. Davis 1975; compare with Cullen and Cullen 1978).

## POWER AND INEQUALITY

In addition to its significance for labeling theory, the story of the Saints and Roughnecks points toward the role that power and control over valued resources can play in defining deviance. Sociologist Richard Quinney (1974, 1979, 1980) is a leading proponent of the view that the criminal justice system serves the interests of the powerful; people with power protect their own interests and define deviance to suit their own needs. Crime, according to Quinney (1970), is defined as such by legislators who may be influenced by the economic elites to advance their interests.

**Race and Class** Looking at crime from this perspective draws our attention to the effects that power and position might have throughout the criminal justice system in the United States. Researchers have found that the system treats suspects differently based on their racial, ethnic, or social class background. In many cases, officials using their own discretion make biased decisions about whether to press charges or drop them, whether to set bail and how much, and whether to offer parole or deny it. Researchers have found that this kind of **differential justice**—differences in the way social control is exercised over different groups—puts African Americans and Latinos at a disadvantage in the justice system, both as juveniles and as adults. On average, White offenders receive shorter sentences than comparable Latino and African American offenders, even when prior arrest records and the relative severity of the crime are taken into consideration (Brewer and Heitzeg 2008; Quinney 1974).

We see this pattern of differential justice at work with death penalty cases. Simply put, poor people cannot afford to hire the best lawyer but must rely on court-appointed attorneys, who typically are overworked and underpaid. With capital punishment in place, these unequal resources may mean the difference between life and death for poor defendants. Indeed, the American Bar Association (1998) has repeatedly expressed concern about the limited defense most defendants facing the death penalty receive. Through mid-2008, DNA analysis and

**social disorganization theory** The theory that attributes increases in crime and deviance to the absence or breakdown of communal relationships and social institutions, such as the family, school, church, and local government.

**labeling theory** An approach to deviance that attempts to explain why certain people are viewed as deviants while others engaged in the same behavior are not.

**societal-reaction approach** Another name for labeling theory.

**differential justice** Differences in the way social control is exercised over different groups.

# Executions by State Since 1976

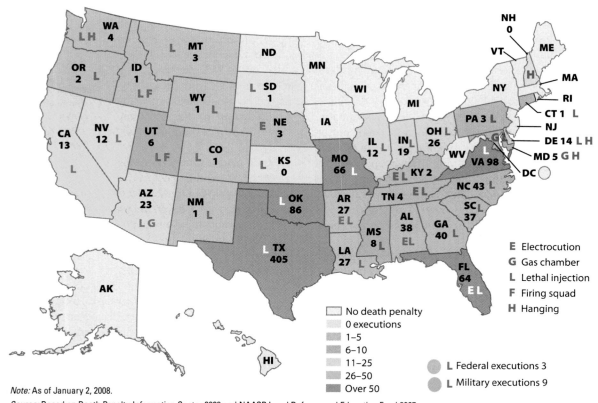

E Electrocution
G Gas chamber
L Lethal injection
F Firing squad
H Hanging

No death penalty
0 executions
1–5
6–10
11–25
26–50
Over 50

L Federal executions 3
L Military executions 9

*Note:* As of January 2, 2008.

*Source:* Based on Death Penalty Information Center 2008 and NAACP Legal Defense and Education Fund 2007.

---

other new technologies had exonerated 16 death row inmates and 217 inmates overall.

Various studies show that defendants are more likely to be sentenced to death if their victims were White rather than Black. About 79 percent of the victims in death penalty cases are White, even though only 50 percent of *all* murder victims are White. There is some evidence that Black defendants, who constituted 42 percent of all death row inmates in 2007, are more likely to face execution than Whites in the same legal circumstances. About 70 percent of those who have been exonerated by DNA testing were members of minority groups. Evidence exists, too, that capital defendants receive poor legal services because of the racist attitudes of their own defense counsel. Apparently, discrimination and racism do not end even when the stakes are life and death (Death Penalty Information Center 2008; Innocence Project 2008; D. Jacobs et al. 2007).

Differential justice is not limited to the United States. In 2007, the people of India were alarmed to learn that police had never investigated a series of killings in the slums of New Delhi. Only after residents found 17 bodies of re-

cently murdered children in a sewer drain on the edge of a slum were police moved to act. For many onlookers, it was just the latest example of the two-tier justice system found in India and many other countries (Gentleman 2007).

Such dramatic differences in social treatment may lead to heightened violence and crime. People who view themselves as the victims of unfair treatment may lash out, not against the powerful so much as against fellow victims. In studying crime in rural Mexico, Andrés Villarreal (2004) found that crime rates were high in the areas where land distribution was most inequitable. In areas where land was distributed more equally, communities appeared to suffer less violence and to enjoy greater social cohesion.

**Gender** Feminist criminologists such as Freda Adler and Meda Chesney-Lind have suggested that many of the existing approaches to deviance and crime were developed with only men in mind. For example, in the United States, for many years any husband who forced his wife to have sexual intercourse—without her consent and against her will—was not legally considered to have committed rape.

> Whenever you find yourself on the side of the majority, it is time to pause and reflect.
>
> Mark Twain

The law defined rape as pertaining only to sexual relations between people who were not married to each other, reflecting the overwhelmingly male composition of state legislatures at the time.

It took repeated protests by feminist organizations to get changes in the criminal law defining

## 5 Movies on ORGANIZED CRIME/CORPORATE CRIME

**The Godfather**
*An organized crime family makes offers you can't refuse.*

**Michael Clayton**
*A law firm has a dark secret.*

**Traffic**
*Organized drug trafficking.*

**The Constant Gardener**
*A pharmaceutical company puts profit above human life.*

**Goodfellas**
*Not so "good"…*

rape. It was not until 1993 that husbands in all 50 states could be prosecuted under most circumstances for the rape of their wives. However, significant exceptions remain in no fewer than 30 states. For example, the husband is exempt when he does not need to use force because his wife is asleep, unconscious, or mentally or physically impaired. These interpretations rest on the notion that the marriage contract entitles a husband to have sex (Bergen 2006).

When it comes to crime and to deviance in general, society tends to treat women in a stereotypical fashion. For example, consider how women who have many and frequent sexual partners are more likely to be viewed with scorn than men who are promiscuous. Cultural views and attitudes toward women influence how they are perceived and labeled. The feminist perspective also emphasizes that deviance, including crime, tends to flow from economic relationships. Traditionally, men have had greater earning power than their wives. As a result, wives may be reluctant to report acts of abuse to the authorities and thereby lose what may be their primary or even sole source of income. In the workplace, men have exercised greater power than women in pricing, accounting, and product control, giving them greater opportunity to engage in such crimes as embezzlement and fraud. But as women have taken more active and powerful roles both in the household and in business, these gender differences in deviance and crime have narrowed (F. Adler 1975; F. Adler et al. 2004; Chesney-Lind 1989).

Together these perspectives on deviance and crime direct our attention to multiple factors that we should consider when seeking to explain such acts. Based only on the theories we looked at—sociologists of crime have more to offer—we need, at the very least, to take into account the following: the extent to which deviance exists for the sake of social order, the degree of opportunity to attain both means and ends, the role of socialization into deviance, the strength of local community networks, the power to administer labels and make them stick, and differential access to valuable resources based on class, race, and gender. As Sudhir Venkatesh found in his research on gangs, if we are to fully understand something, we need to dig deep enough and consider what is going on from enough angles and with sufficient care, concern, and curiosity.

**get involved!**
Observe! If possible, visit your local courthouse to observe a trial in action. Most court proceedings are open to the public, so take advantage of that opportunity to learn more about how our system works.

# For REVIEW

I. **How do groups maintain social control?**
- They use positive and negative sanctions in both formal and informal ways to bring about conformity and obedience.

II. **What is the difference between deviance and crime?**
- Deviance involves violating a group's expected norms, which may lead the offender to be stigmatized. Crime is a form of deviance that involves violating the formal norms administered by the state for which the offender may receive formal sanctions.

III. **How do sociologists explain deviance and crime?**
- Sociologists offer up a number of theories of crime, each of which provides additional factors to be considered—such as the need for social order, the significance of interpersonal relationships and local context, and the importance of power and access to resources—that help us to better understand why deviance and crime occur.

# Pop Quiz

1. Society brings about acceptance of basic norms through techniques and strategies for preventing deviant human behavior. This process is termed
    a. stigmatization.
    b. labeling.
    c. law.
    d. social control.

2. The penalties and rewards we face for conduct concerning a social norm are known as
    a. informal social controls.
    b. stigmas.
    c. sanctions.
    d. conformities.

3. Stanley Milgram used the word *conformity* to mean
    a. going along with peers.
    b. compliance with higher authorities in a hierarchical structure.
    c. techniques and strategies for preventing deviant behavior in any society.
    d. penalties and rewards for conduct concerning a social norm.

4. According to Hirschi's control theory,
    a. deviance involves acceptance and/or rejection of society's goals and means.
    b. our connection to members of society leads us to systematically conform to society's norms.

    c. we come to view ourselves as deviant based on how others view us.
    d. power and access to resources shape whose norms and values determine individual action.

5. Which of the following statements is true of deviance?
    a. Deviance is always criminal behavior.
    b. Deviance is behavior that violates the standards of conduct or expectations of a group or society.
    c. Deviance is perverse behavior.
    d. Deviance is inappropriate behavior that cuts across all cultures and social orders.

6. The FBI reports which two major categories of crime in its annual *Uniform Crime Reports*?
    a. violent crime and property crime
    b. organized crime and white-collar crime
    c. victimless crime and transnational crime
    d. transnational crime and victimization crime

7. Which of the following is *not* one of the basic forms of adaptation specified in Robert Merton's anomie theory of deviance?
    a. conformity
    b. innovation
    c. ritualism
    d. hostility

1. (d); 2. (c); 3. (a); 4. (b); 5. (b); 6. (a); 7. (d);

8. Which sociologist first advanced the idea that an individual undergoes the same basic socialization process whether learning conforming or deviant acts?
   a. Robert Merton
   b. Edwin Sutherland
   c. Travis Hirschi
   d. William Chambliss

9. Which of the following theories contends that criminal victimization increases when communal relationships and social institutions break down?
   a. labeling theory
   b. conflict theory
   c. social disorganization theory
   d. differential association theory

10. Who of the following conducted observation research on two groups of high school males (the Saints and the Roughnecks) and concluded that social class played an important role in the varying fortunes of the two groups?
    a. Richard Quinney
    b. Edwin Sutherland
    c. Émile Durkheim
    d. William Chambliss

8. (b); 9. (c); 10. (d)

# 7

# FAMILIES

# LOVING, MARRYING, AND RAISING FAMILIES

"Do you love me?" This is the question that Tevye asks Golde, his wife, in the musical *The Fiddler on the Roof* (Jewison 1971). They had married 25 years ago in the old-fashioned way—a matchmaker had set them up—and they were not "in love" when they got married. They did not necessarily expect to ever love each other, but times were changing in their small Russian village in the early 1900s, and now Tevye wants to know.

Tevye and Golde's questions about love and marriage arise because their three daughters all reject the matchmaker tradition, believing that their own hearts should drive their matches. Their oldest turns down the matchmaker's choice of an older, wealthy butcher, opting instead for a poor tailor her own age. Their next daughter falls in love with a revolutionary university student from the big city and she seeks Tevye's blessing but not his permission. Finally, their youngest daughter seeks neither blessing nor permission in marrying a Russian who is outside their Jewish faith. Along the way, Tevye asks himself if he can accept such violations of "tradition."

In the story, the daughters' breaks with tradition are tied to the larger social, economic, and historical upheavals in Russia at the time. Tradition has always ruled in the community, and these changes in tradition challenge Tevye and Golde's ability to accept their daughters' relationships and even their ability to understand their own. Tevye and Golde decide that they do, in fact, love each other. But their affirmation of love emerges only with the decline of traditions that have guided village life for generations.

Such forces continue to shape our understanding of marriage and of families. We often think that the way things are is the way that things have always been, but when it comes to love, marriage, and families, there is significant variation over time and across cultures. Understanding our beliefs and actions from within the context of an institution such as the family allows us to better see and understand both the "big picture" of our interconnections and the intimate realities of our everyday interactions.

# As You READ

>>

- What is the family?
- How do people pick partners?
- How do families vary?

## >> Global View of the Family

Among Tibetans, a woman may be married simultaneously to more than one man, usually brothers. This system allows sons to share the limited amount of good land. Among the Betsileo of Madagascar, a man has multiple wives, each one living in a different village where he cultivates rice. Wherever he has the best rice field, that woman is considered his first or senior wife. Among the Yanomami of Brazil and Venezuela, it is considered proper to have sexual relations with one's opposite-sex cousins if they are the children of one's mother's brother or father's sister. But if one's opposite-sex cousins are the children of one's mother's sister or father's brother, the same practice is considered to be incest (Haviland et al. 2005; Kottak 2004).

In the Unites States, the family of today is not what it was a century or even a generation ago. New roles, new gender distinctions, and new child-rearing patterns have all combined to create new forms of family life. Today, for example, more and more women are taking the bread-winner's role, whether as a spouse or as a single parent. Blended families—the result of divorce and remarriage—are common. And many people are seeking intimate rela-

tionships outside marriage, whether in gay or lesbian partnerships or in cohabiting arrangements.

We see such changes reflected in popular culture representations of families. The 1950s U.S. family was epitomized on television by shows such as *Leave It to Beaver* and *Father Knows Best* with a stay-at-home mom, working dad, and assorted kids. Times have changed. *Two and a Half Men* features a father, son, and uncle; *Hannah Montana* depicts a single father with his daughter and son; and then there's *Desperate Housewives*. Perhaps the closest you get these days to the 1950s family is *The Simpsons* with Homer, Marge, Lisa, Bart, and Maggie.

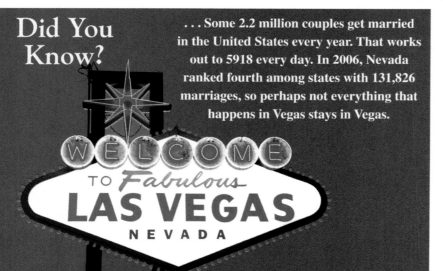

## Did You Know?

...Some 2.2 million couples get married in the United States every year. That works out to 5918 every day. In 2006, Nevada ranked fourth among states with 131,826 marriages, so perhaps not everything that happens in Vegas stays in Vegas.

WELCOME TO *Fabulous* LAS VEGAS NEVADA

This shift in how families are portrayed is consistent with changes we have seen both in practice and in our understanding of what constitutes a family.

Because families as we experience them are varied in structure and style, we need a sociological approach that is sufficiently broad to encompass all those things we experience as family. We will look at two different definitional approaches. The first is a substantive definition that focuses on what a family is, and the second is a functional definition that focuses on what families do.

## SUBSTANCE: WHAT A FAMILY IS

Perhaps the most conventional approach to defining family is the **substantive definition,** which focuses on blood and law. Blood, in this case, means that people are related because they share a biological heritage passed on directly from parent to child, linking people indirectly to grandparents, aunts and uncles, and other biological relatives. Law means the formal social recognition and affirmation of a bond as family, particularly in the form of marriage and adoption.

The primary advantage of this definitional approach is that boundaries are clear; we can tell who is in and who is out. This makes it easier to count such families, so perhaps it is no surprise that the U.S. Census relies on a substantive approach: "A family is a group of two people or more (one of whom is the householder) related by birth, marriage, or adoption and residing together" (U.S. Census Bureau 2004). It also allows us to track who is related to whom over time.

**Kinship Patterns** Many of us can trace our roots by looking at a family tree or by listening to elderly family members talk about their lives—and about the lives of ancestors who died long before we were born. Yet a person's lineage is more than simply a personal history; it also reflects societal traditions that govern descent. In every culture, children encounter relatives to whom they are expected to show an emotional attachment. The state of being related to others is called **kinship.** Kinship is culturally learned, however, and is not totally determined by biological or marital ties. For example, adoption creates a kinship tie that is legally acknowledged and socially accepted.

The family and the kin group are not necessarily one and the same. Whereas the family is a household unit, kin do not always live together or function as a collective body on a daily basis. Kin groups include aunts, uncles, cousins, in-laws, and so forth. In a society such as the United States, the kinship group may come together only rarely, for a wedding or funeral. However, kinship ties frequently involve obligations and responsibilities. We may feel compelled to assist our kin, and we feel free to call upon them for many types of aid, including loans and babysitting.

How do we identify kinship groups? The principle of descent assigns people to kinship groups according to their relationship to a mother or father. There are three primary ways of determining descent. The United States follows the system of **bilateral descent,** which means that both sides of a person's family are regarded as equally important. For example, no higher value is given to the brothers of one's

> **substantive definition of the family** A definition of the family based on blood, meaning shared genetic heritage, and law, meaning social recognition and affirmation of the bond including both marriage and adoption.
>
> **kinship** The state of being related to others.
>
> **bilateral descent** A kinship system in which both sides of a person's family are regarded as equally important.

father than to the brothers of one's mother. However, most societies—according to anthropologist George Murdock, 64 percent of societies—give preference to one side of the family or the other in tracing descent. In **patrilineal** (from the Latin *pater,* "father") **descent,** only the father's relatives are significant in terms of property, inheritance, and emotional ties. Conversely, in societies that favor **matrilineal** (from the Latin *mater,* "mother") **descent,** only the mother's relatives are significant.

# SOCthink

> > > How important are intergenerational kinship networks and extended family members in your family? How has this changed since your parents' and grandparents' generations?

**Family Types** The substantive approach also shapes what we traditionally view as common family types. If we assume that we are connected through blood and law, we can analyze how we structure those relationships. Families might place greater emphasis on immediate family members or on extended family networks. They also are shaped by the number of partners deemed appropriate.

Historically, family connections served as a valuable resource, providing us with access to material, social, and cultural resources. We depended on relatives for food, shelter, opportunities, and knowledge. In fact, historian Stephanie Coontz (2005) argues that, historically, the primary reason to get married was to obtain not a partner but in-laws, thus extending one's network of cooperative relationships. This was the logic of the matchmaker tradition that not only brought Tevye and Golde together in *The Fiddler on the Roof* but brought their families together as well. The matchmaker, as a member of the community, sought to maximize social network connections for the good of the whole.

A family in which relatives—such as grandparents, aunts, or uncles—live in the same household as parents and their children is known as an **extended family.** Although not common, such living arrangements do exist in the United States. The structure of the extended family offers certain advantages over that of the nuclear family. Crises such as death, divorce, and illness put less strain on family members, since more people can provide assistance and emotional support. In addition, the extended family constitutes a larger economic unit than the nuclear family. If the family is engaged in a common enterprise—a farm

**patrilineal descent** A kinship system in which only the father's relatives are significant.
**matrilineal descent** A kinship system in which only the mother's relatives are significant.
**extended family** A family in which relatives—such as grandparents, aunts, or uncles—live in the same household as parents and their children.
**nuclear family** A married couple and their unmarried children living together.

or a small business—the additional family members may represent the difference between prosperity and failure.

With the advent of the Industrial Revolution, the economy shifted away from agricultural production and its corresponding small-town life and toward industrial production in urban areas. Families became smaller and more mobile in response to these structural changes. The obligations of the extended family could hold individuals back, and so we saw a move toward a smaller family unit that came to be known as the nuclear family. The **nuclear family** includes a married couple and their unmarried children living together. The concept of nuclear family builds on the essence or nucleus of the substantive definition of blood and law, including as it does both the parent-to-child and the marriage relationship.

# SOCthink

> > > How often do you communicate with your parents, grandparents, or siblings? How might advances in communications technology, especially the cell phone and the Internet, make it easier to maintain regular contacts with extended family members? What consequences might this have for how we view family?

Most people in the United States see the nuclear family as the preferred family arrangement. Yet by 2000, only about one-third of the nation's family households fit this model. The proportion of households in the United States that is composed of married couples with children at home has decreased steadily over the past 40 years and is expected to continue shrinking. At the same time, the number of single-parent households has increased.

**Types of Marriage** In considering these different family types, we have limited ourselves to the form of marriage that is characteristic of the United States— monogamy. The term **monogamy** describes a form of marriage in which

# U.S. Households by Family Type, 1940–2010

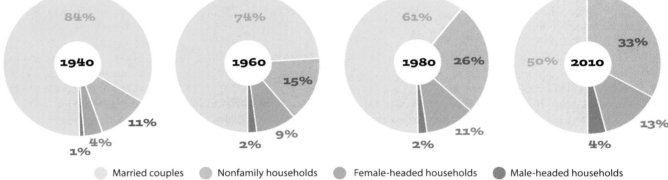

| | | | |
|---|---|---|---|
| **1940** 84% / 11% / 4% / 1% | **1960** 74% / 15% / 9% / 2% | **1980** 61% / 26% / 11% / 2% | **2010** 50% / 33% / 13% / 4% |

● Married couples  ● Nonfamily households  ● Female-headed households  ● Male-headed households

*Note:* Nonfamily households include women and men living alone or exclusively with people to whom they are not related, as in a college dormitory, homeless shelter, or military base.

*Source:* Author's estimate based on Bureau of the Census 1996; Fields 2004; see also McFalls 2003:23.

one woman and one man are married only to each other. Some observers, noting the high rate of divorce in the United States, have suggested that "serial monogamy" is a more accurate description of the form that marriage takes in this country. In **serial monogamy,** a person may have several spouses in his or her lifetime, but only one spouse at a time.

Some cultures allow an individual to have several husbands or wives simultaneously. This form of marriage is known as **polygamy.** In fact, most societies throughout the world, past and present, have preferred polygamy to monogamy. Anthropologist George Murdock (1949, 1957) sampled 565 societies and found that in more than 80 percent, some type of polygamy was the preferred form. While polygamy declined steadily through most of the 20th century, in at least five countries in Africa, 20 percent of men still have polygamous marriages (Population Reference Bureau 1996).

There are two basic types of polygamy. The most common is **polygyny,** which refers to the marriage of a man to more than one woman at the same time. Less common is **polyandry,** in which a woman may have more than one husband at the same time. Such is the case, for example, in the Nyinba culture of Nepal and Tibet, in which brothers share a common wife. This arrangement provides a sufficient number of physical laborers in the difficult farming environment yet minimizes the number of offspring.

Most people assumed that polygamy was a thing of the past in the United States. However, in April 2008, law enforcement officials in Texas received an anonymous phone call purported to be from a 16-year-old girl who claimed

that she had been forced into a polygamous marriage with an adult man. The girl also complained of having been beaten. Shortly thereafter, officials raided the Yearning for Zion ranch where the girl was living, taking a total of 462 children from the ranch and placing them into temporary legal custody. The ranch was run by members of the Fundamentalist Church of Jesus Christ of Latter Day Saints (FLDS), a group that practices polygamy even though it is illegal in the United States and was banned by the mainstream LDS denomination over 100 years ago. The state ordered DNA testing to ascertain who was related to whom. Ultimately, the children were returned to their families as there was insufficient evidence to demonstrate

> **monogamy** A form of marriage in which one woman and one man are married only to each other.
>
> **serial monogamy** A form of marriage in which a person may have several spouses in his or her lifetime but only one spouse at a time.
>
> **polygamy** A form of marriage in which an individual may have several husbands or wives simultaneously.
>
> **polygyny** A form of polygamy in which a man may have more than one wife at the same time.
>
> **polyandry** A form of polygamy in which a woman may have more than one husband at the same time.

## SOCthink

> > > Why do you think that polygamy was the most common form of marriage historically? Why has it given way to monogamy in modern societies?

abuse or the immediate risk of abuse. However, the case did raise awareness of the fact that polygamy continues to exist in the United States.

Once we begin to look at the varieties of family types around the world, we see the main limitation of the substantive definition: There are people who seem to be family but who do not fit neatly into blood or law. For example, the biological parent-to-child tie was expanded by including adoption as part of law. We accept stepparents and stepsiblings as family members even when the children have not been formally adopted by the stepparent. We are currently debating whether to grant same-sex couples legal standing as families. But what about pushing the definition of family still further? Is dad's college friend "Uncle" Bob part of the family? New forms of reproductive technology, involving donated sperm and eggs and surrogate parents, also challenge conventional thinking. Any substantive definition we might come up with runs the risk of excluding those whom we think of as family members. In response sociologists turn toward the more inclusive functionalist definition of families to address such limitations.

> Family isn't about whose blood you have. It's about who you care about.
>
> **Trey Parker and Matt Stone**

## FUNCTIONS: WHAT FAMILIES DO

When we ask people how they would define family, their conception is much more inclusive than the substantive definition implies. People in the United States seem to agree that traditional definitions of family are too restrictive. In one survey, only 22 percent of the respondents defined family in the same way as the U.S. Census Bureau. Instead, 74 percent considered a family to be "any group whose members love and care for one another" (Coontz, 1992:21).

We need a definition of families that is inclusive enough to encompass the broad range of intimate groups that people form, such as extended families, nuclear families, single-parent families, blended or reconstituted or step families, gay and lesbian families, child-free families, racially and ethnically mixed families, commuter marriage families, surrogate or chosen families, and more. One way to avoid getting trapped into overly narrow conceptions of families, and to embrace their diversity is to shift focus from a substantive definition of what families *are* to a **functionalist definition** of what families *do* for society and for their members.

Sociologist William F. Ogburn (Ogburn and Tibbits 1934) identified six primary functions that families perform for us:

- *Reproduction.* For a society to maintain itself, it must replace dying members. Families provide the context within which biological reproduction takes place.
- *Socialization.* Parents and other family members monitor a child's behavior and transmit the norms, values, and language of their culture to the child.
- *Protection.* Unlike the young of other animal species, human infants need constant care and economic security. In all cultures, the family assumes the ultimate responsibility for the protection and upbringing of children.

## From Me to You

*When discussing families in terms of what they do instead of what they are, students inevitably ask, "Do pets count as family?" Some strongly agree, while others think it is the most ridiculous thing they have ever heard. More and more students are coming down on the side of pets as family. When we "adopted" Jessie, our Pembroke Welsh corgi, I better understood why. Owners develop strong emotional bonds with their pets and some refer to them as their "fur kids." Pets provide a source of comfort and companionship. They give us someone to care about and they care for us in their own ways. Isn't that what we want from family?*

**PETS AS FAMILY**

- *Regulation of sexual behavior.* Sexual norms are subject to change both over time (for instance, in the customs for dating) and across cultures (compare strict Saudi Arabia to the more permissive Denmark). However, whatever the time period or cultural values of a society, standards of sexual behavior are most clearly defined within the family circle.

- *Affection and companionship.* Ideally, families provide members with warm and intimate relationships, helping them to feel satisfied and secure. Of course, a family member may find such rewards outside the family —from peers, in school, at work—and may even perceive the home as an unpleasant or abusive setting. Nevertheless, we expect our relatives to understand us, to care for us, and to be there for us when we need them.

- *Provision of social status.* We inherit a social position because of the family background and reputation of

**Hot or Not?**

Should pets, including dogs, cats, birds, or others, count as family?

our parents and siblings. For example, the race, ethnicity, social class, education level, occupation, and religion of our parents all shape the material, social, and cultural resources to which we have access and therefore the options we might have.

No matter how it is composed, any group that fulfills these functions is family to us. We might count teammates, close college dorm mates, or a long-term circle of friends as family. We look to such groups in moments of need for all kinds of support, including care and affection, guidance in how to think and act, dating advice, and sometimes even material support, whether borrowing a car or just some money for pizza. We may use the expression that they are "like family" to convey that sense, or we may even refer to such significant people in our lives as our sister, brother, mom, or dad. In fact, given the survey results above, people may already be defining as family any group that provides sufficient love and care for each other. According to this functionalist definition, a family *is* what a family *does*.

## AUTHORITY PATTERNS: WHO RULES?

Regardless of what a family looks like, within the context of any group we define as family, we will inevitably have to address issues of power. Imagine, for example, that you have recently married and must begin to make decisions about the future of your new family. You and your partner face many questions: Where will you live? How will you furnish your home? Who will do the cooking, shopping, and cleaning? Whose friends will be invited to dinner? Each time a decision must be made, an issue is raised: Who has the power to make the decision? In simple terms, who rules the family?

Societies vary in the way that power is distributed within the family; historically, however, the answer to that question has largely been shaped by gender. A society that expects males to dominate in all family decision making is termed a **patriarchy.** In patriarchal societies, such as Iran, the eldest male often wields the greatest power, although wives are expected to be treated with respect and kindness. An Iranian woman's status is typically defined by her relationship to a male relative, usually as a wife or daughter. In many patriarchal societies, women find it more difficult to obtain a divorce than a man does. In contrast, in a **matriarchy,** women have greater authority than men. Formal matriarchies, which are uncommon, emerged among Native American tribal societies and in nations in which men were absent for long periods because of warfare or food-gathering expeditions (Farr 1999).

> **functionalist definition of families** A definition of families that focuses on what families do for society and for their members.
> **patriarchy** A society in which men dominate in family decision making.
> **matriarchy** A society in which women dominate in family decision making.

Over a century ago, Friedrich Engels ([1884] 1959), a colleague of Karl Marx, went so far as to say that the family is the ultimate source of social inequality because of its role in the transfer of power, property, and privilege. Historically, the family has legitimized and perpetuated male dominance. It has contributed to societal injustice, denied women opportunities that are extended to men, and limited freedom in sexual expression and mate selection. In the United States, it was not until the first wave of contemporary feminism, in the mid-1800s, that there was a substantial challenge to the historical status of wives and children as the legal property of husbands and fathers.

**egalitarian family** An authority pattern in which spouses are regarded as equals.

Due in part to the efforts of women and men in similar movements over the years, we have seen the rise of a third type of authority pattern. In the **egalitarian family,** spouses are regarded as equals. This shift has been driven at least in part by occupational and financial opportunities for women that previously had been denied them (Wills and Risman 2006). That does not mean, however, that all decisions are shared in such families. Wives may hold authority in some spheres, and husbands in others. For example, sociologists have found that, in terms of paid and unpaid labor in two-parent families, the total hours worked by mothers and fathers is roughly equal at about 65 hours per week, though the distribution of tasks varies (Bianchi, Robinson, and Milkie 2006).

Historian Stephanie Coontz (2008) suggests that, when it works, marriage today is better than ever. She writes that it "delivers more benefits to its members—adults and children—than ever before. A good marriage is fairer and more fulfilling for both men and women than couples of the past could ever have imagined." She points to shared decision making and housework, increases in time spent with children, and declines in violence and sexual coercion and in the likelihood of adultery.

While the egalitarian family has become a more common pattern in the United States in recent decades, male dominance over the family has hardly disappeared. Sociologists have found that although married men are increasing their involvement in child care, their wives still perform a disproportionate amount of it. Furthermore, for every stay-at-home dad there are 38 stay-at-home moms (Fields 2004:11–12; Garcia-Moreno et al. 2004; Sayer et al. 2004). And unfortunately, many husbands reinforce their power and control over wives and children through acts of domestic violence.

In addition to the issue of authority within relationships, families also continue to provide a foundation for power within the larger society. Family serves as the basis for transferring power, property, and privilege from one generation to the next. Although the United States is widely viewed as a land of opportunity, social mobility is restricted in important ways. Children inherit the privileged or less-than-privileged social and economic status of their parents (and in some cases, of earlier generations as well). The social class of parents significantly influences children's socialization experiences and the degree of protection they receive. Thus, the socioeconomic status of a child's family will have a marked influence on his or her nutrition, health care, housing, educational opportunities, and in many respects, life chances as an adult. In many ways the family helps to maintain inequality.

## >> Marriage and Family

Currently, over 95 percent of all men and women in the United States marry at least once during their lifetimes. Historically, the most consistent aspect of family life in this country has been the high rate of marriage. In fact, despite the high rate of divorce, there are some indications of a miniboom in marriages of late. When it comes to picking partners, most of us assume that romantic love alone will guide our choice. We learn from sociology, however, that even if we no longer rely on a matchmaker to tell us which particular individual to choose, our social positions shape our choices.

## SOCthink

> > > Matchmaker services still exist in the United States, and some charge as much as $20,000 for a membership with additional annual fees. Why might people turn to matchmaking services today? What are the limitations of relying on our own contacts and judgment when it comes to finding a romantic partner?

## COURTSHIP AND MATE SELECTION

"My rugby mates would roll over in their graves," says Tom Buckley of his online courtship of and subsequent marriage to Terri Muir. But Tom and Terri are hardly alone these days in turning to the Internet for matchmaking services. A generation or two ago, most couples met in high school or college, but now that people are marrying later in life, the Internet has become the new meeting place for the romantically inclined. Today, thousands of websites offer to help people find mates. For example, eHarmony, which claims to be the first to use a "scientific approach" to matching people based on a variety of abilities and interests, says that it "facilitates" 46 marriages a day. A 2005 survey found that 12 percent of couples who visited an online wedding site had met online (Kapos 2005; B. Morris 1999:D1).

*Going* **GLOBAL**

**Percentage of People Ages 20–24 Ever Married, Selected Countries**

Finland
4.7 10.5

Australia
5.5 13

Canada
14 26.7

Poland
14.4 31.4

United States
16.3 27.2

China
21.4 42.5

Mexico
37.8 52.3

India
Men     Women
71.5     94.3

*Source: United Nations Population Division 2005.*

## Ten Questions Couples Should Ask (or Wish They Had) Before Marrying

- Do you want to have children?
- Who will do what when it comes to housework?
- What are your expectations regarding sex?
- What do you think about having a television in the bedroom?
- What do you expect regarding religious training for our children?
- How much money do you owe?
- Do you like and respect my friends?
- What do you really think about my parents?
- What does my family do that annoys you?
- Are there some things you are not willing to give up in the marriage?

*Source: New York Times 2006.*

Internet romance is only the latest courtship practice. Many other traditional cultures, including those of the central Asian nation of Uzbekistan, define courtship largely through the interaction of two sets of parents, who arrange marriages for their children. Typically, a young Uzbekistani woman is socialized to eagerly anticipate her marriage to a man whom she has met only once, when he is presented to her family at the time of the final inspection of her dowry. In the United States, by contrast, courtship occurs primarily by individuals who have a romantic interest in each other. In U.S. culture, courtship often requires these individuals to rely heavily on intricate games, gestures, and signals. Despite such differences, the norms and values of the larger society—whether in the United States,

Uzbekistan, or elsewhere—influence courtship (C. J. Williams 1995).

One unmistakable trend in mate selection is that the process appears to be taking longer today than in the past. A variety of factors, including concerns about financial security and personal independence, has contributed to this delay in marriage. Most people are now well into their 20s before they marry, both in the United States and in other countries. In the United States, the median age at first marriage for women is 25.5, and for men is 27.5. Over the past 30 years, this represents an increase of 4.2 years for women and 3.7 years for men (U.S. Census Bureau 2007a).

Many societies have explicit or unstated rules that define potential mates as acceptable or unacceptable. These norms can be distinguished in terms of endogamy and exogamy. **Endogamy** (from the Greek *endon,* "within") specifies the groups within which a spouse must be found and prohibits marriage with others. For example, in the United States, many people are expected to marry within their own racial, ethnic, or religious group and are strongly discouraged or even prohibited from marrying outside the group. Endogamy is intended to reinforce the cohesiveness of the group by suggesting to the young that they should marry someone "of their own kind."

In contrast, **exogamy** (from the Greek *exo,* "outside") requires mate selection outside certain groups, usually one's own family or certain kinfolk. The **incest taboo,** a social norm common to virtually all societies, prohibits sexual relationships between certain culturally specified relatives. In the United States, this taboo means that we must marry outside the nuclear family. We cannot marry our siblings, and in most states, we cannot marry our first cousins.

Endogamous restrictions may be seen as preferences for one group over another. In the United States, such preferences are most obvious in racial barriers. Some states outlawed interracial marriage, until a 1967 Supreme Court decision overturned such laws. Nevertheless, the number of marriages between African Americans and Whites in the United States has increased more than eight times in recent decades, jumping from 51,000 in 1960 to 403,000 in 2006. Moreover, 25 percent of married Asian American women and 12 percent of married

**endogamy** The restriction of mate selection to people within the same group.
**exogamy** The requirement that people select a mate outside certain groups.
**incest taboo** The prohibition of sexual relationships between certain culturally specified relatives.

**5 Movies on MARRIAGE**

**Green Card**
*The business arrangement of marriage.*

**Arranged**
*Arranged marriages lead to unexpected friendship.*

**The Squid and the Whale**
*How divorce affects children.*

**The Story of Us**
*The ups and downs of marriage.*

**Kramer vs. Kramer**
*A custody battle.*

Asian American men are married to a person who is not of Asian descent. Marriage across ethnic lines is even greater among Hispanics; 27 percent of all married Hispanics have a non-Hispanic spouse. Even though all these examples of racial exogamy are noteworthy, endogamy is still the social norm in the United States (Bureau of the Census 1998, 2007a:Table 59).

Another factor that influences the selection of marriage partner is **homogamy**—the conscious or unconscious tendency to select a mate with personal characteristics similar to one's own. The "like marries like" rule can be seen in couples with similar personalities and interests. Internet dating services depend upon this principle to help find matches. Sociologist Pepper Schwartz, who works as a consultant for PerfectMatch.com, has developed a 48-question survey that covers everything from prospective mates' decision-making style to their degree of impulsivity (Gottlieb 2006). While it is certainly possible that "opposites attract," when it comes to romance, we tend toward people more like ourselves.

## VARIATIONS IN FAMILY LIFE AND INTIMATE RELATIONSHIPS

Within the United States, social class, race, and ethnicity create variations in family life. Studying these variations will give us a more sophisticated understanding of contemporary family styles in our country. The desire to avoid having to negotiate such differences also helps to explain why people often practice homogamy.

**Social Class Differences** Social class differences in family life are less striking today than they once were.

In the past, family specialists agreed that the contrasts in child-rearing practices were pronounced. Poor and working-class families were found to be more authoritarian in rearing children and more inclined to use physical punishment. Middle-class families were more permissive and more restrained in punishing their children. Compared to poor and working-class families, middle-class families tended to schedule more of their children's time, or even to overstructure it. However, these differences may have narrowed as more and more families from all social classes turned to the same books, magazines, and even television talk shows for advice on rearing children (Kronstadt and Favreault 2008; Luster et al. 1989).

Among the poor, women often play a significant role in the economic support of the family. Men may earn low

sharing goods and services. In addition to these strong kinship bonds, Black family life has emphasized deep religious commitment and high aspirations for achievement (F. Furstenberg 2007).

Like African Americans, Native Americans draw on family ties to cushion many of the hardships they face. On the Navajo reservation, for example, teenage parenthood is not regarded as the crisis that it is elsewhere in the United States. The Navajo trace their descent matrilineally. Traditionally, couples reside with the wife's family after marriage, allowing the grandparents to help with the child rearing. While the Navajo do not approve of teenage parenthood, the deep emotional commitment of their extended families provides a warm home environment for fatherless children (Dalla and Gamble 2001).

## The goal in marriage is not to think alike, but to think together.

Robert C. Dodds

wages, may be unemployed, or may be entirely absent from the family. In 2006, 28 percent of all families headed by women with no husband present were below the official poverty line. The rate for married couples was only 4.9 percent (DeNavas-Walt et al. 2007:12). Many racial and ethnic groups appear to have distinctive family characteristics. However, racial and class factors are often closely related. In examining family life among racial and ethnic minorities, keep in mind that certain patterns may result from class as well as cultural factors.

**Racial and Ethnic Differences** The subordinate status of racial and ethnic minorities in the United States profoundly affects their family lives. For example, the lower incomes of African Americans, Native Americans, most Hispanic groups, and selected Asian American groups make creating and maintaining successful marital unions a difficult task. The economic restructuring of the past 50 years, described by sociologist William Julius Wilson (1996) and others, in which blue-collar jobs disappeared from urban areas as companies moved production facilities abroad, has especially affected people living in inner cities and desolate rural areas. Furthermore, the immigration policy of the United States has complicated the successful relocation of intact families from Asia and Latin America.

The African American family suffers from many negative and inaccurate stereotypes. It is true that in a significantly higher proportion of Black than White families, no husband is present in the home. Yet Black single mothers often belong to stable, functioning kin networks, which mitigate the pressures of sexism and racism. Members of these networks—predominantly female kin such as mothers, grandmothers, and aunts—ease financial strains by

Sociologists also have taken note of differences in family patterns among other racial and ethnic groups. For example, Mexican American men have been described as exhibiting a sense of virility, personal worth, and pride in their maleness that is called **machismo.** Mexican Americans are also described as being more familistic than many other subcultures. **Familism** refers to pride in the extended family, expressed through the maintenance of close ties and strong obligations to kinfolk outside the immediate family. Traditionally, Mexican Americans have placed proximity to their extended families above other needs and desires.

These family patterns are changing, however, in response to changes in Latinos' social class standing, educational achievements, and occupations. Like other Americans, career-oriented Latinos in search of a mate but short on spare time are turning to the Internet. As Latinos and other groups assimilate into the dominant culture of the United States, their family lives take on both the positive and the negative characteristics associated with White households (Landale and Orapesa 2007).

> **homogamy** The conscious or unconscious tendency to select a mate with personal characteristics similar to one's own.
> **machismo** A sense of virility, personal worth, and pride in one's maleness.
> **familism** Pride in the extended family, expressed through the maintenance of close ties and strong obligations to kinfolk outside the immediate family.

## CHILD-REARING PATTERNS

Caring for children is a universal function of the family, yet the ways in which different societies assign this function to family members can vary significantly. The Nayars of southern India acknowledge the biological role of fathers, but the mother's eldest brother is responsible for her children. In contrast, uncles play only a peripheral role in child care in the United States. Even within the United States, child-rearing patterns are varied. Just as our conception of families has changed, so also has our practice of child rearing.

**adoption** In a legal sense, a process that allows for the transfer of the legal rights, responsibilities, and privileges of parenthood to a new legal parent or parents.

**Parenthood and Grandparenthood** The socialization of children is essential to the maintenance of any culture. Consequently, parenthood is one of the most important (and most demanding) social roles in the United States. Sociologist Alice Rossi (1968, 1984) has identified four factors that complicate the transition to parenthood and the role of socialization. First, there is little anticipatory socialization for the social role of caregiver. The nor-

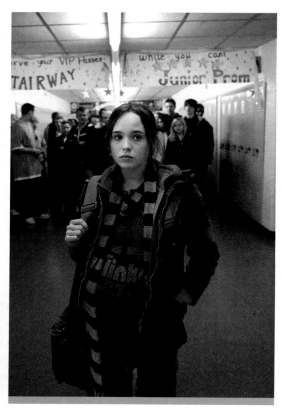

Parenthood has been a frequent source of entertainment in the movies. Examples of such films include *Mr. Mom, Parenthood, Finding Nemo, Freaky Friday, Cheaper by the Dozen, Daddy's Little Girls, Juno, Baby Mama,* and even *Alvin and the Chipmunks.* They all convey messages of what it means to be a parent. What lessons might we learn from an analysis of how mothers and fathers are portrayed in such films? What recurring images and themes occur? How common is the bungling dad or the career mom who wonders if she is making the right choices? What are the consequences of such films for how we practice parenting?

mal school curriculum gives scant attention to the subjects most relevant to successful family life, such as child care and home maintenance. Second, only limited learning occurs during the period of pregnancy itself. Third, the transition to parenthood is quite abrupt. Unlike adolescence, it is not prolonged; unlike the transition to work, the duties of caregiving cannot be taken on gradually. Finally, in Rossi's view, our society lacks clear and helpful guidelines for successful parenthood. There is little consensus on how parents can produce happy and well-adjusted offspring—or even on what it means to be well adjusted. For these reasons, socialization for parenthood involves difficult challenges for most men and women in the United States.

One recent development in family life in the United States has been the extension of parenthood, as adult children continue to live at home or return home after college. In 2006, 53 percent of men and 43 percent of women ages 18–24 lived with their parents. Some of these adult children were still pursuing an education, but in many instances, financial difficulties underlay these living arrangements. While rents and real estate prices have skyrocketed, salaries for younger workers have not kept pace, and many find themselves unable to afford their own homes. Moreover, with many marriages now ending in divorce, divorced sons and daughters often return to live with their parents, sometimes with their own children (Bureau of the Census 2007g:Table A1).

Given that the dominant cultural expectation in the United States remains some form of the nuclear family, in which children are expected to set up households on their own once they reach adulthood, such arrangements present challenges for everybody involved. Social scientists have just begun to examine the phenomenon, sometimes called the "boomerang generation" or the "full-nest syndrome." One survey in Virginia showed that neither the parents nor their adult children were happy about continuing to live together. The children often felt resentful and isolated, but the parents suffered too. Learning to live without children in the home is an essential stage of adult life and may even be a significant turning point for a marriage (*Berkeley Wellness Letter* 1990; Mogelonsky 1996).

In some homes, the full nest holds grandchildren. In 2004, 6.5 million children, or 9 percent of all children in the United States, lived in a household with a grandparent. In about a third of these homes, no parent was present to assume responsibility for the youngsters. Special difficulties are inherent in such relationships, including legal custodial concerns, financial issues, and emotional problems for adults and youths alike. Perhaps not surprisingly, support groups such as Grandparents as Parents have emerged to provide assistance (Kreider 2008).

**Adoption** In a legal sense, **adoption** is a "process that allows for the transfer of the legal rights, responsibilities, and privileges of parenthood" to a new legal parent or parents (E. Cole 1985:638). In many cases, these rights are transferred from a biological parent or parents (often called birth parents) to an adoptive parent or parents.

*Hollywood stars Angelina Jolie and Brad Pitt and several of their children, many from overseas adoptions.*

About 4 percent of all people in the United States are adopted, and about 2 percent by persons not related to them at birth. There are two legal methods of adopting an unrelated person: (1) the adoption may be arranged through a licensed agency, or (2) in some states it may be arranged through a private agreement sanctioned by the courts. Adopted children may come from the United States or from abroad. In 2006, more than 20,000 children entered the United States as the adopted children of U.S. citizens. While the number of international adoptions remains substantial, it has declined in recent years. China, the source for about one-third of overseas adoptions, recently began to tighten the rules for foreigners. Applicants who are single, obese, or older than 50 may now be disqualified automatically (Carr 2007; Gross 2007).

In the United States, one of the limitations historically was that only married couples could adopt. In 1995, an important court decision in New York held that a couple does not have to be married to adopt a child. Under this ruling, unmarried heterosexual couples, lesbian couples, and gay couples can all legally adopt children in New York. Writing for the majority, Chief Justice Judith Kaye argued that by expanding the boundaries of who can be legally recognized as parents, the state may be able to assist more children in securing "the best possible home." With this ruling, New York became the third state (after Vermont and Massachusetts) to recognize the right of unmarried couples to adopt children (Dao 1995).

For every child who is adopted, many more remain the wards of state-sponsored child protective services. At any given time, over half a million children in the United States are living in foster care. About 118,000 of these children are eligible for adoption (Koch 2006).

**Dual-Income Families** The idea of a family consisting of a wage-earning husband and a stay-at-home wife has largely given way to the dual-income household. Among married people ages 25–34, 95 percent of the men and 68 percent of the women were in the labor force in 2006 (Bureau of the Census 2007a:Table 578).

## SOCthink

> > > What are the advantages and disadvantages of the dual-income model for women, for men, for children, and for society as a whole?

Both opportunity and need have driven the rise in the number of dual-income couples. Women now have the chance to pursue careers in a way that previously had been closed due to cultural expectations regarding gender. This has resulted in increased education levels for women and increased participation in occupational fields that had been largely closed. At the same time, however, couples find it harder to make it on a single income. Evidence of this trend can be found in the rise of married couples living apart for reasons other than marital discord. The 3.6 million couples who now live apart represent 1 out of every 33 marriages. More than half live farther than 100 miles apart, and half of those live 1000 or more miles apart. Of course, couples living apart are nothing new; men have worked at transient jobs for generations as soldiers, truck drivers, or traveling salesmen. The existence of such household arrangements reflects an

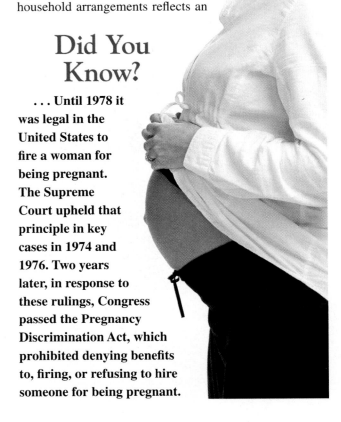

## Did You Know?

... Until 1978 it was legal in the United States to fire a woman for being pregnant. The Supreme Court upheld that principle in key cases in 1974 and 1976. Two years later, in response to these rulings, Congress passed the Pregnancy Discrimination Act, which prohibited denying benefits to, firing, or refusing to hire someone for being pregnant.

acceptance of the egalitarian family type (L. Cullen 2007; Holmes 2006).

**Single-Parent Families** The 2004 *American Idol* winner Fantasia Barrino's song "Baby Mama" offers a tribute to young single mothers—a subject she knows about. Barrino was 17 when she became pregnant with her daughter. Though critics charged that the song sends the wrong message to teenage girls, Barrino says it is not about encouraging teens to have sex. Rather, she sees the song as an anthem for young mothers courageously trying to raise their children alone (Cherlin 2006).

In recent decades, the stigma attached to unwed mothers and other single parents has significantly diminished. **Single-parent families,** in which only one parent is present to care for the children, can hardly be viewed as a rarity in the United States. In 2004, a single parent headed about 20 percent of White families with children under age 18, 29 percent of Hispanic families, and 59 percent of African American families (as we can see in the figure on page 153).

The life of single parents and their children is not inevitably more difficult than that of a traditional nuclear family. It is as inaccurate to assume that a single-parent family is necessarily deprived as it is to assume that a two-parent family is always secure and happy. Nevertheless, to the extent that such families have to rely on a single income

> What greater thing is there for human souls than to feel that they are joined for life—to be with each other in silent unspeakable memories.
>
> ———————
>
> **George Eliot**

or a sole caregiver, life in the single-parent family can be extremely stressful. A family headed by a single mother faces especially difficult problems when the mother is a teenager, especially when she lacks access to significant social and economic resources.

Why might low-income teenage women wish to have children and face the obvious financial difficulties of motherhood? Some theorists argue that these women tend to have low self-esteem and limited options; a child may provide a sense of motivation and purpose for the teenager whose economic worth in our society is limited at best. Given the barriers that many young women face because of their gender, race, ethnicity, and class, many teenagers may believe they have little to lose and much to gain by having a child.

Although 88 percent of single parents in the United States are mothers, the number of households headed by single fathers more than quadrupled between 1980 and 2000. While single mothers often develop social networks, single fathers are typically more isolated. In addition, they must deal with schools and social service agencies that are more accustomed to women as custodial parents (Kreider 2008).

**Stepfamilies** Approximately 45 percent of all people in the United States will marry, divorce, and then remarry. The rising rates of divorce and remarriage have led to a noticeable increase in stepfamily relationships. The exact nature of blended families has social significance for adults and children alike.

*Comedians Tina Fey and Amy Poehler starred in the 2008 film* Baby Mama, *in which Fey played a would-be single mother.*

# Rise of Single-Parent Families in the United States, 1970–2001

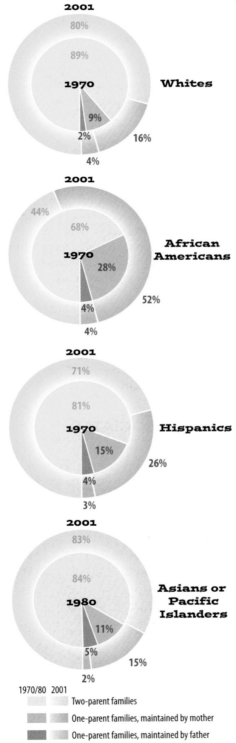

**2001**
80%
89%

**1970**     **Whites**
9%
2%
16%
4%

**2001**
44%
68%

**1970**     **African Americans**
28%
4%
52%
4%

**2001**
71%
81%

**1970**     **Hispanics**
15%
26%
4%
3%

**2001**
83%
84%

**1980**     **Asians or Pacific Islanders**
11%
5%
15%
2%

1970/80  2001
☐ Two-parent families
☐ One-parent families, maintained by mother
☐ One-parent families, maintained by father

*Note:* "Children" refers to children under 18. Early data for Asian Americans are for 1980. Hispanics can be of any race. Not included are unrelated people living together with no children present. All data exclude the 4 percent of children in nonparental households.

*Source:* Bureau of the Census 1994:63; Kreider and Fields 2005:3.

Family members in stepfamilies must deal with resocialization issues when an adult becomes a stepparent or a child becomes a stepchild and stepsibling. In evaluating these stepfamilies, some observers have assumed that children would benefit from remarriage because they would be gaining a second custodial parent and would potentially enjoy greater economic security. However, after reviewing many studies of stepfamilies, sociologist Andrew J. Cherlin (2008:800) concluded that "the well-being of children in stepfamilies is no better, on average, than the well-being of children in divorced, single-parent households."

> **single-parent family** A family in which only one parent is present to care for the children.

Stepparents can and do play valuable and unique roles in their stepchildren's lives, but their involvement does not guarantee an improvement in family life. In fact, standards may decline. Studies suggest that children raised in families with stepmothers are likely to have less health care, education, and money spent on their food than children raised by biological mothers. The measures are also negative for children raised by stepfathers, but only half as negative as in the case of stepmothers. This may be due to the stepmother holding back out of concern for seeming too intrusive or relying on the biological father to carry out parental duties (Schmeeckle 2007; Schmeeckle et al. 2006).

## >> Divorce

"Do you promise to love, honor, and cherish . . . until death do you part?" Every year, people of all social classes and racial and ethnic groups make this legally binding agreement. Yet a significant number of these promises shatter prior to divorce.

### STATISTICAL TRENDS IN DIVORCE

Just how common is divorce? Surprisingly, this is not a simple question to answer; divorce statistics are difficult to interpret. The media frequently report that one out of every two marriages ends in divorce. But that figure is misleading in that many marriages last for decades. It is

So even though she's from an unusual family, we still treat Heather with respect.

What is Diversity?

Heather Has a Mommy and Daddy Who Are Married and Live Together

# Percentage of Marriages to Reach Milestones*

| Men, year of first marriage | Anniversary (percentage still married)* | | | | | | | |
| --- | --- | --- | --- | --- | --- | --- | --- | --- |
| | 5th | 10th | 15th | 20th | 25th | 30th | 35th | 40th |
| 1955–59 | 96.4 | 88.3 | 80.3 | 73.8 | 70.4 | 67.3 | 64.7 | 61.4 |
| 1960–64 | 95.1 | 85.0 | 75.2 | 69.7 | 65.0 | 62.4 | 59.7 | 52.5 |
| 1965–69 | 90.5 | 76.9 | 67.4 | 62.3 | 58.6 | 55.5 | 48.2 | |
| 1970–74 | 88.5 | 74.4 | 64.6 | 58.1 | 53.8 | 46.2 | | |
| 1975–79 | 88.1 | 73.0 | 65.2 | 59.6 | 49.5 | | | |
| 1980–84 | 88.7 | 73.7 | 65.3 | 53.8 | | | | |
| 1985–89 | 89.3 | 76.4 | 60.6 | | | | | |
| 1990–94 | 89.4 | 70.0 | | | | | | |

*Counts marriages ended by divorce, separation, and death

| Women, year of first marriage | Anniversary (percentage still married)* | | | | | | | |
| --- | --- | --- | --- | --- | --- | --- | --- | --- |
| | 5th | 10th | 15th | 20th | 25th | 30th | 35th | 40th |
| 1955–59 | 94.0 | 86.8 | 79.4 | 72.4 | 67.2 | 63.5 | 58.9 | 54.7 |
| 1960–64 | 92.8 | 82.3 | 72.7 | 66.5 | 60.4 | 56.1 | 52.7 | 44.9 |
| 1965–69 | 89.5 | 74.9 | 65.7 | 60.0 | 55.1 | 51.3 | 43.8 | |
| 1970–74 | 87.1 | 71.6 | 61.4 | 55.4 | 50.6 | 42.1 | | |
| 1975–79 | 85.3 | 70.0 | 61.4 | 55.7 | 46.4 | | | |
| 1980–84 | 86.5 | 70.7 | 63.1 | 52.4 | | | | |
| 1985–89 | 85.7 | 73.0 | 56.9 | | | | | |
| 1990–94 | 87.2 | 69.2 | | | | | | |

Source: U.S. Census Bureau 2004:Table 2.

based on a comparison of all divorces that occur in a single year (regardless of when the couples were married) with the number of new marriages in that same year. We get a somewhat more complete picture by looking at marital milestones people reach based on the year they first married (as shown in the table above). These data include marriages that end due to the death of the partner; given that life expectancy has increased, it does provide a sense of shifting patterns. Following either the rows or the columns provides insight into both the generational effect and the impact of changing attitudes and practices over time.

In the United States and many other countries, overall divorce rates began to increase in the late 1960s but then leveled off; since the late 1980s, the divorce rate has declined by 30 percent. This trend is due partly to the aging of the baby boomer generation and the corresponding decline in the proportion of people of marriageable age. But it also indicates an increase in marital stability in recent years (Coontz 2006).

Getting divorced obviously does not sour people on marriage. About 63 percent of all divorced people in the United States have remarried. However, women are less likely than men to remarry because many retain custody of their children after a divorce, which complicates a new adult relationship (Bianchi and Spain 1996; Saad 2004).

Some people regard the nation's high rate of remarriage as an endorsement of the institution of marriage, but it does lead to the new challenges of a kin network characterized by both current and prior marital relationships. Such networks can be particularly complex if children are involved or if an ex-spouse remarries.

## FACTORS ASSOCIATED WITH DIVORCE

One of the major factors shaping the increase in divorce over the past 100 years has been the greater social acceptance of divorce. It is no longer considered necessary to endure an unhappy marriage. Even major religious groups

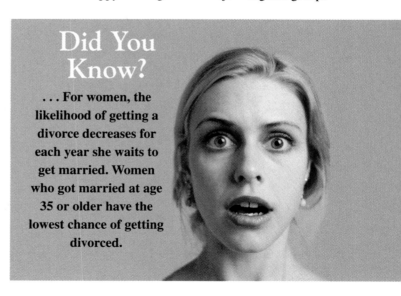

### Did You Know?

... For women, the likelihood of getting a divorce decreases for each year she waits to get married. Women who got married at age 35 or older have the lowest chance of getting divorced.

# Trends in Marriage and Divorce in the United States, 1920–2006

**Rate per 1,000 total population**

Marriage

Divorce

| 16 |
| 14 |
| 12 |
| 10 |
| 8 |
| 6 |
| 4 |
| 2 |
| 0 |
1920  1930  1940  1950  1960  1970  1980  1990  2006

SOCstudies

*Sources:* Bureau of the Census 1975:64; *National Vital Statistics Reports* 2008.

divorce each year. Of course, for some of these children, divorce signals the welcome end to a highly dysfunctional relationship. A national sample conducted by sociologists Paul R. Amato and Alan Booth (1997) showed that in about a third of divorces, the children actually benefited from parental separation because it lessened their exposure to conflict. But in about 70 percent of divorces, the parents engaged in a low level of conflict; in those cases, the realities of divorce appeared to be harder for the children to bear than living with the marital unhappiness.

Other researchers, using differing definitions of conflict, have found greater unhappiness for children living in homes with marital differences. Still, it would be simplistic to assume that children are automatically better off following the breakup of their parents' marriage. The interests of the parents do not necessarily serve children well.

have relaxed what were often negative attitudes toward divorce, commonly having treated it as a sin.

The growing acceptance of divorce is a worldwide phenomenon. Only a decade ago, Sunoo, South Korea's foremost matchmaking service, had no divorced clients. Few Koreans divorced, and those who did felt social pressure to resign themselves to the single life. In one recent seven-year period, South Korea's divorce rate doubled. Today, 15 percent of Sunoo's membership is divorced (Onishi 2003).

In the United States, a variety of factors have contributed to the growing social acceptance of divorce. For instance, most states have adopted less restrictive divorce laws in the past three decades. No-fault divorce laws, which allow a couple to end their marriage without assigning blame (by specifying adultery, for instance), accounted for an initial surge in the divorce rate after they were introduced in the 1970s, though these laws appear to have had little effect beyond that. Additionally, a general increase in family incomes, coupled with the availability of free legal aid to some poor people, has meant that more couples can afford costly divorce proceedings. Also, as society provides greater opportunities for women, more and more wives are becoming less dependent on their husbands, both economically and emotionally. They may feel more able to leave a marriage if it seems hopeless.

## IMPACT OF DIVORCE ON CHILDREN

Divorce is traumatic for all involved, but it has special meaning for the more than 1 million children whose parents

## >> Diverse Lifestyles

Marriage is no longer the presumed route from adolescence to adulthood. In fact, it has lost much of its social significance as a rite of passage. Now, establishing oneself through education and a career has taken precedence (Cherlin 2004). The nation's marriage rate has declined since 1960 because people are postponing marriage until later in life and because more couples, including same-sex couples, are deciding to form partnerships without marriage.

### COHABITATION

In the United States, testing the marital waters by living together before making a commitment is a common practice among marriage-wary 20- and 30-somethings. The tremendous increase in the number of male–female couples who choose to live together without marrying, a practice called **cohabitation,** is one of the most dramatic social trends of recent years.

> **cohabitation** The practice of living together as a male–female couple without marrying.

About half of all currently married couples in the United States say that they lived together prior to marriage. And this percentage is likely to increase. The number of unmarried-couple households in the United States rose sixfold in the 1960s and increased another 72 percent between 1990 and 2000. Presently, over 8 percent of opposite-sex couples are unmarried. Cohabitation is more common among African Americans and American

Indians than among other racial and ethnic groups; it is least common among Asian Americans. The figure below shows how globalization varies by region (Peterson 2003; T. Simmons and O'Connell 2003).

In much of Europe, cohabitation is so common that the general sentiment seems to be "Love, yes; marriage, maybe." In Iceland, 62 percent of all children are born to single mothers; in France, Great Britain, and Norway, the proportion is about 40 percent. Government policies in these countries make few legal distinctions between married and unmarried couples or households (Lyall 2002; M. Moore 2006).

People commonly associate cohabitation only with younger couples, but according to a study done in Los Angeles, working couples are almost twice as likely to cohabit as college students. And census data show that in 2003, 45 percent of unmarried couples had one or more children present in the household. These cohabitants are more like spouses than dating partners. Moreover, in contrast to the common perception that people who cohabit have never been married, researchers report that about half of all people involved in cohabitation in the United States have been previously married. Cohabitation serves as a temporary or permanent alternative to matrimony for many men and women who have experienced their own or their parents' divorces (Fields 2004; Popenoe and Whitehead 1999).

## REMAINING SINGLE

More and more people in the United States are postponing entry into a first marriage. The trend toward maintaining a single lifestyle for a longer period is related to the growing economic independence of young people. This trend is especially significant for women. Freed from financial needs, women don't necessarily need to marry to enjoy a satisfying life. Divorce, late marriage, and longevity also figure into this trend. Even so, fewer than 4 percent of women and men in the United States are likely to remain single throughout their lives (Bureau of the Census 2007a:Table 56).

There are many reasons why a person may choose not to marry. Some singles do not want to limit their sexual intimacy to one lifetime partner. Some men and women do not want to become highly dependent on any one person—and do not want anyone depending heavily on them. In a society that values individuality and self-fulfillment, the single lifestyle can offer certain freedoms that marriage may not.

Remaining single represents a clear departure from societal expectations; indeed, it has been likened to "being single on Noah's Ark." A single adult must confront the inaccurate view that he or she is always

# Unmarried-Couple Households by State, 2000

**Percentage of all couple households**

- 11.0–20.8
- 9.1–10.9
- 8.0–9.0
- 5.2–7.9

Note: Data are for 2000 and include both opposite-sex and same-sex partners. U.S. average is 9.1 percent.

Source: T. Simmons and O'Connell 2003:4.

lonely, is a workaholic, or is immature. These stereotypes help to support the traditional assumption in the United States and most other societies that to be truly happy and fulfilled, a person must get married and raise a family. To counter these societal expectations, singles have formed numerous support groups (Hertz 2006; Lundquist 2006).

## MARRIAGE WITHOUT CHILDREN

There has been a significant increase in childlessness in the United States. According to census data, about 16 to 17 percent of women will now complete their childbearing years without having borne any children, compared to 10 percent in 1980. As many as 20 percent of women in their 30s expect to remain childless (Clausen 2002).

Childlessness within marriage has generally been viewed as a problem that can be solved through such means as adoption and artificial insemination. More and more couples today, however, choose not to have children and regard themselves as child-free rather than childless. They do not believe that having children automatically follows from marriage, nor do they feel that reproduction is the duty of all married couples. Childless couples have formed support groups (with names like No Kidding) and set up websites (K. Park 2005; Terry 2000).

Economic considerations have contributed to this shift in attitudes; having children has become quite expensive. According to a government estimate made for 2004, the average middle-class family will spend $184,320 to feed, clothe, and shelter a child from birth to age 18. If the child attends college, that amount could double, depending on the college chosen. Aware of the financial pressures, some couples are having fewer children than they otherwise might, and others are weighing the advantages of a child-free marriage (Lino 2005).

## LESBIAN AND GAY RELATIONSHIPS

One of the more active political debates about families in recent years has involved marriage of same-sex couples. Such couples highlight the difficulty of defining families in too narrow terms. If we stick with a narrow, substantive definition, such relationships have not counted as families. When we define families in terms of what they do—what

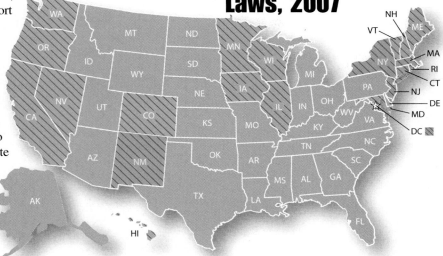

# Discriminatory Marriage and Anti-Gay Discrimination Laws, 2007

■ States that define marriage as a male-female union
■ States that do *not* define marriage as a male-female union
\\\ States that prohibit discrimination based on sexual orientation

*Note:* Current as of June 2007. Vermont prohibits same-sex marriage but provides for same-sex civil union.

*Source:* Human Rights Campaign 2007.

functions they perform—however, we find a growing acceptance that such relationships do constitute families.

The lifestyles of lesbians and gays are varied, just like those of heterosexuals. Some live in long-term, monogamous relationships; others live alone or with roommates. Some remain in "empty shell" heterosexual marriages and do not publicly acknowledge their homosexuality; others live with children from a former marriage or with adopted children. Based on election exit polls, researchers for the National Health and Social Life Survey and the Voter News Service estimate that 2–5 percent of the adult population identify themselves as either gay or lesbian. An analysis of the 2000 U.S. Census shows a minimum of at least 600,000 gay households and a gay and lesbian adult population approaching 10 million (Laumann et al. 1994b:293; Smith and Gates 2001).

Gay and lesbian couples face discrimination on both a personal and a legal level. Their inability to marry in most states denies them many rights that married couples take for granted, from the ability to make decisions for an incapacitated partner to the right to receive government benefits to dependents, such as Social Security payments (see the figures above and on page 158). Though gay couples consider themselves families, legally they are usually treated

> Call it a clan, call it a network, call it a tribe, call it a family. Whatever you call it, whoever you are, you need one.
>
> Jane Howard

as if they are not. Precisely because of such inequities, many gay and lesbian couples are now demanding the right to marry.

Events in three states brought the issue to the forefront. In 1999, Vermont gave gay couples the legal benefits of marriage through civil union but stopped short of calling the arrangement a marriage. Then, in 2003, the Massachusetts Supreme Court ruled 4-3 that under the state's constitution, gay couples have the right to marry—a ruling the U.S. Supreme Court has refused to review. More recently, in May 2008, the California Supreme Court overturned the state's ban on same-sex marriage, becoming the second state to offer full marriage rights to same-sex couples.

In the United States, many local jurisdictions have sought to address the lack of federal and state rights by passing legislation allowing for the registration of domestic partnerships and have extended employee benefits to those relationships. Under such policies, a **domestic partnership** may be defined as two unrelated adults who share a mutually caring relationship, reside together, and agree to be jointly responsible for

# Attitudes Toward Gay Rights Depend on Who You Know

| | Doesn't know someone gay or lesbian | Knows someone gay or lesbian |
|---|---|---|
| Gay couples should be able to adopt | 28% | 50% |
| Gay partners should have Social Security benefits | 43% | 60% |
| Gay and lesbian people should serve openly in the military | 48% | 63% |
| Hate-crime laws should include violence committed against gay and lesbian people | 54% | 69% |
| Gay partners should have inheritance rights | 50% | 73% |
| Gay and lesbian people should have equal rights in employment | 77% | 90% |

**Doesn't know someone gay or lesbian**
**Knows someone gay or lesbian**

Source: www/hrc.org. October 4, 2006.

shown an even split among the public. In 2007, 46 percent of those surveyed felt that marriages between same-sex couples should be considered valid, while 53 percent felt that they should not be recognized. These results reflect the gradual shift in the level of acceptance of gay marriage since 1982, when 34 percent of respondents felt that it should be legal (Gallup 2008b). Typically, people are more opposed to gay marriage than to civil union: About one-fourth of respondents favor legal recognition of gay marriage, while as many as half favor civil union (Saad 2005).

The debates surrounding same-sex families highlight many of the issues sociologists seek to address in their investigation of family life. What families are, what they do, how they do it, and what obstacles they face are issues relevant for all families. In our modern, pluralistic world, the singular traditions of the past can no longer be taken for granted, as Tevye and Golde discovered in *The Fiddler on the Roof.* People come from many different cultures with multiple taken-for-granted assumptions. Sociology investigates such complexity, providing us with tools so that we might better understand how we think and act in the context of families.

domestic partnership Two unrelated adults who share a mutually caring relationship, reside together, and agree to be jointly responsible for their dependents, basic living expenses, and other common necessities.

their dependents, basic living expenses, and other common necessities. Domestic partnership benefits can apply to couples' inheritance, parenting, pensions, taxation, housing, immigration, workplace fringe benefits, and health care. Even though the most passionate support for domestic partnership legislation has come from lesbian and gay activists, the majority of those eligible for such benefits would be cohabiting heterosexual couples.

Recently, national surveys of attitudes toward gay marriage in the United States have

*get* involved!

Volunteer! There are numerous organizations designed to assist children in situations of need, including Big Brothers and Big Sisters, CASA (Court Appointed Special Advocates), and school tutoring programs. Such programs can fulfill some of the functions of families. Seek out one of these organizations, and find out ways that you can help.

Couple getting married in San Francisco after a state Supreme Court ruling to allow same-sex marriage.

# For REVIEW

I. **What is the family?**
- Sociologists define the family in terms of both what a family is, with an emphasis on blood and law, and what families do or what functions they perform, including reproduction, socialization, protection, regulation of sexual behavior, affection and companionship, and provision of social status.

II. **How do people pick partners?**
- Social factors shape the pool of potential partners from which individuals select. People balance selection between someone who is from within their group (endogamy) but not too close (exogamy). People tend to pick people with similar social characteristics (homogamy), including age, education, class, race, and ethnicity.

III. **How do families vary?**
- There is significant variation in terms of proximity (extended versus nuclear), authority (patriarchal, matriarchal, and egalitarian), duration (divorce), and structure (dual-income, single-parent, stepfamilies, cohabitation, singlehood, child-free, and same-sex).

# Pop Quiz

1. Which system of descent is followed in the United States?
   a. matrilineal
   b. patrilineal
   c. bilateral
   d. unilateral

2. Alice, age seven, lives at home with her parents, her grandmother, and her aunt. Alice's family is an example of a(n)
   a. nuclear family.
   b. dysfunctional family.
   c. extended family.
   d. polygynous family.

3. In which form of marriage may a person have several spouses in his or her lifetime but only one spouse at a time?
   a. serial monogamy
   b. monogamy
   c. polygamy
   d. polyandry

4. The marriage of a woman to more than one man at the same time is referred to as
   a. polygyny.
   b. monogamy.
   c. serial monogamy.
   d. polyandry.

5. According to the approach that defines families in terms of what they do, which of the following is *not* one of the paramount functions performed by the family?
   a. mediation
   b. reproduction
   c. regulation of sexual behavior
   d. affection and companionship

6. Which norm requires mate selection outside certain groups, usually one's own family or certain kinfolk?
   a. exogamy
   b. endogamy
   c. matriarchy
   d. patriarchy

7. The principle that prohibits sexual relationships between certain culturally specified relatives is known as
   a. monogamy.
   b. the incest taboo.
   c. polygamy.
   d. endogamy.

8. One recent development in family life in the United States has been the extension of parenthood as adult children continue to live at home or return home after college. The reason for this is
   a. the rising divorce rate.
   b. skyrocketing rent and real estate prices.
   c. financial difficulties.
   d. all of the above.

9. Overall, the divorce rate in the United States in the past 30 years
   a. has risen dramatically.
   b. has risen slowly but steadily.
   c. has declined after having risen significantly in the 1960s and 1970s.
   d. shows no clear pattern.

10. An increasing number of couples are opting not to have children, but instead of referring to themselves as childless, they opt for the alternative expression
    a. kid independent.
    b. baby barren.
    c. patrilineal dissenters.
    d. child-free.

1. (c); 2. (c); 3. (a); 4. (d); 5. (a); 6. (a); 7. (b); 8. (d); 9. (c); 10. (d)

8

EDUCATION&R

# FAITH AND LEARNING

Patrick Henry College, located near Washington, D.C., was founded in 2000 with the explicit intention of competing with Ivy League schools. The elite students it pursues, however, come from a particular niche: Approximately 80 percent of them were home-schooled, and they all share a strong commitment to evangelical Christian faith.

In keeping with the school's expectation of a high level of religious commitment, students must sign a "Statement of Faith" that sets out a series of Christian beliefs, including the virgin birth of Jesus Christ, the existence of Satan, and eternal punishment in hell for non-Christians. Students are required to abide by a strict dress code, attend daily chapel, and abstain from alcohol, smoking, and premarital sex.

The students by and large take these commitments quite seriously. As journalist Hannah Rosin (2007) recounts in her book on Patrick Henry College entitled *God's Harvard,* "To them, a 'Christian' keeps a running conversation with God in his or her head . . . and believes that at any moment God might in some palpable way step in and show He either cares or disapproves" (p. 5).

Student Elisa Muench was something of a trailblazer at Patrick Henry College. She was the first woman to run for a leadership position in student government, in the face of disapproval by students who thought it inappropriate that a woman should serve in such an office. As a junior, she had an internship in the White House. Yet she found herself fearing that what counted as success in the eyes of the dominant society, including a professional career, might conflict with success in the eyes of God (Rosin 2007:85). Elisa struggled to be true to both her educational and religious teachings.

It is within such educational and religious communities that we learn what to believe and how to act. All of us are, in some respects, like Elisa, seeking to balance the sometimes conflicting demands of the various spheres of our lives, including family, education, religion, work, and politics. In this chapter, we focus on the roles education and religion play both for individuals and for society as a whole.

# ELIGION

- How does education help to maintain social order?
- How does education support the existing system of inequality?
- How do sociologists define religion?

## >> Education in Society

Historically, we counted on families to be significant agents of socialization, teaching us the basic knowledge, values, and norms we needed to survive. As societies became more diverse and the division of labor increased, however, our educational needs expanded, and we placed a greater emphasis on more formal socialization. When learning is explicit and formalized—when some people consciously teach, while others adopt the role of learner—the process of socialization is called **education.**

> **education** A formal process of learning in which some people consciously teach, while others adopt the social role of learner.

We invest a significant amount of time and money in education. Why? The simple answer is that we believe the individual and collective benefits are worth it. In schools we investigate the deeper mysteries of life so that we might have a better understanding of ourselves and our world. As sociologist W. E. B. Du Bois ([1903] 1994) put it, "The true college will ever have one goal,—not to earn meat, but to know the end and aim of that life which meat nourishes" (p. 51). As individuals we also acquire skills and credentials that we need to find a good job. In terms of both how we think and what we are capable of doing, education provides pathways for social change.

The history of education in the United States is one of expansion and institutionalization. Expansion is reflected

### SOCthink

> > > Who most influenced you to go to college? Considering people you know who did not go to college, what influenced them to make that choice? How powerful are socialization and social networks in making such decisions?

### Did You Know?

. . . In 2006, 66 percent of high school seniors enrolled in college in the fall semester following their graduation. During the 1970s, the average was about 50 percent.

in the growing percentage of Americans going to school for more years and for higher degrees. The proportion of people age 25 or over with a high school diploma increased from 41 percent in 1960 to more than 86 percent in 2006. The proportion with a college degree rose from 8 percent in 1960 to 29 percent in 2006 (Bureau of the Census 2007a:Table 217). Institutionalization has occurred as education has become more formalized—a distinct part of the public sphere. Educational organizations have become more professional and bureaucratic in their attempt to more efficiently provide services to the whole population.

Early American political leaders such as Benjamin Franklin and Thomas Jefferson advocated public education as an essential component of democratic societies. They argued that public education provides individuals with essential knowledge and skills for development and advancement and that it provides society with informed citizens who can serve as social, economic, and political leaders.

American civic figures have also presented public education as a means to opportunity. Horace Mann, often referred to as the "father of public education," wrote in 1848, "Education, beyond all other devices of human origin, is the great equalizer of the conditions of men,—the balance-wheel of the social machinery" ([1848] 1957). Mann hoped that public education would ensure that those who

## Percentage of Adults Ages 25–64 Who Have Completed Higher Education (BA/BS)

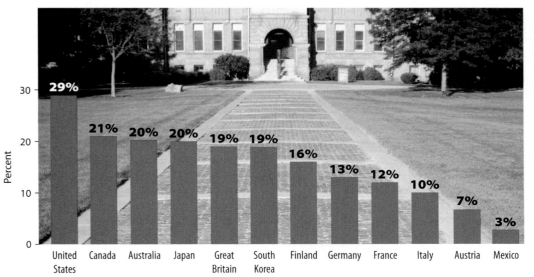

| Country | Percent |
|---|---|
| United States | 29% |
| Canada | 21% |
| Australia | 20% |
| Japan | 20% |
| Great Britain | 19% |
| South Korea | 19% |
| Finland | 16% |
| Germany | 13% |
| France | 12% |
| Italy | 10% |
| Austria | 7% |
| Mexico | 3% |

*Source:* Data for 2002 released in Bureau of the Census 2007a:Table 1312.

were born poor and lacked the means to afford schooling still had the opportunity to develop their knowledge and skills and, in so doing, get ahead in society. Initially, public schools were open only to White males. Over time, due in part to the efforts of sociologists like Du Bois and Jane Addams, public education expanded to include everyone regardless of race, ethnicity, sex, or national origin. As we will see, however, the principle of equal educational opportunity does not necessarily result in the practice of educational equality.

## >> Sociological Perspectives on Education

Sociologists have closely examined the degree to which education actually succeeds in providing social order and individual opportunity. They have found that while it does offer opportunity and help to establish social order, it also perpetuates inequality. Fulfilling the hopes of Jefferson, Franklin, and Mann, it has produced an educated citizenry equipped to take on the challenges of modern life. At the same time, however, it reinforces existing beliefs, values, and norms that justify the status quo and its inequalities. The dominant sociological perspectives on education focus on the role education plays in society.

## EDUCATION AND SOCIAL ORDER

Society needs people with the knowledge and skills to perform the tasks necessary for its continued existence, and individuals need this know-how to survive and prosper. Schools teach students how to read, speak foreign languages, repair automobiles, and much more. In this section, we will look at some of the collective and individual benefits of education that sociologists have identified.

**Transmitting Culture** As a social institution, education preserves and transmits the dominant culture. Schooling exposes each generation of young people to the existing beliefs, norms, and values of their culture. In the United States, we learn respect for existing values and norms and reverence for established institutions, such as the economy, the family, and the presidency. Of course, this is true of many other cultures as well. While schoolchildren in the United States are hearing about the accomplishments of George Washington and Abraham Lincoln, British children are hearing about the distinctive contributions of Queen Elizabeth I and Winston Churchill.

In Great Britain, the transmission of the dominant culture through schools goes beyond traditional content such as learning about monarchs, prime ministers, and generals. In 1996 the government's chief curriculum advisor—noting the need to fill a void left by the diminishing authority of the Church of England—proposed that British schools socialize students into a set of core values. The set included honesty, respect for others, politeness, a sense of fair play, forgiveness, punctuality, nonviolent behavior, patience, faithfulness, and self-discipline

**POPSOC**

Schools have been a source of entertainment in popular culture for a long time. We see examples of this in films like *High School Musical, School of Rock, Legally Blonde, Ferris Bueller's Day Off, The Breakfast Club,* and *Freedom Writers,* and in television programs such as *Saved by the Bell* and *Freaks and Geeks.*

(Charter and Sherman 1996). Similar programs have been established in the United States, such as the Character Counts program, which highlights the Six Pillars of Character: trustworthiness, respect, responsibility, fairness, caring, and citizenship.

## SOCthink

> > > Why do you think there has been a move toward character education in schools? What changes in society might contribute to that perceived need?

Sometimes nations reassess the ways in which they transmit culture to students. Recently, the Chinese government revised the nation's history curriculum. Students are now taught that the Chinese Communist Party, not the United States, played a central role in defeating Japan in World War II. No mention is made of the estimated 30 million Chinese who died from famine because of party founder Mao Zedong's disastrous Great Leap Forward (1958–1962), a failed effort to transform China's agrarian economy into an industrial powerhouse. In urban, Western-oriented areas such as Shanghai, textbooks acknowledge the technological advances made in Western industrial countries but avoid any criticism of past policies of the Chinese government (French 2004b; Kahn 2006b).

### Hot or Not?

Should public schools in the United States offer bilingual education to accommodate non-English-speaking students?

**Promoting Social Integration** Schools seek to bring students together to provide a sense of community. Many colleges and universities require first- and second-year students to live on campus for just this reason. Such programs become more important when students come from diverse backgrounds with different cultural expectations. The goal is to provide experiences that will unify a population composed of diverse racial, ethnic, and religious groups into a community whose members share—to some extent—a common identity. Historically, schools at all levels in the United States have played an important role in socializing the children of immigrants into the norms, values, and beliefs of the dominant culture. The common identity and social integration fostered by education contributes to societal stability and consensus (Touraine 1974).

In the past, the integrative function of education was most obvious in its emphasis on promoting a common language. Immigrant children were expected to learn English. In some instances, they were even forbidden to speak their native language on school grounds. More recently, bilingualism has been defended both for its educational value and as a means of encouraging cultural diversity. However, critics argue that bilingualism undermines the social and political integration that education traditionally has promoted.

## Education Pays

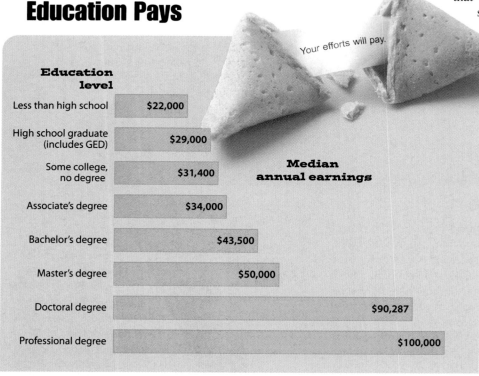

| Education level | Median annual earnings |
|---|---|
| Less than high school | $22,000 |
| High school graduate (includes GED) | $29,000 |
| Some college, no degree | $31,400 |
| Associate's degree | $34,000 |
| Bachelor's degree | $43,500 |
| Master's degree | $50,000 |
| Doctoral degree | $90,287 |
| Professional degree | $100,000 |

*Your efforts will pay.*

**Training and Social Control** Schools teach students how to behave. In the early grades in particular, significant time and effort is spent getting students to do what the teacher wants them to do, when and how the teacher wants them to do it. Through the exercise of social control, schools teach students various skills and values essential to their future positions in the labor force. Students learn punctuality, discipline, scheduling, and responsible work habits, as well as how to negotiate the complexities of a bureaucratic orga-

\* Includes full-time, full-year wage and salary for workers ages 25–34.
*Source:* Planty et al. 2008:30.

Government policies at the national, state, and local levels all influence public education in the United States.

nization. Schools train students for whatever lies ahead, whether it be the assembly line or a physician's office. In effect, then, schools serve as a transitional agent of social control, bridging the gap between parents and employers in the life cycle of most individuals (Bowles and Gintis 1976; M. Cole 1988).

In a society with a complex division of labor, schools help in the essential process of selecting and training individuals for specialized jobs. We expect schools to choose those with the most ability to pursue degrees in fields that demand the greatest skill. For example, we want students with aptitude in math and science to become engineers. We use grades as an indicator of such ability and provide degrees to certify that the graduate has sufficient training to perform the job well. We hold out the promise of higher pay to reward those who make the sacrifices that higher education calls for in terms of time and money. As we will see below, however, many people are concerned about the degree to which this is accomplished fairly.

**Stimulating Cultural Innovation** While schools do preserve and transmit existing culture, education can also stimulate social change. For example, public schools began to offer sex education classes in response to the soaring pregnancy rate among teenagers. Many schools endorse affirmative action in admissions—giving priority to females or minorities—as a means of countering discrimination based on race or sex. Project Head Start, an early-childhood program that serves more than 808,000 children annually, has sought to compensate for the disadvantages in school readiness experienced by children from low-income families (National Center for Education Statistics 2007:Table 370). To ensure school readiness, it provides classes for preschool children from families below a certain income level, working with them on letter recognition, vocabulary, nutrition, and other basic skills.

Colleges and universities are particularly committed to cultural innovation. Faculty members, especially at large universities, must pursue research and publish articles and books. In so doing, they produce new technology, techniques, knowledge, and practices. Cultural innovation on campuses goes beyond such concrete results, however, because college provides a context within which we can challenge existing ideas and try out new practices. Such experimentation sometimes leads people to accuse professors, especially those with innovative or unpopular ideas, of being out of touch or out of line, but we need people to experiment with new ideas so that our culture does not stagnate.

Campuses also provide an environment in which students from around the world with widely divergent ideas and experiences can interact. In 2006–2007, U.S. campuses hosted just over 582,000 international students. Such exposure provides opportunities for cultural innovation as people from various cultures are exposed to and experiment with new and different cultural norms and values.

## EDUCATION AND INEQUALITY

Although education does promote social order and provide individual opportunity, there are significant inequalities in the educational opportunities available to different groups. For example, wide disparities exist in funding and facilities between urban and suburban schools. Jonathan Kozol (2005:321), who has studied educational inequality for decades, reports that, in the same year, Chicago public schools spent $8482 per student while the wealthy northern suburban Highland Park and Deerfield school district spent $17,291. This is just one example among many. Schools in well-off areas have the funding to offer programs and facilities that poor districts cannot hope to match, including high-tech labs, athletic facilities, and elective classes in art, music, and languages. As a former New York City principal, in an interview with Kozol, puts it, "I'll believe money doesn't count the day the rich stop spending so much on their own children" (Kozol 2005:59). In this section, we will look at a number of such ways that the experience of and outcomes from education are not equal for everyone.

## SOCthink

> > > Only about 8 percent of funding for public schools comes from the federal government. In most states, the majority of funding comes from local property taxes. What are the consequences of this model for equitable funding of education? Why might some districts resist changing this model?

**The Hidden Curriculum** One of the ways that schools reinforce the existing system of inequality is through the teaching of what Philip Jackson (1968) has called the **hidden curriculum**—standards of behavior that society deems proper and that teachers subtly communicate to students. It prepares students to submit to authority. For example, children learn not to speak until the teacher calls on them, and they learn to regulate their activities according to the clock or bells. A classroom environment that is overly focused on obedience rewards students for pleasing the teacher and remaining compliant, rather than for creative thought and academic learning. In this way, schools socialize students to submit to authority figures, including bosses and political leaders.

> **hidden curriculum** Standards of behavior that are deemed proper by society and are taught subtly in schools.
> **teacher-expectancy effect** The impact that a teacher's expectations about a student's performance may have on the student's actual achievements.

**Teacher Expectancy** Student outcomes can also become a self-fulfilling prophecy based on how teachers perceive students. Psychologist Robert Rosenthal and school principal Lenore Jacobson (1968) documented what they referred to as a **teacher-expectancy effect**—the impact that a teacher's expectations about a student's performance may have on the student's actual achievements. They conducted experiments to document this effect.

Rosenthal and Jacobson informed teachers that they were administering a verbal and reasoning pretest to children in a San Francisco elementary school. After administering the tests, the researchers told the teachers that some of the students were "spurters"—children who showed particular academic potential. However, rather than using the actual test scores to make this determination, the researchers randomly selected the 20 percent of the students they identified as spurters. When the

PRINCIPAL

## From Me to You

My daughters Emily and Eleanor make me proud. They get good grades and their scores on the standardized exams are sky high. But as a sociologist, I know that it is a whole lot easier to do well in school if your parents are college graduates. Lori and I provide Em and El with economic, social, and cultural resources in the form of books, programs, and even vacations to historic locations. They are privileged compared to many of their classmates who lack such opportunities. I sometimes wonder how this is any different than cheating on their part. Through such exposure and experiences, they are able to bring resources to exams that are not available to all students.

**UNEARNED ADVANTAGES**

students were later retested, the spurters scored not only significantly higher than they had in previous tests but also significantly higher than their peers. Moreover, teachers evaluated the spurters as more interesting, more curious, and better adjusted than their classmates. These results were striking. Apparently, teachers' perceptions that the students were exceptional led to noticeable improvements in the students' performances. Such effects are of particular concern if factors such as race, ethnicity, class, or gender shape teachers' perceptions.

**Bestowal of Status** As we saw above, part of the public school ideal was that education would contribute to the creation of opportunity and the establishment of a more open society. According to sociologists Kingsley Davis and Wilbert E. Moore (1945), all societies have positions that are more important for the society's survival or that require greater skill or knowledge to perform. Ideally, the institution of education selects those with ability and trains

# The Influence of Parents' Education on Test Performance

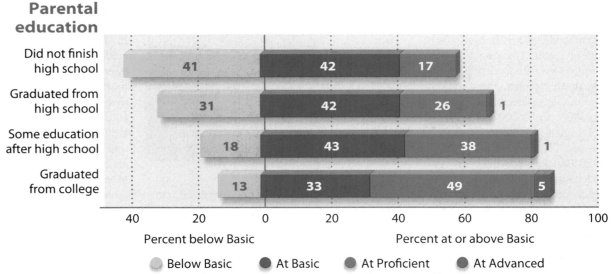

**Parental education**

Note: Percentage distribution of 12th-grade students across NAEP economics achievement levels, by highest level of parental education, 2006.

Source: Planty et al. 2008:25.

them for such positions. We reward people in such positions with social prestige and high pay, Davis and Moore claim, because we value such skills and respect the fact that these individuals sacrificed the time and energy necessary to acquire those skills. For example, not everyone has the skill necessary to become a medical doctor, and in order to encourage people who do have the potential to pursue that path, we promise them sufficient social and economic compensation.

The problem with this model is that, in practice, people apparently are picked for success based not on potential and ability, but on factors such as social class, race, ethnicity, and gender. Although the educational system helps certain poor children to move into middle-class professional positions, it denies most disadvantaged children the same educational opportunities afforded to children of the affluent. In this way, schools tend to preserve social class inequalities in each new generation (Giroux 1988; Pinkerton 2003).

## Did You Know?

. . . Harvard University accepted only 7.1 percent of the 27,462 high school graduates who applied for admission in 2008. Although over 2500 who applied had a perfect score on their SAT, even this was no guarantee of admittance.

Even a single school can reinforce class differences by putting students in tracks. The term **tracking** refers to the practice of placing students in specific curriculum groups on the basis of their test scores and other criteria. Tracking begins very early, often in first-grade reading groups. The practice can reinforce the disadvantages that children from less affluent families may face if they haven't been exposed to reading materials, computers, and other forms of educational stimulation during their early-childhood years. To ignore this connection between tracking and students' race and social class is to fundamentally misunderstand how schools perpetuate the existing social structure.

> **tracking** The practice of placing students in specific curriculum groups on the basis of their test scores and other criteria.

## SOCthink

> > > What experiences have you had with tracking? To what extent do you believe it was effective both for high-track and low-track students? What are its limitations in terms of equal opportunity?

Most recent research on tracking raises questions about its effectiveness, especially for low-ability students. In one study of low-income schools in California, researchers discovered a staggering difference between students who were tracked and those who were not. At one school, all interested students were allowed to enroll in advanced placement (AP) courses, not just those who were selected by the administration. Half the open-enrollment students scored high enough to qualify for college credit—a much higher proportion than in selective programs, in which only 17 percent of students qualified for college credit. Tracking programs do not necessarily identify those students with the potential to succeed (B. Ellison 2008; Sacks 2007).

Sociologists Samuel Bowles and Herbert Gintis (1976) have argued that the educational inequalities produced by tracking are designed to meet the needs of modern capitalist societies. They claim that capitalism requires a skilled, disciplined labor force and that the educational system of the United States is structured with that objective in mind. Citing numerous studies, they offer support for what they call the **correspondence principle.** According to this approach, schools promote the values expected of individuals in each social class and perpetuate social class divisions from one generation to the next. Thus, working-class children, assumed to be destined for subordinate positions, are likely to be placed in high school vocational and general tracks, which emphasize close supervision and compliance with authority. In contrast, young people from more affluent families are likely to be directed to college preparatory tracks, which stress leadership and decision making—the skills they are expected to need as adults.

**Credentialism** Students today also face elevated expectations. When it comes to educational attainment, they now have to go farther just to stay in the same place. Fifty years ago, a high school diploma was the minimum requirement for entry into the paid labor force of the United States. Today, a college diploma is virtually the bare minimum. This change reflects the process of **credentialism**—a term used to describe an increase in the lowest level of education needed to enter a field.

In recent decades, the number of occupations considered professions has risen. Credentialism is one symptom of this trend. Employers and occupational associations typically contend that such changes are a logical response to the increasing complexity of many jobs. However, in many cases, employers raise the degree requirements for a position simply because all applicants have achieved the existing minimum credential (D. Brown 2001; Hurn 1985).

One potential effect of credentialism is to reinforce social inequality. Applicants from poor

**Did You Know?**

>. . . The likelihood of going to college directly after high school varies by family income. For students from high-income families, 81 percent went directly to college; 61 percent went from middle-income families, and 51 percent from low-income families.

and minority backgrounds are especially likely to suffer from the escalation of qualifications, since they lack the financial resources needed to obtain degree after degree. In addition, upgrading of credentials serves the self-interest of the two groups most responsible for this trend. First, educational institutions profit from prolonging the investment of time and money that people make by staying in school. Moreover, as C. J. Hurn (1985) has suggested, current jobholders have a stake in raising occupational requirements, since credentialism can increase the status of an occupation and lead to demands for higher pay. Max Weber anticipated this possibility as early as 1916, concluding that the "universal clamor for the creation of educational certificates in all fields makes for the formation of a privileged stratum in businesses and in offices" (Gerth and Mills 1958:240–41).

**Gender** The educational system of the United States, like many other social institutions, has long been characterized by discriminatory treatment of women. In 1833, Oberlin College became the first institution of higher learning to admit female students—some 200 years after the founding of the first men's college in the United States (Harvard). Oberlin, however, believed that women should aspire to become wives and mothers, not lawyers and intellectuals. In addition to attending classes, female students washed men's clothing, cared for their rooms, and served them meals.

**5 Movies on EDUCATION**

**Dangerous Minds**
*An ex-marine teacher changes an inner-city school.*

**Dead Poets Society**
*An English professor teaches his students to "seize the day."*

**The History Boys**
*An unruly class of gifted boys in search of sex, sports, and higher education.*

**Good Will Hunting**
*A janitor at MIT has a gift for mathematics greater than that of the school's students.*

**Finding Forrester**
*An author mentors a teen writing prodigy.*

**correspondence principle** The tendency of schools to promote the values expected of individuals in each social class and to prepare students for the types of jobs typically held by members of their class.

**credentialism** An increase in the lowest level of education required to enter a field.

In the 20th century, sexism in education showed up in many ways—in textbooks with negative stereotypes of women, in counselors' pressure on female students to prepare for "women's work," and in unequal funding for women's and men's athletic programs. But perhaps nowhere was educational discrimination more evident than in the employment of teachers. The positions of university

Education does establish social order and provide opportunities for individuals to get ahead. At the same time, in preserving the existing order, it reproduces practices of inequality. Sociology allows us to better understand how these seemingly contradictory goals can be accomplished through education. As the experience with Title IX demonstrates, positive social change is possible. Having a better

> Good schools, like good societies and good families, celebrate and cherish diversity.
>
> Deborah Meier

professor and college administrator, which hold relatively high status in the United States, were generally filled by men. Public school teachers, who earn much lower salaries, were largely female.

Today women have much greater educational opportunity, largely as a result of women's movements that worked for social change. Title IX of the Education Amendments of 1972 played a pivotal role in expanding access. It states, "No person in the United States shall, on the basis of sex, be excluded from participation in, be denied the benefits of, or be subjected to discrimination under any education program or activity receiving Federal financial assistance." While Title IX is most commonly associated with equal opportunity for women in athletics, among other things, it also eliminated sex-segregated classes and prohibited sex discrimination in admissions. And women have made the most of this opportunity. The proportion of women who continue their schooling has risen dramatically. As recently as 1969, twice as many men as women received college degrees; today, women outnumber men at college commencements. Moreover, women's access to graduate education and to medical, dental, and law schools has increased significantly in recent decades. In fact, women now regularly outperform men academically.

appreciation of how education functions enables us to more effectively work toward realizing the initial goal of education: to provide opportunity and a more open society.

## >> Schools as Formal Organizations

The early advocates of public education would be amazed at the scale of the education system in the United States in the 21st century. For example, California's public school system, the largest in the nation, currently enrolls as many children as there were in secondary schools nationwide in 1950 (Bureau of the Census 1975:368; 2004a).

In many respects, today's schools, when viewed as an example of a formal organization, are similar to factories, hospitals, and business firms. Like those organizations, schools do not operate autonomously; they are influenced by the market of potential students. This is especially true of private schools, but it could have broader application if adoption of voucher plans and other school choice programs continues to increase. The parallels between schools and other types of formal organizations will become more apparent as we examine the bureaucratic nature of schools, teaching as an occupation, and the student subculture (K. Dougherty and Hammack 1992).

## SOCthink

> > > Women's participation in college athletics has increased over 500 percent since 1972, from 31,852 then to 170,526 in 2005–2006. And high school rates have risen almost 1000 percent, with 2.95 million participants in 2005. To what extent would we have seen such an increase had it not been for a law that mandated increased opportunity? How might increased opportunity for women in athletics have an impact on increased opportunity in other areas?

### THE BUREAUCRATIZATION OF SCHOOLS

It simply is not possible for a single teacher to transmit all the necessary culture and skills to children who will enter many diverse occupations. The growing number of students being served by school systems and the greater degree of specialization required within a technologically complex society have combined to bureaucratize schools.

In many respects, schools put into practice all of Max Weber's principles of bureaucracy that we considered in Chapter 5. When it comes to the division of labor, teachers specialize in particular age levels and specific subjects. Schools are hierarchically organized, with teachers reporting to principals, who are themselves answerable to the superintendent of schools and the board of education. In terms of written rules and regulations, teachers must submit written lesson plans, and students, teachers, and administrators must all adhere to established policies and procedures or face sanctions for not doing so. As schools grow, they become increasingly impersonal, and teachers are expected to treat all students in the same way, regardless of their distinctive personalities and learning needs. Finally, hiring and promotion—and even grading—are based on technical qualifications alone, and standards are established and rubrics created in an effort to ensure this practice.

The trend toward more centralized education particularly affects disadvantaged people, for whom education promises to be a path to opportunity. The standardization of educational curricula, including textbooks, generally reflects the values, interests, and lifestyles of the most powerful groups in our society, and may ignore those of racial and ethnic minorities. In addition, in comparison to the affluent, the disadvantaged often lack the time, financial resources, and knowledge necessary to sort through complex educational bureaucracies and to organize effective lobbying groups. As a result, low-income and minority parents will have even less influence over citywide and statewide

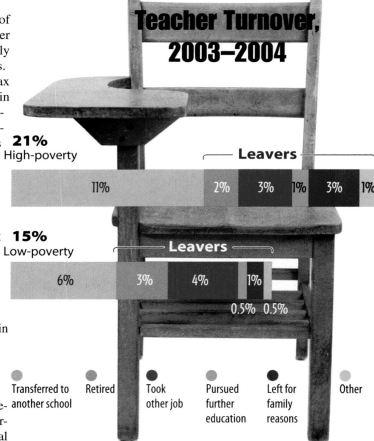

## Teacher Turnover, 2003–2004

**21%**
High-poverty

| 11% | 2% | 3% | 1% | 3% | 1% |

**Leavers**

**15%**
Low-poverty

| 6% | 3% | 4% | 1% | 0.5% | 0.5% |

**Leavers**

- Transferred to another school
- Retired
- Took other job
- Pursued further education
- Left for family reasons
- Other

*Note:* Percentage of public K–12 teachers who did not teach in the same school the following year, by poverty level of school and the reason teachers left.
*Source:* Planty et al. 2008:51.

educational administrators than they have over local school officials (Bowles and Gintis 1976; M. Katz 1971).

## TEACHING AS A PROFESSION

As schools become more bureaucratic, teachers increasingly encounter the conflicts inherent in serving as a professional within the context of a bureaucracy. The organization follows the principles of hierarchy and expects adherence to its rules, but professionalism demands the individual responsibility of the practitioner. While teachers want to practice their craft as professionals, the demands on their time remain diverse and contradictory. Conflicts arise from having to serve simultaneously as instructor, disciplinarian, administrator, and employee of a school district.

As professionals, teachers feel pressure from a number of directions. First, the level of formal schooling required for teaching remains high, and the public has begun to call for new competency examinations. Second, teachers' salaries are significantly lower than those of many comparably educated professionals and skilled workers. Finally, the overall prestige of the teaching profession has declined over the past decade. Many teachers, disappointed and frustrated, have left the

## Average Salaries for Teachers, 2007

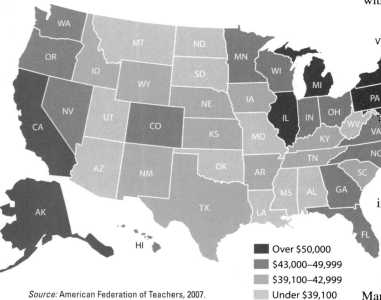

- Over $50,000
- $43,000–49,999
- $39,100–42,999
- Under $39,100

*Source:* American Federation of Teachers, 2007.

educational world for careers in other professions. In fact, between a quarter and a third of new teachers quit within their first three years, and as many as half leave poor urban schools within their first five years (Wallis 2008). Even within a single year, teacher turnover is significant; in high-poverty areas, over 20 percent of teachers did not teach in the same school the following year.

## STUDENT SUBCULTURES

Schools also provide for students' social and recreational needs. Education helps toddlers and young children develop interpersonal skills that are essential during adolescence and adulthood. In their high school and college years, students may meet future spouses and establish lifelong friendships.

School leaders often seek to develop a sense of school spirit and collective identity, but student subcultures are actually complex and diverse. High school cliques and social groups may crop up according to race, social class, physical attractiveness, academic placement, athletic ability, and leadership roles in the school and community. In his classic community study of "Elmtown," August B. Hollingshead (1975) found some 259 distinct cliques in a single high school. The cliques, whose average size was five, were centered on the school itself, on recreational activities, and on religious and community groups.

Amid these close-knit and often rigidly segregated cliques, some students get left out. Historically, gay and lesbian students have been particularly vulnerable to such exclusion. Many have organized to establish their own stronger sense of collective identity, including through the

establishment of gay–straight alliances (GSAs)—school-sponsored support groups that bring gay teens together with sympathetic straight peers. Begun in Los Angeles in 1984, these programs numbered nearly 3000 nationwide in 2005.

We can find a similar diversity of student groups at the college level. Burton Clark and Martin Trow (1966) and, more recently, Helen Lefkowitz Horowitz (1987) have identified four distinctive subcultures among college students:

- The *collegiate* subculture focuses on having fun and socializing. These students define what constitutes a "reasonable" amount of academic work (and what amount of work is "excessive" and leads to being labeled as a "grind"). Members of the collegiate subculture have little commitment to academic pursuits. Athletes often fit into this subculture.

- The *academic* subculture identifies with the intellectual concerns of the faculty and values knowledge for its own sake.

- The *vocational* subculture is interested primarily in career prospects and views college as a means of obtaining degrees that are essential for advancement.

- The *nonconformist* subculture is hostile to the college environment and seeks out ideas that may or may not relate to academic studies. This group may find outlets through campus publications or issue-oriented groups.

Each college student is eventually exposed to these competing subcultures and must determine which (if any) seems most in line with his or her feelings and interests.

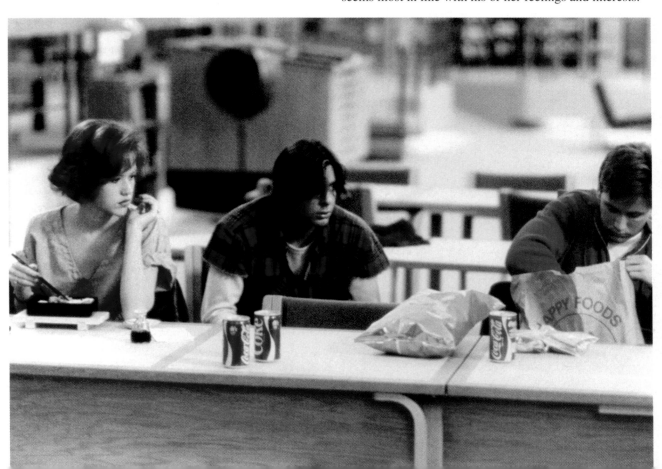

The typology used by the researchers reminds us that the school is a complex social organization—almost like a community with different neighborhoods. Of course, these four subcultures are not the only ones evident on college campuses in the United States. For example, one might find subcultures of Vietnam veterans or former full-time homemakers at community colleges and four-year commuter institutions. As more and more students from minority groups decide to continue their formal education beyond high school, subcultures based on race and ethnicity will cotinue to grow. Future graduating classes are projected to be more diverse.

Sociologist Joe R. Feagin has studied a distinctive collegiate subculture: Black students at predominantly White universities. These students must function academically and socially within universities where there are few Black faculty members or Black administrators, where harassment of Blacks by campus police is common, and where the curricula place little emphasis on Black contributions. Feagin (1989:11) suggests that "for minority students life at a predominantly White college or university means long-term encounters with pervasive whiteness." In Feagin's view, African American students at such institutions experience both blatant and subtle racial discrimination, which has a cumulative impact that can seriously damage the students' confidence (see also Feagin et al. 1996).

## HOMESCHOOLING

Some people have decided to opt out of the formal organization of schools altogether. They look at the state of schools described above and, in conjunction with additional concerns, decide to educate their children themselves. More than 2 million students are now being educated at home—about 4 percent of the K–12 school population (Ray 2006).

After the establishment of public schools in the 1800s, most families that taught their children at home lived in isolated environments or held strict religious views. Religion continues to play a significant role in the decision to homeschool, but increasing numbers of people now are opting to do so for other reasons. Poor academic quality, peer pressure, and school violence are motivating many parents to teach their children at home. Concern about the school environment was cited by 85.4 percent of families that opted to homeschool their children (Princiotta and Bielick 2006). In addition, some immigrants choose homeschooling as a way to ease their children's transition to a new society. For example, increasing numbers of the nation's growing Arab American population have joined the movement toward homeschooling (B. Cooper and Sureau 2007; MacFarquhar 2008).

Critics argue that homeschooled children are isolated from the larger community, which

## Public High School Graduates by Race and Ethnicity, 2019 (projected)

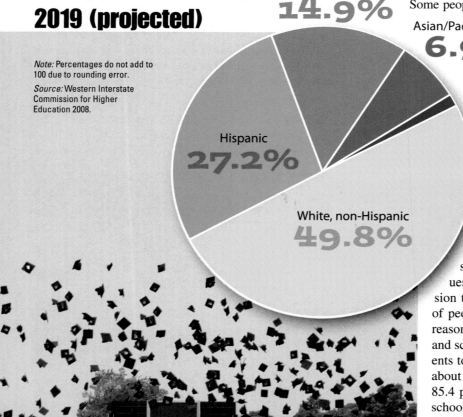

Note: Percentages do not add to 100 due to rounding error.

Source: Western Interstate Commission for Higher Education 2008.

Black, non-Hispanic
**14.9%**

Asian/Pacific Islander
**6.9%**

American Indian/Alaska Native
**1.3%**

Hispanic
**27.2%**

White, non-Hispanic
**49.8%**

causes them to lose the opportunity to improve their socialization skills. Supporters of homeschooling counter that children can do just as well or better in home schools as in public schools. They claim that homeschooled children benefit from contact with others besides their own age group. They also see homeschooling as a good alternative for children who suffer from attention-deficit/hyperactivity disorder (ADHD) and learning disorders (LDs). Such children often do better in smaller classes, which present fewer distractions to disturb their concentration. A study by the Home School Legal Defense Association (2005), a home school advocacy organization, reported that homeschooled students score higher than others on standardized tests, in every subject and every grade.

## SOCthink

> > > What do you think are the advantages and disadvantages of being homeschooled? How might it contribute to a stronger sense of identity? How might it threaten the social order?

The rise in homeschooling points to concerns people have about the institutionalized practice of education. In a sense, this movement represents a rejection of the larger society and its norms and values as institutionalized in education and is part of the trend toward greater individualism and pluralism. In a survey of families that homeschooled their children, 72.3 percent cited providing religious or moral instruction as a factor in their decision to homeschool (Princiotta and Bielick 2006). In such cases, parents are often concerned that the instruction their children receive at school will contradict or undermine the faith they learn at home. Although such new forms of schooling may better meet the individual needs of diverse groups in today's society, they also tend to undermine the historical commitment to education as a means of fostering unity among society as a whole.

# >> Defining Religion

Religion historically has played a powerful role in people's lives, and it continues to shape individual behavior, national policy, and international actions. It has been a central part of social life but, just as we saw with families, religion is not a singular thing. It takes a variety of forms among different peoples and over time. Sociologists have sought to better understand both what it is and what it does.

As with families, sociologists have taken two main approaches to defining religion. The first focuses on the substance of religion, or what it is. The second emphasizes the functions religion performs, or what it does.

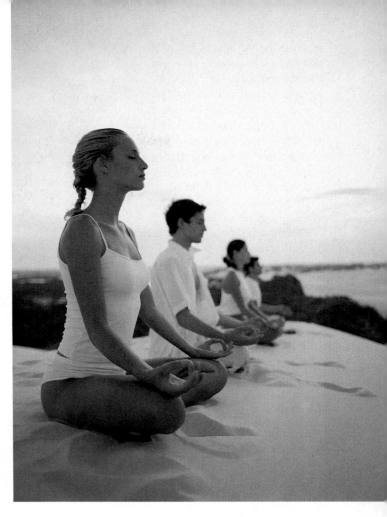

## SUBSTANCE: WHAT RELIGION IS

According to a **substantive definition of religion,** religion has a unique content or substance that separates it from other forms of knowledge and belief. Most commonly, this unique focus involves some conception of a supernatural realm, such as heaven, but it does not have to be outside the physical world. The key is that religion centers around something that goes above and beyond the mundane realities of our everyday existence, that points to something larger, and that calls for some response from us in terms of how we think and act. Sociologist Peter Berger (1969) provided a substantive definition of religion as "the human enterprise by which a sacred cosmos is established" (p. 25). The sacred here refers to that extraordinary realm that becomes the focus of religious faith and practice. It provides believers with meaning, order, and coherence. In describing that sacred realm, people might touch on concepts such as gods and goddess, angels and demons, heaven and hell, nirvana, or other beings or realms. A society with broad agreement about the nature and importance of this sacred realm is, by definition, more religious.

> **substantive definition of religion** The idea that religion has a unique content or substance relating to the sacred that separates it from other forms of knowledge and belief.

Following a substantive approach, sociologists focus on the ways in which religious groups rally around what they define to be sacred. The **sacred** encompasses elements beyond everyday life that inspire respect, awe, and even fear. People interact with the sacred realm through ritual practices, such as prayer or sacrifice. Because believers have faith in the sacred, they accept what they cannot understand. The sacred realm exists in contrast to the **profane,** which includes the ordinary and commonplace.

Different religious groups define their understanding of the sacred or profane in different ways. For example, who or what constitutes "god" varies between Muslims, Christians, and Hindus. Even within a group, different believers may treat the same object as sacred or profane, depending on whether it connects them to the sacred realm. Ordinarily, a piece of bread is profane, but it becomes sacred during the Christian practice of communion because through it believers enter into connection with God. Similarly, a candelabrum becomes sacred to Jews if it is a menorah. For Confucians and Taoists, incense sticks are not mere decorative items, but highly valued offerings to the gods in religious ceremonies that mark the new and full moons.

**sacred** Elements beyond everyday life that inspire respect, awe, and even fear.
**profane** The ordinary and commonplace elements of life, as distinguished from the sacred.
**functionalist definition of religion** The idea that religion unifies believers into a community through shared practices and a common set of beliefs relative to sacred things.

## FUNCTION: WHAT RELIGIONS DO

A functionalist approach focuses less on what religion is than on what religions do, with a particular emphasis on how religions contribute to social order. According to a **functionalist definition of religion,** religion unifies believers into a community through shared practices and a common set of beliefs relative to sacred things. The emphasis here is on the unifying dimension of religion rather than on the substance of that which unifies. For functionalists, the supernatural or something like it is not an essential part of religion. Religion need not have gods or goddesses, an afterlife, or other such conventional elements. In fact, many social practices, such as being a sports fan, can function like religion for the individual and for society.

The functional approach to defining religion has roots in the work of Émile Durkheim. He defined religion as "a unified system of beliefs and practices relative to sacred things, that is to say things set apart and forbidden—beliefs and practices which unite into a single moral community, called a 'church,' all those who adhere to them" ([1887] 1972:224). This definition points to three aspects sociologists should focus on when studying religion: a unified system of beliefs and practices, relative to sacred things, and in the context of community.

The first element of Durkheim's functional approach is the unified system of beliefs and practices. What those beliefs and practices are matters less than the fact that they are shared. Terms historically used to describe religious beliefs include *doctrine, dogma, creeds,* and *scripture,* all representing principles believers share through faith. Practices refer to shared rituals such as attendance at services, prayer, meditation, and fasting. Because beliefs and practices are central to religion, regardless of which definitional approach you take, we will look at them in more detail below.

Unlike the substantive approach, Durkheim's emphasis on sacred things focuses less on the objects themselves than on the believers' attitude toward those objects. Sacred objects and sacred places convey a sense of awe, and religion calls upon believers to treat them with reverence and care. Roman Catholics, for example, treat the bread and wine of communion with respect because they believe that the sacrament transforms those elements into the body and blood of Christ. For Muslims, the Qur'an is a sacred object, and the Kaaba in Mecca is a sacred place. In the functional approach to religion, however, sacredness is in the eyes of the beholders. Any object can be sacred so long as people define it as such and treat it accordingly.

The most important component of Durkheim's definition is this third part: community. It is not the church,

## Hot or Not?

Is it appropriate for religious leaders, such as pastors, priests, rabbis, or imams, to discuss political issues during religious services?

# From Me to You

*I confess to being a Green Bay Packers fan. I follow them religiously. Even though I know better, I practice superstitions in the hope that they will help, including wearing a lucky shirt, not talking on the phone during the game, and though I am embarrassed to admit it, doing a celebratory dance around the dining room table after the Packers score a touchdown, with high-fives for everyone including the dog. I was fortunate enough to be at "the frozen tundra of Lambeau Field" to see Brett Favre play his last game with the Packers, and I have tucked the ticket stub away, preserving it as if it were a sacred object. Now I pray the team didn't make a mistake letting him get away..*

mosque, or temple as a building that matters, but the unification of a body of believers into a shared community. What they believe, what they practice, or what they view as sacred is less important than that they have these beliefs, practices, and shared sacred things in common.

## SOCthink

> > > What other things function like religion for us? How about followers of bands, TV shows, or politics? To what extent might consumerism or even work function like religion?

As suggested above, according to this approach, religion need not look like what we conventionally think of as religion. Anything that does what Durkheim's three elements do can function as religion. Just as our understanding of what families are has expanded to include people who are "like family" to us, so also has the definition of religion expanded to include things that function like religion. Sports provides a classic example. When it comes to beliefs and practices, sports fans—short for *fanatics,* a term that his-

torically had religious connotations—share beliefs about the superiority of their team and regularly practice rituals in hopes that it will help their team win. They may wear the same jersey to watch the game, sit in the same chair, or do a touchdown dance after their team scores, all out of superstitious fear that failure to do so will lead to a negative outcome for the game. In terms of sacred things, there are autographs, jerseys, balls, and so on. In terms of a sacred place, there is the stadium where the team plays, often referred to by fans as a shrine. Finally, fans are united into a community with other fans of the team. Being a fan of the team becomes part of their identity. It provides them with joy, satisfaction, and even a sense of purpose. In a personal essay recounting his obsession with soccer, Michael Elliott (2005) put it this way: "What does being a fan mean? It means you will never walk alone" (p. 76).

## >> Components of Religion

In studying religion, regardless of which definitional approach they take, sociologists investigate components of religion that are common to most groups. Their goal is to gain a more complete picture of the role religion plays for both individuals and groups. Sociologists using both approaches focus on how religious groups organize beliefs, rituals, experience, and community. We will look at some examples of what they learn about religion by focusing on each in turn.

### BELIEFS

Some people believe in life after death, in supreme beings with unlimited powers, or in supernatural forces. **Religious beliefs** are statements to which members of a particular religion adhere. These views can vary dramatically from religion to religion.

In the late 1960s, a significant shift occurred in the nature of religious belief in the United States. Denominations that held to relatively liberal interpretations of religious scripture (such as the Presbyterians, Methodists, and Lutherans) declined in membership, while those that held to more conservative interpretations and sought a return to the fundamentals of the faith grew in numbers. The term **fundamentalism** refers to a rigid adherence to core religious doctrines. Often, fundamentalism is accompanied by a literal application of scripture or historical beliefs to today's world. Fundamentalism grows out of a sense that the world is falling apart due to a decline in true religious belief and practice. Fundamentalists see themselves as presenting a positive vision for the future through a return to the purity of the original religious message.

> **religious belief** A statement to which members of a particular religion adhere.
> **fundamentalism** Rigid adherence to core religious doctrines, often accompanied by a literal application of scripture or historical beliefs to today's world.

The phrase "religious fundamentalism" was first applied to Protestants in the United States who took a literal interpretation of the Bible, but fundamentalism is found worldwide among most major religious groups, including Roman Catholicism, Islam, and Judaism. Fundamentalists vary immensely in their beliefs and behavior. Some stress the need to be strict in their own personal faith but take little interest in broad social issues. Others are watchful of societal actions, such as government policies, that they see as conflicting with fundamentalist doctrine.

Christian fundamentalists in the United States have fought against the teaching of evolution in public schools because they believe not only that it represents a threat to their beliefs but also that it is itself a type of religious faith in naturalism (as opposed to the supernaturalism of God). The first, and most famous, court case over the teaching of evolution in public schools occurred in 1925 and is often referred to as the "Scopes Monkey Trial." In that trial, high school biology teacher John T. Scopes was convicted of violating a Tennessee law that made it a crime to teach the scientific theory of evolution in public schools. Since that time there have been numerous other court challenges. The most recent major case, known as the "Dover Case," occurred in Pennsylvania in 2005. Those opposed to the teaching of evolution sought to force schools to teach the "science" of intelligent design—the idea that life is so complex that there had to be some form of intelligence behind its creation. The judge ruled that intelligent design was a variation on creationism, the teaching of which in a public school would violate the separation of church and state.

## RITUALS

**Religious rituals** are practices required or expected of members of a faith. Rituals usually honor the divine power (or powers) worshiped by believers; they also remind adherents of their religious duties and responsibilities. Rituals and beliefs can be interdependent; rituals generally affirm beliefs, as in a public or private statement confessing a sin. Like any social institution, religion develops distinctive norms to structure people's behavior. Moreover, sanctions are attached to religious rituals, in the form of either rewards (such as bar mitzvah gifts) or penalties (such as expulsion from a religious institution for violation of norms).

Rituals may be very simple, such as saying grace at a meal or observing a moment of silence to commemorate someone's death. Other rituals, such as the process of canonizing a saint, are quite elaborate. Most religious rituals in the United States focus on services conducted at houses of worship. Attendance at a service, silent and spoken prayers, communion, and the singing of hymns and chants are common forms of ritual behavior that generally take place in group settings. These rituals serve as important face-to-face encounters in which people reinforce their religious beliefs and their commitment to their faith. Religious participation varies widely from country to country.

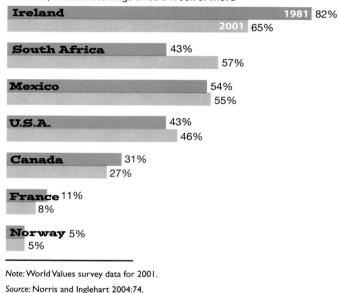

## Going GLOBAL

### Religious Participation in Selected Countries, 1981 and 2001

Percentage attending religious services other than weddings, funerals, and christenings once a week or more

| Country | 1981 | 2001 |
|---|---|---|
| Ireland | 82% | 65% |
| South Africa | 43% | 57% |
| Mexico | 54% | 55% |
| U.S.A. | 43% | 46% |
| Canada | 31% | 27% |
| France | 11% | 8% |
| Norway | 5% | 5% |

*Note:* World Values survey data for 2001.

*Source:* Norris and Inglehart 2004:74.

For Muslims, a very important ritual is the *hajj*—a pilgrimage to the Grand Mosque in Mecca, Saudi Arabia. Every Muslim who is physically and financially able is expected to make this trip at least once. Each year 2 million pilgrims go to Mecca during the one-week period indicated by the Islamic lunar calendar. Muslims from all over the world make the *hajj*, including those in the United States, where many tours are arranged to facilitate the trip.

## EXPERIENCE

In the sociological study of religion, the term **religious experience** refers to the feeling or perception of being in direct contact with the ultimate reality, such as a divine

**Did You Know?**

...About two-thirds of incoming first-year college students say that they gain spiritual strength by trusting in a higher power. Almost one-half "frequently" feel loved by God.

being, or of being overcome with religious emotion. A religious experience may be rather slight, such as the feeling of exaltation a person might receive from hearing a choir sing Handel's "Hallelujah Chorus." Many religious experiences, however, are more profound, such as a Muslim's experience on a *hajj*. In his autobiography, the late African American activist Malcolm X (1964:338) wrote of his *hajj* and how deeply moved he was by the way that Muslims in Mecca came together across racial and color lines. For Malcolm X, the color blindness of the Muslim world "proved to me the power of the One God."

Another profound religious experience for many Christians is being "born again," which involves making a personal commitment to Jesus Christ, marking a major turning point in one's life. According to a 2006 national survey, 43 percent of people in the United States claim they have had a born-again Christian experience at some time in their lives. An earlier survey found that Southern Baptists (75 percent) were the most likely to report such experiences; in contrast, only 21 percent of Catholics and 24 percent of Episcopalians stated that they had been born again.

The collective nature of religion, as emphasized by Durkheim, is evident in these statistics. The beliefs and rituals of a particular faith can create an atmosphere either friendly toward or less conducive to this type of religious experience. Thus, a Baptist would be encouraged to "come forward" to make such a commitment and then to share her or his experience with others. An Episcopalian who claimed to have been born again, on the other hand, would receive much less attention within his or her church (Gallup 2008c; Gallup Opinion Index 1978).

## COMMUNITY

Religious communities organize themselves in varieties of ways. Specific structures such as churches and synagogues have been constructed for religious worship; individuals have been trained for occupational roles within various fields. These developments make it possible to distinguish clearly between the sacred and secular parts of one's life— a distinction that could not be made easily in earlier times, when religion was largely a family activity carried out in the home.

Sociologists find it useful to distinguish between four basic forms of organization: the ecclesia, the denomination, the sect, and the new religious movement, or cult. We can see differences among these four forms of organization in their size, power, degree of commitment expected from members, and historical ties to other faiths.

**Ecclesiae** When studying how groups organize their communities, sociologists have used the term **ecclesia** (plural, *ecclesiae*) to describe a religious organization that claims to include most or all members of a society and is recognized as the national or official religion. Since virtually everyone belongs to the faith, membership is by birth rather than conscious decision. The classic example in sociology was the Roman Catholic Church in medieval Europe. Contemporary examples of ecclesiae include Islam in Saudi Arabia and Buddhism in Thailand. However, significant differences exist within this category. In Saudi Arabia's Islamic regime, leaders of the ecclesia hold vast power over actions of the state. In contrast, the historical state church in Sweden, Lutheranism, holds no such power over the Riksdag (parliament) or the prime minister.

Generally, ecclesiae are conservative, in that they do not challenge the leaders of a secular government. In a society with an ecclesia, the political and religious institutions often act in harmony and reinforce each other's power in their relative spheres of influence. In the modern world, ecclesiae are declining in power.

> **religious ritual** A practice required or expected of members of a faith.
> **religious experience** The feeling or perception of being in direct contact with the ultimate reality, such as a divine being, or of being overcome with religious emotion.
> **ecclesia** A religious organization that claims to include most or all members of a society and is recognized as the national or official religion.
> **denomination** A large, organized religion that is not officially linked to the state or government.

**Denominations** A **denomination** is a large, organized religion that is not officially linked to the state or government. Like an ecclesia, it tends to have an explicit set of beliefs, a defined system of authority, and a generally respected position in society. Denominations often claim large segments of a population as members. Generally, children accept the denomination of their parents and give little thought to membership in other faiths. Although considered respectable and not viewed as a challenge to the secular government, unlike ecclesia, denominations lack the

# Major Religious Traditions in the United States

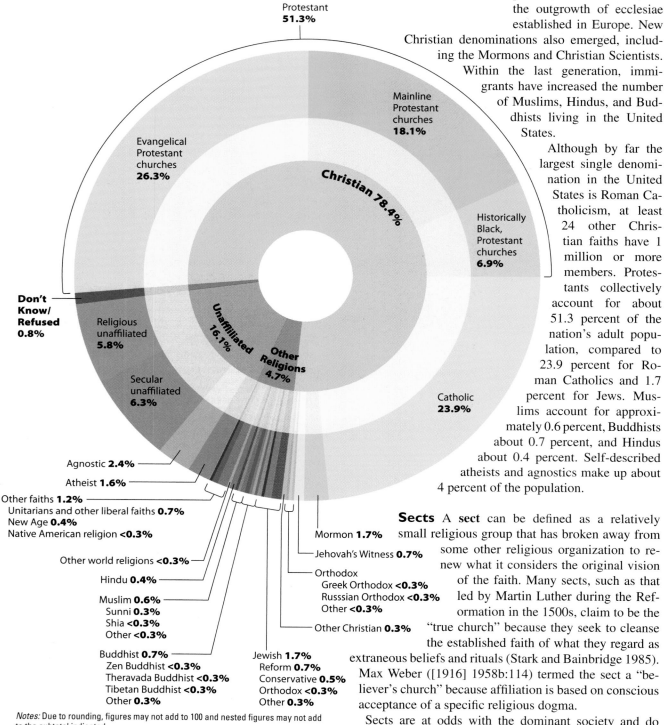

**Protestant 51.3%**

Mainline Protestant churches **18.1%**

Evangelical Protestant churches **26.3%**

Christian 78.4%

Historically Black, Protestant churches **6.9%**

**Don't Know/ Refused 0.8%**

Religious unaffiliated **5.8%**

Unaffiliated 16.1%

Other Religions 4.7%

Secular unaffiliated **6.3%**

Catholic **23.9%**

Agnostic **2.4%**

Atheist **1.6%**

Other faiths **1.2%**
Unitarians and other liberal faiths **0.7%**
New Age **0.4%**
Native American religion **<0.3%**

Other world religions **<0.3%**

Hindu **0.4%**

Muslim **0.6%**
Sunni **0.3%**
Shia **<0.3%**
Other **<0.3%**

Buddhist **0.7%**
Zen Buddhist **<0.3%**
Theravada Buddhist **<0.3%**
Tibetan Buddhist **<0.3%**
Other **0.3%**

Jewish **1.7%**
Reform **0.7%**
Conservative **0.5%**
Orthodox **<0.3%**
Other **0.3%**

Other Christian **0.3%**

Orthodox
Greek Orthodox **<0.3%**
Russsian Orthodox **<0.3%**
Other **<0.3%**

Jehovah's Witness **0.7%**

Mormon **1.7%**

*Notes:* Due to rounding, figures may not add to 100 and nested figures may not add to the subtotal indicated.

*Source:* http://religions.pewforum.org/pdf/report-religious-landscap-study-full.pdf.

Roman Catholics, Episcopalians, and Lutherans, are the outgrowth of ecclesiae established in Europe. New Christian denominations also emerged, including the Mormons and Christian Scientists. Within the last generation, immigrants have increased the number of Muslims, Hindus, and Buddhists living in the United States.

Although by far the largest single denomination in the United States is Roman Catholicism, at least 24 other Christian faiths have 1 million or more members. Protestants collectively account for about 51.3 percent of the nation's adult population, compared to 23.9 percent for Roman Catholics and 1.7 percent for Jews. Muslims account for approximately 0.6 percent, Buddhists about 0.7 percent, and Hindus about 0.4 percent. Self-described atheists and agnostics make up about 4 percent of the population.

**Sects** A **sect** can be defined as a relatively small religious group that has broken away from some other religious organization to renew what it considers the original vision of the faith. Many sects, such as that led by Martin Luther during the Reformation in the 1500s, claim to be the "true church" because they seek to cleanse the established faith of what they regard as extraneous beliefs and rituals (Stark and Bainbridge 1985). Max Weber ([1916] 1958b:114) termed the sect a "believer's church" because affiliation is based on conscious acceptance of a specific religious dogma.

Sects are at odds with the dominant society and do not seek to become established national religions. Unlike ecclesiae and denominations, they require intensive commitments and demonstrations of belief by members. Partly owing to their outsider status, sects frequently exhibit a higher degree of religious fervor and loyalty than more established religious groups. They actively recruit adults as new members, and acceptance comes through conversion.

Sects are often short-lived. Those that are able to survive may become less antagonistic to society over time and

official recognition and power held by an ecclesia (Doress and Porter 1977).

The United States is home to a large number of denominations. This diversity is largely the result of the nation's immigrant heritage. Many settlers brought with them the religious commitments native to their homelands. Some Christian denominations in the United States, such as the begin to resemble denominations. In a few instances, sects have been able to endure over several generations while remaining fairly separate from society. Sociologist J. Milton Yinger (1970:226–73) uses the term **established sect** to describe a religious group that is the outgrowth of a sect, yet remains isolated from society. The Hutterites, Jehovah's Witnesses, Seventh-Day Adventists, and Amish are contemporary examples of established sects in the United States.

Throughout the world, including the United States, Muslims are divided into a variety of sects, such as Sunni and Shia (or Shiite). The great majority of Muslims in the United States are Sunni Muslims—literally, those who follow the *Sunnah,* or way of the Prophet. Compared to other Muslims, Sunnis tend to be more moderate in their religious orthodoxy. The Shia, who come primarily from Iraq and Iran, are the second-largest group. Shia Muslims are more attentive to guidance from accepted Islamic scholars than are Sunnis. About two-thirds of Muslims in the United States are native-born citizens.

**Cults or New Religious Movements** Historically, sociologists have used the term *cult* to describe alternative religious groups with unconventional religious beliefs. Partly as a result of the notoriety generated by some of these more extreme groups—such as the Heaven's Gate cult members who committed mass suicide in 1997 so that their spirits might be freed to catch a ride on the spaceship hidden behind the Hale-Bopp comet—many sociologists have abandoned the use of the term. In its place they have adopted the expression "new religious movement."

A **new religious movement (NRM)** or **cult** is generally a small, alternative religious group that represents either a new faith community or a major innovation in an existing faith. NRMs are similar to sects in that they tend to be small and are often viewed as less respectable than more established faiths. Unlike sects, however, NRMs normally do not result from schisms or breaks with established ecclesiae or denominations. Some cults, such as those focused on UFO sightings, may be totally unrelated to existing faiths. Even when a cult does accept certain fundamental tenets of a dominant faith—such as a belief in Jesus as divine or in Mohammad as a messenger of God—it will offer new revelations or insights to justify its claim to being a more advanced religion (Stark and Bainbridge 1979, 1985).

> **sect** A relatively small religious group that has broken away from some other religious organization to renew what it considers the original vision of the faith.
> **established sect** A religious group that is the outgrowth of a sect, yet remains isolated from society.
> **new religious movement (NRM)** or **cult** A small, alternative faith community that represents either a new religion or a major innovation in an existing faith.

Like sects, NRMs may be transformed over time into other types of religious organization. An example is the Christian Science Church, which began as a new religious movement under the leadership of Mary Baker Eddy. Today, this church exhibits the characteristics of a denomination. In fact, most major religions, including Christianity, began as cults. NRMs may be in the early stages of developing into a denomination or new religion, or they may just as easily fade away through the loss of members or weak leadership (Schaefer and Zellner 2007).

### Comparing Forms of Religious Organization

How can we determine whether a particular religious group falls into the sociological category of ecclesia, denomination, sect, or NRM? As we have seen, these types of religious organization have somewhat different relationships to society. Ecclesiae are recognized as national churches; denominations, although not officially approved by the state, are generally widely respected. In contrast, sects and NRMs are much more likely to be at odds with the larger culture.

Still, ecclesiae, denominations, and sects are best viewed as types along a continuum in terms of their level of accommodation with the larger society. With ecclesiae, church and state merge together as one. On the other end, however, sects find themselves at odds with the dominant society. Denominations fall between the two. Because they offer an alternative to the mainstream, NRMs might fall close to sects.

secularization Religion's diminishing influence in the public sphere, especially in politics and the economy.

But NRMs could be said to lie outside the continuum because they define themselves in terms of a new view of life rather than in terms of existing religious faiths. Since the United States has no ecclesiae, sociologists studying this country's religions have focused on denominations, sects, and NRMs.

## >> World Religions

Early sociologists predicted that modern societies would experience widespread **secularization,** which involves religion's diminishing influence in the public sphere, especially in politics and the economy. Nevertheless, religion continues to play a significant role. Worldwide, tremendous diversity exists in religious beliefs and practices.

Overall, about 85 percent of the world's population adheres to some religion; only about 15 percent is nonreligious. This level of adherence changes over time and also varies by country and age group. In the United States today, those who are nonreligious account for about 10–14 percent of the population; in 1900, however, they consti-

tuted a mere 1.3 percent of all Americans. In 2006, 19 percent of incoming U.S. college students had no religious preference compared to 10 percent of their mothers (Hout and Fischer 2002; Pryor et al. 2006; Winseman 2005).

Christianity is the largest single faith in the world; the second largest is Islam (see the table on page 184). Although global news events often suggest an inherent conflict between Christians and Muslims, the two faiths are similar in many ways. Both are monotheistic (that is, based on a single deity), and both include a belief in prophets, an afterlife, and a judgment day. In fact, Islam recognizes Jesus as a prophet, though not as the son of

## *Going* GLOBAL

### Religions of the World

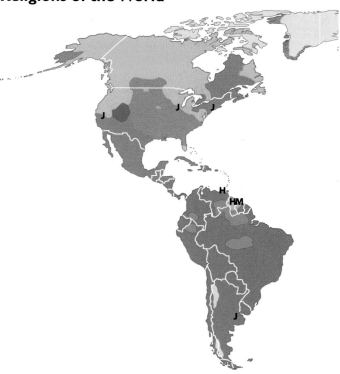

Religious adherence is one of the defining social characteristics of a culture.

*Source:* J. Allen, 2008.

God. Both faiths impose a moral code on believers, which varies from fairly rigid proscriptions for fundamentalists to relatively relaxed guidelines for liberals.

The followers of Islam, called Muslims, believe that the prophet Muhammad received Islam's holy scriptures from Allah (God) nearly 1400 years ago. They see Muhammad as the last in a long line of prophets, preceded by Adam, Abraham, Moses, and Jesus. Islam is more communal in its expression than Christianity, particularly the more individualistic Protestant denominations. Consequently, in countries that are predominantly Muslim, the separation of religion and the state is not considered necessary or even desirable. In fact, Muslim governments often reinforce Islamic practices through their laws. Muslims do vary sharply in their interpretation of several traditions, some of which—such as the wearing of veils by women—are more cultural than religious in origin.

Like Christianity and Islam, Judaism is monotheistic. Jews believe that God's true nature is revealed in the Torah, which Christians know as the first five books of the Old Testament. According to these scriptures, God formed a covenant, or pact, with Abraham and Sarah, the ancestors of the twelve tribes of Israel. Even today, Jews believe, this covenant holds them accountable to God's will. If they follow both the letter and the spirit of the Torah, a long-awaited Messiah will one day bring paradise to earth. Although Judaism has a relatively small following compared to other major faiths, it forms the historical foundation for both Christianity and Islam. That is why Jews revere many of the same sacred Middle Eastern sites as Christians and Muslims.

Two other major faiths developed in a different part of the world—India. The earliest, Hinduism, originated around 1500 B.C. Hinduism differs from Judaism, Christianity, and Islam in that it embraces a number of gods and minor gods, although most worshipers are devoted primarily to a single deity, such as Shiva or Vishnu. Hinduism is also distinguished by a belief in reincarnation, or the perpetual rebirth of the soul after death. Unlike Judaism, Christianity, and Islam, which are based largely on sacred texts, Hindu beliefs have been preserved mostly through oral tradition.

Buddhism developed in the sixth century B.C. as a reaction against Hinduism. This faith is founded on the teachings of Siddhartha (later called Buddha, or "The Enlightened One"). Through meditation, followers of Buddhism strive to overcome selfish cravings for physical or material pleasures, with the goal of reaching a state of enlightenment, or nirvana. Buddhists created the first monastic orders, which are thought to be the models for monastic orders in other religions, including Christianity. Though Buddhism emerged in India, its followers were eventually driven out of that country by the Hindus. It is now found primarily in other parts of Asia.

Although the differences among religions are striking, they are exceeded by variations within faiths. Consider the differences within Christianity, from relatively liberal de-

**Predominant Religions**

**Christianity (C)***
- Roman Catholic
- Protestant
- Mormon (LDS)
- Eastern Churches
- Mixed Sects

**Islam (M)**
- Sunni
- Shi'a

**Buddhism (B)**
- Hinayanistic
- Lamaistic

**Hinduism (H)**
**Judaism (J)**
**Sikhism**
**Animism (Tribal)**
**Chinese Complex**
(Confucianism, Taoism, and Buddhism)

**Korean Complex**
(Buddhism, Confucianism, Christianity, and Chondogyo)

**Japanese Complex**
(Shinto and Buddhism)

**Vietnamese Complex**
(Buddhism, Taoism, Confucianism, and Cao Dai)

**Unpopulated Regions**

* Capital letters indicate the presence of locally important minority adherents of nonpredominant faiths.

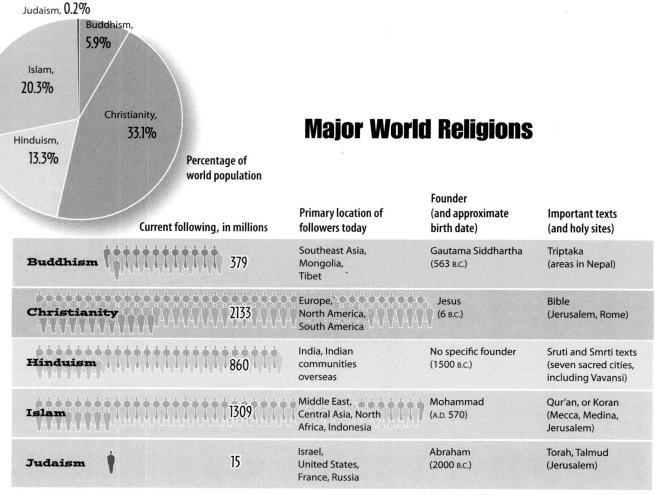

# Major World Religions

| | Current following, in millions | Primary location of followers today | Founder (and approximate birth date) | Important texts (and holy sites) |
|---|---|---|---|---|
| **Buddhism** | 379 | Southeast Asia, Mongolia, Tibet | Gautama Siddhartha (563 B.C.) | Triptaka (areas in Nepal) |
| **Christianity** | 2133 | Europe, North America, South America | Jesus (6 B.C.) | Bible (Jerusalem, Rome) |
| **Hinduism** | 860 | India, Indian communities overseas | No specific founder (1500 B.C.) | Sruti and Smrti texts (seven sacred cities, including Vavansi) |
| **Islam** | 1309 | Middle East, Central Asia, North Africa, Indonesia | Mohammad (A.D. 570) | Qur'an, or Koran (Mecca, Medina, Jerusalem) |
| **Judaism** | 15 | Israel, United States, France, Russia | Abraham (2000 B.C.) | Torah, Talmud (Jerusalem) |

*Sources:* Based on Barrett et al. 2006; Swatos 1998.

nominations such as Presbyterians or Episcopalians to the more conservative Mormons and Greek Orthodox Catholics. Similar divisions exist within Hinduism, Islam, and other world religions (Barrett et al. 2006; Swatos 1998).

# >> Sociological Perspectives on Religion

Sociology emerged as a discipline in the 19th century in the context of significant intellectual, political, and economic upheaval. Intellectuals at the time felt that the religious teachings that had guided society in times of crisis in the past were failing. Auguste Comte and other early sociologists sought to provide a science of society that would tap the ways of knowing built into the scientific method and apply them to the study of society. They recognized the significant role that religion had played in maintaining social order in the past and believed it essential to understand how it had accomplished this, so the study of religion became a significant topic in early sociology. Among classical theorists, for example, Émile Durkheim concluded that

religion promoted social order; Max Weber maintained that it helped generate social change; and Karl Marx argued that it reinforced the interests of the powerful.

## INTEGRATION

Durkheim viewed religion as an integrative force in human society. He sought to answer a perplexing question: "How can human societies be held together when they are generally composed of individuals and social groups with diverse interests and aspirations?" In his view, religious bonds often transcend these personal and divisive forces.

How does religion provide this "societal glue"? Religion, whether it be Buddhism, Islam, Christianity, or Judaism, gives meaning and purpose to people's lives. It offers certain ultimate values and ends to hold in common. Although they are subjective and not always fully accepted, these values and ends help society to function as an integrated social system. For example, funerals, weddings, bar and bat mitzvahs, and confirmations serve to integrate people into larger communities by reaffirming shared beliefs and values related to the ultimate questions of life.

Religion also serves to bind people together in times of crisis and confusion. Immediately after the terrorist attacks of September 11, 2001, on New York City and Washington, D.C., attendance at worship services in the United States increased dramatically. Muslim, Jewish, and Christian clerics made joint appearances to honor the dead and to urge citizens not to retaliate against those who looked, dressed, or sounded different from others. A year later, however, attendance levels had returned to normal (D. Moore 2002).

The integrative power of religion can be seen, too, in the role that churches, synagogues, and mosques have traditionally played and continue to play for immigrant groups in the United States. For example, Roman Catholic immigrants may settle near a parish church that offers services in their native language, such as Polish or Spanish. Similarly, Korean immigrants may join a Presbyterian church that has many Korean American members and follows religious practices similar to those of churches in Korea. Like other religious organizations, these Roman Catholic and Presbyterian churches help to integrate immigrants into their new homeland.

Religion also strengthens feelings of social integration within specific faiths and denominations. In many faiths, members share certain characteristics that help to bind them together, including their race, ethnicity, and social class.

Such integration, while unifying believers, can come at the expense of outsiders. In this sense, religion can contribute to tension and even conflict between groups or nations. During the Second World War, Nazi Germany attempted to exterminate the Jewish people; approximately 6 million European Jews were killed. In modern times, nations such as Lebanon (Muslims versus Christians), Israel (Jews versus Muslims, as well as Orthodox versus secular Jews), Northern Ireland (Roman Catholics versus Protestants), and India (Hindus versus Muslims and, more recently, Sikhs) have been torn by clashes that are in large part based on religion. Such conflicts often do, however, have the effect of drawing the believers closer together.

## SOCIAL CHANGE

Max Weber sought to understand how religion, which so often seems conservative in that it works to maintain order, might also contribute to social change. To do so, he focused on the relationship between religious faith and the rise of capitalism. Weber's findings appeared in his sociology classic, *The Protestant Ethic and the Spirit of Capitalism* ([1904] 2009).

**The Weberian Thesis** Weber noted that in European nations with both Protestant and Catholic citizens, an overwhelming number of business leaders, owners of capital, and skilled workers were Protestant. In his view, this was no mere coincidence. Weber explained it as a consequence of what he called the **Protestant ethic**—a disciplined commitment to worldly labor driven by a desire to

# Income and Education Levels, Selected Denominations

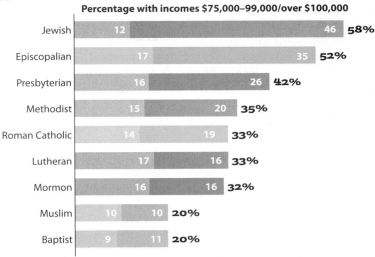

**Percentage with incomes $75,000–99,000/over $100,000**

| Denomination | | |
|---|---|---|
| Jewish | 12 / 46 | 58% |
| Episcopalian | 17 / 35 | 52% |
| Presbyterian | 16 / 26 | 42% |
| Methodist | 15 / 20 | 35% |
| Roman Catholic | 14 / 19 | 33% |
| Lutheran | 17 / 16 | 33% |
| Mormon | 16 / 16 | 32% |
| Muslim | 10 / 10 | 20% |
| Baptist | 9 / 11 | 20% |

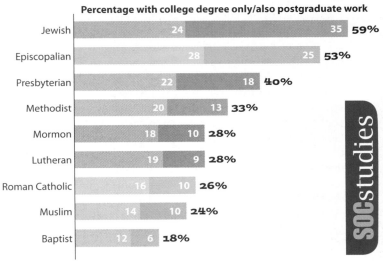

**Percentage with college degree only/also postgraduate work**

| Denomination | | |
|---|---|---|
| Jewish | 24 / 35 | 59% |
| Episcopalian | 28 / 25 | 53% |
| Presbyterian | 22 / 18 | 40% |
| Methodist | 20 / 13 | 33% |
| Mormon | 18 / 10 | 28% |
| Lutheran | 19 / 9 | 28% |
| Roman Catholic | 16 / 10 | 26% |
| Muslim | 14 / 10 | 24% |
| Baptist | 12 / 6 | 18% |

*Source:* Pew Research Center, 2008.

SOCstudies

bring glory to God that was shared by followers of Martin Luther and John Calvin. Weber argued that this emphasis on hard work and self-denial provided capitalism with an approach toward labor that was essential to capitalism's development.

To explain the impact of the Protestant ethic on the rise of capitalism, Weber looked to Luther's concept of a calling, Calvin's concept of predestination, and Protestant believers' resulting experience of "salvation panic." According to Protestant reformer Martin Luther (1483–1546), God called believers to their position in life,

> **protestant ethic** Max Weber's term for the disciplined commitment to worldly labor driven by a desire to bring glory to God, shared by followers of Martin Luther and John Calvin.

and they had to work hard in that calling so as to bring glory to God, regardless of whether they were rich or poor. Protestant Reformer John Calvin (1509–1564) added to this the concept of predestination, according to which

God, before the beginning of time, picked who would go to heaven and who would go to hell, and there was nothing anyone could do to change their fate. It was impossible to earn salvation through good works; salvation was totally dependent upon the grace of God. Complicating this was the fact that no individual could ever know for sure that he or she was saved because none could presume to know the mind of God. Weber concluded that this created a sense of salvation panic among believers who wanted to know if they were going to heaven or not.

## SOCthink

> > > To what extent do you think religion can be a force for social change? What examples have you seen in your lifetime?

Weber theorized that believers would seek to resolve this uncertainty by leading the kinds of lives they thought God would expect godly people to lead. This meant hard work, humility, and self-denial, not for the sake of salvation or individual gain, but for the sake of God. Although doing so would not earn them salvation, to do otherwise would be an almost certain sign that they were not among the chosen. But they could never fully be sure, so they could never let up in their commitment to do God's will. Thus they worked hard not because they had to (either for subsistence or because they were forced) but because they wanted to in response to the call they hoped would come from God. It was precisely this kind of worker, internally motivated to work hard and willing to show up every day even after getting paid, that capitalism needed if it was to engage in rationally planned production. This "spirit of capitalism," to use Weber's phrase, contrasted with the moderate work hours, leisurely work habits, and lack of ambition that Weber saw as typical of traditional labor.

In this way, religion contributed, through the Protestant Reformation, to one of the most significant examples of social change, in the form of the rise of capitalism and its effects, in human history. Weber's argument has been hailed as one of the most important theoretical works in the field and as an excellent example of macrolevel analysis. Like Durkheim, Weber demonstrated that religion is not solely a matter of intimate personal beliefs. He stressed that the collective nature of religion has consequences for society as a whole.

**liberation theology** Use of a church, primarily Roman Catholicism, in a political effort to eliminate poverty, discrimination, and other forms of injustice from a secular society.

**Liberation Theology** A more contemporary example of religion serving as a force for social change came through liberation theology, in which the clergy were at the forefront. Many religious activists, especially in the Roman Catholic Church in Latin America, support **liberation theology**—the use of a church in a political effort to eliminate poverty, discrimination, and other forms of injustice from a secular society. Advocates of this religious movement sometimes sympathize with Marxism. Many believe that radical change, rather than economic development in itself, is the only acceptable solution to the desperation of the masses in impoverished developing countries. Activists associated with liberation theology believe that organized religion has a moral responsibility to take a strong public stand against the oppression of the poor, racial and ethnic minorities, and women (C. Smith 1991).

The *term liberation theology* dates back to the publication in 1973 of the English translation of *A Theology of Liberation*. The book was written by a Peruvian priest, Gustavo Gutiérrez, who lived in a slum area of Lima in the early 1960s. After years of exposure to the vast poverty around him, Gutiérrez concluded that "in order to serve the poor, one had to move into political action" (R. M. Brown 1980:23; Gutiérrez 1990). Eventually, politically committed Latin American theologians came under the influence of social scientists who viewed the domination of capitalist multinational

**Little Buddah**
The story of the Buddah interwoven with a tale of reincarnation.

**The Chosen**
Two Jewish boys with very different ways of life become friends.

**The Passion of the Christ**
The story of Jesus Christ.

**Monsoon Wedding**
A traditional Hindu wedding ceremony.

**Malcolm X**
A biography of Malcolm X and his conversion to Islam.

5 Movies on RELIGION

corporations as central to the hemisphere's problems. One result was a new approach to theology that built on the cultural and religious traditions of Latin America rather than on models developed in Europe and the United States.

## SOCIAL CONTROL

Liberation theology is a relatively recent phenomenon that marks a break with the traditional role of churches. It was this traditional role that Karl Marx opposed. In his view, religion inhibited social change by encouraging oppressed people to focus on otherworldly concerns rather than on their immediate poverty or exploitation.

**Marx on Religion** Marx described religion as an "opiate" that was particularly harmful to oppressed peoples. He felt that religion often, in essence, drugged the masses into submission by offering a consolation for their harsh lives on earth: the hope of salvation in an ideal afterlife. For example, during the period of slavery in the United States, White masters forbade Blacks to practice native African religions. Instead, they encouraged slaves to adopt Christianity, which taught that obedience would lead to salvation and eternal happiness in the hereafter. Viewed from this perspective, Christianity may have pacified certain slaves and blunted the rage that often fuels rebellion.

Marx acknowledged that religion plays an important role in propping up the existing social structure. The values of religion, as already noted, tend to reinforce other social institutions and the social order as a whole. From Marx's perspective, however, religion's promotion of social stability only helps to perpetuate patterns of social inequality. According to Marx, the dominant religion reinforces the interests of those in power.

From a Marxist perspective, religion keeps people from seeing their lives and societal conditions in political terms—for example, by obscuring the overriding significance of conflicting economic interests. Marxists suggest that by inducing a "false consciousness" among the disadvantaged, religion lessens the possibility of collective political action that could end capitalist oppression and trans-

> But the poor person does not exist as an inescapable fact of destiny. . . . The poor are a by-product of the system in which we live and for which we are responsible.
>
> **Liberation Theologian Gustavo Gutierrez**

form society. Sociological analysis in this tradition seeks to reveal the ways in which religion serves the interests of the powerful at the expense of others.

**Gender and Religion** Drawing on the feminist approach, researchers and theorists point to the fundamental role women play in religious socialization. Most people develop their allegiance to a particular faith in their childhood, with their mothers playing a critical role in the process. Yet when it comes to positions of leadership, women generally take a subordinate role in religious governance. Indeed, most faiths have a long tradition of exclusively male spiritual leadership. Furthermore, because most religions are patriarchal, they tend to reinforce men's dominance in secular as well as spiritual matters. Women do play a vital role as volunteers, staff, and religious educators, but even today, religious decision making and leadership typically fall to the men. Exceptions to this rule, such as the Shakers and Christian Scientists, as well as Hinduism with its long goddess heritage, are rare (Schaefer and Zellner 2007).

In the United States, women compose 12.8 percent of the clergy, even though they account for 51 percent of students enrolled in theological institutions. Female clerics typically have shorter careers than men, often in related fields that do not involve congregational leadership, such as counseling. In faiths that restrict leadership positions to men, women still serve unofficially. For example, about 4 percent of Roman Catholic congregations are led by women who hold nonordained pastoral positions—a necessity in a church that faces a shortage of male priests (Adams 2007; Banerjee 2006; Bureau of the Census 2007a:Table 598).

In this chapter, we have looked at both education and religion. In both cases we find institutions that play a powerful role in shaping how we think and act. Each provides opportunity and reinforces the status quo, including its system of inequality. Sociologists believe that by having a better appreciation for both the opportunities and constraints such institutions present, we can better act both individually and collectively to bring about positive social change.

**get involved!**

Visit! Attend at least two religious services for a group that is significantly different from what you might have experienced in the past. Interview the religious leader of the group to gain a better understanding of their beliefs and practices and their reasons for faith

# For REVIEW

I. **How does education help to maintain social order?**
   - Education transmits culture, promotes social integration, provides training and social control, and contributes to cultural innovation.

II. **How does education support the existing system of inequality?**
   - Education reinforces the status quo, and therefore its existing inequalities, through the hidden curriculum, teacher expectancy, bestowal of status, and credentialism.

III. **How do sociologists define religion?**
   - One approach focuses on the substance of what religion is, defining religion as knowledge and beliefs relating to the sacred realm. The other approach looks at what religions do for society in terms of social order and integration. Both approaches analyze common components including belief, ritual, experience, and community.

# Pop Quiz

1. Horace Mann, often referred to as the "father of public education," refers to education as
   a. the great equalizer.
   b. the opiate of the masses.
   c. an instrument for social control.
   d. an opportunity engine.

2. One of the ways education contributes to social order is by providing an environment within which we can challenge existing ideas and experiment with new norms and values. This is known as
   a. transmitting culture.
   b. promoting social integration.
   c. training and social control.
   d. cultural innovation.

1. (a); 2. (d),

3. Samuel Bowles and Herbert Gintis have argued that capitalism requires a skilled, disciplined labor force and that the educational system of the United States is structured with that objective in mind. Citing numerous studies, they offer support for what they call

   a. tracking.

   b. credentialism.

   c. the correspondence principle.

   d. the teacher-expectancy effect.

4. Fifty years ago, a high school diploma was the minimum requirement for entry into the paid labor force of the United States. Today, a college diploma is virtually the bare minimum. This change reflects the process of

   a. tracking.

   b. credentialism.

   c. the hidden curriculum.

   d. the correspondence principle.

5. The college student subculture that focuses on having fun and socializing and doesn't take its studies too seriously is the

   a. collegiate subculture.

   b. academic subculture.

   c. vocational subculture.

   d. nonconformist subculture.

6. The approach to defining religion that emphasizes the significance of the sacred, most often supernatural, realm is known as the

   a. functionalist approach.

   b. component approach.

   c. substantive approach.

   d. ecclesiae approach.

7. Religious rituals are

   a. statements to which members of a particular religion adhere.

   b. the feelings or perceptions of being in direct contact with the ultimate reality, such as a divine being.

   c. the religious structures through which faith communities organize themselves.

   d. practices required or expected of members of a faith.

8. Looking at world religions, the religion with the most followers around the world is

   a. Buddhism.

   b. Islam.

   c. Judaism.

   d. Christianity.

9. Sociologist Max Weber pointed out that the followers of John Calvin emphasized a disciplined work ethic, worldly concerns, and a rational orientation to life. Collectively, this point of view has been referred to as

   a. capitalism.

   b. the Protestant ethic.

   c. the sacred.

   d. the profane.

10. The use of a church, primarily Roman Catholic, in a political effort to eliminate poverty, discrimination, and other forms of injustice evident in a secular society is referred to as

    a. creationism.

    b. ritualism.

    c. religious experience.

    d. liberation theology.

3. (c); 4. (b); 5. (a); 6. (c); 7. (d); 8. (d); 9. (b); 10. (d)

9

GOVERNI

# ADAPTING AND SURVIVING IN A MULTINATIONAL WORLD

**In 2002, Jim Wier headed to Wal-Mart's corporate headquarters in Bentonville, Arkansas, to tell their executives that he would no longer be selling his company's Snapper lawn mowers in Wal-Mart stores.** This was highly unusual for a Wal-Mart supplier. Most would go to great lengths to get their products on Wal-Mart shelves because, with 127 million U.S. customers per week, the possibilities for high-volume sales are immense. In fact, when they pulled their mowers from Wal-Mart, Snapper's sales dropped 20 percent (Fishman 2006).

Wal-Mart began as a single store in 1962, and there are now over 4,000 U.S. stores and 2,800 abroad. In fact, Wal-Mart is the largest corporation in the world, with a total of $378 billion in revenues in 2007. It is also the world's largest private employer, with 1.3 million U.S. workers and a total of 1.9 million worldwide.

Wier understood the appeal of gaining access to all those Wal-Mart customers, but as he put it, "Once you get hooked on the volume, it's like getting hooked on cocaine" (Fishman 2006:117). The need to maintain volume, he argued, would change the character of the company, requiring it to cut corners and change operating procedures. He opted instead to sell to a different kind of customer, one who wants quality, durability, and service more than up-front savings.

Ironically, to compete with Wal-Mart, Snapper had to adopt similar business techniques. To maximize efficiency, Wal-Mart measures everything. Snapper, too, now tracks every step of the production process to increase efficiency. Their productivity is three times what it was a decade ago with a workforce half the size. Though they continue to thrive, Snapper still faces an uphill fight.

Companies and workers have no choice but to adapt to compete with huge multinational corporations such as Wal-Mart and with firms and workers globally. When a company's revenues are greater than the gross national income for the majority of the world's nations—Wal-Mart would rank 21st out of 209 nations—it cannot help but have economic and political consequences (World Bank 2008). In this chapter we will look at both the economy and politics to better understand how both shape our lives.

# As You READ >>

- How is economic and political power organized?
- How does power operate?
- How has the economy changed over time?

## >> Power and Authority

Sociologists have been concerned about the exercise of power since the birth of the discipline in the 1800s. In the context of those times, traditional forms of power were changing even as economic and political contexts were shifting. The movement away from agricultural to industrial economies, and from the rule of monarchs to more democratic forms of government, meant that the taken-for-granted processes of power were shifting. Early sociologists sought to develop theories of power that were sufficiently broad to explain the success of companies such as Wal-Mart or the outcomes of international conflicts, yet sufficiently narrow to explain who gets their way within interpersonal relationships.

### POWER

According to Max Weber, **power** is the ability to exercise one's will over others, even if they resist. To put it another way, if you can make people do what you want them to do—whether that is to go to war, coordinate a business meeting, clean their

room, or even take an exam—you have power. Power relations can involve large organizations, small groups, or even people in an intimate association.

There are three basic sources of power within any political system: force, influence, and authority. **Force** is the actual or threatened use of coercion to impose one's will on others. When leaders imprison or even execute political dissidents, they are applying force; so, too, are terrorists when they seize or bomb an embassy or assassinate a political leader. **Influence,** on the other hand, refers to the exercise of power through a process of persuasion. A citizen may change his or her view of a Supreme Court nominee because of a newspaper editorial, the expert testimony of a law school dean before the Senate Judiciary Committee, or a stirring speech by a political activist at a rally. In each case, sociologists would view such efforts to persuade people as examples of influence. Now let's take a look at the third source of power—authority.

### TYPES OF AUTHORITY

**Authority** refers to institutionalized power that is recognized by the people over whom it is exercised. Sociologists commonly use the term in connection with those who hold legitimate power through elected or publicly acknowledged positions. A person's authority is often limited by her or his position. Thus, a referee has the authority to decide whether a penalty should be called during a football game but has no authority over the price of tickets to the game.

Max Weber ([1913] 1947) developed a classification system for authority that has become one of the most useful and fre-

# From Me to You

*My daughters, Emily and Eleanor, mostly do what I ask, accepting my authority as legitimate. The fact that I am their father is usually enough to get them to obey. When they resist, however, they face the prospect of "sitting in the green chair" until I say they can get out. Just the threat of being sent there usually has the desired effect. It is not much of a punishment, really. It's a rocker that we have in the living room that is used as a normal chair at all other times; it's in full view of the television and is not isolated from the rest of the family. As a parent, I am constantly amazed at the power of traditional authority.*

## SOCthink

> > > Which of these three forms of power do parents, bosses, or professors most rely on? Are there times when each of those groups use each of the three types of power?

quently cited contributions of early sociology. He identified three ideal types of authority: traditional, rational-legal, and charismatic. Weber did not insist that only one type applies to a given society or organization. All can be present, but their relative importance will vary. Sociologists have found Weber's typology valuable in understanding different manifestations of legitimate power within a society.

**Traditional Authority** Until the middle of the 20th century, Japan was ruled by a revered emperor whose absolute power was

passed down from generation to generation. In a political system based on **traditional authority,** legitimate power is conferred by custom and accepted practice. The past is a justification of the present. A king or queen is accepted as ruler of a nation simply by virtue of inheriting the crown; a tribal chief rules because that is the accepted practice. The ruler may be loved or hated, competent or destructive; in terms of legitimacy, that does not matter. For the traditional leader, authority rests in custom, not in personal characteristics, technical competence, or even written law. People accept the ruler's authority because that is how things have always been done. Traditional authority is absolute when the ruler has the ability to determine laws and policies.

> **power** The ability to exercise one's will over others even if they resist.
> **force** The actual or threatened use of coercion to impose one's will on others.
> **influence** The exercise of power through a process of persuasion.
> **authority** Institutionalized power that is recognized by the people over whom it is exercised.
> **traditional authority** Legitimate power conferred by custom and accepted practice.
> **rational-legal authority** Authority based on formally agreed-upon and accepted rules, principles, and procedures of conduct that are established in order to accomplish goals in the most efficient manner possible.
> **charismatic authority** Power made legitimate by a leader's exceptional personal or emotional appeal to his or her followers.

## Rational-Legal Authority

The U.S. Constitution gives Congress and the president the authority to make and enforce laws and policies. Power made legitimate by law is a form of rational-legal authority. **Rational-legal authority** involves formally agreed-upon and accepted rules, principles, and procedures of conduct that are established in order to accomplish goals in the most efficient manner possible. Such authority extends beyond governments to include any organization. Bureaucracies are the purest form of rational-legal authority. Generally, in societies based on rational-legal authority, leaders are thought to have specific areas of competence and authority, but are not thought to be endowed with divine inspiration, as in certain societies with traditional forms of authority.

**Charismatic Authority** Joan of Arc was a simple peasant girl in medieval France, yet she was able to rally the French people and lead them into major battles against English invaders despite having no formally recognized position of power. How was this possible? As Weber observed, power can be legitimized by the charisma of an individual. **Charismatic authority** refers to power made legitimate by a leader's exceptional personal or emotional appeal to his or her followers.

Charisma lets a person such as Joan of Arc lead or inspire without relying on set rules or traditions. In fact, charismatic authority is derived more from the beliefs of followers than from the actual qualities of leaders. So long as people perceive a charismatic leader such as Jesus, Joan of Arc, Gandhi, Malcolm X, or Martin Luther King, Jr., as having qualities that set him or her apart from ordinary citizens, that leader's authority will remain secure and often unquestioned. That unfortunately is also the case with malevolent figures such as Adolf Hitler, whose charismatic appeal turned people toward violent and destructive ends in Nazi Germany.

The expansion of the electronic media facilitated the development of charismatic authority (Couch 1996). During the 1930s and 1940s, the heads of state of the United States, Great Britain, and Germany all used radio to issue direct appeals to citizens; President Franklin Delano Roosevelt's fireside chats are a prime example. Now, television and the Internet allow leaders to "visit" people's homes and communicate with them via broadcasts, email, blogposts, and YouTube videos. In both Taiwan and South Korea in 1996, troubled political leaders facing reelection campaigns spoke frequently to national audiences and exaggerated military threats from neighboring China and North Korea, respectively.

## >> Economic Systems

Out of the Industrial Revolution grew a new kind of political and economic structure known as the **industrial society,** a society that depends on mechanization to produce its goods and services. People left their rural agricultural communities and migrated to the cities to work in factories. Chicago saw explosive growth as a result of this revolution. The city had a population of about 300 when it was founded in 1833. By 1850 it had grown to about 30,000; in 1890 it broke the 1-million barrier; and by 1900 it was the fifth-largest city in the world, with a population of 1.7 million. Such changes, driven by economic transformations and opportunities, had radical impacts on the lives of its residents. In fact, we cannot

**industrial society** A society that depends on mechanization to produce its goods and services.

**economic system** The social institution through which goods and services are produced, distributed, and consumed.

**capitalism** An economic system in which the means of production are held largely in private hands and the main incentive for economic activity is the accumulation of profits.

fully understand what happens in the context of families or education without taking into account such economic change.

This new, more global economy of the industrial age called for large-scale systems of power and authority. The term **economic system** refers to the social institution through which goods and services are produced, distributed, and consumed. Two basic types of economic system distinguish contemporary industrial societies: capitalism and socialism. As described in the following sections, capitalism and socialism serve as ideal types of economic systems. In practice, no nation fully embodies either model. Instead, the economy of each individual state represents a mixture of capitalism and socialism, although one type or the other is generally more useful in describing a society's economic structure.

### CAPITALISM

In preindustrial societies based on an agricultural economy, land functioned as the source of virtually all wealth. The Industrial Revolution changed all that. It required that certain individuals and institutions be willing to take substantial monetary risks in order to finance new inventions, machinery, and business enterprises. Eventually, bankers, industrialists, and other holders of large sums of money replaced landowners as the most powerful economic force. These people invested their funds in the hope of realizing even greater profits and thereby became owners of property and business firms.

The transition to private ownership of business was accompanied by the emergence of **capitalism**—an economic system in which the means of production are held largely in private hands and the main incentive for economic activity is the accumulation of profits. In practice, capitalist systems vary in the degree to which the government regulates private ownership and economic activity (D. Rosenberg 1991).

Immediately following the Industrial Revolution, the prevailing form of capitalism was what is termed **laissez-faire** ("let them do [as they choose]"). Under the principle of laissez-faire, as expounded and endorsed by British economist Adam Smith (1723–1790), people could compete freely, with minimal government intervention in the economy. Business retained the right to regulate itself and operated essentially without fear of government interference (Smelser 1963).

In principle, through competition in the free market, capitalist economies should reach a natural balance between what consumers demand and what producers supply. In practice, capitalism produces monopolistic conditions. A **monopoly** exists when a single business firm controls the market. Domination of an industry allows the firm to effectively control a commodity by dictating pricing, quality standards, and availability. Buyers have little choice but to yield to the firm's decisions; there is no other place to purchase the product or service. Monopolistic practices violate the ideal of free competition cherished by Adam Smith and other supporters of laissez-faire capitalism.

and Microsoft, owner of the dominant operating system for personal computers, illustrates the uneasy relationship between the government and private monopolies in capitalistic countries.

Globalization and the rise of multinational corporations have spread the capitalistic pursuit of profits around the world. Especially in developing countries, governments are not always prepared to deal with the sudden influx of foreign capital and its effects on their economies. One particularly striking example of how unfettered capitalism can harm developing nations is found in the Democratic Republic of Congo (formerly Zaire). The Congo has significant deposits of the metal columbite-tantalite—coltan, for short—which is used in the production of electronic circuit boards. Until the market for cell phones, pagers, and laptop computers heated up recently, U.S. manufacturers obtained most of their coltan from Australia. But at the height of consumer demand, they turned to miners in the Congo to increase their supply.

Predictably, the escalating price of the metal—as much as $400 per kilogram at one point, or more than three times the average Congolese worker's yearly wages—attracted undesirable attention. Soon the neighboring countries of Rwanda, Uganda, and Burundi, at war with one another and desperate for resources to finance the conflict, were raiding the Congo's national parks, slashing and burning to expose the coltan underneath the forest floor. Indirectly, the sudden increase in the demand for coltan was financing war and the rape of the environment. U.S. manufacturers have since cut off their sources in the Congo in an effort to avoid abetting the destruction. However, their action has only penalized legitimate miners in the impoverished country (Austin 2002; Delawala 2002).

Some capitalistic nations, such as the United States, outlaw monopolies through antitrust legislation. Such laws prevent any business from taking over so much of the competition in an industry that it controls the market. The U.S. federal government allows monopolies to exist only in certain exceptional cases, such as the utility and transportation industries. Even then, regulatory agencies scrutinize these officially approved monopolies to protect the public. The protracted legal battle between the Justice Department

## SOCIALISM

In their writings, Karl Marx and Friedrich Engels developed and refined socialist theory. They were disturbed by the exploitation of the working class during the Industrial Revolution. In their view, capitalism forced large numbers of people to exchange their labor for low wages. Marx and Engels argued that the owners of industry profit from the labor of workers primarily by paying workers less than the value of the goods produced.

**laissez-faire** A form of capitalism under which people compete freely, with minimal government intervention in the economy.

**monopoly** Control of a market by a single business firm.

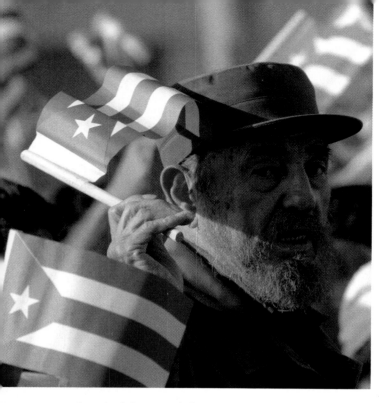

munist economic systems. However, this usage represents an incorrect application of a term with sensitive political connotations. All nations known as communist in the 20th century actually fell far short of the ideal type.

By the early 1990s, Communist parties were no longer ruling the nations of Eastern Europe. As of 2007, however, China, Cuba, Laos, and Vietnam remained socialist societies ruled by Communist parties. Even in those countries, however, capitalism has begun to make inroads. By 2000, fully 25 percent of China's production originated in the private business sector.

## THE MIXED ECONOMY

In practice, national economic systems combine elements of both capitalism and socialism. A **mixed economy** features elements of more than one economic system. Moving from a capitalist ideal toward a mixed economy typically involves removing some goods and services from the competitive free market and providing them for all or subsidizing them to assure broader access. In the United States, we do this with goods and services such as police and fire protection, roads, and public schools. We argue that all people should have access to such public goods without regard for their ability to pay. Perhaps the most active current debate about extending this status further involves whether healthcare should be considered a similar public good.

Also in contrast to the laissez-faire ideal, capitalism today features government regulation of economic relations. Without regulation, business firms would be more likely to mislead consumers, endanger workers' safety, and even defraud the companies' investors—all in the pursuit

In principle, a socialist economic system attempts to eliminate such economic exploitation. Under **socialism,** the means of production and distribution in a society are collectively rather than privately owned. Marx predicted that technological advances would make it possible for society to produce enough for everyone, and a socialist system would ensure that everyone got enough. Socialists reject the laissez-faire philosophy that free competition benefits the general public. Instead, they believe that the central government, acting as the representative of the people, should make basic economic decisions. Therefore, government ownership of all major industries—including steel production, automobile manufacturing, and agriculture—is a primary feature of socialism as an ideal type.

> **socialism** An economic system under which the means of production and distribution are collectively owned.
>
> **communism** As an ideal type, an economic system under which all property is communally owned and no social distinctions are made on the basis of people's ability to produce.

Marx believed further that socialist states would eventually "wither away" and evolve into communist societies. In principle, **communism** is an economic system under which all property is communally owned and no social distinctions are made on the basis of people's ability to produce. In recent decades, the former Soviet Union, the People's Republic of China, Vietnam, Cuba, and the nations of Eastern Europe were popularly thought of as examples of com-

# Fifty Years of Growth, 1970–2020

**Percent GDP increases (trillions of dollars)**

Countries (left to right): United Kingdom, Japan, United States, Canada, Spain, Mexico, Brazil, India, China

Scale: 0, 500, 1000, 1500, 2000, 2500, 3000

■ Percent GDP increase, 1970–2007     ▪ Percent GDP increase, 2007–2020 (projected)

*Source:* U.S. Department of Agriculture 2007.

of greater profits. That is why governments in capitalist nations often monitor prices, set safety and environmental standards for industries, protect the rights of consumers, and regulate collective bargaining between labor unions and management. Yet, under capitalism, government rarely takes over ownership of an entire industry.

Starting from a socialist ideal and moving toward a mixed economy means opening up some aspects of the economy to competition and the free market. When communists assumed leadership of China in 1949, they cast themselves as the champions of workers and peasants and the enemies of those who exploited workers, namely landlords and capitalists. Profit making was outlawed, and those who engaged in it were arrested. By the 1960s, China's economy was dominated by huge state-controlled enterprises, such as factories. Peasants essentially worked for the government, receiving payment in goods based on their contribution to the collective good. It did not work well economically.

In the 1980s, party leaders in China began to make market-oriented reforms, revising the nation's legal structure to promote private business. For the first time, private entrepreneurs were allowed to compete with some state-controlled businesses. By the mid-1990s, party officials had begun to hand some ailing state-controlled businesses over to private entrepreneurs, in hopes that the firms could be turned around. Today, those entrepreneurs are among the nation's wealthiest citizens, and some even hold positions on government advisory boards. For Chinese workers, the loosening of state control over the economy has opened up opportunities for occupational mobility.

However, critics in China point to the negative consequences of taking this path. For one thing, the accumulation of wealth by a few violates a core socialist principle. Further, workers often receive minimal pay and face poor working conditions; wages average $120–200 for a six-day week. They also suffer from high injury rates, and harsh working conditions contribute to rapid turnover in the labor force. In addition, there is no pension system in China, so retirees must struggle to find other ways to support themselves. Further, pollution is common in urban areas, and environmental problems are extensive (Barboza 2008; French 2008). Finally, Chinese women traditionally have been relegated to subservient roles in the patriarchal family structure, and despite recent economic changes, women receive lower wages than men who work in the same job sectors, not unlike what we see in the United States (Wang and Cai 2006).

## THE INFORMAL ECONOMY

An informal economy operates within the confines of the dominant macroeconomic system in many countries, whether capitalist or socialist. In this **informal economy,** transfers of money, goods, or services take place but are not reported to the government. Examples of the informal economy include bartering in which people trade goods and services with someone (say, exchanging a haircut for a computer lesson), selling goods on the street, and engaging in illegal transactions, such as gambling or drug deals. Participants in this type of economy avoid taxes and government regulations.

> **mixed economy** An economic system that combines elements of both capitalism and socialism.
> **informal economy** Transfers of money, goods, or services that are not reported to the government.

In the developing world, governments often create burdensome business regulations that overworked bureaucrats must administer. When requests for licenses and permits pile up, delaying business projects, legitimate entrepreneurs find that they need to "go underground" to get anything done. Despite its apparent efficiency, this type of informal economy is dysfunctional for a country's overall political and economic well-being. Since informal firms typically operate in remote locales to avoid detection, they cannot easily expand when they become profitable. And given the limited protection for their property and contractual rights, participants in the informal economy are less likely than others to save and invest their income.

Informal economies can also be dysfunctional for workers. Working conditions in these businesses are often unsafe or dangerous, and the jobs rarely provide any benefits to those who become ill or cannot continue to work. Perhaps more significant, the longer a worker remains in the informal economy, the less likely he or she is to make the transition to the regular economy. No matter how efficient or productive a worker may be, employers expect to see experience in the formal economy on a job application. Experience as a successful street vendor or self-employed cleaning person does not carry much weight with interviewers (Venkatesh 2006).

**Hot or Not?**

Should the United States guarantee health care coverage for all?

## SOCthink

> > > When doing jobs in the informal economy such as babysitting, lawn mowing, house cleaning, or construction, it can be nice to get cash under the table without having to pay taxes, Social Security, and so on. What are the long-term disadvantages of doing so for the individual? What about for society? Why might someone opt to do so anyway?

# >> Changing Economies

Economies are not static. Just as they changed due to the impact of the Industrial Revolution, economies continue to adapt to new contexts. Increased opportunity for workers, regardless of race, ethnicity, or gender—made possible in part by various social movements—has made the workforce more diverse. Technological innovation and globalization have reduced the number of traditional blue-collar jobs through deindustrialization. Microfinancing has opened up opportunities for poor people, especially women, around the world.

> **deindustrialization** The systematic, widespread withdrawal of investment in basic aspects of productivity, such as factories and plants.

## THE CHANGING FACE OF THE WORKFORCE

The workforce in the United States is constantly changing. During World War II, when men were mobilized to fight abroad, women entered the workforce in large numbers. With the coming of the civil rights movement in the 1960s, minorities found numerous job opportunities opening to them. While predictions are not always reliable, sociologists and labor specialists foresee a workforce increasingly composed of women and racial and ethnic minorities. In 1960 there were twice as many men in the labor force as women. By 2014, however, 54 percent of new workers are expected to be women. The dynamics for minority group workers are even more dramatic, as the number of Black, Latino, and Asian American workers continues to increase at a faster rate than the number of White workers (Toossi 2005:26).

More and more, then, the workforce reflects the diversity of the population, as ethnic minorities enter the labor force and immigrants and their children move from marginal jobs or employment in the informal economy to positions of greater visibility and responsibility. The impact of this changing labor force is not merely statistical. A more diverse workforce means that relationships between workers are more likely to cross gender, racial, and ethnic lines. People will soon find themselves supervising and being supervised by people very different from themselves. In response to these changes, 75 percent of businesses had instituted some type of cultural diversity training program as of 2000 (Melia 2000).

## DEINDUSTRIALIZATION

In recent decades, the U.S. economy has moved away from its industrial base through the process of **deindustrialization,** which refers to the systematic, widespread withdrawal of investment in basic aspects of productivity, such as factories and plants. Giant corporations that deindustrialize are not necessarily refusing to invest in new economic opportunities. Rather, the targets and locations of investment change, and the need for labor decreases as advances in technology continue to automate production. First, companies may move their plants from the nation's central cities to the suburbs. The next step may be relocation from suburban areas of the Northeast and Midwest to the South, where labor laws place more restrictions on unions. Finally, a corporation may simply relocate outside the United States to a country with a lower rate of prevailing wages. General Motors, for example, decided to build a multibillion-dollar plant in China rather than in Kansas City or even in Mexico (Lynn 2003).

Although deindustrialization often involves relocation, it can also take the form of corporate restructuring known as **downsizing,** which involves reducing the size of a company's workforce. The goal is to increase efficiency and reduce costs in the face of growing worldwide competition. When such restructuring occurs, the impact on the bureaucratic hierarchy

## Workforce Diversity: Past, Present, and Future

### Percentage of the workforce

White, non-Hispanic 64.6% | Hispanic 16.4% | Black 12.3% | Asian 5.3% | Other — **2016**

Men 53.4% | Women 46.6% — **2016**

69.1% | 13.7% | 11.4% | 4.4% — **2006**

53.7% | 46.3% — **2006**

81.3% | 6.1% | 10.3% | 2.5% — **1982**

56.7% | 43.3% — **1982**

*Source:* Fullerton 1995; Toossi 2007.

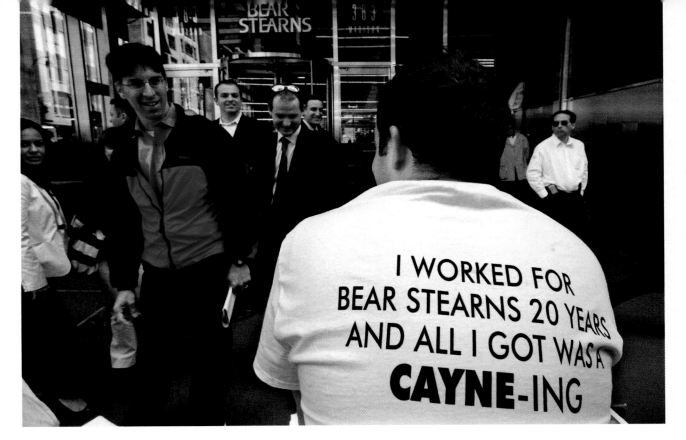

The deeply troubled investment bank Bear Stearns underwent layoffs before being sold to another investment bank. The tee shirt of a downsized employee places the blame at the hands of former CEO and Chairman Jimmy Cayne.

## SOCthink

> > > If you were the CEO of an American manufacturing company that was facing declining profits due to international competition, and Wal-Mart insisted that you reduce the price of your products another 5 percent this year, what would you do? To what extent does the system within which companies operate shape the choices that are available to them?

of formal organizations can be significant. A large corporation may choose to sell off or entirely abandon less productive divisions and to eliminate layers of management it views as unnecessary. Wages and salaries may be frozen and fringe benefits cut—all in the name of restructuring. Increasing reliance on automation also spells the end of work as we have known it.

> Majority rule only works if you're also considering individual rights. Because you can't have five wolves and one sheep voting on what to have for supper.
>
> **Larry Flynt**

U.S. firms have been outsourcing certain types of work for generations. For example, moderate-sized businesses such as furniture stores and commercial laundries have long relied on outside trucking firms to make deliveries to their customers. The new trend toward **offshoring** carries this practice one step further by transferring other types of work to foreign contractors. Now, even large companies are turning to overseas firms, many of them located in developing countries. Offshoring has become the latest tactic in the time-worn business strategy of raising profits by reducing costs.

Offshoring began when U.S. companies started transferring manufacturing jobs to foreign factories, where wage rates were much lower. But the transfer of work from one country to another is no longer limited to manufacturing. Office and professional jobs are being exported, too, thanks to advanced telecommunications and the growth of skilled, English-speaking labor forces in developing nations with relatively low wage scales. The trend includes even those jobs that require considerable training, such as accounting and financial analysis, computer programming, claims adjustment, telemarketing, and hotel and airline reservations. Today, when you call a toll-free num-

> **downsizing** Reductions in a company's workforce as part of deindustrialization.
> **offshoring** The transfer of work to foreign contractors.

While this shift has brought jobs and technology to nations such as India, there is a downside to offshoring for foreign workers as well. Although outsourcing is a significant source of employment for India's upper middle class, hundreds of millions of other Indians have benefited little if at all from the trend. Most households in India do not possess any form of high technology: only about 1 out of 10 have a telephone, and just 3 out of 1000 a computer. Instead of improving these people's lives, the new business centers have siphoned water and electricity away from those who are most in need. Even the high-tech workers are experiencing negative consequences. Many suffer from stress disorders such as stomach problems and difficulty sleeping; more than half quit their jobs before the end of a year (Waldman 2004a, 2004b, 2004c).

ber to reach a customer service representative, chances are that the person who answers the phone will not be speaking from the United States.

The social costs of deindustrialization and downsizing cannot be overemphasized. Plant closings lead to substantial unemployment in a community, which can have a devastating impact on both the micro and macro levels. On the micro level, the unemployed person and his or her family must adjust to a loss of spending power. Painting or re-siding the house, buying health insurance or saving for retirement, even thinking about having another child—all must be put aside. Both marital happiness and family cohesion may suffer as a result. Although many dismissed workers eventually reenter the paid labor force, they often must accept less desirable positions with lower salaries and fewer benefits. Unemployment and underemployment are tied to many of the social problems discussed throughout this textbook, among them the need for child care and the controversy over welfare.

**politics** In Harold Lasswell's words, "who gets what, when, and how."

**political system** The social institution that is founded on a recognized set of procedures for implementing and achieving society's goals.

Alan S. Blinder (2006), former vice chair of the Federal Reserve, predicts that offshoring will become the "third Industrial Revolution"—a life-altering shift in the way goods and services are produced and consumed. Blinder says we have barely seen the "tip of the offshoring iceberg." While offshoring may not lead to large-scale unemployment, it will likely produce a shift in Western labor markets. Jobs that are easily outsourced, like accounting and computer programming, will migrate to developing countries, leaving those that must be done on site, like nursing and construction, at home.

## MICROFINANCING

Economic development can, however, have a significant positive impact on people's lives around the globe. Microfinancing, for example, involves lending small sums of money to the poor so that they can work their way out of poverty. Borrowers use the money to get small businesses off the ground—to buy the tools, equipment, and bamboo to make stools, the yarn to weave into cloth, or cows to produce milk. They then sell the products they produce in local shops. The typical microloan is less than $100, and often as little as $12. The recipients are people who ordinarily would not be able to qualify for banking services.

Sometimes referred to as "banking the unbanked," microfinancing was the brainchild of Bangladeshi economist Muhammad Yunus. In 1976, in the midst of a devastating famine in Bangladesh, Yunus founded the Grameen (meaning "village") Bank. The idea came to him when he reached into his pocket to lend $27 to a group of villagers who had asked him for help. Working through local halls or meeting places, the Grameen Bank has now extended credit to nearly 7 million people. The idea has spread, and microloans have even been underwritten by multinational organizations such as the International Monetary Fund and for-profit banks like Citigroup. Estimates suggest that by 2007 microfinancing had reached 60 million people.

Microfinancing works well in countries that have experienced economic devastation. For example, in 2002, after decades of conflict and military occupation, Afghanistan did not have a single functioning bank. Five years later, with the help of the World Bank and other donors, Afghans could get microloans and other financial services in 22 of the country's 34 provinces. The new microlenders are the first evidence of a formal financial sector that Afghanistan has seen in years. Their funds have helped to start businesses and allowed farmers to convert from opium growing to other crops.

Because an estimated 90 percent of the recipients of microcredit are women, feminist theorists are especially interested in the growth of microfinancing. Women's economic status has been found to be critical to the well-being of their children, and the key to a healthy household environment. In developing countries, where women often are not treated as well as men, being entrusted with credit is particularly empowering to them. In recognition of these social and economic benefits of microfinancing, the United Nations proclaimed 2005 the International Year of Microcredit (Dugger 2006; Flynn 2007; World Bank 2006c).

## >> Types of Government

Just as new economic systems developed in response to broader historical changes, political systems also adapted. In all societies, someone or some group—whether it be a tribal chief, a dictator, a council, or a parliament—makes important decisions about how to use resources and allocate goods. Inevitably, the struggle for power and authority involves **politics,** which political scientist Harold Lasswell (1936) tersely defined as "who gets what, when, and how." Politics takes place within the context of a **political system,** which is the social institution that is founded on a recognized set of procedures for implementing and achieving society's goals, such as the allocation of valued resources.

Government represents an institutionalized form of authority. Given the scope of international relations and the globalization of national economies, these formal systems of authority make a significant number of critical political decisions. Such systems take a variety of forms, including monarchy, oligarchy, dictatorship, totalitarianism, and democracy.

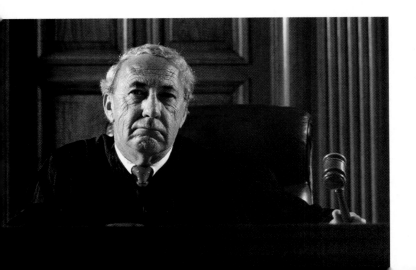

## MONARCHY

A **monarchy** is a form of government headed by a single member of a royal family, usually a king, queen, or some other hereditary ruler. In earlier times, many monarchs claimed that God had granted them a divine right to rule. Typically, they governed on the basis of traditional forms of authority, sometimes accompanied by the use of force. By the beginning of the 21st century, however, monarchs held genuine governmental power in only a few nations, such as Monaco. Most monarchs, such as Queen Elizabeth II in England, now have little practical power; they serve primarily ceremonial purposes.

> **monarchy** A form of government headed by a single member of a royal family, usually a king, queen, or some other hereditary ruler.
> **oligarchy** A form of government in which a few individuals rule.

## OLIGARCHY

An **oligarchy** is a form of government in which a few individuals rule. A venerable method of governing that flourished in ancient Greece and Egypt, oligarchy now often takes

### Did You Know?

. . . One of Queen Elizabeth's official duties is to appoint the prime minister. Given that political power rests with Parliament, however, this too has become largely a ceremonial duty.

the form of military rule. In developing nations in Africa, Asia, and Latin America, small factions of military officers may forcibly seize power, either from legally elected regimes or from other military cliques.

Strictly speaking, the term *oligarchy* is reserved for governments that are run by a few selected individuals. However, the People's Republic of China can be classified as an oligarchy if we stretch the meaning of the term. In China, power rests in the hands of a large but exclusive ruling *group,* the Communist Party. In a similar vein, we might argue that many industrialized nations of the West should be considered oligarchies (rather than democracies), since only a powerful few—leaders of big business, government, and the military—actually rule. Later in this chapter, we will examine the "elite model" of the U.S. political system in greater detail.

> **dictatorship** A government in which one person has nearly total power to make and enforce laws.
>
> **totalitarianism** Virtually complete government control and surveillance over all aspects of a society's social and political life.
>
> **democracy** In a literal sense, government by the people.
>
> **representative democracy** A form of government in which certain individuals are selected to speak for the people.

## DICTATORSHIP AND TOTALITARIANISM

A **dictatorship** is a government in which one person has nearly total power to make and enforce laws. Dictators rule primarily through the use of coercion, which often includes imprisonment, torture and executions. Typically, they *seize* power rather than being freely elected (as in a democracy) or inheriting power (as in a monarchy). Some dictators are quite charismatic and manage to achieve a certain popularity, although their supporters' enthusiasm is almost certainly tinged with fear. Other dictators are bitterly hated by the people over whom they rule.

Frequently, dictators develop such overwhelming control over people's lives that their governments are called totalitarian. (Monarchies and oligarchies may also achieve

## SOCthink

> > > In 2001, expressing a sentiment shared by many past presidents, George W. Bush joked that, when it came to working with Congress, "a dictatorship would be a heck of a lot easier." In what ways is the U.S. system of government intentionally inefficient? Why might that be on purpose?

this type of dominance.) **Totalitarianism** involves virtually complete government control and surveillance over all aspects of a society's social and political life. Germany during Hitler's reign, the Soviet Union under Stalin in the 1930s, and North Korea today are classified as totalitarian states.

## DEMOCRACY

In a literal sense, **democracy** means government by the people. The word comes from two Greek roots—*demos,* meaning "the populace" or "the common people," and *kratia,* meaning "rule." Of course, in large, populous nations such as the United States, government by the people is impractical at the national level. Americans cannot vote on every important issue that comes before Congress. Consequently, popular rule is generally maintained through **representative democracy,** a form of government in which certain individuals are selected to speak for the people.

## SOCthink

> > > The United States is commonly classified as a representative democracy, since the elected members of Congress and state legislatures make our laws. However, critics have questioned how representative our democracy really is. Do Congress and the state legislatures genuinely represent the masses? Are the people of the United States legitimately self-governing, or has our government become a forum for powerful elites?

# *Going* GLOBAL

**Voter Turnout Worldwide**

**Percent turnout at all parliamentary elections since 1945**

| Country | Turnout |
|---------|---------|
| Italy | 92.5 |
| Cambodia | 90.5 |
| Australia | 84.4 |
| Germany | 80.6 |
| Canada | 68.4 |
| India | 60.7 |
| Russia | 55.0 |
| United States | 48.3 |
| Mexico | 48.1 |
| Thailand | 47.4 |
| Colombia | 36.2 |
| Egypt | 24.6 |

*Source:* International Institute for Democracy and Electoral Assistance 2006.

## >> Political Behavior in the United States

Citizens of the United States take for granted many aspects of their political system. They are accustomed to living in a nation with a Bill of Rights, two major political parties, voting by secret ballot, an elected president, state and local governments distinct from the national government, and so forth. Because it is, in principle, a representative democracy, the system depends upon all individuals having equal access to and input into the political process in order to be fully responsive. In practice, two particular concerns—voter participation and race and gender representation—raise questions about the degree to which this is happening.

### PARTICIPATION AND APATHY

In the United States, virtually all citizens are familiar with the basics of the political process, and most tend to identify to some extent with a political party. In 2007, about 34 percent of registered voters in the United States saw themselves as Democrats, 36 percent as independents, and 29 percent as Republicans. However, only a small minority of citizens, often members of the higher social classes, actually participate in political organizations at the local, state, or national level. Studies reveal that only 8 percent of Americans belong to a political club or organization. Not more than one in five has ever contacted an official of national, state, or local government about a political issue or problem (Gallup 2007a; Orum 2001).

By the 1980s, it had become clear that many people in the United States were beginning to be turned off by political parties, politicians, and big government. The most dramatic indication of this growing alienation came from voting statistics. Today, voters of all ages and races appear to be less enthusiastic than ever about elections, even presidential contests. For example, in the presidential election of 1896, almost 80 percent of eligible voters in the United States went to the polls; in the 2004 election, only 64 percent of all eligible voters did so. Obviously, even modestly higher voter turnout could dramatically change election outcomes, as we saw in the razor-thin margin in the 2000 presidential election (Holder 2006).

While a few nations still command high voter turnout, it is increasingly common to hear national leaders of other countries complain of voter apathy. Still, among the 140 countries that have held parliamentary elections since 1945, the United States

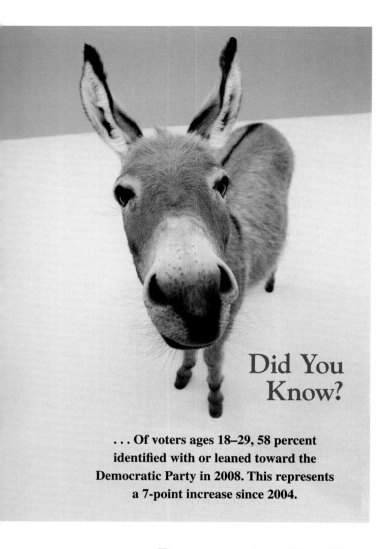

## Did You Know?

... Of voters ages 18–29, 58 percent identified with or leaned toward the Democratic Party in 2008. This represents a 7-point increase since 2004.

ranks only 114th in voter turnout. No other industrialized nation has recorded a lower average turnout.

Political participation makes government accountable to the voters. If participation declines, government operates with less of a sense of accountability to society. This issue is most serious for the least powerful individuals and groups in the United States. Voter turnout has been particularly low among members of racial and ethnic minorities. In postelection surveys, fewer African Americans and Hispanics than Whites report that they actually voted. And many more potential voters fail to register to vote. The poor—whose focus understandably is on survival—are traditionally underrepresented among voters as well. The low turnout found among these groups is due at least in part to their common feeling of powerlessness. By the same token, by declining to vote, they encourage political power brokers to continue to ignore the interests of the less affluent and the nation's minorities. The segment of the voting population that has shown the most voter apathy is the young (Holder 2006).

## RACE AND GENDER IN POLITICS

Because politics is synonymous with power and authority, we should not be surprised that marginalized groups, such as women and racial and ethnic minorities, lack political strength. Nationally, women did not get the vote until 1920. Most Chinese Americans were turned away from the polls until 1926. American Indians did not win the right to vote until 1954. And African Americans were disenfranchised until 1965, when national voting rights legislation was passed. Predictably, it has taken these groups some time to develop their political power and begin to exercise it effectively.

# Reasons for Not Voting, 18- to 24-Year Olds

Too busy, conflicting schedule
Don't know or refused
Out of town
Other reason
Not interested
Registration problems
Forgot to vote
Illness or disability
Did not like candidates or campaign issues
Inconvenient polling place
Transportation problems
Bad weather conditions

0  5  10  15  20  25
**Percent**

Source: U.S. Census Bureau, Current Population Survey, May 25, 2005.

## Going GLOBAL

### Women in National Legislatures, Selected Countries, 2007

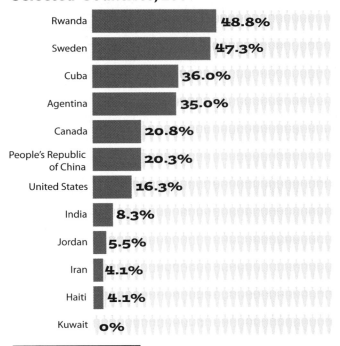

| Country | Percentage |
|---|---|
| Rwanda | 48.8% |
| Sweden | 47.3% |
| Cuba | 36.0% |
| Agentina | 35.0% |
| Canada | 20.8% |
| People's Republic of China | 20.3% |
| United States | 16.3% |
| India | 8.3% |
| Jordan | 5.5% |
| Iran | 4.1% |
| Haiti | 4.1% |
| Kuwait | 0% |

*Note:* Data are for lower legislative houses only, as of March 31, 2007; data on upper houses, such as the U.S. Senate or the U.K. House of Lords, are not included. In 2005, the all-male Kuwati Parliament granted women the right to vote and serve in elected offices, which could allow women to run for office as soon as 2007.

*Source:* Inter-Parliamentary Union 2007.

Progress toward the inclusion of minority groups in government has been slow as well. As of mid-2007, only 16 out of 100 U.S. senators were women. One senator was an African American, 3 were Latinos, and 2 were Asian Americans, leaving 78 White non-Hispanic men. Among the 435 members of the U.S. House of Representatives, 314 were White non-Hispanic men. Seventy were women, 40 were African Americans (including 10 women), 23 were Latinos (including 7 Latinas), 4 were Asian Americans, and 1 was an American Indian. These numbers, though low, represent a high-water mark for these groups.

## Percentages of Minorities and Women in 110th Congress as Compared to Overall Population

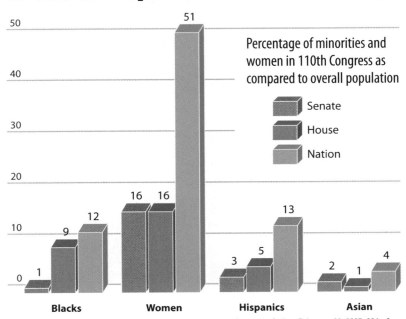

Percentage of minorities and women in 110th Congress as compared to overall population

Senate · House · Nation

*Source:* Greg Giroux, "An Old Boys Club with New Twists," *CQ Weekly Online,* February 26, 2007: 604–8. Accessed online at http://library.cqpress.com on June 14, 2007.

Many critics within minority communities decry what they term "fiesta politics." This refers to the tendency of white power brokers to visit racial and ethnic minority communities only when they need electoral support, making a quick appearance on a national or ethnic holiday to get their picture taken and then vanishing. When the election is over, they too often forget to consult the residents who supported them about community needs and concerns.

Female politicians may be enjoying more electoral success now than in the past, but there is evidence that the media cover them differently than male politicians. A content analysis of newspaper coverage of recent gubernatorial races showed that reporters wrote more often about a female candidate's personal life, appearance, or personality than a male candidate's, and less often about her political viewpoints and voting record. Furthermore, when political issues were raised in newspaper articles, reporters were more likely to illustrate them with statements made by male candidates than by female candidates (Devitt 1999; Jost 2008).

While the proportion of women in national legislatures has increased in the United States and many other nations, women still do not account for half the members of the national legislature in any country. The African Republic of Rwanda ranks the highest, with 48.8 percent of its legislative seats held by women. Overall, the United States ranked 85th among 188 nations in the proportion of women serving as national legislators in 2007 (Paxton et al. 2007).

> **elite model** A view of society as being ruled by a small group of individuals who share a common set of political and economic interests.
> **power elite** A small group of military, industrial, and government leaders who control the fate of the United States.

To remedy this situation, many countries have adopted quotas for female representatives. In some, the government sets aside a certain percentage of seats for women, usually 10–30 percent. In others, political parties have decided that 20–40 percent of their candidates should be women. Thirty-two countries now have some kind of quota system (Vasagar 2005).

## >> The Power Structure in the United States

The issue of power extends beyond just politics and the people who occupy formally recognized offices. Over the years, sociologists repeatedly have sought to discover who really holds power in the United States. Do "we the people" genuinely run the country through our elected representatives? Or does a small elite behind the scenes control both the government and the economic system? It is difficult to determine the location of power in a society as complex as the United States. In exploring this critical question, social scientists have developed two basic views of our nation's power structure: the power elite and the pluralist models.

## POWER ELITE MODELS

Karl Marx believed that 19th-century representative democracy was essentially a sham. He argued that industrial societies were dominated by relatively small numbers of people who owned the factories and controlled natural resources. In Marx's view, government officials and military leaders were essentially servants of this capitalist class and followed their wishes. Therefore, any key decisions made by politicians inevitably reflected the interests of the dominant business owners. Like others who hold an **elite model** of power relations, Marx believed that society is ruled by a small group of individuals who share political and economic interests.

**Mills' Model** Sociologist C. Wright Mills, who developed the concept of the sociological imagination that we looked at in Chapter 1, put forth a model similar to Marx's in his pioneering work *The Power Elite* ([1956] 2000b). Mills described a small group of military, industrial, and government leaders who controlled the fate of the United States—the **power elite.** Power rested in the hands of a few, both inside and outside government.

A pyramid illustrates the power structure of the United States in Mills' model. The power elite rests at the top and includes the corporate rich, leaders of the executive branch of government, and heads of the military (whom Mills called the "warlords"). Directly below are local opinion leaders, members of the legislative branch of government, and leaders of special-interest groups. Mills contended that these individuals and groups basically follow the wishes of

**Power Elite Models**

SOCstudies

THE POWER ELITE

Corporate rich
Executive branch
Military leaders

Interest group leaders
Legislators
Local opinion leaders

Unorganized, exploited masses

**C. Wright Mills's model, 1956**

Social upper class

THE POWER ELITE

Corporate community

Policy-formation organizations

**G. William Domhoff's model, 2006**

*Source:* Left, based on C. W. Mills (1956) 2000b; right, Domhoff 2006:105.

# Which Interests Are Best Represented?

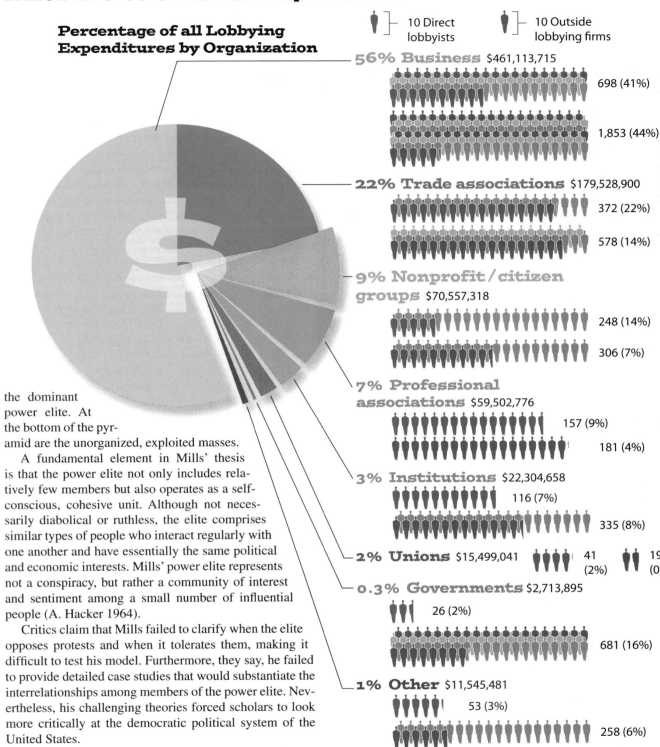

**Percentage of all Lobbying Expenditures by Organization**

10 Direct lobbyists | 10 Outside lobbying firms

**56% Business** $461,113,715
698 (41%)
1,853 (44%)

**22% Trade associations** $179,528,900
372 (22%)
578 (14%)

**9% Nonprofit/citizen groups** $70,557,318
248 (14%)
306 (7%)

**7% Professional associations** $59,502,776
157 (9%)
181 (4%)

**3% Institutions** $22,304,658
116 (7%)
335 (8%)

**2% Unions** $15,499,041
41 (2%)   19 (0)

**0.3% Governments** $2,713,895
26 (2%)
681 (16%)

**1% Other** $11,545,481
53 (3%)
258 (6%)

*Source:* Compiled from Frank Baumgartner and Beth L. Leech, "Interest Niches and Policy Bandwagons: Patterns of Interest Group Involvement in National Politics," *Journal of Politics* 63 (4) 2001, Table 1, p. 1195, and Table 3, p. 1197.

the dominant power elite. At the bottom of the pyramid are the unorganized, exploited masses.

A fundamental element in Mills' thesis is that the power elite not only includes relatively few members but also operates as a self-conscious, cohesive unit. Although not necessarily diabolical or ruthless, the elite comprises similar types of people who interact regularly with one another and have essentially the same political and economic interests. Mills' power elite represents not a conspiracy, but rather a community of interest and sentiment among a small number of influential people (A. Hacker 1964).

Critics claim that Mills failed to clarify when the elite opposes protests and when it tolerates them, making it difficult to test his model. Furthermore, they say, he failed to provide detailed case studies that would substantiate the interrelationships among members of the power elite. Nevertheless, his challenging theories forced scholars to look more critically at the democratic political system of the United States.

In commenting on the scandals that have rocked major corporations such as Enron and Arthur Andersen over the past decade, observers have noted that members of the business elite are closely interrelated. In a study of the members of the boards of directors of Fortune 1000 corporations, researchers found that each director can reach *every* other board of directors in just 3.7 steps. That is, by consulting acquaintances of acquaintances, each director

can quickly reach someone who sits on each of the other 999 boards. Furthermore, the face-to-face contact directors regularly have in their board meetings makes them a highly cohesive elite. Finally, the corporate elite not only is wealthy, powerful, and cohesive but also is overwhelmingly White and male (G. Davis 2003, 2004; Kentor and Jang 2004; Mizruchi 1996; Strauss 2002).

**Domhoff's Model** Sociologist G. William Domhoff (2006) agrees with Mills that a powerful elite runs the United States. Domhoff stresses the role played by elites from within networks of organizations including the corporate community; policy formation organizations such as think tanks, chambers of commerce, and labor unions; and the social upper class. Membership in these groups overlaps, and members with connections in more than one of these spheres have more power and influence. Domhoff finds that those in this latter group are still largely White, male, and upper class, but he notes the presence of a small number of women and minority men in key positions—groups that were excluded from Mills' top echelon and are still underrepresented today (Zweigenhaft and Domhoff 2006).

Although the three groups in Domhoff's power elite model do overlap, they do not necessarily agree on specific policies. Domhoff notes that in politics, two different coalitions have exercised influence. A corporate-conservative coalition has played a large role in both political parties, generating support for particular candidates through direct-mail appeals. A liberal-labor coalition is based in unions, local environmental organizations, a segment of the minority group community, liberal churches, and the university and arts communities (Zweigenhaft and Domhoff 2006). This suggests that the interests of members of the power elite are not always singular or uniform but that overall they do work together to advance their larger interests.

**Hot or Not?**

Is there a relatively small and unified group of powerful people in the United States who, in effect, rule the country through their power and influence?

## THE PLURALIST MODEL

Other theorists argue that power in the United States is shared more widely, that there is no core group at the top who are able to advance their common interests. In their view, a pluralist model more accurately describes the nation's power structure. According to the **pluralist model,** many competing groups within the community have access to government, so that no single group is dominant.

The pluralist model suggests that a variety of groups play a significant role in decision making. Typically, pluralists make use of intensive case studies or community studies based on observation research. One of the most famous—an investigation of decision making in New Haven, Connecticut—was reported by Robert Dahl (1961). Dahl found that, although the number of people involved in any important decision was rather small, community power was nonetheless diffuse. Few political actors exercised decision-making power on all issues, and no one group got its way all the time. One individual or group might be influential in a battle over urban renewal but have little impact on educational policy.

The pluralist model, too, has its critics. Domhoff (1978, 2006) reexamined Dahl's study of decision making in New Haven and argued that Dahl and other pluralists had failed to trace how local elites who were prominent in decision making belonged to a larger national ruling class. In addition, studies of community power, such as Dahl's work in New Haven, can examine decision making only on issues that become part of the political agenda. They fail to address the potential power of elites to keep certain matters entirely out of the realm of political debate.

Dianne Pinderhughes (1987) has criticized the pluralist model for failing to account for the exclusion of African Americans from the political process. Drawing on her studies of Chicago politics, Pinderhughes points out that the residential and occupational segregation of Blacks and their long political disenfranchisement violate the logic of pluralism—which would hold that such a substantial minority should always have been influential in community decision making. This critique applies to many cities across the United States, where other large racial and ethnic minorities, among them Asian Americans, Puerto Ricans, and Mexican Americans, are relatively powerless.

Historically, pluralists have stressed ways in which large numbers of people can participate in or influence governmental decision making. New communications technologies like the Internet are increasing the opportunity to be heard, not just in countries like the United States but in developing countries the world over. The ability to communicate with political leaders via email, for example, increases the opportunity for the average citizen to have a voice in politics.

## >> War and Peace

When it comes to political power, perhaps no decision is as weighty as the decision to go to war. Conflict is a central aspect of social relations. Sociologists Theodore Caplow and Louis Hicks (2002:3) have defined **war** as conflict between organizations that possess trained combat forces equipped with deadly weapons. This meaning is broader than the legal definition, which typically requires a formal declaration of hostilities.

### WAR

Sociologists approach war in three different ways. Those who take a global view study how and why two or more nations

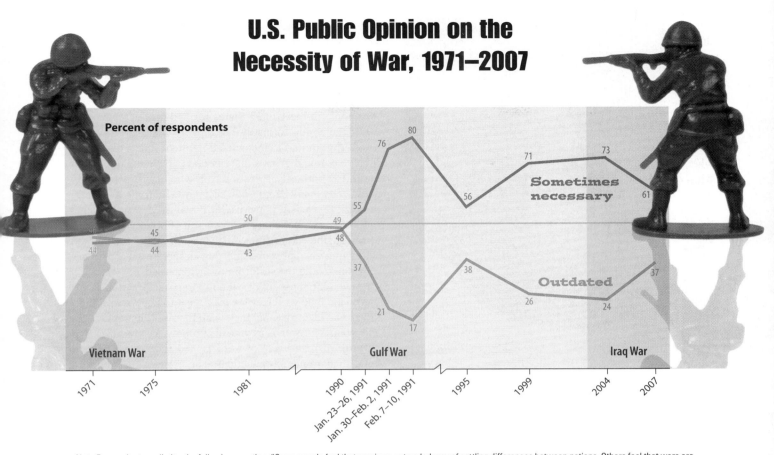

# U.S. Public Opinion on the Necessity of War, 1971–2007

**Percent of respondents**

Sometimes necessary: 46, 45, 50, 49, 55, 76, 80, 56, 71, 73, 61

Outdated: 44, 44, 43, 48, 37, 21, 17, 38, 26, 24, 37

Vietnam War     Gulf War     Iraq War

1971, 1975, 1981, 1990, Jan. 23–26, 1991, Jan. 30–Feb. 2, 1991, Feb. 7–10, 1991, 1995, 1999, 2004, 2007

*Note:* Respondents replied to the following question: "Some people feel that war is an outmoded way of settling differences between nations. Others feel that wars are sometimes necessary to settle differences. With which point of view do you agree?"

*Sources:* Arora 2004; www.gallup.com/poll/1666/military-national-defense.aspx.

become engaged in military conflict. Those who take a nation-state view stress the interaction of internal political, socioeconomic, and cultural forces. And those who take a micro view focus on the social impact of war on individuals and the groups to which they belong (Kiser 1992).

Analysis at the global level focuses on macro issues such as the distribution of resources, struggles over political philosophies, and debates about boundaries. Often it involves nations with competing political and economic systems, as was the case in World War I, World War II, and the Cold War. Some have argued that the conflict in Iraq is about bringing freedom and democracy to the Middle East, while others argue it was motivated by oil and profits.

Sociologists have devoted much effort to studying the internal decision-making process that leads to war. During the Vietnam War, Presidents Johnson and Nixon both misled Congress, painting a falsely optimistic picture of the likely outcome. Based on their intentional distortions, Congress appropriated the military funds the two administrations requested. However, in 1971, *The New York Times* published a set of classified documents now known as "The Pentagon Papers," which revealed that many members of both administrations had knowingly distorted the real prospects for the war. Two years later—over Nixon's veto—Congress passed the War Powers Act, which requires the president to notify Congress of the reasons for committing combat troops to a hostile situation (Patterson 2003).

Even though government leaders make the decision to go to war, public opinion plays a significant role in its execution. By 1971, the number of U.S. soldiers killed in Vietnam had surpassed 50,000, and antiwar sentiment was strong. Surveys done at that time showed that the public was split roughly equally on the question of whether war was an appropriate way to settle differences between nations (see the figure above). This division in public opinion continued until the United States led the charge in the Gulf War following Iraq's invasion of Kuwait in 1990. Since then, U.S. sentiment has been more supportive of war as a means of resolving disputes.

A major change relating to the conduct of war involves the composition of the U.S. military. Women represent a growing presence among the troops. Over 195,000 women, or about 18 percent of U.S. military forces, are now in uniform, serving not just as support personnel but as an integral part of combat units. The first casualty of the war in Iraq, in fact, was Private First Class Lori Piestewa, a member of the Hopi tribe and a descendant of Mexican

> **pluralist model** A view of society in which many competing groups within the community have access to government, so that no single group is dominant.
> **war** Conflict between organizations that possess trained combat forces equipped with deadly weapons.

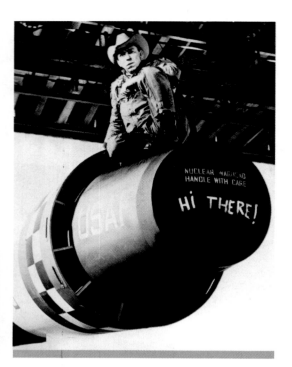

During World War II, the U.S. government sponsored films to garner support for the war effort, boost people's morale, and even demonize the enemy. From cartoons featuring Mickey Mouse and Donald Duck to films including *This Is the Army* (which starred Ronald Reagan), Hollywood cooperated in getting the message out in the 1940s. In more recent years, antiwar films have also raised difficult questions that governments would sometimes rather not be aired. During the Cold War, *Dr. Strangelove* called into question the insanity of the nuclear standoff; in 1970, the film version of *M*A*S*H,* though set in Korea, raised questions about the conflict in Vietnam. More recently, there have been numerous films about the war in Iraq, including Michael Moore's *Fahrenheit 9/11, No End in Sight, Stop-Loss,* and *War, Inc.*

settlers in the Southwest (Bureau of the Census 2007a: Table 503).

At the level of interpersonal interaction, war can bring out the worst as well as the best in people. In 2004, graphic images of the abuse of Iraqi prisoners by U.S. soldiers at Iraq's Abu Ghraib prison shocked the world. For social scientists, the deterioration of the guards' behavior brought to mind Philip Zimbardo's mock prison experiment, done in 1971. Though the results of the experiment have been applied primarily to civilian correctional facilities, Zimbardo's study was actually funded by the Office of Naval Research. In July 2004, the U.S. military began using a documentary film about the experiment to train military interrogators to avoid mistreatment of prisoners (Zarembo 2004; Zimbardo 2004).

## TERRORISM

As people in the United States learned on September 11, 2001, the ability to instill fear through large-scale violent acts is not limited to recognized political states, and it can involve political groups that operate outside the bounds of legitimate authority. Acts of terror, whether perpetrated by a few or by many people, can be a powerful force. Formally defined, **terrorism** is the use or threat of violence against random or symbolic targets in pursuit of political aims. For terrorists, the end justifies the means. They believe that the status quo is oppressive and that desperate measures are essential to end the suffering of the deprived.

An essential aspect of contemporary terrorism involves use of the media. Terrorists may wish to keep secret their individual identities, but they want their political messages and goals to receive as much publicity as possible. The purpose of many acts of terrorist violence is more symbolic than strategic or tactical. These attacks represent a statement made by people who feel that the world has gone awry, that accepted political paths to problem resolution are ineffective or blocked, and that there is a larger or cosmic struggle going on, raising the stakes and so justifying the means (Juergensmeyer 2003). Whether through calls to the media, anonymous manifestos, or other means, terrorists typically admit responsibility for and defend their violent acts.

Terrorism is a global concern. Since September 11, 2001, governments around the world have renewed their efforts to fight terrorism. Even though the public generally regards increased surveillance and social control as a nec-

*Aftermath of a terrorist attack.*

essary evil, these measures have nonetheless raised governance issues. For example, some citizens in the United States and elsewhere have expressed concern that measures such as the USA Patriot Act of 2001 threaten civil liberties. Citizens also complain about the heightened anxiety created by the vague "terror alerts" the federal government issues from time to time. Worldwide, immigration and the processing of refugees have slowed to a crawl, separating families and preventing employers from filling job openings. As these efforts to combat political violence illustrate, the term *terrorism* is an apt one (R. Howard and Sawyer 2003; Lee 1983; R. Miller 1988).

## PEACE

Sociologists have considered **peace** both as the absence of war and as a proactive effort to develop cooperative relations among nations. While

will focus here on international relations, we should note that in the 1990s, 90 percent of the world's armed conflicts occurred *within* rather than between states. Often, outside powers became involved in these internal conflicts, either as supporters of particular factions or as brokers of a potential peace accord. In at least 28 countries where such conflicts occurred—none of which would be considered core nations in world systems analysis—at least 10,000 people died (Kriesberg 1992; Dan Smith 1999).

> **terrorism** The use or threat of violence against random or symbolic targets in pursuit of political aims.
> **peace** The absence of war, or more broadly, a proactive effort to develop cooperative relations among nations.

Sociologists and other social scientists who draw on sociological theory and research have tried to identify conditions that deter war. One of their findings is that international trade may act as a deterrent to armed conflict. As countries exchange goods, people, and then cultures, they become more integrated and less likely to threaten each other's security. Viewed from this perspective, not just trade but also immigration and foreign exchange programs have a beneficial effect on international relations.

Another means of fostering peace is the activity of international charities and activist groups, or nongovernmental

### *Going* GLOBAL

### The Global Reach of Terrorism

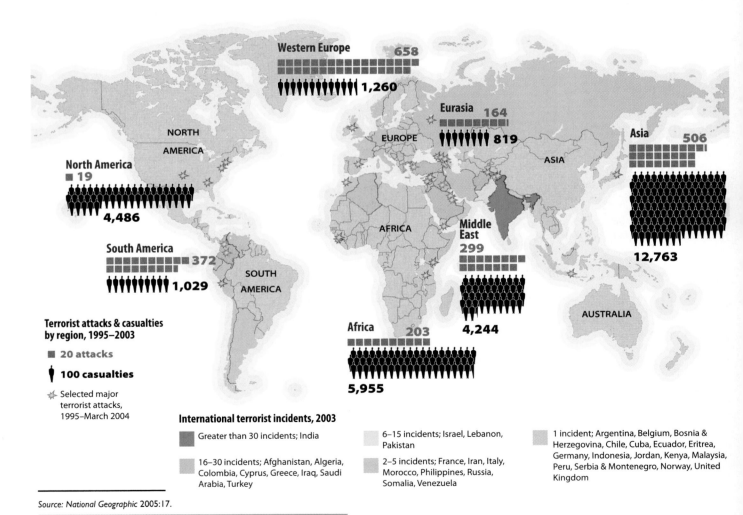

Terrorist attacks & casualties
by region, 1995–2003

■ 20 attacks

| 100 casualties

✴ Selected major terrorist attacks, 1995–March 2004

**International terrorist incidents, 2003**

Greater than 30 incidents; India

16–30 incidents; Afghanistan, Algeria, Colombia, Cyprus, Greece, Iraq, Saudi Arabia, Turkey

6–15 incidents; Israel, Lebanon, Pakistan

2–5 incidents; France, Iran, Italy, Morocco, Philippines, Russia, Somalia, Venezuela

1 incident; Argentina, Belgium, Bosnia & Herzegovina, Chile, Cuba, Ecuador, Eritrea, Germany, Indonesia, Jordan, Kenya, Malaysia, Peru, Serbia & Montenegro, Norway, United Kingdom

Source: National Geographic 2005:17.

organizations (NGOs). The Red Cross and Red Crescent, Doctors Without Borders, and Amnesty International donate their services wherever they are needed, without regard to nationality. In the past decade or so, these NGOs have been expanding in number, size, and scope. By sharing news of local conditions and clarifying local issues, they often prevent conflicts from escalating into violence and war. Some NGOs have initiated cease-fires, reached settlements, and even ended warfare between former adversaries.

Finally, many analysts stress that nations cannot maintain their security by threatening violence. Peace, they contend, can best be maintained by developing strong mutual security agreements among potential adversaries (Etzioni 1965; Shostak 2002). Following this path involves active diplomacy and, to the extent that it involves negotiations with countries viewed as enemies, can be controversial.

From Snapper mowers to microloans to peace movements, stories such as these provide hope. Even though large-scale economic trends can have negative impacts on companies, communities, and individuals and can shape political outcomes, positive social change is possible. Sociological analysis helps us to see the underlying processes at work in the economy and politics, and in so doing can assist us in recognizing places in those systems where opportunities for bringing about such change exist.

*get involved!*

Investigate! Who contributed and how much to the senators and representatives in your state? What interests do those contributors represent? OpenSecrets.org provides an easily searchable database to track down who gives what to whom.

# For REVIEW

I. **How is economic and political power organized?**

- The two major economic systems are capitalism and socialism, though in practice most economies are some mix of the two. Political systems of government include monarchy, oligarchy, dictatorship, totalitarianism, and democracy. A debate exists when looking at formal power in the United States about the degree to which there is a small, cohesive group of power elites who effectively rule or if leadership is more diverse and pluralistic, operating through democratic processes.

II. **How does power operate?**

- Power involves the capacity to get others to do what you want, which can involve force, influence, and authority. In the case of authority, followers accept your power as legitimate, whether based on a traditional, rational-legal, or charismatic foundation.

III. **How has the economy changed over time?**

- The rise of a global economy has brought with it a changing composition of the national and international workforce, deindustrialization, and in the form of microfinancing, economic opportunities for people who are poor.

# Pop Quiz

1. What are the three basic sources of power within any political system?
   a. force, influence, and authority
   b. force, influence, and democracy
   c. force, legitimacy, and charisma
   d. influence, charisma, and bureaucracy

2. Which of the following is *not* part of the classification system of authority developed by Max Weber?
   a. traditional authority
   b. pluralist authority
   c. legal-rational authority
   d. charismatic authority

3. Under capitalism, laissez-faire means that
   a. the means of production and distribution in a society are collectively held.
   b. people should compete freely, with minimal government intervention in the economy.
   c. a single business firm controls the market.
   d. society depends on mechanization to produce its goods and services.

4. Transfers of money, goods, and services that take place but are not reported to the government are best described as
   a. globalization.
   b. the mixed economy.
   c. laissez-faire capitalism.
   d. the informal economy.

5. The systematic, widespread withdrawal of investment in basic aspects of productivity such as factories and plants is called
   a. deindustrialization.
   b. downsizing.
   c. postindustrialization.
   d. gentrification.

6. Political scientist Harold Lasswell defined *politics* as
   a. the struggle for power and authority.
   b. the allocation of valued resources.
   c. who gets what, when, and how.
   d. a cultural universal.

7. The type of government in which a few individuals rule is known as
   a. a monarchy.
   b. a democracy.
   c. a dictatorship.
   d. an oligarchy.

8. Comparing voter turnout in the United States to that of other nations, the United States ranks
   a. first with the highest level of turnout.
   b. in the top 10 internationally.
   c. at about the middle of the nations.
   d. lowest of all industrial nations (and in the bottom quarter of all nations).

9. According to C. Wright Mills, power rests in the hands of the
   a. people.
   b. power elite.
   c. aristocracy.
   d. representative democracy.

10. The use or threat of violence against random or symbolic targets in pursuit of political aims is referred to as
    a. politics.
    b. power.
    c. terrorism.
    d. authority.

1. (a); 2. (b); 3. (b); 4. (d); 5. (a); 6. (c); 7. (d); 8. (d); 9. (b); 10. (c)

# SOCIAL C

# LIVING THE GOOD LIFE– OR NOT

Grayer is four years old. He takes lessons in French, Latin, music, swimming, ice skating, karate, and physical education—in addition to attending preschool. When he failed to get into the elite kindergarten of her choice, his mother hired a grief counselor for him. He lives on Park Avenue in Manhattan with his mother and father, but the person with whom he spends most of his time is his nanny.

Grayer's fictional character was drawn from the real-life experiences of Emma McLaughlin and Nicola Kraus (2002), who worked as nannies to help pay their way through college. They told their stories in the book *The Nanny Diaries,* which later became a film (2007). They depict a world in which, like ours, social class matters.

Sima, one of the nannies in the novel, was an engineer in her home country of El Salvador. She came to the United States with her husband and children, but when he was unable to obtain a green card her husband went back to El Salvador with the kids. Nan, the main nanny character in the book, refers to Sima as "a woman who has a higher degree than I will ever receive, in a subject I couldn't get a passing grade in, and who has been home [to see her husband and children] less than one month in the last twenty-four" (p. 173).

The story of women leaving behind their own children to raise the children of others, effectively "on the clock" 24 hours a day with minimum pay and benefits, going for months or years without seeing their own children, is hardly unique (Ehrenreich and Hochschild 2003). In the United States, we often act as if social class does not matter. Stories like *The Nanny Diaries,* or more significantly, the real-life stories we get from sociological studies, tell a very different tale. As we will see in this chapter, one of the most significant structural determinants shaping our individual lives grows out of our economic position and involves the distribution of economic resources. However, we will see that social class involves more than just unequal economic resources; it also reflects significant social and cultural differences.

# As You READ >>

- What is social class?
- How does social class operate?
- What are the consequences of social class?

## >> Understanding Stratification

Social class was among the earliest interests of sociologists and remains so to this day. Marx, Weber, and Durkheim all highlighted the significance of class differences and sought to understand both their causes and consequences. Du Bois and Addams carried this a step further, actually working to ameliorate the excesses of social stratification.

In the United States, however, social class has long been a touchy subject (DeMott 1990). When the topic of social class does come up here, many people's first response is to deny that it exists. Some even angrily argue that opportunity is open to everyone and that individual effort alone determines one's life outcome. From a sociological perspective, however, we must understand the consequences of social class differences if we are to understand why we think and act the way we do. This is especially true in capitalist societies, in which the significance of economic position is heightened. To provide context, we begin by considering the varieties of ways in which societies are stratified.

### SYSTEMS OF STRATIFICATION

Ever since people first began to speculate about the nature of human society, they have focused on the differences between individuals and groups within society. The term **social inequality** describes a condition in which members of society have different amounts of wealth, prestige, or power. Some degree of social inequality characterizes every society. Sociologists refer to social inequality that

is built into the structure of society as **stratification**—the structured ranking of entire groups of people that perpetuates unequal economic rewards and power in a society.

Stratification shapes individual opportunity based on the position that one occupies in the system. Certain groups of people stand higher in social rankings, control scarce resources, wield power, and receive special treatment. Unequal rewards include income and wealth, but they are also related to the power conveyed by social networks (who you know) and knowledge (what you know). Control over such resources enables one generation to pass on social advantages to the next, producing groups of people arranged in rank order, from low to high.

Sociologists focus on four major systems of stratification: slavery, caste, estate, and class. To understand these systems better, it is helpful to recall the distinction between achieved status and ascribed status from Chapter 5. **Ascribed status** is a social position assigned to a person by society without regard for his or her unique talents or characteristics. In contrast, **achieved status** is a social position that a person attains largely through his or her own efforts. Members of the two are closely linked. The nation's most affluent families generally inherit wealth and status, while many members of racial and ethnic minorities inherit disadvantaged status. Age and gender are additional ascribed statuses that influence a person's wealth and social position.

**Slavery** The most extreme form of legalized social inequality for individuals and groups is **slavery.** Enslaved individuals are the property of other people, who have the right to treat them as they please, as if they were tools or draft animals.

The practice of slavery has varied over different times and places. Most of the slaves in ancient Greece were prisoners of war or individuals captured and sold by pirates. Although succeeding generations could inherit slave status, it was not necessarily permanent. A person's status might change, depending on which city-state happened to triumph in a military conflict. In effect, all citizens had the potential to become slaves or gain freedom, depending on the historical circumstances. By contrast, slavery in the United States and Latin America was an ascribed status, and slaves faced racial and legal barriers to freedom.

Today, the Universal Declaration of Human Rights, which is binding on all members of the United Nations, prohibits slavery in all its forms. Yet around the world, millions of people still live as slaves. In many developing countries, bonded laborers are imprisoned in virtual lifetime employment; in some countries, human beings are owned outright. Though slavery is outlawed in the United States and Europe, guest workers and illegal immigrants have been forced to labor for years under terrible conditions, either to pay off debts or to avoid being turned over to immigration authorities. In 2007 a wealthy couple from New York was convicted of holding two Indonesian women as slaves in their home for four years (Eltman 2007; S. Greenhouse 2007).

**Castes** Castes are hereditary ranks, usually dictated by religion, that tend to be fixed and immobile. The caste system is generally associated with Hinduism in India and other countries. In India there are four major castes, or *varnas*: priests (*Brahman*), warriors (*Kshatriya*), merchants (*Vaishya*), and artisans/farmers (*Shudra*). A fifth category of outcastes, referred to as the *dalit,* or untouchables, is considered to be so lowly and unclean as to have no place within this system of stratification. There are also many minor castes. Caste membership is an ascribed status (at birth, children automatically assume the same position as their parents). Each caste is quite sharply defined, and members are expected to marry within that caste.

In 1950, after gaining independence from Great Britain, India adopted a new constitution that formally outlawed

> **social inequality** A condition in which members of society have different amounts of wealth, prestige, or power.
> **stratification** A structured ranking of entire groups of people that perpetuates unequal economic rewards and power in a society.
> **ascribed status** A social position assigned to a person by society without regard for the person's unique talents or characteristics.
> **achieved status** A social position that a person attains largely through his or her own efforts.
> **slavery** A system of enforced servitude in which some people are owned by others as property.
> **caste** A hereditary rank, usually religiously dictated, that tends to be fixed and immobile.

tion largely defined the estate system. The nobles inherited their titles and property; the peasants were born into a subservient position within an agrarian society.

As the estate system developed, it became more differentiated. Nobles began to achieve varying degrees of authority. By the 12th century, a priesthood had emerged in most of Europe, along with classes of merchants and artisans. For the first time, there were groups of people whose wealth did not depend on land ownership or agriculture. This economic change had profound social consequences as the estate system ended and a class system of stratification came into existence.

**Social Classes** A **class system** is a social ranking based primarily on economic position in which achieved characteristics can influence social mobility. In contrast to slavery and caste systems, in a class system the boundaries between classes are imprecisely defined, and one can move from one stratum, or level, of society to another. Even so, class systems maintain stable stratification hierarchies and patterns of class divisions, and they, too, are marked by an unequal distribution of wealth and power. Class standing, though it can be achieved, is heavily dependent on family and on ascribed factors such as race and ethnicity.

Sociologist Daniel Rossides (1997) uses a five-class model to describe the class system of the United States: the upper class, the upper-middle class, the lower-middle class, the working class, and the lower class. Although the lines separating social classes in his model are not as sharp as the divisions between castes, members of the five classes differ significantly in ways other than just income level.

the caste system. Over the past decade or two, however, urbanization and technological advances have brought more change to India's caste system than the government has in more than half a century. The anonymity of city life tends to blur caste boundaries, allowing the *dalit* to pass unrecognized in temples, schools, and workplaces. The globalization of high technology also has opened up India's social order, bringing new opportunities to those who possess the skills and ability to capitalize on them, regardless of caste.

Rossides categorizes about 1–2 percent of the people of the United States as upper class, a group limited to the very wealthy. These people associate in exclusive clubs and social circles. In contrast, the lower class, consisting of approximately 20–25 percent of the population, disproportionately consists of Blacks, Hispanics, single mothers with dependent children, and people who cannot find regular work or must make do with low-paying work. This class lacks both wealth and income and is too weak politically to exercise significant power.

**Estates** A third type of stratification system developed within the feudal societies of medieval Europe. Under the **estate system,** or feudalism, nobles owned the land, which they leased to peasants who worked it and lived on it. The peasants turned over a portion of what they produced to the landowner, who in return offered the peasants military protection against bandits and rival nobles. The basis for the system was the nobles' ownership of land, which was critical to their superior and privileged status. As in systems based on slavery and caste, inheritance of one's posi-

## SOCthink

> > > People with incomes well above average often prefer to identify themselves as middle class. Why might they do this? How might this tendency be an outgrowth of the dominant American values of equality and democracy?

Sandwiched between the upper and lower classes in this model are the upper-middle class, the lower-middle class, and the working class. The upper-middle class, numbering about 10–15 percent of the population, is composed of professionals such as doctors, lawyers, and architects. They participate extensively in politics and take leadership roles in voluntary associations. The lower-middle class, which accounts for approximately 30–35 percent of the population, includes less affluent professionals (such as elementary school teachers and nurses), owners of small businesses, and a sizable number of clerical workers. While not all members of this varied class hold a college degree, they share the goal of sending their children to college.

Rossides describes the working class—about 40–45 percent of the population—as people who hold regular manual or blue-collar jobs. Certain members of this class, such as electricians, may have higher incomes than people in the lower-middle class. Yet even if they have achieved some degree of economic security, they tend to identify with manual workers and their long history of involvement in the labor movement of the United States. Of the five classes, the working class is declining noticeably in size. In the U.S. economy of today, service and technical jobs are replacing those involved in the actual manufacturing or transportation of goods.

## SOCthink

> > > Into which class would you place most of the people in your community? Are there relatively clear boundaries between class neighborhoods there?

## SOCIAL MOBILITY

A key component of each of these systems of stratification is **social mobility**—the degree to which one can change

the social stratum into which one is born. The ascent of a person from a poor background to a position of prestige, power, or financial reward—such as in the movie *Maid in Manhattan*—is an example of social mobility. In the film, Jennifer Lopez plays a chambermaid in a big-city hotel who rises to become a company supervisor and the girlfriend of a well-to-do politician. While stories in which the commoner marries the prince truly were fairy tales in the era of the estate system, today they are metaphors for the seeming permeability of modern class boundaries.

### Open Versus Closed Stratification Systems

Sociologists distinguish between stratification systems that are open versus closed to indicate the degree of social mobility in a society. An **open system** implies that a person's achieved status influences his or her social position. Such a system encourages competition among members of society. The United States has sought to move toward this ideal by removing once-legal barriers faced by women, racial and ethnic minorities, and people born in lower social classes.

At the other extreme is the **closed system,** which allows little or no possibility of individual social mobility. Slavery and caste systems are examples of closed systems. In such societies, social placement is based on ascribed statuses, such as race or family background, which cannot be changed.

**Types of Social Mobility** Sociologists also distinguish between mobility within a social class versus movement between social classes. For example, a bus driver who becomes a hotel clerk moves from one social position to another of approximately the same rank. Sociologists call this

**estate system** A system of stratification under which peasants were required to work land leased to them by nobles in exchange for military protection and other services. Also known as feudalism.

**class system** A social ranking based primarily on economic position in which achieved characteristics can influence social mobility.

**social mobility** Movement of individuals or groups from one position in a society's stratification system to another.

**open system** A social system in which the position of each individual is influenced by his or her achieved status.

**closed system** A social system in which there is little or no possibility of individual social mobility.

**horizontal mobility** The movement of an individual from one social position to another of the same rank.

**vertical mobility** The movement of an individual from one social position to another of a different rank.

**intergenerational mobility** Changes in the social position of children relative to their parents.

**intragenerational mobility** Changes in social position within a person's adult life.

**capitalism** An economic system in which the means of production are held largely in private hands and the main incentive for economic activity is the accumulation of profits.

kind of movement **horizontal mobility.** However, if the bus driver were to become a lawyer, he or she would experience **vertical mobility**—the movement of an individual from one social position to another of a different rank (Sorokin [1927] 1959). Vertical mobility can also involve moving downward in a society's stratification system, as would be the case if the lawyer became a bus driver.

Sociologists also consider the differences between intergenerational and intragenerational mobility when evaluating mobility. **Intergenerational mobility** involves changes in the social position of children relative to their parents. Thus, a plumber whose father was a physician provides an example of downward intergenerational mobility. A film star whose parents were both factory workers illustrates upward intergenerational mobility. Because education contributes significantly to upward mobility, any barrier to the pursuit of advanced degrees can definitely limit intergenerational mobility (Isaacs et al. 2008).

**Intragenerational mobility**, on the other hand, involves changes in social position within a person's adult life. Thus, a woman who enters the paid labor force as a teacher's aide and eventually becomes superintendent of the school district experiences upward intragenerational mobility. A man who becomes a cab driver after his accounting firm goes bankrupt undergoes downward intragenerational mobility.

## SOCthink

> > > What is the story of social mobility in your family? To what extent have there been shifts both across and within generations? What factors, such as family connections or historical events, contributed to the social mobility that occurred?

In the United States, one way to define the "American Dream" is as upward vertical mobility that is intragenerational. In other words, a person could experience a significant shift in social class position over the course of her or his career, from a relatively low-level position to one of significant wealth and power. While this does happen, as we will see below, the "American reality" is that we tend to end up in positions relatively close to where we began.

## SOCIOLOGICAL PERSPECTIVES ON STRATIFICATION

Sociologists have examined the relative significance of key resources that shape social stratification. Early in the development of sociology, Karl Marx argued that material resources were most important, especially ownership of the means of production. Max Weber, who sought to extend Marx's model and make it more broadly applicable, argued that three primary resources shape social position: class, status, and party. More recently, Pierre Bourdieu has highlighted the significance of culture as an additional resource. We will look at each of their models in turn.

**Marx on Class** Karl Marx has been aptly described as both a revolutionary and a social scientist. Marx was concerned with stratification in all types of human societies, beginning with primitive agricultural tribes and continuing into feudalism. But his main focus was on the effects of economic inequality on all aspects of his own society—19th-century Europe. The plight of the working class made him feel that it was imperative to strive for changes in the class structure of society (Beeghley 1978:1).

In Marx's view, social relations during any period of history depend on who controls the

**Water**
An Indian widow attempts to escape the social restrictions of her position.

**The Departed**
A man from a family of crooks wants to become a cop.

**Save the Last Dance**
An upper-class White girl at an inner city Chicago school.

**Atonement**
Two people from two classes fall in love and face the consequences.

**Titanic**
A first-class and third-class love affair.

**5 Movies on SOCIAL CLASS**

primary mode of economic production, such as land or factories. Differential access to scarce resources shapes the relationship between groups. Thus, under the feudal estate system, most production was agricultural, and the nobility owned the land. Peasants had little choice but to work according to terms dictated by the landowners.

Using this type of analysis, Marx examined social relations within **capitalism**—the economic system in which private individuals control the means of production and the main incentive for economic activity is the accumulation of profits (D. Rosenberg 1991). Marx focused on

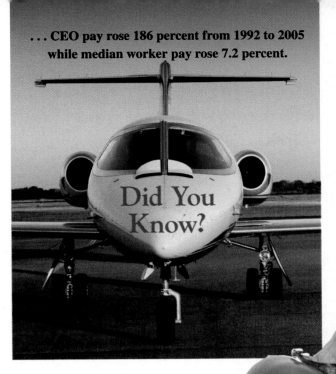

**... CEO pay rose 186 percent from 1992 to 2005 while median worker pay rose 7.2 percent.**

Did You Know?

**Hot or Not?**

Is a classless society possible?

the two classes that began to emerge as the feudal estate system declined: the bourgeoisie and the proletariat. The **bourgeoisie,** or capitalist class, owns the means of production, such as factories and machinery; the **proletariat** is the working class. In capitalist societies, the members of the bourgeoisie maximize profit in competition with other firms. In the process, they exploit workers, who must exchange their labor for subsistence wages. In Marx's view, members of each class share a distinctive culture. Marx was most interested in the culture of the proletariat, but he also examined the ideology of the bourgeoisie, through which that class justifies its dominance over workers.

According to Marx, exploitation of the proletariat would inevitably lead to the destruction of the capitalist system, because the workers would revolt. Two keys help us to understand why: the problem of scarcity and the capitalist system of social relations. Marx believed that humans had to produce in order to survive, but as we saw in Chapter 1, how we do so is not narrowly determined by our genes. Our natural creative capacity, Marx believed, would lead to technological innovation that made it possible for us to produce enough food, clothes, shelter, and other goods that eventually everyone would have more than enough. Capitalism actually encourages such technological innovation in the context of the competitive marketplace.

Once this technological obstacle to providing for all our needs was solved, Marx felt that the only obstacle to an equitable society would be the capitalist system of so-

cial relations. Its emphasis on private property enabled the few at the top, the bourgeoisie, to own and control much more than they could ever hope to need or want while the majority at the bottom, the proletariat, struggled. Eventually, Marx argued, the proletariat would see that they had no real interest in the existing set of social relations. They would develop **class consciousness**—a subjective awareness of common vested interests and the need for collective political action to bring about social change. This would lead to the overthrow of capitalism in favor of a system of more equitable distribution in the form of socialism and then communism.

A question that often arises in response to Marx's work is this: Why hasn't that revolution happened? One answer is that Marx thought capitalists would work against the development of such class consciousness by shaping society's accepted values and norms. The term **dominant ideology** describes a set of cultural beliefs and practices that helps to maintain powerful social, economic, and political interests. Private property is a core principle of this ideology, but our failure to recognize the collective efforts that go into the production of any products and services contributes as well. For Marx, the bourgeoisie controlled not only material resources but also the means of producing beliefs about reality through religion, education, and the media (Abercrombie et al. 1980, 1990; Robertson 1988). As a result, workers had to overcome what Marx termed **false consciousness**—an attitude held by members of a class that does not accurately reflect their objective position. A worker with false consciousness may adopt an individualistic viewpoint toward capitalist exploitation ("*I* am being exploited by *my* boss"). In contrast, the class-conscious worker realizes that all workers are being exploited by the bourgeoisie and have a common stake in revolution.

**Weber's Multidimensional Model** Unlike Marx, Max Weber insisted that class does not totally define a person's position within the stratification system. Instead, writing in 1916, he identified three distinct components of stratification: class, status, and party (Weber [1916] 1958). These three point to the importance of material, social, and organizational resources in shaping how much power people have.

Weber used the term **class** to refer to a group of people who have a similar level of economic resources. He agreed with Marx that this includes ownership of

**bourgeoisie** Karl Marx's term for the capitalist class, comprising the owners of the means of production.

**proletariat** Karl Marx's term for the working class in a capitalist society.

**class consciousness** In Karl Marx's view, a subjective awareness held by members of a class regarding their common vested interests and need for collective political action to bring about social change.

**dominant ideology** A set of cultural beliefs and practices that helps to maintain powerful social, economic, and political interests.

**false consciousness** A term used by Karl Marx to describe an attitude held by members of a class that does not accurately reflect their objective position.

**class** A group of people who have a similar level of economic resources.

the means of production, but he went further than Marx, adding income, wealth, and skill knowledge to the equation. Regarding such knowledge, Marx thought that mechanization and extreme division of labor would make skill less significant under capitalism. But Weber argued that skill would continue to be a valuable commodity in the labor market and that by developing our skill knowledge—for example, by going to college—we could enhance our class position. For Weber, people who shared similar economic positions, such as workers in minimum-wage jobs, were in the same class. Although Weber agreed with Marx on the importance of this economic dimension of stratification, he argued that the actions of individuals and groups cannot be understood solely in economic terms.

Weber used the term **status group** to refer to people who have the same prestige or lifestyle. While class is an economic resource, status represents a social resource. Status is, to some extent, in the eye of the beholder. A person has status because others recognize the position that she or he occupies as distinctive relative to other positions, whether higher or lower. Association with a group, such as medical doctors or schoolteachers, conveys status. Being part of such groups can limit our social interactions with others whom the group sees as outsiders. Such memberships are also often associated with a particular lifestyle, including the kind of car you drive or vacations you take, but status is not the same as economic class standing. In our culture, a successful pickpocket may belong to the same income class as a college professor. Yet the thief is widely regarded as a member of a low-status group, whereas the professor holds high status.

For Weber, the third major component of stratification involved organizational resources. **Party** refers to the capacity to organize to accomplish some particular goal. This is what we mean when we talk of a political party, but such organization extends beyond politics to all spheres of life. As we have seen before with Weber, bureaucracies represent the ideal form of this resource because they are organized explicitly to maximize available resources and to accomplish their goals in the most efficient manner possible. For Weber, party was a potential resource, available to any individuals or groups who would seize it. The civil rights movement in the United States provides a classic example. With minimal class or status resources as defined by the larger society, organization was critical to the success of this movement.

## SOCthink

> > > How might a group coordinate their class, status, and party resources to accomplish their goals? Pick a group on campus or in your community that is seeking to bring about social change, and imagine how you might advise them using Weber's principles.

Weber maintained that, in practice, these three resources work together to shape individual and group power. Each factor influences the other two, and in fact the rankings on these three dimensions often tend to coincide. For example, John F. Kennedy came from an extremely wealthy family, attended exclusive preparatory schools, graduated

## From Me to You

As a professor, I have seen that grades are shaped by more than just effort and intellectual ability. Students with more cultural capital, including significant background educational resources, simply do not have to work as hard. Seniors, for example, know the rules of the game. First-year students, on the other hand, often have a hard time distinguishing what is important from what is secondary. These are the students who, when they read the textbook, highlight virtually every word (I know because I was one myself). Students who come to college with the kinds of cultural capital that professors value have an edge over those who lack such resources.

from Harvard University, and went on to become president of the United States. Like Kennedy, many people from affluent backgrounds achieve high status and demonstrate impressive political organization.

**Bourdieu and Cultural Capital** While Marx emphasized material resources and Weber highlighted the significance of social resources in the form of both status and party, sociologist Pierre Bourdieu added to these the significance of cultural resources. Bourdieu introduced the concept of **cultural capital,** by which he meant our tastes, knowledge, attitudes, language, and ways of thinking that we exchange in interaction with others. Often associated with artistic or literary preferences, cultural capital goes much deeper than this as it is rooted in our perception of reality itself. For Bourdieu, because culture is hierarchically valued, it is a form of power.

Bourdieu argued that people in different social class positions possess different types of cultural capital. From NASCAR to Mozart, for example, the tastes of the working class differ from those of the upper class. Symphonic concerts, operas, and foreign films for instance, are considered "high culture," while "pop culture," including popular movies, TV shows, and music CDs, are considered

"middle-brow" or below. People draw distinctions, for example, between watching *Masterpiece Theatre* versus *I Survived a Japanese Game Show* and listening to Pavarotti versus Britney Spears. Such judgments are based on a certain level of cultural elitism in which those at the top are able to define their preferences as apparently superior to those of the masses. The cultural capital of people who are working class, often disparaged as redneck or ghetto, is often valued least of all—until it is claimed by others as their own, as was the case with jazz, blues, rock and roll, and rap (Gans 1971).

> **status group** People who have the same prestige or lifestyle, independent of their class positions.
> **party** The capacity to organize to accomplish some particular goal.
> **cultural capital** Our tastes, knowledge, attitudes, language, and ways of thinking that we exchange in interaction with others.

When we interact with others, we draw on the cultural capital resources we possess. Such interaction is fairly easy with others who share the same basic set of resources. When interaction occurs with others who possess a different stock of cultural capital, however, it becomes more complex. We see these kinds of difficulties when executives try to interact casually with workers on the factory floor or when we find ourselves dining in a place where we aren't quite sure what the rules are. If this were only a matter of social difference between various subcultures, it might not be a big deal. But the cultural capital of the elite is also tied to their control over economic and social resources. As a result, cultural capital can be used as a form of exclusion

Whether it is the rags-to-riches dreams of *American Idol,* the glitz and glamour of *Dancing with the Stars,* the upper-middle-class aspirations of *The Apprentice,* or the conspicuous consumption of *Pimp My Ride,* TV shows have found social class lifestyle differences a tempting topic. Perhaps no program uses the contrast between class preferences as effectively, however, as does *Wife Swap* on ABC. In this show, two wives/mothers switch families for two weeks, frequently pitting families from different social classes against each other. The tension between their cultural capital resources is on display, highlighting the contrast between the two family environments.

from jobs, organizations, and opportunities. For example, a qualified applicant may lose out on a job during the interview due to inappropriate syntax or inadequate familiarity with cultural references, such as current news events or the latest in the world of golf. Employers tend to hire people they feel comfortable with, and cultural capital plays a significant role in that process (Kanter 1993).

Compounding this problem of cultural inequality is the fact that our preferences and perceptions often pass down from parent to child in the same way that material capital is inherited. Parents teach their children linguistic patterns and cultural tastes, from the use of double negatives to the appreciation of literature. Cultural capital is also reproduced in the next generation in the context of schools, where class distinctions within the community shape the curriculum and patterns of discipline. Jonathan Kozol (2005), for example, in his most recent study on how education perpetuates inequality, told the story of an inner-city high school student who wanted to take an AP class in preparation for college but was placed in a sewing class instead. As a friend of hers put it, the factory owners need workers, and it won't be their kids: "You're ghetto—so you sew!" (2005:180). Such transmission increases the likelihood that social advantage will be passed from one generation to the next.

Social mobility from this perspective involves more than just acquiring more money and better social connections. Winning the lottery, for example, does not transform a person at the bottom of the hierarchy into one at the top, or, as Bourdieu put it, "having a million does not in itself make one able to live like a millionaire" (1984:374). Such movement requires a social and cultural transformation as well. For mobility to happen, the individual must earn and learn a different set of knowledge and skills, as well as a whole new lifestyle: new tastes, attitudes, language, and thoughts. The same goes for someone who would drop from a higher rank into a lower one.

**Material, Social, and Cultural Resources** We can point to three critical categories of resources that shape the positions we occupy and influence our likelihood for social mobility. Material resources refer to economic resources that we own or control, including money, property, and land. Social resources include prestige based on the position we occupy and connections based on the social networks we are a part of. It turns out that the old saying "It's not what you know; it's who you know" has some truth to it. Position and connections make it possible for us to increase the likelihood of accomplishing our goals. Finally, cultural resources include our tastes, language, and way of looking at the world. They represent our knowledge

> Anyone who has ever struggled with poverty knows how extremely expensive it is to be poor.
>
> James A. Baldwin

of cognitive, normative, and material elements of culture that we can draw on when acting to accomplish our goals. A simple but classic example involves knowing which fork to use for the various courses of a formal dinner. But it also includes knowing how to respond when we are put on the spot, whether in a business meeting, at a rock concert, or in class. Viewing social class in terms of material, social, and cultural resources makes social class a much more useful concept when trying to map our social lives or figure out why we think and act as we do.

All societies have some degree of stratification, and tracking these three resources helps us to better understand how stratification works. As we saw in Chapter 8 on education, Davis and Moore (1945) suggested that, especially in societies with a complex division of labor, some positions are more important or require more skill. Perhaps we need to hold out the promise of high pay and prestige as a reward so that those with the necessary skill and determination take the time and money required to develop their talents. Even if we accept the principle that a certain degree of inequality is inevitable, however, questions remain about the extent of inequality that is practiced. In addition, if inequality is to be tied to ability and effort, we need to investigate the degree to which positions are earned versus inherited. We turn next to an analysis of the degree of inequality that exists in the United States.

## >> Social Class in the United States

Social class dividing lines in the United States are not as clear-cut or firm as they were in historically in, say, England. When we take a step back, however, we see that social class differences do impact our everyday lives. We may not label them as such, and we might want to dismiss their significance. Nevertheless, when we look through the lens of class as highlighted by these three resources, we bring to the surface differences that we already recognize as important.

### CULTURAL CAPITAL

In some ways it is easiest to look first at cultural resources because, while we recognize that such differences exist, we may feel that they are not such a big deal. If one person likes Chopin while another likes Kenny Chesney, what difference does that make? As indicated above, however, such tastes do not exist in isolation; rather, they are tied to social and material resources as well and can serve as a means of exclusion (Halle 1993). Looking at just a few examples, we can appreciate the degree to which we already see class, even if we don't usually recognize it as such.

We can recognize class in the clothes we wear, and even in the terms we use to describe them, such as "business casual" or "blue collar." Some people would not be caught dead wearing a suit and tie (or maybe that's the only way they will wear them), while others are incapable of being comfortable in blue jeans and a T-shirt. And brands can matter, whether it's Lilly Pulitzer, Sean Jean, J. McLaughlin, Gap, Rocawear, Juicy Couture, Wrangler, Calypso, Abercrombie & Fitch, Coach, or Gucci. Even the fabrics clothes are made of suggest class differences, with higher classes more likely to wear clothes made out of organic materials (such as wool, silk, or cotton) and lower classes more likely to wear synthetic fabrics (including nylon, rayon, and orlon). This is likely driven not only by the initial cost differences for such materials but also by the long-term care costs for dry-cleaning.

## SOCthink

> > > Paul Fussell, in his book *Class: A Guide Through the American Status System,* argued that the writing on our clothes says a lot about our social class. What story do the logos, brands, and writing on your clothes tell about you? How might your clothing choices have differed had you been in a different class position?

We also see class differences when it comes to houses. Just driving through neighborhoods we recognize class indicators of houses: the distance they are located from the street; the composition of a driveway, if there is one; the fastidiousness of lawn care; the existence of flamingoes, gnomes, or gazing balls; and the presence of pillars or fountains. When it comes to where we live, expressions such as "the wrong side of the tracks," "snob hill," and "McMansion" point to our recognition that class matters.

Similarly, class makes a difference when it comes to vacations. Elites might head to Martha's Vineyard or the Hamptons, or they might "summer" in Nepal or Istanbul. Middle-class people are more likely to head to Disney World or perhaps go on a cruise, though either dream vacation may be possible only after having saved for some time or going into debt. Because money and vacation time are often limited, working-class families are more likely to go on a one-week trip, probably not too far from home, to which they are more likely to drive, and it might involve camping.

> **prestige** The respect and admiration that an occupation holds in a society.
> **esteem** The reputation that a specific person has earned within an occupation.

We could look at other areas too, including what we eat (fast food versus haute cuisine), what we drink (Bud Light versus fine wine), and what sports we watch (NASCAR and professional wrestling versus tennis and America's Cup yachting). In all kinds of ways, our preferences are shaped by our social class positions. Yet we seldom take seriously the source of such preferences or their effect on the choices we make and the doors that these choices may open or close to us.

## STATUS AND PRESTIGE

We have a sense of where people fit relative to each other. Some we see as higher, while others we see as lower. We have seen as much already with regard to cultural preferences, but when it comes to status, it is not just what people like that we rank, but who they are. Sociologists seek to describe those systems of ranking and the advantages and disadvantages they convey.

**Occupational Prestige** One way sociologists describe the relative social class positions people occupy is by focusing on their occupational prestige. The term **prestige** refers to the respect and admiration that an occupation holds in a society. Fairly or not, "my daughter, the physicist" connotes something very different from "my daughter, the waitress." Prestige is independent of the particular individual who occupies a job, a characteristic that distinguishes it from esteem. **Esteem** refers to the reputation that a specific person has earned within an occupation. Therefore, we can say that the position of president of the United States has high prestige even though it has been occupied by people with varying degrees of esteem. A hairdresser may have the esteem of his clients, but he lacks the prestige of a corporate executive.

Using the results from a series of national surveys, sociologists have identified prestige rankings for about 500 occupations. They created a scale with 0 as the lowest possible score and 100 as the highest, and ranked the occupations based on the results of their surveys. Surgeon, physician, lawyer, dentist, and college professor were among the most highly regarded occupations, while bartender, farmworker, janitor, newspaper vendor, prostitute, and

**Did You Know?**

...According to Harris polls, the status of teachers has risen more than any other occupational category they have tracked over the past 30 years. In 2007, 54 percent of respondents identified teachers as having "very great prestige" compared with 29 percent in 1977.

# Prestige Rankings of Occupations

| Occupation | Score |
|---|---|
| Surgeon | 87 |
| Physician | 86 |
| Lawyer | 75 |
| Dentist | 74 |
| College professor | 74 |
| Architect | 73 |
| Psychiatrist | 72 |
| Clergy | 69 |
| Pharmacist | 68 |
| Registered nurse | 66 |
| High school teacher | 66 |
| Accountant | 65 |
| Optician | 65 |
| Elementary school teacher | 64 |
| Banker | 63 |
| Veterinarian | 62 |
| Legislator | 61 |
| Airline pilot | 60 |
| Police officer or detective | 60 |
| Prekindergarten teacher | 55 |
| Librarian | 54 |
| Firefighter | 53 |
| Social worker | 52 |
| Dental hygienist | 52 |
| Electrician | 51 |
| Funeral director | 49 |
| Farm manager | 48 |
| Mail carrier | 47 |
| Secretary | 46 |
| Insurance agent | 45 |
| Bank teller | 43 |
| Nurse's aide | 42 |

| Occupation | Score |
|---|---|
| Farmer | 40 |
| Correctional officer | 40 |
| Receptionist | 39 |
| Carpenter | 39 |
| Barber | 36 |
| Child care worker | 35 |
| Hotel clerk | 32 |
| Bus driver | 32 |
| Auto body repairer | 31 |
| Truck driver | 30 |
| Salesworker (shoes) | 28 |
| Garbage collector | 28 |
| Waiter and waitress | 28 |
| Cook in a pizza shop | 27 |
| Bartender | 25 |
| Farm worker | 23 |
| Janitor | 22 |
| Newspaper vendor | 19 |
| Prostitute | 14 |
| Panhandler | 11 |

Note: 100 is the highest and 0 the lowest possible prestige score.

Source: J. Davis et al. 2007; see also Nakao and Treas 1994.

istics, while the reverse is true for someone from a lower position.

**Socioeconomic Status** As a single variable, occupation provides us with a sense of where people stand, but status involves more than just occupational prestige. In their research, sociologists add variables to the mix to gain a more complete picture of social class standing. These include such things as the value of homes, sources of income, assets, years in present occupations, neighborhoods, and considerations regarding dual careers. Adding these variables will not necessarily paint an alternative picture of class differentiation in the United States, but it does allow sociologists to measure class in a more complex and multidimensional way. When researchers use multiple measures, they typically speak of **socioeconomic status (SES),** a measure of social class that is based on income, education, occupation, and related variables.

One of the lessons we learn from SES research is that society often undervalues, in terms of prestige and pay, work that is essential for our individual and collective survival. In an effort to make the value of women's contribution to the economy more visible, for example, the International Women Count Network, a global grassroots feminist organization, has sought to give a monetary value to women's unpaid work. Besides providing symbolic recognition of women's contributions to society, they propose that this value also be used to calculate pension and other benefits that are based on wages received. The United Nations has placed an $11-*trillion* price tag on unpaid labor by women, largely in child care, housework, and agriculture. Whatever the figure, the continued undercounting of many workers' contributions to both family and the economy means that focusing only on prestige when it comes to evaluating status is insufficient. We must also consider the significance of other factors, especially income (United Nations Development Programme 1995; Wages for Housework Campaign 1999).

panhandler were at the bottom. Sociologists have found a significant amount of stability in such rankings from 1925 to the present (Nakao and Treas 1994:11). This suggests that we do confer status to people based on the positions they occupy. Someone with a higher status is more likely to get the benefit of the doubt because of the position she or he occupies, regardless of her or his individual character-

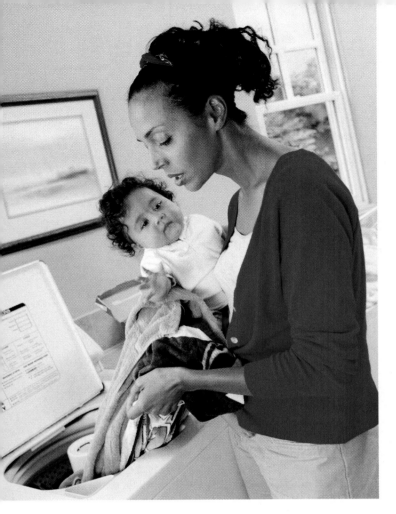

We gain additional insight into this inequality by looking at the relative placement of households from bottom to top. One of the most common ways to present income dispersion is to line up all income-earning households from low to high and then break them into quintiles, or blocks of 20 percent. There are approximately 116 million households in the United States, so each quintile would include an equal number of about 23.2 million households. Doing so allows us to get a sense of what the average income is within each of these quintiles, along with the percentage of the total income pie that each quintile earns.

> **socioeconomic status (SES)** A measure of class that is based on income, education, occupation, and related variables.
> **income** Wages and salaries measured over some period, such as per hour or year.
> **wealth** The total of all a person's material assets, including savings, land, stocks, and other types of property, minus his or her debt at a single point in time.

## INCOME AND WEALTH

While cultural capital and status provide a clearer picture of how we perceive social class, income and wealth serve as its material foundation. **Income** refers to wages and salaries measured over some period, such as per hour or year. **Wealth** encompasses all a person's material assets, including savings, land, stocks, and other types of property, minus his or her debts at a single point in time. If you were to sell everything you own and pay off all your debts, what you had left would be the value of your wealth. These material resources make our class-based lifestyles possible (Bourdieu 1986). As such, if we are to understand social class in the United States, we need a clear picture of their distribution.

**Income** Income inequality is a basic characteristic of a class system. In 2006, the median household income in the United States was $48,201. In other words, half of all households had higher incomes in that year, and half had lower incomes. But this fact does not fully convey the income disparities in our society. We get some sense of income inequality by contrasting the median (middle) score with the mean (arithmetic average), which in 2006 was $66,570 (U.S. Census 2007e). The mean is so much higher because some people make a lot more money than others, which draws the mean up, making it a less useful statistic for describing "average" or typical income.

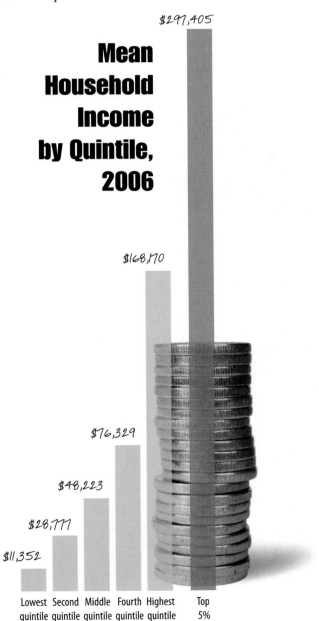

**Mean Household Income by Quintile, 2006**

$297,405

$168,170

$76,329

$48,223

$28,777

$11,352

| Lowest quintile | Second quintile | Middle quintile | Fourth quintile | Highest quintile | Top 5% |

Source: U.S. Census 2007d.

# The Income Pie: Percent Share of Total Income, 2006

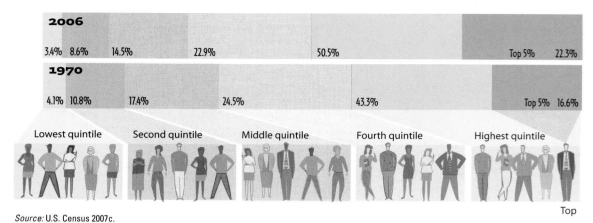

**2006**

3.4% | 8.6% | 14.5% | 22.9% | 50.5% | Top 5% | 22.3%

**1970**

4.1% | 10.8% | 17.4% | 24.5% | 43.3% | Top 5% | 16.6%

Lowest quintile | Second quintile | Middle quintile | Fourth quintile | Highest quintile

Top

*Source:* U.S. Census 2007c.

As we can see in the accompanying graphs, looking at the population in this way shows a significant degree of income inequality. Focusing on the extremes, the mean income for households in the lowest quintile is $11,352, while households in the top quintile average $168,170. Those households in the top 5 percent, the ones most responsible for bringing up the arithmetic mean, average $297,405. Those in the bottom quintile earn just 3.4 percent of the nation's total income, while those in the top quintile earn 50.5 percent. In fact, the top 5 percent earns a significantly greater percent of total income than the bottom 40 percent combined.

By all measures, income in the United States is distributed unevenly. In 2003, about 181,000 tax returns reported incomes in excess of $1 million. At the same time, over 23 million households reported incomes under $9000 (Bureau of the Census 2006a:317; DeNavas-Walt et al. 2007). Nobel Prize–winning economist Paul Samuelson has described the situation in the following way: "If we made an income pyramid out of building blocks, with each layer portraying $500 of income, the peak would be far higher than Mount Everest, but most people would be within a few feet of the ground" (P. Samuelson and Nordhaus 2005:383). The top 400 taxpayers in 2005 earned an average of $214 million each (Herman 2008).

Income inequality has increased steadily since 1970. Former Federal Reserve Board Chair Alan Greenspan was referring to this trend when he told Congress that the gap between the rich and the poor in the United States has become so wide that a democratic society must address it (Furman 2007; Greenblatt 2005; Grier 2005). Just how dramatic has this growth in inequality been? As the "Income Pie" chart above shows, the share earned by each of the bottom quintiles has decreased since 1970, while the top quintile now earns over one-half of total income. This represents the greatest degree of income inequality since before the Great Depression.

Americans do not appear to be seriously concerned about income and wealth inequality in the United States. In a comparison of opinions about social inequality in 27 different countries, respondents in the United States were less aware than those in other countries of the extent of inequality of the income distribution. Americans would prefer to "level down" the top of the nation's earning distribution, but compared to people in other countries, they are less concerned about reducing income differentials at the bottom of the distribution (Osberg and Smeeding 2006).

## SOCthink

> > > Why do you think that most Americans do not seem to be aware of or concerned about the degree of income inequality in the United States? To what extent might it be due to the power of the American Dream, the influence of the media, or the working of the dominant ideology?

**Wealth** Wealth in the United States is much more unevenly distributed than income. The median wealth for families in 2004 was $93,100. Contrast this with the mean of $448,200 and, just as with income, we see significant inequality. Comparing the top end to the bottom, we get a sense of the scale of difference. On the low end, the bottom 25 percent of wealth-holding families had a median wealth of $1700 and mean wealth of –$1400, meaning that, on average, they owed more than they owned. The top 10 percent, on the other hand, had a median wealth of $1.4 million and a mean wealth of $3.1 million (Bucks et al. 2006:A8).

We can get a better sense of the degree of difference by looking at how total wealth is distributed. As the accompanying chart shows, the top 1 percent owns 33.4 percent of all wealth in the United States. By contrast, the bottom 50 percent owns just 2.5 percent. In fact, the top 1 percent owns more than the bottom 90 percent combined. The concentration of ownership is even more extreme when it comes to stocks, with the top 1 percent owning 50.9 percent of their total value, and business assets, of which they own 62.3 percent. In fact, the only place where the bottom 50 percent comes close to matching its share of wealth relative to its portion of the population is with debt. The bottom 50 percent owes 46.2 percent of all installment debt and 45.7 percent of outstanding credit card debt (Kennickell 2006:27–29).

## Percentage of Wealth Owned, by Percentile

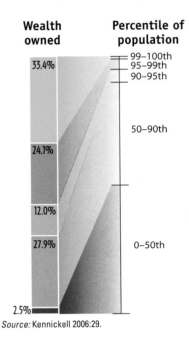

| Wealth owned | Percentile of population |
| --- | --- |
| 33.4% | 99–100th / 95–99th / 90–95th |
| 24.1% | 50–90th |
| 12.0% | |
| 27.9% | 0–50th |
| 2.5% | |

*Source:* Kennickell 2006:29.

**The Shrinking Middle Class** The cherished belief that the poor can rise to middle-class status has long been central to the United States' reputation as a land of opportunity. However, according to economics professor Lester C. Thurow, the American middle class is shrinking. Using a common definition of a middle-class household as one whose income falls between 75 and 125 percent of the nation's median household income (that is, between $36,150 and $60,250), only about 22 percent of American households qualified as middle class in 2006, compared to 28 percent in 1967 (DeNavas-Walt et al. 2007; Witte 2005).

Of those who relinquished their middle-class standing during this period, about half rose to a higher ranking in the social class system while half dropped to a lower posi-

tion. These data suggest that the United States is moving toward a bipolar income distribution. That is, a broadly based middle class is slowly being replaced by two growing groups of rich and poor (Greenblatt 2005).

Sociologists and other scholars have identified several factors that have contributed to the shrinking size of the middle class:

- *Disappearing opportunities for those with little education.* Today, increasing numbers of jobs require formal schooling, yet fewer than a third of adults ages 35–44 have a college degree.

- *Global competition and rapid advances in technology.* These two trends, which began several decades ago, have rendered workers more replaceable than they once were. Increasingly, these trends are affecting the more complex jobs that were once the bread and butter of middle-class life. Experts disagree on whether they represent a permanent setback to the workforce or the foundation for new industries that will someday generate millions of new jobs. In the meantime, however, U.S. households are struggling.

- *Growing dependence on the temporary workforce.* Some workers depend on temporary jobs for a second income, in order to maintain their middle-class lifestyle. For those workers who have no other job, these positions are tenuous at best, because they rarely offer health care coverage or retirement benefits.

- *The rise of new-growth industries and nonunion workplaces.* In the past, workers in heavy industry were able to achieve middle-class incomes through the efforts of strong labor unions. But today, the growth areas in the economy are fast-food restaurants and large retail outlets. Though these industries have added employment opportunities, they are at the lower end of the wage scale.

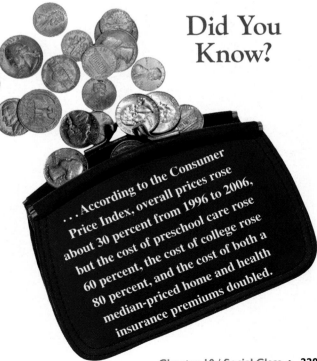

Did You Know?

... According to the Consumer Price Index, overall prices rose about 30 percent from 1996 to 2006, but the cost of preschool care rose 60 percent, the cost of college rose 80 percent, and the cost of both a median-priced home and health insurance premiums doubled.

In response to these concerns, observers note that living standards in the United States are improving. Middle-class families want large homes, college degrees for their children, and high-quality health care—the cost of which has been rising faster than inflation. Accomplishing these goals, however, has often meant becoming a dual-income family, working longer hours, or taking multiple jobs (Leonhardt 2007; Massey 2007).

## POVERTY

In 2006, 36.5 million people in the United States—12.3 percent of the population—were living in poverty. The problem of insufficient income, however, affects more people than these official numbers indicate. A recent Bureau of the Census report showed that one in five households has trouble meeting basic needs, from paying the utility bills to buying food (Bauman 1999; DeNavas-Walt et al. 2007).

**Defining Poverty** The efforts of sociologists and other social scientists to better understand poverty are complicated by the difficulty of defining it. This problem is evident even in government programs that conceive of poverty in either absolute or relative terms.

**Absolute poverty** refers to a minimum level of subsistence that no family should be expected to live below. One commonly used measure of absolute poverty is the federal government's poverty line. This is a money income figure that the government adjusts annually to reflect the consumption requirements of families based on their size and composition. It serves as an official definition of who is poor. In

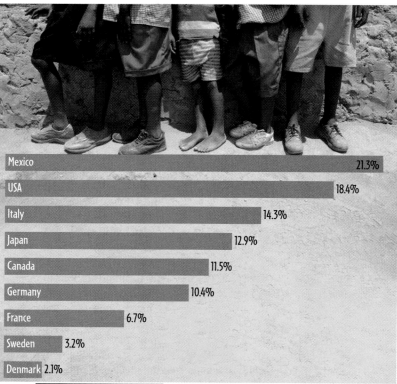

*Going* GLOBAL

**The Poverty Rate in Households with Children, Selected Countries**

| Country | Rate |
|---------|------|
| Mexico | 21.3% |
| USA | 18.4% |
| Italy | 14.3% |
| Japan | 12.9% |
| Canada | 11.5% |
| Germany | 10.4% |
| France | 6.7% |
| Sweden | 3.2% |
| Denmark | 2.1% |

*Note:* Data are for 2000 except for Germany (2001) and Mexico (2002). Poverty threshhold is 50 percent of nation's median income.

*Source:* Förster and d'Ercole 2005:36.

2006, a family consisting of two adults and two children with a combined income of $20,444 or less fell below the poverty line. By contrast, a single person under the age of 65 must earn less than $10,488 to be considered officially poor (DeNavas-Walt et al. 2007). These cutoffs determine which individuals and families will be eligible for certain government benefits.

Although by absolute standards, poverty has declined in the United States—for example, it was 22.4 percent in 1959—it remains higher than in many other industrial nations. As we can see in the accompanying graph, a comparatively high proportion of U.S. households are poor, meaning that they are unable to purchase basic consumer goods. If anything, this cross-national comparison understates the extent of poverty in the United States, since U.S. residents are likely to pay more for housing, health care, child care, and education than residents of other countries, where such expenses are often subsidized.

In contrast, **relative poverty** is a floating standard of deprivation by which people at the bottom of a society, whatever their lifestyles, are judged to be disadvantaged in comparison with the nation as a whole. Therefore, even if the poor today are better off in absolute terms than the poor of the 1930s or 1960s, they are still seen as poor relative to those above them. Someone who would be considered poor by U.S. standards would be well off by global standards of poverty; hunger and starvation are daily realities in many regions of the world.

Since the 1990s, debate has grown over the adequacy of the federal government's measure of poverty. If noncash benefits such as Medicare, Medicaid, food stamps, public housing, and health care and other employer-provided fringe benefits were included, the reported poverty rate would be lower. On the other hand, if out-of-pocket medical expenses and mandatory work expenses for transportation and child care were included, the poverty rate would be higher. The Census Bureau estimates that on balance, if both these recommendations were followed, the official poverty rate would be 2 percent higher, and 5 million more people would fall below the poverty line (Bernasek 2006).

> **Civilization is unbearable,**
> **but it is less unbearable at the top.**
>
> Timothy Leary

**absolute poverty** A minimum level of subsistence that no family should be expected to live below.

**relative poverty** A floating standard of deprivation by which people at the bottom of a society, whatever their lifestyles, are judged to be disadvantaged in comparison with the nation as a whole.

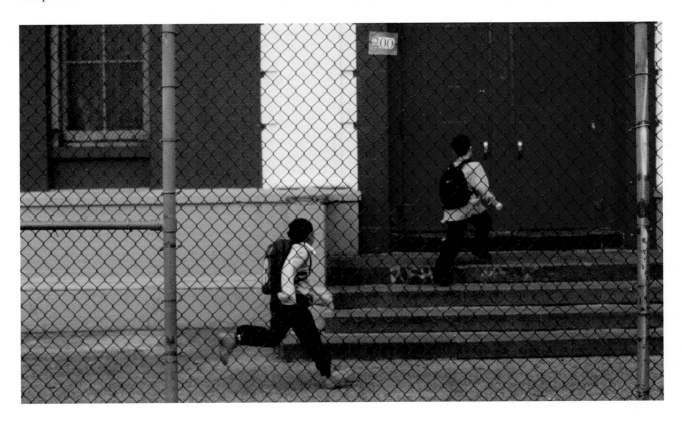

# Who Are the Poor in the United States?

| | Percentage of the population of the United States | Percentage of the poor of the United States |
|---|---|---|
| **Age** | | |
| Under 18 years old | 26 | 35 |
| 18 to 64 years old | 61 | 56 |
| 65 years and older | 13 | 9 |
| **Race/Ethnicity** | | |
| Whites (non-Hispanic) | 83 | 44 |
| Blacks | 12 | 25 |
| Hispanics | 11 | 25 |
| Asians and Pacific Islanders | 4 | 4 |
| **Households** | | |
| Married couples and families with male householders | 82 | 47 |
| Families with female householders | 18 | 53 |

*Note:* Data for 2006, as reported by the Bureau of the Census in 2007.
*Source:* DeNavas-Walt et al. 2007.

**Who Are the Poor?** One of the lessons that we learn by analyzing those who fall below the poverty line is that our stereotypes about poverty are flawed. For example, many people in the United States believe that the vast majority of the poor are able to work but will not. Yet of the 36.5 million people in poverty, 16.2 million are either under age 18 or 65 years old or older. Many working-age adults who are poor do work outside the home, although often in part-time positions. In 2006, about 31 percent of all poor adults worked full-time, compared to 66 percent of all adults. Of those poor adults who do not work, most are ill or disabled, or are occupied in maintaining a home. As we can see in the accompanying table, the likelihood of being in poverty is also shaped by factors such as age, race, ethnicity, and family type.

> **underclass** The long-term poor who lack training and skills.

Since World War II, an increasing proportion of the poor people of the United States have been women, many of whom are divorced or never-married mothers. In 1959, female householders accounted for 26 percent of the nation's poor; by 2006, that figure had risen to 53 percent. This alarming trend, known as the feminization of poverty, is evident not just in the United States but around the world.

About half of all women living in poverty in the United States are in transition, coping with an economic crisis caused by the departure, disability, or death of a husband. The other half tend to be economically dependent either on the welfare system or on friends and relatives living nearby. A major factor in the feminization of poverty has been the increase in families with women as single heads of household. In 2006, 28.3 percent of households headed by single mothers lived in poverty, compared to 13.2 percent for single-father households and 4.9 percent for married couples. Contributing to such rates are factors such as the difficulty in finding affordable child care and sex discrimination in the labor market.

In 2006, 43 percent of poor people in the United States were living in big cities. These urban residents are the focus of most governmental efforts to alleviate poverty. Yet according to many observers, the plight of the urban poor is growing worse, owing to the devastating interplay of inadequate education and limited employment prospects. Traditional employment opportunities in the industrial sector are largely closed to the unskilled poor. Past and present discrimination heightens these problems for those low-income urban residents who are Black and Hispanic (DeNavas-Walt et al. 2007:12).

Along with other social scientists, sociologist William Julius Wilson (1980, 1987, 1989, 1996), and his colleagues (2004) have used the term **underclass** to describe the long-term poor who lack training and skills. According to an analysis of Census 2000 data, 7.9 million people live in high-poverty neighborhoods. About 30 percent of the population in these neighborhoods is Black, 29 percent Hispanic, and 24 percent White. In central cities, about 49 percent of the underclass is African American, 29 percent Hispanic, 17 percent White, and 5 percent "other" (Jargowsky and Yang 2006; O'Hare and Curry-White 1992).

Analyses of the poor in general reveal that they are, however, not a static social class. The overall composition of the poor changes continually, because some individuals and families move above the poverty level after a year or two, while others slip below it. Still, hundreds of thousands of people remain in poverty for many years at a time. African Americans and Latinos are more likely than Whites to be persistently poor. Over a 21-year period, 15 percent of African Americans and 10 percent of Latinos were persistently poor, compared to only 3 percent of Whites. Both Latinos and Blacks are less likely than Whites to leave the welfare rolls as a result of recent welfare reform (Mangum et al. 2003).

In late 1996, in a historic shift in federal policy, Congress passed the Personal Responsibility and Work Opportunity Reconciliation Act, ending the longstanding federal guarantee of assistance to every poor family that meets eligibility requirements. The law sets a lifetime limit of five years of welfare benefits and requires all able-bodied adults to work after receiving two years of benefits (although hardship exceptions are allowed). The federal government gives block grants to the states to use as they wish in assisting poor and needy residents, and it permits states to experiment with ways to move people off welfare.

Other countries vary widely in their commitment to social service programs. But most industrialized nations devote higher proportions of their expenditures to housing, social security, welfare, health care, and unemployment compensation than the United States does. Data available in 2004 indicated that in Great Britain, 86 percent of health care expenditures were paid for by the government; in Sweden, 85 percent; in Canada, 70 percent; but in the United States, only 45 percent (World Bank 2007a:92–94).

The issue of poverty is ultimately about more than just money. It is also tied to social and cultural resources. Poor people often lack the social

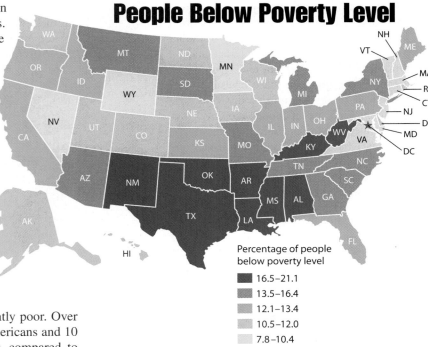

## People Below Poverty Level

Percentage of people below poverty level

- ■ 16.5–21.1
- ■ 13.5–16.4
- ■ 12.1–13.4
- ■ 10.5–12.0
- □ 7.8–10.4

*Source:* 2006 census data presented in Bureau of the Census 2007d: Tables R1701, 1901.

**Hot or Not?**

Should welfare recipients be required to work? If so, what should happen to their children while they are at work?

network connections to help them get good jobs, not to mention having to overcome the negative prestige associated with being poor. When it comes to cultural capital, they also often lack the same kind of educational credentials that can serve as a valuable cultural resource. Journalist David Shipler (2004), in his in-depth study titled *The Working Poor: Invisible in America,* referred to the combination of factors that poor people must overcome as the "interlocking deficits of poverty." As Shipler put it, "Breaking away and moving a comfortable distance from poverty seems to require a perfect lineup of favorable conditions. A set of skills, a good starting wage, and a job with the likelihood of promotion are prerequisites. But so are clarity of purpose, courageous self-esteem, a lack of substantial debt, freedom from mental illness or addiction, a functional family, a network of upstanding friends, and the right help from private or governmental agencies" (2004:4–5). To deal with poverty as a social problem, we must address all three of the major resource areas, because mobility out of poverty is a difficult task. The truth is, however, most of us end up near where we start.

## SOCIAL MOBILITY

The belief in upward mobility is an important value in the United States. As we saw above, social class systems are more open than other stratification systems, but this does not mean that the principle of opportunity necessarily matches the practice of mobility. For such mobility to be possible, ascribed statuses and inherited positions, along with the resources to which they provide access, should not play a significant role in shaping outcomes.

**Occupational Mobility** Two sociological studies conducted a decade apart offered insight into the degree of mobility in the nation's occupational structure (Blau and Duncan 1967; Featherman and Hauser 1978). Taken together, these investigations lead to several noteworthy conclusions. First, occupational mobility (both intergenerational and intragenerational) has been common among males. Approximately 60–70 percent of sons are employed in higher-ranked occupations than their fathers. Second, although there is a great deal of mobility in the United States, much of it is minor. That is, people who reach an occupational level above or below that of their parents usually advance or fall back only one or two out of a possible eight occupational levels. Thus, the child of a laborer may become an artisan or a technician, but he or she is less likely to become a manager or professional. The odds of reaching the top are extremely low unless one begins from a relatively privileged position.

**Income and Wealth** More recent studies focusing on income and wealth mobility show much the same results. Mobility does occur, but most people do not move very far. In comparing father's and son's income, researchers found that sons of low-income fathers do have about a 60 percent chance of rising above the lowest quintile, but only a 20 percent chance of reaching the median and a 4.5 percent chance of breaking into the top quintile (Mishel et al. 2007:95). Similarly, as we can see in the accompanying graph when looking at wealth, 36 percent of children with parents in the lowest quintile end up there themselves while only 7 percent make it to the top quintile. On the other end of the scale, 36 percent of children with parents in the top wealth quintile stay there while only 11 percent drop down into the bottom quintile (Haskins 2008:8). In fact, the likelihood of ending up in the same position as your parents has been rising since about 1980 (Aaronson and Mazumder 2007).

**Education** Studies also conclude that education plays a critical role in mobility. The impact of formal schooling on adult status is even greater than that of family background (although, as we have seen, family background influences the likelihood that one will receive higher education). Furthermore, education represents an important means of intergenerational mobility. A person who was born into a poor family but who graduates from college has a one in five chance of entering the top quintile of all income earners as an adult (Isaacs et al. 2008).

Education is a critical factor in the development of cultural capital. As such, access to higher education plays an important role in social mobility. In 2004, 40 percent of first-year students at major state universities came from families with incomes of more than $100,000 a year. In other words, close to half of all students came from high-income families. This statistic should not be surprising, given the high cost of tuition and room and board at state universities. For students from families with the lowest incomes, the cost can be prohibitive. Only 11 percent of children from the poorest families in the United States have earned college degrees, compared to 53 percent of children from the top fifth of the population. Those moderate-income students who do graduate, and even those who fail to complete their degrees, are often saddled with heavy postgraduate debt (Isaacs et al. 2008).

## Did You Know?

**. . . Although 67 percent of families make more money than their parents, only half of those earn enough to jump them into the next income quintile.**

## SOCthink

> > > The percentage of financial aid in the form of grants has gone down while the percentage of loan aid has increased. Why do you think that has occurred? What are the consequences of such a shift for social mobility?

The impact of education on mobility has diminished somewhat over the past decade. An undergraduate degree—a BA or BS—serves less as a guarantee of upward mobility now than it did in the past, simply because more and more entrants into the job market hold such a degree.

**Parental wealth quintile**

# Wealth Mobility:
## Percentage of Children in Each Wealth Quintile Compared to Parental Wealth Quintile

**Child wealth quintile**

- Top
- Fourth
- Middle
- Second
- Bottom

*Source:* Haskins 2008.

nation plays a significant role in the disparity between the two groups' experiences. Compared to White households, the relatively modest wealth of African American households means that adult Black children are less likely than adult White children to receive financial support from their parents. Indeed, young Black couples are much more likely than young White couples to be assisting their parents—a sacrifice that hampers their social mobility.

The African American middle class has grown over the past few decades, due to economic expansion and the benefits of the civil rights movement of the 1960s. Yet many of these middle-class households have little savings, a fact that puts them in danger during times of crisis. Studies have consistently shown that downward mobility is significantly higher for Blacks than it is for Whites (Oliver and Shapiro 1995; Sernau 2001; W. J.Wilson 1996).

The Latino population is not doing much better. The typical Hispanic has less than 10 percent of the wealth that a White person enjoys. A 2004 study suggests that in recent years Latinos have even lost ground. Their continuing immigration accounts for part of the disparity: Most of the

Moreover, intergenerational mobility is declining, since there is no longer such a stark difference between generations. In earlier decades, many high school–educated parents managed to send their children to college, but today's college students are increasingly likely to have college-educated parents (Economic Mobility Project 2007).

**Race and Ethnicity** Sociologists have long documented the fact that the class system is more rigid for African Americans than it is for members of other racial groups. Black men who have good jobs, for example, are less likely than White men to see their adult children attain the same status. The cumulative disadvantage of discriminew arrivals are destitute. But even the wealthiest 5 percent of Latino households have only a third as much net worth as the top 5 percent of White households (Kochhar 2004).

**Gender** Studies of mobility, even more than those of class, have traditionally ignored the significance of gender, but some research findings are now available that explore the relationship between gender and mobility. Women's employment opportunities are much more limited than men's. Moreover, according to recent research, women whose skills far exceed the jobs offered them are more likely than men to withdraw entirely from the paid labor force. Their withdrawal violates an assumption common to traditional mobility studies: that most people will aspire to upward mobility and seek to make the most of their opportunities.

In contrast to men, women have a rather large range of clerical occupations open to them. But the modest salary ranges and limited prospects for advancement in many of these positions reduce the possibility of upward mobility. Self-employment as shopkeepers, entrepreneurs, independent professionals, and the like—an important road to upward mobility for men—is more difficult for women, who find it harder to secure the necessary financing. Although sons commonly follow in the footsteps of their fathers, women are less likely to move into their fathers' positions. Consequently, gender remains an important factor in shaping social mobility. Women in the United States (and in other parts of the world) are especially likely to be trapped in poverty, unable to rise out of their low-income status (Heilman 2001).

## Education Pays:
## Full-Time, Year-Round Workers,
## Ages 25–64, 2006

| Education level | Median annual earnings |
| --- | --- |
| Professional degree | $100,000 |
| Doctorate degree | $90,287 |
| Master's degree | $62,085 |
| Bachelor's degree | $51,842 |
| Associate's degree | $40,812 |
| Some college, no degree | $38,008 |
| High school graduate (includes GED) | $31,935 |
| Less than high school | $22,000 |

*Source:* U.S. Census 2007f.

On the positive side, although today's women lag behind men in employment, their earnings have increased faster than their mothers' did at a comparable age, so that their incomes are substantially higher. The one glaring exception to this trend involves the daughters of low-income parents. Because these women typically care for children—many as single parents—and sometimes for other relatives as well, their mobility is severely restricted (Isaacs 2007b).

## >> Life Chances

One of the lessons we learn from sociology is that class matters. Max Weber saw class as being closely related to people's **life chances**—that is, their opportunities to provide themselves with material goods, positive living conditions, and favorable life experiences (Gerth and Mills 1958). Life chances are reflected in measures such as housing, education, and health. Occupying a higher position in a society improves individuals' life chances and brings greater access to social rewards. In contrast, people in the lower social classes are forced to devote a larger proportion of their limited resources to the necessities of life.

In fact, our very survival can be at stake. When the supposedly unsinkable British ocean liner *Titanic* hit an iceberg in 1912, it was not carrying enough lifeboats to accommodate all passengers. Plans had been made to evacuate only first- and second-class passengers. About 62 percent of the first-class passengers survived the disaster. Despite a rule that women and children would go first, about

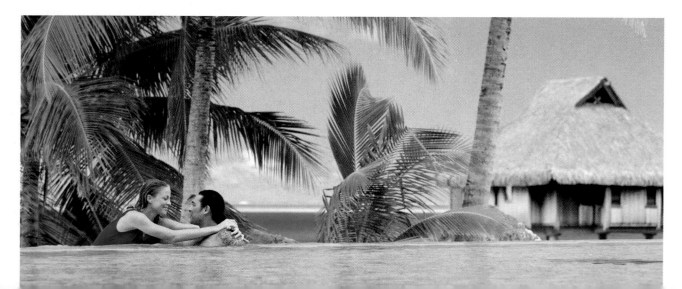

a third of those passengers were male. In contrast, only 25 percent of the passengers in third class survived. The first attempt to alert them to the need to abandon ship came well after other passengers had been notified (D. A. Butler 1998; Crouse 1999; Riding 1998).

## SOCthink

> > > What factors have shaped your life chances? What kinds of resources have you inherited from others? What resources might you have lacked access to?

Class position also affects people's vulnerability to natural disasters. When Hurricane Katrina hit the Gulf Coast of the United States in 2005, affluent and poor people alike became its victims. However, poor people who did not own automobiles (100,000 of them in New Orleans alone) were less able than others to evacuate in advance of the storm. Those who survived its fury had no nest egg to draw on, and thus were more likely than others to accept relocation wherever social service agencies could place them—sometimes hundreds or even thousands of miles from home (Department of Homeland Security 2006).

Some people have hoped that the Internet revolution would help to level the playing field by making information and markets uniformly available. Unfortunately, however, not everyone can get onto the information superhighway, so yet another aspect of social inequality has emerged— the **digital divide.** The poor, minorities, and those who live in rural communities and inner cities are not getting connected at home or at work. A recent government study found that despite falling computer prices, the Internet gap between the haves and have-nots has not narrowed. For ex-

ample, while 70 percent of all people in the United States could access the Internet at home in 2006, that group included 93 percent of people with incomes over $100,000 but fewer than 49 percent of people with incomes less than $30,000. As wealthier people switch to high-speed Internet connections, they will be able to take advantage of even more sophisticated interactive services, and the digital divide will grow even wider (Pew Internet Project 2007).

**life chances** The opportunities people have to provide themselves with material goods, positive living conditions, and favorable life experiences.
**digital divide** The relative lack of access to the latest technologies among low-income groups, racial and ethnic minorities, rural residents, and the citizens of developing countries.

Wealth, status, and power may not ensure happiness, but they certainly provide additional ways of coping with problems and disappointments. For this reason, the opportunity for advancement—for social mobility—is of special significance to those at the bottom of society. These people want the rewards and privileges that are granted to high-ranking members of a culture.

If we are to better understand why we think and act the way we do, we must consider the impact of social class. The positions we occupy shape our access to material, social, and cultural resources, which in turn shapes our future positions. In the United States, part of the American Dream is that anyone who is willing to work hard can get ahead. The principle of meritocracy—that we earn our positions—is at the heart of that faith which represents a rejection of aristocracy in which positions are inherited. Class patterns in the United States call into question the degree to which principle and practice meet.

## Did You Know?

. . . **Warren Buffet, who in 2008 beat out Bill Gates as the richest man in the world, pays a far lower percentage of his income for payroll, Social Security, and Medicare taxes than do the secretaries and clerks who work for him. He used this information to argue that wealthy people such as him unfairly benefit from the current tax system.**

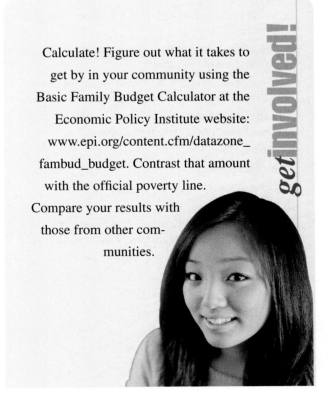

Calculate! Figure out what it takes to get by in your community using the Basic Family Budget Calculator at the Economic Policy Institute website: www.epi.org/content.cfm/datazone_fambud_budget. Contrast that amount with the official poverty line. Compare your results with those from other communities.

get**involved!**

I. What is social class?

- Like slavery, caste, and estate, it is a stratification system in which people and groups are ranked, but it places them based primarily on economic position.

II. How does social class operate?

- Three categories of resources are key: material, including income and wealth; social, including social networks and prestige; and, cultural, including tastes, education, and knowledge. Power is based on access to and control over these resources.

III. What are the consequences of social class?

- While class-based systems are more open than the others, our life chances are shaped by our inherited class position and the material, social, and cultural resources that go with it. For most people, the social mobility that does occur, whether in terms of occupation, income, or wealth, is of a relatively short distance.

# Pop Quiz

1. Social inequality refers to
   a. the structured ranking of entire groups of people that perpetuates unequal economic rewards and power in a society.
   b. social ranking based primarily on economic position.
   c. the positive or negative reputation an individual has in the eyes of others.
   d. a condition in which members of society have different amounts of wealth, prestige, or power.

2. The stratification system in which hereditary ranks are usually religiously dictated is the
   a. class system.
   b. estate system.
   c. caste system.
   d. slave system.

3. According to Daniel Rossides' model of the class system in the United States, the class that includes the most people is the
   a. lower class.
   b. working class.
   c. upper-middle class.
   d. upper class.

4. A plumber whose father was a physician is an example of
   a. downward intergenerational mobility.
   b. upward intergenerational mobility.
   c. downward intragenerational mobility.
   d. upward intragenerational mobility.

5. According to Karl Marx, the class that owns the means of production is the
   a. nobility.
   b. proletariat.
   c. Brahman.
   d. bourgeoisie.

6. Which of the following were viewed by Max Weber as distinct components of stratification?
   a. conformity, deviance, and social control
   b. class, status, and party
   c. class, caste, and age
   d. class, prestige, and esteem

7. According to Pierre Bourdieu, our tastes, our education, the way we talk, and the things we like all represent forms of
   a. social capital.
   b. esteem.
   c. cultural capital.
   d. intelligence.

1. (d); 2. (c); 3. (b); 4. (a); 5. (d); 6. (b); 7. (c);

8. The respect or admiration that an occupation holds in a society is referred to as
   a. status.
   b. esteem.
   c. prestige.
   d. ranking.

9. Approximately how much wealth does the top 1 percent of families own in the United States?
   a. 20 percent
   b. 33 percent
   c. 50 percent
   d. 80 percent

10. Approximately what percentage of the U.S. population lived in poverty in 2006?
   a. 2.1 percent
   b. 8.6 percent
   c. 12.3 percent
   d. 19.4 percent

11

# GLOBAL INEQ

# STRUGGLING TO SURVIVE IN A WORLD OF PLENTY

**In spring of 2008, riots broke out in countries around the world in response to a global food crisis.** From sub-Saharan African nations to countries including Egypt, India, and Yemen, people took to the streets in response to skyrocketing prices and food shortages. Hit hardest by the effects of this crisis were people in the poorest countries, where the margin between survival and starvation is razor-thin.

In Haiti, where more than three-quarters of the population live on less than $2 a day, price increases have been devastating. Georges Jean Wesner gets up every day at 4:00 A.M. to walk two hours to get two small pails of rice and beans from a charity food kitchen—the only source of food he and his family have had for weeks. "I'm 52 years old, I have lots of energy and I want to work," he says, "but I can't work because there is no work" (Williams 2008). People are turning to patties made of mud, oil, and sugar, about which Olwich Louis Jeune, 24, says, "It's salty and it has butter, and you don't know you're eating dirt. . . . It makes your stomach quiet down" (Lacey 2008).

In the Darfur region of Sudan, Khamisa Tafaela worried because her 10-month-old son was vomiting and suffering from diarrhea. She had already lost one son who had the same symptoms. She, along with her husband and their five children, had been living in a camp in West Darfur for over four years with thousands of others forced from their homes in Sudan. For the second month in a row, she had been living on halved food rations, not because there was insufficient food, but because it was too dangerous to get the food from the warehouses to the camps (*Sudan Tribune* 2008).

We see in this Darfur story that the food crisis may be due not only to insufficient food but also to insufficient access to food. Dominique Strauss-Kahn, the Managing Director of the International Monetary Fund, says, "There is enough food to feed the world . . . the problem is that prices have risen and many people cannot afford food. So we need to get food—or the money to buy food—to those most in need" (IMF 2008). In other words, we produce enough globally so that everyone can have enough, but we do not allocate resources in such a way that people now facing starvation can gain access to the food they need to survive.

UALITY

# As You
# READ >>

- How did the global divide develop?
- How significant is global stratification?
- Why did the global movement for universal human rights develop?

## >> The Global Divide

When it comes to resources, the global divide is immense. Millions of people struggle on the very edge of survival even as others around the world lead lives of relative comfort and leisure. A few centuries ago, most people were poor. There was a significant divide between the few who were extremely wealthy and the many who lacked significant resources, with little concept of a middle class between the nobility and the peasants. In much of Europe, life was as difficult as it was in Asia or South America. This was true until the Industrial Revolution and increased agricultural productivity resulted in explosive economic growth. However, the ensuing rise in living standards was not evenly distributed across the world.

We get a glimpse of the relative share of resources, and their consequences, by looking at splits between developing and industrial nations. For example, the likelihood of dealing with the death of a child or the burden of disease is much greater for those in developing nations. At the same time, the industrial nations of the world, with a much smaller share of the total population, have much higher incomes and many more exports than the developing nations. People in industrial nations also receive better health care and have greater security due to what those nations spend on health care and the military (Sachs 2005a; Sutcliffe 2002). As we will see, the divide within countries in terms of income, wealth, poverty, and social mobility is also significant.

Average income varies significantly across the nations of the world along a continuum from those that are the richest in natural resources to those that are the poorest. The contrast between those at the top and those at the bottom is stark. For example, in 2006, per capita gross national prod-

> If it's far away, it's news; but if it's close at home, it's sociology.

James Reston

# Gross National Income per Capita, 2007

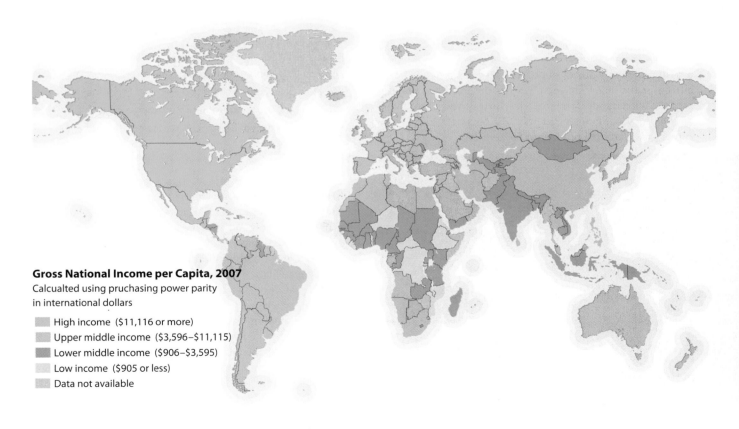

**Gross National Income per Capita, 2007**
Calcualted using pruchasing power parity
in international dollars

High income ($11,116 or more)
Upper middle income ($3,596–$11,115)
Lower middle income ($906–$3,595)
Low income ($905 or less)
Data not available

# *Going* GLOBAL

**Fundamental Global Inequality**

Deaths of children — Developing nations — 99% | 1%
Rural population — 94% | 6%
Total births — 94% | 6%
The burden of disease — 93% | 7%
TOTAL POPULATION — 85% | 15%
Cultivated land — 74% | 26%
Urban population — 73% | 27%
Income — 46% | 54%
CO$_2$ emissions — 36% | 64%
Health spending — 24% | 76%
Exports — 22% | 78%
Military spending — 12% | 88% — Industrial nations

*Note:* In this comparison, industrial nations include the United States and Canada, Japan, western Europe, and Australasia. Developing nations include Africa, Asia (except for Japan), Latin America, eastern Europe, the Caribbean, and the Pacific.

*Source:* Adapted from Sutcliffe 2002:18.

uct (the average value of goods and services produced per citizen) in the industrialized countries of the United States, Japan, Switzerland, Belgium, and Norway was more than $31,000. By comparison, at least 10 countries had a per capita gross national product of $900 or less.

## >> Perspectives on Global Stratification

Theorists have taken a step back to look at this global system from a top-down, macro perspective. In so doing, they provide us with insights into how the world system developed and how the various parts fit together. We will focus on three areas of analysis, including the rise of modernization, the legacy of colonialism, and the growth of multinational corporations.

### THE RISE OF MODERNIZATION

Early sociologists often assumed that society was progressing toward some common positive future. We certainly get that sense from both Karl Marx and Émile Durkheim, who believed that societies would all inevitably evolve along a similar path, ending up in some shared version of the good society. For Durkheim this meant a natural balance between interdependence and individual freedom; for Marx it meant some form of socialism. For his part, though his vision was not as hopeful, Max Weber also believed that all societies would move toward a rational-legal form of authority.

## SOCthink

> > > Early sociologists were optimistic that positive social change was inevitable. To what extent do you think people today share this vision of the inevitable rise of the good society? How might cynicism about the possibility for change contribute to the maintenance of the status quo?

This notion that the present was superior to the past, with its petty tyrannies and irrational superstitions, and that the future would unite us all, shaped how people viewed the world throughout much of the twentieth century. Many people supposed that, through **modernization,** nations would move from traditional forms of social organization toward forms characteristic of post–Industrial Revolution societies. Features of the latter include a complex division of labor in which work is specialized; the separation of institutions including family, economy, government, education, and religion into specialized spheres, each with their own experts; the decline of the local and the rise of a societal or global orientation; the rise of rational decision making in the public sphere and a corresponding decline in public religious authority; and the spread of both cultural

PUBLISHED BY CURRIER & IVES    Copyright 1876 by Currier & Ives, N.Y.    125 NASSAU ST. NEW YORK.

### THE PROGRESS OF THE CENTURY.
THE LIGHTNING STEAM PRESS.    THE ELECTRIC TELEGRAPH.    THE LOCOMOTIVE.    THE STEAMBOAT.

diversity, as more peoples from different backgrounds come into contact with each other, and a corresponding growth in egalitarianism as a value that embraces such diversity (Bruce 2000).

From this modernization perspective, countries such as China and India are in the process of becoming modern societies. Even if the transition from traditional to mod-

ern is difficult for many, the presupposition is that their people will benefit in the long term. According to these theorists, just as many people in the United States and Europe experienced displacement and poverty in the early years of the Industrial Revolution, only later to lead more comfortable lives, the same future awaits people in such developing nations.

> **modernization** The far-reaching process by which nations pass from traditional forms of social organization toward those characteristic of post–Industrial Revolution societies.

Many sociologists today are quick to note that terms such as *modernization* and even *development* contain an ethnocentric bias. There is an implicit sense in this model that people in such nations are more "primitive" and that modern Western culture is more advanced, more "civilized." The unstated assumption is that what "they" (people living in developing countries) really want is to become more like "us" (people in modern industrialized nations). According to this vision, they want both our economic development and our cultural values including democracy, freedom, and consumerism. Such modernization, then, represents a form of cultural imperialism. Many groups around the world reject this path, viewing such "development" as an attack on their way of life including their core values and norms.

When it comes to the portrayal of people from around the world in U.S. television shows and films, we often see negative stereotypes reinforced, which perpetuate a sense of U.S. cultural superiority. In 2004, nearly half of all Middle Eastern characters shown on television were criminals compared to only 5 percent of White characters. And in an analysis of about 1000 films over 20 years, communications professor Jack Shaheen found that only 5 percent of Arab and Muslim characters were presented in a positive light. The good news, he said, is that that figure has risen to about 30 percent in recent films; he pointed to *Syriana* and *Babel* as examples.

## THE LEGACY OF COLONIALISM

An alternative perspective to modernization focuses on colonialism as a model for better understanding the expansion of our interconnected world. **Colonialism** occurs when a foreign power maintains political, social, economic, and cultural domination over a people for an extended period. In simple terms, it is rule by outsiders. The long reign of the British Empire over much of North America, parts of Africa, and India is an example of colonial domination. The same can be said of French rule over Algeria, Tunisia, and other parts of North Africa. Relations between the colonial nation and the colonized people are similar to those between the dominant capitalist class and the proletariat, as described by Marx.

> **colonialism** The maintenance of political, social, economic, and cultural dominance over a people by a foreign power for an extended period.
> **neocolonialism** Continuing dependence of former colonies on foreign countries.
> **world systems analysis** A view of the global economic system as one divided between certain industrialized nations that control wealth and developing countries that are controlled and exploited.

By the 1980s, such global political empires had largely disappeared. Most of the nations that were colonies prior to World War I had achieved political independence and established their own governments. However, for many of these countries, the transition to genuine self-rule was not yet complete. Colonial domination had established patterns of economic exploitation that continued even after nationhood was achieved—in part because the former colonies were unable to develop their own industry and technology. Their dependence on more industrialized nations, including their former colonial masters, for managerial and technical expertise, investment capital, and manufactured goods kept the former colonies in a subservient position. Such continuing dependence and foreign domination are referred to as **neocolonialism**.

Sociologist Immanuel Wallerstein (1974, 1979a, 2000) views the global economic system as being divided between nations that control wealth and nations from which resources are taken. Through his **world systems analysis,** Wallerstein has described the unequal economic and political relationships in which certain industrialized nations (among them the United States, Japan, and Germany) and their global corporations dominate the core of this system. At the semiperiphery of the system are countries with marginal economic status, such as Israel, Ireland, and South Korea. Wallerstein suggests that the poor developing countries of Asia, Africa, and Latin America are on the periphery of the world economic system. The key to Wallerstein's analysis is the exploitative relationship of core nations toward noncore nations. Core nations and their corporations control and exploit noncore nations' economies. Unlike other nations, they are relatively independent of outside control (Chase-Dunn and Grimes 1995).

The division between core and periphery nations is both significant and remarkably stable. A study by the International Monetary Fund (2000) found little change over the past century for the 42 economies studied. The only changes were Japan's movement up into the group of core nations and China's movement down toward the margins of the semiperiphery nations. Yet Wallerstein (2000) speculates that the world system as we currently understand it may soon undergo unpredictable changes. The world is becoming increasingly urbanized, a trend that is gradually

# World Systems Analysis at the Beginning of the 21st Century

| Core | Semiperiphery | Periphery |
|---|---|---|
| Canada | China | Afghanistan |
| France | India | Bolivia |
| Germany | Ireland | Chad |
| Japan | Mexico | Dominican Republic |
| United Kingdom | Pakistan | Egypt |
| United States | Panama | Haiti |
| | | Philippines |
| | | Vietnam |

*Note:* Figure shows only a partial listing of countries.

**SOC**studies

# Did You Know?

. . . Jamaica spends 27.9 percent of its government budget on debt relief and 16.1 percent on health and education. Such ratios are not uncommon in developing nations, although Lebanon spends 52.1 percent on debt service.

eliminating the large pools of low-cost workers in rural areas. In the future, core nations will have to find other ways to reduce their labor costs. The exhaustion of land and water resources through clear-cutting and pollution is also driving up the costs of production.

Wallerstein's world systems analysis is the most widely used version of **dependency theory.** According to this theory, even as developing countries make economic advances, they remain weak and subservient to core nations and corporations in an increasingly intertwined global economy. This interdependency allows industrialized nations to continue to exploit developing countries for their own gain.

According to world systems analysis and dependency theory, a growing share of the human and natural resources of developing countries is being redistributed to the core industrialized nations. This redistribution happens in part because developing countries owe huge sums of money to industrialized nations as a result of foreign aid, loans, and trade deficits. The global debt crisis has intensified the Third World dependency rooted in colonialism, neo-colonialism, and multinational investment. International financial institutions are pressuring indebted countries to take severe measures to meet their interest payments. The result is that developing nations may be forced to devalue their currencies, freeze workers' wages, increase privatization of industry, and reduce government services and employment.

Closely related to these problems is **globalization**—the worldwide integration of government policies, cultures, social movements, and financial markets through trade and the exchange of ideas. Because the forces of world financial markets transcend governance by conventional nation-states, international organizations such as the World Bank and the International Monetary Fund have emerged as major players in the global economy. The function of these institutions, which are heavily funded and influenced by core nations, is to encourage trade and development and to ensure the smooth operation of international financial markets. As such, they are seen as promoters of globalization

and defenders primarily of the interests of core nations. Critics call attention to a variety of related issues, including violations of workers' rights, the destruction of the environment, the loss of cultural identity, and discrimination against minority groups in periphery nations.

## THE GROWTH OF MULTINATIONAL CORPORATIONS

Worldwide, corporate giants have played a key role in the rise of globalization. The term **multinational corporations** refers to commercial organizations that are headquartered in one country but do business around the world. Such private trade and lending relationships are not new; merchants have conducted business abroad for hundreds of years, trading gems, spices, garments, and other goods. Today's multinational giants are not merely buying and selling overseas; they are also producing goods all over the world (I. Wallerstein 1974). Through deindustrialization, corporate executives also have relocated production jobs around the globe.

Increasingly, it is not just production jobs that are being relocated. Today's global factories may now have the "global office" alongside them. Multinationals based in core nations are beginning to establish reservation services and centers for processing data and insurance claims in the periphery nations. As service industries become a more important part of the international marketplace, many companies are concluding that the low costs of overseas operations more than offset the expense of transmitting information around the world.

> **dependency theory** An approach contending that industrialized nations continue to exploit developing countries for their own gain.
> **globalization** The worldwide integration of government policies, cultures, social movements, and financial markets through trade and the exchange of ideas.
> **multinational corporation** A commercial organization that is headquartered in one country but does business throughout the world.

## SOCthink

> > > How has the rise of multinational corporations and the trend toward globalization affected you, your family, and your community, both positively and negatively?

These multinational corporations are huge, with total revenues on a par with the total value of goods and services exchanged in entire nations. Foreign sales represent an important source of profit for multinational corporations, encouraging them to expand into other countries (in

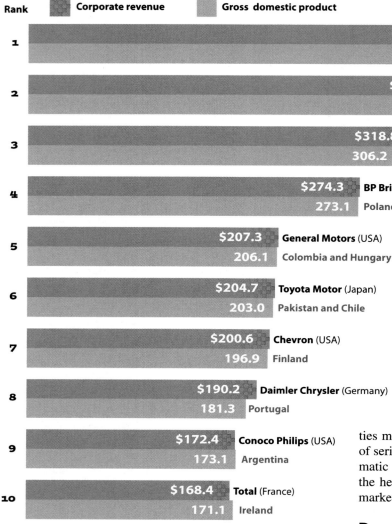

## Going GLOBAL

### Multinational Corporations Compared to Nations

**Rank**   ■ **Corporate revenue**   ■ **Gross domestic product**   **Millions of dollars**

| Rank | Corporate revenue | GDP |
|---|---|---|
| 1 | $351.1 **Wal-Mart** (USA) | 369.1 Sweden |
| 2 | $347.2 **Exxon Mobil** (USA) | 342.0 Turkey |
| 3 | $318.8 **Royal Dutch Petroleum** (Britain/Netherlands) | 306.2 Austria |
| 4 | $274.3 **BP British Petroleum** (Britain) | 273.1 Poland |
| 5 | $207.3 **General Motors** (USA) | 206.1 Colombia and Hungary |
| 6 | $204.7 **Toyota Motor** (Japan) | 203.0 Pakistan and Chile |
| 7 | $200.6 **Chevron** (USA) | 196.9 Finland |
| 8 | $190.2 **Daimler Chrysler** (Germany) | 181.3 Portugal |
| 9 | $172.4 **Conoco Philips** (USA) | 173.1 Argentina |
| 10 | $168.4 **Total** (France) | 171.1 Ireland |

*Note:* Total is an oil, petroleum, and chemical company. Where two nations are listed, the country with the larger GDP is listed first.

*Sources:* For corporate data, *Fortune* 2007; for GDP data, World Bank 2007a14–16.

### SOCthink

> > > Multinational corporations have become so big that they have more economic resources than do some nations. What consequences arise from the fact that they can relocate their headquarters, offices, and production facilities anywhere in the world? How might this affect a nation's political power?

many cases, the developing nations). The U.S. economy is heavily dependent on foreign commerce, much of which is conducted by multinationals. Over one-fourth of all goods and services in the United States involve either the export of goods to foreign countries or the import of goods from abroad (U.S. Trade Representative 2003).

### Modernization

Consistent with the modernization approach, some analysts believe that the relationship between the corporation and the developing country is mutually beneficial. Multinational corporations can help the developing nations of the world by bringing industries and jobs to areas where subsistence agriculture once served as the only means of survival. Multinationals also promote rapid development through the diffusion of inventions and innovations from industrial nations. The combination of skilled technology and management provided by multinationals and the relatively cheap labor available in developing nations benefits the corporation. Multinationals can take maximum advantage of technology while reducing costs and boosting profits. Through their international ties, multinationals also make the nations of the world more interdependent. These ties may prevent certain disputes from reaching the point of serious conflict. A country cannot afford to sever diplomatic relations or engage in warfare with a nation that is the headquarters for its main business suppliers or a key market for its exports.

**Dependency** Critics of multinational expansion challenge this favorable evaluation of the impact of corporations. They argue that multinationals exploit local workers to maximize profits. For example, Starbucks—the international coffee retailer based in Seattle—gets some of its coffee beans from farms in Guatemala. But to earn enough money to buy a pound of Starbucks coffee, a Guatemalan farm worker would have to pick 500 pounds of beans, representing five days of work (Entine and Nichols 1996).

The pool of cheap labor in the developing world prompts multinationals to move factories out of core countries. Workers in these developing countries do not have the same kinds of legal protections and also lack unions to fight on their behalf. In industrialized countries, organized labor insists on decent wages and humane working conditions, but governments seeking to attract or keep multinationals may develop a "climate for investment," including repressive antilabor laws that restrict union activity and collective bargaining. If labor's demands become too threatening, the multinational firm will simply move its plant elsewhere, leaving a trail of unemployment behind. Nike, for example, has moved its factories from the United States to Korea to Indonesia to Vietnam in search of the lowest labor costs.

Workers in the United States and other core countries are beginning to recognize that their own interests are served by helping to organize workers in developing nations. As long as multinationals can exploit cheap labor abroad, they will be in a strong position to reduce wages and benefits in industrialized countries. With this in mind, in the 1990s, labor unions, religious organizations, campus groups, and other activists began to mount public relations campaigns to pressure companies such as Nike, Starbucks, Reebok, Gap, and Wal-Mart to improve wages and working conditions in their overseas operations (Global Alliance for Workers and Communities 2003; Gonzalez 2003).

Sociologists studying the effects of foreign investment by multinationals have found that, although it initially may contribute to a host nation's wealth, such investment eventually increases economic inequality within developing nations. This finding holds for both income and ownership. The upper and middle classes ben-

efit most from economic expansion; the lower classes are less likely to benefit. And because multinationals invest in limited economic sectors and restricted regions of a nation, only some sectors benefit. The expansion of such sectors of the host nation's economy, such as hotels and high-end restaurants, appears to retard growth in agriculture and other economic sectors. Moreover, multinational corporations often buy out or force out local entrepreneurs and companies, thereby increasing economic and cultural dependence (Chase-Dunn and Grimes 1995; Kerbo 2009; I. Wallerstein 1979b).

## >> Stratification Around the World

As these economic investments by multinationals suggest, at the same time that the gap between rich and poor nations is widening, so too is the gap between rich and poor citizens within nations. As discussed earlier, stratification in developing nations is closely related to their relatively weak and dependent position in the global economy. Local elites work hand in hand with multinational corporations and prosper from such alliances. At the same time, the economic system creates and perpetuates the exploitation of industrial and agricultural workers. That's why foreign investment in developing countries tends to increase economic inequality (Bornschier et al. 1978; Kerbo 2009).

### INCOME AND WEALTH

Global inequality is staggering, as the graphs on page 250 suggest. In at least 22 nations around the world, the most affluent 10 percent of the population receives at least 40 percent of all income. Among these countries are the African nation

**Hot or Not?**

Do CEOs owe anything to local communities, either here or abroad, when they make the decision to move jobs overseas?

# Percent Shares of Global Household Wealth

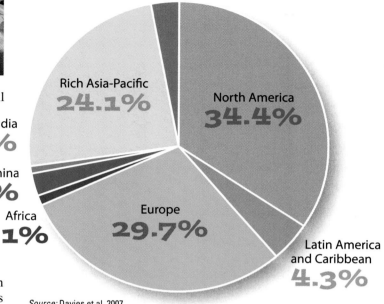

Other Asia-Pacific
## 2.9%

Rich Asia-Pacific
## 24.1%

India
## 0.9%

China
## 2.6%

Africa
## 1%

North America
## 34.4%

Europe
## 29.7%

Latin America and Caribbean
## 4.3%

*Source:* Davies et al. 2007.

of Namibia (the leader, at 65 percent of all income) as well as Colombia, Mexico, Nigeria, and South Africa (Shorrocks et al. 2006).

When it comes to wealth, the top 10 percent of the world's population own 85 percent of global household wealth, and the top 1 percent own 40 percent. On the other end of the spectrum, the bottom 50 percent of the world's population combined own 1 percent of global wealth. Median household wealth globally is estimated to be $2129 per adult. To make it into the top 1 percent takes $510,000. Analyzing the distribution globally, the bulk of the wealth is held by countries in North America, Europe, and the rich Asia-Pacific nations (Davies et al. 2007).

Looking in more detail at the world's top 10 percent of wealth holders, 25 percent come from the United States, 21 percent come from Japan, and Germany, Italy, Britain, France, and Spain combine for 29 percent. Within nations, the amount of wealth held by the top 10 percent varies. Denmark demonstrates the most significant amount of wealth inequality, with the top 10 percent of wealth holders there owning 76.4 percent of household wealth—significantly more than Japan, where the top 10 percent hold 39.3 percent of the wealth.

Women in developing countries often face significant obstacles, making it difficult for them to attain economic assets. Karuna Chanana Ahmed, an anthropologist from India who has studied women in developing nations, calls women the most exploited of oppressed people. Beginning at birth, women face sex discrimination. They are commonly fed less than male children, are denied educational opportunities, and often are hospitalized only when they are critically ill. Only one-third of Pakistan's sexually segregated schools are for women, and one-third of those schools have no buildings. Inside or outside the home, women's work is devalued. And when economies fail, as they did in Asian countries in the late 1990s, women are the first to be laid off from work (J. Anderson and Moore 1993; Kristof 1998). In Kenya and Tanzania, it is illegal for a woman to own a house.

In Saudi Arabia, women are prohibited from driving, walking alone in public, and socializing with men outside their families (C. Murphy 1993).

## Distribution of Income in Nine Nations

Percent

Brazil — 61.3 | 2
Mexico — 55.4 | 3
Jamaica — 52.5 | 7
USA — 46 | 5
Great Britain — 44 | 6
Bangladesh — 43.9 | 9
Canada — 40 | 7
Sweden — 37 | 9
Japan — 36 | 11

Highest 20%

Lowest 20%

*Note:* Data are considered comparable although based on statistics covering 1993 to 2001.
*Source:* World Bank 2007a:66–68.

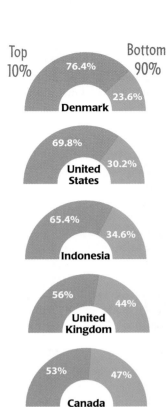

76.4% 23.6%
**Denmark**

69.8% 30.2%
**United States**

65.4% 34.6%
**Indonesia**

56% 44%
**United Kingdom**

53% 47%
**Canada**

52.9% 47.1%
**India**

45% 55%
**Australia**

43.1% 56.9%
**South Korea**

42.3% 57.7%
**Ireland**

41.9% 58.1%
**Spain**

41.4% 58.6%
**China**

39.3% 60.7%
**Japan**

# Amount of Wealth Held by the Top 10 Percent

*Source:* Davies et al. 2007.

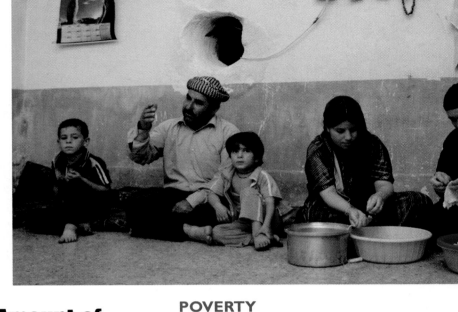

## POVERTY

In developing countries, any deterioration in the economic well-being of the least well-off threatens their very survival. Poverty is a worldwide problem that blights the lives of billions of people, but it, too, is distributed unequally. If we drew a map in which the size of each country was based on the number of poor people there, Africa and Asia would appear huge compared to the relatively affluent areas of industrialized North America and Europe.

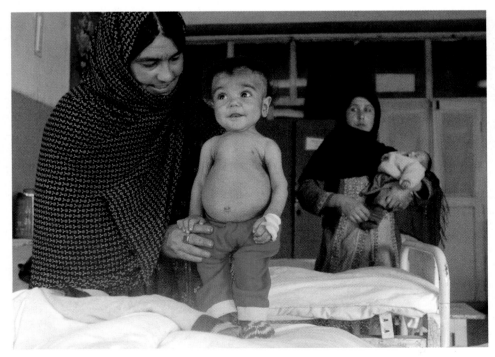

In 2000, the United Nations launched the Millennium Project, whose objective is to eliminate extreme poverty worldwide by the year 2015. While 15 years may seem a long time, the challenge was great. Today, almost 3 billion people subsist on $2 a day or less. To accomplish the project's goal, planners estimate that industrial nations must set aside 0.7 percent of their **gross national product (GNP)**—the value of a nation's goods and services—for aid to developing nations.

At the time the Millennium Project was launched, only five countries were giving at that target rate: Denmark, Luxembourg, the Netherlands, Norway, and Sweden. To match their contribution proportionally, the United States would need to multiply its present aid level by 45. Although the U.S. government delivers far more aid to foreign countries and multinational organizations than any other nation, a number of countries give a much larger percentage of their wealth. In terms of per capita giving, the United States ranks 12th among the 22 most advanced industrial countries—behind countries such as Great Britain, France, and Norway (Kerbo 2009; Sachs 2005a; World Bank 2007a).

Direct government-to-government foreign aid is only one way of alleviating poverty, however. While per capita aid from the U.S. government may not be high, private spending by U.S. residents is. Rates of individual charitable giving are much higher in the United States than in other industrial nations. Even more significant are remittances—the money that immigrants to the United States send home to relatives. In 2006, remittances from the United States to developing countries were estimated at $199 billion—twice the total of foreign aid from all countries (*The Economist* 2007a; World Bank 2006b).

> In a world of increasing inequality, the legitimacy of institutions that give precedence to the property rights of the Haves over the human rights of the Have Nots is inevitably called into serious question.
>
> **David Korten**

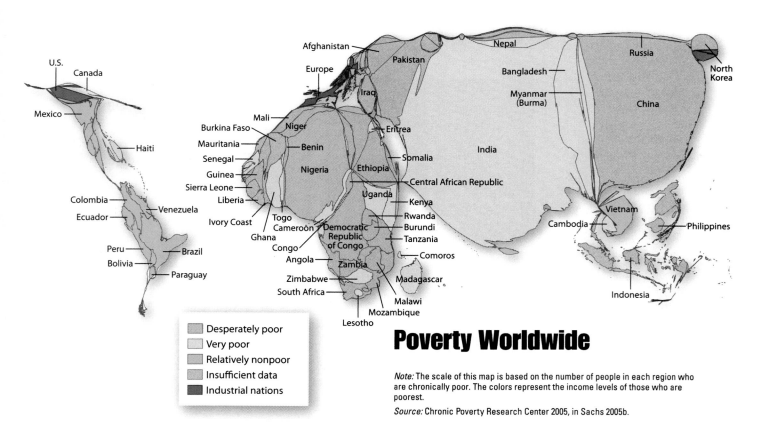

## Poverty Worldwide

Desperately poor
Very poor
Relatively nonpoor
Insufficient data
Industrial nations

*Note:* The scale of this map is based on the number of people in each region who are chronically poor. The colors represent the income levels of those who are poorest.

*Source:* Chronic Poverty Research Center 2005, in Sachs 2005b.

## Millennium Project Goals by 2015

*Source:* www.unmillenniumproject.org.

Eradicate extreme poverty and hunger

Achieve universal primary education

Promote gender equality and empower women

Reduce child mortality

Improve maternal health

Combat HIV/AIDS, malaria, and other diseases

Ensure environmental sustainability

Develop a global partnership for development

When it comes to aid, even a small amount of capital can make a big difference. Microfinance programs, which involve relatively small grants or loans, have encouraged marginalized people to invest not in livestock, which may die, or jewelry, which may be stolen, but in technological improvements such as small cooking stoves.

### 5 Movies on GLOBAL INEQUALITY

**Babel**
*Four stories on hardship from around the globe.*

**Born into Brothels**
*Children are forced into prostitution due to poverty.*

**Life and Debt**
*The IMF exploits Jamaica.*

**Maria Full of Grace**
*A factory worker is forced to transport heroin to the United States.*

**Invisible Children**
*Ugandan children go unnoticed.*

In Indonesia, for example, some 60,000 microloans have enabled families who once cooked their food in a pit to purchase stoves. Improvements like these not only enable people to cook more food at a more consistent temperature but can become the basis of small-scale home businesses (*The Economist* 2005g).

## SOCIAL MOBILITY

Although significant global inequality exists, perhaps sufficient social mobility exists to provide hope for those born without significant access to resources. As we saw in the previous chapter, mobility can and does happen in the United States, though the majority of such movement is over only short distances. Here we will look at the possibility for mobility in both industrial nations and developing nations, as well as consider the impact gender has on mobility.

> **gross national product (GNP)** The value of a nation's goods and services.

**Intergenerational Mobility Across Nations** Intergenerational mobility varies across countries; for example, the amount of income advantage passed from fathers to sons is significantly higher in the United Kingdom, the United States, and France than in Denmark, Norway, or Finland (Corak 2006). What this means, in contrast to the classic vision of the American Dream, is that there is less chance for intergenerational mobility in the United States than in those Scandinavian countries.

In developing nations, macrolevel social and economic changes often overshadow microlevel movement from one occupation to another. For example, there is typically a substantial wage differential between rural and urban areas, which leads to high levels of migration to the cities. Yet the urban industrial sectors of developing countries generally cannot provide sufficient employment for all those seeking work.

# Foreign Aid per Capita in Eight Countries

| Country | Total aid in $ millions of dollars | Per capita aid in dollars |
|---|---|---|
| Australia | 1.4 | $72 |
| USA | 25.8 | $87 |
| Canada | 2.8 | $88 |
| Germany | 9.2 | $113 |
| Japan | 17.3 | $135 |
| Great Britain | 8.5 | $142 |
| France | 8.9 | $145 |
| Norway | 2.0 | $407 |

*Note:* Data for bilateral aid in 2005 released by World Bank in 2007.

*Source:* World Bank 2007a:14–16, 346.

## Intergenerational Earnings Mobility by Country

| Country | Percentage of earning advantage passed from fathers to sons |
|---|---|
| Denmark | 15 |
| Norway | 17 |
| Finland | 18 |
| Canada | 19 |
| Sweden | 27 |
| Germany | 32 |
| France | 41 |
| United States | 47 |
| United Kingdom | 50 |

*Source:* Corak 2006.

In large developing nations, the most socially significant mobility is the movement out of poverty. This type of mobility is difficult to measure and confirm, however, because economic trends can differ from one area of a country to another. For instance, China's rapid income growth has been accompanied by a growing disparity in income between urban and rural areas and among different regions. Similarly, in India during the 1990s, poverty declined in urban areas but may have remained static at best in rural areas. Around the world, social mobility is also dramatically influenced by catastrophes such as crop failure and warfare (World Bank 2000).

**Gender Differences and Mobility** Only recently have researchers begun to investigate the impact of gender on the mobility patterns of developing nations. Many aspects of the development process—especially modernization in rural areas and the rural-to-urban migration just described—may result in the modification or abandonment of traditional cultural practices and even marital systems. The effects on women's social standing and mobility are not necessarily positive. As a country develops and modernizes, women's vital role in food production deteriorates, jeopardizing both their autonomy and their material well-being. Moreover, the movement of families to the cities weakens women's ties to relatives who can provide food, financial assistance, and social support.

In the Philippines, however, women have moved to the forefront of the indigenous peoples' struggle to protect their ancestral land from exploitation by outsiders. Having established their right to its rich minerals and forests, members of indigenous groups had begun to feud among themselves over the way in which the land's resources should be developed. Aided by the United Nations Partners in Development Programme, women volunteers established the Pan-Cordillera Women's Network for Peace and Development, a coalition of women's groups dedicated to resolving local disputes. The women mapped boundaries, prepared development plans, and negotiated more than 2000 peace pacts among community members. They have also run in elections, campaigned on issues related to social problems, and organized residents to work together for the common good (United Nations Development Programme 2000:87).

## SOCIAL STRATIFICATION IN MEXICO

To get a more complete picture of these global stratification issues, it helps to look at a particular case. Here we will focus on the dynamics of stratification in Mexico, a country of 102 million people.

In May 2003, on a stretch of highway in southern Arizona, the open doors of an abandoned tractor trailer revealed the dead bodies of 19 Mexicans. The truck had been carrying a group of about 75 men, women, and children across the Sonoran Desert illegally into the United States when the people hidden inside began to suffer from the intense desert heat. Their story is not unusual. In recent years, as many as 500 people per year have died trying to cross the U.S.–Mexican border. From October 2007 through June 2008, according to border patrol officials in Arizona, 61 died in the Tucson sector alone.

Why do Mexicans risk their lives crossing the dangerous desert that lies between the two countries? The answer to this question can be found primarily in the income disparity between the two nations—one an industrial giant and the other a partially developed country still recovering from a history of colonialism and neocolonialism. Since the early 20th century, there has been a close cultural, economic, and political relationship between Mexico and the United States, one in which the United States is the dominant party. According to Immanuel Wallerstein's analysis, the United States is at the core while neighboring Mexico is still on the semiperiphery of the world economic system.

**Mexico's Economy** If we compare Mexico's economy to that of the United States, differences in the standard of living and in life chances are quite dramatic, even though Mexico is considered a semiperiphery nation. Gross national income is a commonly used measure of an average resident's economic well-being. In 2007, the gross national income per person in the United States came to $44,260; in Mexico, it was a mere $11,330. About 87 percent of adults in the United States have a high school education, compared to only 13 percent of those in Mexico. And fewer than 7 of every 1000 infants in the United States die in the first year of life, compared to about 21 per 1000 in Mexico (Bureau of the Census 2007a:Table 1312; Haub 2005).

Not only is Mexico unquestionably a poor country, but the gap between its richest and poorest citizens is one of the widest in the world. The top quintile earns 55.4 percent of total income while the bottom earns just 3 percent. The

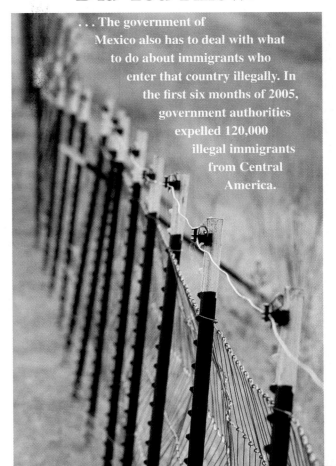

World Bank reports that, in 2006, 20 percent of Mexico's population survived on just $2 per day. At the same time, the wealthiest 10 percent of Mexico's people accounted for 39 percent of the nation's income. According to a *Forbes* magazine portrait of the world's wealthiest individuals, that year Mexico ranked 11th in terms of the number of residents who were among the world's wealthiest people (Kroll and Fass 2006; World Bank 2007a:67).

Political scientist Jorge Castañeda (1995:71) calls Mexico a "polarized society with enormous gaps between rich and poor, town and country, north and south, white and brown (or *criollos* and *mestizos*)." He adds that the country is also divided along lines of class, race, religion, gender, and age. To better understand the nature of the stratification within Mexico, we will examine race relations and the plight of Mexican Indians, the status of Mexican women, and immigration to the United States and its impact on the U.S.–Mexican borderlands.

**borderlands** The area of common culture along the border between Mexico and the United States.

### Race Relations in Mexico: The Color Hierarchy
Mexico's indigenous Indians account for an estimated 14 percent of the nation's population. More than 90 percent of them live in houses without sewers, compared to 21 percent of the population as a whole. And whereas just 10 percent of Mexican adults are illiterate, the proportion for Mexican Indians is 44 percent (Boudreaux 2002; *The Economist* 2004b; G. Thompson 2001b).

The subordinate status of Mexico's Indians is but one reflection of the nation's color hierarchy, which links social class status to the appearance of racial purity. At the top of this hierarchy are the *criollos,* the 10 percent of the population who are typically White, well-educated members of the business and intellectual elites, with familial roots in Spain. In the middle is the large, impoverished *mestizo* majority, most of whom have brown skin and a mixed racial lineage as a result of intermarriage. At the bottom of the color hierarchy are the destitute, full-blooded Mexican Indian minority and a small number of Blacks, some descended from 200,000 African slaves brought to Mexico. This color hierarchy is an important part of day-to-day life—enough so that some Mexicans in the cities use hair dyes, skin lighteners, and blue or green contact lenses to appear more White and European. Ironically, however, nearly all Mexicans are considered part Indian because of centuries of intermarriage (Castañeda 1995; DePalma 1995).

## SOCthink

> > > How might racial categories in Mexico differ from those in the United States? Why might such differences arise?

Many observers take note of widespread denial of prejudice and discrimination against people of color in Mexico. Schoolchildren are taught that the election of Benito Juárez, a Zapotec Indian, as president of Mexico in the 19th century proves that all Mexicans are equal. Yet there has been a marked growth in the past decade of formal organizations and voluntary associations representing indigenous Indians (Escárcega 2008; Stavenhagen 1994; Utne 2003).

### The Status of Women in Mexico
In 1975, Mexico City hosted the first international conference on the status of women, convened by the United Nations. Much of the discussion concerned the situation of women in developing countries; in that regard, the news is mixed. Women now constitute 45 percent of the labor force—an increase from 31 percent in 1980, but still less than in industrial countries. Unfortunately, Mexican women are even more mired in the lowest-paying jobs than their counterparts in industrial nations. In the political arena, though they rarely occupy top decision-making positions, women have significantly increased their representation in the national legislature, to 23 percent. Mexico now ranks 39th among 189 nations in female representation—well ahead of Great Britain and France (Bureau of the Census 2007a:Table 133; Inter-Parliamentary Union 2007).

Even when Mexican women work outside the home, they often are not recognized as active and productive household members, whereas men are typically viewed as heads of the household. As one consequence, women find it difficult to obtain credit and technical assistance in many parts of the country and to inherit land in rural areas. Within the manufacturing and service industries, women generally receive little training and tend to work in the least-automated and least-skilled jobs. This occurs in large part because there is little expectation that women will pursue career advancement, organize for better working conditions, or become active in labor unions (Kopinak 1995; Martelo 1996; see also Young 1993).

In recent decades, Mexican women have begun to organize to address an array of economic, political, and health issues. Since women continue to serve as the household managers for their families, even when they work outside the home, they are well aware of the consequences of the inadequate public services in lower-income urban neighborhoods. As far back as 1973, women in Monterrey—the nation's third-largest city—began protesting the continuing disruptions of the city's water supply. After individual complaints to city officials and the water authority proved fruitless, social networks of female activists began to emerge. These activists sent delegations to confront politicians, organized protest rallies, and blocked traffic as a means of gaining media attention. Though their efforts brought improvements in Monterrey's water service, the issue of reliable and safe water remains a concern in Mexico and many other developing countries (Bennett 1995).

## From Me to You

One of the most effective ways to more fully understand international issues and global inequality, whether in Mexico, Guatemala, Malawi, Bangladesh, or China, is to go there and spend some time with people inside the culture. If it is at all possible during your educational career, seek out an opportunity to study abroad. Most of us, unless we choose to emigrate, never get the chance to spend a significant amount of time in another country except through higher education. If you do go, step off the tourist path and pursue interaction with everyday people so as to better understand their world from within.

**The Borderlands** Growing recognition of the borderlands reflects the increasingly close and complex relationship between Mexico and the United States. The term **borderlands** refers to the area of common culture along the border between Mexico and the United States. Legal and illegal emigration from Mexico to the United States, day laborers crossing the border regularly to go to work in the United States, the implementation of the North American Free Trade Agreement (NAFTA), the exchange of media across the border—all make the notion of separate Mexican and U.S. cultures obsolete in the borderlands.

The economic position of the borderlands is rather complicated, as demonstrated by the emergence of *maquiladoras*. These are foreign-owned factories established just across the border in Mexico, where the companies that own them do not have to pay taxes or provide insurance and benefits to workers. As of 2006, *maquiladoras* employed 1.1 million people, paying entry-level workers between $4 and $5 per day. Since many of these firms come from the United States and sell their products to Mexico's vast domestic market, their operations deepen the impact of U.S. consumer culture on Mexico's urban and rural areas (Federal Reserve Bank of Dallas 2006; *Migration News* 2005c).

The *maquiladoras* have contributed to Mexico's economic development, but not without some cost. Their unregulated growth allows owners to exploit workers with jobs that lack security, possibilities for advancement, and decent wages. Moreover, many of the U.S.-owned factories require female job applicants to take a urine test to screen out those who are pregnant—a violation of Mexican law as well as of NAFTA, and the source of numerous cases of sex discrimination (Dillon 1998; Dougherty and Holthouse 1999).

# The Borderlands

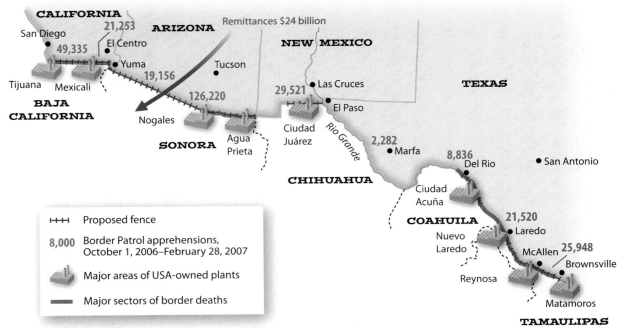

*Source:* Prepared by Schaefer 2009 based on Marosi 2007; Romano and Ramirez 2007; G. Thompson 2001a.

Ironically, the *maquiladoras* are now experiencing the same challenge from global trade as U.S. manufacturing plants did. Beginning in 2001, some companies began shifting their operations to China. Average Mexican labor costs (wages plus benefits) are just $2 to $2.50 an hour, but Chinese labor costs are even lower—50 cents to $1 an hour. Of the 700,000 new *maquiladora* jobs created in NAFTA's first seven years, 43 percent were eliminated between 2000 and 2003 (*Migration News* 2002c, 2004).

**Emigration to the United States** From the Mexican point of view, the United States too often regards Mexico simply as a reserve pool of cheap labor, encouraging Mexicans to cross the border when workers are needed but discouraging and cracking down on them when they are not. Some people, then, see immigration more as a labor market issue than a law enforcement issue. Viewed from the perspective of Wallerstein's world systems analysis and dependency theory, it is yet another example of a core industrialized nation exploiting a developing country.

## SOCthink

> > > How do U.S. consumers benefit from the buildup of factories along the U.S.–Mexican border? What impact might they have on U.S. workers?

The social impact of immigration to the United States is felt throughout Mexico. According to sociological research, the earliest emigrants were typically married men

*Mass grave site in Srebrenica, Bosnia-Herzegovina.*

of working age from the middle of the stratification system. They had sufficient financial resources to afford the costs and risks of immigration, yet were experiencing enough financial strain that entering the United States was attractive to them. Over time, kinship ties to emigrants multiplied, and immigration became less class-selective, with entire families making the trek to the United States. More recently, the occupational backgrounds of Mexican emigrants have widened further, reflecting not only changes in U.S. immigration policy but the continuing crisis in the Mexican economy (Massey 1998, 2008).

Many Mexicans who have come to the United States send some part of their earnings back across the border to family members in Mexico. This substantial flow of money, sometimes referred to as **remittances,** or *migradollars,* is estimated at a minimum of $24 billion a year. It is second only to oil as a source of foreign revenue for Mexico. If these funds went solely into the purchase of consumer goods, they would underscore the view of dependency theory—that Mexico's economy is little more than an extension of the U.S. economy. In fact, however, some of these migradollars are used by Mexicans to establish and maintain small business enterprises, such as handicraft workshops and farms. Consequently, the transfer of migradollars does stimulate the local and national economies of Mexico (*Migration News* 2008a).

## >> Universal Human Rights

As globalization has spread, impacting more and more peoples around the world, a movement toward ensuring universal human rights has arisen. Recognizing the harmful effects of such global expansion, activists in this move-

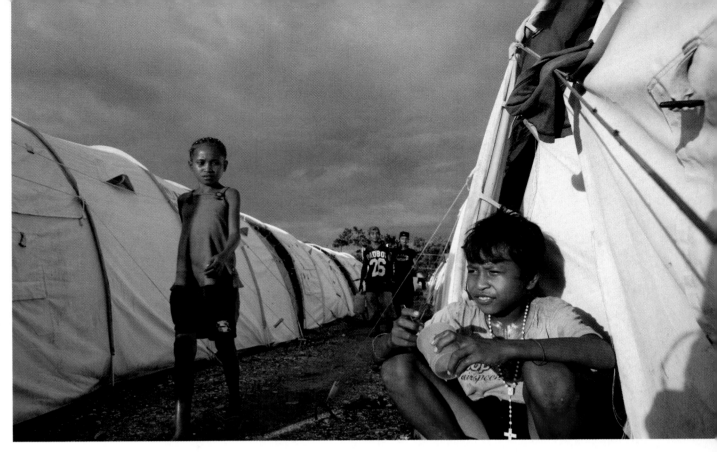

*Ongoing violence in East Timor has driven children like these to seek safety in refugee camps in the country.*

ment fight to preserve and protect the interests of people who lack significant power or access to resources. The sheer size and economic might of multinational corporations, along with their freedom to move jobs and plants around the world without regard for the impact on national populations, encouraged the establishment of universal human rights as a countervailing source of power. The goal of human rights activists is to establish a nonnegotiable and inviolable foundation of rights that applies no matter where people are or which governments or multinational corporations are involved.

## DEFINING HUMAN RIGHTS

The term **human rights** refers to universal moral rights that all people possess by virtue of being human. The most important elaboration of human rights appears in the Universal Declaration of Human Rights, adopted by the United Nations in 1948. This declaration prohibits slavery, torture, and degrading punishment; grants everyone the right to a nationality and its culture; affirms freedom of religion and the right to vote; proclaims the right to seek asylum in other countries to escape persecution; and prohibits arbitrary interference with one's privacy and the arbitrary seizure of a person's property. It also emphasizes that mothers and children are entitled to special care and assistance.

At first, the United States opposed a binding obligation to the Universal Declaration of Human Rights. The government feared loss of national sovereignty—the right to rule over its people without external interference. This concern was driven in part by the existence of racial segregation laws that were still common at the time the UN issued the Universal Declaration and that violated the human rights principles. By the early 1960s, however, the United States had begun to use the declaration to promote democracy abroad (Forsythe 1990).

In the 1990s, concerns about human rights brought the term *ethnic cleansing* into the world's vocabulary as a euphemism for forcible expulsion and murder. In the former Yugoslavia, Serbs initiated a policy intended to "cleanse" Muslims from parts of Bosnia-Herzegovina and ethnic Albanians from the province of Kosovo. Hundreds of thousands of people were killed in fighting there, while many others were uprooted from their homes. Moreover, reports surfaced of Serbian soldiers raping substantial numbers of Muslim, Croatian, and Kosovar women. Regrettably, ethnic cleansing has since spread to other parts of the world, including East Timor, Iraq, Kenya, and Sudan.

**remittances** The monies that immigrants return to their families of origin. Also called *migradollars*.
**human rights** Universal moral rights possessed by all people because they are human.

An ongoing human rights concern is the transnational crime of trafficking in humans. Each year an estimated 600,000–800,000 men, women, and children are transported across international borders for slavery or sexual exploitation, In 2000, Congress passed the Trafficking Vic-

# Human Trafficking Report

| Tier 1<br>Full Compliance | Tier 2<br>Significant Effort | Tier 2 Watch<br>Some Effort, but Trafficking<br>Remains a Concern | Tier 3<br>Noncompliant,<br>No Effort |
| --- | --- | --- | --- |
| Australia | Afghanistan | Armenia | Algeria |
| Canada | Azerbaijan | Bahrain | Burma |
| Columbia | Brazil | Cambodia | Cuba |
| Denmark | Greece | China | Iran |
| France | Israel | Dominican Republic | Kuwait |
| Germany | Japan | Egypt | Malaysia |
| Hong Kong | Nicaragua | Honduras | North Korea |
| Italy | Nigeria | India | Qatar |
| Morocco | Philippines | Mexico | Saudi Arabia |
| Norway | Romania | Mozambique | Sudan |
| Poland | Turkey | Russia | Syria |
| South Korea | Vietnam | South Africa | Uzbekistan |
| Spain | Yemen | Ukraine | Venezuela |

*Note:* Table is incomplete; each tier lists only sample nations.

*Sources:* Ribando 2008:22 for the Department of State.

tims Protection Act, which established minimum standards for the elimination of human trafficking. The act requires the State Department to monitor other countries' efforts to vigorously investigate, prosecute, and convict individuals who participate in trafficking—including government officials. Each year the department reports its findings, dividing countries into three groups, or tiers, depending upon their level of compliance. Tier-1 countries are thought to be largely in compliance with the act. Tier-2 nations are making a significant effort to comply, while tier-2 "watch" nations are making efforts to comply, though trafficking remains a real concern. Tier-3 countries are not compliant (Kapstein 2006; Kempadoo and Doezema 1998).

## PRINCIPLE AND PRACTICE

When it comes to human rights, the balance between principle and practice can be problematic. In the wake of the terrorist attacks of September 11, 2001, increased police personnel and surveillance at U.S. airports and border crossings caused some observers to wonder whether human rights were not being jeopardized in the name of security. At the same time, thousands of noncitizens of Arab and south Asian descent were questioned for no other reason than their ethnic and religious backgrounds. A few were placed in custody, sometimes without access to legal assistance. And as the war on terror moved overseas, human rights concerns escalated. In 2005, Secretary-General Kofi Annan of the UN criticized the United States and Britain for equating people who were resisting the presence of foreign troops in Afghanistan and Iraq with terrorists (Parker 2004; Steele 2005).

## SOCthink

> > > To what extent do you think violations of human rights are excusable in a time of war? At such times, how might our perception of the balance between rights and security alter what we think of as universal?

What this points to is the significance of perspective even when it comes to something that appears to be a fundamental principle. Cultural insiders and outsiders can disagree about what constitutes a violation. For example, was India's caste system an inherent violation of human rights? What about the many cultures of the world that view the subordinate status of women as an essential element in their traditions? Should human rights be interpreted differently in different parts of the world?

We can consider, as an example, female genital mutilation, a practice that is common in more than 30 countries around the world but that has been condemned in Western nations as a human rights abuse. This controversial practice often involves removal of the clitoris, in the belief that its excision will inhibit a young woman's sex drive, making her chaste and thus more desirable to her future husband. Though some countries have passed laws against the practice, they have gone largely unenforced. Emigrants from countries where genital mutilation is common often insist that their daughters undergo the procedure, to protect them from Western cultural norms that allow premarital sex (Religious Tolerance 2008). To what extent should outside nations have the power to dictate such internal laws? In this sense, the movement for universal human rights also represents a form of cultural imperialism.

## SOCthink

> > > How active should the U.S. government be in addressing violations of human rights in other countries? At what point, if any, does concern for human rights turn into ethnocentrism through failure to respect the distinctive norms, values, and customs of another culture?

In 1993, the United States opted for an absolute definition of human rights, insisting that the Universal Declaration of Human Rights set a single standard for acceptable behavior around the world. In practice, however, interpretation still plays a role. Some have argued that the United States practices selective enforcement of human rights. Critics contend, for example, that officials in the United States are more likely to become concerned about human rights abuses when oil is at stake, as in the Middle East, or when military alliances come into play, as in Europe.

### HUMAN RIGHTS ACTIVISM

Efforts to protect and ensure human rights seldom come from inside governments but arise out of social movements that organize to generate economic, social, and political pressure in an effort to force change. For example, in June 2008, Human Rights Watch (www.hrw.org), a premier international human rights organization, called for other African nations to impose sanctions on Zimbabwe after what they called the sham reelection of President Robert Mugabe. They monitor human rights abuses around the world, including calling upon U.S. officials to end abuses against prisoners in the Guantanamo Bay detention camps.

In Sudan, the Save Darfur Coalition (www .savedarfur.org) fights for justice and relief for refugees who were attacked, driven off their land and out of the country, and often killed by the Janjaweed, a group of armed gunmen backed by the Sudanese government. Their cause was helped significantly with the release of the film *The Devil Came on Horseback*—translated from the Janjaweed—in which ex-marine Brian Steidle, who was hired as a human rights

observer by the African Union, documented genocide in Darfur with photos and video. He ultimately testified before Congress and at the UN, providing his documentation to support the genocide claims. In addition to numerous other organizational efforts, the Save Darfur Coalition also coordinated an agreement on May 28, 2008, in which presidential candidates Barack Obama, John McCain, and Hillary Clinton issued a joint statement demanding an end to the violence in Darfur.

*Médecins sans Frontières* (Doctors Without Borders), the world's largest independent emergency medical aid organization, won the 1999 Nobel Peace Prize for its work in countries worldwide. Founded in 1971 and based in Paris, the organization has 5000 doctors and nurses working in 80 countries. "Our intention is to highlight current upheavals, to bear witness to foreign tragedies and reflect on the principles of humanitarian aid," explains Dr. Rony Brauman, the organization's president (Spielmann 1992:12; see also Daley 1999).

In recent years, awareness has been growing of lesbian and gay rights as an aspect of universal human rights. In 1994, Amnesty International (1994:2) published a pioneering report in which it acknowledged that "homosexuals in many parts of the world live in constant fear of government persecution." The report examined abuses in Brazil, Greece, Mexico, Iran, the United States, and other countries, including cases of torture, imprisonment, and extrajudicial execution. Later in 1994, the United States issued an order that would allow lesbians and gay men to seek political asylum in the United States if they could prove they had suffered government persecution in their home countries solely because of their sexual orientation (Johnston 1994).

One of the things we learn from sociology is that we are embedded in larger networks in which decisions and events that happen far away, and about which we may know little or nothing, shape our daily life experiences.

> **Hot or Not?**
>
> Should outside nations, including the UN, have the power to force the United States to change its laws to comply with human rights principles?

> There can be no peace as long as there is grinding poverty, social injustice, inequality, oppression, environmental degradation, and as long as the weak and small continue to be trodden by the mighty and powerful.
>
> **the Dalai Lama**

Ethnic cleansing in the former Yugoslavia, human rights violations in Iraq and Afghanistan, increased surveillance in the name of counterterrorism, violence against women inside and outside the family, governmental torture of lesbians and gay men—all these are vivid reminders that social inequality can have life-and-death consequences. In each case, people recognized the consequences of global inequality, and individuals, groups, and nations took steps to address the problems. By developing a more fully formed sociological imagination, we can more readily see such issues and take necessary steps toward addressing them.

**get involved!**

Donate! Give of your time and your money. It can be something as simple as going to www.freerice.com to donate rice to the UN World Food Program or giving clothes to a local shelter. Or perhaps it might include volunteering time at a local organization that works with international immigrants or donating money to organizations that seek to alleviate global poverty, such as OxFam.

# For REVIEW

I. **How did the global divide develop?**
- Theorists emphasizing modernization argue that it is part of the natural evolution of societies as they pass through the effects of the Industrial Revolution and beyond. Dependency theorists argue that it is due to a fundamental power struggle between wealthy nations at the core and developing nations at the periphery.

II. **How significant is global stratification?**
- Analyses of wealth, income, poverty, and social mobility demonstrate a wide gap both within and between nations.

III. **Why did the global movement for universal human rights develop?**
- As global inequality became more apparent, activists worked to establish a foundational set of human rights that would protect people regardless of who or where they were.

## Pop Quiz

1. Which of the following terms is used by contemporary social scientists to describe the far-reaching process by which nations pass from traditional forms of social organization toward those characteristic of post–Industrial Revolution societies?
   a. dependency
   b. globalization
   c. industrialization
   d. modernization

2. The maintenance of political, social, economic, and cultural domination over a people by a foreign power for an extended period of time is referred to as
   a. neocolonialism.
   b. government-imposed stratification.
   c. colonialism.
   d. dependency.

3. Immanuel Wallerstein's world systems analysis focuses on
   a. the unequal access to and control of resources between core and periphery nations.
   b. the natural evolutionary development of all societies toward the modern ideal.
   c. the rise of multinational corporations.
   d. the global pattern of inequality faced by women.

4. Companies that are headquartered in one country but do business throughout the world are known as
   a. global corporations.
   b. multinational corporations.
   c. *maquiladoras*.
   d. international agencies.

1. (d); 2. (c); 3. (a); 4. (b);

5. In at least 22 nations around the world, the most affluent 10 percent of the population receive at least what percentage of all income?
   a. 20 percent
   b. 30 percent
   c. 40 percent
   d. 50 percent

6. How much of total global wealth do the bottom 50 percent of the world's population own?
   a. 1 percent
   b. 6 percent
   c. 23 percent
   d. 47 percent

7. Karuna Chanana Ahmed, an anthropologist from India who has studied developing nations, calls which group the most exploited of oppressed people?
   a. children
   b. women
   c. the elderly
   d. the poor

8. Globally, approximately how many people subsist on less than $2 per day?
   a. 500 million
   b. 1 billion
   c. 2 billion
   d. 3 billion

9. Which of the following terms is used to refer to Mexico's large, impoverished majority, most of whom have brown skin and a mixed racial lineage due to intermarriage?
   a. *criollo*
   b. *indio*
   c. *mestizo*
   d. *zapatista*

10. Which of the following terms refers to the foreign-owned factories established just across the border in Mexico, where the companies that own them don't have to pay taxes or high wages, or provide insurance or benefits for their workers?
    a. *maquiladoras*
    b. *hombres*
    c. *mujeres*
    d. *toreadors*

5. (c); 6. (a); 7. (b); 8. (d); 9. (c); 10. (a)

# GENDER &

# RAISING WOMEN'S CONSCIOUSNESS

Betty Friedan was living the American dream. She came from a solid middle-class background and graduated from Smith College, a prestigious liberal arts college. Friedan worked as a journalist before marrying and settling into life as a 1950s suburban housewife and mother. However, she continued to work as a freelance journalist, writing articles for magazines such as *Redbook* and *Cosmopolitan.*

Fifteen years after her college graduation, Friedan surveyed her college classmates about their lives for a story she planned to write. During her research, she heard a consistent message from well-educated, middle-class suburban housewives: They shared a sense of nameless, aching dissatisfaction which she famously labeled "the problem that has no name." The message they received from educators, psychologists, and the mass media was of one voice: They should be happy. And yet, something was missing. They mostly blamed themselves for this feeling of emptiness or incompleteness, and when they sought help, doctors and psychiatrists would prescribe charity work, community activities, or perhaps tranquilizers.

In her best-selling classic *The Feminine Mystique,* Friedan argued that the problem was not with women as individuals, but with the position they occupied in American society at the time. Friedan's realization that this was not a private trouble but a public issue represents a classic case of using the sociological imagination (Mills [1959] 2000a). Women were cut off from the public sphere, and their lack of access to valued economic, social, and cultural resources—including money and power in the workplace—was the real problem. (Friedan herself attributed part of her relative happiness to the fact that she retained dual status as both journalist and housewife.) In order to challenge this structural problem, they had to challenge the cultural assumption that the primary and most "natural" goal for women was to be a wife and mother in the private sphere. As Friedan put it, "We can no longer ignore that voice within women that says: 'I want something more than my husband and my children and my home.'" ([1963] 1983: 32).

# AGE

# As You READ >>

- How has opportunity for women in the United States changed over time?
- To what extent does gender still shape access to resources?
- How do sociologists approach the study of aging?

## >> The Social Construction of Gender

We tend to take for granted that differences between men and women must be "natural." Historically, however, things that we took for granted as natural often turned out not to be so. Unfortunately, in the meantime, such differences may have been used to justify unequal opportunity in education, employment, politics, and more. Members of groups defined as inferior in some way, including women but also racial and ethnic minorities and the elderly, have consistently had to fight against such characterizations in order to pursue equal opportunity.

sex The biological differences between males and females.

It was once thought, for example, that women were incapable of succeeding at college because their biological makeup limited them. At the Jefferson Medical College in Philadelphia in 1847, Professor Charles Meigs, in a famous speech delivered to an all-male class of gynecology students, said of women, "She has a head almost too small for intellect and just big enough for love . . . She reigns in the heart . . . the household altar is her place of worship and service" (quoted in Collins 2003:89–90). In 1874, at Harvard University, Dr. Edward Clarke, a member of their board of overseers, wrote that women were too delicate to handle the rigors of college education. The increased effort needed for thinking would sap energy from a woman's uterus and ovaries, leading these reproductive organs to shrink (Clarke 1874). In fact, Harvard did not formally admit women to its undergraduate program until the early 1970s.

When they were given the opportunity, however, women excelled in college. They now have a higher overall grade point average and outnumber men among college graduates. Just as Friedan found with the feminine mystique, our cultural presuppositions are more often rooted in our social constructions of what is natural than in biological limitations themselves. In this chapter, we will examine how such constructions develop and what their consequences are in terms of opportunity. We will then do the same for the issue of age.

### SEX AND GENDER

To better understand the nature of social realities for men and women, sociologists typically make a distinction between sex and gender. **Sex** refers to biological differences between males and females. **Gender** involves the social and cultural significance that we attach to those presumed biological differences.

Sex includes variation that occurs at the cellular level (chromosomes and sex-specific genes), the hormonal level (estrogen and testosterone), and the anatomical level (genitals and secondary sexual characteristics). In the taken-for-granted biological model of sex, females have XX chromosome patterns, estrogen hormones, ovaries, and a vagina, while males have XY chromosome patterns, androgen hormones, testicles, and a penis. This definition of sex assumes a simple, two-sex, or "dimorphic," model in which the line between females and males is distinct and absolute. In fact, however, there is no absolute biological dividing line; we find a range of

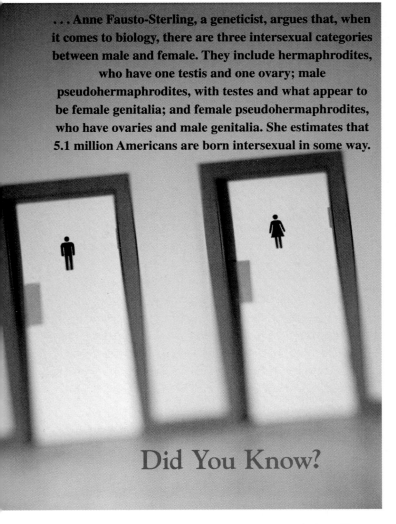

... Anne Fausto-Sterling, a geneticist, argues that, when it comes to biology, there are three intersexual categories between male and female. They include hermaphrodites, who have one testis and one ovary; male pseudohermaphrodites, with testes and what appear to be female genitalia; and female pseudohermaphrodites, who have ovaries and male genitalia. She estimates that 5.1 million Americans are born intersexual in some way.

## Did You Know?

these characteristics throughout the population (Fausto-Sterling 2000).

Gender, on the other hand, varies across time and place. We construct gender by attaching social and cultural significance to the presumed biological differences between the sexes. Sex refers to who we are as males and females; gender refers to what we become as men and women. This process of becoming occurs through socialization, in which we learn the appropriate cognitive, normative, and material culture information assumed to be natural in our social worlds.

## GENDER ROLES
## IN THE UNITED STATES

In studying gender, sociologists are interested in the gender-role socialization that leads females and males to behave differently. In Chapter 4 on socialization, we defined gender roles as expectations regarding the proper behavior, attitudes, and activities of males and females. The application of dominant gender roles leads to many forms of differentiation between women and men. Both sexes are physically capable of learning to cook and sew, yet in most Western societies, women predominantly perform those tasks. Both men and women are capable of learning to weld and to fly airplanes, but men generally fill those jobs. We learn such expectations through our interactions with others.

**Gender-Role Socialization** Male babies get blue blankets; females get pink ones. Boys are expected to play with trucks, blocks, and toy soldiers; girls receive dolls and kitchen goods. Boys must be masculine—active, aggressive, tough, daring, and dominant—but girls must be feminine—soft, emotional, sweet, and submissive. These traditional gender-role patterns have been influential in the socialization of children in the United States.

> **gender** The social and cultural significance that we attach to the biological differences of sex.
> **homophobia** Fear of and prejudice against homosexuality.

Children learn these preferences primarily from adults, who play a critical role in guiding them into those gender roles that a society deems appropriate. Parents are normally the first and most crucial agents of socialization. However, other adults, along with older siblings, the mass media, and religious and educational institutions, also exert an important influence on gender-role socialization, in the United States and elsewhere.

The prevalence in U.S. society of **homophobia**—the fear of and prejudice against homosexuality—gives us a sense of how important maintaining a clear line between masculinity and femininity is in our culture. Homophobia contributes significantly to rigid gender-role socialization, since many people stereotypically associate male homosexuality with femininity, and lesbianism with masculinity. Consequently, men and women who deviate from traditional expectations about gender roles are often presumed to be gay. Despite the advances made by the gay liberation movement, the continuing stigma attached to homosexuality in the United States becomes a mechanism for reinforcing narrow "masculine" and "feminine" characteristics for men and women (Seidman 1994; see also Lehne 1995).

It is not hard to test how rigid

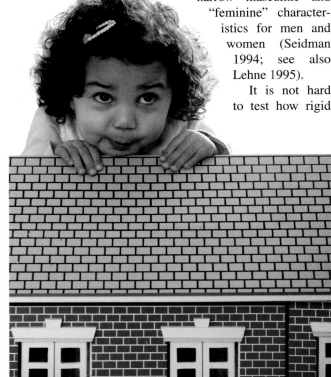

gender-role socialization can be. Just try transgressing some gender norm—say, by smoking a cigar in public if you are female, or by carrying a purse if you are male. That was exactly the assignment given to sociology students at the University of Colorado and at Luther College in Iowa. Professors asked students to behave in ways that they thought violated the norms of how a man or woman should act. The students had no trouble coming up with gender-norm transgressions, and they kept careful notes on others' reactions to their behavior, ranging from amusement to disgust (Nielsen et al. 2000).

### Women's Gender Roles

How does a girl come to develop a feminine self-image, while a boy develops one that is masculine? Socialization from parents, school, friends, and the mass media all contribute to a person's sense of what kind of thoughts, actions, and appearance are appropriate. We receive from these agents of socialization images of what society considers ideal, and we face positive and negative sanctions for deviating from such standards.

In 2004, Dove launched a series of ads in what they called the Campaign for Real Beauty (www.campaignforrealbeauty.com). In preparation for this campaign, they conducted a formal research project in which they hired academic re-

## From Me to You

When they were little, our refrigerator was covered with pictures of our family drawn by Emily and Eleanor. In the pictures, the girls wore dresses while I wore pants. They had long eyelashes and I did not. They had long hair and I had what looked like a plate on my head. I asked Eleanor, "What about the women we know with short hair and the men we know with long hair?" She replied, "Yeah, but women have long hair and men have short hair." She recognized evidence disproving her hair theory, but she had already come to accept an image in which the line between men and women was obvious, important, and inevitable.

searchers to conduct surveys of women from 10 countries around the world, including the United States. They found that only 2 percent of women around the world feel comfortable describing themselves as beautiful. This was in spite of the fact that these women distinguished between beauty (which they maintain involves happiness, confidence, dignity, and humor) and physical attractiveness (which involves how a person looks). Regarding their weight and body shape, overall, just 13 percent of women said they were very satisfied. In the survey, 68 percent strongly agreed that "the media and advertising set an unrealistic standard of beauty that most women can't ever achieve." Dove set out to address this through an advertising campaign that featured a wide range of body types and highlighted an expanded definition of beauty.

While television consistently portrays youth, thinness, and beauty as essential to this ideal, it is far from alone in stereotyping women. Studies of children's books published in the United States in the

## An Experiment in Gender Norm Violation by College Students

**SOCstudies**

Norm Violations by Men

Wear fingernail polish
Needlepoint in public
Throw Tupperware party
Cry in public
Have pedicure
Apply to baby-sit
Shave body hair

Norm Violations by Women

Send men flowers
Spit in public
Use men's bathroom
Buy jockstrap
Talk knowledgeably about cars
Buy/chew tobacco
Open doors for men

Source: Nielsen et al. 2000:287.

1940s, 1950s, and 1960s found that females were significantly underrepresented in central roles and in illustrations. The books portrayed virtually all female characters as helpless, passive, incompetent, and in need of a strong male caretaker. Studies of picture books published from the 1970s through the 1990s found some improvement, but males still dominated the central roles. While authors portrayed males as a variety of characters, they tended to show females primarily in traditional roles, such as mother, grandmother, or volunteer —even if they also held nontraditional roles, such as working professional (Etaugh 2003).

The pervasiveness of these traditional gender roles extends even to unpaid labor as volunteers. Sociologists Thomas Rotolo and John Wilson (2007), drawing on a representative national sample of over 90,000 adults, found that men and women are equally likely to volunteer, but male volunteers from high-prestige occupations are much more likely than women to serve on boards and committees. An exception to this was men who work in traditionally "feminine" fields such as education and the fine arts. Female volunteers, in contrast, are disproportionately involved in direct charitable service as caregivers, nurturers, and food preparers. A significant exception is involvement in political campaigns, where gender roles are not pronounced among volunteers.

**Men's Gender Roles** How about stay-at-home fathers? Until recent decades, such an idea was unthinkable. Yet, in a nationwide survey conducted in 2002, 69 percent of respondents said that if one parent stays home with the children, it makes no difference whether that parent is the mother or the father. Only 30 percent thought that the mother should be the one to stay home. Although people's conceptions of gender roles are obviously changing, the fact is that men who stay home to care for their children is still an unusual phenomenon. For every stay-at-home dad, there are 38 stay-at-home moms (Fields 2004a:11–12; Robison 2002).

While attitudes toward parenting may be changing, studies show little change in the traditional male gender role. Men's roles are

## Going GLOBAL

### Satisfaction with Body Weight and Shape

| | Very/somewhat satisfied ■ + ■ | Very satisfied | Somewhat satisfied | Neither | Very/somewhat dissatisfied | DK/Refused |
|---|---|---|---|---|---|---|
| USA | 55% | 16% | 39% | 8% | 36% | 1% |
| Canada | 69% | 20% | 49% | 8% | 23% | |
| UK | 50% | 16% | 34% | 14% | 36% | |
| Italy | 63% | 12% | 51% | 19% | 18% | |
| France | 57% | 2% | 55% | 18% | 24% | 1% |
| Netherlands | 64% | 21% | 43% | 11% | 25% | |
| Portugal | 65% | 7% | 58% | 17% | 18% | |
| Brazil | 63% | 9% | 54% | | 37% | |
| Argentina | 69% | 26% | 43% | 4% | 27% | |
| Japan | 20% | 3% | 17% | 20% | 59% | 1% |

0%   20%   40%   60%   80%   100%

*Source:* Etcoff et al. 2004.

socially constructed in much the same way as women's. Family, peers, and the media all influence how a boy or man comes to view his appropriate role in society. The male gender role includes proving one's masculinity at work and in sports—often by using force in dealing with others—as well as initiating and controlling sexual relations.

Males who do not conform to the socially constructed gender role often face criticism and even humiliation. Boys who deviate from expected patterns of masculinity risk being called a "chicken," "sissy," or "fag" even by fathers or brothers (Katz 1999). And grown men who pursue nontraditional occupations, such as preschool teaching or nursing, must constantly deal with others' misgivings and strange looks. In one study, interviewers found that such men frequently had to alter their behavior in order to minimize others' negative reactions. One 35-year-old nurse reported that he had to claim he was "a carpenter or something like that" when he "went clubbing," because women weren't interested in getting to know a male nurse. The subjects made similar accommodations in casual exchanges with other men (Cross and Bagilhole 2002:215).

There may be a price to pay for such narrow conceptions of manhood. Boys who successfully adapt to cultural standards of masculinity may grow up to be inexpressive men who cannot share their feelings with others. They remain forceful and tough, but they are also closed and isolated. In fact, a small but growing body of scholarship suggests that these traditional gender roles may be putting men at a disadvantage. Today girls outdo boys in high school, grabbing a disproportionate share of the leadership positions, from valedictorian to class president to yearbook editor—everything, in short, except captain of the boys' athletic teams. And their advantage continues after high school. In the 1980s, girls in the United States became more likely than boys to go to college. By 2005, women accounted for over 57 percent of college students nationwide. And in 2002, for the first time, more women than men in the United States earned doctoral degrees (Bureau of the Census 2007a:Table 214).

In the past 40 years, inspired in part by the contemporary women's movement that Betty Friedan helped start, increasing numbers of men in the United States have criticized the restrictive aspects of the traditional male gender role. Australian sociologist R. W. Connell (1987, 2002, 2005) has written about **multiple masculinities,** meaning that men

learn and play a range of gender roles. These may include a nurturing-caring role, an effeminate-gay role, or their more traditional role. Sociologist Michael Kimmel gave voice to this broader conception of what it means to be a man when he was sitting with his newborn son in the park. When a woman came up to him and said that he was expressing his "femi-

## Did You Know?

. . . Women are more likely to perform unpaid volunteer work in the United States. A total of 36 million women volunteer, which includes 30 percent of all women. This compares to 23 percent for men.

nine side," he responded, "I'm not expressing anything of the sort, ma'am. I'm being tender and loving and nurturing toward my child. As far as I can tell, I'm expressing my *masculinity*" (Kimmel 2004:290–91).

## GENDER ACROSS CULTURES

We have already seen that our conception of gender shifts over time. We turn next to ways that gender varies across cultures. If biology alone determined gender categories, we would expect to find universal agreement about the definitions of the sexes. What we find instead is that not all cultures divide people into female and male in the same way.

Some cultures assume the existence of three or four gender categories. Judith Lorber (1994) notes that "male women," biological males who live for the most part as women, and "female men," biological females who live for the most part as men, can be found in various societies. "Female men" can be found in some African and Native American societies, where they take on male work and family roles. "Male women" include the *berdaches* of the Native Americans of the Great Plains and *hijras* of India. Michael Kimmel (2004) describes the *xanith* of Oman in the Middle East:

They work as skilled domestic servants, dress in men's tunics (but in pastel shades more associated with feminine colors), and sell themselves in passive homosexual relationships. They are permitted to speak with women on the street (other men are prohibited). At sex-segregated public events, they sit with the women. However, they can change their minds. (p. 65)

These gender categories are a well-accepted part of their social lives. Individuals who fill them are not simply tolerated or viewed as deviant. The *berdache,* for example, have high status because they are thought to have special powers (Kimmel, 2004).

Beginning with the path-breaking work of Margaret Mead ([1935] 2001) and continuing through contemporary fieldwork, these scholars have shown that gender roles can vary greatly from one physical environment, economy, and political system to the next. Peggy Reeves Sanday's (2002, 2008) work in West Sumatra, Indonesia, for example, describes the 4-million-member Minangkabau society as one in which men and women are not competitors but partners for the common good. This society is characterized by a nurturing approach to the environment, blended with Islamic religious ethics. Women control the land through inheritance; in the event of a divorce, the ex-husband leaves with only his clothes. The larger community may be governed by men, women, or both men and women working together. Sanday's findings, together with Mead's, confirm the influential role of culture and socialization in gender-role differentiation.

## SOCthink

> > > Given that our understandings of gender vary across time and place, why are we so committed to the notion that gender differences are narrowly determined by biology?

## >> Gender and Inequality

Although the work of early sociologists such as Harriet Martineau, Charlotte Perkins Gilman, and Ida B. Wells-Barnett highlighted the significance of gender inequality, in the 1950s, sociologists Talcott Parson and Robert Bales (1955) argued that families needed both an instrumental and an expressive leader. The **instrumental leader** is the person in the family who bears responsibility for completion of tasks, focuses on more distant goals, and manages the external relationship between the family and other social institutions. The **expressive leader** is the person in the family who bears responsibility for the maintenance of harmony and internal emotional affairs. According to their theory, women's interest in expressive goals frees men for instrumental tasks, and vice versa. Women become naturally anchored in the family as wives, mothers, and household man-

agers; men become anchored in the occupational world outside the home.

As a result of insights from feminist theorists and findings from further research, sociologists now argue that such separate abilities are not innate but are instead social constructs. The key sociological task is to analyze how gender expectations are created and maintained—for example, through gender-role socialization—and then to investigate the consequences of such constructs. We turn next to how resources are distributed based on gender.

**multiple masculinities** The idea that men learn and play a full range of gender roles.
**instrumental leader** The person in the family who bears responsibility for the completion of tasks, focuses on more distant goals, and manages the external relationship between one's family and other social institutions.
**expressive leader** The person in the family who bears responsibility for the maintenance of harmony and internal emotional affairs.

### WOMEN IN THE UNITED STATES

More than 30 years ago, the U.S. Commission on Civil Rights (1976) concluded that the phrase in the Declaration of Independence proclaiming that "all men are created equal" had been taken literally for too long. They found that women in the United States experienced a consistent pattern of inequality. Looking at the workplace, income, housework, politics, and more, we can see that their concern is still valid.

**Labor Force Participation** The labor market has opened up significantly since Betty Friedan published *The Feminine Mystique* in 1963. Today, millions of women—married or single, with or without children, pregnant or recently having given birth—are in the labor force. Overall, 57 percent of adult women in the United States were in the labor force in 2006, compared to 41 percent in 1970. By contrast, in 2006, 70 percent of adult men in the United States were in the labor force, compared to 76 percent in 1970. Presently, 57 percent of women who are pregnant with their first child work full-time, compared to less than 40 percent in the early 1960s. Among married mothers, 41

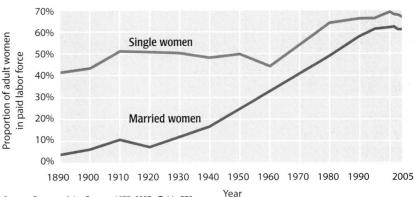

# Trends in U.S. Women's Participation in the Paid Labor Force, 1890–2005

*Source:* Bureau of the Census 1975; 2007a:Table 578.

percent of those with children under age 6 were in the labor force in 2006, compared to 30 percent in 1970 (Bureau of the Census 2007a:Tables 571, 580; T. Johnson 2008).

**glass ceiling** An invisible barrier that blocks the promotion of a qualified individual in a work environment because of the individual's gender, race, or ethnicity.

Still, women entering the job market find their options restricted in important ways. Particularly damaging is occupational segregation, or confinement to sex-typed "women's jobs." For example, in 2006, women accounted for 99 percent of all dental hygienists and 84 percent of all librarians. Entering such sex-typed occupations often places women in "service" roles that parallel the traditional gender-role standard.

Women are underrepresented in occupations historically defined as "men's jobs," which often offer much greater financial rewards and prestige than women's jobs. For example, in 2005, women accounted for approximately 45 percent of the paid labor force of the United States, yet they constituted only 12 percent of civil engineers, 23 percent of all dentists, and 32 percent of all computer systems analysts and physicians.

When it comes to getting promotions, women sometimes encounter attitudinal or organizational bias that prevents them from reaching their full potential. The term **glass ceiling** refers to an invisible barrier that blocks the promotion of a qualified individual in a work environment because of the individual's gender, race, or ethnicity. A 2007 study showed that women held less than 15 percent of the seats on the boards of directors of the 500 largest corporations in the United States. Furthermore, only 11 of those corporations had a female CEO while 489 had a male in that post (Catalyst 2007; Guerrera and Ward 2007).

**Income** He works. She works. Both are physicians—a high-status occupation with considerable financial rewards. He makes $140,000. She makes $88,000.

The Census Bureau released these median earnings for physicians in the United States in 2004. They are typical of the findings of the bureau's detailed study of occupations and income. Among air traffic controllers, for example, men average $67,000 while women earn $56,000. Among housekeepers, he makes $19,000 while she earns $15,000. Among teacher's assistants, he makes $20,000 while she earns $15,000. Statisticians at the bureau looked at the median earnings for 821 occupations ranging from dishwasher to chief executive. After adjusting for workers' age, education, and work experience, they came to an unmistakable conclusion: across the board, there is a substantial gender gap in the median earnings of full-time workers.

Men do not always earn more than women for doing the same work. Researchers at the Census Bureau found 2 occupations out of the 821 in which women on average earn more than men: hazardous materials recovery and telecommunications line installation. The income advantage for women in both was about 1 percent. However, these two occupations employed less than 1 out of every 1000 workers the bureau studied (Weinberg 2004).

# U.S. Women in Selected Occupations, 2006: Women as a Percentage of All Workers in the Occupation

| Underrepresented | | Overrepresented | |
|---|---|---|---|
| Aircraft pilots | 2 | High school teachers | 56 |
| Firefighters | 4 | Cashiers | 75 |
| Civil engineers | 12 | File clerks | 79 |
| Police officers | 13 | Elementary teachers | 82 |
| Clergy | 13 | Social workers | 83 |
| Photographers | 16 | Librarians | 84 |
| Dentists | 23 | Tellers | 85 |
| Chefs and head cooks | 24 | Registered nurses | 91 |
| Computer systems analysts | 32 | Word processors and typists | 91 |
| Physicians | 32 | Receptionists | 93 |
| Lawyers | 33 | Child care workers | 94 |
| Mail carriers | 36 | Dental hygienists | 99 |

*Note:* Women constitute 45 percent of the entire labor force.

*Source:* Data for 2006 reported in Bureau of the Census 2007a: Table 598.

# Actual and Projected Wage Gaps Between Male and Female Earnings

## 1994 2001 2011 2031

| | 1994 | 2001 | 2011 | 2031 |
|---|---|---|---|---|
| **Percentage gap between men's and women's earnings** | | | | |
| **All ages** | 27.5 | 29.2 | 26.5 | 21.9 |
| **Age 25–44** | 20.9 | 21.3 | 17.6 | 16.9 |
| **Age 45–64** | 42.9 | 43.6 | 38.8 | 29.0 |

*Source:* Kelly Rathie, "Male Versus Female Earnings—Is the Gender Gap Converging?" *Economist Ltd.,* Spring 2002, vol. 7, no. 1.

What accounts for these wage gaps between men and women in the same occupation? The Census Bureau studied the following characteristics of men and women in the same occupation:

- Age and degree of formal education
- Marital status and the presence of children at home
- Specialization within the occupation (for example, family practice versus surgical practice)
- Years of work experience
- Hours worked per year

Taking all these factors into consideration reduced the pay gap between men and women by only 3 cents. Even taking such factors into account, women still earned 80 cents for every dollar earned by men. In sum, the disparity in pay between men and women cannot be explained by pointing to women's career choices (Government Accountability Office 2003; Weinberg 2004, 2007).

While women are at a disadvantage in male-dominated occupations, the same is not true for men in female-dominated occupations. Sociologist Michelle Budig (2002) examined a national database containing career information on more than 12,000 men, collected over the course of 15 years. She found that men were uniformly advantaged in female occupations. Although male nurses, grade school teachers, and librarians may experience some scorn in the larger society, they get paid more than women in those jobs, and they are more likely to be encouraged to become administrators. Observers of the labor force have termed this advantage for men in female-dominated occupations the *glass escalator,* in contrast to the glass ceiling (J. Jacobs 2003; C. L. Williams 1992, 1995).

**Home and Work** Today, many women face the challenge of trying to juggle work and family. Who does the housework when women become productive wage earners? Studies indicate that there is a clear gender gap in the performance of housework, although it has been narrowing.

## Did You Know?

**. . . Married mothers spend about twice as much time per week on child care and housework as married fathers. Mothers spend about 13 hours per week on child care and 19 hours on housework compared to 7 and 10, respectively, for fathers.**

## Why Leave Work?

### Five Top Reasons for Leaving

| Women | | Men |
|---|---|---|
| 44% | Family time | 12% |
| 16% | Change in career | 29% |
| 23% | Earn a degree, other training | 25% |
| 17% | Work not enjoyable, satisfying | 24% |
| * | Not interested in field | 18% |
| 17% | Moved away | * |

\* Not one of top 5 reasons

*Note:* Based on a representative Harris interactive survey of "highly qualified" workers, defined as those with a graduate degree, a professional degree, or a high honors undergraduate degree.

*Source:* Figure adapted from Sylvia Ann Hewlett and Carolyn Buck Luce, "Off-Ramps and On-Ramps: Keeping Talented Women on the Road to Success," *Harvard Business Review,* March 2005. Copyright © 2005 by the Harvard Business School Publishing Corporation, all rights reserved. Reprinted by permission of Harvard Business Review.

housework—that many women face and few men share equitably. On the basis of interviews with and observations of 52 couples over an eight-year period, Hochschild reported that the wives (and not their husbands) drive home from the office while planning domestic schedules and play dates for children—and then begin their second shift. Drawing on national studies, she concluded that women spend 15 fewer hours each week in leisure activities than their husbands. In a year, these women work an extra month of 24-hour days because of the second shift; over a dozen years, they work an extra year of 24-hour days. Hochschild found that the married couples she studied were fraying at the edges, and so were their careers and their marriages. With such reports in mind, many feminists have advocated greater governmental and corporate support for child care, more flexible family leave policies, and other reforms designed to ease the burden on the nation's families (Moen and Roehling 2005).

Women do more housework and spend more time on child care than men, whether on a workday or a nonworkday (Sayer et al. 2004).

Sociologist Arlie Hochschild (1989, 1990, 2005) has used the phrase **second shift** to describe the double burden—work outside the home followed by child care and

**Politics** Turning to political involvement, after years of struggle, women won the right to vote with the passage of the 19th Amendment in 1920. Looking at voter participation rates we can see that they have taken advantage of that opportunity. In fact, a higher percentage of women turn out to vote than do men. This has been true in every presidential election since 1980. In 2004, for example, 60.1 percent of voting-age women reported having voted, compared with 56.3

© Baby Blues Partnership. King Features Syndicate.

## Young Women and Men Voters (18–29) in Presidential Elections

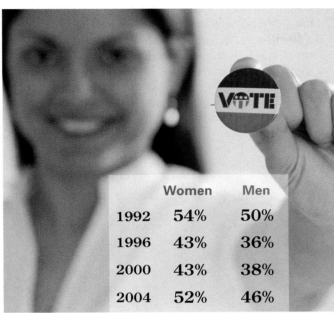

|      | Women | Men |
|------|-------|-----|
| 1992 | 54%   | 50% |
| 1996 | 43%   | 36% |
| 2000 | 43%   | 38% |
| 2004 | 52%   | 46% |

Source: www.civicyouth.org.

percent of men (Center for American Women and Politics 2005c).

When it comes to holding elected office, however, we find the same kind of underrepresentation in positions of power by women as is evident in the workplace. Even though women make up slightly more than half of the population, they make up a significantly smaller proportion of elected officials. As of mid-2008, for example, only 8 of the nation's 50 states had a female governor (Alaska, Arizona, Connecticut, Delaware, Hawaii, Kansas, Michigan, and Washington).

Women have made slow but steady progress in certain political arenas. In 1981, out of 535 members of Congress, only 21 were women: 19 in the House of Representatives and 2 in the Senate. In contrast, the Congress that held office in mid-2008 had 88 women: 72 in the House and 16 in the Senate. Yet even with the election of Nancy Pelosi as Speaker of the House—the first woman ever to serve in that role —the membership and leadership of Congress remain overwhelmingly male. Since 1789, 11,582 men have served as members of Congress compared to only 240 women—a mere 2 percent of the total (Center for American Women and Politics 2008).

In the Supreme Court, Sandra Day O'Connor was sworn in as the nation's first female justice in October 1981. She has since retired, and Ruth Bader Ginsburg remains as the only other woman to have served in this position. No woman has ever served as chief justice of the Supreme Court. In the executive branch, no woman has ever been elected either vice president or president of the United States.

## WOMEN AROUND THE WORLD

Even as inequality continues to be a concern in the United States, a detailed overview of the status of the world's women, issued by the United Nations in 2000, noted that women and men live in different worlds. Their worlds differ in terms of access to education and work opportunities, as well as in health, personal security, and human rights. The Hindu culture of India, for example, makes life especially harsh for widows. When Hindu women marry, they join their husband's family. If the husband dies, the widow is the "property" of that family. In many cases, she ends up working as an unpaid servant; in others, she is simply abandoned and left penniless. Ancient Hindu scriptures portray widows as "inauspicious" and advise that "a wise man should avoid her blessings like the poison of a snake" (Burns 1998:10).

> **second shift** The double burden—work outside the home followed by child care and housework—that many women face and few men share equitably.

When it comes to the economy, it is estimated that women grow half the world's food, but they rarely own land. They constitute one-third of the world's paid labor force but are generally found in the lowest-paying jobs. Women perform much of the exploited labor in developing nations, especially in the nonindustrial sector. Female workers typically toil long hours for low pay, but they still contribute significantly to their families' incomes (Jacobson 1993). Single-parent households headed by women, which appear to be on the rise in many nations, are typically found in the poorest sections of the population. The feminization of poverty has become a global phenomenon.

*Somalian-born author Ayaan Hirsi Ali, now a Dutch feminist and activist, and named by TIME magazine in 2005 as one of the 100 most influential people in the world.*

# *Going* GLOBAL

## Gender Inequality in Industrial Nations

Striking differences exist in women's empowerment—that is, the percentage of women in leadership positions—from one country to the next (right). Yet there is much less difference in the division of housework, even in the same countries (left).

| | Division of Housework | Empowerment |
|---|---|---|
| Canada | 3.70 | 0.81 |
| United States | 3.72 | 0.68 |
| Norway | 3.73 | 1.00 |
| Great Britain | 3.92 | 0.46 |
| Czech Republic | 4.07 | 0.28 |
| Italy | 4.24 | 0.26 |
| Japan | 4.49 | 0.13 |

**Division of Housework**
(includes laundry, grocery shopping, dinner preparation, and care for sick family members)

5   4   3   2   1
wife                    husband
always does        always does

**Empowerment**
(includes the proportions of women in parliament, in management, and in professional/technical positions)

0   0.20   0.40   0.60   0.80   1.00
least                              most
equality                      equality

*Source:* Adapted from Fuwa 2004:757.

but 40 percent representation by 2008. The percentage in Norway now stands at 36—much higher than Europe's average of 9 percent (Center for Corporate Diversity 2008; Fouché 2008; Goering 2008).

Women in other industrial nations also struggle with the balance between home and work, especially regarding housework. According to one survey, 30 percent of the couples in U.S. households share most of the housework, compared to 4 percent in Japan, 25 percent in Great Britain, 27 percent in Sweden, and 32 percent in Canada (C. Geist 2005). Sociologist Makiko Fuwa (2004) analyzed gender inequality in 22 industrial countries using data from the International Social Survey Programme. Fuwa compared how couples divided their housework to society-wide measures of women's presence in high-status occupations, as well as their wages relative to men's. A pattern emerged in which those countries that placed greater emphasis on empowerment for women tended to have more balanced housework loads between men and women.

## SEXISM AND DISCRIMINATION

Both in the United States and around the world, this systematic pattern of inequality in income, occupation, housework, and politics points to the existence of institutional sexism. **Sexism** is the ideology that claims one sex is superior to the other. The term generally refers to male prejudice and discrimination against women. It is not enough, however, to understand gender inequality only by looking at the attitudes and practices of individuals, such as sexist remarks and acts of aggression. We must analyze it as a characteristic of the social system itself. Sociologists refer to such patterns of treatment that, as part of a society's normal operations, systematically deny a group access to resources and opportunities as **institutional discrimination.**

All the major institutions of our society—including the government, the armed forces, large corporations, the media, uni-

As is the case in the United States, women in other industrialized nations also experience occupational segregation. In Great Britain, for example, only 29 percent of computer analysts are women, while 81 percent of cashiers and 90 percent of nurses are women (Cross and Bagilhole 2002). Worldwide, women hold less than 1 percent of corporate managerial positions.

In recognition of the underrepresentation of women on boards of directors, the Norwegian legislature established minimum quotas for the number of female board members. As the architects of the plan put it, "Instead of assuming what people *can't* do at work, provide opportunities for employees to prove what they can do." The goal was not complete equity for women,

**sexism** The ideology that one sex is superior to the other.
**institutional discrimination** A pattern of treatment that systematically denies a group access to resources and opportunities as part of society's normal operations.
**feminism** The belief in social, economic, and political equality for women.

versities, and the medical establishment—are controlled by men. These institutions, in their normal, day-to-day routines, often discriminate against women and perpetuate sexism. For example, if the central office of a nationwide bank sets a policy that single women are a bad risk for loans—regardless of their incomes and investments—that bank will discriminate against women in state after state. It will do so even at branches where loan officers hold no personal biases toward women but are merely obeying company policy.

## >> Working for Change: Women's Movements

One of the lessons we learn from research on gender is that change is possible. As we saw with college education for women, past norms need not determine future practices. Change, however, seldom comes without a fight. People have fought against existing cultural assumptions about what is natural in order to advance opportunity for women in politics, the economy, and other spheres of public and private life. **Feminism** is the term for this belief in social, economic, and political equality for women.

### THE FIRST WAVE

The feminist movement in the United States was born in upstate New York, in the town of Seneca Falls, in the summer of 1848. On July 19, the first women's rights convention began, attended by Elizabeth Cady Stanton, Lucretia Mott, and other pioneers in the struggle for women's rights. This first wave of feminists, as they are currently known, faced ridicule and scorn as they fought for legal and political equality for women. They were not afraid to risk controversy on behalf of their cause; in 1872, Susan B. Anthony was arrested for attempting to vote in that year's presidential election.

Ultimately, the early feminists won many victories. As indicated above, among them was the passage and ratification of the 19th Amendment to the Constitution, which granted women the right to vote in national elections beginning in 1920. However, suffrage did not lead to other reforms related to women's social and economic position, and in the early and mid-20th century, the women's movement became a much less powerful force for social change.

### THE SECOND WAVE

The second wave of feminism in the United States emerged in the 1960s and came into full force in the 1970s. Betty

... When the 19th Amendment finally passed in 1920, it did so by a single vote. Having passed the House and Senate in 1919, it still needed to win approval in 36 state legislatures. It reached this milestone when Tennessee legislator Harry T. Burn switched his vote and broke the tie after receiving a letter from his mother that said, "Don't forget to be a good boy and help Mrs. [Carrie Chapman] Catt put the 'Rat' in ratification."

## Did You Know?

Friedan's book *The Feminine Mystique* played a crucial part, as did two other pioneering books that argued for women's rights: Simone de Beauvoir's *The Second Sex* and Kate Millett's *Sexual Politics*. In addition, the general political activism of the 1960s led women—many of whom were working for Black civil rights or against the war in Vietnam—to reexamine their own powerlessness. The sexism they often found within allegedly progressive and radical political circles convinced many women that they needed to establish their own movement for women's liberation (Breines 2007; Freeman 1973, 1975).

In 1966, Friedan helped found the National Organization for Women (NOW) in order to fight for equality for women; she served as its president until 1970. In addition to political and legal battles, one of the organization's tools was "consciousness-raising groups." Among other things, these groups sought to elevate awareness among women of the degree to which they shared "the problem that has no name." This shared consciousness could then lead to collective action and the development of a new structure with enhanced opportunities. Choice was a core value at the center of these efforts. NOW contended that women should be able to choose their own paths and should not be cut off from opportunity in society simply because they are women.

> Gender equality is more than a goal in itself. It is a precondition for meeting the challenge of reducing poverty, promoting sustainable development and building good governance.
>
> **Kofi Annan**

cumstances. These findings have held fairly steady for the past 35 years (Gallup 2008a).

As more and more women became aware of sexist attitudes and practices—including attitudes they themselves had accepted through socialization into traditional gender roles—they began to challenge male dominance. A sense of sisterhood, much like the class consciousness that Marx hoped would emerge in the proletariat, became evident. Individual women identified their interests with women as a whole, and they rejected the principle that their happiness depended upon their acceptance of submissive and subordinate roles.

**Hot or Not?**

What does it mean to be a feminist?

## FEMINISM TODAY

Current national surveys show that while women generally endorse feminist positions, they do not necessarily accept the label "feminist." In 1987, 57 percent of U.S. women considered themselves feminists; the proportion had dropped to about 25 percent by 2001. Both women and men prefer to express their views on complex issues such as abortion, sexual harassment, pornography, and welfare individually rather than under the banner of feminism. Still, feminism is very much alive in the growing acceptance of women in nontraditional roles and even the basic acknowledgment that a married mother not only can work outside the home but perhaps belongs in the labor force. A majority of women say that, given the choice, they would prefer to work outside the home rather than stay home and take care of a house and family, and about one-quarter of women prefer "Ms." to "Miss" or "Mrs." (Feminist Majority Foundation 2007; J. Robison 2002).

While women still face inequality, much has changed. In 2008, for example, Senator Hillary Clinton came extremely close to securing the Democratic nomination for president and Sarah Palin was selected as John McCain's running mate. While there are still people who believe that women are not suited to such positions of power, they are in the minority. Our dominant cultural values now suggest that we believe women should not be denied opportunity based on their

The issue of choice—the question of whether women should have control over their reproductive rights and their bodies—has been at the heart of the battle over abortion. In the United States, most people support a woman's right to a legal abortion, but with reservations. According to a 2007 national survey, 18 percent oppose a woman's right to a legal abortion under all circumstances. However, 26 percent feel that abortion should be legal under any cir-

*Nancy Pelosi, Democrat from California, and the first female Speaker of the U.S. House of Representatives.*

sex. The only way for these values to be realized in practice is if people continue to fight to make them a reality.

## >> Aging and Society

In addition to *The Feminine Mystique,* Betty Friedan (1993) wrote another book later in life in which she addressed many of the stereotypes about aging. In *The Fountain of Age,* she argued that, just as was the case with gender, cultural presuppositions related to aging were limiting people's opportunity. In so doing, she contributed to the movement to change our cultural perceptions about what it means to be elderly and opened up more opportunities for older citizens.

Like gender stratification, age stratification varies from culture to culture. One society may treat older people with reverence, while another sees them as unproductive and "difficult." The Sherpas—a Tibetan-speaking Buddhist people in Nepal—live in a culture that idealizes old age. Almost all elderly members of the Sherpa culture own their homes, and most are in relatively good physical condition. Typically, older Sherpas value their indepen-

dence and prefer not to live with their children. Among the Fulani of Africa, however, older men and women move to the edge of the family homestead. Since that is where people are buried, the elderly sleep over their own graves, for they are viewed socially as already dead (M. Goldstein and Beall 1981; Stenning 1958; Tonkinson 1978).

Understandably, all societies have some system of age stratification that associates certain social roles with distinct periods in life. Some of this age differentiation seems inevitable; it would make little sense to send young children off to war or to expect older citizens to handle physically demanding tasks, such as loading freight at shipyards. However, as is the case with stratification by gender, in the United States, age stratification goes far beyond the physical constraints on human beings at different ages.

"Being old" is a master status that commonly overshadows all others in the United States. Once people have been labeled "old," the designation has a major impact on how others perceive them, and even on how they view themselves. Negative stereotypes of the elderly contribute to their position as a minority group subject to discrimination. There is one crucial difference between older people and other subordinate groups, such as racial and ethnic minorities or women: All of us who live long enough will eventually assume the ascribed status of older person.

Around the world, there are more than 453 million people age 65 and over, representing about 7 percent of the world's population. By 2050, one in three people will be over 65. In an important sense, the aging of the world's population represents a major success story that unfolded during the latter 20th century. Through the efforts of both national governments and international agencies, many societies have drastically reduced the incidence of disease and the rate of death. Consequently, these nations—especially the industrialized countries of Europe and North America—now have increasingly higher proportions of older members (Haub 2005; He et al. 2005; Kinsella and Phillips 2005; Vidal 2004).

### *Going* GLOBAL

**World's "Oldest" Countries Versus the United States, 2006**

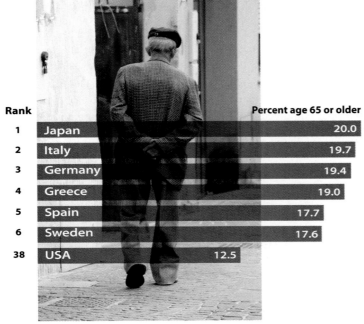

| Rank | | Percent age 65 or older |
|---|---|---|
| 1 | Japan | 20.0 |
| 2 | Italy | 19.7 |
| 3 | Germany | 19.4 |
| 4 | Greece | 19.0 |
| 5 | Spain | 17.7 |
| 6 | Sweden | 17.6 |
| 38 | USA | 12.5 |

*Source:* Bureau of the Census 2005d (projected).

## >> Perspectives on Aging

Aging is one important aspect of socialization throughout the life course—the lifelong process through which an individual learns the cultural norms and values of a particular society. There are no clear-cut definitions for different periods of the aging cycle in the United States. In the recent past, old age has been regarded as beginning at 65, which corresponds to the retirement age for many workers, but not everyone in the United States accepts that definition. With increases in life expectancy, writers are beginning to refer to people in their 60s as the "young old," to distinguish them from those in their 80s and beyond—the "old old."

**gerontology** The study of the sociological and psychological aspects of aging and the problems of the aged.

The particular problems of the elderly have become the focus of a specialized field of research and inquiry known as **gerontology**—the study of the sociological and psychological aspects of aging and the problems of the aged. It originated in the 1930s, as an increasing number of social scientists became aware of the plight of the elderly.

Gerontologists rely heavily on sociological principles and theories to explain the impact of aging on the individual and society. They also draw on psychology, anthropology, physical education, counseling, and medicine in their study of the aging process. Three perspectives on aging—disengagement theory, activity theory, and age discrimination—arise out of these studies.

## SOCthink

> > > What do you think about getting old? Can you picture yourself at age 65? What might your life look like?

### DISENGAGEMENT THEORY

After studying elderly people in good health and relatively comfortable economic circumstances, Elaine Cumming and William Henry (1961) introduced their **disengagement theory,** which implicitly suggests that society and the aging individual mutually sever many of their relationships. Highlighting the significance of social order in society, disengagement theory emphasizes that passing social roles on from one generation to another ensures social stability.

According to this theory, the approach of death forces people to drop most of their social roles—including those of worker, volunteer, spouse, hobby enthusiast, and even reader. Younger members of society then take on these functions. The aging person, it is held, withdraws into an increasing state of inactivity while preparing for death. At the same time, society withdraws from the elderly by segregating them residentially (in retirement homes and communities), educationally (in programs designed solely for senior citizens), and recreationally (in senior citizens' centers). Implicit in disengagement theory is the view that society should help older people to withdraw from their accustomed social roles.

Since it was first outlined more than four decades ago, disengagement theory has generated considerable controversy. Some gerontologists have objected to the implication that older people want to be ignored and put away—and even more to the idea that they should be encouraged to withdraw from meaningful social roles. Critics of disengagement theory insist that society forces the elderly into an involuntary and painful withdrawal from the paid labor force and from meaningful social relationships. Rather than voluntarily seeking to disengage, older employees find themselves pushed out of their jobs—in many instances, even before they are entitled to maximum retirement benefits (Boaz 1987).

People who are elderly have been fighting that trend, and postretirement employment has been increasing in recent decades. In the United States, fewer than half of all employees actually retire from their career jobs. Instead, most move into a "bridge job"—employment that spans the period between the end of their career and their retirement. Unfortunately, the elderly can easily be victimized in such bridge jobs. Psychologist Kathleen Christensen (1990), warning of "bridges over troubled water," emphasizes that older employees do not want to end their working days as minimum-wage jobholders engaged in activities unrelated to their careers (Doeringer 1990; Hayward et al. 1987).

## SOCthink

> > > Consider people over the age of 65 that you have known well, such as grandparents or great-grandparents. How did their lifestyle change after they crossed that age barrier? To what extent did they remain connected in close-knit social networks?

## ACTIVITY THEORY

Ask Ruth Vitow if she would like to trade her custom lampshade business in New York City for a condo

### 5 Movies on GENDER AND AGE

**Thelma and Louise**
*Two women have had enough.*

**Transamerica**
*A male-to-female transsexual travels the country with her son.*

**4 Months, 3 Weeks, 2 Days**
*Illegal abortion and gender inequality.*

**Cocoon**
*Florida retirees meet E.T.*

**Magnolia**
*A man holds motivational seminars on masculinity.*

in Florida, and you will get a quick response: "Deadly! I'd hate it." Vitow, in her 90s, vows to give up her business "when it gives me up." James Russell Wiggins has been working at a weekly newspaper in Maine since 1922. At age 95, he remains as the editor. Vitow and Wiggins are among the 9 percent of men and 3 percent of women age 75 years or older who are still participating in the nation's labor force (Himes 2001).

How important is it for older people to stay actively involved, whether at a job or in other pursuits? A tragic disaster in Chicago in 1995 showed that it can be a matter of life and death. An intense heat wave lasting more than a week—with a heat index exceeding 115 degrees on two consecutive days—resulted in 733 heat-related deaths. About three-fourths of the deceased were 65 or older. Subsequent analysis showed that older people who lived alone had the highest risk of dying, suggesting that support networks for the elderly literally help to save lives. Older Hispanics and Asian Americans had lower death rates from the heat wave than other racial and ethnic groups. Their stronger social networks probably resulted in more regular contact with family members and friends (Klinenberg 2002; Schaefer 1998a).

Often seen as the opposite of disengagement theory, **activity theory** suggests that those elderly people who remain active and socially involved will be best adjusted. Proponents of this perspective acknowledge that a 70-year-old person may not have the ability or desire to perform various social roles that he or she had at age 40. Yet they contend that old people have essentially the same need for social interaction as any other group.

The improved health of older people—sometimes overlooked by social scientists— has strengthened the arguments of activity theorists. Illness and chronic disease are no longer quite the scourge of the elderly that they once were. The recent emphasis on fitness, the availability of better medical care, greater control of in-

**disengagement theory** A theory of aging that suggests that society and the aging individual mutually sever many of their relationships.
**activity theory** A theory of aging that suggests that those elderly people who remain active and socially involved will be best adjusted.

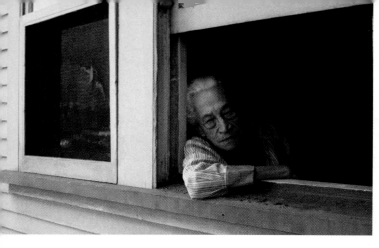

fectious diseases, and the reduction in the number of fatal strokes and heart attacks have combined to reduce the traumas of growing old.

Accumulating medical research also points to the importance of remaining socially involved. Among those who decline in their mental capacities later in life, deterioration is most rapid in those who withdraw from social relationships and activities. Fortunately, the aged are finding new ways to remain socially engaged, as evidenced by their increasing use of the Internet, especially to keep in touch with family and friends (Korczyk 2002).

Admittedly, many activities open to the elderly involve unpaid labor, for which younger adults may receive salaries. Unpaid elderly workers include hospital volunteers (versus aides and orderlies), drivers for charities such as the Red Cross (versus chauffeurs), tutors (as opposed to teachers), and craftspeople for charity bazaars (as opposed to carpenters and dressmakers). However, some companies have recently begun programs to hire retirees for full- or part-time work.

Though disengagement theory suggests that older people find satisfaction in withdrawal from society, con-

**POPSOC**

In 2002, the Senate Special Committee on Aging convened a panel on the media's portrayal of older people and sharply criticized media and marketing executives for bombarding audiences with negative images of the aged. How many characters on top TV shows today can you think of who are over 65? How does that compare to the number of characters you can think of who are under 30?

veniently receding into the background and allowing the next generation to take over, proponents of activity theory view such withdrawal as harmful to both the elderly and society. Activity theorists focus on the potential contributions of older people to the maintenance of society. In their opinion, aging citizens will feel satisfied only when they can be useful and productive in society's terms—primarily by working for wages (Civic Ventures 1999; Crosnoe and Elder, Jr., 2002; Dowd 1980; Quadagno 2005).

## AGEISM AND DISCRIMINATION

Physician Robert Butler (1990) became concerned 30 years ago when he learned that a housing development near his home in metropolitan Washington, D.C., barred the elderly. Butler coined the term **ageism** to refer to prejudice and discrimination based on a person's age. For example, we may choose to assume that someone cannot handle a rigorous job because he is "too old," or we may refuse to give someone a job with authority because she is "too young."

In order to more fully understand issues regarding aging, it is important to also consider the impact of social structure on patterns of aging. Critics argue that neither disengagement nor activity theory answers the question of *why* social interaction must change or decrease in old age. The low status of older people is seen in prejudice and discrimination against them, in age segregation, and in unfair job practices—none of which are directly addressed by either disengagement or activity theory. In addition, these theories often ignore the impact of social class on the lives of the elderly.

The privileged upper class generally enjoys better health and vigor and has less likelihood of dependency in old age. Affluence cannot forestall aging indefinitely, but it can soften the economic hardships people face in later years. Although pension plans, retirement packages, and insurance benefits may be developed to assist older people, those whose wealth allows them access to investment funds can generate the greatest income for their later years.

In contrast, the working class often faces greater health hazards and a greater risk of disability; aging is particularly difficult for those who suffer job-related injuries or illnesses. Working-class people also depend more heavily on Social Security benefits and private pension programs. And during inflationary times, their relatively fixed incomes from these sources barely keep pace with the escalating costs of food, housing, utilities, and other necessities (Atchley and Barusch 2004).

## >> Aging in the United States

Just as women face institutional discrimination because they are female, people who are elderly face discrimination because they are old. While these trends may change as the average age of the population increases, we still see a pattern of unequal treatment.

## THE GRAYING OF AMERICA

At age 82, Lenore Schaefer decided to bring her dancing shoes out of retirement and enter the world of competitive ballroom dancing. Having been a successful dancer in her youth, she decided it was time. She competed for the rest of her life, winning over 200 awards. When she was 101, she won a dance competition, leading to her appearance on the *Tonight Show with Jay Leno*. Stories such as Lenore's are becoming less uncommon in our society. Today, people over 100 constitute, proportionately, the country's fastest-growing age group (Himes 2001; Rimer 1998).

In 1900, men and women age 65 or older constituted only 4.1 percent of the nation's population, but by 2010, that age group is expected to grow to 13.0 percent. According to current projections, the over-65 segment will continue to increase throughout this century. As the decades pass, the population of "old old" (people who are 85 or older) will increase at an ever-faster rate.

In 2010, 15.9 percent of non-Hispanic Whites are projected to be older than 65, compared to 8.7 percent of Af-

*"Good news, honey—seventy is the new fifty."*

rican Americans, 9.6 percent of Asian Americans, and 5.9 percent of Hispanics. In part, these differences reflect the shorter life spans of the latter groups. They also stem from immigration patterns among Asians and Hispanics, who tend to be young when they enter the country (Bureau of the Census 2005a:17).

The highest proportions of older people are found in Florida, Pennsylvania, Rhode Island, Iowa, West Virginia, and Arkansas. However, that will soon change. In 2000, Florida was the state most populated by the elderly, with 17.6 percent of the population over age 65. In another 25 years or so, more than half the states will have an even greater proportion of elderly than Florida does now. The graying of the United States is a phenomenon that can no longer be ignored, either by social scientists or by government policy makers. Advocates for the elderly have spoken out on a wide range of issues. Politicians court the votes of older people, since they are the age group most likely to register and vote. In fact, in the 2004 presidential race, though they made up 30 percent of the total population, people 55 or older accounted for 35 percent of the total vote. Among this group, 72 percent turned out to vote compared to 47 percent of those ages 18–24 (Holder 2006).

> **ageism** Prejudice and discrimination based on a person's age.

On a local scale, one of the more recent residential patterns we find among senior citizens has been the tendency to congregate together. Many do not reside in nursing homes or planned retirement communities. Instead, they congregate in areas that gradually become informal centers for senior citizens. Social scientists have dubbed such areas "naturally occurring retirement communities" (NORCs). NORCs can be as small as a single apartment building or as large as a neighborhood in a big city. The larger they are, the more likely they are to attract business establishments that cater to the elderly, such as pharmacies, medical supply outlets, and small restaurants, making them even more attractive to older citizens.

## Actual and Projected Growth of the Elderly Population of the United States

**Proportion of population**

- ■ 65–84 years
- ▓ 85 years and older

| Year | 65–84 years | 85 years and older |
|------|-------------|---------------------|
| 1900 | 3.9% | 0.2% |
| 1930 | 5.1% | 0.2% |
| 1980 | 10.3% | 1.0% |
| 2010 | 11.0% | 2.0% |
| 2050 (projection) | 15.5% | 4.8% |

*Source:* Bureau of the Census 2004a:113; He et al. 2005:9.

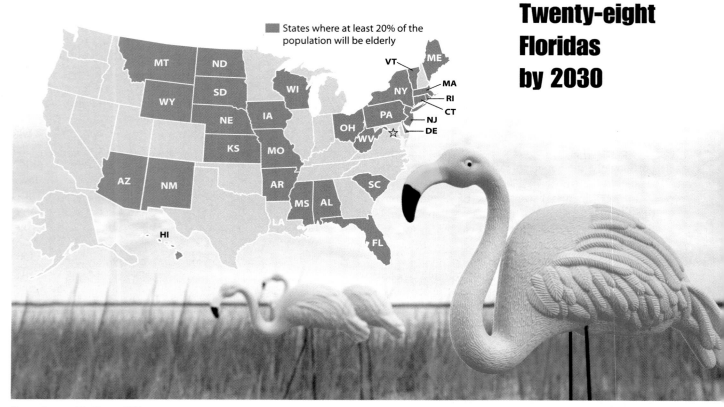

Source: Bureau of the Census 2005c.

The largest known NORC in the United States is Co-op City, a high-rise apartment complex in the Bronx, north of Manhattan. Built in the 1960s, the huge community was meant to house low-income workers and their families in apartments that were relatively spacious by New York City's standards. More than three decades later, many of the buildings' first residents are still there, "aging in place," as the social workers say. Today, roughly 8000 of Co-op City's 50,000 residents are 65 or older (A. Feuer 2002; Lansprey 1995; Perry 2001).

## WEALTH AND INCOME

There is significant variation in wealth among the nation's older people. Some individuals and couples find themselves poor in part because of fixed pensions and skyrocketing health care costs. Nevertheless, as a group, older people in the United States are neither homogeneous nor poor. The typical elderly person enjoys a standard of living that is much higher now than at any point in the nation's past. Class differences among the elderly remain evident but tend to narrow somewhat. Those older people who enjoyed middle-class incomes while younger tend to remain better off after retirement, but less so than before (Denise Smith and Tillipman 2000).

To some extent, older people owe their overall improved standard of living to a greater accumulation of wealth—in the form of home ownership, private pensions, and other financial assets. But much of the improvement is due to more generous Social Security benefits. While modest when compared with other countries' pension programs, Social Security nevertheless provides 39 percent of all income received by older people in the United States. Still, in 2006, 9.4 percent of people age 65 or older lived below the poverty line (DeNavas-Walt 2007; He et al. 2005).

Members of groups who face a greater likelihood of income inequality earlier in their lives, including women and members of racial and ethnic minorities, continue to do so when they are older. For women age 65 or older, the poverty rate is 11.5 percent compared to the rate for elderly men of 6.6 percent. Considering race and ethnicity, in 2006, 19.4 percent of Latinos age 65 or older had incomes below the poverty level, which was more than twice the rate of 7.0 percent for non-Hispanic Whites. The 22.7 percent poverty rate for elderly African Americans was more than three times as high (DeNavas-Walt et al. 2007; U.S. Census Bureau 2007g).

## COMPETITION IN THE LABOR FORCE

Participation in paid work is not typical after the age of 65, but that is changing. In 2007, 34 percent of men ages 65–69 participated in the paid labor force, as did 26 percent of women of the same age. This represents a 28 percent increase for men and a 44 percent increase for women since 1994. While some people view these workers as experienced contributors to the labor force, others see them as "job stealers," a biased judgment similar to that directed against illegal immigrants. This mistaken belief not only intensifies age conflict but leads to age discrimination (Gendell 2008).

# Rising Labor Force Participation Rates Among the Elderly

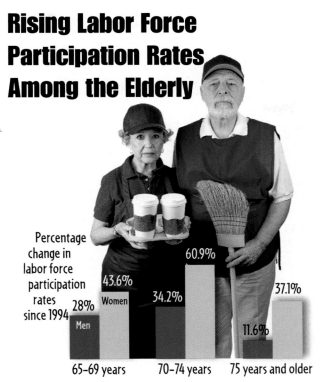

Percentage change in labor force participation rates since 1994

- Men
- Women

| 65-69 years | 70-74 years | 75 years and older |
|---|---|---|
| 28% (Men) | 34.2% | 11.6% |
| 43.6% (Women) | 60.9% | 37.1% |

*Source:* Gendell 2008:47.

Although firing people simply because they are old violates federal law, courts have upheld the right to lay off older workers for economic reasons. Critics contend that, later, the same firms hire young, cheaper workers to replace experienced older workers. When economic growth began to slow in 2001 and companies cut back on their workforces, the number of complaints of age bias rose sharply as older workers began to suspect they were bearing a disproportionate share of the layoffs. According to the Equal

around the United States. In situations for which positions were actually available, the younger applicant received a favorable response 43 percent of the time. By contrast, the older applicant received favorable responses only 17 percent of the time. One Fortune 500 corporation asked the younger applicant for more information while informing the older applicant that no appropriate positions were open (Bendick et al. 1993; Neumark 2008).

Perhaps in part due to the rising numbers of people who continue to work, some companies have come to realize that older workers can be an asset. One study found that older workers can be retrained in new technologies, have lower rates of absenteeism than younger employees, and are often more effective salespeople. The study focused on two corporations based in the United States (the hotel chain Days Inns of America and the holding company Travelers Corporation of Hartford) and a British retail chain—all of which have long-term experience in hiring workers age 50 or over. More and more U.S. corporations, from Borders to Home Depot, are actively trying to recruit retired people, recognizing their comparatively lower turnover rates and often superior work performance (Freudenheim 2005; Telsch 1991).

## DEATH AND DYING

In the film *The Bucket List,* Morgan Freeman and Jack Nicholson play the two main characters, who are diagnosed with terminal cancer and have less than one year to live. They make a list of all the things they would like to do before they "kick the bucket." On the list are things they had never dared to do, such as traveling the world and sky-diving, but it also includes reconciling broken relationships.

Until recently, death was a taboo topic in the United States. Death represents a fundamental disruption that cannot be undone, so we often find it easier to live with a sense

> First you are young; then you are middle-aged; then you are old; then you are wonderful.
>
> Lady Diana Cooper

Employment Opportunity Commission, between 1999 and 2007, complaints of age discrimination rose more than 35 percent. However, evidence of a countertrend has emerged. Some firms have been giving larger raises to older workers, to encourage their retirement at the higher salary—a tactic that prompts younger workers to complain of age discrimination (EEOC 2008; Novelli 2004; Uchitelle 2003).

A controlled experiment conducted by the AARP (formerly known as the American Association of Retired Persons) confirmed that older people often face discrimination when applying for jobs. Comparable résumés for two applicants—one 57 years old and the other 32 years old—were sent to 775 large firms and employment agencies

of denial about our mortality. In the words of sociologist Peter Berger, "Death presents society with a formidable problem . . . because it threatens the basic assumptions of order on which society rests" (1969:23). However, psychologist Elisabeth Kübler-Ross (1969), through her pioneering book *On Death and Dying,* greatly encouraged open discussion of the process of dying. Drawing on her work with 200 cancer patients, Kübler-Ross identified five stages of the experience: denial, anger, bargaining, depression, and finally acceptance.

While we may still be uncomfortable with the topic, *The Bucket List*'s portrayal of a "good death" represents one of the ways we have become more open about it. Gerontologist Richard Kalish (1985) laid out some of the issues people must face in order to have a "good death." These included completing unfinished business, such as settling insurance and inheritance matters; restoring harmony to social relationships and saying farewell to friends and family; dealing with medical needs; and making funeral plans and other arrangements for survivors. In accomplishing these tasks, the dying person actively contributes to smooth intergenerational transitions, role continuity, compliance with medical procedures, and minimal disruption of the social system, despite the loss of a loved one.

We have also begun to create institutions to facilitate our wishes for a good death. The practice of **hospice care**, introduced in England in the 1960s, is devoted to easing this final transition. Hospice workers seek to improve the quality of a dying person's last days by offering comfort and by helping the person to remain at home, or in a homelike setting at a hospital or other special facility, until the end. Currently, there are more than 3200 hospice programs serving over 880,000 people a year.

**hospice care** Treatment of the terminally ill in their own homes, or in special hospital units or other facilities, with the goal of helping them to die comfortably, without pain.

Recent studies in the United States suggest additional ways in which people have broken through the historical taboos about death. For example, bereavement practices— once highly structured—are becoming increasingly varied and therapeutic. More and more people are actively addressing the inevitability of death by making wills, leaving "living wills" (health care proxies that explain their feelings about the use of life support equipment), donating organs, and providing instructions for family members about funerals, cremations, and burials. Given medical and technological advances and increasingly open discussion and negotiation regarding death and dying, it is possible that good deaths may become a social norm in the United States (La Ganga 1999; J. Riley 1992).

Resist! There are growing resources out there that encourage new ways to attain healthier body images for women and men. The website of the organization About-Face (www.about-face.org) brings public awareness to negative stereotypes of women in the media. Visit the site and explore the lists of "winners" and "offenders" in the media.

get involved!

Sociology often confronts us with things that can make us uncomfortable. Whether that is gender inequality, age inequality, or even death, the point of doing so is a more complete understanding of what we do and why we do it. Such knowledge can lead us to new and better practices that provide greater understanding, fairness, equality, and opportunity. Through practicing the sociological imagination, as Betty Friedan did in the case of gender and age, we can make the world a better place.

# For REVIEW

I.  **How has opportunity for women in the United States changed over time?**
    *   In the 1950s, women's primary roles were wife and mother. Since that time, largely due to the efforts of the second wave of the women's movement, their labor force participation and income have risen significantly.

II. **To what extent does gender still shape access to resources?**
    *   Women continue to be paid less than men in the same occupations, tend to be segregated into a narrower range of female-dominated occupations, bear greater responsibility for housework, and are underrepresented as elected officials.

III. **How do sociologists approach the study of aging?**
    *   There is a debate about the degree to which old age represents a stage during which elderly people are expected to fade away, making way for the next generation, versus a stage when they are denied opportunities and face discrimination. Increased willingness to talk about death shows that we are becoming more open about discussing aging and its consequences.

# Pop Quiz

1. Both males and females are physically capable of learning to cook and sew, yet most Western societies determine that women should perform these tasks. This illustrates the operation of
   a. gender roles.
   b. sociobiology.
   c. homophobia.
   d. comparable worth.

2. An important element shaping traditional views of proper "masculine" and "feminine" behavior is fear of homosexuality. This fear, along with accompanying prejudice, is referred to as
   a. lesbianism.
   b. femme fatalism.
   c. homophobia.
   d. claustrophobia.

3. What is the expression used when claiming that gender for men is not narrowly limited to traditional conceptions of masculinity?
   a. disengagement
   b. gender modification
   c. sex
   d. multiple masculinities

4. Cross-cultural research by anthropologists Margaret Mead and Peggy Reeves Sanday has shown that
   a. biology is the most important factor in determining the social roles of males and females.
   b. cultural conditioning is the most important factor in defining the social roles of males and females.
   c. biology and cultural conditioning have an equal impact in determining the social roles of males and females.
   d. biology and cultural conditioning have a negligible impact in determining the social roles of males and females.

5. As of 2006, what percentage of adult women were in the labor force?
   a. 28 percent
   b. 41 percent
   c. 57 percent
   d. 76 percent

6. After adjusting for the effects of factors such as age, education, occupation, and years of experience, how many cents do women earn for every dollar earned by a man?
   a. 65 cents
   b. 80 cents
   c. 94 cents
   d. There no longer is a wage gap between men and women.

7. The expression "second shift" refers to
   a. doing the emotional work of maintaining family relationships.
   b. maintaining the household including housework in addition to a job outside the home.
   c. having a work shift ranging approximately between 4:00 P.M. and midnight.
   d. doing paid labor at the workplace.

8. The primary accomplishment of the first wave of the women's movement was
   a. making women citizens.
   b. gaining the right to an abortion.
   c. earning the right to nondiscrimination in the workplace.
   d. winning the right to vote.

9. Which theory argues that elderly people have essentially the same need for social interaction as any other group and that those who remain active and socially involved will be best adjusted?
   a. disengagement theory
   b. institutional discrimination theory
   c. activity theory
   d. ageism theory

10. In recent years, labor force participation rates for people over age 65 have
    a. gone down for both men and women.
    b. gone up for both men and women.
    c. gone down for men but up for women.
    d. stayed about the same for both men and women.

1. (a); 2. (c); 3. (d); 4. (b); 5. (c); 6. (b); 7. (b); 8. (d); 9. (c); 10. (b)

13

RACE AND ET

## COMING TO AMERICA

On May 12, 2008, Santiago Cordero was on a high school field trip when he got an urgent text message. The Immigration and Customs Enforcement agency (ICE) had raided the meat processing plant where his mother worked. ICE had arrested 389 people, and his mother was one of them (Fuson 2008).

The raid occurred at Agriprocessors, Inc., in Postville, a rural Iowa town with a population of about 2500. It was the largest such raid in U.S. history. The plant employed 968 people, and ICE agents had warrants for the arrest of 697 of them.

Santiago's immigration story is not uncommon. His dad was the first in the family to come from Mexico. He gained legal work documentation and now serves as a custodian in the local school district. Santiago arrived a year later, and his mom and siblings arrived after that. They had no such papers.

In high school, Santiago served as an interpreter for student–teacher conferences, started on the varsity football team, and organized the school's first soccer team, which included 28 students from five nationalities. As a senior he won the class volunteer award and received two scholarships. He graduated on May 25 and faced the possibility of arrest and deportation as soon as he walked across the stage to receive his diploma (Fuson 2008).

The Postville workers represented the latest in a long line of immigration stories. Earlier immigrants arrived from Germany, Italy, Poland, Lithuania, China, Vietnam, or Laos, but the obstacles and opposition they faced were similar. A decade before, the Postville workers would have likely been from Mexico or Bosnia. Now many of those workers had moved on to better jobs. Of the 389 workers arrested, 295 were from Guatemala. Other processing plants were employing increasing numbers of immigrants from Somalia and Sudan. People immigrate because conditions in their homelands are so poor. Like every other immigration stream in U.S. history, they were looking for opportunity (Leys 2008).

Postville represents a microcosm of the United States. It has a diverse population from around the world, both rich and poor. In a small community like this, face-to-face interaction with people from other cultures is inevitable. Such contact can break down some barriers and lead to greater understanding on all sides. As Postville's school superintendent, David Strudthoff, put it, "It's harder than hell to hate people when you get to know them" (Fuson 2008).

**INICITY**

# As You READ >>

- How do sociologists define race and ethnicity?
- What are prejudice and discrimination, and how do they operate?
- What are the consequences of race and ethnicity for opportunity?

## >> Racial and Ethnic Groups

Since European colonists established their first permanent settlement at Jamestown in 1607, first-generation immigrants to what later became the United States have struggled, facing economic hardships and hostile relations with existing groups. Those early European immigrants ultimately survived in part because they received assistance from members of the na-

**minority group** A subordinate group whose members, even if they represent a numeric majority, have significantly less control or power over their own lives than the members of a dominant or majority group have over theirs.

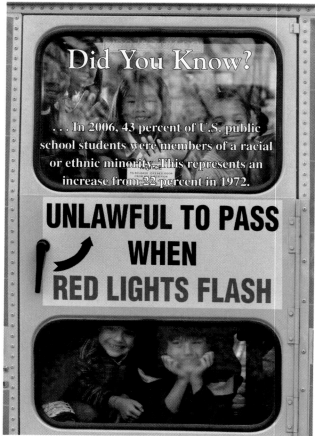

**Did You Know?**

. . . In 2006, 43 percent of U.S. public school students were members of a racial or ethnic minority. This represents an increase from 22 percent in 1972.

**UNLAWFUL TO PASS WHEN RED LIGHTS FLASH**

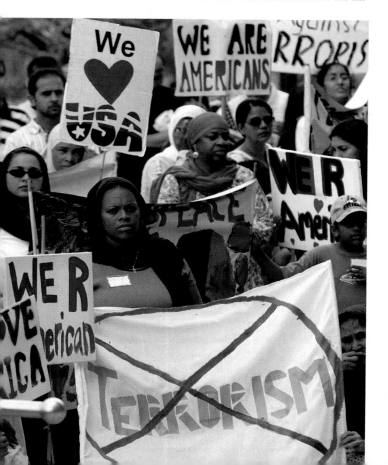

tive Powhatan tribe, but there was still antagonism between the two groups. In time the Europeans came to dominate the region—and ultimately the entire continent—using their control over resources to subjugate other groups. Settlers pushed Native Americans off their lands, Dutch traders brought the first African slaves to America in 1619, and emigrants from other nations struggled to establish a foothold. Since those beginnings, intergroup relations based on ethnic and racial background have played a powerful role in shaping both interaction and opportunity.

# Racial and Ethnic Groups in the United States, 2006

| Classification | Number in Thousands | Percentage of Total Population |
|---|---|---|
| **Racial Groups** | | |
| Whites (non-Hispanic) | 198,744 | 66.3% |
| Blacks/African Americans | 37,051 | 12.4 |
| Native Americans, Alaskan Native | 2,369 | 0.8 |
| Asian Americans | 13,100 | 4.4 |
|   Chinese | 3,090 | 1.0 |
|   Asian Indians | 2,482 | 0.8 |
|   Filipinos | 2,328 | 0.8 |
|   Vietnamese | 1,476 | 0.5 |
|   Koreans | 1,335 | 0.4 |
|   Japanese | 830 | 0.3 |
|   Pacific Islanders and other | 1,559 | 0.5 |
| **Ethnic Groups** | | |
| White ancestry (single or mixed, non-Hispanic) | | |
|   Germans | 50,764 | 17.0 |
|   Irish | 35,976 | 12.0 |
|   English | 28,290 | 9.4 |
|   Italians | 17,829 | 6.0 |
|   Scottish and Scotch-Irish | 11,400 | 3.8 |
|   Poles | 10,025 | 3.3 |
|   French | 9,651 | 3.2 |
|   Jews | 6,452 | 2.2 |
| Hispanic (or Latinos) | 44,252 | 14.8 |
|   Mexican Americans | 28,339 | 9.5 |
|   Puerto Ricans | 3,988 | 1.3 |
|   Cubans | 1,520 | 0.5 |
|   Salvadorans | 1,300 | 0.4 |
|   Dominicans | 1,100 | 0.4 |
|   Other Hispanics | 8,005 | 2.7 |
| **Total (all groups)** | **299,398** | |

*Note:* Percentages do not total 100 and subtotals do not add up to totals in major categories because of overlap between groups (for example, Polish American Jews or people of mixed ancestry, such as Irish and Italian). White ancestry is for the year 2000, and percentages are based on total population in that year.

*Source:* Author estimates based on American Community Survey 2006, Tables DP-1 and R0203, in Bureau of the Census 2007d; Sheskin and Dashefsky 2006.

One of the factors shaping outcomes was access to valued material, social, and cultural resources, a factor strongly influenced by the social status of the group to which one belonged. A **minority group** is a subordinate group whose members have significantly less control or power over their own lives than the members of the dominant or majority group have over theirs. Sociologists consider groups that lack power to be minority groups even if they represent a numeric majority of the population in a society.

Race and ethnicity historically have served as markers of minority group status. The term **racial group** describes a group that is set apart from others because of physical differences that have taken on social significance. Whites, African Americans, and Asian Americans are all considered racial groups in the United States. Although the construct of race emphasizes the significance of external physical differences, it is the culture of a particular society that identifies and attaches social significance to those differences. An **ethnic group** is one that is set apart from others primarily because of its national origin or distinctive cultural patterns. In the United States, Puerto Ricans, Jews, and Polish Americans are all categorized as ethnic groups. As a nation comprised primarily of immigrants and their descendants, the United States has a significant amount of racial and ethnic diversity.

> **racial group** A group that is set apart from others because of physical differences that have taken on social significance.
> **ethnic group** A group that is set apart from others primarily because of its national origin or distinctive cultural patterns.

## RACE

We tend to think of race as strictly a biological category, but researchers for the Human Genome Project (HGP), who mapped the entire genetic code, concluded that race as we understand it does not exist. Craig Venter (2000), one of the project's lead scientists, declared in his presentation of the HGP results that "the concept of race has no genetic or scientific basis," and in a later interview, he said, "Race is a social concept, not a scientific one" (Angier 2000). The researchers found that all humans share the same basic genetic material, and physical manifestations such as skin color represent different combinations, in greater or lesser degrees, of the same shared genes.

When it comes to genetic variation, the biological differences within what we think of as racial groups are actually greater than the differences between those groups. Genetic researchers Luca Cavalli-Sforza, Paolo Menozzi, and Alberto Piazza (1994), for example, point out that people from northeast China are genetically closer to Europeans, Eskimos, and North American Indians than they are to people from south China (p. 78). In fact, the overall degree of human genetic variation is quite small when compared with genetic variation among other large mammals—

due primarily to the fact that communities of human beings have always interacted, even across great distances (MacEachern 2003:20).

**Social Construction of Race** The racial categories that we typically take for granted grow out of sociocultural traditions and historical experiences that are specific to various groups. If we look cross-culturally, we see that different groups define racial categories in different ways at different times. Each society defines which differences are important while ignoring other characteristics that could serve as a basis for social differentiation. In the United States, we see differences in both skin color and hair color. Yet people learn informally that differences in skin color have a dramatic social and political meaning while differences in hair color do not.

When observing skin color, many people in the United States tend to lump others rather casually into the traditional categories of "Black," "White," and "Asian." More subtle differences in skin color often go unnoticed. In many nations of Central America and South America, by contrast, people recognize color gradients on a continuum from light to dark skin color. Brazil has approximately 40 color groupings, while in other countries people may be described as "Mestizo Honduran," "Mulatto Colombian," or "African Panamanian." What we see as "obvious" differences, then, are subject to each society's social definitions.

Racial definitions are crystalized through what Michael Omi and Howard Winant (1994) have called **racial formation**—a sociohistorical process in which racial categories are created,

**racial formation** A sociohistorical process in which racial categories are created, inhibited, transformed, and destroyed.

**stereotype** An unreliable generalization about all members of a group that does not recognize individual differences within the group.

. . . In a 2007 survey of African Americans, 37 percent said that, due to increased diversity within their community, Blacks should no longer be thought of as a single race. Just over half—53 percent—thought that they still should be.

inhibited, transformed, and destroyed. In this process, those who have power define groups of people according to a racist social structure. The creation of a reservation system for Native Americans in the late 1800s is one example of racial formation. Federal officials combined what were distinctive tribes into a single racial group, which we refer to today as Native Americans. The extent to which and frequency with which peoples are subject to racial formation is such that no one escapes it.

Another example of racial formation from the 1800s involves what was known as the "one-drop rule." If a person had even a single drop of "Black blood"—that is, if any of his or her ancestors, no matter how remote, were Black—society defined and viewed that person as Black, even if he or she appeared to be White. Clearly, race had social significance, enough so that White legislators established official standards about who was "Black" and who was "White."

The one-drop rule was a vivid example of the social construction of race—the process by which people come to define a group as a race based in part on physical characteristics, but also on historical, cultural, and economic factors. For example, in the 1800s, immigrant groups such as Italian Americans and Irish Americans were seen not as "White" but as members of another race who were not necessarily trustworthy (Ignatiev 1995). The social construction of race is an ongoing process that is subject to debate, especially in a diverse society such as the United

*Like many Americans, champion golfer Tiger Woods is of mixed racial heritage. His father's ancestry was African American, Chinese, and Native American, while his mother is of Thai, Chinese, and Dutch descent. Woods is shown here with his wife, Swedish model Elin Nordgegren.*

**292** • SOC 2009

States, where each year increasing numbers of children are born to parents of different racial backgrounds.

Even though these differences are socially constructed, their consequences are no less real. Race is often used to justify unequal access to economic, social, and cultural resources based on the assumption that such inequality is somehow "natural." This can happen through the use of **stereotypes,** for example, which are unreliable generalizations about all members of a group that do not recognize individual differences within the group. Anthropologist Ashley Montagu (1997), who was at the forefront of the movement to use scientific evidence to demonstrate the socially constructed nature of race, suggested that "the very word (*race*) is racist; that the idea of 'race,' implying the existence of significant biologically determined mental differences rendering some populations inferior to others, is wholly false" (p. 31).

## SOCthink

> > > To what extent does the race you belong to shape opportunities you face? How conscious are you of your race and its impact?

**Multiple Identities** In recognition of the growing diversity of the nation's population, the 2000 census gave people the option of identifying themselves with multiple racial categories for the first time. With the addition of this multirace option, 63 total race combinations are possible. Over 7 million people in the United States (or about 2.6 percent of the population) reported that they were of two or more races. Half the people classified as multiracial were under age 18, suggesting that this segment of the population will grow in the years to come. People who claimed both White and American Indian ancestry were the largest group of multiracial residents (Bonilla-Silva 2004; N. Jones 2005). Racial categories used by the Census Bureau have themselves varied over time, providing additional support for the notion that our definition of race is not so much determined by biology as it is subject to historical and cultural forces.

The historical approach to racial classification of including only a handful of choices is part of a long history that dictates single-race identities. This move by the Census Bureau to expand choice points toward a growing awareness of population diversity. It also reflects the struggle by many individuals, especially young adults, against social pressure to choose a single identity, and instead openly embrace multiple heritages. The classic case is Tiger Woods, the world's best-known golfer. Woods created his own racial category, referring to himself as "Cablinasian," a combination of his Caucasian, Black, American Indian, and Asian (Chinese and Thai) ancestry.

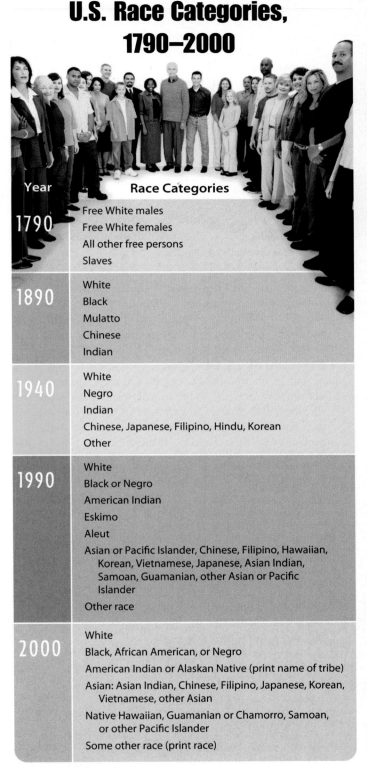

# U.S. Race Categories, 1790–2000

| Year | Race Categories |
|---|---|
| 1790 | Free White males<br>Free White females<br>All other free persons<br>Slaves |
| 1890 | White<br>Black<br>Mulatto<br>Chinese<br>Indian |
| 1940 | White<br>Negro<br>Indian<br>Chinese, Japanese, Filipino, Hindu, Korean<br>Other |
| 1990 | White<br>Black or Negro<br>American Indian<br>Eskimo<br>Aleut<br>Asian or Pacific Islander, Chinese, Filipino, Hawaiian, Korean, Vietnamese, Japanese, Asian Indian, Samoan, Guamanian, other Asian or Pacific Islander<br>Other race |
| 2000 | White<br>Black, African American, or Negro<br>American Indian or Alaskan Native (print name of tribe)<br>Asian: Asian Indian, Chinese, Filipino, Japanese, Korean, Vietnamese, other Asian<br>Native Hawaiian, Guamanian or Chamorro, Samoan, or other Pacific Islander<br>Some other race (print race) |

*Source:* Nobles 2000: 1739.

## ETHNICITY

An ethnic group is set apart from others explicitly because of its national origin or cultural patterns. Distinctive characteristics can include language, diet, sports, and religious beliefs, along with various traditions, norms, and values.

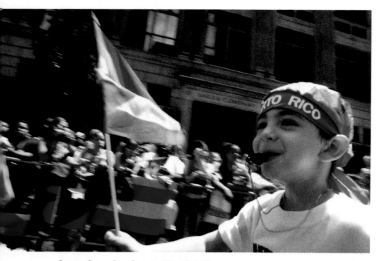

*Puerto Rican Day Parade, New York City.*

Among the ethnic groups in the United States are peoples with a Spanish-speaking background, referred to collectively as Latinos or Hispanics, such as Puerto Ricans, Mexican Americans, and Cuban Americans. Other ethnic groups in this country include Jewish, Irish, Italian, and Norwegian Americans.

The distinction between racial and ethnic minorities is not always clear-cut. As the socially constructed nature of race becomes clearer, factors such as the significance of national origin and cultural traditions become more important in our understanding of racial groups. Despite categorization problems, however, sociologists maintain that

# Did You Know?

**. . . Of the Muslims in the United States, 65 percent are foreign born. Of those who were born here,**

**about one-half are African American. Approximately one-fourth of all U.S. Muslims are third generation.**

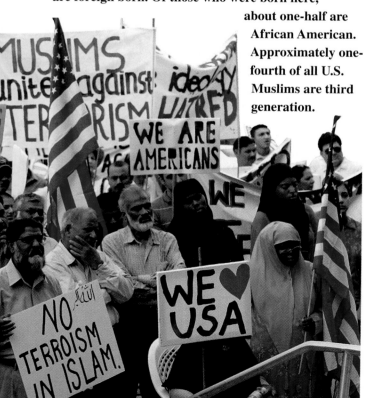

the distinction between racial groups and ethnic groups is socially significant. The fact that race is constructed makes it no less real in terms of how it shapes our identities, how we have defined it historically, how we have experienced it individually, and how it has been used politically and economically.

Although we will look at various ethnic and racial groups in more detail later in the chapter, it is important to understand the significance such categories have in society. As we have already seen, often they are used to justify exclusion from critical resources. This exclusion is rooted in both values and norms, that is, in how we think and how we act. When it comes to race and ethnicity, the terms that describe such practices are *prejudice* and *discrimination*.

# >> Prejudice and Discrimination

In recent years, college campuses across the United States have been the scene of bias-related incidents. Student-run newspapers and radio stations have ridiculed racial and ethnic minorities; threatening literature has been stuffed under the doors of minority students; and graffiti endorsing the views of White supremacist organizations such as the Ku Klux Klan have been scrawled on university walls. In some cases, there have even been violent clashes between groups of White and Black students (Bunzel 1992; Schaefer 2008a). Such acts grow out of attitudes people have about other groups.

## PREJUDICE

**Prejudice** is a negative attitude toward an entire category of people, often an ethnic or racial minority. If you resent your roommate because he or she is sloppy, you are not necessarily guilty of prejudice. However, if you immediately stereotype your roommate on the basis of such characteristics as race, ethnicity, or religion, that is a form of prejudice. Prejudice tends to perpetuate false definitions of individuals and groups.

Sometimes prejudice results from **ethnocentrism**—the tendency to assume that one's own culture and way of life represent the norm or are superior to all others. Ethnocentric people judge other cultures by the standards of their own group. This leads quite easily to prejudice against cultures they view as inferior.

One important and widespread ideology that reinforces prejudice is **racism**—the belief that one race is supreme and all others are innately inferior. When racism prevails in a society, members of subordinate groups generally experience prejudice, discrimination, and exploitation. In 1990, as concern mounted about racist attacks in the United States, Congress passed the Hate Crimes Statistics Act. A **hate crime** is a criminal offense committed because

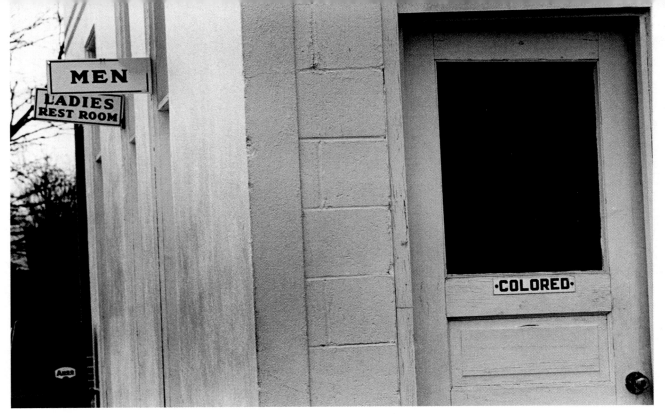

Before passage of the Civil Rights Act in 1964, segregation of public accommodations was the norm throughout the South.

## Categorization of Reported Hate Crimes

15.5%
Sexual orientation

18.9%
Religion

12.7%
Ethnicity

Disability
1.1%

Race
51.8%

Source: Department of Justice 2007b.

of the offender's bias against an individual based on race, religion, ethnicity, national origin, or sexual orientation. In 2006 alone, more than 7400 hate crimes were reported to authorities. More than half those crimes against persons involved racial bias.

Over the past three generations, nationwide surveys have consistently shown growing support among Whites for integration, interracial dating, and the election of minority group members to public office—including even the presidency of the United States. Nevertheless, there are persistent patterns of unequal treatment. People claim not to be prejudiced, affirming principles such as equal opportunity, yet many fail to put these ideals into practice.

Some suggest that **color-blind racism,** which uses the principle of race neutrality to perpetuate a racially unequal status quo, is at work. In such cases, commitment to the principle of equality actually serves to perpetuate inequality. In a system where inequality based on race and ethnicity is built into the structure of society, unwillingness to address these issues explicitly in those terms serves to perpetuate the status quo. Although it might seem counter to the principle of equality, some

**prejudice** A negative attitude toward an entire category of people, often an ethnic or racial minority.

**ethnocentrism** The tendency to assume that one's own culture and way of life represent the norm or are superior to all others.

**racism** The belief that one race is supreme and all others are innately inferior.

**hate crime** A criminal offense committed because of the offender's bias against an individual based on race, religion, ethnicity, national origin, or sexual orientation.

**color-blind racism** The use of race-neutral principles to perpetuate a racially unequal status quo.

Members of the Ku Klux Klan, masked in white robes and hoods, used night-time cross-burnings to instill terror.

nations have established quotas in political representation and hiring to force the social structure to provide greater opportunity, a practice that is controversial in the United States.

## DISCRIMINATION

Prejudice often leads to **discrimination**—the denial of opportunities and equal rights to individuals and groups because of prejudice or other arbitrary reasons. While prejudice is a way of thinking, discrimination involves action. Imagine that a White corporate president with a prejudice against Asian Americans has to fill an executive position, and the most qualified candidate for the job is a Vietnamese American. If the president refuses to hire this candidate and instead selects an inferior White candidate, he or she is engaging in an act of racial discrimination.

**Discriminatory Behavior** Prejudiced attitudes should not be equated with discriminatory behavior. Although the two are generally related, they are not identical; either condition can be present without the other. A prejudiced person does not always act on his or her biases. The White president, for example, might choose—despite his or her prejudices—to hire the Vietnamese American because that person is the most qualified. That would be prejudice without discrimination. On the other hand, a White corporate president with a completely respectful view of Vietnamese Americans might refuse to hire them for executive posts out of fear that biased clients would take their business else-

*Federal troops were needed to support the Supreme Court decision that led to the integration of schools in the 1950s.*

where. In that case, the president's action would constitute discrimination without prejudice.

Sometimes racial and ethnic discrimination is overt. Internet forums like Craigslist.org or Roommate.com feature classified ads that state "African Americans and Arabians tend to clash with me" or "Clean, Godly Christian men only." While antidiscrimination laws prevent such notices from being published in the newspapers, existing law has not caught up with online bigotry in hiring and renting (Liptak 2006).

In sociologist Devah Pager's 2003 experiment investigating racial discrimination in hiring, a White job applicant with a prison record received slightly more callbacks than a Black applicant with no criminal record. Over time, the cumulative impact of such differential behavior contributes to significant differences in access to critical resources. For example, income varies significantly based on race and ethnicity in the United States.

**The Glass Ceiling** Discrimination persists even for the most educated and qualified minority group members

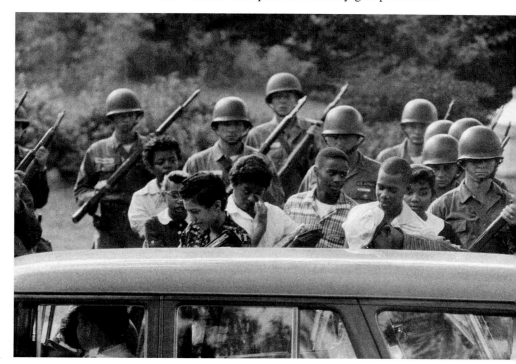

# U.S. Median Income by Race, Ethnicity, and Gender

Median income (thousands of dollars)

| | |
|---|---|
| Asian American men | $51,997 |
| White men | $50,606 |
| Asian American women | $40,164 |
| White women | $36,735 |
| Black men | $36,070 |
| Native American men | $33,744 |
| Black women | $30,823 |
| Hispanic men | $30,754 |
| Native American women | $27,685 |
| Hispanic women | $25,990 |

*Note:* Includes only people working full-time, year-round, 25 years and older. White refers to non-Hispanic Whites.

*Sources:* DeNavas-Walt et al. 2007; for Native Americans, author's estimate based on Bureau of the Census 2003b.

from the best family backgrounds. Despite their talent and experience, they sometimes encounter attitudinal or organizational bias that prevents them from reaching their full potential. Recall that the term *glass ceiling* refers to an invisible barrier that blocks the promotion of a qualified individual in a work environment because of the individual's gender, race, or ethnicity (Schaefer 2006; Yamagata et al. 1997).

In early 1995, the federal Glass Ceiling Commission issued the first comprehensive study of barriers to promotion in the United States. The commission found that glass ceilings continue to block women and minority group men from top management positions in the nation's industries. For example, in 2006, 72 percent of the members on the boards of directors for Fortune 100 companies were White men, compared to 13 percent White women, 11 percent minority males, and 4 percent minority females (Catalyst 2008). The existence of the glass ceiling often results from the fears and prejudices of many middle- and upper-level White male managers, who believe that the inclusion of women and minority group men in management circles will threaten their own prospects for advancement (Bureau of the Census 2007a; Department of Labor 1995a, 1995b; Hickman 2002).

**Racial Profiling** Another form of discrimination involves **racial profiling,** which is any arbitrary action initiated by an authority based on race, ethnicity, or national origin rather than on a person's behavior. Generally, racial profiling occurs when law enforcement officers, including customs officials, airport security, and police, assume that people who fit a certain description are likely to engage in illegal activities. With the emergence of crack cocaine in the 1980s, skin color became a key characteristic in racial profiling. This practice is often based on very explicit stereotypes. For example, one federal antidrug initiative encouraged officers to look specifically for people with dreadlocks and for Latino men traveling together.

> **discrimination** The denial of opportunities and equal rights to individuals and groups because of prejudice or other arbitrary reasons.
>
> **racial profiling** Any police-initiated action based on race, ethnicity, or national origin rather than on a person's behavior.

Today, authorities continue to rely on racial profiling despite overwhelming evidence that race is not a valid predictor of criminal behavior. A recent study showed that African Americans are still more likely than Whites to be frisked and handled with force when they are stopped. Yet Whites are more likely than Blacks to possess weapons, illegal drugs, and stolen property (Ridgeway 2007).

Research on the ineffectiveness of racial profiling, coupled with complaints by minority communities about the stigmatization it fosters, has led to growing demands to end the practice. However, these efforts came to an abrupt halt after the September 11, 2001, terrorist attacks on the United States, in the face of widespread suspicion toward Muslim and Arab immigrants. Federal authorities

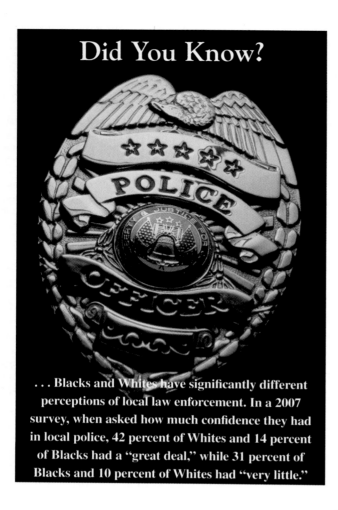

## Did You Know?

... Blacks and Whites have significantly different perceptions of local law enforcement. In a 2007 survey, when asked how much confidence they had in local police, 42 percent of Whites and 14 percent of Blacks had a "great deal," while 31 percent of Blacks and 10 percent of Whites had "very little."

other social scientists are becoming increasingly interested in what it means to be "White," for White privilege is the other side of the proverbial coin of racial discrimination.

The feminist scholar Peggy McIntosh (1988) became interested in White privilege after noticing that most men would not acknowledge the privileges attached to being male—even if they would agree that being female had its disadvantages. She wondered whether White people suffer from a similar blind spot regarding their own racial privilege. Intrigued, McIntosh began to list all the ways in which she benefited from her Whiteness. She soon realized that the list of unspoken advantages was long and significant.

McIntosh found that as a White person, she rarely needed to step out of her comfort zone, no matter where she went. If she wished to, she could spend most of her time with people of her own race. She could find a good place to live in a pleasant neighborhood, buy the foods she liked to eat from almost any grocery store, and get her hair styled in almost any salon. She could attend a public meeting without feeling that she did not belong, that she was different from everyone else.

McIntosh discovered, too, that her skin color opened doors for her. She could cash checks and use credit cards without suspicion, and she could browse through stores without being shadowed by security guards. She could be seated without difficulty in a restaurant. If she asked to see the manager, she could assume he or she would be of her own race. If she needed help from a doctor or a lawyer, she could get it.

> ### Whites of course have the privilege of not caring, of being colorblind. Nobody else does.
> Ursula K. LeGuin

subjected foreign students from Arab countries to special questioning, and they scrutinized legal immigrants identified as Arab or Muslim for possible illegal activity. They also prosecuted Arab and Muslim detainees for violations that were routinely ignored among immigrants of other ethnicities and faiths (Withrow 2006).

## THE PRIVILEGES OF THE DOMINANT

One often-overlooked aspect of discrimination is the privileges that dominant groups enjoy at the expense of others. For instance, we tend to focus more on the difficulty women have balancing career and family than on the ease with which men avoid household chores and advance in the workplace. Similarly, we concentrate more on discrimination against racial and ethnic minorities than on the advantages members of the White majority enjoy. Indeed, most White people rarely think about their "Whiteness," taking their status for granted. However, sociologists and

McIntosh also realized that her Whiteness made the job of parenting easier. She did not need to worry about protecting her children from people who didn't like them. She could be sure that their books would show pictures of people who looked like them and that their history texts would describe White people's achievements. She knew that the television programs they watched would include White characters.

Finally, McIntosh had to admit that others did not constantly evaluate her in racial terms. When she appeared in public, she didn't need to worry that her clothing or behavior might reflect poorly on White people. If she was recognized for an achievement, it was seen as her own accomplishment, not that of an entire race. And no one ever assumed that the personal opinions she voiced should be those of all White people. Because McIntosh blended in with the people around her, she wasn't always onstage.

# SOCthink

> > > McIntosh recommends that we all step back and consider unearned advantages we inherit due to the positions we may occupy. What would be on your list? What disadvantages might you inherit?

These are not all the privileges White people take for granted as a result of their membership in the dominant racial group in the United States. As Devah Pager's study showed, White job seekers enjoy a tremendous advantage over equally well-qualified—even better-qualified—Blacks. Whiteness *does* carry privileges—to a much greater extent than most White people realize.

## INSTITUTIONAL DISCRIMINATION

Such persistent patterns of inequality suggest that discrimination is practiced not only by individuals in one-to-one encounters but also by institutions in their daily operations. Social scientists are particularly concerned with the ways in which structural factors such as employment, housing, health care, and government operations maintain the social significance of race and ethnicity. **Institutional discrimination** refers to the denial of opportunities and equal rights to individuals and groups that results from the normal operations of a society. This kind of discrimination consistently affects certain racial and ethnic groups more than others.

A recent example of institutional discrimination occurred in the wake of the September 11, 2001, terrorist attacks on the United States. Under pressure to prevent terrorist takeovers of commercial airplanes, Congress passed the Aviation and Transportation Security Act, which was intended to strengthen airport screening procedures. The law stipulated that all airport screeners must be U.S. citizens. Nationally, 28 percent of all airport screeners were legal residents but not citizens of the United States; as a group, they were disproportionately Latino, Black, and Asian. Many observers noted that other airport and air-

line workers, including pilots, cabin attendants, and even armed National Guardsmen stationed at airports, need not be citizens. Currently, the constitutionality of the act is being challenged. Even well-meant legal measures can have disastrous consequences for racial and ethnic minorities (H. Weinstein 2002).

# SOCthink

> > > Why might institutional discrimination be an even greater concern than interpersonal discrimination?

In some cases, even ostensibly neutral institutional standards can have discriminatory effects. African American students at a midwestern state university protested a policy under which fraternities and sororities that wished to use campus facilities for a dance were required to post a $150 security deposit to cover possible damages. The Black students complained that the policy had a discriminatory impact on minority student organizations. Campus police countered that the university's policy applied to all student groups interested in using the facilities. However, since the overwhelmingly White fraternities and sororities at the school had their own houses, which they used for dances, the policy indeed affected only African American and other minority organizations.

> **institutional discrimination** The denial of opportunities and equal rights to individuals and groups that results from the normal operations of a society.

Attempts have been made to eradicate or compensate for discrimination in the United States. The 1960s saw the passage of many pioneering civil rights laws, including the landmark 1964 Civil Rights Act, which prohibits discrimination in public accommodations and publicly owned facilities on the basis of race, color, creed, national origin, and gender. In two important rulings in 1987, the Supreme Court held that federal prohibitions

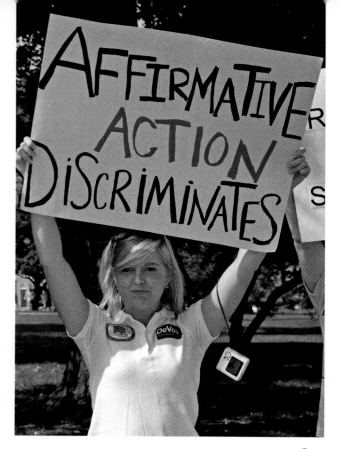

against racial discrimination protect members of all ethnic minorities—including Hispanics, Jews, and Arab Americans—even though they may be considered White.

For more than 40 years, government, schools, and industry have instituted affirmative action programs to overcome past discrimination. **Affirmative action** refers to positive efforts to recruit minority group members or women for jobs, promotions, and educational opportunities. Many people resent these programs, arguing that advancing one group's cause merely shifts the discrimination to another group. By giving priority to African Americans in admissions, for example, schools may deny more qualified White candidates. In many parts of the country and many sectors of the economy, affirmative action is being rolled back, even though it was never fully implemented.

Discriminatory practices continue to pervade nearly all areas of life in the United States. In part, that is because various individuals and groups actually benefit from racial and ethnic discrimination in terms of money, status, and influence. Discrimination permits members of the majority to enhance their wealth, power, and prestige at the expense of others. Less qualified people get jobs and promotions simply because they are members of the

**affirmative action** Positive efforts to recruit minority group members or women for jobs, promotions, and educational opportunities.

**exploitation theory** A belief that views racial subordination in the United States as a manifestation of the class system inherent in capitalism.

dominant group. Such individuals and groups will not surrender these advantages easily.

## >> Sociological Perspectives on Race and Ethnicity

Sociologists seek to understand and explain why prejudice and discrimination develop and persist and what might be done to address them. As we have seen, often such negative characteristics exist because they serve certain interests. Here we will look at how prejudice and discrimination contribute to the maintenance of the existing social order by reinforcing the dominant culture.

### SOCIAL ORDER AND INEQUALITY

One of the ways we see such beliefs and practices perpetuated is through acceptance of the dominant ideology that supports them. Prejudice and discrimination are rooted in fundamental beliefs about the natural order of the world. Such values provide a moral justification for maintaining an unequal society that routinely deprives minority groups of their rights and privileges. Southern Whites, for example, justified slavery by asserting that Africans were physically and spiritually subhuman and devoid of souls. It is easy in retrospect to find such beliefs appalling, but they became part of what people assumed was natural and were therefore difficult to challenge.

This does not mean, however, that certain groups do not intentionally promote such beliefs at the expense of others. Prejudice and discrimination help to preserve the existing system of inequality. **Exploitation theory,** for example, argues that such practices are a basic part of the capitalist economic system (Blauner 1972; Cox 1948; Hunter 2000). Racism keeps minorities in low-paying jobs, thereby supplying the capitalist ruling class with a pool of cheap labor. Moreover, by forcing racial minorities to accept low wages, capitalists can restrict the wages of all members of the proletariat. Business owners can always replace workers from the dominant group who demand higher wages with minorities who have no choice but to accept low-paying jobs. This increases the likelihood that working-class members of the majority group will develop racist attitudes toward working-class members of minority groups, whom they view as threats to their jobs. As a result they direct their hostilities not toward the capitalists, but toward other workers, thereby not challenging the structure of the existing system.

**Hot or Not?**

Should companies establish hiring quotas based on race, ethnicity, or gender to ensure greater opportunity?

# Perceptions of Discrimination

**Black respondents**

**Hispanic respondents**

**White respondents**

**How often do Blacks face discrimination when . . . ?**

- (college icon) Applying to a college or university
- (people icon) Applying for a job
- (light shade) Almost always/frequently
- (house icon) Renting an apartment or buying a house
- (fork icon) Eating at a restaurant or shopping in a retail store
- (dark shade) Not often/hardly ever

*Source:* Pew Research Center 2007:30.

**SOC**studies

Maintaining these practices, however, comes at significant cost to society. For example, a society that practices discrimination fails to use the resources of all individuals. Discrimination limits the search for talent and leadership to the dominant group. Advocates for the children whose parents were caught up in the Postville immigration raid, for example, bemoaned the loss of creativity and talent that those kids would take with them when they left the country

with their deported parents. Discrimination also aggravates social problems such as poverty, delinquency, and crime. Such effects require the investment of a good deal of time and money in which the primary goal is to maintain barriers to the full participation of all members (Rose 1951).

Challenging prejudice and discrimination, however, involves questioning taken-for-granted views of the world in which people have invested their faith and trust. Women in the 1950s in the United States had to do just that. They challenged the idea that it was "natural" for women to stay at home and have babies rather than get an education and enter the paid labor force. At the same time, workers in the civil rights movement faced a similar challenge in confronting social attitudes that represented barriers to the full participation of African Americans in U.S. society.

## THE CONTACT HYPOTHESIS

At its heart, racism is about division, separating the human population into us versus them. As society becomes more global and pluralistic, more people from diverse cultural backgrounds have increased opportunities to interact with others unlike themselves on a daily basis. This is precisely what the school superintendent from Postville gave voice to. When people interact with others as people, rather than as stereotypes or distant others, the possibility arises for prejudice and discrimination to decrease.

Take, for example, a Hispanic woman who is transferred from a job on one part of an assembly line to a similar position working next to a White man. At first, the White man is patronizing, assuming that she must be incompetent. For her part, the Latina is cold and resentful; even when she needs assistance, she refuses to admit it. After a week, the growing tension between the two leads to a bitter quarrel. Yet over time, each slowly comes to appreciate the other's strengths and talents. A year after they begin working together, these two workers become respectful friends. This story is an example of the contact hypothesis in action.

*Civil rights activist Rosa Parks being fingerprinted upon her arrest in 1955 for her act of civil disobedience in refusing to give up her seat on a bus to a White man.*

The **contact hypothesis** states that in cooperative circumstances, interracial contact between people of equal status will cause them to become less prejudiced and to abandon old stereotypes. People begin to see one another as individuals and to discard the broad generalizations characteristic of stereotyping. Note the phrases "equal status" and "cooperative circumstances." In our assembly line example, if the two workers had been competing for one vacancy as a supervisor, the racial hostility between them might have worsened, highlighting the significance of power and position when it comes to the issue of racism (Allport 1979; Fine 2008).

**contact hypothesis** The theory that in cooperative circumstances interracial contact between people of equal status will reduce prejudice.
**genocide** The deliberate, systematic killing of an entire people or nation.
**expulsion** The systematic removal of a group of people from society.
**amalgamation** The process through which a majority group and a minority group combine to form a new group.
**assimilation** The process through which a person forsakes his or her own cultural tradition to become part of a different culture.

As Latinos and other minorities slowly gain access to better-paying and higher-responsibility jobs, the contact hypothesis may take on even greater significance. The trend in our society is toward increasing contact between individuals from dominant and subordinate groups. That may be one way of eliminating—or at least reducing—racial and ethnic stereotyping and prejudice. Another may be the establishment of interracial coalitions, an idea suggested by sociologist William Julius Wilson (1999). To work, such coalitions would obviously need to provide an equal role for all members.

## PATTERNS OF INTERGROUP RELATIONS

The possibility of equal status, however, is shaped by how societies handle racial and ethnic differences. Some are more open to diverse groups maintaining their cultural traditions. Others pressure groups to abandon their beliefs and practices in favor of those of the dominant society. We will focus on six characteristic patterns of intergroup relations: genocide, expulsion, amalgamation, assimilation, segregation, and pluralism. Each pattern defines the dominant group's actions and the minority group's responses. The first two are relatively rare, though their consequences are extreme; the final four are more common.

**Genocide** The most devastating pattern of intergroup relations is **genocide**—the deliberate, systematic killing of an entire people or nation. This is precisely what happened when Turkish authorities killed 1 million Armenians beginning in 1915. The term is most commonly associated with Nazi Germany's extermination of 6 million European Jews, along with gays, lesbians, and the Romani people ("Gypsies"), during World War II. The term also describes the United States' policies toward Native Americans in the 19th century. In 1800, the Native American (or American Indian) population of the United States was about 600,000; by 1850, warfare with the U.S. cavalry, disease, and forced relocation to inhospitable environments had reduced it to 250,000.

**Expulsion** Another extreme response is **expulsion**—the systematic removal of a group of people from society. In 1979, Vietnam expelled nearly 1 million ethnic Chinese, partly as a result of centuries of hostility between Vietnam and neighboring China. Similarly, Serbian forces began a program of "ethnic cleansing" in 1991, in the newly independent states of Bosnia and Herzegovina. Throughout the former Yugoslavia, the Serbs drove more than 1 million Croats and Muslims from their homes. Some they tortured and killed; others they abused and terrorized, in an attempt to "purify" the land (Cigar 1995; Petrovic 1994). More recently, the government of Sudan has pushed people off their land and out of the country in Darfur.

**Amalgamation** When a majority group and a minority group combine to form a new group, **amalgamation** results. This often occurs through intermarriage over several generations. This pattern can be expressed as A + B + C → D, where A, B, and C represent different groups in a society, and D signifies the end result, a unique cultural-racial group unlike any of the initial groups (Newman 1973).

The belief in the United States as a "melting pot" became compelling in the early 20th century, particularly since that image suggested that the nation had an almost divine mission to amalgamate various groups into one peo-

POPSOC

In a survey about media portrayals of African Americans, the majority of Whites and Hispanics felt that the way Blacks are portrayed in television and films is better today than it was 10 years ago. Among African Americans, however, 43 percent agreed. Blacks were also more likely than the other groups to say that negative portrayals have a negative impact on society's views of Blacks. Both Blacks and Whites agreed, at almost identical levels, that hip hop and rap have a bad influence on society today.

ple. In actuality, however, many residents were not willing to include Native Americans, Jews, Blacks, Asians, and Irish Roman Catholics in the melting pot. Therefore, this pattern does not adequately describe dominant-subordinate relations in the United States.

**Assimilation** In India, many Hindus complain about Indian citizens who emulate the traditions and customs of the British. In France, people of Arab and African origin, many of them Muslim, complain they are treated as second-class citizens—a charge that provoked riots in 2005. In Australia, Aborigines who have become part of the dominant society refuse to acknowledge their darker-skinned grandparents on the street. All of these cases are examples of the effects of **assimilation**—the process through which a person forsakes his or her own cultural tradition to become part of a different culture. Generally, it is practiced by minority group members who want to conform to the standards of the dominant group. Assimilation can be described as a pattern in which A + B + C → A. The majority, A, dominates in such a way that members of minorities B and C imitate it and attempt to become indistinguishable from it (Newman 1973).

Assimilation can strike at the very roots of a person's identity. In the United States, some immigrants have changed their ethnic-sounding family names to names that better fit into the dominant White Protestant culture. Jennifer Anastassakis, for example, changed her name to Jennifer Aniston, Ralph Lipschitz became Ralph Lauren, Natalie Portman switched from Natalie Hershlag, and the Academy Award–winning British actress Helen Mirren gave up her birth name of Ilyena Vasilievna Mironova. Name changes, switches in religious affiliation, and the dropping of native languages can obscure one's roots and

heritage. Especially across generations, assimilation can lead to the virtual death of a culture in that family's history. It is not uncommon for grandchildren of immigrants who have not learned the language or the cultural traditions of their ancestors to regret this loss.

**Segregation** Separate schools, separate seating on buses and in restaurants, separate washrooms, even separate drinking fountains—these were all part of the lives of African Americans in the South when segregation ruled early in the 20th century. **Segregation** refers to the physical separation of two groups of people in terms of residence, workplace, and social events. Generally, a dominant group imposes this pattern on a minority group. Segregation is rarely complete, however. Intergroup contact inevitably occurs, even in the most segregated societies.

From 1948 (when it received its independence) to 1990, the Republic of South Africa severely restricted the movement of Blacks and other non-Whites by means of a wide-ranging system of segregation known as **apartheid.** Apartheid even included the creation of separate homelands where Blacks were expected to live. However, decades of local resistance to apartheid, combined with international pressure, led to marked political changes in the 1990s. In 1994, a prominent Black activist, Nelson Mandela, became South Africa's president

> **segregation** The physical separation of two groups of people in terms of residence, workplace, and social events; often imposed on a minority group by a dominant group.
> **apartheid** A former policy of the South African government, designed to maintain the separation of Blacks and other non-Whites from the dominant Whites.

*Former South African President Nelson Mandela oversaw that country's transition from a segregated society.*

spite federal laws that forbid housing discrimination, residential segregation is still the norm. Across the nation, neighborhoods remain divided along both racial and ethnic lines. The average White person lives in an area that is at least 83 percent White, while the average African American lives in a neighborhood that is mostly Black. The typical Latino lives in an area that is 42 percent Hispanic. Overall, segregation flourishes at the community and neighborhood levels, despite the increasing diversity of the nation as a whole (Lewis Mumford Center 2001).

Whatever the country, residential segregation directly limits people's economic opportunity. Sociologists Douglas Massey and Nancy Denton (1993), in a book aptly titled *American Apartheid,* noted that segregation separates poor people of color from job opportunities and isolates them from successful role models. This pattern repeats itself the world over, from South Central Los Angeles to Oldham, England, and Soweto, South Africa.

**Composition of Neighborhoods by Racial and Ethnic Groups**
**June 6–25, 2005**

|  | % of non-Hispanic whites who say there are "many" of each group in area | % of blacks who say there are "many" of each group in area | % of Hispanics who say there are "many" of each group in area |
|---|---|---|---|
| Whites | 86% | 45% | 52% |
| Blacks | 28% | 66% | 32% |
| Hispanics | 32% | 26% | 61% |
| Asians | 12% | 6% | 13% |
| Recent immigrants | 14% | 18% | 30% |

Source: *Who Are the People in Your Neighborhood?* Gallup Organization July 12, 2005.

in the first election in which Blacks (the majority of the nation's population) were allowed to vote. Mandela had spent almost 28 years in South African prisons for his anti-apartheid activities. His election was widely viewed as the final blow to South Africa's oppressive policy of segregation.

Long-entrenched social patterns are difficult to change, however. A recent analysis of living patterns in U.S. metropolitan areas shows that, de-

**pluralism** Mutual respect for one another's cultures among the various groups in a society, which allows minorities to express their own cultures without experiencing prejudice.

**Pluralism** In a pluralistic society, a subordinate group does not have to forsake its lifestyle and traditions. **Pluralism** is based on mutual respect for one another's cultures among the various groups in a society. This pattern allows a minority group to express its own culture and still participate without prejudice in the larger society. Earlier, we described amalgamation as A + B + C → D, and assimilation as A + B + C → A. Using this same approach, we can conceive of pluralism as A + B + C → A + B + C; that is, all the groups coexist in the same society (Newman 1973).

In the United States, pluralism is more of an ideal than a reality. There are distinct instances of pluralism—the ethnic neighborhoods in major cities, such as Koreatown, Little Tokyo, Andersonville (Swedish Americans), and Spanish Harlem—yet there are also limits to cultural freedom. To survive, a society must promote a certain consensus among its members regarding basic ideals, values, and beliefs. Thus, if a Romanian immigrant to the United States wants to move up the occupational ladder, he or she cannot avoid learning English.

Switzerland exemplifies the modern pluralistic state. There the absence of both a national language and a dominant religious faith leads to a tolerance for cultural diversity. In addition, various political devices safeguard the interests of ethnic groups in a way that has no parallel in the United States. By contrast, Great Britain has had difficulty achieving cultural pluralism in a multiracial society. East Indians, Pakistanis, and Blacks from the Caribbean and Africa experience prejudice and discrimination within the dominant White society there. Some British advocate cutting off all Asian and Black immigration, and a few even call for expulsion of those non-Whites currently living in Britain.

## >> Race and Ethnicity in the United States

Few societies have a more diverse population than the United States; the nation is truly a multiracial, multiethnic society. Of course, this has not always been the case. The population of what is now the United States has changed dramatically since the arrival of European settlers in the 1600s. Immigration, colonialism, and, in the case of Blacks, slavery determined the racial and ethnic makeup of our present-day society.

### RACIAL GROUPS

The largest racial minorities in the United States are African Americans, Native Americans, and Asian Americans.

**African Americans** "I am an invisible man," wrote Black author Ralph Ellison in his novel *Invisible Man* (1952:3). "I am a man of substance, of flesh and bone, fiber and liquids—and I might even be said to possess a mind. I am invisible, understand, simply because people refuse to see me."

Over five decades later, many African Americans still feel invisible. Despite their large numbers, they have long been treated as second-class citizens. As of 2006, according to official government statistics, 24.3 percent of African Americans were in poverty compared to 8.2 percent for Whites (DeNavas-Walt 2007).

Contemporary institutional discrimination and individual prejudice against African Americans are rooted in the

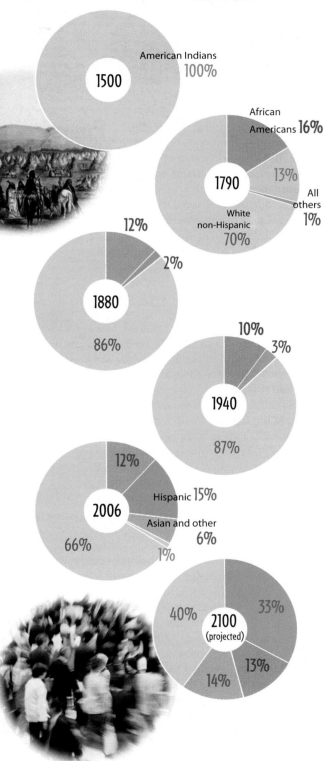

# Racial and Ethnic Groups in the United States, 1500–2100 (Projected)

1500 — American Indians 100%

1790 — African Americans 16%; 13%; All others 1%; White non-Hispanic 70%

1880 — 12%; 2%; 86%

1940 — 10%; 3%; 87%

2006 — 12%; Hispanic 15%; Asian and other 6%; 66%; 1%

2100 (projected) — 33%; 13%; 14%; 40%

*Source:* Author's estimate; American Community Survey 2006 in Bureau of the Census 2004a, 2007d. Data for 2006 and 2100, African Americans and Asian and other are for non-Hispanics.

history of slavery in the United States. Many other subordinate groups had little wealth and income, but as sociologist W. E. B. Du Bois (1909) and others have noted, enslaved Blacks were in an even more oppressive situation because they could not own property legally and could not pass on the benefits of their labor to their children. In spite of generations of slavery with its long-term economic consequences, African Americans never received slave reparations to compensate for the historical injustices of forced servitude (Williams and Collins 2004).

The end of the Civil War did not bring genuine freedom and equality for Blacks. Whites were able to maintain their dominance formally through legalized segregation and informally by means of vigilante terror and violence. The southern states passed "Jim Crow" laws to enforce official segregation, and the Supreme Court in the case of *Plessy v. Ferguson* upheld them as constitutional in 1896. In addition, Blacks faced the danger of lynching campaigns, often led by the Ku Klux Klan, during the late 1800s and early 1900s (Franklin and Moss 2000).

During the 1950s and 1960s, a vast civil rights movement emerged, with many competing factions and strategies for change. The Southern Christian Leadership Conference (SCLC), founded by Dr. Martin Luther King, Jr., used nonviolent civil disobedience to oppose segregation. The National Association for the Advancement of Colored People (NAACP) favored use of the courts to press for equality for African Americans. Many younger Black leaders, most notably Malcolm X, turned toward an ideology of Black power. Proponents of **Black power** rejected the goal of assimilation into White middle-class society. They defended the beauty and dignity of Black and African cultures and supported the creation of Black-controlled politi-

## Poverty Rates by Race and Ethnicity, 2006

20.6% **Hispanic, any race**

10.3% **Asian**

24.3% **Black**

8.2% **White, non-Hispanic**

*Source:* DeNavas-Walt 2007:12.

cal and economic institutions (Ture and Hamilton 1992).

Despite numerous courageous actions to achieve Black civil rights, Black and White citizens are still separate, still unequal. From birth to death, Blacks suffer in terms of their life chances (see the graph below). Life remains difficult for millions of poor Blacks, who must attempt to survive in areas with high unemployment and substandard housing. The median household income of Blacks is still only 60 percent that of Whites, and the unemployment rate among Blacks is more than twice that of Whites.

Some African Americans—especially middle-class men and women—have made economic gains over the past 50 years. For example, data compiled by the Department of Labor show that the number of African Americans in management increased nationally from 2.4 percent of the total in 1958 to 6.0 percent in 2005. Yet Blacks still represent only 6 percent or less of all physicians, engineers, scientists, lawyers, judges, and marketing managers. In another occupation important to developing role models, Af-

## Life Expectancy by Race and Sex, 1950–2005

**Life expectancy at birth**

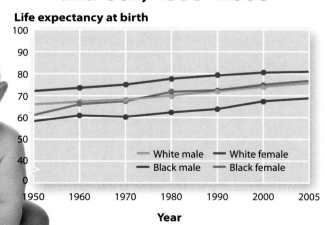

Legend: — White male  — White female  — Black male  — Black female

Year

*Source:* National Center for Health Statistics 2007:175.

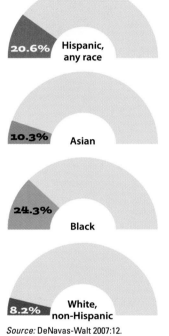

rican Americans and Hispanics together account for less than 9 percent of all reporters in the United States (Bureau of the Census 2007a:Table 598).

In many respects, the civil rights movement of the 1960s left institutionalized discrimination against African Americans untouched. Consequently, in the 1970s and 1980s, Black leaders worked to mobilize African American political power as a force for social change. Between 1970 and 2007, the number of African American elected officials increased sixfold. Yet today, Blacks remain significantly underrepresented, despite Barack Obama's visibility as a national political figure. Their underrepresentation is especially distressing in view of sociologist W. E. B. Du Bois' observation over a century ago that Blacks could not expect to achieve equal social and economic opportunity without first gaining political rights (Bureau of the Census 2007a:64).

**Native Americans** Today about 2.4 million Native Americans represent a diverse array of cultures distinguishable by language, family organization, religion, and livelihood. The outsiders who came to the United States—European settlers and their descendants—came to know these native peoples' forebears as "American Indians." By the time the Bureau of Indian Affairs (BIA) was organized as part of the War Department in 1824, Indian–White relations had featured three centuries of hostility that had led to the virtual elimination of native peoples. During the 19th century, many bloody wars wiped out a significant part of the nation's Indian population. By the end of the century, schools for Indians—operated by the BIA or by church missions—prohibited the practice of Native American cultures. Yet at the same time, such schools did little to make the children effective competitors in White society.

Today, life remains difficult for members of the 554 tribal groups in the United States, whether they live in urban areas or on reservations. For example, one Native American teenager in six has attempted suicide—a rate four times higher than the rate for other teenagers. Over time, some Native Americans have chosen to assimilate and abandon all vestiges of their tribal cultures to escape certain forms of prejudice. However, by the 1990s, an increasing number of people in the United States were openly claiming a Native American identity. Since 1960, the federal government's count of Native Americans has tripled. According to the 2000 census, the Native American population increased 26 percent during the 1990s. Demographers believe that more and more Native Ameri-

# Major Asian American Groups in the United States, 2006

Source: Author's analysis of American Community Survey 2006 in Bureau of the Census 2007d.

cans who previously concealed their identity are no longer trying to pass as White (Grieco and Cassidy 2001).

The introduction of gambling on Indian reservations has transformed the lives of some Native Americans. Native Americans got into the gaming industry in 1988, when Congress passed the Indian Gambling Regulatory Act. The law stipulates that states must negotiate agreements with tribes interested in commercial gaming; they cannot prevent tribes from engaging in gambling operations even if state law prohibits such ventures. The income from these lucrative operations is not evenly distributed, however. About two-thirds of recognized Indian tribes are not involved in gambling ventures. And those tribes that earn substantial revenues from gambling constitute only a small fraction of Native Americans (J. Taylor and Kalt 2005).

> **black power** A political philosophy, promoted by many younger Blacks in the 1960s, that supported the creation of Black-controlled political and economic institutions.

## Did You Know?

... Including Barack Obama, there have been a total of 5 African American senators in the history of the United States. There have also been 111 African Americans who have served in the House of Representatives.

**Asian Americans** Asian Americans are a diverse group, one of the fastest-growing segments of the U.S. population (up 69 percent between 1990 and 2000). Among the many groups of Americans of Asian descent are Vietnamese Americans, Chinese Americans, Japanese Americans, and Korean Americans.

Asian Americans are often held up as a **model** or **ideal minority** group, supposedly because they have succeeded economically, socially, and educationally despite past prejudices and discrimination. Yet this picture minimizes the degree of diversity among Asian Americans. There are rich and poor Japanese Americans, rich and poor Filipino Americans, and so on. In fact, Southeast Asians living in the United States have the highest rate of welfare dependency of any racial or ethnic group. Even though Asian Americans have substantially more schooling than other ethnic groups, their median income is only slightly higher than that of Whites, and their poverty rate is higher as well. In 2006, for every Asian American family with an annual income of $100,000 or more, there was another earning less than $35,000 a year (DeNavas-Walt et al. 2007:33).

The fact that as a group Asian Americans work in the same occupations as Whites suggests that they have been successful—and many have. However, there are some differences between the two groups. Asian immigrants, like other minorities and immigrants, are found disproportionately in low-paying service occupations. At the same time, better-educated Asian Americans are concentrated near the top in professional and managerial positions, although they rarely reach the pinnacle. Instead, they hit the glass ceiling, or try to "climb a broken ladder," as some put it. In 2002, only 2 percent of the 11,500 people who served on the boards of the nation's 1000 largest corporations were Asian American (Strauss 2002).

**model** or **ideal minority**
A subordinate group whose members supposedly have succeeded economically, socially, and educationally despite past prejudice and discrimination.

One day our descendants will think it incredible that we paid so much attention to things like the amount of melanin in our skin or the shape of our eyes or our gender instead of the unique identities of each of us as complex human beings.

Franklin Thomas

*Vietnamese Americans* Each Asian American group has its own history and culture. Vietnamese Americans, for instance, came to the United States primarily during and after the Vietnam War—especially after the U.S. withdrawal from the region in 1975. Assisted by local agencies, refugees from communist Vietnam settled throughout the United States, tens of thousands of them in small towns. Over time, Vietnamese Americans have gravitated toward the larger urban areas, establishing ethnic enclaves featuring Vietnamese restaurants and grocery stores.

In 1995, the United States resumed normal diplomatic relations with Vietnam. Gradually, the *Viet Kieu,* or Viet-namese living abroad, began to return to their old country to visit, but usually not to take up permanent residence. Today, more than 30 years after the end of the Vietnam War, sharp differences of opinion remain among Vietnamese Americans, especially the older ones, concerning the war and the present government of Vietnam (Pfeifer 2008).

*Chinese Americans* Unlike African slaves and Native Americans, the Chinese were initially encouraged to immigrate to the United States. From 1850 to 1880, thousands of Chinese immigrated to this country, lured by job opportunities created by the discovery of gold. However, as employment possibilities decreased and competition for mining jobs grew, the Chinese became the target of a bitter campaign to limit their numbers and restrict their rights. Chinese laborers were exploited, then discarded.

In 1882, Congress enacted the Chinese Exclusion Act, which prevented Chinese immigration and even forbade Chinese in the United States to send for their families. As a result, the Chinese population declined steadily until after World War II. More recently, the descendants of the 19th-century immigrants have been joined by a new influx from Hong Kong and Taiwan. These groups may contrast sharply in their degree of assimilation, desire to live in Chinatowns, and feelings about this country's relations with the communist People's Republic of China.

Currently, about 3.1 million Chinese Americans live in the United States. Some Chinese Americans have entered lucrative occupations, yet many immigrants struggle to survive under living and working conditions that belie the model-minority stereotype. New York City's Chinatown district is filled with illegal sweatshops in which recent immigrants—many of them Chinese women—work for minimal wages. Even in legal factories in the garment industry, hours are long and rewards are limited. A seamstress typically works 11 hours per day, 6 days a week, and earns $10,000–15,000 a year (Finder 1995; Louie 2001; Lum and Kwong 1989; Shipler 2004).

*Japanese Americans* Approximately 830,000 Japanese Americans live in the United States. As a people, they are relatively recent arrivals. In 1880, only 148 Japanese lived in the United States, but by 1920, there were more than 110,000. Japanese immigrants—called the *Issei,* or first generation—were usually males seeking employment opportunities. Many Whites saw them (along with Chinese immigrants) as a "yellow peril" and subjected them to prejudice and discrimination.

# Census 2000: The Image of Diversity

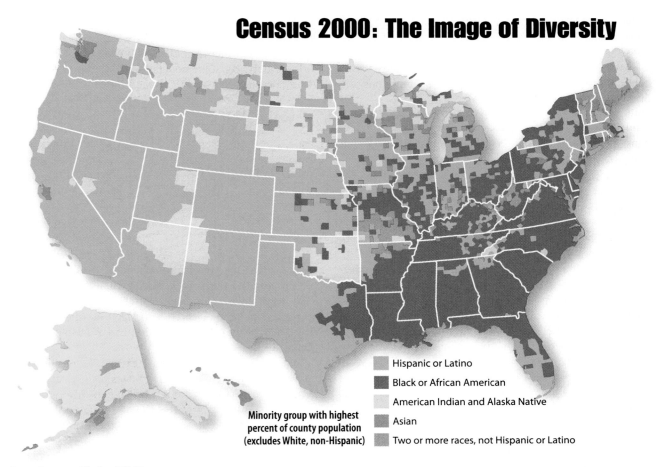

**Minority group with highest percent of county population (excludes White, non-Hispanic)**

- Hispanic or Latino
- Black or African American
- American Indian and Alaska Native
- Asian
- Two or more races, not Hispanic or Latino

*Source:* Brewer and Suchan 2001:20.

In 1941, the attack on Hawaii's Pearl Harbor by Japan had severe repercussions for Japanese Americans. The federal government decreed that all Japanese Americans on the West Coast had to leave their homes and report to "evacuation camps." Japanese Americans became, in effect, scapegoats for the anger that other people in the United States felt concerning Japan's role in World War II. By August 1943, 113,000 Japanese Americans had been forced into hastily built camps. In striking contrast, only a few German Americans and Italian Americans were sent to such camps (Hosokawa 1969).

This mass detention was costly for Japanese Americans. The Federal Reserve Board estimates their total income and property losses at nearly half a billion dollars. Moreover, the psychological effect on these citizens—including the humiliation of being labeled "disloyal"—was immeasurable. Eventually, children born in the United States to the *Issei,* called *Nisei,* were allowed to enlist in the army and serve in Europe in a segregated combat unit. Others resettled in the East and Midwest to work in factories.

In 1983, a federal commission recommended government payments to all surviving Japanese Americans who had been held in detention camps. The commission reported that the detention was motivated by "race prejudice, war hysteria, and a failure of political leadership." It added that "no documented acts of espionage, sabotage, or fifth-column activity were shown to have been committed" by Japanese Americans. In 1988, President Ronald Reagan signed the Civil Liberties Act, which required the federal government to issue individual apologies for all violations of Japanese Americans' constitutional rights and established a $1.25-billion trust fund to pay reparations to the approximately 77,500 surviving Japanese Americans who had been detained (Department of Justice 2000).

## SOCthink

> > > There is significant variation among numerous Asian nations and the billions of people they represent. Why do you think there is a tendency to lump people of Asian descent into a single category? How might factors such as geographical region and immigration history influence this perception?

*Korean Americans* At 1.3 million, the population of Korean Americans now exceeds that of Japanese Americans. Yet Korean Americans are often overshadowed by other groups from Asia. Today's Korean American community is the result of three waves of immigration. The initial wave arrived between 1903 and 1910, when Korean laborers migrated to Hawaii. The second wave followed the end of the Korean War in 1953; most of those immigrants were wives of U.S. servicemen and war orphans. The third wave, continuing to the present, has reflected the admissions priorities established by the 1965 Immigration Act. These well-educated immigrants arrive in the United States with professional skills, though they often must settle, at least initially, for positions of lower responsibility than those they held in Korea.

In the early 1990s, the apparent friction between Korean Americans and another subordinate racial group, African Americans, attracted nationwide attention. In New York City, Los Angeles, and Chicago, Korean American merchants confronted Blacks who were allegedly threatening them or robbing their stores. Black neighborhoods responded with hostility to what they perceived as the disrespect and arrogance of Korean American entrepreneurs. In South Central Los Angeles, the only places to buy groceries, liquor, and gas were owned by Korean immigrants, who had largely replaced White businesspeople. African Americans were well aware of the dominant role that Korean Americans played in their local retail markets. During the 1992 riots in South Central, small businesses owned by Koreans were a particular target. More than 1800 Korean businesses were looted or burned during the riots (Kim 1999).

Conflict between the two groups was dramatized in Spike Lee's 1989 movie *Do the Right Thing*. The situation stems from Korean Americans' position as the latest immigrant group to cater to the needs of inner-city populations abandoned by those who have moved up the economic ladder. This type of friction is not new; generations of Jewish, Italian, and Arab merchants have encountered similar hostility from another oppressed minority that to outsiders might seem an unlikely source.

**Arab Americans** Arab Americans are immigrants and their descendants who hail from the 22 nations of the Arab world. As defined by the League of Arab States, these are the nations of North Africa and what is commonly known as the Middle East. Not all residents of those countries are Arab; for example, the Kurds of northern Iraq are not Arab. And some Arab Americans may have immigrated to the United States from non-Arab countries such as Great Britain or France, where their families have lived for generations.

The Arabic language is the single most unifying force among Arabs, although not all Arabs, and certainly not all Arab Americans, can read and speak Arabic. Moreover, the language has evolved over the centuries so that people in different parts of the Arab world speak different dialects. The fact that the Muslim holy book the Qur'an (or Koran) was originally written in Arabic gives the language special importance to Muslims.

Estimates of the size of the Arab American community differ widely. By some counts, up to 3 million people of Arab ancestry now reside in the United States. Among those who identify themselves as Arab Americans, the most common country of origin is Lebanon, followed by Syria, Egypt, and Palestine. In 2000, these four countries of origin accounted for two-thirds of all Arab Americans. As with other racial and ethnic groups, the Arab American population is concentrated in certain areas of the United States. Their rising numbers have led to the development of Arab retail centers in several cities, including Dearborn and Detroit, Michigan; Los Angeles; Chicago; New York City; and Washington, D.C. (David 2008).

As a group, Arab Americans are extremely diverse. Many families have lived in the United States for several generations; others are foreign born. Their points of origin range from the metropolis of Cairo, Egypt, to the rural villages of Morocco. Despite the stereotype, most Arab Americans are *not* Muslim, and not all practice religion. The majority of Arab Americans are Christian (see the accompany-

> A fully functional multiracial society cannot be achieved without a sense of history and open, honest dialogue.
>
> **Cornel West**

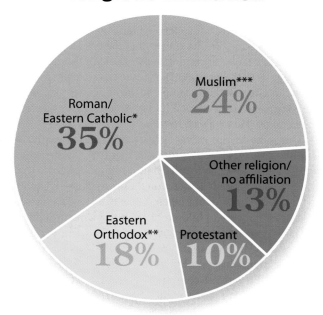

## Arab American Religious Affiliation

- Roman/ Eastern Catholic* **35%**
- Muslim*** **24%**
- Other religion/ no affiliation **13%**
- Protestant **10%**
- Eastern Orthodox** **18%**

*Catholic includes Roman Catholic, Maronite, and Melkite (Greek Catholic).

**Orthodox includes Antiochian, Syrian, Greek, and Coptic.

***Muslim includes Sunni, Shi'a, and Druze.

*Source:* Arab American Institute 2008.

ing figure). Nor can Arab Americans be characterized as having a specific family type, gender role, or occupational pattern (David 2004).

For years, airport personnel and law enforcement authorities used appearance and ethnic-sounding names to identify Arab Americans and search their belongings. After the terrorist attacks of September 2001, criticism of this practice declined as concern for the public's safety mounted.

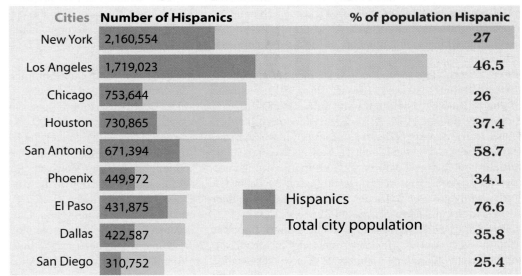

# Cities with Large Numbers of Hispanics

| Cities | Number of Hispanics | % of population Hispanic |
|---|---|---|
| New York | 2,160,554 | 27 |
| Los Angeles | 1,719,023 | 46.5 |
| Chicago | 753,644 | 26 |
| Houston | 730,865 | 37.4 |
| San Antonio | 671,394 | 58.7 |
| Phoenix | 449,972 | 34.1 |
| El Paso | 431,875 | 76.6 |
| Dallas | 422,587 | 35.8 |
| San Diego | 310,752 | 25.4 |

■ Hispanics
■ Total city population

*Source:* www.anthro.palomor.edu.

## ETHNIC GROUPS

Unlike racial minorities, members of subordinate ethnic groups may not be hindered by physical differences from assimilating into the dominant culture of the United States. However, members of ethnic minority groups still face many forms of prejudice and discrimination. Take, for instance, the country's largest ethnic groups—Latinos, Jews, and White ethnics.

**Latinos** Together, the various groups included under the general category Latinos represent the largest minority in the United States. In 2006, there were more than 44 million Hispanics in this country, including 28 million Mexican Americans, almost 4 million Puerto Ricans, and smaller numbers of Cuban Americans and people of Central and South American origin. The latter group represents the fastest-growing and most diverse segment of the Hispanic community.

According to Census Bureau data, the Latino population now outnumbers the African American population in 6 of the 10 largest cities of the United States: Los Angeles, Houston, Phoenix, San Diego, Dallas, and San Antonio (see the accompanying graph). Hispanics are now the majority of residents in cities such as Miami, Florida; El Paso, Texas; and Santa Ana, California. The rise in the Hispanic population of the United States—fueled by comparatively high birthrates and levels of immigration—has intensified debates over public policy issues such as bilingualism and immigration.

The various Latino groups share a heritage of Spanish language and culture, which can cause serious problems in their assimilation. An intelligent student whose first language is Spanish may be presumed to be slow or even unruly by English-speaking schoolchildren, and frequently by English-speaking teachers as well. The labeling of Latino children as underachievers, as learning disabled, or as emotionally disturbed can act as a self-fulfilling prophecy for some children. Bilingual education aims at easing the educational difficulties experienced by Hispanic children and others whose first language is not English.

The educational difficulties of Latino students certainly contribute to Hispanics' generally low economic status. In 2006, about 16 percent of all Hispanic households earned less than $15,000, compared to 11 percent of White non-Hispanic households. Only 12 percent of Hispanic adults had completed college, compared to 28 percent of White Americans, and the Hispanic poverty rate was 20.6 percent, compared to only 8.2 percent for White non-Hispanics. Overall, Latinos are not as affluent as White non-Hispanics, but a middle class is beginning to emerge (Bureau of the Census 2007a:Table 217; DeNavas-Walt et al. 2007:31, 34, 46, 48; Tienda and Mitchell 2006).

*Mexican Americans* The largest Latino population is Mexican American (see the figure on page 312), who can be further subdivided into those descended from residents of the territories annexed after the Mexican-American War of 1848 and those who have emigrated from Mexico to the United States. The opportunity for a Mexican to earn in one hour what it would take an entire day to earn in Mexico has pushed millions of immigrants, legal and illegal, north.

Aside from the family, the most important social institution in the Mexican American community is the church—specifically, the Roman Catholic Church. This strong identification with the Catholic faith has reinforced the already formidable barriers between Mexican Americans and their predominantly White and Protestant neighbors in the Southwest. At the same time, the Catholic Church helps many immigrants to develop a sense of identity and assists their assimilation into the dominant culture of the United States. The complexity of the Mexican American community is underscored by the fact that Protestant churches—especially those that endorse expressive, open worship—have attracted increasing numbers of Mexican Americans.

*Puerto Ricans* The second-largest segment of Latinos in the United States is Puerto Ricans. Since 1917, residents of Puerto Rico have held the status of American citizens; many have migrated to New York and other eastern cities. Puerto Ricans have experienced serious poverty both in the United States and on the island. Those who live in the continental United States earn barely half the family income of Whites. As a result, a reverse migration began in the 1970s, with more Puerto Ricans leaving for the island than coming to the mainland (Torres 2008).

Politically, Puerto Ricans in the United States have not been as successful as Mexican Americans in organizing for their rights. For many mainland Puerto Ricans—as for many residents of the island—the paramount political issue is the destiny of Puerto Rico itself. Should it continue in its present commonwealth status, petition for admission to the United States as the 51st state, or attempt to become an independent nation? This question has divided Puerto Rico for decades and remains a central issue in Puerto Rican elections. In a 1998 referendum, voters supported a "none of the above" option, effectively favoring continuation of the commonwealth status over statehood or independence.

*Cuban Americans* Cuban immigration to the United States dates back as far as 1831, but it began in earnest following Fidel Castro's seizure of power in the Cuban revolution of 1959. The first wave of 200,000 Cubans included many professionals with relatively high levels of schooling; these men and women were largely welcomed as refugees from communist tyranny. However, more recent waves of immigrants have aroused growing concern, partly because they were less likely to be skilled professionals. Throughout these waves of immigration, Cuban Americans have been encouraged to locate around the United States. Nevertheless, many continue to settle in (or return to) metropolitan Miami, Florida, with its warm climate and proximity to Cuba.

**Jewish Americans** Jews constitute about 2.2 percent of the population of the United States. They play a prominent role in the worldwide Jewish community, because the United States has the world's largest concentration of Jews. Like the Japanese, many Jewish immigrants came to this country and became white-collar professionals in spite of prejudice and discrimination.

**Anti-Semitism**—that is, anti-Jewish prejudice—has often been vicious in the United States, although rarely so widespread and never so formalized as in Europe. In many cases, Jews have been used as scapegoats for other people's failures. Given such attitudes, Jews have not achieved equality in the United States. Despite high levels of education and professional training, they are still conspicuously absent from the top management of large corporations (except for the few firms founded by Jews). Until the late 1960s, many prestigious universities maintained restrictive quotas that limited Jewish enrollment. Private social clubs and fraternal groups frequently limit membership to gentiles (non-Jews), a practice upheld by the Supreme Court in the 1964 case *Bell v. Maryland.*

The Anti-Defamation League (ADL) of B'nai B'rith funds an annual tally of reported anti-Semitic incidents. Although the number has fluctuated, the 1994 tabulation reached the highest level in the 19 years the ADL had been recording them. In 2007, the total reported incidents of harassment, threats, vandalism, and assaults came to 1337. Some incidents were inspired and carried out by neo-Nazi skinheads—groups of young people who champion racist and anti-Semitic ideologies. Such threatening behavior

# Major Hispanic Groups in the United States, 2006

Other Hispanic
**5.1%**

Other Central and South American
**13.1%**

Dominican **2.5%**

Salvadoran **2.9%**

Cuban **3.4%**

Mexican
**64%**

Puerto Rican **9%**

*Source:* Author's analysis of American Community Survey 2006 in Bureau of the Census 2007d.

## From Me to You

I live in Pella, Iowa, a small town in Iowa with a strong Dutch heritage. The first weekend in May, Pella holds its annual Tulip Time festival (www .pellatuliptime.com). Hundreds of thousands of tourists come to the three-day celebration to watch the parades, eat the food, and see people scrub streets in their Dutch costumes. Even though I have no Dutch ancestors, I regularly put on my costume and take part. I have carved wooden shoes in the historical museum, peddled the Jaarsma Bakery cart in the two daily parades, and more. Like other ethnic celebrations in other communities, Tulip Time plays a significant role in fostering a sense of community solidarity.

life in the United States—intermarriage or anti-Semitism—only 41 percent of respondents chose intermarriage; 50 percent selected anti-Semitism (American Jewish Committee 2001; United Jewish Communities 2003).

**White Ethnics** A significant segment of the population of the United States is made up of White ethnics whose ancestors arrived from Europe within the past century. The nation's White ethnic population includes about 43 million people who claim at least partial German ancestry, 31 million Irish Americans, 16 million Italian Americans, and 9 million Polish Americans, as well as immigrants from other European nations. Some of these people continue to live in close-knit ethnic neighborhoods, while others have largely assimilated and left the "old ways" behind (Brittingham and de la Cruz 2004).

> **anti-Semitism** Anti-Jewish prejudice.
> **symbolic ethnicity** An ethnic identity that emphasizes concerns such as ethnic food or political issues rather than deeper ties to one's ethnic heritage.

Many White ethnics today identify only sporadically with their heritage. **Symbolic ethnicity** refers to an emphasis on concerns such as ethnic food or political issues rather than on deeper ties to one's ethnic heritage. It is reflected in the occasional family trip to an ethnic bakery, the celebration of a ceremonial event such as St. Joseph's Day among Italian Americans, or concern about the future of Northern Ireland among Irish Americans. Except in cases in which new immigration reinforces old traditions, symbolic ethnicity tends to decline with each passing generation (Alba 1990; Winter 2008).

White ethnics and racial minorities have often been antagonistic to one another because of economic competition. As Blacks, Latinos, and Native Americans emerge from the lower class, they must compete with working-class Whites for jobs, housing, and educational opportunities. In times of high unemployment or inflation, any such competition can easily generate intense intergroup conflict.

In many respects, the plight of White ethnics involves the same basic issues as that of other subordinate people

only intensifies the fears of many Jewish Americans, who remember the Holocaust—the extermination of 6 million Jews by Nazi Germany during World War II (Anti-Defamation League 2008).

As is true for other minorities discussed in this chapter, Jewish Americans face the choice of maintaining ties to their long religious and cultural heritage or becoming as indistinguishable as possible from gentiles. Many Jews have

> ## Race hate isn't human nature; race hate is the abandonment of human nature.
>
> Orson Welles

tended to assimilate, as is evident from the rise in the rate of marriages between Jews and Christians. A study released in 2003 found that 47 percent of Jews who had married in the past five years chose to marry a non-Jew. Many people in the Jewish community worry that intermarriage will lead to a rapid decline in those who identify themselves as "Jewish." Yet when asked which was the greater threat to Jewish

in the United States. How ethnic can people be—how much can they deviate from an essentially White, Anglo-Saxon, Protestant norm—before society responds to their desire to be different? The United States does seem to reward people for assimilating. Yet, as we have seen, assimilation is no easy process. In the years to come, more and more people will face the challenge of fitting in, not only in the United States but around the world, as the flow of immigrants from one country to another continues to increase.

## >> Immigration

Worldwide, immigration is at an all-time high. Each year, about 2.3 percent of the world's population, or 146 million people, move from one country to another. One million of them enter the United States legally, to join the 12 percent of the population who are foreign born. Globally, these mass migrations have had a tremendous social impact. The constantly increasing numbers of immigrants and the pressure they put on employment opportunities and welfare capabilities in the countries they enter raise troubling questions for many of the world's economic powers. Who should be allowed in? At what point should immigration be curtailed (Schmidley and Robinson 2003; Stalker 2000)?

### IMMIGRATION TRENDS

The migration of people is not uniform across time or space. At certain times, war or famine may precipitate large movements of people, either temporarily or permanently. Temporary dislocations occur when people wait until it is safe to return to their home ar-

eas. However, more and more migrants who cannot eke out an adequate living in their home nations are making permanent moves to developed nations. The major migration streams flow into North America, the oil-rich areas of the Middle East, and the industrial economies of western Europe and Asia. Currently, seven of the world's wealthiest nations (including Germany, France, the United Kingdom, and the United States) shelter about one-third of the world's migrant population but less than one-fifth of the world's total population. As long as disparities in job opportunities exist among countries, there is little reason to expect this international trend to reverse.

Even though the sending nation loses a significant source of labor and talent due to emigration, the process does contribute to its economy. For example, it reduces the size of the population that an economy with limited resources has a difficult time supporting, and it leads to an economic infusion in the form of remittances—monies that immigrants send back to their home nations. Worldwide, immigrants send more than $300 billion a year back home to their relatives—an amount that represents a major source of income for developing nations. In Guatemala, for example, the home country of the majority of workers at the Postville meat packing plant, $3.6 billion was sent back home in 2006, representing 9 percent of Guatemala's economy (DeParle 2007; Leys 2008).

Immigrants continue to face obstacles due to their relative lack of resources. Immigrant women, for example, face all the challenges that immigrant men do, plus some additional ones. Typically, they bear the responsibility for obtaining services for their families, particularly their children. Women are often left to navigate the bureaucratic tangle of schools, city services, and health care, as well as the unfamiliar stores and markets they must shop at to feed their families. Women who need special medical services

*Going* **GLOBAL**

**World Immigration
Since 1500**

Source: J. Allen 2008.

or are victims of domestic violence are often reluctant to seek outside help. Finally, because many new immigrants view the United States as a dangerous place to raise a family, women must be especially watchful over their children's lives (Hondagneu-Sotelo 2003).

One consequence of global immigration has been the emergence of transnationals—people or families who move across borders multiple times in search of better jobs and education. The industrial tycoons of the early 20th century, whose power outmatched that of many nation-states, were among the world's first transnationals. Today, however, millions of people, many of very modest means, move back and forth between countries much as commuters do between city and suburbs. More and more of these people have dual citizenship. Rather than being shaped by allegiance to one country, their identity is rooted in their struggle to survive—and in some instances prosper—by transcending international borders (Croucher 2004; Sassen 2005).

## IMMIGRATION POLICIES

Countries that have long been a destination for immigrants, such as the United States, usually have policies to determine who has preference to enter. Often, clear racial and ethnic biases are built into these policies. In the 1920s, U.S. policy gave preference to people from western Europe while making it difficult for residents of southern and eastern Europe, Asia, and Africa to enter the country. During the late 1930s and early 1940s, the federal government refused to loosen restrictive immigration quotas in order to allow Jewish refugees to escape the terror of Nazi Germany. In line with this policy, the SS *St. Louis,* with more than 900 Jewish refugees on board, was denied permission to dock in the United States in 1939. The ship was forced to sail back to Europe, where at least a few hundred of its passengers later died at the hands of the Nazis (Morse 1967; G. Thomas and Witts 1974).

Since the 1960s, U.S. policy has encouraged the immigration of relatives of U.S. residents and of people who have desirable skills. This policy has significantly altered the pattern of sending nations. Previously, Europeans dominated, but for the past 40 years, immigrants have come primarily from Latin America and Asia. Thus, an ever-growing proportion of the U.S. population will be Asian or Hispanic. To a large degree, fear and resentment of racial and ethnic diversity is a key factor in opposition to immigration. In many nations, people are concerned that the new arrivals do not reflect and will not embrace their own cultural and racial heritage.

The long border with Mexico provides ample opportunity for illegal immigration into the United States. Throughout the 1980s, the public perception grew that the United States had lost control of its borders. Feeling pressure to control immigration, Congress ended a decade of debate by approving the Immigration Reform and

# *Going* GLOBAL

## Legal Migration to the United States, 1820–2010

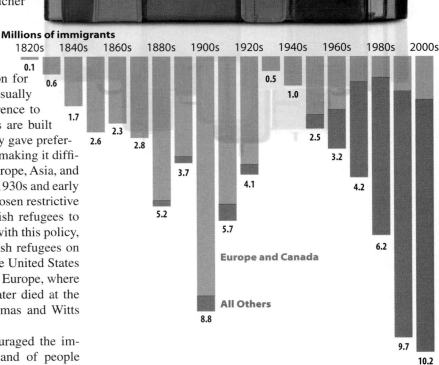

**Millions of immigrants**

1820s 1840s 1860s 1880s 1900s 1920s 1940s 1960s 1980s 2000s

0.1
0.6
1.7
2.6 2.3
2.8
3.7
5.2
5.7
8.8
0.5
1.0
4.1
2.5
3.2
4.2
6.2
9.7
10.2

Europe and Canada

All Others

*Source:* Author's estimates for the period 2000–2010; Office of Immigration Statistics, 2007.

Control Act of 1986. The act marked a historic change in the nation's immigration policy. For the first time, the hiring of illegal aliens was outlawed, and employers caught violating the law became subject to fines and even prison. Just as significant a change was the extension of amnesty and legal status to many illegal immigrants already living in the United States. Almost 20 years later, however, the act appears to have had mixed results. Substantial numbers of illegal immigrants continue to enter the country each year, with an estimated 11 million present now at any given time—a marked increase since 2000 (Hoefer et al. 2006).

Recently, immigrants have staged massive marches to pressure Congress to speed the naturalization process and develop ways for illegal immigrants to gain legal residency. Opponents of illegal immigration have called for more resources with which to track down and deport illegal immigrants and close up the U.S.-Mexican border. Despite this widespread public dissatisfaction with the nation's immigration policy, little progress has been made. Congress has had difficulty reaching a bipartisan compromise that pleases both sides.

In the wake of the September 11, 2001, attacks on the World Trade Center and the Pentagon, immigration procedures were complicated by the need to detect potential terrorists. Illegal immigrants especially, but even legal immigrants, have faced increased scrutiny by government officials around the world. For would-be immigrants to many nations, the wait to receive the right to enter a country—even to join relatives—has increased substantially, as immigration officials scrutinize what were once routine applications more closely.

The intense debate over immigration reflects deep value conflicts in the cultures of many nations. One strand of our culture, for example, has traditionally emphasized egalitarian principles and a desire to help people in time of need. At the same time, hostility to potential immigrants and refugees—whether the Chinese in the 1880s, European Jews in the 1930s and 1940s, or Mexicans, Haitians, and Arabs today—reflects not only racial, ethnic, and religious prejudice but a desire to maintain the dominant culture of the in-group by excluding those viewed as outsiders.

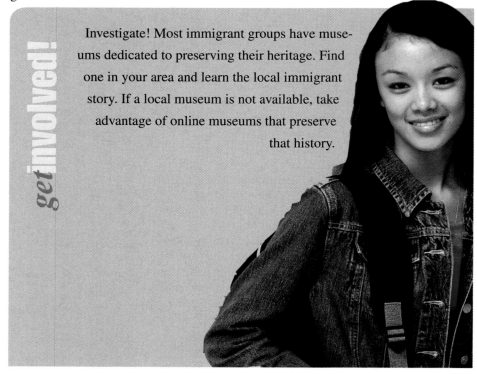

get involved!

Investigate! Most immigrant groups have museums dedicated to preserving their heritage. Find one in your area and learn the local immigrant story. If a local museum is not available, take advantage of online museums that preserve that history.

# For REVIEW

I. **How do sociologists define race and ethnicity?**

- Race is shaped by biological differences but is defined by the social significance that groups attach to external physical characteristics. Ethnicity is rooted in cultural and national traditions that define a population. Sociologists emphasize the significance of culture and its consequences for both.

II. **What are prejudice and discrimination, and how do they operate?**

- Prejudice involves attitudes and beliefs while discrimination involves actions. In both cases, they represent a negative response to a group of people that denies them full equality as persons. Institutional discrimination is built in to the structure of society itself, systematically denying some groups access to key resources.

III. **What are the consequences of race and ethnicity for opportunity?**

- Racial and ethnic groups in the United States—including African Americans, Native Americans, Asian Americans, Latino Americans, Jewish Americans, and White ethnic Americans—face differing levels of opportunity based on their relative position in society. Groups within each of these categories continue to face significant structural inequality.

# Pop Quiz

1. A group that is set apart because of its national origin or distinctive cultural patterns is a(n)
   a. assimilated group.
   b. ethnic group.
   c. minority group.
   d. racial group.

2. According to the findings of the Human Genome Project, race
   a. determines intellectual ability.
   b. is a biological, not a social, concept.
   c. explains significant social outcomes.
   d. has no genetic or scientific basis.

3. Starting with the 2000 census, there were a total of _____ possible race combinations you could choose to identify yourself.
   a. 3
   b. 6
   c. 27
   d. 63

4. Suppose that a White employer refuses to hire a Vietnamese American and selects an inferior White applicant. This decision is an act of
   a. prejudice.
   b. ethnocentrism.
   c. discrimination.
   d. stigmatization.

5. The term that Peggy McIntosh uses to describe the unearned advantages that those in the majority take for granted is
   a. privilege.
   b. discrimination.
   c. racism.
   d. institutional discrimination.

6. Working together as computer programmers for an electronics firm, a Hispanic woman and a Jewish man overcome their initial prejudices and come to appreciate each other's strengths and talents. This scenario is an example of
   a. the contact hypothesis.
   b. a self-fulfilling prophecy.
   c. amalgamation.
   d. reverse discrimination.

7. Intermarriage over several generations, resulting in various groups combining to form a new group, would be an example of
   a. pluralism.
   b. assimilation.
   c. segregation.
   d. amalgamation.

8. Jennifer Anastassakis changed her name to Jennifer Aniston. Her action was an example of
   a. expulsion.
   b. assimilation.
   c. segregation.
   d. pluralism.

9. The largest racial minority group in the United States is
   a. Asian Americans.
   b. African Americans.
   c. Native Americans.
   d. Jewish Americans.

10. Which of the following is the largest overall minority group in the United States?
    a. African Americans
    b. Asian Americans
    c. Latinos
    d. Arab Americans

1. (b); 2. (d); 3. (d); 4. (c); 5. (a); 6. (a); 7. (d); 8. (b); 9. (b); 10. (c)

**14**

# HEALTH, ME
# EN

# ICINE, AND RONMENT

## LIVING ON MOTHER EARTH

**Earth is alive. At least it functions as if it is.** So claims scientist James Lovelock, the originator of Gaia theory, which analyzes the planet and its interdependent parts as if it were a single, living organism. Today, Lovelock claims, humans are in danger of pushing this living system out of balance.

Gaia (pronounced "GUY-uh") is the ancient Greek earth goddess. Lovelock chose this name for his theory to emphasize that all living things represent a single interdependent system. He believes that we must develop an integrated vision of life to better understand the environment and our relationship with it.

Lovelock argues that Gaia maintains conditions on earth suitable for life through feedback loops. The oxygen cycle, in which humans and other animals breathe in oxygen and exhale carbon dioxide while plants do the reverse, is one simple example. Lovelock and his colleagues demonstrate that temperature, the salinity of oceans, and oxygen and methane levels are regulated by similar systems. Balance is maintained through natural evolution in which life responds to environmental conditions in ways that perpetuate its survival. If things get out of balance, organisms respond in ways that seek a return to balance.

Like all living things, however, Gaia can become sick and potentially even die. Lovelock has already played a significant role in averting an environmental crisis. In 1957, Lovelock invented the electron capture detector (ECD), which measures minute traces of particles. The ECD provided marine biologist Rachel Carson with data she used in her book *Silent Spring* (1962), which helped give birth to the modern environmental movement. Carson found that cancer-causing pesticides, such as DDT, were distributed around the world far from their sources of origin. She argued that our local actions have global consequences.

Gaia theory tells us we are globally interconnected. By looking at the planet as if it were a single organism, we can recognize how the various parts affect each other. Such a perspective is akin to that of the sociologist who looks at society and the way its various parts work together. We ignore such interdependent processes, and any cues that they may be out of balance, at our peril.

# As You READ >>

- What does sociology contribute to something as seemingly biological as health?
- What is social epidemiology?
- What environmental lessons do we learn from sociology?

## >> Culture, Society, and Health

In the same way, when it comes to health and illness, we must take seriously the interdependent connections that shape our likely outcomes. To understand health, we cannot focus on biology alone. We must consider relationships, contexts, and the significance and impact of culture and society. The communities in which we live shape how we think about health and the body, as do our access to health care and our exposure to health risks.

> **health** As defined by the World Health Organization, a state of complete physical, mental, and social well-being, and not merely the absence of disease and infirmity.

We can begin, however, with a general definition of health from the preamble to the 1946 constitution of the World Health Organization. The WHO defined **health** as a "state of complete physical, mental, and social well-being, and not merely the absence of disease and infirmity" (Leavell and Clark 1965:14). This absolute standard provides an ideal type of what constitutes health, although in practice most people fall somewhere along a continuum between this ideal on one extreme and death on the other.

Our culture influences where we place ourselves along that continuum. Different places present us with differing levels of health risk. The type of health care available and our access to it also influences what we come to count as essential care, as do the risks we face. In rural areas, for example, residents must travel many miles to see a doctor. On the other hand, people who live in the country may escape many of the stresses and strains, along with environmental risks, that plague people who live in cities. Similarly, in Japan, organ transplants are rare. The Japanese do not generally favor harvesting organs from brain-dead donors. As a result, they forgo the health benefits that such transplants provide.

Researchers have shown that diseases, too, are rooted in the shared meanings of particular cultures. The term **culture-bound syndrome** refers to a disease or illness that cannot be understood apart from some specific social context. This means that there is something particular about the culture—how it is organized, what it believes, what is expected of members—that contributes to that malady (Shepherd 2003; U.S. Surgeon General 1999b).

*Anorexia is not a new disease, though it is discussed much more openly today. Seventies rock star Karen Carpenter died from anorexia in 1983.*

## Did You Know?

**. . . The average American woman is 5 feet 4 inches tall, weighs 155 pounds, and wears a size 14 dress, while the average model is 5 feet 9 inches tall, weighs 110 pounds, and wears a size 0 or 2.**

In the United States, a culture-bound syndrome known as anorexia nervosa has received increasing attention in recent decades. First described in England in the 1860s, this condition is characterized by an intense fear of becoming obese and a distorted image of one's body. Those who suffer from anorexia nervosa (primarily young women in their teens or 20s) lose weight drastically through self-induced semistarvation. Anorexia nervosa is best understood in the context of Western culture, which typically views the slim, youthful individual as healthy and beautiful, and the fat person as ugly and lacking in self-discipline.

Until recently, U.S. researchers dealt with the concept of culture-bound syndromes only in cross-cultural studies. However, recent increases in immigration, along with efforts by the medical establishment to reach out to immigrant communities, have led to a belated recognition that not everyone views medicine in the same way. Medical practitioners are now being trained to recognize cultural beliefs that are related to medicine. For example, people from Central America may consider pain a consequence of the imbalance of nature, and Muslim women are particularly concerned about personal modesty. Health care professionals are increasingly incorporating such knowledge into their practices.

Culture can also influence the relative incidence of a disease or disorder. In her book *The Scalpel and the Silver Bear,* Dr. Lori Arviso Alvord, the first Navajo woman to become a surgeon, writes of the depression and alcoholism that attend life on the reservation. These diseases, she says, are born from "historical grief": "Navajo children are told of the capture and murder of their forefathers and mothers, and then they too must share in the legacy." Not just for the Navajo, Alvord writes, but for African Americans as well, the weight of centuries of suffering, injustice, and loss too often manifests itself in despair and addiction. The rate of alcoholism mortality among Native Americans served by the Indian Health Service is five times that of the general U.S. population (Alvord and Van Pelt 1999:12).

## >> Sociological Perspectives on Health and Illness

Whether we are considered "healthy" or "ill" is not our decision alone to make. Family, friends, co-workers, physicians, and others all shape how we perceive the state of our own and others' health. To fully understand the scope of health and illness in society, we have to consider how society defines illness, what the consequences of such definitions are, and how social position and access to resources shape health outcomes.

> **culture-bound syndrome** A disease or illness that cannot be understood apart from some specific social context.

### ILLNESS AND SOCIAL ORDER

Illness represents a threat to the social order. If too many people are sick at the same time, it not only presents a problem for those who are ill but also undercuts our collective ability to perform tasks necessary for the continued operation of society. This can result in debates over what constitutes being "sick enough" to be considered truly ill. At what point, for example, do we stay home from school or work due to illness, and who gets to decide? All of us have likely faced this dilemma, sometimes dragging ourselves out of bed and going anyway because we felt we needed to be there, whether for the sake of ourselves or for others.

When people cross the line into illness, they take on what sociologists call the **sick role,** a term that refers to societal expectations about the attitudes and behavior of a person labeled as ill (Parsons 1951, 1975). Fit members of society exempt the sick from normal, day-to-day responsibilities and generally do not blame them for their condition. Yet the sick are obligated to attempt recovery, which includes seeking competent professional care. This obligation arises from the sense of responsibility we have to perform our normal roles in society, whether as student, worker, parent, or more. It also is motivated by the reality that we may well face sanctions from others for failing to return to those normal roles quickly. In fact, especially in the context of competitive work environments, we often look down on those who seem to get sick too easily or frequently, suspecting that they are either lazy or weak. Such attitudes present significant difficulties for those facing chronic health problems.

# SOCthink

> > > What factors shape your likelihood of doing all you can to avoid "being sick"? How might the power others have over you influence your actions? What positions do they occupy relative to you?

Physicians and nurses have the power to label people as healthy or sick and, thus, to function as gatekeepers for the sick role. For example, instructors often require students to get a note from a health care professional to verify a claim of illness as a legitimate excuse for missing a paper or an exam. The ill person becomes dependent on the doctor or nurse, because the latter control the resources the patient needs, whether it be a note for a professor or a prescription for medication. We look to such professionals to solve our health care needs, trusting that they have sufficient expertise and experience to diagnose and treat our problems.

Factors such as gender, age, social class, and ethnic group all influence patients' judgments regarding their own state of health. Younger people may fail to detect the warning signs of a dangerous illness, while the elderly may focus too much on the slightest physical malady. Whether one is employed also seems to affect one's willingness to assume the sick role—as does the impact of socialization into a particular occupation or activity. For example, from an early age, athletes learn to define certain ailments as "sports injuries" and so do not regard themselves as "sick" when suffering from such maladies.

## POWER, RESOURCES, AND HEALTH

The faith we place in physicians to heal what ails us has helped them attain significant levels of prestige and power.

# From Me to You

There may be nothing more natural than childbirth. Yet when Lori was pregnant with our daughter Emily, the doctor sent us to a series of "natural" child birth classes. They were held in a hospital and were taught by a health care professional. We even had homework, which included breathing exercises. Although there has been a movement toward home births and the use of midwives, as of 2006, 99 percent of all births in the United States took place in hospitals. This is in spite of the fact that there is no significant difference in the neonatal death rates between the two. In the Netherlands, by contrast, 30 percent of births take place at home.

Sociologist Eliot Freidson (1970:5) has likened the status of medicine today to that of state religions in the past—it has an officially approved monopoly on the right to define health and to treat illness. Theorists use the phrase "medicalization of society" to refer to the growing role of medicine as a major institution of social control (Conrad 2007; McKinlay and McKinlay 1977; Zola 1972, 1983).

**The Medicalization of Society** Social control involves techniques and strategies for regulating behavior in order to enforce the distinctive norms and values of a culture. How does medicine manifest its social control? First, medicine has greatly expanded its domain of expertise in recent decades. Physicians now examine a wide range of issues in addition to basic health, among them sexuality, old age, anxiety, obesity, child development, alcoholism, and drug addiction. We tolerate this expansion of the boundaries of medicine because we hope that these experts can provide factual and effective cures to complex human problems, as they have to various infectious diseases.

The social significance of this expanding medicalization is that once a problem is viewed from a medical model framework—once medical experts become influential in proposing and assessing relevant public policies—it becomes more difficult for common people to join the dis-

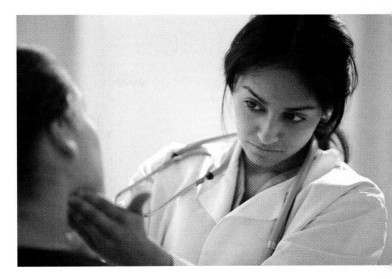

cussion and exert influence on decision making. It also becomes more difficult to view these issues as being shaped by social, cultural, or psychological factors, rather than simply by physical or medical factors (Caplan 1989; Conrad 2007; Starr 1982).

A second way that medicine serves as an agent of social control is by retaining absolute jurisdiction over many health care procedures. It has even attempted to guard its jurisdiction by placing health care professionals such as chiropractors and nurse-midwives outside the realm of acceptable medicine. Despite the fact that midwives first brought professionalism to child delivery, they have been portrayed as having invaded the "legitimate" field of obstetrics, in both the United States and Mexico. Nurse-midwives have sought licensing as a way to achieve professional respectability, but physicians continue to exert power to ensure that midwifery remains a subordinate occupation (Scharnberg 2007).

**Inequities in Health Care** Another serious concern regarding power and resources in the context of contemporary medicine involves the glaring inequities that exist in health care. Around the world, poor areas tend to be underserved because medical services concentrate where the wealth is. The United States, for example, has about 27 physicians per 10,000 people, while African nations have less than 1 per 10,000.

The supply of health care in poorer countries is further reduced by what is referred to as **brain drain**—the immigration to the United States and other industrialized nations of skilled workers, professionals, and technicians who are desperately needed in their home countries. As part of this brain drain, physicians, nurses, and other health care professionals have come to the United States from developing countries such as India, Pakistan, and various African states. Their emigration out of the Third World represents yet another way in which the world's core industrialized nations enhance their quality of life at the expense of developing countries (Bureau of the Census 2007a:Table154; World Bank 2007a:92–94).

Such inequities in health care have clear life-and-death consequences. For example, there are dramatic differences in infant mortality rates between developing countries such as Afghanistan, Sierra Leone, and Pakistan and industrial nations like Iceland, Japan, and Australia. The **infant mortality rate** is the number of deaths of infants under one year old per 1000 live births in a given year. This measure is an important indicator of a society's level of health care; it reflects prenatal nutrition, delivery procedures, and infant screening measures. Such differences in infant mortality reflect unequal distribution of health care resources based on the wealth or poverty of various nations. Surprisingly, despite our national wealth and the huge amounts spent on health care in the United States, at least 42 nations have lower infant mortality rates. An additional way that developing countries suffer the consequences of health care inequality is in reduced life expectancy. In Africa and much of Latin America and Asia, life expectancy is far lower than in the industrialized nations.

> **sick role** Societal expectations about the attitudes and behavior of a person viewed as being ill.
> **brain drain** The immigration to the United States and other industrialized nations of skilled workers, professionals, and technicians who are desperately needed in their home countries.
> **infant mortality rate** The number of deaths of infants under one year old per 1000 live births in a given year.

**Labeling and Power** Sometimes the power to label and the power to oppress go hand in hand. A historical example illustrates perhaps the ultimate extreme in labeling social behavior as a sickness. As enslavement of Africans in the United States came under increasing attack in the 19th century, medical

**5 Movies on HEALTH AND MEDICINE**

**The Diving Bell and the Butterfly**
*A man suddenly becomes completely paralyzed.*

**I Am Legend**
*A virus destroys humankind while one man looks for a cure.*

**Philadelphia**
*One man's battle with AIDS and the society that shuns him.*

**Sicko**
*A documentary criticizing the U.S. health care system.*

**Pride of the Yankees**
*The story of Lou Gehrig and his disease.*

# Going GLOBAL

## Infant Mortality Rates in Selected Countries

Infant deaths per 1,000 live births

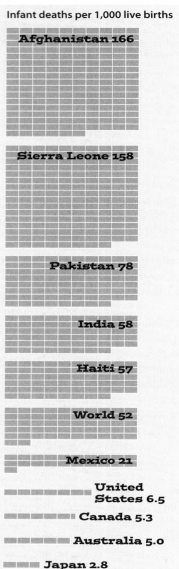

| Country | Rate |
| --- | --- |
| Afghanistan | 166 |
| Sierra Leone | 158 |
| Pakistan | 78 |
| India | 58 |
| Haiti | 57 |
| World | 52 |
| Mexico | 21 |
| United States | 6.5 |
| Canada | 5.3 |
| Australia | 5.0 |
| Japan | 2.8 |
| Iceland | 2.4 |

Source: Haub 2007.

remedy for this "disease" was to treat slaves kindly, as one might treat children. Apparently, these medical authorities would not entertain the view that it was healthy and sane to flee slavery or join in a slave revolt (Szasz 1971).

By the late 1980s, the power of one particular label—"person with AIDS"—had become quite evident. This label often functions as a master status that overshadows all other aspects of a person's life. Once someone is told that he or she has tested positive for HIV, the virus associated with AIDS, that person is forced to confront immediate and difficult questions: Should I tell my family members? My sex partners? My friends? My co-workers? My employer? How will these people respond? People's intense fear of the disease has led to prejudice and discrimination—even social ostracism—against those who have (or are suspected of having) AIDS. A person who has AIDS must deal not only with the serious medical consequences of the disease but also with the distressing social consequences associated with the label.

AIDS caught major social institutions—particularly the government, the health care system, and the economy—by surprise when it was first noticed by medical practitioners in the 1970s. It has since spread around the world, with the first U.S. cases of AIDS reported in 1981. Rather than being a distinct disease, AIDS is actually a predisposition to various diseases that is caused by a virus, the human immunodeficiency virus (HIV). The virus gradually destroys the body's immune system, leaving the carrier vulnerable

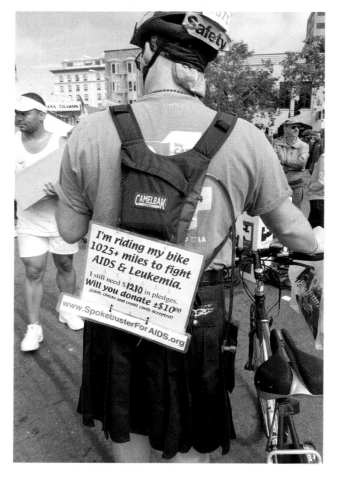

authorities provided new rationalizations for the oppressive practice. Noted physicians published articles stating that the skin color of Africans deviated from "healthy" white skin coloring because Africans suffered from congenital leprosy. Moreover, physicians classified the continuing efforts of enslaved Africans to escape from their White masters as an example of the "disease" of drapetomania (or "crazy runaways"). The prestigious *New Orleans Medical and Surgical Journal* suggested that the

## Going GLOBAL

### HIV/AIDS Cases, 2007

**Eastern Europe/Central Asia**
1.6 million
55,000 ■

**East Asia**
800,000
32,000 ■

**North America**
1.3 million
▌21,000

**Western/Central Europe**
760,000
12,000 ▎

**Caribbean**
230,000
▎11,000

**North Africa/Middle East**
380,000
25,000 ■

**South/Southeast Asia**
4 million
270,000 ■■■■

**Latin America**
1.6 million
■ 58,000

**Sub-Saharan Africa**
22.5 million
1.6 million

**Oceania (Australia/New Zealand)**
75,000
1,400 ▎

▨ People living with HIV
■ Deaths from AIDS in 2007
⊤ 100,000 people

*Sources:* Centers for Disease Control and Prevention 2007a; UNAIDS 2007.

*Note:* Midpoint estimates for December 2007. Total number of adults and children living with HIV, 33.2 million; total number of estimated adult and child deaths during 2007, 2.1 million.

to infections such as pneumonia that those with healthy immune systems generally can resist.

While the numbers of new cases and deaths have recently shown some evidence of decline, more than a million people in the United States were living with AIDS or HIV as of December 2007. Globally, an estimated 33.2 million people are now infected; however, the disease is not evenly distributed. Those areas least equipped to deal with it—the developing nations of sub-Saharan Africa—face the greatest challenge (Centers for Disease Control and Prevention 2007c).

Because those in high-risk groups—gay men and IV drug users—were comparatively powerless, and labeled as such, policy makers were slow to respond to the AIDS crisis in the United States. Over time, however, the response has improved, and today people with HIV or AIDS who receive appropriate medical treatment are living longer than they did in the past. The high cost of drug treatment programs has generated intensive worldwide pressure on the major pharmaceutical companies to lower the prices to patients in developing nations, especially in sub-Saharan Africa. Bowing to this pressure, several of the companies have agreed to make the combination therapies available at cost. As a result, the accessibility of HIV treatment has in-creased steadily, though inequalities remain. By the beginning of 2008, only 11 percent of mothers who need therapy to prevent transmission of the virus to their babies were receiving it (R. Wolf 2008).

According to labeling theorists, we can view a variety of life experiences as illnesses or not. Recently, the medical community has recognized premenstrual syndrome, posttraumatic disorders, and hyperactivity as medical disorders. Probably the most noteworthy medical example of labeling is the case of homosexuality. For years, psychiatrists classified being gay or lesbian not as a lifestyle but as a mental disorder subject to treatment. This official sanction by the psychiatry profession became an early target of the growing gay and lesbian rights movement in the United States. In 1974, members of the American Psychiatric Association voted to drop homosexuality from the standard manual on mental disorders (Conrad 2007).

## NEGOTIATING CURES

In practice, we seek to strike a balance between the authority of the physician and the agency of the patient. Physicians use cues to reinforce their prestige and power. According to medical sociologist Brenda Beagan (2001), the technical language students learn in medical school becomes the basis for the script they follow as novice physicians. The familiar white coat and stethoscope is their costume—one that helps them to appear confident and professional at the same time that it identifies them as doctors to patients

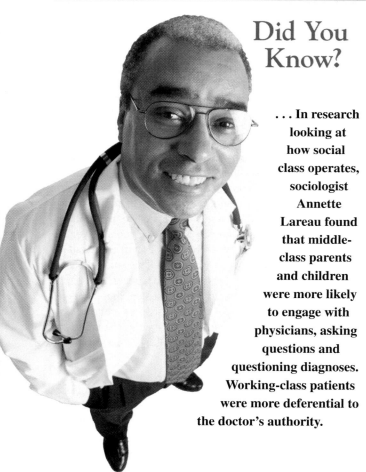

Patients, on the other hand, are not passive. Sometimes patients play an active role in health care by failing to follow a physician's advice. For example, some patients stop taking medications long before they should. Some take an incorrect dosage on purpose, and others never even fill their prescriptions. Such noncompliance results in part from the prevalence of self-medication in our society; many people are accustomed to self-diagnosis and -treatment.

Patients' active involvement in their health care can have very positive consequences. Some patients consult books, magazines, and websites about preventive health care techniques, attempt to maintain a healthful and nutritious diet, carefully monitor any side effects of medication, and adjust the dosage based on perceived side effects. Recognizing this change, pharmaceutical firms are advertising their prescription drugs directly to potential customers. For their part, medical professionals are understandably suspicious of these new sources of information. A study published in the *Journal of the American Medical Association* in 2001 found that health information on the Internet is often incomplete and inaccurate, even on the best sites. Nevertheless, there is little doubt that Internet research is transforming patient–physician encounters (Berland 2001; Gerencher 2007).

## >> Social Epidemiology

By looking at patterns of health and illness throughout society, we can better understand which factors are at work in shaping health outcomes. **Social epidemiology** is the study of disease distribution, impairment, and general health status across a population. Initially, epidemiology concentrated on the scientific study of epidemics, focusing on how they started and spread. Contemporary social epi-

and other staff members. Beagan found that many medical students struggle to project the appearance of competence they think their role demands, but over time most become accustomed to expecting respect and deference.

demiology is much broader in scope, concerned not only with epidemics but also with nonepidemic diseases, injuries, drug addiction and alcoholism, suicide, and mental illness. Recently, epidemiologists took on the new role of tracking bioterrorism. In 2001, they mobilized to trace an anthrax outbreak and prepare for any terrorist use of smallpox or other lethal microbes. Epidemiologists draw on the work of a wide variety of scientists and researchers, among them physicians, sociologists, public health officials, biologists, veterinarians, demographers, anthropologists, psychologists, and meteorologists.

Researchers in social epidemiology commonly use two concepts: incidence and prevalence. **Incidence** refers to the number of new cases of a specific disorder that occur within a given population during a stated period, usually a year. For example, the incidence of AIDS in the United States in 2005 was 40,608 cases. In contrast, **prevalence** refers to the total number of cases of a specific disorder that exist at a given time. The prevalence of AIDS in the United States through 2006 was about 1 million cases (Centers for Disease Control and Prevention 2007b).

When disease incidence figures are presented as rates—for example, the number of reports per 100,000 people—they are called **morbidity rates.** This is distinct from the **mortality rate,** which refers to the incidence of death in a given population. Sociologists find morbidity rates useful because they can reveal whether a specific disease occurs more frequently among one segment of a population than another. As we shall see, social class, race, ethnicity, gender, and age can all affect a population's morbidity rates.

## SOCIAL CLASS

Social class is clearly associated with differences in morbidity and mortality rates. Studies in the United States and other countries have consistently shown that people in the lower classes have higher rates of mortality and disability

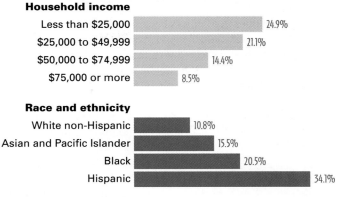

# Percentage of People Without Health Insurance, 2006

**Household income**

| | |
|---|---|
| Less than $25,000 | 24.9% |
| $25,000 to $49,999 | 21.1% |
| $50,000 to $74,999 | 14.4% |
| $75,000 or more | 8.5% |

**Race and ethnicity**

| | |
|---|---|
| White non-Hispanic | 10.8% |
| Asian and Pacific Islander | 15.5% |
| Black | 20.5% |
| Hispanic | 34.1% |

*Source:* DeNavas-Walt et al. 2007:21.

strains are certainly a major factor in the health problems of less affluent people.

People who are poor—many of whom belong to racial and ethnic minorities—are less able than others to afford quality medical care (see the accompanying graph). Not surprisingly, those with high incomes are significantly more likely to have health insurance, either because they can afford it or because they have jobs that provide it. The middle class has been particularly hard hit by the decision of companies to eliminate employer-provided coverage (the most common form of health insurance). Such rates declined steadily from 2000 to 2004 (DeNavas-Walt et al. 2007:20; E. Gould 2006).

> **social epidemiology** The study of the distribution of disease, impairment, and general health status across a population.
> **incidence** The number of new cases of a specific disorder that occur within a given population during a stated period.
> **prevalence** The total number of cases of a specific disorder that exist at a given time.
> **morbidity rate** The incidence of disease in a given population.
> **mortality rate** The incidence of death in a given population.

> ## It is a lot harder to keep people well than it is to just get them over a sickness.
>
> DeForest Clinton Jarvis

than others. One study concluded that Americans whose family income was less than $10,000 could expect to die seven years sooner than those with an income of at least $25,000 (Pamuk et al. 1998).

A number of factors appear to influence the effect class has on health. Crowded living conditions, substandard housing, poor diet, and stress all contribute to the ill health of many low-income people in the United States. In certain instances, poor education may lead to a lack of awareness of measures necessary to maintain good health. Financial

The ultimate price to pay for a lack of health insurance is the increased risk of early death. Uninsured women who develop breast cancer tend to be diagnosed later—when treatment is less effective—than insured women. Uninsured men who develop high blood pressure are more likely than others to forgo screenings and medication, a decision that jeopardizes their health. According to estimates, 22,000 deaths among the uninsured could have been prevented in 2006 (Dorn 2008).

What is particularly troubling about social class differences is that they appear to be cumulative. Little or no health care in childhood or young adulthood is likely to mean more illness later in life. The longer that low income presents a barrier to adequate health care, the more chronic and difficult to treat illness becomes (Prus 2007).

Karl Marx would have argued, and some contemporary sociologists agree, that capitalist societies such as the United States care more about maximizing profits than they do about the health and safety of industrial workers.

*curanderismo* Latino folk medicine, a form of holistic health care and healing.

As a result, government agencies do not take forceful action to regulate conditions in the workplace, and workers suffer many preventable job-related injuries and illnesses. As we will see later in this chapter, research also shows that the lower classes are more vulnerable to environmental pollution, another consequence of capitalist production, than are the affluent, not only where they work but where they live.

## RACE AND ETHNICITY

The health profiles of many racial and ethnic minorities reflect the social inequality evident in U.S. society. The poor economic and environmental conditions of groups such as African Americans, Hispanics, and Native Americans are manifested in high morbidity and mortality rates for these groups. It is true that some afflictions, such as sickle-cell anemia among Blacks, are influenced by genetics, but in most instances, environmental factors contribute to the differential rates of disease and death.

As noted earlier, infant mortality is regarded as a primary indicator of health care. There is a significant gap in the United States between the infant mortality rates of African Americans and Whites. On average, the rate of infant death is more than twice as high among Blacks. African Americans account for 15 percent of all live births in the nation but 29 percent of infant deaths. Puerto Ricans and Native Americans have infant mortality rates that are lower than African Americans' but higher than Whites' (MacDorman et al. 2005).

Considering mortality rates, Blacks have higher death rates from heart disease, pneumonia, diabetes, and cancer than do Whites. The death rate from stroke is twice as high among African Americans. Such epidemiological findings are related to the social class effects noted previously—the fact that average income for African Americans is lower than that for Whites. The effect of these factors can be seen in terms of life expectancy. According to the National Center for Health Statistics for 2007, Whites can expect to live 78.3 years; in contrast, life expectancy for Blacks is 73.1 years.

The medical establishment is not exempt from institutional discrimination. There is evidence that minorities receive inferior care even when they are insured. Despite having access to care, Blacks, Latinos, and American Indians are treated unequally as a result of differences in the quality of various health care plans. Furthermore, national clinical studies have shown that even allowing for differences in income and insurance coverage, racial and ethnic minorities are less likely than other groups to receive both standard health care and life-saving treatment (Dressler et al. 2005; A. Green et al. 2007).

Numerous examples in the history of African American health care demonstrate that such institutional discrimination has been around for a long time. For example, in the notorious Tuskegee syphilis study, begun by the federal government in 1932, doctors knowingly infected Black men from Alabama with syphilis in order to observe the disease's progression. Another study, conducted from 1992 to 1997, was designed to determine whether there is a biological or genetic basis for violent behavior. Researchers misled the parents of young subjects, all of whom were Black males, by telling them that the children would undergo a series of tests and questions. In fact, the boys were given potentially risky doses of the same drug found in the now-banned Fen-phen weight-loss pill, which causes heart irregularities.

# Infant Motality Rates in the United States, 2002–2004

| Race/Ethnicity | Infant deaths per 1,000 live births |
|---|---|
| Black, non-Hispanic | 13.7 |
| American Indian or Alaska Native | 8.6 |
| White, non-Hispanic | 5.7 |
| Hispanic | 5.6 |
| Asian or Pacific Islander | 4.8 |

*Source:* National Center for Health Statistics 2007:166–167.

## SOCthink

> > > Studies such as the Tuskegee syphilis experiment seem to clearly violate ethical principles of research. How do you think that researchers justify studies involving race that appear to violate the ethical guidelines they are bound to follow?

Having to deal with the effects of racism may itself contribute to the medical problems of Blacks (Waitzkin

1986). The stress that results from racial prejudice and discrimination helps to explain the higher rates of hypertension found among African Americans (and Hispanics) compared to Whites. Hypertension—twice as common in Blacks as in Whites—is believed to be a critical factor in Blacks' high mortality rates from heart disease, kidney disease, and stroke (Morehouse Medical Treatment and Effectiveness Center 1999).

Mexican Americans and many other Latinos adhere to cultural beliefs that make them less likely to use the established medical system. They may interpret their illnesses according to traditional Latino folk medicine, or *curanderismo*—a form of holistic health care and healing. *Curanderismo* influences how one approaches health care and even how one defines illness. Although most Hispanics use folk healers, or *curanderos,* infrequently, perhaps 20 percent rely on home remedies. Some define such illnesses as *susto* (fright sickness) and *atague* (fighting attack) according to folk beliefs. Because these complaints often have biological bases, sensitive medical practitioners need to deal with them carefully in order to diagnose and treat illnesses accurately.

Also affecting Latino morbidity rates is the fact that Latinos are much more likely to wait to seek treatment. Due in part to a lack of health insurance, they seek treatment for pressing medical problems at clinics and emergency rooms rather than receiving regular preventive care through a family physician. Such delays in treatments increase the severity of the consequences of illness and disease (Council on Scientific Affairs 1999; Durden and Hummer 2006; Trotter and Chavira 1997).

## GENDER

A large body of research indicates that compared with men, women experience a higher prevalence of many illnesses, although they do have a longer life expectancy. There are some variations—for example, men are more likely to have parasitic diseases, whereas women are more likely to become diabetic—but as a group, women appear to be in poorer health than men.

The apparent inconsistency between the ill health of women and their greater longevity appears to be tied to lifestyle differences between men and women that grow out of gendered norms. Women's lower rate of cigarette smoking (reducing their risk of heart disease, lung cancer, and emphysema), lower consumption of alcohol (reducing the risk of auto accidents and cirrhosis of the liver), and lower rate of employment in dangerous occupations explain about one-third of their greater longevity than men. Researchers argue that women are much more likely than men to seek treatment, to be diagnosed as having a disease, and thus to have their illnesses reflected in the data examined by epidemiologists.

With everything from birth to beauty being treated in an increasingly medical context, women have been particularly vulnerable to the medicalization of society. Ironically, even given the increased power of the medical establishment in women's lives, medical researchers have often excluded them from clinical studies. Female physicians and researchers charge that sexism lies at the heart of such research practices and insist there is a desperate need for studies of female subjects (Rieker and Bird 2000).

## AGE

Health is the overriding concern of the elderly. Most older people in the United States report having at least one chronic illness, but only some of those conditions are potentially life threatening or require medical care. The quality of life among older people is of particular concern in the face of potentially escalating health problems. Almost half of older people in the United States are troubled by arthritis, and many have visual or hearing impairments that can interfere with the performance of everyday tasks.

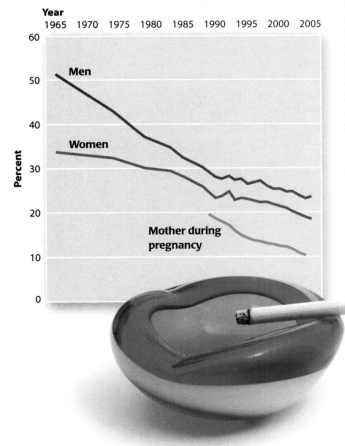

## Smoking Rates by Gender, 1965–2005

Year

Percent

Men

Women

Mother during pregnancy

*Source:* National Center for Health Statistics 2007.

Older people are also especially vulnerable to certain mental health problems. Alzheimer's disease, the leading cause of dementia in the United States, afflicts an estimated 5 million older people. While some individuals with Alzheimer's exhibit only mild symptoms, the risk of severe problems resulting from this disease rises substantially with age (Alzheimer's Association 2008:9).

Due to their increased health risks, older people in the United States (age 75 or older) are five times more likely to use health services than younger people (ages 15–24). This heightened use level is tied to health insurance coverage, with people over age 65 the most likely to be covered (see the graph below). The disproportionate use of the U.S. health care system by older people is a critical factor in all discussions about the cost of health care and possible reforms of the health care system (Bureau of the Census 2007a:Table 157).

A person's odds of good health are shaped by her or his class, race and ethnicity, gender, and age. Even geography matters, as there are significant differences in the number of physicians from one state to the next. Health care professionals and program advisors need to take such differential effects into account when considering what constitutes equitable health care coverage. Any attempts to do so, however, are constrained by the cost of health care.

## Availability of Physicians by State, 2005

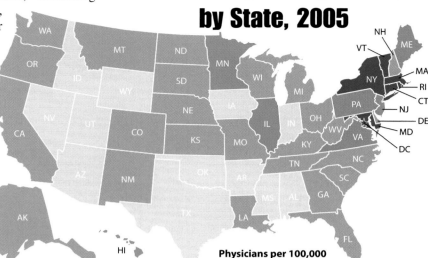

Source: Bureau of the Census 2007a:Table 154.

**Physicians per 100,000**
National average 266

- 315 and over
- 314–267
- 266–217
- Under 216

## Health Insurance Rates by Age, 2006

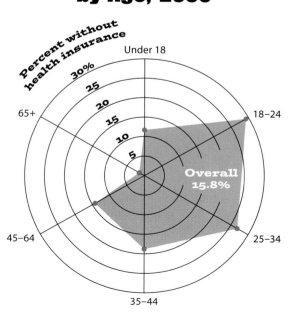

Source: DeNavas-Walt et al. 2007:21.

## Total Health Care Expenditures in the United States, 1970–2017 (projected)

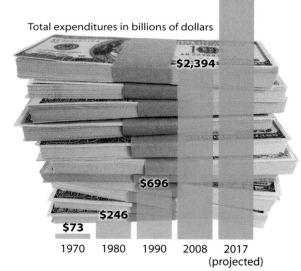

Total expenditures in billions of dollars

$4,277

$2,394

$696

$246

$73

| 1970 | 1980 | 1990 | 2008 | 2017 (projected) |

Source: Centers for Medicare and Medicaid Services 2008:Table 1 (2008–2017 data); Health Care Financing Administration 2001 (1979–1990 data).

## >> Health Care in the United States

The costs of health care have skyrocketed in the past 35 years. In 1997, total expenditures for health care in the United States crossed the trillion-dollar threshold—more than four times the 1980 figure. In 2000, the amount spent on health care equaled what we spent on education, defense, prisons, farm subsidies, food stamps, and foreign aid combined. By the year 2017, total expenditures for health care in the United States are expected to exceed $4.2 trillion. The costs of medical care are especially burdensome in the event of catastrophic illnesses or confinement to a nursing home. Bills of tens of thousands of dollars are not unusual in the treatment of cancer, Alzheimer's, and other chronic illnesses requiring custodial care.

The health care system of the United States has moved far beyond the days when general practitioners living in a neighborhood or community typically made house calls and charged modest fees for their services. Over time health care became a big business involving nationwide hospital chains and marketing campaigns. These changes have influenced the nature of relationships between doctors, nurses, and patients.

## A HISTORICAL VIEW

Today, state licensing and medical degrees confer a widely recognized level of authority on medical professionals.

Our perception of doctors and health care is shaped by the media. For a long time, E.R. was the king of the hospital heap on television. In recent years, Grey's Anatomy has taken the lead. If such programs were our only source of information about backstage life among doctors and nurses, what would we conclude about the nature of health care in the United States?

This was not always the case. The "popular health movement" of the 1830s and 1840s emphasized preventive care and what is termed "self-help." It voiced strong criticism of "doctoring" as a paid occupation. New medical philosophies or sects established their own medical schools and challenged the authority and methods of more traditional doctors. By the 1840s, most states had repealed medical licensing laws, and the health care field was largely unregulated.

In response, through the leadership of the American Medical Association (AMA), founded in 1848, "regular" doctors marginalized lay practitioners, sectarian doctors, and female physicians in general. They institutionalized their authority through standardized programs of education and licensing. These served as gatekeeping mechanisms. Only those who successfully completed AMA programs gained legitimate authority as medical practitioners. The authority of the physician no longer depended on lay attitudes or on the person occupying the sick role; increasingly, it was built into the structure of the medical profession and the health care system.

As the institutionalization of health care proceeded, the medical profession gained control over both the market for its services and the various organizational hierarchies that govern medical practice, financing, and policy making. By the 1920s, physicians controlled hospital technology, the division of labor of health personnel, and indirectly, other professional practices such as nursing and pharmaceutical services (R. Coser 1984). It was through such expansion that the medicalization of society was born.

## THE ROLE OF GOVERNMENT

Not until the 20th century did health care receive federal aid in conjunction with the expansion of medicine as a social institution. The first significant government involvement was the 1946 Hill-Burton Act, which provided subsidies for building and improving hospitals, especially in rural areas. An even more important development was the enactment in 1965 of two wide-ranging government assistance programs: Medicare, which is essentially a compulsory health insurance plan for the elderly, and Medicaid, which is a noncontributory federal and state insurance plan for the poor. These programs greatly expanded federal involvement in health care financing for needy men, women, and children.

Given the high rates of illness and disability among the elderly, Medicare has had a huge impact on the health care system. Initially, Medicare simply reimbursed health care providers such as physicians and hospitals for the billed costs of their services. However, in 1983, as the overall costs of Medicare increased dramatically, the federal government introduced a price control system. Under this system, in a process known as "dumping," private hospitals often transfer patients whose treatment may be unprofitable to public facilities. In fact, many private hospitals have be-

## Rising Medicare Expenses, 1970–2006

| Year | Expenditures |
|------|--------------|
| 1970 | $7.5 |
| 1980 | $36.8 |
| 1990 | $111 |
| 2000 | $221.5 |
| 2006 | $408.3 |

**Expenditures (billions of dollars)**

*Source:* National Center for Health Statistics 2007:408.

gun to investigate the financial status of potential patients, with those judged undesirable refused admission or dumped. Although a federal law passed in 1987 made it illegal for any hospital receiving Medicare funds to dump patients, the practice continues (E. Gould 2007; Light 2004; Quadagno 2005).

## PHYSICIANS, NURSES, AND PATIENTS

The power of medicine and the prestige of doctors have risen together. As the occupation became more professional and training became more standardized, some of the depersonalizing effects of working in bureaucratic organizations came to influence role performance. This was true in regard to doctors' relationships with both nurses and patients.

Considering doctors' relationships with patients, and reflecting on the training she received, Dr. Lori Arviso Alvord writes, "I had been trained by a group of physicians who placed much more emphasis on their technical abilities and clinical skills than on their abilities to be caring and sensitive" (Alvord and Van Pelt 1999:13). Despite many efforts to formally introduce a humanistic approach to patient care into the medical school curriculum, patient overload and cost cutting by hospitals have tended to undercut positive relations. Moreover, widespread publicity about malpractice suits and high medical costs have further strained the physician–patient relationship.

Just as physicians have maintained dominance in their interactions with patients, they have controlled interac-

tions with nurses. Despite their training and professional status, nurses commonly take orders from physicians. Traditionally, the relationship between doctors and nurses has paralleled the male dominance of the United States: Most physicians have been male, while virtually all nurses have been female.

Like other women in subordinate roles, nurses have been expected to perform their duties without challenging the authority of men. Psychiatrist Leonard Stein (1967) referred to this process as the "doctor–nurse game." According to the rules of this game, the nurse must never openly disagree with the physician. When she has recommendations concerning a patient's care, she must communicate them indirectly, in a deferential tone. For example, if asked by a hospital's medical resident, "What sleeping medication has been helpful to Mrs. Brown in the past?" (an indirect request for a recommendation), the nurse will respond with a disguised recommendation, such as "Pentobarbital 100 mg was quite effective night before last." Her careful response allows the physician to authoritatively restate the same prescription as if it were his idea.

In an occupation that was once predominantly male, increasing numbers of women are becoming physicians. In fall 2006, 48 percent of all new medical school students in the United States were female. An equivalent pattern in nursing has not occurred, however. While there are more male nurses now than in the past, the overwhelming majority continue to be female (Association of American Medical Colleges 2007, 2008).

A study of male and female medical residents suggests that the increasing number of women physicians may alter the traditional doctor–patient relationship. The study found male residents to be more focused on the intellectual challenges of medicine and the prestige associated with certain medical specialties. In contrast, female residents were more likely to express a commitment to caring for patients and devoting time to them. As women continue to enter and move higher in the hierarchies of the medical profession, sociological studies will surely be done to see whether these apparent gender differences persist.

### Hot or Not?

Is the way doctors act due more to the fact that they are mostly male or to their level of prestige and power?

## ALTERNATIVES TO TRADITIONAL HEALTH CARE

In traditional forms of health care, people rely on physicians and hospitals for the treatment of illness. Yet a significant proportion of adults in the United States attempt to maintain good health or respond to illness through the use of alternative health care techniques. For example, in recent decades, interest has been growing in holistic (sometimes spelled wholistic) medical principles, first developed in China. **Holistic medicine** refers to therapies in which the health care practitioner considers the person's physical, mental, emotional, and spiritual characteristics. The individual is regarded as a totality rather than a collection of interrelated organ systems. Treatment methods include massage, chiropractic medicine, acupuncture (which involves the insertion of fine needles into surface points), respiratory exercises, and the use of herbs as remedies. Nutrition, exercise, and visualization may also be used to treat ailments that traditionally are addressed through medication or hospitalization (Sharma and Bodeker 1998).

## SOCthink

> > > What do you think about alternative medicine? Would you be willing to get assistance from a holistic healer? What background factors, such as age, race and ethnicity, or gender, might play a role in your willingness or unwillingness to do so?

Practitioners of holistic medicine do not necessarily function totally outside the traditional health care system. Some have medical degrees and rely on X-rays and EKG machines for diagnostic assistance. Others who staff holistic clinics, often referred to as wellness clinics, reject the use of medical technology. The recent resurgence of holistic medicine comes amid widespread recognition of the value of nutrition and the dangers of overreliance on prescription drugs (especially those used to reduce stress, such as Valium).

# Complementary and Alternative Medicine Use

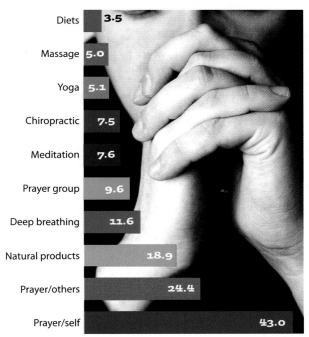

| | |
|---|---|
| Diets | 3.5 |
| Massage | 5.0 |
| Yoga | 5.1 |
| Chiropractic | 7.5 |
| Meditation | 7.6 |
| Prayer group | 9.6 |
| Deep breathing | 11.6 |
| Natural products | 18.9 |
| Prayer/others | 24.4 |
| Prayer/self | 43.0 |

*Source:* Barnes et al. 2004.

The medical establishment—professional organizations, research hospitals, and medical schools—continues to zealously protect its authority. However, a major breakthrough occurred in 1992 when the federal government's National Institutes of Health (NIH)—the nation's major funding source for biomedical research—opened an Office of Alternative Medicine and empowered it to accept grant requests. A 2002 NIH-sponsored national study found that 36 percent of adults in the United States had used some form of "complementary and alternative medicine" within the previous year. Examples included practices such as acupuncture, folk medicine, meditation, yoga, homeopathic treatment, megavitamin therapy, and chiropractic treatment. When prayer was included as an alternative form of medicine, the number rose to 62.1 percent (Barnes et al. 2004).

> **holistic medicine** Therapies in which the health care practitioner considers the person's physical, mental, emotional, and spiritual characteristics.

On the international level, the World Health Organization (WHO) has begun to monitor the use of alternative medicine around the world. According to the WHO, 80 percent of people who live in the poorest countries in the world use alternative medicine, from herbal treatments to the services of a faith healer. In most countries, these treatments are largely unregulated, even though some of them can be fatal. For example, Kava Kava, an herbal tea used in the Pacific Islands to relieve anxiety, can be toxic to the liver in concentrated form. Other alternative treatments have been found to be effective in the treatment of serious diseases, such as malaria and sickle-cell anemia. The WHO's goal is to compile a list of such practices, as well as to encourage the development of universal training programs and ethical standards for practitioners of alternative medicine. To date, the organization has published findings on about 100 of the 5000 plants believed to be used as herbal remedies (McNeil 2002).

Sociological analysis of health and illness suggests that if we are to understand sickness we must look beyond biology. Society and culture, family and friends, the medical profession, and social position all help shape medical outcomes. Given the increasing costs of health care, and the fact that different groups experience different outcomes, this issue becomes one of equality and fairness. To what extent, for example, are we willing to accept that a child will live or die due to his or her income, race, or ethnicity? Or that one's life expectancy is shaped by such factors? It is precisely such concerns that drive debates about the expansion of health care coverage as a social right.

## >> Sociological Perspectives on the Environment

We have seen that the environment people live in has a noticeable affect on their health. Those who live in stressful, overcrowded places suffer more from disease than those who do not. Likewise, people have a noticeable effect on their environment. Around the world, increases in population, together with the economic development that accompanies them, have had serious environmental consequences. We can see signs of despoliation almost everywhere: our air, our water, and our land are being polluted, whether we live in St. Louis; Mexico City; or Lagos, Nigeria. Although environmental problems may be easy to identify, devising socially and politically acceptable solutions to them is much more difficult. Sociologists provide us with some models to better understand the issues we must consider.

### HUMAN ECOLOGY

**Human ecology** is an area of study that is concerned with interrelationships between people and their environment. As the environmentalist Barry Commoner (1971:39) put it, "Everything is connected to everything else." Human ecologists focus on how the physical environment shapes people's lives and on how people influence the surrounding environment.

In an application of the human ecological perspective, sociologists and environmentalists have identified

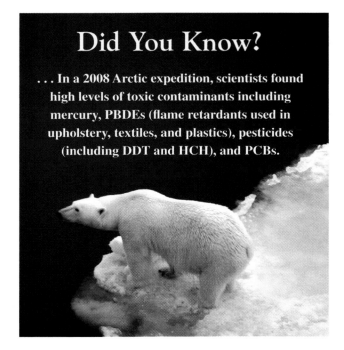

**Did You Know?**

. . . In a 2008 Arctic expedition, scientists found high levels of toxic contaminants including mercury, PBDEs (flame retardants used in upholstery, textiles, and plastics), pesticides (including DDT and HCH), and PCBs.

several relationships between the environment and people. Among them are the following:

- *The environment provides the resources essential for life.* These include air, water, and materials used to create shelter, transportation, and needed products. If human societies exhaust these resources—for example, by polluting the water supply or cutting down rain forests—the consequences could be dire.

- *The environment serves as a waste repository.* More so than other living species, humans produce a huge quantity and variety of waste products—bottles, cans, boxes, paper, sewage, garbage, and so on. Various types of pollution have become more common because human societies are generating more wastes than the environment can safely absorb.

- *The environment "houses" our species.* It is our home, our living space, the place where we reside, work, and play. At times we take this truism for granted, but not when day-to-day living conditions become unpleasant and problematic. If our air is "heavy," if our tap water turns brown, or if toxic chemicals seep into our neighborhood, we remember why it is vital to live in a healthful environment.

There is no shortage of illustrations of the interconnectedness of humans and the environment. For example, scientific research has linked pollutants in the environment to people's health and behavior. The increasing prevalence of asthma, lead poisoning, and cancer has been tied to human alterations to the environment. Similarly, the rise in melanoma (skin can-

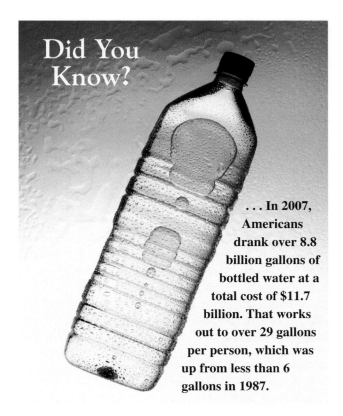
cer) diagnoses has been linked to global warming. And ecological changes in our food and diet have been related to early obesity and diabetes.

With its view that "everything is connected to everything else," human ecology stresses the trade-offs inherent in every decision that alters the environment. In facing the environmental challenges of the 21st century, government policy makers and environmentalists must determine how they can fulfill humans' pressing needs for food, clothing, and shelter while preserving the environment as a source of resources, a waste repository, and a home.

## POWER, RESOURCES, AND THE ENVIRONMENT

Analyzing environmental issues from a world systems approach allows us to better understand the global consequences of differential access to resources. This approach highlights the difference in relative power between core nations, which control wealth and so dominate the global economy, and developing countries, which lack control and whose resources are exploited. This process only intensifies the destruction of natural resources in poorer regions of the world. Less affluent nations are being forced to exploit their mineral deposits, forests, and fisheries in order to meet their debt obligations. People in developing nations often end up turning to the only means of survival available to them, including plowing mountain slopes, burning sections of tropical forests, and overgrazing grasslands (Livernash and Rodenburg 1998).

Brazil exemplifies this interplay between economic troubles and environmental destruction. Each year more than 5.7 million acres of rain forest are cleared for crops and livestock. The elimination of the rain forest affects worldwide weather patterns, heightening the gradual warming of the earth. These socioeconomic patterns, with their harmful environmental consequences, are evident not only in Central and South America but in many regions of Africa and Asia.

**human ecology** The area of study concerned with the interrelationships between people and their environment.

Although destruction of the rain forest has long been a concern, only in the past few years have policy makers begun to listen to the indigenous peoples who live in these areas. Preservation of the rain forests may make sense at the global level, but for many local peoples, it limits their ability to cultivate crops or graze cattle. Even though it harms the global environment, they feel they have no choice but to take advantage of their available resources. In 2008, native peoples from Brazil to the Congo to Indonesia convened to make the case that wealthier countries should compensate them for conservation of the tropical rain forests (Barrionuevo 2008).

There is, in fact, a certain amount of ethnocentrism involved when people in industrialized countries insist that those developing nations change their practices to save the planet. In calling for the poverty-stricken and "food-hungry" populations of the world to sacrifice, they should also consider the lifestyle consequences for the "energy-hungry" nations. The industrialized nations of North America and Europe account for only 12 percent of the world's population but are responsible for 60 percent of worldwide consumption. The money their residents spend on ocean cruises each year could provide clean drinking water for everyone on the planet. Ice cream expenditures in Europe alone could be used to immunize every child in the world. The global consumer represents a serious environmental threat, but it is often difficult to look in the mirror and blame ourselves because our individual contribution to the problem seems so small. Collectively, however, the

along racial and social class lines. In general, poor people and people of color are much more likely than others to be victimized by the everyday consequences of economic development, including air pollution from expressways and incinerators.

Sociologists Paul Mohai and Robin Saha (2007) examined over 600 hazardous waste treatment, storage, and disposal facilities in the United States. They found that

**Suburbia is where the developer bulldozes out the trees, then names the streets after them.**

Bill Vaughn

choices we make have a significant global impact (G. Gardner et al. 2004).

The rise in global consumption is tied to a capitalist system that depends upon growth for its survival. Capitalism creates a "treadmill of production" (Schnaiberg 1994). Cutting back on consumption means cutting back on purchases, which leads to reduced production and the loss of profits and jobs. This treadmill necessitates creating an increasing demand for products, obtaining natural resources at minimal cost, and manufacturing products as quickly and cheaply as possible—no matter what the long-term environmental consequences.

## ENVIRONMENTAL JUSTICE

In autumn 1982, nearly 500 African Americans participated in a six-week protest against a hazardous waste landfill containing cancer-causing chemicals in Warren County, North Carolina. Their protests and legal actions continued until 2002, when decontamination of the site finally began. This 20-year battle can be seen as yet another "not-in-my-backyard" (NIMBY) event in which people desire the benefits of growth but want someone else to pay for its negative effects. In any event, the Warren County struggle is viewed as a transformative moment in contemporary environmentalism: the beginning of the environmental justice movement (Bullard 1993; McGurty 2000; North Carolina Department of Environment and Natural Resources 2008).

**Environmental justice** is a legal strategy based on claims that racial minorities are subjected disproportionately to environmental hazards. Some observers have heralded environmental justice as the "new civil rights of the 21st century" (Kokmen 2008:42). Since the advent of the environmental justice movement, activists and scholars have identified other environmental disparities that break

**environmental justice** A legal strategy based on claims that racial minorities are subjected disproportionately to environmental hazards.

non-Whites and Latinos make up 43 percent of the people who live within one mile of these dangerous sites. There are two possible explanations for this finding. One is that racial and ethnic minorities possess less power than others, so that they cannot prevent toxic sites from being located in their backyards. The other is that they end up settling near the sites after they are constructed, because economics and the forces of discrimination push them into the least desirable living areas.

Following reports from the Environmental Protection Agency (EPA) and other organizations documenting the discriminatory location of hazardous waste sites, President Bill Clinton issued an executive order in 1994 requiring all federal agencies to ensure that low-income and minority communities have access to better information about their environment, as well as an opportunity to participate in shaping government policies that affect their health. Initial efforts to implement the policy, along with increased activity by the environmental justice movement, aroused widespread opposition because of the delays the policy imposes in establishing new industrial sites. Some observers question the wisdom of an order that slows economic development in areas that are in dire need of employment opportunities. Others counter that such businesses employ few unskilled or less skilled workers and only make the environment less livable (Stretesky 2006; D. Taylor 2000).

Meanwhile, the poor and oppressed continue to bear the brunt of environmental pollution. In the 1990s, the federal government, unable to find a disposal site for spent

**SOC**think

> > > It took 20 years for the Warren County protest to succeed. Why do you think it took so long? How might access to resources shape the length of such struggles?

nuclear fuel, turned to tribal reservations. Agents eventually persuaded a tiny band of Goshute Indians in Skull Valley, Utah, to accept more than 44,000 barrels of the highly radioactive substance, which will remain dangerous for an estimated 10,000 years. The government dropped the plan only after opposition from surrounding towns and

cities, whose residents objected to the movement of the material through their communities. This was not the first time the government had attempted to persuade the impoverished tribe to accept environmentally objectionable installations. The military's nerve gas storage facility resides on or near the reservation, along with the Intermountain Power Project, which generates coal-fired electrical power for consumers in California (Eureka County 2006; Foy 2006).

In considering environmental issues, sociologists have emphasized the interconnectedness of humans and the environment, as well as the divisiveness of race and social class. Scientific findings can also play a role in our understanding of the nature and scope of environmental concerns. Of course, when such findings affect government policy and economic regulations, they become highly politicized. Such struggles are inevitable when core values and differential access to resources are at stake.

## >> Environmental Problems

Unfortunately, as we have already seen, the environmental problems caused by development have effects far beyond the places where they are created. Witness Muhammad Ali, a Bangladeshi man who has had to flee floodwaters five times in the last decade. Scientists believe that global warming is to blame both for worsening monsoons and for the raging waters of the Iamuna River, swollen by abnormally high glacier melt from the Himalayas. Every time the river floods, Ali tears down his house, made of tin and bamboo, and moves to higher ground. But he is running out of land to move to. "Where we are standing, in five days it will be gone," he says. "Our future thinking is that if this problem is not taken care of, we will be swept away" (Goering 2007).

Increasingly, people are recognizing the need to address such challenges to the environment. In a 2008 survey, 63

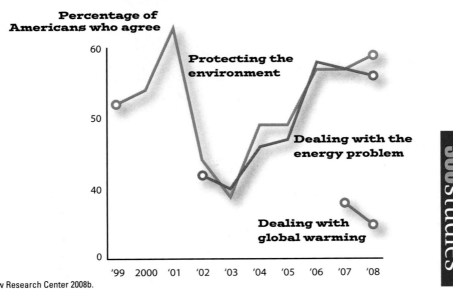

## Should Environmental Issues Be Top Priorities of Congress?

**Percentage of Americans who agree**

Protecting the environment

Dealing with the energy problem

Dealing with global warming

'99 2000 '01 '02 '03 '04 '05 '06 '07 '08

*Source:* Pew Research Center 2008b.

SOCstudies

percent agreed that the effects of global warming are already manifest or will occur within five years. Of those surveyed, 49 percent of adults said that protection of the environment should be given priority. This contrasted with 42 percent who said that the government should pursue economic growth even if the environment suffers (Gallup 2008c; Jacobe 2008). Three environmental areas are of particular concern: air pollution, water pollution, and global warming.

## AIR POLLUTION

Worldwide, more than 1 billion people are exposed to potentially health-damaging levels of air pollution. Unfortunately, in cities around the world, residents have come to accept smog and polluted air as normal. Urban air pollution is caused primarily by emissions from automobiles and secondarily by emissions from electric power plants and heavy industries. Smog not only limits visibility but can lead to health problems as uncomfortable as eye irritation and as deadly as lung cancer. Such problems are especially severe in developing countries. The WHO estimates that up to 700,000 premature deaths per year could be prevented if pollutants were brought down to safer levels (Carty 1999; World Resources Institute 1998).

People are capable of changing their behavior, but they are also often unwilling to make such changes permanent. During the 1984 Olympics in Los Angeles, authorities asked residents to carpool and stagger their work hours to relieve traffic congestion and improve the quality of the air athletes would breathe. These changes resulted in a remarkable 12 percent drop in ozone levels. After the Olympics ended, however, people reverted to their normal behavior, and the ozone levels climbed once again. Similarly, China took drastic action to ensure that Beijing's high levels of air pollution did not mar the 2008 Olympic Games. Construction work in the city ceased, polluting factories and power plants closed down, and workers swept roads and sprayed them with water several times a day. This temporary solution, however, has not solved China's ongoing pollution problem (*The Economist* 2008b).

## WATER POLLUTION

Throughout the United States, waste materials dumped by industries and local governments have polluted streams, rivers, and lakes. Consequently, many bodies of water have become unsafe for fishing and swimming, let alone drinking. Around the world, pollution of the oceans is an issue of growing concern. Such pollution results regularly from waste dumping and is made worse by fuel leaks from shipping and occasional oil spills. When the oil tanker *Exxon Valdez* ran aground in Prince William Sound, Alaska, in 1989, its cargo of 11 million gallons of crude oil spilled into the sound and washed onto the shore, contaminating 1285 miles of shoreline. Altogether, about 11,000 people joined in a massive cleanup effort that cost over $2 billion. Globally, oil spills occur regularly. In 2002, the oil tanker *Prestige* spilled twice as much fuel as the *Valdez,* greatly damaging coastal areas in Spain and France (ITOPF 2006).

Less dramatic than large-scale accidents or disasters, but more common in many parts of the world, are problems with the basic water supply. Worldwide, over 1.1 bil-

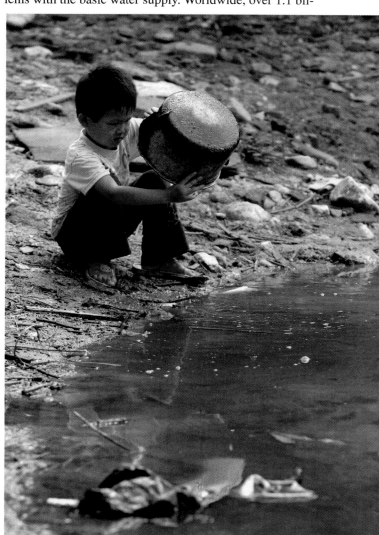

lion people lack safe and adequate drinking water, and 2.6 billion have no acceptable means of sanitation—a problem that further threatens the quality of water supplies. The health costs of unsafe water are enormous (United Nations Development Programme 2006).

Given such water shortages, it should not come as a surprise that water is now a highly contested commodity in many parts of the world. In the United States, competition over water is intense, especially in booming Las Vegas and the Southwest. In the Middle East, the immense political challenges posed by ethnic and religious conflict are often complicated by battles over water. There, competing nations accuse each other of taking unfair advantage

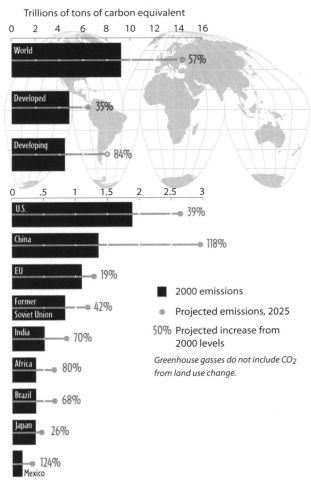

## *Going* GLOBAL

### Projected Emissions of Greenhouse Gases, 2025

Trillions of tons of carbon equivalent

| | 0 | 2 | 4 | 6 | 8 | 10 | 12 | 14 | 16 |

World ● 57%
Developed ● 35%
Developing ● 84%

| | 0 | .5 | 1 | 1.5 | 2 | 2.5 | 3 |

U.S. ● 39%
China ● 118%
EU ● 19%
Former Soviet Union ● 42%
India ● 70%
Africa ● 80%
Brazil ● 68%
Japan ● 26%
Mexico ● 124%

■ 2000 emissions
● Projected emissions, 2025
50% Projected increase from 2000 levels

*Greenhouse gasses do not include CO₂ from land use change.*

In 2000, the United States was the largest emitter of $CO_2$ from fossil fuels. China is expected to take the lead by 2025.

*Source:* Baumert 2005.

of existing water supplies, and water tanks are a likely target for both military forces and terrorists (Carmichael 2007).

## GLOBAL WARMING

The scientific evidence for global warming is clear, consistent, and compelling, yet we continue to struggle with how seriously we should take it. "Global warming" refers to the significant rise in the earth's surface temperatures that occurs when industrial gases like carbon dioxide turn the planet's atmosphere into a virtual greenhouse. Even one additional degree of warmth in the globe's average surface temperature can increase the likelihood of wildfires, shrinkage of rivers and lakes, expansion of deserts, and torrential downpours, including typhoons and hurricanes. Scientists now track carbon dioxide emissions around the world and can map the current and projected $CO_2$ contribution each country makes. Such analyses show the sizable and growing contribution of the United States to the problem (Lynas 2008).

MIKELUCKOVICH ATLANTA JOURNAL-CONSTITUTION © AJC.COM 8-4-6

THAT EXPLAINS THE POLAR BEAR...

ICECAPS MELTING

Although scientific concern over global warming has heated up, climate change remains low on policy makers' list of concerns. For some politicians, the problem seems too abstract and distant. Others recognize that effective solutions demand a difficult-to-manage multinational response, and they fear that their nation may bear too much of the cost. The Kyoto Protocol was intended to provide a unified response in which the nations of the world would take collective responsibility to reduce global emissions of greenhouse gases. To date, 169 countries have signed the accord, but the United States, which produces 24 percent of the world's carbon dioxide, has failed to ratify it. Opponents of the protocol argue that doing so would place the nation at a disadvantage in the global marketplace (Landler 2005; United Nations Development Programme 2007:59).

We can again draw on world systems analysis when it comes to seeing who pays the highest price for global warming. Historically, core nations have been the major emitters of greenhouse gases. Today, much manufacturing has moved to semiperiphery and periphery nations, where greenhouse gas emissions are escalating. Ironically, many of those who are now calling for a reduction in the human activity that contributes to global warming are located in core nations, which have contributed disproportionately to the problem. We want our hamburgers, but we decry the destruction of the rain forests to create grazing land for cattle. We want inexpensive clothes and toys, but we condemn developing countries for depending on coal-fired power plants, the number of which are expected to in-

# Estimated Time for Each Successive Increase of 1 Billion People in World Population

| Population Level | Time taken to reach new population level | Year of Attainment |
|---|---|---|
| First billion | Human history before 1800 | 1804 |
| Second billion | 123 years | 1927 |
| Third billion | 32 years | 1959 |
| Fourth billion | 15 years | 1974 |
| Fifth billion | 13 years | 1987 |
| Sixth billion | 12 years | 1999 |
| Seventh billion | 13 years | 2012 |
| Eighth billion | 14 years | 2026 |
| Ninth billion | 17 years | 2043 |

*Source:* Bureau of the Census 2008b.

crease 46 percent by 2030. The challenge of global warming, then, is closely tied to global inequality (M. Jenkins 2008; J. Roberts et al. 2003).

One of the primary factors causing this global environmental crisis is the rise in global population (Ehrlich and Ehrlich 1990). As of July 2008, there were 6.7 billion people on the planet, an increase of 1.7 billion since 1987. To put this in terms of the human ecology model, the more people there are on the planet, the more resources we need to use to sustain them, the more waste they produce that we must process, and the more strain we place on our capacity to house us all (Ehrlich 1968; Ehrlich and Ehrlich 1990; Ehrlich and Ellison 2002).

Technological advances also contribute to increased environmental concerns. At least since the Industrial Revolution and the invention of the steam engine, the automobile, coal-burning power plants, and more, the environmental effects of technological innovation have been extreme. Biologist Barry Commoner argues that additional contributors to the probem include plastics, detergents, synthetic fibers, pesticides, herbicides, and chemical fertilizers. We appreciate the lifestyles that such innovations allow us to experience, but we pay a significant price for their benefits (Commoner 1971, 1990).

## THE GLOBAL RESPONSE

Globalization can be both good and bad for the environment. On the negative side, it can create a race to the bottom, as polluting companies relocate to countries with less stringent environmental standards. Also of concern is that globalization allows multinationals to exploit the resources of developing countries for short-term profit. From Mexico to China, the industrialization that often accompanies globalization has increased pollution of all types.

Yet globalization can have a positive impact as well. As barriers to the international movement of goods, services, and people fall, multinational corporations have an incentive to carefully consider the cost of natural resources.

## Percentage of People Citing Pollution and Environmental Problems as a Top Global Threat

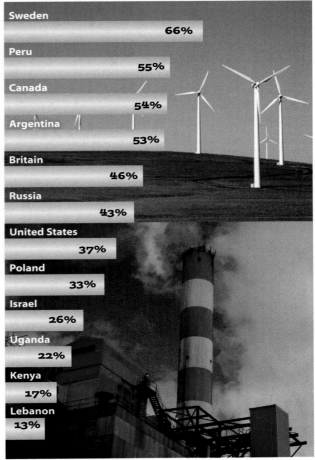

| | |
|---|---|
| Sweden | 66% |
| Peru | 55% |
| Canada | 54% |
| Argentina | 53% |
| Britain | 46% |
| Russia | 43% |
| United States | 37% |
| Poland | 33% |
| Israel | 26% |
| Uganda | 22% |
| Kenya | 17% |
| Lebanon | 13% |

*Source:* Pew Research Center 2007b.

Overusing or wasting resources makes little sense, especially when they are in danger of depletion (Kwong 2005). Perhaps, as Émile Durkheim might have argued long ago, by recognizing the negative effects of our global expansion, along with our mutual interdependence, we will take the steps necessary to bring about positive social change.

There are signs that individuals, countries, and corporations are beginning to understand and appreciate our interdependence. In response, individuals are taking greater responsibility for their global impact by recycling and switching to fluorescent light bulbs. Increasing numbers of corporations are "going green" and even finding profits in doing so. Sociology helps us to better see the ways we are interconnected by highlighting the significance of the system as a whole, as well as raising awareness about the inequalities that are a consequence of the global system we have constructed. Such analysis can prepare us to more effectively respond to the global challenges we face.

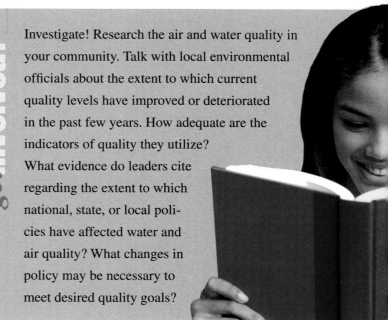

*get involved!*

Investigate! Research the air and water quality in your community. Talk with local environmental officials about the extent to which current quality levels have improved or deteriorated in the past few years. How adequate are the indicators of quality they utilize? What evidence do leaders cite regarding the extent to which national, state, or local policies have affected water and air quality? What changes in policy may be necessary to meet desired quality goals?

# For
# REVIEW

I. **What does sociology contribute to something as seemingly biological as health?**

- Our understanding of what counts as health and illness is shaped by the society to which we belong. Similarly, control over resources shapes our likelihood of exposure to illness and our access to health care.

II. **What is social epidemiology?**

- Social epidemiology involves the study of factors that shape the health status of various groups within a population. In the United States and elsewhere, social class, race and ethnicity, gender, and age all have an impact.

III. **What environmental lessons do we learn from sociology?**

- The natural environment represents our human home, within which all social interaction occurs, and the way we organize our social relations shapes the impact we have on the environment. Countries that control a larger amount of resources have a bigger impact and therefore bear a greater responsibility for those effects.

# Pop Quiz

1. A disease that cannot be understood apart from its specific social context is an example of
   a. human ecology.
   b. culture-bound syndrome.
   c. the sick role.
   d. social epidemiology.

2. The expansion of medicine's domain of expertise and its assertion of absolute jurisdiction over many health care procedures are examples of
   a. labeling and power.
   b. social epidemiology.
   c. the medicalization of society.
   d. human ecology.

3. Which one of the following nations has the lowest infant mortality rate?
   a. the United States
   b. Sierra Leone
   c. Canada
   d. Japan

4. Compared with Whites, Blacks have higher death rates from
   a. heart disease.
   b. diabetes.
   c. cancer.
   d. all of the above.

5. The age group that is most likely to be covered by some form of health insurance is
   a. under 18.
   b. 18–34.
   c. 35–64.
   d. 65 and older.

6. Which program is essentially a compulsory health insurance plan for the elderly?
   a. Medicaid
   b. Blue Cross
   c. Medicare
   d. HealthPac

7. Not counting prayer, what percentage of Americans reported using some form of complementary or alternative medicine in a 2002 survey?
   a. 17
   b. 36
   c. 62
   d. 84

8. The sociological perspective that emphasizes the interrelationships between people and their environment is known as
   a. human ecology.
   b. resource allocation.
   c. environmental justice.
   d. labeling theory.

9. The industrialized nations of North America and Europe account for 12 percent of the world's population. What percentage of worldwide consumption are they responsible for?
   a. 15 percent
   b. 30 percent
   c. 45 percent
   d. 60 percent

10. What is the international treaty that sought to reduce global emissions of greenhouse gases?
    a. the Valdez Treaty
    b. the Kyoto Protocol
    c. the Port Huron Statement
    d. the Gore Accord

1. (b); 2. (c); 3. (d); 4. (d); 5. (d); 6. (c); 7. (b); 8. (a); 9. (d); 10. (b)

15

SOCIAL CH

## CHANGING THE WORLD ONE CAMPUS AT A TIME

In the summer of 1964, college students traveled to Mississippi to change the world. As volunteers in Freedom Summer, their goal was to make a difference in the lives of African Americans who had been systematically denied the right to vote, quality education, and legal and political representation. The volunteers—mostly upper-middle-class White students from northern colleges—registered Black voters, established Freedom Schools, and provided legal advice and medical assistance. By the end of the summer, they had registered 17,000 voters and taught 3000 children. In 1964, 6.7 percent of voting age African Americans in Mississippi were registered, but by 1967, 66.5 percent were (Colby 1986; McAdam 1988).

From April 18 to May 8, 2001, students at Harvard University occupied Massachusetts Hall, the location of the president's and provost's offices, as part of their Living Wage Campaign. The city of Cambridge, where Harvard is located, had passed a living wage ordinance ensuring a minimum wage of $10 per hour, adjustable for inflation. Students argued that a school with a multibillion-dollar endowment could do better than the $6.50 many employees were receiving. After numerous attempts at negotiation, students decided to make a statement. During the sit-in, students organized daily pickets and rallies involving thousands of people. After three weeks, the administration agreed to establish a committee to implement living wage principles (Progressive Student Labor Movement 2008).

In January 2007, students at Middlebury College in Vermont convinced their board of trustees to invest in an $11 million biomass power plant and pushed officials to attain net carbon neutrality on campus. Catherine McEachern, who is involved in a similar student movement at Cornell University in New York, says, "Global warming has been neglected by the previous generation, and we see it as an injustice that needs to be changed" (James 2008).

College students continue to fight for and bring about significant change on campuses around the world. Max Weber argued that all of us have the potential power to change our worlds. In fact, change will happen whether we like it or not. A key question is this: Will we be active agents seeking the change we desire or passive recipients who accept the change enacted by others?

# As You READ

>>

- How and why does social change happen?
- What factors shape the success of a social movement?
- What does it mean to practice sociology?

## >> Global Social Change

We are at a truly dramatic era in history in terms of global social change. Within the past two decades, we have witnessed the computer revolution and the explosion of Internet connectivity; the collapse of communism; major regime changes and severe economic disruptions in Africa, the Middle East, and Eastern Europe; the spread of AIDS; the first verification of the cloning of a complex animal, Dolly the sheep; and the first major terrorist attack on U.S. soil. Today we continue to face global challenges including international terrorism, skyrocketing energy costs, and global warming along with other environmental threats.

**social change** Significant alteration over time in behavior patterns and culture, including norms and values.

The transformation of society has been a fundamental concern of sociologists from the very beginning. At the time of sociology's birth, social life was undergoing dramatic change. The taken-for-granted norms and values that made sense in a traditional agricultural society no longer fit with the lived experience of most people. The Industrial Revolution, the rise of capitalism, and the transformation from aristocratic to democratic rule all challenged traditional practices and beliefs. Sociological theory and research provide us with tools that allow us to make sense of where we are now and where we are headed.

The collapse of communist regimes in the former Soviet Union and the nations of Eastern Europe in the late 1980s and early 1990s, for example, took many people by surprise. Yet prior to the collapse, sociologist Randall Collins (1986, 1995) had observed a crucial sequence of events that most observers missed. Long before it happened, Collins had argued that Soviet expansionism had resulted in an overextension of resources, including disproportionate spending on the military. Such overextension strains a regime's stability. Moreover, geopolitical theory suggests that nations in the middle of a geographic region, such as the Soviet Union, tend to fragment into smaller units over time. Collins predicted that the confluence of social crises on several frontiers would precipitate the collapse of the Soviet Union.

History ultimately followed the path Collins predicted it might. In 1979, the success of the Iranian revolution spurred an upsurge of Islamic fundamentalism in nearby Afghanistan, as well as in Soviet republics with substantial Muslim populations. At the same time, resistance to communist rule was growing both throughout Eastern Europe and within the Soviet Union itself. In addition, as Collins predicted, a dissident form of communism arose within the Soviet Union, facilitating the breakdown of the regime. Beginning in the late 1980s, Soviet leader Mikhail Gorbachev chose not to use military power and other types of repression to crush dissidents in Eastern Europe. Instead, he offered plans for democratization and social reform of Soviet society, and he seemed willing to reshape the Soviet Union into a loose federation of somewhat autonomous states. In 1991,

### Did You Know?

. . . In the mid-1980s, the Soviet Union was spending as much as 25 percent of its annual gross domestic product on the military while the United States was spending about 6 percent. By 1997, well after the collapse of the USSR, Russia's spending had fallen to about one-tenth of that amount. Currently, the United States spends more on national defense than does the rest of the world combined, which represents approximately 4 percent of its GDP.

six republics on the western periphery declared their independence, and within months, the entire Soviet Union had formally disintegrated into Russia and a number of other independent nations.

Sociology helps us to understand such shifts by paying attention both to large-scale, or macro, shifts that alter the basic landscape of society and the relationships among groups, and to the small-scale, or micro, changes in social interaction within which decisions are made that can alter the course of history. We construct society through our everyday actions. As such, we have the power to change society by altering the choices we make. Of course, some people, due to their control over valued resources, have more power than do others. Sociology can better focus our attention so that we might understand which direction change might follow.

## >> Sociological Perspectives on Social Change

As humans, we are creative beings. We continually innovate and experiment, developing new technologies, ideas, and ways of doing things. Each of these represents an example of **social change,** which involves significant alteration over time in behavior patterns and culture. Social change can occur so slowly as to be almost undetectable to those it affects, but it can also happen with breathtaking rapidity. In the past century or so, for example, the U.S. population has more than doubled, the percentage of people finishing high school and attending college has skyrocketed, women have entered the paid labor force in significant numbers, life ex-

# The United States: A Changing Nation

| Population | 1850 | 1940 | 1950 | 2010 |
|---|---|---|---|---|
| Total in millions | 23.2 | 132.1 | 180.7 | 308.9 |
| Percentage under age 15 | 41% | 25% | 31% | 20% |
| **Education** | **1850** | **1940** | **1960** | **2005** |
| Percentage not completing high school | 88% | 18% | 13% | 15% |
| Percentage ages 19–24 enrolled in higher education | < 1% | 8% | 40% | 46% |
| **Labor Force Participation** | **1850** | **1940** | **1960** | **2005** |
| Men working in their 20s | 94% | 88% | 86% | 86% |
| Women working in their 20s | 22% | 39% | 74% | 72% |
| **Health** | **1850** | **1940** | **1960** | **2010** |
| Physicians per 100,000 population | 176 | 133 | 150 | 265 |
| Life expectancy at birth, in years | 38 | 63 | 70 | 78.5 |
| **Technology** | **1870** | **1940** | **1960** | **2005** |
| Copyrights issued | 5,600 | 176,997 | 243,926 | 157,700 |
| Patents issued | 12,127 | 42,238 | 47,170 | 121,600 |
| **Family** | **1890** | **1940** | **1960** | **2006** |
| Median age at first marriage | | | | |
| Men | 26 | 24 | 23 | 28 |
| Women | 22 | 22 | 20 | 26 |
| Number of children born per family | 3.25 | 2.7 | 3.65 | 2.04 |

*Note:* Data are comparable, although definitions vary. Definition of the United States changes between 1850 and 1940 and between 1940 and 1960. Earliest date for children born per family is 1905.

*Source:* U.S. Census Bureau 2007.

SOCstudies

pectancy has risen, technological innovation has exploded, men and women have been marrying later, and family size has shrunk. In our global, interdependent world, there is no reason to suspect that such changes will cease, and many future changes will be difficult to predict.

Explaining social change is clearly a challenge in the diverse and complex world we inhabit. Nevertheless, theo-

simple to more complex forms of social organization. Both believed that by gaining an understanding of the principles of order and change in such societies, we would be able to more effectively shape the direction our modern, more complex societies would take.

Since that time, we have learned that the idea that societies will follow a singular path from simple to complex,

> ## All change is not growth, as all movement is not forward.
>
> Ellen Glasgow

rists from several disciplines have sought to analyze social change. In some instances, they have examined historical events to arrive at a better understanding of contemporary changes. We will look at change from three perspectives so that we might better identify issues we should include when considering how and why change happens.

## THE EVOLUTION OF SOCIETIES

One approach to understanding how societies change draws upon the principle of evolution. It was inspired, in part, by Charles Darwin's (1809–1882) work on the biological evolution of species. Darwin's approach stresses a continuing progression of successive generations of life forms as they adapt to their environment. For example, human beings came at a later stage of evolution than reptiles and represent a more complex form of life. Social theorists seeking an analogy to this biological model proposed **evolutionary theory,** in which society is viewed as moving in a definite direction. Early evolutionary theorists generally agreed that society was progressing from the simple to the complex, which they assumed was superior.

Early sociologists and anthropologists believed it was possible to study what they referred to at that time as simple or "primitive" societies for clues about the essential building blocks that serve as the foundation for all societies. August Comte (1798–1857), a founder of sociology, was an evolutionary theorist of change. He saw human societies as moving forward in their thinking, from mythology to the scientific method. Similarly, Émile Durkheim ([1893]1933) maintained that society progressed from

from primitive to modern, is flawed. The notion that traditional societies are simple or primitive has proven to be both incorrect and ethnocentric. Such societies demonstrate significant levels of sophistication and innovation, in terms of both social relations and technological adaptation to their environments. In addition, there is no single path of social evolution that all societies must pass through. Social change can impact one area of social life, such as politics, while leaving other areas of life relatively unchanged, such as work and the economy. For example, a society might move toward a democratic form of government, but the traditional nature of work, primarily small-scale and agricultural, might stay the same.

Though there are limits to the evolutionary model of social change, it does provide a helpful metaphor when thinking about how change happens. For example, we can look to past practices to better understand where new ways of thinking and acting come from. In addition, it highlights the role that context or environment plays in shaping change. In biology, when the environment changes, mutations in species can occur, making them more fit to survive in that new context than were past generations. For Darwin, however, this did not mean that the new was superior to the old; it was simply more likely that the new would survive given changed environmental circumstances. The danger when applying this analogy to society is to assume that those who adapt to changed circumstances are superior. The truth is that all societies must adapt to change. Sometimes it comes fast and is thus easier to recognize, and other times it is gradual. Sometimes that change comes from within, and other times it is a product of environmental forces, whether social or natural.

## SOCthink

> > > Why would early theorists have thought of traditional societies as "primitive"? How is this a reflection of the evolutionary theoretical paradigm they adopted?

## EQUILIBRIUM AND SOCIAL ORDER

Another approach to understanding social change is rooted in the principle that societies naturally seek to attain stability or balance. Any social change that occurs represents necessary adjustments as society seeks to return to that state of equilibrium. For example, sociologist Talcott Parsons (1902–1979), an advocate of this approach, viewed even prolonged labor strikes or civilian riots as temporary disruptions in the status quo rather than as significant alterations in the social structure. According to his **equilibrium model,** as changes occur in one part of society, adjustments must be made in other parts. If not, society's equilibrium will be threatened, and strains will occur.

Parsons (1966) maintained that four processes of social change are inevitable. The first, differentiation, refers to the increasing complexity of social organization. We see this in the form of job specialization as is evident in more bureaucratic systems. The transition from a healer—a

## 5 Movies on SOCIAL MOVEMENTS AND SOCIAL CHANGE

**Ghandi**
*His story.*

**Erin Brockovich**
*How one person can affect major business.*

**Norma Rae**
*Union! Union!*

**V for Vendetta**
*One man defeats a totalitarian government.*

**Miracle**
*How a game of hockey brought about the symbolic end of the Cold War.*

single person who handles all your health care needs—to a series of positions, including physician, anesthetist, nurse, and pharmacist, is an illustration of differentiation in the field of medicine. This process is accompanied by adaptive upgrading, in which social institutions become more specialized in their purposes. The division of physicians into obstetricians, internists, surgeons, and so forth is an example of adaptive upgrading.

The third process Parsons identified is the inclusion of groups that were previously excluded because of their gender, race, ethnicity, and social class. Recently, medical schools have practiced inclusion by admitting increasing numbers of women and African Americans. Finally, Parsons contended that societies experience value generalization—the development of new values that legitimate a broader range of activities. The acceptance of preventive and alternative medicine is an example of value generalization: Society has broadened its view of health care. All four processes identified by Parsons stress consensus—societal agreement on the nature of social organization and values (B. Johnson 1975; Wallace and Wolf 1980).

## SOCthink

> > > Why might the equilibrium model have a difficult time addressing issues such as inequality and poverty as social problems to be solved?

One of the sources of potential strain that can lead to such social adaptation involves technological innovation. For example, sociologist William F. Ogburn (1922) distinguished between material and nonmaterial aspects of culture. Material culture includes inventions, artifacts, and technology; nonmaterial culture encompasses ideas, norms, communications, and social organization. Ogburn pointed out that technology often changes faster than do the ideas and values with which we make sense of such change. Thus, the nonmaterial culture typically must respond to changes in the material culture. Ogburn introduced the term **culture lag** to refer to the period of adjustment when the nonmaterial culture is still struggling to adapt to new material conditions. One example is the Internet. Its rapid uncontrolled growth raises questions about whether to regulate it, and if so, how much.

In certain cases, the changes in the material culture can strain the relationships between social institutions. For example, new means of birth control have been developed in recent decades. Large families are no longer economically necessary, nor are they commonly endorsed by social norms. But certain religious faiths, among them Roman Catholicism, continue to extol large families and to disapprove methods of limiting family size, such as contraception and abortion. This issue represents a lag between aspects of the material culture (technology) and nonmaterial culture (religious beliefs). Conflicts may also emerge between religion and other social institutions, such as government and the educational system, over the dissemination of birth control and family-planning information (M. Riley et al. 1994a, 1994b).

From Parsons's point of view, such tensions represent little more than normal adjustments needed to maintain the inevitable balance that is the natural state of all societies. Though his approach explicitly incorporates the evolutionary notion of continuing progress, the dominant theme in this model is stability. Society may change, but it remains stable through new forms of integration. For example, in place of the kinship ties that provided social cohesion in the past, people develop laws, judicial processes, and new values and belief systems. Parsons and other theorists would argue that those parts of society that

**evolutionary theory** A theory of social change that holds that society is moving in a definite direction.
**equilibrium model** The view that society tends toward a state of stability or balance.
**culture lag** A period of adjustment when the nonmaterial culture is still struggling to adapt to new material conditions.

persist, even including crime, terrorism, and poverty, do so because they contribute to social stability. Critics note, however, that his approach virtually disregards the use of coercion by the powerful to maintain the illusion of a stable, well-integrated society (Gouldner 1960).

## RESOURCES, POWER, AND CHANGE

Such theories are helpful, but it is not enough to look at change as part of the natural evolution or equilibrium of societies. Some groups in society, because they control valued resources, are able either to inhibit or to facilitate social change more effectively than are others. Although Karl Marx, for example, accepted the evolutionary argument that societies develop along a particular path, he did not view each successive stage as an inevitable improvement over the previous one. History, according to Marx, proceeds through a series of stages, and within each stage, those who control the means of production exploit an entire class of people. Thus, ancient society exploited slaves, the estate system of feudalism exploited serfs, and modern capitalist society exploits the working class. Ultimately, through a socialist revolution led by the proletariat, human society would move toward the final stage of development: a classless communist society, or "community of free individuals," as Marx described it in 1867 in *Das Kapital* (see Bottomore and Rubel 1956:250).

> **vested interests** Those people or groups who will suffer in the event of social change and who have a stake in maintaining the status quo.
> **technology** Cultural information about how to use the material resources of the environment to satisfy human needs and desires.

Marx argued that conflict is a normal and desirable aspect of social change. In fact, change must be encouraged as a means of eliminating social inequality. In his view, people are not restricted to a passive role in responding to inevitable cycles or changes in the material culture. Rather, Marxist theory offers a tool for those who wish to seize control of the historical process and gain their freedom from injustice (Lauer 1982). Efforts to promote social change are, however, likely to meet with resistance.

Certain individuals and groups have a stake in maintaining the existing state of affairs. Social economist Thorstein Veblen (1857–1929) coined the term **vested interests** to refer to those people or groups who will suffer in the event of social change. For example, the American Medical Association (AMA) has taken strong stands against national health insurance and the professionalization of midwifery. National health insurance could lead to limits on physicians' income, and a rise in the status of midwives could threaten the preeminent position of doctors as deliverers of babies. In general, those with a disproportionate share of society's wealth, status, and power, such as members of the AMA, have a vested interest in preserving the status quo (Starr 1982; Veblen 1919).

Economic factors play an important role in resistance to social change. For example, it can be expensive for manufacturers to meet mandated standards for the safety of products and workers and for the protection of the environment. In the pursuit of both profit and survival, many firms seek to avoid the costs of meeting strict safety and environmental standards. If they have sufficient power in society, they can effectively pass the costs of such practices on to others who must bear the consequences. To battle against such influence requires a countervailing source of power. Government regulations, for example, force all companies to bear the common burden of such costs, and labor unions can present the unified power of workers as a group.

Communities, too, protect their vested interests, often in the name of "protecting property values." The abbreviation NIMBY stands for "not in my backyard," a cry often heard when people protest landfills, prisons, nuclear power facilities, and even bike trails and group homes for people with developmental disabilities. The targeted community may not challenge the need for the facility, but may simply insist that it be located elsewhere. The NIMBY attitude has become so common that it is almost impossible for policy makers to find acceptable locations for facilities such as hazardous waste dumps. Unfortunately, it is often those

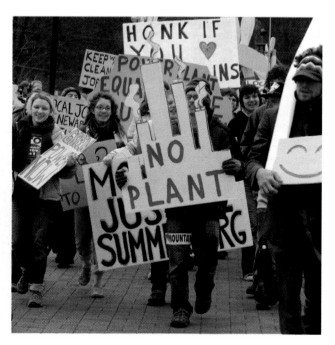

with the fewest resources who end up on the losing end of such battles (Jasper 1997).

In today's world, change is inevitable. From sociology we learn that we need to watch for the ways in which change evolves out of existing practices. We also must be aware of the ways in which societies perpetuate existing social order by seeking an acceptable level of balance between stability and change. Finally, we recognize the role that power and control over resources plays in shaping what changes do or do not occur. In all these cases, because of the ways it both enables and constrains, we must be aware of the role that technology plays in affecting the nature and direction of social change.

## >> Technology and the Future

**Technology** is cultural information about how to use the material resources of the environment to satisfy human needs and desires. Technological advances—the telephone, the automobile, the airplane, the television, the atomic bomb, and more recently, the computer, digital media, and the cellular phone—have brought striking changes to our culture, our patterns of socialization, our social institutions, and our day-to-day social interactions. Technological innovations are, in fact, emerging and being accepted with remarkable speed.

In the past generation alone, industrial countries have seen a major shift in consumer technologies. We no longer buy electronic devices to last for 10 years. Increasingly, we buy them with the expectation that within three years or less, we will need to upgrade to an entirely new technology, whether it be a handheld device or a home computer. These technologies have both positive and negative consequences. They enable us to maintain contacts with friends and family around the world, but they can cut us off from the person right next to us. Take, for example, the iPod-wearing, cell-phone-talking person we encounter who barely seems to notice we exist.

## Adopting Technology

**Omnivores:** 8% of American adults constitute the most active participants in the information society, consuming information goods and services at a high rate and using them as a platform for participation and self-expression.

**The Connectors:** 7% of the adult population surround themselves with technology and use it to connect with people and digital content. They get a lot out of their mobile devices and participate actively in online life.

**Lackluster Veterans:** 8% of American adults make up a group who are not at all passionate about their abundance of modern information and communication technologies (ICTs). Few like the intrusiveness their gadgets add to their lives and not many see ICTs adding to their personal productivity.

**Productivity Enhancers:** 9% of American adults happily get a lot of things done with information technology, both at home and at work.

**Mobile Centrics:** 10% of the general population are strongly attached to their cell phones and take advantage of a range of mobile applications.

**Connected but Hassled:** 9% of American adults fit into this group. They have invested in a lot of technology, but the connectivity is a hassle for them.

**Inexperienced Experimenters:** 8% of adults have less ICT on hand than others. They feel competent in dealing with technology, and might do more with it if they had more.

**Light but Satisfied:** 15% of adults have the basics of information technology, use it infrequently, and it does not register as an important part of their lives.

**Indifferents:** 11% of adults have a fair amount of technology on hand, but it does not play a central role in their daily lives.

**Off the Net:** 15% of the population, mainly older Americans, are off the modern information network.

*Note:* From a Pew Internet and American Life Project Survey conducted in April 2006.

*Source:* Horrigan 2007:vii.

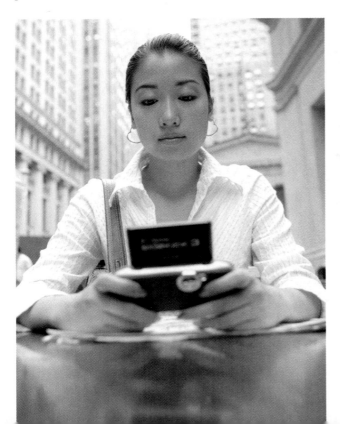

## COMPUTER TECHNOLOGY

In the past decade, computer access has gone global, and Internet access along with it. While the revolutions in transportation and communication have brought us together since the Industrial Revolution, the Internet provides a potential for immediate global connection that previously was virtually and physically impossible. In 2008, the Internet reached 1.3 billion users, compared to just 50 million in 1996.

The Internet evolved from a computer system built in 1962 by the U.S. Defense Department to enable scholars and military researchers to continue their government work, even if part of the nation's communications system were destroyed by nuclear attack. Until recently, it was difficult to gain access to the Internet without holding a position at a university or a government research laboratory. Today, however, virtually anyone with sufficient resources can reach the Internet with a phone line, a computer, and a modem. People buy and sell cars, trade stocks, auction off items, research new medical remedies, vote, and track down long-lost friends online, to mention just a few of the thousands of possibilities (Reddick and King 2000).

If we look at global Internet use, the regions with the greatest number of users are Asia and Europe. Asia alone represents approximately 400 million users. However, a larger proportion of the population in North America—over 70 percent—has access to the Internet than in any other continent. Even though Asia has the greatest number of users, only about 14 percent of the population there has Internet access. Another sign of the global nature of this expansion has been the increase in languages used on the Internet. While English continues to lead, Chinese usage increased 470 percent between 2000 and 2008 compared to only 167 percent for English (Internet World Stats 2008).

Unfortunately, a digital divide persists, and not everyone can get onto the information highway, especially not the less affluent. Moreover, this pattern of inequality is global. In Africa, for example, only 3.6 percent of the population has access to the Internet. The core nations that Immanuel Wallerstein described in his world systems analysis have a virtual monopoly on information technology; the peripheral nations of Asia, Africa, and Latin America depend on the core nations both for technology and for the information it provides. For example, North America, Europe, and a few industrialized nations in other regions

# Internet Use and Penetration by World Region

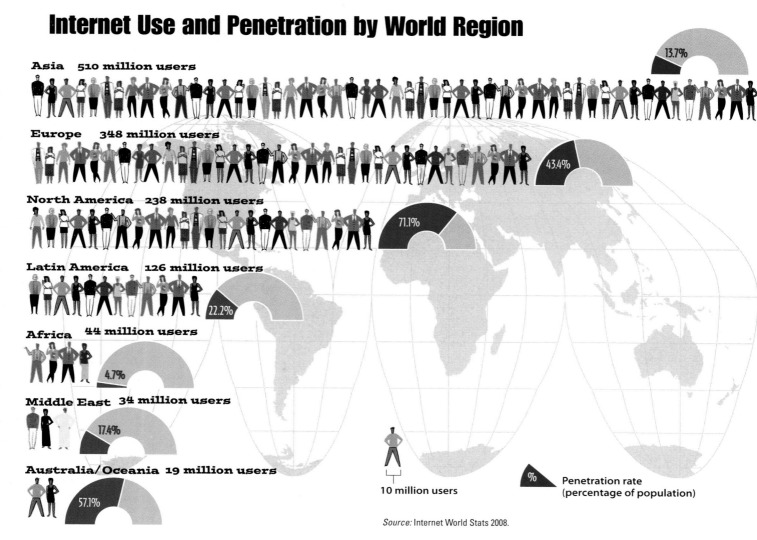

Source: Internet World Stats 2008.

possess almost all the world's Internet hosts—computers that are connected directly to the worldwide network.

One way to address this divide is to provide computing technology to those people who do not have it. The "One Laptop per Child" (OLPC) campaign seeks to do just that (http://laptop.org). In January 2005, Nicholas Negroponte of the Massachusetts Institute of Technology announced his revolutionary idea for just such a giveaway. For several years, he had been trying to develop a low-cost computer, called the XO, for the 1.2 billion children of the developing world. Negroponte's goal was to sell the laptop for $100, complete with a wireless hookup and a battery with a five-year life span. His intention was to persuade foundations and the governments of industrial countries to fund the distribution, so that the laptop would be available to the children for free. As of June 2008, OLPC had distributed almost 700,000 computers around the world to children in Peru, Haiti, Cambodia, Mexico, Rwanda, Iraq, and more.

## SOCthink

> > > From a purely business point of view, what would be the pros and cons of giving a free XO to every needy child in the developing world? Would the social benefits of doing so outweigh the business costs and benefits?

## PRIVACY AND CENSORSHIP IN A GLOBAL VILLAGE

In addition to the digital divide, sociologists have also raised concerns about threats to privacy and the possibility of censorship. Recent advances have made it increasingly easy for business firms, government agencies, and even criminals to retrieve and store information about everything from our buying habits to our Web-surfing pat-

## Internet Top 10 Languages

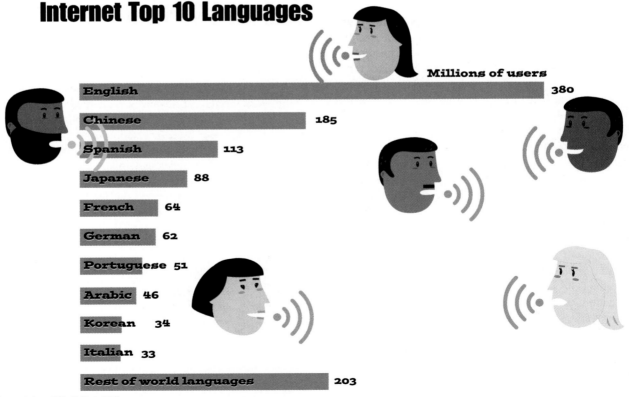

**Millions of users**

| Language | Millions of users |
|---|---|
| English | 380 |
| Chinese | 185 |
| Spanish | 113 |
| Japanese | 88 |
| French | 64 |
| German | 62 |
| Portuguese | 51 |
| Arabic | 46 |
| Korean | 34 |
| Italian | 33 |
| Rest of world languages | 203 |

*Source:* Internet World Stats 2008.

terns. In public places, at work, and on the Internet, surveillance devices now track our every move, be it a keystroke or an ATM withdrawal. As technology spreads, so does the exposure to risk. In 2006, for example, the theft of a laptop computer from the home of an employee of the Veterans' Administration compromised the names, social security numbers, and dates of birth of up to 26.5 million veterans.

At the same time that these innovations have increased others' power to monitor our behavior, they have raised fears that they might be misused for undemocratic purposes. In short, new technologies threaten not just our privacy but our freedom from surveillance and censorship (O'Harrow, Jr. 2005). There is, for example, the danger that the most powerful groups in a society will use technology to violate the privacy of the less powerful. Indeed, officials in the People's Republic of China have attempted to censor online discussion groups and web postings that criticize the government. Civil liberties advocates remind us that the same abuses can occur in the United States if citizens are not vigilant in protecting their right to privacy (Magnier 2004).

In the United States, legislation regulating the surveillance of electronic communications has not always upheld citizens' right to privacy. In 1986, the federal government passed the Electronic Communications Privacy Act, which outlawed the surveillance of telephone calls except with the permission of both the U.S. attorney general and a federal judge. Telegrams, faxes, and email did not receive the same degree of protection, however. In 2001, one month after the terrorist attacks of September 11, Congress passed the USA PATRIOT Act, which relaxed existing legal checks on surveillance by law enforcement officers. Federal agencies are now freer to gather data electronically, including credit card receipts and banking records (Eckenwiler 1995).

If anything, however, people seem to be less vigilant today about maintaining their privacy than they were prior to the information age. Young people who have grown up browsing the Internet seem to accept the existence of the "cookies" and "spyware" they may pick up while surfing. They have become accustomed to adult surveillance of their conversations in electronic chat rooms. Many see no risk in providing personal information about themselves to the strangers they meet online. Such attitudes represent a shift from the fears that sharing such information opens one up to risk (Turkle 2004).

## BIOTECHNOLOGY AND THE GENE POOL

Another field in which technological advances have spurred global social change is biotechnology. Sex selection of fetuses, genetically engineered organisms, the cloning of animals—these have been among the significant yet controversial scientific advances in the field of biotechnology in recent years. No phase of life now seems exempt from therapeutic or medical intervention. In fact, sociologists view many aspects of biotechnology as as an extension of the recent trend toward the medicalization of society. Through genetic manipulation, the medical profession is expanding its turf still further (Clarke et al. 2003).

One area of genetic modification that has raised concern involves genetically modified (GM) food. This issue arose in Europe but has since spread to other parts of the world, including the United States. The idea behind the technology is to increase food production and make agriculture more efficient and economical. But critics use the term *frankenfood* (as in Frankenstein) to refer to everything from breakfast cereals

# Cloning Milestones

**Dolly,** Sheep Feb. '97

**Cumulina,** Mouse Oct. '97

**Mira,** Goat Oct. '98

**Gene,** Calf Aug. '97

**Millie, Christa, Alexis, Carrel, & Dotcom,** Piglets Mar. '00

**CC,** Cat Dec. '01

**Taz,** Mule **Dewey,** Deer **Prometea,** Horse May '03

**Ralph,** Rat Sep. '03

**Snuppy,** Dog Aug. '05

1997　1998　1999　2000　2001　2002　2003　2004　2005

made from genetically engineered grains to "fresh" GM tomatoes. Members of the antibiotech movement object to tampering with nature and are concerned about the possible health effects of GM food. Supporters of GM food include not just biotech companies but those who see the technology as a way to help feed the growing populations of Africa and Asia (Golden 1999; Schurman 2004).

Even as the genetic modification of plants continues to be a concern, the debate about the genetic manipulation of animals escalated in 1997 when scientists in Scotland announced that they had cloned a sheep, which they named Dolly. After many unsuccessful attempts, they were finally able to replace the genetic material of a sheep's egg with DNA from an adult sheep, creating a lamb that was a clone of the adult. Shortly thereafter, Japanese researchers successfully cloned cows. Since then many other species have been successfully cloned (see the timeline above), and it is now even possible to get your pet cat or dog cloned. Such accomplishments point to the possibility that in the near future, scientists may be able to clone human beings.

Manipulation that goes even further than cloning involves potentially altering species through genetic engineering. Fish and plant genes have already been mixed to create frost-resistant potato and tomato crops. More recently, human genes have been implanted in pigs to provide humanlike kidneys for organ transplants. Geneticists working with mouse fetuses have managed to disable genes that carry an undesirable trait and replace them with genes carrying a desirable trait. Such advances raise staggering possibilities for altering animal and human life forms (Kolata 1999). But they also raise ethical concerns related to applying such engineering to humans to eliminate disease or infirmities or to enhance physical abilities such as sight or strength.

Today's biotechnology holds itself out as totally beneficial to human beings, but it is in constant need of monitoring. Biotechnological advances have raised many difficult ethical and political questions. Among them is the desirability of tinkering with the gene pool, which could alter our environment in unexpected and unwanted ways (D. Weinstein and Weinstein 1999). William F. Ogburn probably could not have anticipated such scientific developments when he wrote about culture lag 70 years earlier.

### RESISTANCE TO TECHNOLOGY

Given such consequences, it should come as no surprise that, through the ages, there have been those who questioned whether such technological innovation equals progress. Inventions that grew out of the Industrial Revolution, for example, led to strong resistance in some countries. In England, beginning in 1811, masked craft workers took extreme measures: They mounted nighttime raids on factories and destroyed some of the new machinery. The government hunted these rebels, known as **Luddites,** and ultimately banished or hanged them. In a similar effort in France, angry workers threw their wooden shoes *(sabots)* into factory machinery to destroy it, giving rise to the term *sabotage.* While the resistance of the Luddites and the French workers was short-lived and unsuccessful, they have come to symbolize resistance to technology.

It would be a mistake, however, to simply dismiss their actions as antitechnology. Their primary concern was with the impact such technology had on their employment, their communities, and their way of life. They recognized that it would undercut taken-for-granted norms and values and fought against such threats. Today we often uncritically adopt the latest technologies without taking time to

**Hot or Not?**

If you could modify your children's genes to protect them from genetic diseases, would you do it? How about enhance abilities such as eyesight, strength, or intelligence?

# Five Questions to Ask When Adopting New Technology

- What is the problem to which this technology is the solution?

- Whose problem is it?

- What new problems might be created because we solve the problem?

- Which people and institutions might be most seriously harmed?

- Which people and institutions might acquire special economic and political power?

*Source:* Postman 1988.

# From Me to You

*I confess to having mixed emotions about technology. I love my iPhone, but worry about the consequences such technologies have on community and the environment. One of the first sociologists who had a significant influence on me was Jacques Ellul. In college I read his book* The Technological Society, *which raised questions not so much about technology itself, but about the way technological approaches to nature, objects, and each other—what he referred to as "technique"—shaped how we thought and what we did. While technology can enhance communication, might it be that our quest for efficiency and productivity undercuts community and relationships?*

**TECHNOLOGY AND SOCIETY**

step back and ask what consequences they have for social order and meaning.

Just as the Luddites resisted the Industrial Revolution, people in many countries today continue to resist postindustrial technological changes. The term *neo-Luddites* refers to those who are wary of technological innovations and who question the incessant expansion of industrialization, the increasing destruction of the natural and agrarian world, and the "throw-it-away" mentality of contemporary capitalism with its resulting pollution of the environment. Whether it is TiVo, the iPhone, or even the latest microwave oven or digital camera, many consumers are critical of these so-called must-have items. Neo-Luddites insist that whatever the presumed benefits of industrial and postindustrial technology, such technology has distinctive social costs and may represent a danger to the future of both the human species and the planet (Bauerlein 1996; Rifkin 1995; Sale 1996; Snyder 1996).

## >> Social Movements

We do have the power to resist change even when it seems inevitable. More than that, we also have the power to bring about positive social change. Although factors such as the physical environment, population, technology, and social inequality serve as sources of change, it is the collective effort of individuals organized in social movements that ultimately leads to change. Sociologists use the term **social movements** to refer to organized collective activities to bring about or resist fundamental change in an existing group or society (Benford 1992). Herbert Blumer (1955:19) recognized the special importance of social movements when he defined them as "collective enterprises to establish a new order of life."

In many nations, including the United States, social movements have had a dramatic impact on the course of history and the evolution of the social structure. Consider the actions of abolitionists, suffragists, civil rights workers, and anti–Vietnam War activists. Members of each social movement stepped outside traditional channels for bringing about social change, yet they had a noticeable influence on public policy. In Eastern Europe, equally dramatic collective efforts helped to topple communist regimes in a largely peaceful manner, in nations that many observers had thought were "immune" to such social change (Ramet 1991).

Social movements change how we think and act. Even if they initially fail to accomplish their explicit goals, social movements can influence cultural attitudes and expectations in ways that open people up to future change. Initially, people viewed the ideas of Margaret Sanger and other early advocates of birth control as radical, yet contraceptives are now widely available in the United States. Similarly, protests—whether against the practices of multinational corporations, the unethical treatment of animals, environmental destruction, or war—challenge us to question our taken-for-granted understandings of what is happening and why. This holds true even if we never formally participate ourselves or do not fully subscribe to all the beliefs and practices of the protesters.

At least since the work of Karl Marx, sociologists have studied how and why social movements emerge. Obviously, one factor is that people become discontented with the way things are. To explain how this develops and is transformed into action, sociologists rely on two primary explanations: relative deprivation and resource mobilization.

## RELATIVE DEPRIVATION

Those members of a society who feel most frustrated with and disgruntled by social and economic conditions are not necessarily the worst off in an objective sense. Social scientists have long recognized that what is most significant is how people perceive their situation. As Marx pointed out, although the misery of the workers was important to their perception of their oppressed state, so was their position in relation to the capitalist ruling class (Marx and Engels [1847] 1955).

The term **relative deprivation** refers to the conscious feeling of a negative discrepancy between legitimate expectations and present actualities (J. Wilson 1973). In other words, things aren't as good as one hoped they would be. Such a state may be characterized by scarcity rather than a complete lack of necessities. A relatively deprived person is dissatisfied because he or she feels downtrodden relative to some appropriate reference group. Thus, blue-collar workers who live in two-family houses on small plots of land—though hardly destitute—may nevertheless feel deprived in comparison to corporate managers and professionals who live in lavish homes in exclusive suburbs.

In addition to the feeling of relative deprivation, however, two other elements must be present before discontent will be channeled into a social movement. First, people must feel that they have a right to their goals, that they deserve better than what they have. For example, the struggle against European colonialism in Africa intensified when growing numbers of Africans decided that it was legitimate for them to have political and economic independence. Second, the disadvantaged group must perceive that its goals cannot be attained through conventional means. This belief may or may not be correct. In any case, the group will not mobilize into a social movement unless there is a shared perception that members can end their relative deprivation only through collective action (Morrison 1971).

Critics of this approach have noted that people don't need to feel deprived to be moved to act. In addition, this approach fails to explain why certain feelings of deprivation are transformed into social movements, whereas in other, similar situations, no collective effort is made to re-

**Did You Know?**

. . . In 1916, Margaret Sanger opened a family planning and birth control clinic. Nine days later, it was raided by police, and she served 30 days in jail as a result. She was undeterred and continued working to dispense birth control information.

**Luddites** Rebellious craft workers in 19th-century England who destroyed new factory machinery as part of their resistance to the Industrial Revolution.

**social movement** An organized collective activity to bring about or resist fundamental change in an existing group or society.

**relative deprivation** The conscious feeling of a negative discrepancy between legitimate expectations and present actualities.

shape society. Consequently, in recent years, sociologists have paid increasing attention to the forces needed to bring about the emergence of social movements (Alain 1985; Finkel and Rule 1987; Orum 1989).

## RESOURCE MOBILIZATION APPROACH

It takes more than desire to start a social movement. It helps to have money, political influence, access to the media, and personnel. The term **resource mobilization** refers to the ways in which a social movement utilizes such resources. The success of a movement for change will depend in good part on what resources it has and how effectively it mobilizes them (Gamson 1989; J. Jenkins 2004).

Sociologist Anthony Oberschall (1973:199) has argued that to sustain social protest or resistance, there must be an "organizational base and continuity of leadership." As people become part of a social movement, norms develop to guide their behavior. Members of the movement may be expected to attend regular meetings of organizations, pay dues, recruit new adherents, and boycott "enemy" products or speakers. In forming a distinct identity, an emerging social movement may give rise to special language or new words for familiar terms. In recent years, social movements have been responsible for new terms of self-reference such as *Blacks* and *African Americans* (to replace *Negroes*), *senior citizens* (to replace *old folks*), *gays* (to replace *homosexuals*), and *people with disabilities* (to replace the *handicapped*).

Leadership is a central factor in the mobilization of the discontented into social movements. Often, a movement will be led by a charismatic figure, such as occurred in the civil rights movement with Dr. Martin Luther King, Jr. As Max Weber described it in 1904, charisma is that quality of an individual that sets him or her apart from ordinary people. Of course, charisma can fade abruptly, which helps to account for the fragility of certain social movements (A. Morris 2000).

Yet many social movements do persist over long periods because their leadership is well organized and ongo-

ing. Ironically, as Robert Michels (1915) noted, political movements that are fighting for social change eventually may take on some of the aspects of the bureaucracy that they were organized to protest. Leaders tend to dominate the decision-making process without directly consulting followers. The bureaucratization of social movements is not inevitable, however. More radical movements that advocate major structural change in society and embrace mass actions tend not to be hierarchical or bureaucratic (Fitzgerald and Rodgers 2000).

One of the tasks such movements face is to raise consciousness among those who would be inclined to support the movement but who may lack the language or the sense of solidarity with others to mount a systematic critique of the existing system. Marx, for example, recognized the importance of recruitment when he called on workers to become aware of their oppressed status and to develop a class consciousness. Like theorists of the resource mobilization approach, Marx held that a social movement would require leaders to sharpen the awareness of the oppressed. They would need to help workers to overcome feelings of **false consciousness**—attitudes that do not reflect workers' objective position—in order to organize a revolutionary movement.

## GENDER AND SOCIAL MOVEMENTS

Betty Friedan's publication of *The Feminine Mystique* in 1963 gave voice to a sense that many women had at the time that something was wrong, but they did not know that others felt the same way. The book alone, however, was not enough. One of the challenges faced by women's liberation activists of the late 1960s and early 1970s was to convince women that they were being deprived of their rights and of socially valued resources. Consciousness-raising groups represented a critical tool used by women's liberation activists in the 1960s and 1970s. In these groups, women gathered to discuss topics relevant to their experience in the home, at work, in politics, and more. This helped to create a popular base that contributed to significant political and social change.

Sociologists point out that gender continues to be an important element in understanding social movements. In our male-dominated society, women continue to find themselves cut off from leadership positions in social movement organizations. Though women often serve disproportionately as volunteers in these movements, their contributions are not always recognized, nor are their voices as easily heard as men's. Gender bias causes the real extent of their influence to be overlooked. Indeed, traditional examination of the sociopolitical system tends to focus on such

> I cannot say whether things will get better if we change; what I can say is they must change if they are to get better.
>
> George Christoph Lichtenberg

male-dominated corridors of power as legislatures and corporate boardrooms, to the neglect of more female-dominated domains such as households, community-based groups, and faith-based networks. But efforts to influence family values, child rearing, relationships between parents and schools, and spiritual values are clearly significant to a culture and society (Ferree and Merrill 2000; V. Taylor 1999, 2004).

Scholars of social movements now recognize that gender can affect even the way we view organized efforts to bring about or resist change. For example, an emphasis on using rationality and logic to achieve goals helps to obscure the importance of emotion in successful social movements. It would be difficult to find any movement—from labor battles to voting rights to animal rights—in which passion was not part of the consensus-building force. Yet calls for a more serious study of the role of emotion are frequently seen as applicable only to the women's movement, because emotion is traditionally thought of as being characteristics of females (Ferree and Merrill 2000; V. Taylor 1995).

## NEW SOCIAL MOVEMENTS

Beginning in the late 1960s, European social scientists observed a change in both the composition and the targets of emerging social movements. Previously, traditional social movements had focused on economic issues, often led by labor unions or by people who shared the same occupation. However, many social movements that have become active in recent decades—including the contemporary women's movement, the peace movement, and the environmental

movement—do not have the social class roots typical of the labor movements in the United States and Europe over the past century (Tilly 1993, 2004).

The term **new social movements** refers to organized collective activities that address values and social identities, as well as improvements in the quality of life. These movements may be involved in developing collective identities. Many have complex agendas that go beyond a single issue and even cross national boundaries. Educated, middle-class people are significantly represented in some of these new social movements, such as the women's movement and the movement for lesbian and gay rights.

New social movements generally do not view government as their ally in the struggle for a better society. While they typically do not seek to overthrow the government, they may criticize, protest, or harass public officials. Researchers have found that members of new social movements call into question the legitimacy of arguments made by established authorities. Even scientific or technical claims, they argue, do not simply represent objective facts, but often serve specific interests. This characteristic is especially evident in the environmental and anti–nuclear power movements, whose activists present their own experts to

**resource mobilization** The ways in which a social movement utilizes such resources as money, political influence, access to the media, and personnel.
**false consciousness** A term used by Karl Marx to describe an attitude held by members of a class that does not accurately reflect their objective position.
**new social movement** An organized collective activity that addresses values and social identities, as well as improvements in the quality of life.

## Did You Know?

**. . . Women played an active role in the civil rights movement but were often blocked from positions of leadership. Symbolizing this exclusion perhaps better than any other example was Student Nonviolent Coordinating Committee leader Stokely Carmichael's infamous line "The only position for women in SNCC is prone." Such sexism and discrimination led women to start their own organizations to fight for women's rights.**

counter those of government or big business (Garner 1996; Polletta and Jasper 2001; A. Scott 1990).

The environmental movement is one of many new social movements with a worldwide focus. In their efforts to reduce air and water pollution, curtail global warming, and protect endangered animal species, environmental activists have realized that strong regulatory measures within a single country are not sufficient. Similarly, labor union leaders and human rights advocates cannot adequately address exploitative sweatshop conditions in a developing country if a multinational corporation can simply move the factory to another country, where workers earn even less. Whereas traditional views of social movements tended to emphasize resource mobilization on a local level, new social movement theory offers a broader, global perspective on social and political activism.

### COMMUNICATION AND THE GLOBALIZATION OF SOCIAL MOVEMENTS

Although technological advances have contributed to some of the problems people in social movements have raised, new technologies also facilitate activism and social movement formation. Through global text messaging and the Internet, social activists can reach a large number of people around the world almost instantaneously, with relatively little effort and expense. The Internet's listservs, forums, and chat rooms, along with social networking sites such as Facebook and MySpace, allow organizers of social movements to enlist like-minded people without face-to-face contact or simultaneous interaction. In fact, significant social action can occur without the participants ever having met in person (Calhoun 1998; Kavada 2005).

Electronic communication strengthens a group's solidarity, allowing fledgling social movements to grow and develop faster than they might otherwise. Through the instantaneous communication that is possible over the Internet, Mexican Zapatistas and other groups of indigenous peoples can transform their cause into an international lobbying effort, and Greenpeace organizers can link environmental activists throughout the world. Thus, the face-to-face contact that once was critical to a social movement is no longer essential for recruitment and organization (Castells 1997; Niezen 2005).

Through such interaction, people are able to create virtual bonds with like-minded individuals around the world. They can tap into the collective economic, social, and cultural resources that this diverse membership controls. Through fund-raising efforts, email and letter-writing campaigns, and coordinated old-fashioned collective action, such groups are able to alter the social and political landscape. For example, in politics, so-called netroots campaigns solicit small contributions from hundreds of thousands of people to counteract the large donations from a small group of the political and economic elite (Safire 2006). Such networking possibilities have, however, raised concerns, as the Internet is also used by terrorist and hate groups to bring such like-minded individuals together.

## >> Sociology Is a Verb

Ultimately, social change happens because we begin to act in new ways. It involves our stepping off expected paths and, in doing so, creating new sets of norms. Although external changes in our technological and environmental contexts do influence social change, it still takes people willing to do things differently to bring about such shifts.

Sociology is a tool that helps open up new pathways for us. By enabling us to see things we might have missed before, it helps us to view ourselves and the world around us differently. Sociology allows us to recognize how the dis-

**SOC**think

> > > Online sites such as Changemakers.net serve as information clearinghouses and networking hubs for social activists. How might the existence of such resources shape social activism both positively and negatively?

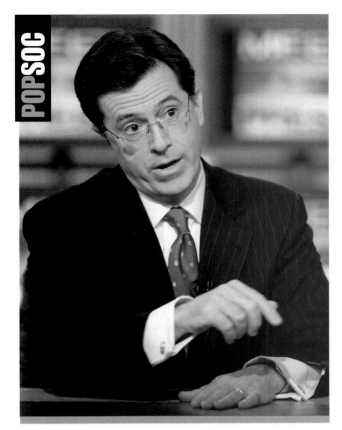

Stephen Colbert worked for several years as a sarcastic correspondent on *The Daily Show* on Comedy Central, but he became famous doing his cynical spoof of a TV talking head on his show *The Colbert Report*. He was quite serious, however, when he gave advice in a 2006 commencement speech at Knox College. He challenged students not to give in to cynicism, telling them, "Cynicism masquerades as wisdom, but it is the farthest thing from it. Because cynics don't learn anything. Because cynicism is a self-imposed blindness, a rejection of the world because we are afraid it will hurt us or disappoint us. Cynics always say 'no.' But saying 'yes' begins things. Saying 'yes' is how things grow. Saying 'yes' leads to knowledge. 'Yes' is for young people. So for as long as you have the strength to, say 'yes.'"

tribution of social, cultural, and material resources gives advantage to some and disadvantage to others. It helps us to understand whether the things we do are consistent with what we claim to believe. It can inform our conversation of whether we are headed where we want to go. It does these things by getting us to pay attention to the world around us in a new way.

We need to move from thinking of sociology as only something we learn about to thinking of sociology as something we *do*. In our daily lives, sociology can help us to better understand our own individual actions and the actions of those around us. In the context of our larger society and the world, it also enables us to better appreciate the forces at work shaping outcomes—knowledge that we can then use to act in ways that make the world a better place.

In both our personal and public lives, we need to practice sociology in the same way that doctors practice medicine.

## PERSONAL SOCIOLOGY

Sociology should be something we use in the present, in our everyday lives, to understand our beliefs and actions and to make more informed choices. We learn from sociology that we are in society and society is in us. Self and society are not two separate things. Being an individual necessitates understanding the importance of place, of position, of connection, and of interaction. Theoretically, any choice is available to us; but in reality, only limited paths are open to us.

Practicing sociology means asking uncomfortable questions and not settling for easy answers. It means considering the significance of both the individual and society, of both action and structure, of both freedom and constraint. It means recognizing the significance of power and the impact that access to material, social, and cultural resources has on the choices available to us. In short, doing **personal sociology** means recognizing the impact our individual position has on who we are and how we think and act, and taking responsibility for the impacts our actions have on others.

From the beginning, sociologists wanted to understand our constraints so that we might be able to change them. As Pierre Bourdieu put it, "To those who always tax the sociologist with determinism and pessimism, I will only say that if people became fully aware of them, conscious action aimed at controlling the structural mechanisms that engender moral failure would be possible" (1998b:56). In other words, we need to be honest with ourselves about the degree to which society limits our choices so that we might be empowered to make choices that are more informed and therefore more effective in helping us to attain our goals.

> **personal sociology** The process of recognizing the impact our individual position has on who we are and how we think and act, and of taking responsibility for the impacts our actions have on others.

As individuals, we need to see the degree to which we follow visible and invisible rules. We need to ask whether our current paths represent the values, norms, and goals that we really want to follow. As we have seen, the shows we watch, the things we buy, our likelihood for suicide, our chances of facing a wage gap, our perception of reality, our very selves—all are shaped by the positions we occupy. Understanding these influences empowers us to change.

## PUBLIC SOCIOLOGY: TOOLS FOR CHANGE

Beyond providing a more informed understanding of why we as individuals act and think the way we do, sociology calls on us to look beyond ourselves to the world around us and ask, What might we do to make the world a better place? Sociologists since the very beginning have sought

# Citizen Activities in a Democratic Society

| PRIVATE LIFE | CIVIC LIFE | |
| --- | --- | --- |
| **Individual activity** | **Civic engagement activities** | |
| | Nonpolitical activities | Political participation |
| Family<br>School<br>Work | Recycling<br>Fellowship meetings<br>Service activities | Voting<br>Attending political meetings<br>Political campaigning |
| Cultivates personal relationships, serves individual needs—e.g., getting an education, earning a living | Provides community services and acts as a training ground for political participation | Fulfills demands of democratic citizenship |

*(left margin: Functions)*

to understand and explain social processes for the purpose of shaping the future of society. **Public sociology** involves bringing the insights gained through sociological observation and analysis into the public sphere, thereby seeking to bring about positive social change. As Michael Burawoy, former president of the American Sociological Association, put it, public sociology seeks to speak to a wide audience, aiming to "enrich public debate about moral and political issues by infusing them with sociological theory and research" (Burawoy 2004:1603).

Because we construct the existing social structures through our collective and recurring actions, we bear responsibility for their consequences. Existing systems—the structure and culture we create—are not inevitable. We can choose to change them; we can act differently, as the accompanying table suggests. It can be difficult to step off the "paths of least resistance" that support the existing system (Johnson, 1997), and the consequences for action and belief that run counter to the status quo can be severe. But we can do so.

**public sociology** The process of bringing the insights gained through sociological observation and analysis into the public sphere, thereby seeking to bring about positive social change.

What we cannot do is absolve ourselves of responsibility for the systems we end up with. In fact, to not act differently is to support the existing system of inequality. As sociologist Scott Schaffer (2004) points out, we can no longer ignore practices that violate our basic beliefs, trying to wash our hands of responsibility:

> Our hands are already dirty; the question I leave here is whether our hands will be dirtied through action intended to bring concrete, actual, enacted freedom into the world, or through our choice to preserve ourselves at the cost of all others in the here and now and in the future. (pp. 271–272)

Our cynicism and resignation only reinforce systems of oppression and violence. To not act to bring about positive change still represents a choice, and our hands are dirty either way.

By helping us to see why we think and act as we do, by helping us to clarify the relationship between belief and practice, and by helping us to better understand the con-

sequences of difference, personal and public sociology can encourage discussion that can lead to a better future. We can use the tools of sociology to allow ourselves to enter into conversations in which we share our stories with others (both positive and negative), clarifying places where we agree and disagree, and opening ourselves up to our blind spots. We often want to avoid uncomfortable conflict, opting instead for polite discourse, but to fail to be more genuinely engaged in our cultural and structural differences virtually ensures a lack of progress toward implementing our core principles (Schaffer, 2004).

## PRACTICING SOCIOLOGY

Change comes because people continue not only to believe that it is possible but also to act on their hopes and dreams (see the figure on page 363). As ethnographer Studs Terkel put it, "In all epochs, there were at first doubts and the fear of stepping forth and speaking out, but the attribute that spurred the warriors on was hope. And the *act*" (2003:xviii). We can change the world for the better. We can do so by becoming more informed about ourselves and others, and then acting on that knowledge. Here are some possibilities for action:

- *Practice personal sociology.* Become more conscious of the factors that shape your beliefs and actions.

- *Become more aware of privilege.* Identify the advantages you have, especially relative to the rest of the world; you likely have sufficient food, clothes, and shelter; you can read this; you can plan for the future; and so on.

- *Become more informed.* We have access to more information about our worlds now than ever. Seek it out; find out what's going on.

- *Interpret what you learn.* Analyze the information you receive. Remember that data never speak for themselves; they aren't just facts but are embedded in networks and systems that have their own interests.

- *Vote.* Elected leaders in a democracy, whether local, state, or national, are chosen by voters. It may not seem like your individual vote is significant, but the simple fact is that all those votes still add up to a winner. And even if your candidate cannot win, you can still make a statement; for example, if you don't think any of the candidates would make a good choice, write in someone who would.

- *Participate in local politics.* Think of politics as a contact sport: Go to rallies, protests, school board meetings, city council meetings, and more. You might be surprised how much of a difference a single voice can make, especially on the local level.

- *Run for office.* Don't assume that such positions of leadership are only for others who are somehow better or more informed than you. We need more people to believe that they can lead so that we get more diversity in our leaders.

- *Volunteer.* There are local organizations in every community seeking to bring about positive social change. You might contact a local school to see if you can read to kids, work at a homeless shelter, or help build houses with Habitat for Humanity.

- *Join.* There are many organizations that provide long-term outreach opportunities, such as AmeriCorps, the Peace Corps, and the American Red Cross, in which you provide assistance to people with varieties of needs, in communities near and far.

- *Organize.* Work to bring about the world you envision; there are undoubtedly others out there who share your views. Find them and work with them, both inside and outside existing institutions, to bring about change.

- *Fight for change.* Regardless of where you are, whether in your relationships, your family, your workplace, your community, or elsewhere, work to bring about positive social change. We have the power to change the world; we can't do so in a vacuum, but if sociologists are at all correct about the social construction of reality, things could be otherwise.

As Comte wrote at sociology's very founding, "Science leads to foresight, and foresight leads to action" (quoted in Bourdieu 1998b:55). It is only by seeing those things that limit us that we can move toward freedom.

We learn a lesson from sociology that is reminiscent of the one Ebenezer Scrooge learns in Charles Dickens' *A Christmas Carol,* written in 1843. Scrooge, a miserly businessman, thinks only of himself, caring little if anything for others, including his employee, his family, and the poor. But on Christmas Eve, he is visited by three ghosts: the Ghost of Christmas Past, the Ghost of Christmas Present, and the Ghost of Christmas Yet to Come. After each of these spirits shows him visions of their time, Scrooge repents, promising to live "an altered life" in which he will reaffirm relationships and reconnect to those around him. What is particularly interesting sociologically is the way he phrases that promise: "I will live in the Past, the Present, and the Future! The Spirits of all Three shall strive within me."

# Do You Believe You Can Effect Political Change?

## External political efficacy index 1952–2004

*Source:* The American National Election Studies, November 30, 2005.

and future together in our minds, we can act to make the world a better place to live.

Sociology is more than just a noun. Sociology is a verb. It is something we do, not something we possess. Our overreliance on individualistic models, and our failure to appreciate the impact of social forces, presents a distorted picture of our freedom. An appreciation of the relationship between self and society and of the consequences of difference allows us to make more informed choices and to shape the future. It allows us to provide answers to the questions Why do we think the way we think? and Why do we act the way we act? Sociology shouldn't be something confined to college classrooms. It shouldn't be left only to professionals. We are all sociologists now, and there is work to be done.

Investigate. Learn. Vote. Organize. Run for office. Fight for change. Practice sociology. Make a difference.

At its core, Scrooge's resolution represents what we are called to do by the sociological imagination. Just as history and biography intersect, so also do we need to understand that the past, created by the actions of ourselves and those who came before us, has shaped who we are now. As American novelist and essayist James Baldwin wrote, "The great force of history comes from the fact that we carry it within us, are unconsciously controlled by it in many ways, and history is literally *present* in all that we do" ([1965] 1985:410). Further, our present actions shape the future directions of both our lives and the lives of others in the worlds around us and of those of yet to come. Like Scrooge, we can reject the myth of the isolated individual and affirm the significance of relationships and companionship (to return to one of the root word meanings of sociology). By simultaneously holding the past, present,

# For REVIEW

I. How and why does social change happen?

- Social change evolves out of past social practices; it represents a response by those in society to maintain social order by seeking an acceptable level of balance between stability and change; and it is influenced by the distribution of power and control over resources, which shapes what changes do or do not occur. Technological innovation has played a powerful role causing social change.

II. What factors shape the success of a social movement?

- There needs to be a sense of relative deprivation in which people have a sense that injustice exists that can and should be challenged. In addition, people must have the capacity to mobilize resources to bring about the change they seek.

III. What does it mean to practice sociology?

- Personal sociology involves better understanding the influence social factors have on our thoughts and actions and using this information to our advantage. Public sociology means taking responsibility for the collective impacts our individual actions have in shaping society and opportunity and working for positive social change.

## Pop Quiz

1. According to the definition, what is social change?
   a. tumultuous, revolutionary alterations that lead to changes in leadership
   b. a significant alteration over time in behavior patterns and culture
   c. regular alterations in a consistent social frame of reference
   d. subtle alterations in any social system

2. Nineteenth-century theories of social change reflect the pioneering work in biological evolution done by
   a. Albert Einstein.
   b. Harriet Martineau.
   c. James Audubon.
   d. Charles Darwin.

3. According to Talcott Parsons' equilibrium model, during which process do social institutions become more specialized in their purposes?
   a. differentiation
   b. adaptive upgrading
   c. inclusion
   d. value generalization

4. Which of the following did William F. Ogburn use to describe the period of maladjustment during which the nonmaterial culture is still struggling to adapt to new material conditions?
   a. economic shift
   b. political turmoil
   c. social change
   d. culture lag

5. The One Laptop per Child campaign was designed to overcome the problem of
   a. relative deprivation.
   b. social change.
   c. the digital divide.
   d. vested interests.

6. You are a student and do not own a car. All your close friends who are attending your college or university have vehicles of their own. You feel downtrodden and dissatisfied. You are experiencing
   a. relative deprivation.
   b. resource mobilization.
   c. false consciousness.
   d. depression.

1. (b); 2. (d); 3. (b); 4. (d); 5. (c); 6. (a);

7. It takes more than desire to start a social movement; it helps to have money, political influence, access to the media, and workers. The ways in which a social movement uses such things are referred to collectively as

a. relative deprivation.

b. false consciousness.

c. resource mobilization.

d. economic independence.

8. Karl Marx held that leaders of social movements must help workers overcome feelings of

a. class consciousness.

b. false consciousness.

c. socialist consciousness.

d. surplus value.

9. Organized collective activities that promote autonomy and self-determination, as well as improvements in the quality of life, are referred to as

a. new social movements.

b. social revolutions.

c. resource mobilizations.

d. crazes.

10. Recognizing the impact our individual position has on who we are and how we think and act, and taking responsibility for the impacts our actions have on others is known as

a. resource mobilization.

b. false consciousness.

c. public sociology.

d. personal sociology

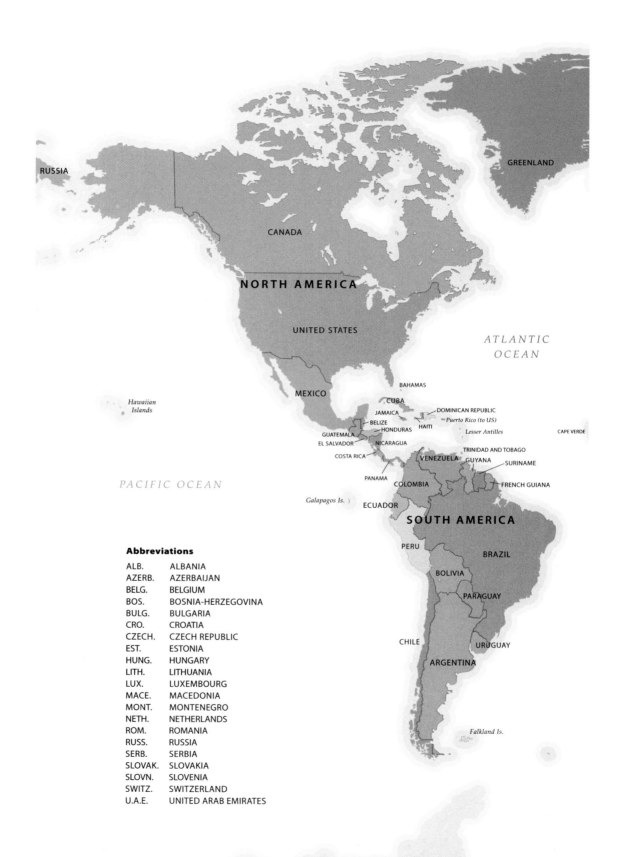

RUSSIA

GREENLAND

CANADA

**NORTH AMERICA**

UNITED STATES

*ATLANTIC OCEAN*

*Hawaiian Islands*

MEXICO

BAHAMAS

CUBA

DOMINICAN REPUBLIC

JAMAICA

*Puerto Rico (to US)*

BELIZE

HAITI

*Lesser Antilles*

CAPE VERDE

GUATEMALA

HONDURAS

EL SALVADOR

NICARAGUA

TRINIDAD AND TOBAGO

COSTA RICA

VENEZUELA

GUYANA

SURINAME

*PACIFIC OCEAN*

PANAMA

COLOMBIA

FRENCH GUIANA

*Galapagos Is.*

ECUADOR

**SOUTH AMERICA**

PERU

BRAZIL

BOLIVIA

PARAGUAY

CHILE

URUGUAY

ARGENTINA

*Falkland Is.*

### Abbreviations

| | |
|---|---|
| ALB. | ALBANIA |
| AZERB. | AZERBAIJAN |
| BELG. | BELGIUM |
| BOS. | BOSNIA-HERZEGOVINA |
| BULG. | BULGARIA |
| CRO. | CROATIA |
| CZECH. | CZECH REPUBLIC |
| EST. | ESTONIA |
| HUNG. | HUNGARY |
| LITH. | LITHUANIA |
| LUX. | LUXEMBOURG |
| MACE. | MACEDONIA |
| MONT. | MONTENEGRO |
| NETH. | NETHERLANDS |
| ROM. | ROMANIA |
| RUSS. | RUSSIA |
| SERB. | SERBIA |
| SLOVAK. | SLOVAKIA |
| SLOVN. | SLOVENIA |
| SWITZ. | SWITZERLAND |
| U.A.E. | UNITED ARAB EMIRATES |

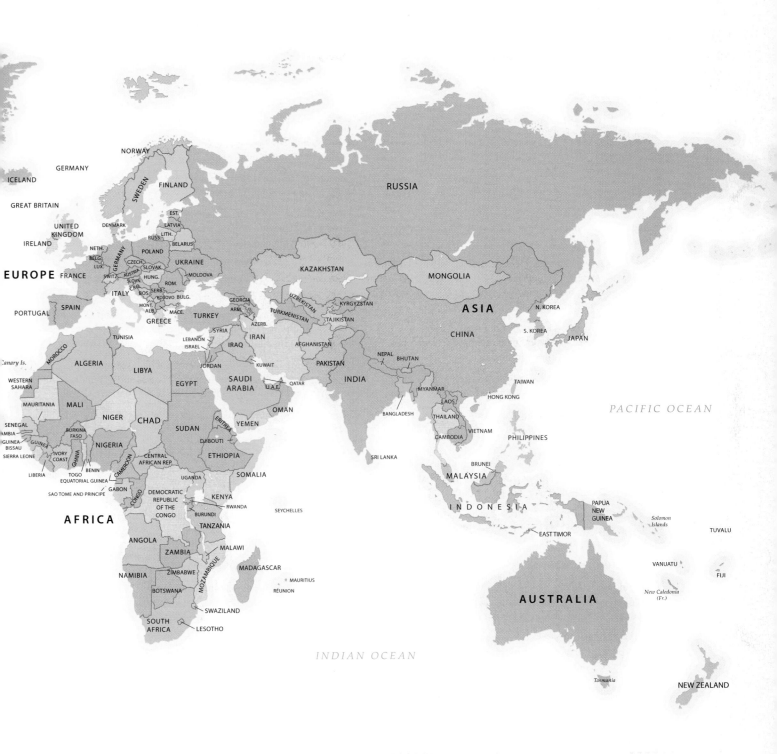

**Absolute poverty**   A minimum level of subsistence that no family should be expected to live below.

**Achieved status**   A social position that a person attains largely through his or her own efforts.

**Activity theory**   A theory of aging that suggests that those elderly people who remain active and socially involved will be best adjusted.

**Adoption**   In a legal sense, a process that allows for the transfer of the legal rights, responsibilities, and privileges of parenthood to a new legal parent or parents.

**Affirmative action**   Positive efforts to recruit minority group members or women for jobs, promotions, and educational opportunities.

**Ageism**   Prejudice and discrimination based on a person's age.

**Agency**   The freedom individuals have to choose and to act.

**Agrarian society**   The most technologically advanced form of preindustrial society. Members are engaged primarily in the production of food, but they increase their crop yields through technological innovations such as the plow.

**Alienation**   Loss of control over our creative human capacity to produce, separation from the products we make, and isolation from our fellow producers.

**Amalgamation**   The process through which a majority group and a minority group combine to form a new group.

**Anomie**   Durkheim's term for the loss of direction felt in a society when social control of individual behavior has become ineffective.

**Anomie theory of deviance**   Robert Merton's theory of deviance as an adaptation of socially prescribed goals or of the means governing their attainment, or both.

**Anticipatory socialization**   Processes of socialization in which a person "rehearses" for future positions, occupations, and social relationships.

**Anti-Semitism**   Anti-Jewish prejudice.

**Apartheid**   A former policy of the South African government, designed to maintain the separation of Blacks and other non-Whites from the dominant Whites.

**Applied sociology**   The use of the discipline of sociology with the specific intent of yielding practical applications for human behavior and organizations.

**Argot**   Specialized language used by members of a group or subculture.

**Ascribed status**   A social position assigned to a person by society without regard for the person's unique talents or characteristics.

**Assimilation**   The process through which a person forsakes his or her own cultural tradition to become part of a different culture.

**Authority**   Institutionalized power that is recognized by the people over whom it is exercised.

**Avatar**   A person's online representation as a character, whether in the form of a 2-D or 3-D image or simply through text.

**Bilateral descent**   A kinship system in which both sides of a person's family are regarded as equally important.

**Black power**   A political philosophy, promoted by many younger Blacks in the 1960s, that supported the creation of Black-controlled political and economic institutions.

**Borderlands**   The area of common culture along the border between Mexico and the United States.

**Bourgeoisie**   Karl Marx's term for the capitalist class, comprising the owners of the means of production.

**Brain drain**   The immigration to the United States and other industrialized nations of skilled workers, professionals, and technicians who are desperately needed in their home countries.

**Bureaucracy**   A component of formal organization that uses rules and hierarchical ranking to achieve efficiency.

**Bureaucratization**   The process by which a group, organization, or social movement increasingly relies on technical-rational decision making in the pursuit of efficiency.

**Capitalism**   An economic system in which the means of production are held largely in private hands and the main incentive for economic activity is the accumulation of profits.

**Caste**   A hereditary rank, usually religiously dictated, that tends to be fixed and immobile.

**Causal logic**   The relationship between a condition or variable and a particular consequence, with one event leading to the other.

**Charismatic authority**   Power made legitimate by a leader's exceptional personal or emotional appeal to his or her followers.

**Class**   A group of people who have a similar level of economic resources.

**Class consciousness**   In Karl Marx's view, a subjective awareness held by members of a class regarding their common vested interests and need for collective political action to bring about social change.

**Class system**   A social ranking based primarily on economic position in which achieved characteristics can influence social mobility.

**Classical theory**   An approach to the study of formal organizations that views workers as being motivated almost entirely by economic rewards.

**Clinical sociology**   The use of the discipline of sociology with the specific intent of altering social relationships or restructuring social institutions.

**Closed system**   A social system in which there is little or no possibility of individual social mobility.

**Coalition**   A temporary or permanent alliance geared toward a common goal.

**Code of ethics**   The standards of acceptable behavior developed by and for members of a profession.

**Cognitive theory of development**   The theory that children's thought progresses through four stages of development.

**Cohabitation**   The practice of living together as a male–female couple without marrying.

**Colonialism**   The maintenance of political, social, economic, and cultural dominance over a people by a foreign power for an extended period.

**Color-blind racism**   The use of race-neutral principles to perpetuate a racially unequal status quo.

**Communism**   As an ideal type, an economic system under which all property is communally owned and no social distinctions are made on the basis of people's ability to produce.

**Conflict perspective**   A sociological approach that assumes that social behavior is best understood in terms of tension between groups over power or the allocation of resources, including housing, money, access to services, and political representation.

**Conformity**   The act of going along with peers—individuals of our own status who have no special right to direct our behavior.

**Contact hypothesis**   The theory that in cooperative circumstances interracial contact between people of equal status will reduce prejudice.

**Content analysis**   The systematic coding and objective recording of data, guided by some rationale.

**Control group**   The subjects in an experiment who are not introduced to the independent variable by the researcher.

**Control theory**   A view of conformity and deviance that suggests that our connection to members of society leads us to systematically conform to society's norms.

**Control variable**   A factor that is held constant to test the relative impact of an independent variable.

**Corporate welfare**   Tax breaks, direct payments, and grants that the government makes to corporations.

**Correlation**   A relationship between two variables in which a change in one coincides with a change in the other.

**Correspondence principle**   The tendency of schools to promote the values expected of individuals in each social class and to prepare students for the types of jobs typically held by members of their class.

**Counterculture**   A subculture that deliberately opposes certain aspects of the larger culture.

**Credentialism**   An increase in the lowest level of education required to enter a field.

**Crime**   A violation of criminal law for which some governmental authority applies formal penalties.

**Cross-tabulation**   A table that shows the relationship between two or more variables.

**Cultural capital**   Our tastes, knowledge, attitudes, language, and ways of thinking that we exchange in interaction with others.

**Cultural relativism**   The viewing of people's behavior from the perspective of their own culture.

**Cultural transmission**   A school of criminology that argues that criminal behavior is learned through social interactions.

**Cultural universal**   A common practice or belief shared by all societies.

**Culture lag**   A period of adjustment when the nonmaterial culture is still struggling to adapt to new material conditions.

**Culture shock**   The feelings of disorientation, uncertainty, and even fear that people experience when they encounter unfamiliar cultural practices.

**Culture**   The totality of our shared language, knowledge, material objects, and behavior.

**Culture-bound syndrome**   A disease or illness that cannot be understood apart from some specific social context.

**Curanderismo**   Latino folk medicine, a form of holistic health care and healing.

**Death rate**   The number of deaths per 1000 population in a given year. Also known as the *crude death rate*.

**Degradation ceremony**   An aspect of the socialization process within some total institutions, in which people are subjected to humiliating rituals.

**Deindustrialization**   The systematic, widespread withdrawal of investment in basic aspects of productivity, such as factories and plants.

**Democracy**   In a literal sense, government by the people.

**Denomination**   A large, organized religion that is not officially linked to the state or government.

**Dependency theory**   An approach that contends that industrialized nations continue to exploit developing countries for their own gain.

**Dependent variable**   The variable in a causal relationship that is subject to the influence of another variable.

**Deviance**   Behavior that violates the standards of conduct or expectations of a group or society.

**Dictatorship**   A government in which one person has nearly total power to make and enforce laws.

**Differential association**   A theory of deviance that holds that violation of rules results from exposure to attitudes favorable to criminal acts.

**Differential justice**   Differences in the way social control is exercised over different groups.

**Diffusion**   The process by which a cultural item spreads from group to group or society to society.

**Digital divide**   The relative lack of access to the latest technologies among low-income groups, racial and ethnic minorities, rural residents, and the citizens of developing countries.

**Discovery**  The process of making known or sharing the existence of an aspect of reality.

**Discrimination**  The denial of opportunities and equal rights to individuals and groups because of prejudice or other arbitrary reasons.

**Disengagement theory**  A theory of aging that suggests that society and the aging individual mutually sever many of their relationships.

**Domestic partnership**  Two unrelated adults who share a mutually caring relationship, reside together, and agree to be jointly responsible for their dependents, basic living expenses, and other common necessities.

**Dominant ideology**  A set of cultural beliefs and practices that helps to maintain powerful social, economic, and political interests.

**Downsizing**  Reductions in a company's workforce as part of deindustrialization.

**Dramaturgical approach**  A view of social interaction in which people are seen as theatrical performers.

**Ecclesia**  A religious organization that claims to include most or all members of a society and is recognized as the national or official religion.

**Economic system**  The social institution through which goods and services are produced, distributed, and consumed.

**Education**  A formal process of learning in which some people consciously teach while others adopt the social role of learner.

**Egalitarian family**  An authority pattern in which spouses are regarded as equals.

**Elite model**  A view of society as being ruled by a small group of individuals who share a common set of political and economic interests.

**Endogamy**  The restriction of mate selection to people within the same group.

**Environmental Justice**  A legal strategy based on claims that racial minorities are subjected disproportionately to environmental hazards.

**Equilibrium model**  The view that society tends toward a state of stability or balance.

**Established sect**  A religious group that is the outgrowth of a sect, yet remains isolated from society.

**Estate system**  A system of stratification under which peasants were required to work land leased to them by nobles in exchange for military protection and other services. Also known as feudalism.

**Esteem**  The reputation that a specific person has earned within an occupation.

**Ethnic group**  A group that is set apart from others primarily because of its national origin or distinctive cultural patterns.

**Ethnocentrism**  The tendency to assume that one's own culture and way of life represent the norm or are superior to all others.

**Ethnography**  The study of an entire social setting through extended systematic observation.

**Evolutionary theory**  A theory of social change that holds that society is moving in a definite direction.

**Exogamy**  The requirement that people select a mate outside certain groups.

**Experiment**  An artificially created situation that allows a researcher to manipulate variables.

**Experimental group**  The subjects in an experiment who are exposed to an independent variable introduced by a researcher.

**Exploitation theory**  A belief that views racial subordination in the United States as a manifestation of the class system inherent in capitalism.

**Expressive leader**  The person in the family who bears responsibility for the maintenance of harmony and internal emotional affairs.

**Expulsion**  The systematic removal of a group of people from society.

**Extended family**  A family in which relatives—such as grandparents, aunts, or uncles—live in the same household as parents and their children.

**Face-work**  The efforts people make to maintain a proper image and avoid public embarrassment.

**False consciousness**  A term used by Karl Marx to describe an attitude held by members of a class that does not accurately reflect their objective position.

**Familism**  Pride in the extended family, expressed through the maintenance of close ties and strong obligations to kinfolk outside the immediate family.

**Feminism**  The belief in social, economic, and political equality for women.

**Folkway**  Norms governing everyday behavior, whose violation raises comparatively little concern.

**Force**  The actual or threatened use of coercion to impose one's will on others.

**Formal norm**  A norm that generally has been written down and that specifies strict punishments for violators.

**Formal organization**  A group designed for a special purpose and structured for maximum efficiency.

**Formal social control**  Social control that is carried out by authorized agents, such as police officers, judges, school administrators, and employers.

**Functionalist definition of families**  A definition of families that focuses on what families do for society and for their members.

**Functionalist definition of religion**  The idea that religion unifies believers into a community through shared practices and a common set of beliefs relative to sacred things.

**Functionalist perspective**   A sociological approach that emphasizes the way in which the parts of a society are structured to maintain its stability.

**Fundamentalism**   Rigid adherence to core religious doctrines, often accompanied by a literal application of scripture or historical beliefs to today's world.

*Gemeinschaft*   A close-knit community, often found in rural areas, in which strong personal bonds unite members.

**Gender role**   Expectations regarding the proper behavior, attitudes, and activities of males or females.

**Gender**   The social and cultural significance that we attach to the biological differences of sex.

**Generalized other**   The attitudes, viewpoints, and expectations of society as a whole that a child takes into account in his or her behavior.

**Genocide**   The deliberate, systematic killing of an entire people or nation.

**Gerontology**   The study of the sociological and psychological aspects of aging and the problems of the aged.

*Gesellschaft*   A community, often urban, that is large and impersonal, with little commitment to the group or consensus on values.

**Glass ceiling**   An invisible barrier that blocks the promotion of a qualified individual in a work environment because of the individual's gender, race, or ethnicity.

**Globalization**   The worldwide integration of government policies, cultures, social movements, and financial markets through trade and the exchange of ideas.

**Goal displacement**   Overzealous conformity to official regulations of a bureaucracy.

**Gross national product (GNP)**   The value of a nation's goods and services.

**Group**   Any number of people with similar norms, values, and expectations who interact with one another on a regular basis.

**Hate crime**   A criminal offense committed because of the offender's bias against an individual based on race, religion, ethnicity, national origin, or sexual orientation.

**Hawthorne effect**   The unintended influence that observers of experiments can have on their subjects.

**Health**   As defined by the World Health Organization, a state of complete physical, mental, and social well-being, and not merely the absence of disease and infirmity.

**Hidden curriculum**   Standards of behavior that are deemed proper by society and are taught subtly in schools.

**Holistic medicine**   Therapies in which the health care practitioner considers the person's physical, mental, emotional, and spiritual characteristics.

**Homogamy**   The conscious or unconscious tendency to select a mate with personal characteristics similar to one's own.

**Homophobia**   Fear of and prejudice against homosexuality.

**Horizontal mobility**   The movement of an individual from one social position to another of the same rank.

**Horticultural society**   A preindustrial society in which people plant seeds and crops rather than merely subsist on available foods.

**Hospice care**   Treatment of the terminally ill in their own homes, or in special hospital units or other facilities, with the goal of helping them to die comfortably, without pain.

**Human ecology**   The area of study concerned with the interrelationships between people and their environment.

**Human relations approach**   An approach to the study of formal organizations that emphasizes the role of people, communication, and participation in a bureaucracy and tends to focus on the informal structure of the organization.

**Human rights**   Universal moral rights possessed by all people because they are human.

**Hunting-and-gathering society**   A preindustrial society in which people rely on whatever foods and fibers are readily available in order to survive.

**Hypothesis**   A testable statement about the relationship between two or more variables.

**I**   The acting self that exists in relation to the Me.

**Ideal type**   A construct or model for evaluating specific cases.

**Impression management**   The altering of the presentation of the self in order to create distinctive appearances and satisfy particular audiences.

**Incest taboo**   The prohibition of sexual relationships between certain culturally specified relatives.

**Incidence**   The number of new cases of a specific disorder that occur within a given population during a stated period.

**Income**   Wages and salaries measured over some period of time, such as per hour or year.

**Independent variable**   The variable in a causal relationship that causes or influences a change in a second variable.

**Index crimes**   The eight types of crime reported annually by the FBI in the *Uniform Crime Reports:* murder, forcible rape, robbery, aggravated assault, burglary, larceny-theft, motor vehicle theft, and arson.

**Industrial society**   A society that depends on mechanization to produce its goods and services.

**Infant mortality rate**   The number of deaths of infants under one year old per 1000 live births in a given year.

**Influence**   The exercise of power through a process of persuasion.

**Informal economy**   Transfers of money, goods, or services that are not reported to the government.

**Informal norm**   A norm that is generally understood but not precisely recorded.

**Informal social control**   Social control that is carried out casually by ordinary people through such means as laughter, smiles, and ridicule.

**In-group**   Any group or category to which people feel they belong.

**Innovation**   The process of introducing a new idea or object to a culture through discovery or invention.

**Institutional discrimination**   The denial of opportunities and equal rights to individuals and groups that results from the normal operations of a society.

**Instrumental leader**   The person in the family who bears responsibility for the completion of tasks, focuses on more distant goals, and manages the external relationship between one's family and other social institutions.

**Interactionist perspective**   A sociological approach that generalizes about everyday forms of social interaction in order to explain society as a whole.

**Intergenerational mobility**   Changes in the social position of children relative to their parents.

**Interview**   A face-to-face or telephone questioning of a respondent to obtain desired information.

**Intragenerational mobility**   Changes in social position within a person's adult life.

**Invention**   The combination of existing cultural items into a form that did not exist before.

**Iron law of oligarchy**   A principle of organizational life under which even a democratic organization will eventually develop into a bureaucracy ruled by a few individuals.

**Kinship**   The state of being related to others.

**Labeling theory**   An approach to deviance that attempts to explain why certain people are viewed as deviants while others engaged in the same behavior are not.

**Laissez-faire**   A form of capitalism under which people compete freely, with minimal government intervention in the economy.

**Language**   A system of shared symbols; it includes speech, written characters, numerals, symbols, and nonverbal gestures and expressions.

**Law**   Formal norms enforced by the state.

**Liberation theology**   Use of a church, primarily Roman Catholicism, in a political effort to eliminate poverty, discrimination, and other forms of injustice from a secular society.

**Life chances**   The opportunities people have to provide themselves with material goods, positive living conditions, and favorable life experiences.

**Life course approach**   A research orientation in which sociologists and other social scientists look closely at the social factors that influence people throughout their lives, from birth to death.

**Looking-glass self**   A concept that emphasizes the self as the product of our social interactions.

**Luddites**   Rebellious craft workers in 19th-century England who destroyed new factory machinery as part of their resistance to the Industrial Revolution.

**Machismo**   A sense of virility, personal worth, and pride in one's maleness.

**Macrosociology**   Sociological investigation that concentrates on large-scale phenomena or entire civilizations.

**Master status**   A status that dominates others and thereby determines a person's general position in society.

**Material culture**   The physical or technological aspects of our daily lives.

**Matriarchy**   A society in which women dominate in family decision making.

**Matrilineal descent**   A kinship system in which only the mother's relatives are significant.

**McDonaldization**   The process by which the principles of efficiency, calculability, predictability, and control shape organization and decision making, in the United States and around the world.

**Me**   The socialized self that plans actions and judges performances based on the standards we have learned from others.

**Mean**   A number calculated by adding a series of values and then dividing by the number of values.

**Mechanical solidarity**   Social cohesion based on shared experiences, knowledge, and skills in which things function more or less the way they always have, with minimal change.

**Median**   The midpoint, or number that divides a series of values into two groups of equal numbers of values.

**Microsociology**   Sociological investigation that stresses the study of small groups and the analysis of our everyday experiences and interactions.

**Midlife crisis**   A stressful period of self-evaluation that begins at about age 40.

**Minority group**   A subordinate group whose members, even if they represent a numeric majority, have significantly less control or power over their own lives than the members of a dominant or majority group have over theirs.

**Mixed economy**   An economic system that combines elements of both capitalism and socialism.

**Mode**   The single most common value in a series of scores.

**Model or ideal minority**   A subordinate group whose members supposedly have succeeded economically, socially, and educationally despite past prejudice and discrimination.

**Modernization**   The far-reaching process by which nations pass from traditional forms of social organization toward those characteristic of post-Industrial Revolution societies.

**Monarchy**   A form of government headed by a single member of a royal family, usually a king, queen, or some other hereditary ruler.

**Monogamy**   A form of marriage in which one woman and one man are married only to each other.

**Monopoly**   Control of a market by a single business firm.

**Morbidity rate**   The incidence of disease in a given population.

**Mores**   Norms deemed highly necessary to the welfare of a society.

**Mortality rate**   The incidence of death in a given population.

**Multinational corporation**   A commercial organization that is headquartered in one country but does business throughout the world.

**Multiple masculinities**   The idea that men learn and play a full range of gender roles.

**Natural science**   The study of the physical features of nature and the ways in which they interact and change.

**Neocolonialism**   Continuing dependence of former colonies on foreign countries.

**New religious movement (NRM)** or **cult**   A small, alternative faith community that represents either a new religion or a major innovation in an existing faith.

**New social movement**   An organized collective activity that addresses values and social identities, as well as improvements in the quality of life.

**Nonmaterial culture**   Ways of using material objects, as well as customs, ideas, expressions, beliefs, knowledge, philosophies, governments, and patterns of communication.

**Nonverbal communication**   The use of gestures, facial expressions, and other visual images to communicate.

**Norm**   An established standard of behavior maintained by a society.

**Nuclear family**   A married couple and their unmarried children living together.

**Obedience**   Compliance with higher authorities in a hierarchical structure.

**Objective method**   A technique for measuring social class that assigns individuals to classes on the basis of criteria such as occupation, education, income, and place of residence.

**Observation**   A research technique in which an investigator collects information through direct participation and/or by closely watching a group or community.

**Offshoring**   The transfer of work to foreign contractors.

**Oligarchy**   A form of government in which a few individuals rule.

**Open system**   A social system in which the position of each individual is influenced by his or her achieved status.

**Operational definition**   Transformation of an abstract concept into indicators that are observable and measurable.

**Organic solidarity**   A collective consciousness that rests on mutual interdependence, characteristic of societies with a complex division of labor.

**Organized crime**   The work of a group that regulates relations among criminal enterprises involved in illegal activities, including prostitution, gambling, and the smuggling and sale of illegal drugs.

**Out-group**   A group or category to which people feel they do not belong.

**Party**   The capacity to organize to accomplish some particular goal.

**Patriarchy**   A society in which men dominate in family decision making.

**Patrilineal descent**   A kinship system in which only the father's relatives are significant.

**Peace**   The absence of war, or more broadly, a proactive effort to develop cooperative relations among nations.

**Personal sociology**   The process of recognizing the impact our individual position has on who we are and how we think and act, and of taking responsibility for the impacts our actions have on others.

**Personality**   A person's typical patterns of attitudes, needs, characteristics, and behavior.

**Peter principle**   A principle of organizational life according to which every employee within a hierarchy tends to rise to his or her level of incompetence.

**Pluralism**   Mutual respect for one another's cultures among the various groups in a society, which allows minorities to express their own cultures without experiencing prejudice.

**Pluralist model**   A view of society in which many competing groups within the community have access to government, so that no single group is dominant.

**Political system**   The social institution that is founded on a recognized set of procedures for implementing and achieving society's goals.

**Politics**   In Harold Lasswell's words, "who gets what, when, and how."

**Polyandry**   A form of polygamy in which a woman may have more than one husband at the same time.

**Polygamy**   A form of marriage in which an individual may have several husbands or wives simultaneously.

**Polygyny**   A form of polygamy in which a man may have more than one wife at the same time.

**Postindustrial society**   A society whose economic system is engaged primarily in the processing and control of information.

**Postmodern society**   A technologically sophisticated, pluralistic, interconnected, globalized society.

**Power elite**   A small group of military, industrial, and government leaders who control the fate of the United States.

**Power**   The ability to exercise one's will over others even if they resist.

**Prejudice**   A negative attitude toward an entire category of people, often an ethnic or racial minority.

**Prestige**   The respect and admiration that an occupation holds in a society.

**Prevalence**   The total number of cases of a specific disorder that exist at a given time.

**Primary group**   A small group characterized by intimate, face-to-face association and cooperation.

**Private troubles**   Obstacles that individuals face as individuals rather than as a consequence of their social position.

**Profane**   The ordinary and commonplace elements of life, as distinguished from the sacred.

**Proletariat**   Karl Marx's term for the working class in a capitalist society.

**Protestant ethic**   Max Weber's term for the disciplined commitment to worldly labor driven by a desire to bring glory to God, shared by followers of Martin Luther and John Calvin.

**Public issues**   Obstacles that individuals in similar positions face; also referred to by sociologists as "social problems."

**Public sociology**   The process of bringing the insights gained through sociological observation and analysis into the public sphere, thereby seeking to bring about positive social change.

**Qualitative research**   Research that relies on what is seen in field or naturalistic settings more than on statistical data.

**Quantitative research**   Research that collects and reports data primarily in numerical form.

**Questionnaire**   A printed or written form used to obtain information from a respondent.

**Racial formation**   A sociohistorical process in which racial categories are created, inhibited, transformed, and destroyed.

**Racial group**   A group that is set apart from others because of physical differences that have taken on social significance.

**Racial profiling**   Any police-initiated action based on race, ethnicity, or national origin rather than on a person's behavior.

**Racism**   The belief that one race is supreme and all others are innately inferior.

**Random sample**   A sample for which every member of an entire population has the same chance of being selected.

**Rational-legal authority**   Authority based on formally agreed upon and accepted rules, principles, and procedures of conduct that are established in order to accomplish goals in the most efficient manner possible.

**Reference group**   Any group that individuals use as a standard for evaluating themselves and their own behavior.

**Relative deprivation**   The conscious feeling of a negative discrepancy between legitimate expectations and present actualities.

**Relative poverty**   A floating standard of deprivation by which people at the bottom of a society, whatever their lifestyles, are judged to be disadvantaged in comparison with the nation as a whole.

**Reliability**   The extent to which a measure produces consistent results.

**Religious belief**   A statement to which members of a particular religion adhere.

**Religious experience**   The feeling or perception of being in direct contact with the ultimate reality, such as a divine being, or of being overcome with religious emotion.

**Religious ritual**   A practice required or expected of members of a faith.

**Remittances**   The monies that immigrants return to their families of origin; also called *migradollars.*

**Representative democracy**   A form of government in which certain individuals are selected to speak for the people.

**Research design**   A detailed plan or method for obtaining data scientifically.

**Resocialization**   The process of discarding former behavior patterns and accepting new ones as part of a transition in one's life.

**Resource mobilization**   The ways in which a social movement utilizes such resources as money, political influence, access to the media, and personnel.

**Rite of passage**   A ritual marking the symbolic transition from one social position to another.

**Role conflict**   The situation that occurs when incompatible expectations arise from two or more social positions held by the same person.

**Role exit**   The process of disengagement from a role that is central to one's self-identity in order to establish a new role and identity.

**Role strain**   The difficulty that arises when the same social position imposes conflicting demands and expectations.

**Role taking**   The process of mentally assuming the perspective of another and responding from that imagined viewpoint.

**Sacred**   Elements beyond everyday life that inspire respect, awe, and even fear.

**Sample**   A selection from a larger population that is statistically representative of that population.

**Sanction**   A penalty or reward for conduct concerning a social norm.

**Sandwich generation**   The generation of adults who simultaneously try to meet the competing needs of their parents and their children.

**Sapir-Whorf hypothesis**   The idea that the language a person uses shapes his or her perception of reality and therefore his or her thoughts and actions.

**Science**   The body of knowledge obtained by methods based on systematic observation.

**Scientific management approach**   Another name for the classical theory of formal organizations.

**Scientific method**   A systematic, organized series of steps that ensures maximum objectivity and consistency in researching a problem.

**Second shift**   The double burden—work outside the home followed by child care and housework—that many women face and few men share equitably.

**Secondary analysis**   A variety of research techniques that make use of previously collected and publicly accessible information and data.

**Secondary group**   A formal, impersonal group in which there is little social intimacy or mutual understanding.

**Sect**   A relatively small religious group that has broken away from some other religious organization to renew what it considers the original vision of the faith.

**Secularization**   Religion's diminishing influence in the public sphere, especially in politics and the economy.

**Segregation**   The physical separation of two groups of people in terms of residence, workplace, and social events; often imposed on a minority group by a dominant group.

**Self**   A distinct identity that sets us apart from others.

**Serial monogamy**   A form of marriage in which a person may have several spouses in his or her lifetime, but only one spouse at a time.

**Sex**   The biological differences between males and females.

**Sexism**   The ideology that one sex is superior to the other.

**Sick role**   Societal expectations about the attitudes and behavior of a person viewed as being ill.

**Significant other**   An individual who is most important in the development of the self, such as a parent, friend, or teacher.

**Single-parent family**   A family in which only one parent is present to care for the children.

**Slavery**   A system of enforced servitude in which some people are owned by others as property.

**Social change**   Significant alteration over time in behavior patterns and culture, including norms and values.

**Social control**   The techniques and strategies for preventing deviant human behavior in any society.

**Social disorganization theory**   The theory that attributes increases in crime and deviance to the absence or breakdown of communal relationships and social institutions, such as the family, school, church, and local government.

**Social epidemiology**   The study of the distribution of disease, impairment, and general health status across a population.

**Social inequality**   A condition in which members of society have different amounts of wealth, prestige, or power.

**Social institution**   An organized pattern of beliefs and behavior centered on basic social needs.

**Social interaction**   The ways in which people respond to one another.

**Social mobility**   Movement of individuals or groups from one position in a society's stratification system to another.

**Social movement**   An organized collective activity to bring about or resist fundamental change in an existing group or society.

**Social network**   A series of social relationships that links individuals directly to others, and through them indirectly to still more people.

**Social role**   A set of expectations for people who occupy a given social position or status.

**Social science**   The study of the social features of humans and the ways in which they interact and change.

**Social structure**   The way in which a society is organized into predictable relationships.

**Socialism**   An economic system under which the means of production and distribution are collectively owned.

**Socialization**   The lifelong process through which people learn the attitudes, values, and behaviors appropriate for members of a particular culture.

**Societal-reaction approach**   Another name for *labeling theory.*

**Society**   The structure of relationships within which culture is created and shared through regularized patterns of social interaction.

**Sociobiology**   The systematic study of how biology affects human social behavior.

**Socioeconomic status (SES)**   A measure of class that is based on income, education, occupation, and related variables.

**Sociological imagination**   An awareness of the relationship between an individual and the wider society.

**Sociology**   The systematic study of the relationship between the individual and society and of the consequences of difference.

**Status**   A term used by sociologists to refer to any of the full range of socially defined positions within a large group or society.

**Status group**   People who have the same prestige or lifestyle, independent of their class positions.

**Stereotype**   An unreliable generalization about all members of a group that does not recognize individual differences within the group.

**Stigma**   A label used to devalue members of certain social groups.

**Stratification**   A structured ranking of entire groups of people that perpetuates unequal economic rewards and power in a society.

**Subculture**   A segment of society that shares a distinctive pattern of mores, folkways, and values that differs from the pattern of the larger society.

**Substantive definition of religion**   The idea that religion has a unique content or substance relating to the sacred that separates it from other forms of knowledge and belief.

**Substantive definition of the family**   A definition of the family based on blood, meaning shared genetic heritage, and law, meaning social recognition and affirmation of the bond including both marriage and adoption.

**Survey**   A study, generally in the form of an interview or questionnaire, that provides researchers with information about how people think and act.

**Symbol**   A gesture, object, or word that forms the basis of human communication.

**Symbolic ethnicity**   An ethnic identity that emphasizes concerns such as ethnic food or political issues rather than deeper ties to one's ethnic heritage.

**Teacher-expectancy effect**   The impact that a teacher's expectations about a student's performance may have on the student's actual achievements.

**Technology**   "Cultural information about how to use the material resources of the environment to satisfy human needs and desires."

**Terrorism**   The use or threat of violence against random or symbolic targets in pursuit of political aims.

**Theory**   In sociology a set of statements that seeks to explain problems, actions, or behavior.

**Total institution**   An institution that regulates all aspects of a person's life under a single authority, such as a prison, the military, a mental hospital, or a convent.

**Totalitarianism**   Virtually complete government control and surveillance over all aspects of a society's social and political life.

**Tracking**   The practice of placing students in specific curriculum groups on the basis of their test scores and other criteria.

**Traditional authority**   Legitimate power conferred by custom and accepted practice.

**Trained incapacity**   The tendency of workers in a bureaucracy to become so specialized that they develop blind spots and fail to notice potential problems.

**Transnational crime**   Crime that occurs across multiple national borders.

**Underclass**   The long-term poor who lack training and skills.

**Validity**   The degree to which a measure or scale truly reflects the phenomenon under study.

**Value**   A collective conception of what is considered good, desirable, and proper—or bad, undesirable, and improper—in a culture.

**Value neutrality**   Max Weber's term for objectivity of sociologists in the interpretation of data.

**Variable**   A measurable trait or characteristic that is subject to change under different conditions.

**Vertical mobility**   The movement of an individual from one social position to another of a different rank.

**Vested interests**   Those people or groups who will suffer in the event of social change and who have a stake in maintaining the status quo.

**Victimization survey**   A questionnaire or interview given to a sample of the population to determine whether people have been victims of crime.

**Victimless crime**   A term used by sociologists to describe the willing exchange among adults of widely desired, but illegal, goods and services.

**War**   Conflict between organizations that possess trained combat forces equipped with deadly weapons.

**Wealth**   The total of all a person's material assets, including savings, land, stocks, and other types of property, minus their debt at a single point in time.

**White-collar crime**   Illegal acts committed by affluent, "respectable" individuals in the course of business activities.

**World systems analysis**   A view of the global economic system as one divided between certain industrialized nations that control wealth and developing countries that are controlled and exploited.

## A

Aaronson, Daniel, and Bhashkar Mazumder. 2007. "Intergenerational Economic Mobility in the U.S., 1940 to 2000." FRB Chicago Working Paper No. WP 2005-12, revised February, 2007. Federal Reserve Bank of Chicago. Accessed June 21, 2008 (http://ssrn.com/abstract=869435).

AARP. 1999. "New AARP Study Finds Boomers Vary in Their Views of the Future and Their Retirement Years." AARP news release, June 1. Washington, DC.

———— 2004. "Baby Boomers Envision Retirement II: Survey of Baby Boomers' Expectations for Retirement." Prepared for AARP Environmental Analysis by Roper ASW. Washington, DC: AARP. Accessed May 13, 2008 (http://assets.aarp.org/rgcenter/econ/boomers_envision.pdf).

ABC News. 2007. "Iraq: Where Things Stand: March 19, 2007." Accessed March 30 (http://abc.go.com/).

ABC Radio Australia. 2006. "China: Crackdown in Air Pollution ahead of 2008 Beijing Olympics." Accessed May 2 (www.abc.net.au).

Abercrombie, Nicholas, Bryan S. Turner, and Stephen Hill, eds. 1990. *Dominant Ideologies.* Cambridge, MA: Unwin Hyman.

Abercrombie, Nicholas, Stephen Hill, and Bryan S. Turner. 1980. *The Dominant Ideology Thesis.* London: George Allen and Unwin.

———— 2000. *The Penguin Dictionary of Sociology,* 4th ed. New York: Penguin Books.

Aberle, David E., A. K. Cohen, A. K. Davis, M. J. Leng, Jr., and F. N. Sutton. 1950. "The Functional Prerequisites of a Society." *Ethics* 60 (January): 100–111.

Acosta, R. Vivian, and Linda Jean Carpenter. 2001. "Women in Intercollegiate Sport: A Longitudinal Study: 1977–1998." Pp. 302–308 in *Sport in Contemporary Society: An Anthology,* 6th ed., ed. D. Stanley Eitzen. New York: Worth.

Adams, Jimi. 2007. "Stained Glass Makes the Ceiling Visible: Organizational Opposition to Women in Congregational Leadership." *Gender and Society* 21 (February) :80–115.

Addams, Jane. 1910. *Twenty Years at Hull-House.* New York: Macmillan.

————. 1930. *The Second Twenty Years at Hull-House.* New York: Macmillan.

Adler, Freda. 1975. *Sisters in Crime: The Rise of the New Female Criminal.* New York: McGraw-Hill.

Adler, Freda, Gerhard O. W. Mueller, and William S. Laufer. 2004. *Criminology and the Criminal Justice System,* 5th ed. New York: McGraw-Hill.

Adler, Patricia A. 1993. *Wheeling and Dealing: An Ethnography of an Upper-Level Drug Dealing and Smuggling Community,* 2d ed. New York: Columbia University Press.

Adler, Patricia A., and Peter Adler. 1985. "From Idealism to Pragmatic Detachment: The Academic Performance of College Athletes." *Sociology of Education* 58 (October): 241–250.

———— 1988. "Intense Loyalty in Organizations: A Case Study of College Athletics." *Administrative Science Quarterly* 33: 401–417.

———— 1991. *Backboards and Blackboards.* New York: Columbia University Press.

———— 1995. "Dynamics of Inclusion and Exclusion in Preadolescent Cliques." *Social Psychology Quarterly* 58 (3): 145–162.

———— 1996. "Preadolescent Clique Stratification and the Hierarchy of Identity." *Sociological Inquiry* 66 (2): 111–142.

———— 1998. *Peer Power: Preadolescent Culture and Identity.* New Brunswick, NJ: Rutgers University Press.

———— 2003. "The Promise and Pitfalls of Going into the Field." *Contexts* (Spring): 41–47.

———— 2004. *Paradise Laborers: Hotel Work in the Global Economy.* Ithaca, NY: Cornell University Press.

———— 2005. "Self-Injurers as Loners: The Social Organization of Solitary Deviance." *Deviant Behavior.*

———— 2007. "The Demedicalization of Self-Injury: From Psychopathology to Sociological Deviance." *Journal of Contemporary Ethnography* 36 (October):537–570.

———— 2008. "The Cyber Worlds of Self-Injurers: Deviant Communities, Relationships, and Selves." *Symbolic Interaction* 31 (1): 33–56.

Adler, Patricia A., Peter Adler, and John M. Johnson. 1992. "Street Corner Society Revisited." *Journal of Contemporary Ethnography* 21 (April): 3–10.

Adler, Patricia A., Steve J. Kless, and Peter Adler. 1992. "Socialization to Gender Roles: Popularity Among Elementary School Boys and Girls." *Sociology of Education* 65 (July): 169–187.

Alain, Michel. 1985. "An Empirical Validation of Relative Deprivation." *Human Relations* 38 (8): 739–749.

Alba, Richard D. 1990. *Ethnic Identity: The Transformation of White America.* New Haven, CT: Yale University Press.

Allen, John L. 2008. *Student Atlas of World Politics.* 8th ed. New York: McGraw-Hill.

Allport, Gordon W. 1979. *The Nature of Prejudice,* 25th anniversary ed. Reading, MA: Addison-Wesley.

Alter, Alexandria. 2007. "Is This Man Cheating on His Wife?" *The Wall Street Journal,* August 10, p. W1. Accessed June 3, 2008 (http://online.wsj.com/article/SB118670164592393622.html).

Alvord, Lori Arviso, and Elizabeth Cohen Van Pelt. 1999. *The Scalpel and the Silver Bear.* New York: Bantam.

Alzheimer's Association. 2008. *2008 Alzheimer's Disease Facts and Figures.* Chicago: Alzheimer's Association.

Amato, Paul R. 2001. "What Children Learn from Divorce." *Population Today,* January, pp. 1, 4.

American Academy of Cosmetic Surgery. 2007. "2006 Procedural Survey Shows 3% Increases in Men Seeking Cosmetic Surgery." Accessed February 17, 2007 (www.medicalnewstoday.com).

American Bar Association. 1998. *Section of Individual Rights and Responsibilities. Section of Litigation (Capital Punishment).* Chicago: Division for Policy Administration, ABA.

American Federation of Teachers. 2007. *Survey and Analysis of Teacher Salary Trends 2005.* Washington, DC: AFT.

American Jewish Committee. 2001. "2000 Annual Survey of American Jewish Opinion." Accessed October 25 (www.ajc.org/pre/survey2000.htm).

American Lung Association. 2003. "Scenesmoking." Accessed December 19 (www.scenesmoking.org).

American Sociological Association. 1997. *Code of Ethics.* Washington, DC: American Sociological Association (www.asanet.org/ members/ecoderev.html).

————. 2001. *Data Brief: Profile of ASA Membership.* Washington, DC: American Sociological Association.

————. 2005a. "Need Today's Data Yesterday." Accessed December 17 (www.asanet.org).

————. 2005b. "Careers and Jobs Home." Accessed December 17 (www.asanet.org/page.ww? section=careers+and+Jobs&name=Careers+and+ Jobs+Home).

————. 2006. "Current Sections." Accessed May 18 (www.asanet.org/page.ww?section=Sections& name=Overview).

————. 2006a. *Careers in Sociology with an Undergraduate Degree in Sociology,* 7th ed. Washington, DC: ASA.

————. 2006b. "What Can I Do with a Bachelor's Degree in Sociology." *A National Survey of Seniors Majoring in Sociology: First Glances: What Do They Know and Where are They Going?* Washington DC: American Sociological Association.

Accessed August 2, 2008 (http://www.asanet.org/galleries/default-file/b&b_first_report_final.pdf).

———. 2007. *2006 Guide to Graduate Departments of Sociology.* Washington, DC: ASA.

Amnesty International. 1994. *Breaking the Silence: Human Rights Violations Based on Sexual Orientation.* New York: Amnesty International.

———. 2006. "Amnesty International: Facts and Figures on the Death Penalty." Accessed February 19 (www.amnesty.org).

———. 2007. "Amnesty International: Facts and Figures on the Death Penalty." Accessed February 17 (www.amnesty.org).

Anderson, Elijah. 1990. *Streetwise: Race, Class, and Change in an Urban Community.* Chicago: University of Chicago Press.

Anderson, John Ward, and Molly Moore. 1993. "The Burden of Womanhood. "*Washington Post National Weekly Edition* 10 (March 22–28): 6–7.

Angier, Natalie. 2000. "Do Races Differ? Not Really, Genes Show." *New York Times,* August 22, p. F6. Accessed June 30, 2008 (http://query.nytimes.com/gst/fullpage.html?res=9E07E7DF1E3EF931A1575BC0A9669C69B63&scp=2&sq=natalie+angier&st=nyt).

Anti-Defamation League. 2008. "Anti-Semitic Incidents Decline for Third Straight Year in U.S., According to Annual ADL Audit." Accessed March 5 (www.adl.org).

Arab American Institute. 2008. "Arab Americans: Demographics." Accessed July 1, 2008 (http://www.aaiusa.org/arab-americans/22/demographics).

Arias, Elizabeth. 2004. "United States Life Tables, 2002." *National Vital Statistics Report,* November 10.

Arora, Raksha. 2004. "Is War Still Necessary in the 21st Century?" Gallup Poll Tuesday Briefing, May 11 (www.gallup.com).

Associated Press. 2007. "Exxon Mobil Appealing $2.5 Billion Compensation for *Valdez* Spill." *Anchorage Daily News,* January 17.

Association of American Medical Colleges. 2007. *Facts Applicants, Matriculates and Graduates.* Accessed March 31, 2008 (www.aamc.org/data/facts/start.htm).

———. 2008. *U.S. Medical School Faculty, 2006.* Accessed March 31 (www.aamc.org/data/facultyroster/usmsfø6/start.htm).

Astin, Alexander, Sarah A. Parrott, William S. Korn, and Linda J. Sax. 1994. *The American Freshman: Thirty Year Trends.* Los Angeles: Higher Education Research Institute.

Atchley, Robert C. 1976. *The Sociology of Retirement.* New York: Wiley.

Atchley, Robert C., and Amanda S. Barusch. 2004. *Social Forces and Agency: An Introduction to Social Gerontology,* 10th ed. Belmont, CA: Thompson.

Austin, April. 2002. "Cellphones and Strife in Congo." *Christian Science Monitor,* December 5, p. 11.

## B

Babad, Elisha Y., and P. J. Taylor. 1992. "Transparency of Teacher Expectancies Across Language, Cultural Boundaries." *Journal of Educational Research* 86: 120–125.

Baby Name Wizard. 2008. "NameVoyager." Accessed August 2, 2008 (www.babynamewizard.com).

Bainbridge, William Sims. 2007. "The Scientific Research Potential of Virtual Worlds." *Science* 317 (July 27): 472–476.

Baker, Therese L. 1999. *Doing Social Research.* 3d ed. New York: McGraw-Hill.

Baldwin, James. [1965] 1985. "White Man's Guilt." Pp. 409–414 in *The Price of the Ticket: Collected Non-Fiction, 1948–1985.* New York: St. Martin's Press.

Banerjee, Neela. 2006. "Clergywomen Find Hard Path to Bigger Pulpit." *New York Times,* August 26, pp. A1, A11.

Barboza, David. 2006. "Citing Public Sentiment, China Cancels Release of 'Geisha.'" *New York Times,* February 1, p. B6.

Barnes, Patricia M., Eve Powell-Griner, Kim McFann, and Richard L. Nahin. 2004. *Complimentary and Alternative Medicine Use Among Adults, United States, 2002.* Advance Data from Vital and Health

Statistics, No. 343. Hyattsville, MD: National Center for Health Statistics. Accessed July 5, 2008 (http://nccam.nih.gov/news/camsurvey_fs1.htm).

Barrett, David B., Todd M. Johnson, and Peter F. Crossing. 2005. "Worldwide Adherents of All Religions, Mid-2004" and "Religions Adherents in the United States of America 1900–2005." P. 282 in *Encyclopedia Britannica, Yearbook 2005.* Chicago: Encyclopedia Britannica.

———. 2006. "The 2005 Annual Megacensus of Religions." Pp. 282–283 in 2006 *Book of the Year.* Chicago: Encyclopedia Britannica.

Barrionuevo, Alexei. 2008. "Amazon's 'Forest Peoples' Seek a Role in Striking Global Climate Agreements." *New York Times,* April 6, p. 6.

Basso, Keith H. 1972. "Ice and Travel Among the Fort Norman Slave: Folk Taxonomies and Cultural Rules." *Language in Society* 1 (March): 31–49.

Baudrillard, Jean. [1981] 1994. *Simulacra and Simulation.* Ann Arbor: The University of Michigan Press.

Bauerlein, Monika. 1996. "The Luddites Are Back." *Utne Reader* (March/April): 24, 26.

Baum, Katrina. 2006. "Identity Theft, 2004." *Bureau of Justice Statistics Bulletin* (April).

Bauman, Kurt J. 1999. "Extended Measures of Well-Being: Meeting Basic Needs." *Current Population Reports,* Ser. P. 70, No. 67. Washington, DC: U.S. Government Printing Office.

BBC. 2006. "Madrid Bans Waifs from Catwalks." September 13. Accessed June 7, 2008 (http://news.bbc.co.uk/2/hi/europe/5341202.stm).

Beagan, Brenda L. 2001. " 'Even If I Don't Know What I'm Doing I Can Make It Look Like I Know What I'm Doing': Becoming a Doctor in the 1990s." *Canadian Review of Sociology and Anthropology* 38: 275–292.

Bearman, Peter S., James Moody, and Katherine Stovel. 2004. "Chains of Affection: The Structure of Adolescent Romantic and Sexual Networks." *American Journal of Sociology* 110 (July): 44–91.

Becker, Howard S. 1952. "Social Class Variations in the Teacher–Pupil Relationship." *Journal of Educational Sociology* 25 (April): 451–465.

———. 1963. *The Outsiders: Studies in the Sociology of Deviance.* New York: Free Press.

———, ed. 1964. *The Other Side: Perspectives on Deviance.* New York: Free Press.

———. 1973. *The Outsiders: Studies in the Sociology of Deviance,* rev. ed. New York: Free Press.

Beeghley, Leonard. 1978. *Social Stratification in America: A Critical Analysis of Theory and Research.* Santa Monica, CA: Goodyear.

Bell, Daniel. 1953. "Crime as an American Way of Life." *Antioch Review* 13 (Summer): 131–154.

———. 1999. *The Coming of Post-Industrial Society: A Venture in Social Forecasting.* With new foreword. New York: Basic Books.

Bendick, Marc, Jr., Charles W. Jackson, and J. Horacio Romero. 1993. *Employment Discrimination Against Older Workers: An Experimental Study of Hiring Practices.* Washington, DC: Fair Employment Council of Greater Washington.

Benford, Robert D. 1992. "Social Movements." Pp. 1880–1887 in *Encyclopedia of Sociology,* vol. 4, ed. Edgar F. Borgatta and Marie Borgatta. New York: Macmillan.

Bennett, Vivienne. 1995. "Gender, Class, and Water: Women and the Politics of Water Service in Monterrey, Mexico." *Latin American Perspectives* 22 (September): 76–99.

Bergen, Raquel Kennedy. 2006. *Marital Rape: New Research and Directions.* Harrisburg, PA: VAW Net.

Berger, Peter. 1969. *The Sacred Canopy: Elements of a Sociological Theory of Religion.* Garden City, NY: Anchor Books.

Berger, Peter, and Thomas Luckmann. 1966. *The Social Construction of Reality.* New York: Doubleday.

*Berkeley Wellness Letter.* 1990. "The Nest Refilled" (February): 1–2.

Berland, Gretchen K. 2001. "Health Information on the Internet: Accessibility, Quality, and Readability in English and Spanish."

*Journal of the American Medical Association* 285 (March 23): 2612–2621.

Berlin, Brent, and Paul Kay. 1991. *Basic Color Terms: Their Universality and Evolution.* Berkeley: University of California Press.

Bernasek, Anna. 2006. "A Poverty Line That's Out of Date and Out of Favor." *New York Times,* August 14, p. 8.

Bernstein, Basil. 1962. "Social Class, Linguistic Codes and Grammatical Elements." *Language and Speech* 5: 221–240.

Bianchi, Suzanne M., and Daphne Spain. 1996. "Women,Work, and Family in America." *Population Bulletin* 51 (December).

Bianchi, Suzanne M., John P. Robinson, and Melissa A. Milkie. 2006. *Changing Rhythms of American Family Life.* New York: Russell Sage Foundation.

Biddlecom, Ann, and Steven Martin. 2006. "Childless in America." *Contexts* 5 (Fall): 54.

Black, Donald. 1995. "The Epistemology of Pure Sociology." *Law and Social Inquiry* 20 (Summer): 829–870.

Blau, Peter M., and Otis Dudley Duncan. 1967. *The American Occupational Structure.* New York: Wiley.

Blau, Peter M., and Marshall W. Meyer. 1987. *Bureaucracy in Modern Society,* 3d ed. New York: Random House.

Blauner, Robert. 1972. *Racial Oppression in America.* New York: Harper and Row.

Blinder, Alan S. 2006. "Offshoring: The Next Industrial Revolution." *Foreign Affairs* (March/April).

Blow, Charles M. 2008. "All Atmospherics, No Climate." New York Times, April 19. Accessed July 4, 2008 (http://www.nytimes.com/2008/04/19/opinion/19blow.html).

Blumer, Herbert. 1955. "Collective Behavior." Pp. 165–198 in *Principles of Sociology,* 2d ed., ed. Alfred McClung Lee. New York: Barnes and Noble.

———. 1969. *Symbolic Interactionism: Perspective and Method.* Englewood Cliffs, NJ: Prentice Hall.

Boaz, Rachel Floersheim. 1987. "Early Withdrawal from the Labor Force." *Research on Aging* 9 (December): 530–547.

Bonilla-Silvia, Eduardo. 2004. "From Bi-Racial to Tri-Racial: Towards a New System of Racial Stratification in the USA." *Ethics and Racial Studies* 27 (November): 931–950.

Bornschier, Volker, Christopher Chase-Dunn, and Richard Rubinson. 1978. "Cross-National Evidence of the Effects of Foreign Investment and Aid on Economic Growth and Inequality: A Survey of Findings and a Reanalysis." *American Journal of Sociology* 84 (November): 651–683.

Bottomore, Tom, and Maximilien Rubel, eds. 1956. *Karl Marx: Selected Writings in Sociology and Social Philosophy.* New York: McGraw-Hill.

Boudreaux, Richard. 2002. "Indian Rights Law Is Upheld in Mexico." *Los Angeles Times,* September 7, p. A3.

Bourdieu, Pierre. 1962. *The Algerians.* Preface by Raymond Aron. Boston: Beacon Press.

———. 1984. *Distinction: A Social Critique of the Judgment of Taste.* Cambridge, MA: Harvard University Press.

———. 1986. "The Forms of Capital." Pp. 241–258 in *Handbook of Theory and Research for the Sociology of Education,* ed. J. G. Richardson. New York: Greenwood Press.

———. 1998a. *Acts of Resistance: Against the Tyranny of the Market.* New York: New Press.

———. 1998b. *On Television.* New York: New Press.

Bowles, Samuel, and Herbert Gintis. 1976. *Schooling in Capitalistic America: Educational Reforms and the Contradictions of Economic Life.* New York: Basic Books.

Breines, Winifred. 2007. "Struggling to Connect: White and Black Feminism in the Movement Years." *Contexts* 6 (Winter): 18–24.

Brewer, Cynthia A., and Trudy A. Suchan. 2001. *Mapping Census 2000: The Geography of U.S. Diversity.* Washington, DC: U.S. Government Printing Office.

Brewer, Rose M., and Nancy A. Heitzeg. 2008. "The Racialization of Criminal Punishment." *American Behavioral Scientist* 51 (January): 625–644.

Brittingham, Angela, and G. Patricia de la Cruz. 2004. *Ancestry: 2000.* Census Brief C2KBR-35. Washington, DC: U.S. Government Printing Office.

Brown, David K. 2001. "The Social Sources of Educational Credentialism: Status Cultures, Labor Markets, and Organizations." *Sociology of Education* 74 (Extra Issue): 19–34.

Brown, Robert McAfee. 1980. *Gustavo Gutierrez.* Atlanta: John Knox.

Bruce, Steve. 2000. *Choice and Religion: A Critique of Rational Choice Theory.* New York: Oxford University Press.

Budig, Michelle J. 2002. "Male Advantage and the Gender Composition of Jobs: Who Rides the Glass Escalator?" *Social Problems* 49 (2): 258–277.

Bucks, B. K., A. B. Kennickell, and K. B. Moore. 2006. *Recent Changes in U.S. Family Finances: Evidence from the 2001 and 2004 Survey of Consumer Finances.* Washington, DC: The Federal Reserve Board of Governors. Accessed March 17 (www.federalreserve.gov/pubs/bulletin/2006/financesurvey.pdf).

Bullard, Robert, D. 1993. *Dumping in Dixie: Race, Class, and Environmentalist Quality,* 2d ed. Boulder, CO: Westview Press.

Bulle,Wolfgang F. 1987. *Crossing Cultures? Southeast Asian Mainland.* Atlanta: Centers for Disease Control and Prevention.

Bunzel, John H. 1992. *Race Relations on Campus: Stanford Students Speak.* Stanford, CA: Portable Stanford.

Burawoy, Michael. 2004. "Public Sociologies: Contradictions, Dilemmas, and Possibilities." *Social Forces* 82: 1603–1618.

Bureau of Labor Statistics. 2006. "Number of Jobs Held, Labor Market Activity, and Earnings Growth Among the Youngest Baby Boomers: Results from a Longitudinal Survey." *News,* August 25. Washington, DC: BLS.

———. 2007. "Labor Force (Demographic) Data." February 13. Accessed February 28 (www.bls.gov).

Bureau of the Census. 1975. *Historical Statistics of the United States, Colonial Times to 1970.* Washington, DC: U.S. Government Printing Office.

———. 1994. *Statistical Abstract of the United States, 1994.* Washington, DC: U.S. Government Printing Office.

———. 1998. "Race of Wife by Race of Husband." Internet release of June 10.

———. 2003a. *Statistical Abstract of the United States, 2003.* Washington, DC: U.S. Government Printing Office.

———. 2003b. *Characteristics of American Indians and Alaska Natives, by Tribe and Language: 2000.* Washington, DC: U.S. Government Printing Office.

———. 2004. *Statistical Abstract of the United States, 2004–2005.* Washington, DC: U.S. Government Printing Office.

———. 2005a. *Statistical Abstract of the United States, 2006.* Washington, DC: U.S. Government Printing Office.

———. 2005b. "Total Midyear Population for the World: 1950–2050." Updated April 26. Accessed June 1 (www.census.gov/ipc/www/worldpop. html).

———. 2005c. *Florida, California and Texas Future Population Growth.* Census Bureau Reports, CB05-52. Washington, DC: U.S. Government Printing Office.

———. 2005d. "International Data Base." Accessed April 26 (www.census.gov/ipc/www/idbnew. html).

———. 2005e. "World Population: 1950–2050." April 2005 version. Accessed May 3, 2006 (www. census.gov/ipc/www/img/worldpop. gif).

———. 2005f. "American Fact Finder: Places with United States." Accessed December 12 (http:// factfinder.census.gov).

———. 2005g. "Hurricane Katrina Disaster Area." Accessed December 15 (www.census.gov).

———. 2006a. *Statistical Abstract of the United States, 2007.* Washington, DC: U.S. Government Printing Office.

———. 2006b. "American Community Survey 2006: Table R1601. Percent of People 5 Years and Over Who Speak a Language Other Than English at Home." Accessed October 14, 2007 (http:// Factfinder.census.gov).

————. 2007a. *Statistical Abstract of the United States, 2008.* Washington, DC: U.S. Government Printing Office.

————. 2007b. "American Community Survey 2006" (www.census.gov).

————. 2007c. "Current Population Survey, 2005 to 2007. Annual Social and Economic Supplements." Accessed December 29 (www.census.gov/hhes/www/income/income06/statemhi3.html).

————. 2007d. "America's Families and Living Arrangements: 2006." Current Population Survey (www.census.gov).

————. 2008a. *Statistical Abstract of the United States.* Washington, DC: U.S. Government Printing Office.

————. 2008b. "Total Midyear Population for the World: 1900–2050." Data updated March 27, 2008. Accessed April 9 (www.census.gov).

————. 2008c. "Nearly Half of Preschoolers Receive Child Care from Relatives." Press Release, February 28 (www.census.gov).

Burkeman, Oliver. 2007. "Virtual World Wakes Up to Violent Protest." *Manchester Guardian,* February 16, p. 6.

Burns, John R. 1998. "Once Widowed in India, Twice Scorned." *New York Times,* March 29, p. A1.

Butler, Daniel Allen. 1998. *"Unsinkable: The Full Story."* Mechanicsburg, PA: Stackpole Books.

Butler, Robert N. 1990. "A Disease Called Ageism." *Journal of American Geriatrics Society* 38 (February): 178–180.


## C

Caplan, Ronald L. 1989. "The Commodification of American Health Care." *Social Science and Medicine* 28 (11): 1139–1148.

Caplow, Theodore, and Louis Hicks. 2002. *Systems of War and Peace,* 2d ed. Lanham, MD: University Press of America.

Calhoun, Craig. 1998. "Community Without Propinquity Revisited." *Sociological Inquiry* 68 (Summer): 373–397.

Call, V. R., and J. D. Teachman. 1991. "Military Service and Stability in the Family Life Course." *Military Psychology* 3: 233–250.

Carey, Anne R., and Elys A. McLean. 1997. "Heard It Through the Grapevine?" *USA Today,* September 15, p. B1.

Carmichael, Mary. 2007. "Troubled Waters." *Newsweek* 149 (June 4), pp. 52–56.

Carr, Deborah. 2007. "Baby Blues." *Contexts* (Spring): 62.

Carroll, Joseph. 2005. "Who Supports Marijuana Legalization?" November 1. Accessed January 19, 2007 (www.galluppoll.com).

Carson, Rachel. 1962. *Silent Spring.* Boston: Houghton Mifflin.

Carty, Win. 1999. "Greater Dependence on Cars Leads to More Pollution in World's Cities." *Population Today* 27 (December): 1–2.

Castañeda, Jorge G. 1995. "Ferocious Differences." *Atlantic Monthly* 276 (July): pp. 68–69, 71–76.

Castells, Manuel. 1983. *The City and the Grass Roots.* Berkeley: University of California Press.

————. 1997. *The Power of Identity.* Vol. 1 of *The Information Age: Economy, Society and Culture.* London: Blackwell.

————. 1998. *End of Millennium.* Vol. 3 of *The Information Age: Economy, Society and Culture.* London: Blackwell.

————. 2000. *The Information Age: Economy, Society and Culture* (3 vols.), 2d ed. Oxford and Malden, MA: Blackwell.

————. 2001. *The Internet Galaxy: Reflections on the Internet, Business, and Society.* New York: Oxford University Press.

Catalano, Shannon M. 2005. *Criminal Victimization, 2004.* Washington, DC: U.S. Government Printing Office.

Catalyst. 2007. *2007 Catalyst Census of Women Board Directors, Corporate Officers, and Top Earners.* New York: Catalyst.

————. 2008. "Women and Minorities on Fortune 100 Boards." The Prout Group, the Executive Leadership Council, and the Hispanic Association on Corporate Responsibility. Accessed June 30 (http://www.catalyst.org/file/86/1-17-08%20abd%20study.pdf).

Cavalli-Sforza, L. Luca, Paolo Menozzi, and Alberto Piazza. 1994. *The History and Geography of Human Genes.* Princeton, NJ: Princeton University Press.

CBS News. 1979. Transcript of *Sixty Minutes* segment, "I Was Only Following Orders." March 31, pp. 2–8.

Center for American Women and Politics. 2008. *Fact Sheet: Women in the U.S. Congress 2008 and Statewide Elective Women 2007.* Rutgers, NJ: CAWP. Accessed August 13 (http://www.cawp.rutgers.edu/fast_facts/index.php).

Center for Corporate Diversity. 2008. "Nordic 500, 2006–2008." Accessed March 17 (www.managementwomen.no).

Centers for Disease Control and Prevention. 2007a. *HIV/AIDS Surveillance Report.* Revised June 2007. Atlanta, GA: CDC.

————. 2007b. "U.S. Public Health Service Syphilis Study at Tuskegee." Accessed April 25 (www.cdc.gov).

————. 2007c. "HIV/AIDS Among Women." Revised June 2007. Accessed March 21 (www.cdc.gov.hiv.topics/women/resources/factsheets/women.htm).

Centers for Medicare and Medicaid Services. 2008. "NHE Projections 2007–2017." Accessed March 23 (www.cms.hhs.gov).

Chambliss, William. 1973. "The Saints and the Roughnecks." *Society* 11 (November/December): 24–31.

Charter, David, and Jill Sherman. 1996. "Schools Must Teach New Code of Values." *London Times,* January 15, p. 1.

Chase-Dunn, Christopher, and Peter Grimes. 1995. "World-Systems Analysis." Pp. 387–417 in *Annual Review of Sociology, 1995,* ed. John Hagan. Palo Alto, CA: Annual Reviews.

Cheng, Shu-Ju Ada. 2003. "Rethinking the Globalization of Domestic Service." *Gender and Society* 17 (2): 166–186.

Cherlin, Andrew. 2004. "The Deinstitutionalization of American Marriage." *Journal of Marriage and the Family* 66: 848–861.

————. 2006. "On Single Mothers 'Doing' Family." *Journal of Marriage and Family* 68 (November): 800–803.

————. 2008. *Public and Private Families: An Introduction,* 5th ed. New York: McGraw-Hill.

————. 2008. "Can the Left Learn the Lessons of Welfare Reform?" *Contemporary Sociology* 37 (March): 101–104.

Chesney-Lind, Meda. 1989. "Girls' Crime and Women's Place: Toward a Feminist Model of Female Delinquency." *Crime and Delinquency* 35: 5–29.

*China Daily.* 2004. "Starbucks Takes Aim at China Chain." Accessed July 21 (www2.chinadaily. com.cn).

Christensen, Kathleen. 1990. "Bridges over Troubled Water: How Older Workers View the Labor Market." Pp. 175–207 in *Bridges to Retirement,* ed. Peter B. Doeringer. Ithaca, NY: IRL Press.

Cigar, Norman. 1995. *Genocide in Bosnia: The Policy of "Ethnic Cleansing."* College Station: Texas A&M University Press.

Civic Ventures. 1999. *The New Face of Retirement: Older Americans, Civic Engagement, and the Longevity Revolution.* Washington, DC: Peter D. Hart Research Associates.

Clark, Burton, and Martin Trow. 1966. "The Organizational Context." Pp. 17–70 in *The Study of College Peer Groups,* ed. Theodore M. Newcomb and Everett K. Wilson. Chicago: Aldine.

Clarke, Adele E., Janet K. Shim, Laura Maro, Jennifer Ruth Fusket, and Jennifer R. Fishman. 2003. "Bio Medicalization: Technoscientific Transformations of Health, Illness, and U.S. Biomedicine." *American Sociological Review* 68 (April): 161–194.

Clarke, Edward H. 1874. *Sex in Education; or, A Fair Chance for Girls.* Boston: James R. Osgood.

Clausen, Christopher. 2002. "To Have . . . or Not to Have." *Utne Reader* (July–August): 66–70.

Clinard, Marshall B., and Robert F. Miller. 1998. *Sociology of Deviant Behavior,* 10th ed. Fort Worth, TX: Harcourt Brace.

CNN. 2006. "Skinny Models Banned from Catwalk." September 13. Accessed June 7, 2008 (http://www.cnn.com/2006/WORLD/europe/09/13/spain.models/index.html).

Colby, David C. 1986. "The Voting Rights Act and Black Registration in Mississippi." *Publius* 16 (Fall): 123–137.

Cole, Elizabeth S. 1985. "Adoption, History, Policy, and Program." Pp. 638–666 in *A Handbook of Child Welfare,* ed. John Laird and Ann Hartman. New York: Free Press.

Cole, Mike. 1988. *Bowles and Gintis Revisited: Correspondence and Contradiction in Educational Theory.* Philadelphia: Falmer.

Coleman, Isobel. 2004. "The Payoff from Women's Rights." *Foreign Affairs* 83 (May/June): 80–95.

Coleman, James William. 2006. *The Criminal Elite: Understanding White-Collar Crime,* 6th ed. New York: Worth.

Collins, Gail. 2003. *America's Women.* New York: HarperCollins.

Collins, Randall. 1975. *Conflict Sociology: Toward an Explanatory Sociology.* New York: Academic Press.

———. 1980. "Weber's Last Theory of Capitalism: A Systematization." *American Sociological Review* 45 (December): 925–942.

———. 1986. *Weberian Sociological Theory.* New York: Cambridge University Press.

———. 1995. "Prediction in Macrosociology: The Case of the Soviet Collapse." *American Journal of Sociology* 100 (May): 1552–1593.

Collura, Heather. 2007. "Roommate Concerns Fed by Facebook." *USA Today,* August 8, p. D6.

Commission on Civil Rights. 1976. *A Guide to Federal Laws and Regulations Prohibiting Sex Discrimination.* Washington, DC: U.S. Government Printing Office.

———. 1981. *Affirmative Action in the 1980s: Dismantling the Process of Discrimination.* Washington, DC: U.S. Government Printing Office.

Commoner, Barry. 1971. *The Closing Circle.* New York: Knopf.

———. 1990. *Making Peace with the Planet.* New York: Pantheon Books.

Connell, R. W. 1987. *Gendered Power: Society, the Person, and Sexual Politics.* Stanford, CA: Stanford University Press.

———. 2002. *Gender.* Cambridge, UK: Polity Press.

———. 2005. *Masculinities,* 2d ed. Berkeley: University of California Press.

Cooley, Charles. H. 1902. *Human Nature and the Social Order.* New York: Scribner.

Coontz, Stephanie. 1992. *The Way We Never Were: American Families and the Nostalgia Trap.* New York: Basic Books.

———. 2005. *Marriage, a History: From Obedience to Intimacy or How Love Conquered Marriage.* New York: Viking.

———. 2006. "A Pop Quiz on Marriage." *New York Times,* February 19, p. 12.

———. 2008. "The Future of Marriage." *Cato Unbound,* January 14. Accessed June 9 (http://www.cato-unbound.org/2008/01/14/stephanie-coontz/the-future-of-marriage/).

Corak, Miles. 2006. "Do Poor Children Become Poor Adults? Lessons from a Cross Country Comparison of Generational Earnings Mobility." Institute for the Study of Labor (IZA) Discussion Paper No. 1993, March. Accessed June 24, 2008 (http://papers.ssrn.com/sol3/papers.cfm?abstract_id=889034).

Conrad, Peter, ed. 2005. *The Sociology of Health and Illness: Cultural Perspectives,* 7th ed. New York: Worth.

———. 2007. *The Medicalization of Society: On the Transformation of Human Conditions into Treatable Disorders.* Baltimore, MD: Johns Hopkins University Press.

Cooper, Bruce S., and John Sureau. 2007. "The Politics of Home-schooling: New Developments, New Challenges." *Educational Policy* 21 (January and March): 110–131.

Cooper, K., S. Day, A. Green, and H. Ward. 2007. "Maids, Migrants and Occupational Health in the London Sex Industry. *Anthropology and Medicine* 14 (April) 41–53.

Coser, Rose Laub. 1984. "American Medicine's Ambiguous Progress." *Contemporary Sociology* 13 (January): 9–13.

Côté, James E. 2000. *Arrested Adulthood: The Changing Nature of Identity and Maturity in the Late World.* New York: New York University.

Couch, Carl J. 1996. *Information Technologies and Social Orders.* Edited with an introduction by David R. Maines and Shing-Ling Chien. New York: Aldine de Gruyter.

Council on Scientific Affairs. 1999. "Hispanic Health in the United States." *Journal of the American Medical Association* 265 (January 9): 248–252.

Cox, Oliver C. 1948. *Caste, Class, and Race: A Study in Social Dynamics.* Detroit: Wayne State University Press.

Crosnoe, Robert, and Glen H. Elder, Jr. 2002. "Successful Adaptation in the Later Years: A Life Course Approach to Aging." *Social Psychology Quarterly* (4): 309–328.

Cross, Simon, and Barbara Bagilhole. 2002. "Girls' Jobs for the Boys? Men, Masculinity and Non-traditional Occupations." *Gender, Work, and Organization* 9 (April):204–226.

Croucher, Sheila L. 2004. *Globalization and Belonging: The Politics of Identity in a Changing World.* Lanham, MD: Rowman and Littlefield.

Crouse, Kelly. 1999. "Sociology of the Titanic." *Teaching Sociology Listserv,* May 24.

Cullen, Francis T., Jr., and John B. Cullen. 1978. *Toward a Paradigm of Labeling Theory,* Ser. 58. Lincoln: University of Nebraska Studies.

Cullen, Lisa Takevchi. 2007. "Till Work Do Us Part." *Time,* October 8, pp. 63–64.

Cumming, Elaine, and William E. Henry. 1961. *Growing Old: The Process of Disengagement.* New York: Basic Books.

Currie, Elliot. 1985. *Confronting Crime: An American Challenge.* New York: Pantheon Books.

———. 1998. *Crime and Punishment in America.* New York: Metropolitan Books.

Curtiss, Susan. 1977. *Genie: A Psycholinguistic Study of a Modern Day "Wild Child."* New York: Academic Press.

———. 1985. "The Development of Human Cerebral Lateralization." Pp. 97–116 in *The Dual Brain,* ed. D. Frank Benson and Eran Zaidel. New York: Guilford Press.

# D

Dahl, Robert A. 1961. *Who Governs?* New Haven, CT: Yale University Press.

Daisey, Mike. 2002. *21 Dog Years: Doing Time @ Amazon.com.* New York: Free Press.

Daley, Suzanne. 1999. "Doctors' Group of Volunteers Awarded Nobel." *New York Times,* October 16, pp. A1, A6.

Dalla, Rochelle L., and Wendy C. Gamble. 2001. "Teenage Mothering and the Navajo Reservation: An Examination of Intergovernmental Perceptions and Beliefs." *American Indian Culture and Research Journal* 25 (1): 1–19.

Daniszewski, John. 2003. "Al-Jazeera TV Draws Flak Outside—and Inside—the Arab World." *Los Angeles Times,* January 5, pp. A1, A5.

Dao, James. 1995. "New York's Highest Court Rules Unmarried Couples Can Adopt." *New York Times,* November 3, pp. A1, B2.

Darwin, Charles. 1859. *On the Origin of Species.* London: John Murray.

David, Gary. 2004. "Scholarship on Arab Americans Distorted Past 9/11." *Al Jadid* (Winter/Spring): 26–27.

———. 2008. "Arab Americans." Pp. 84–87 in *Encyclopedia of Race, Ethnicity, and Society,* vol. 1, ed. Richard T. Schaefer. Thousands Oaks, CA: Sage.

Davies, Christie. 1989. "Goffman's Concept of the Total Institution: Criticisms and Revisions." *Human Studies* 12 (June): 77–95.

Davis, James A., Tom W. Smith, and Peter V. Marsden. 2007. *General Social Surveys, 1972–2006: Cumulative Codebook.* Chicago: National Opinion Research Center.

Davis, James Allan, and Tom W. Smith. 2007. *General Social Surveys, 1972–2006.* Storrs, CT: Roper Center.

Davies, James B., Anthony Shorrocks, Susanna Sandstrom, and Edward N. Wolff. 2007. "The World Distribution of Household Wealth." Center for Global, International and Regional Studies. Mapping Global Inequalities—conference papers. Paper mgi-5, presented November 28. Accessed June 23, 2008 (http://repositories.cdlib.org/cgirs/mgi/mgi-5).

Davis, Gerald. 2003. *America's Corporate Banks Are Separated by Just Four Handshakes.* Accessed March 7 (www.bus.umich.edu/ research/ davis.html).

———. 2004. "American Cronyism: How Executive Networks Inflated the Corporate Bubble." *Contexts* (Summer): 34–40.

Davis, Kingsley. 1940. "Extreme Social Isolation of a Child." *American Journal of Sociology* 45 (January): 554–565.

———. 1947. "A Final Note on a Case of Extreme Isolation." *American Journal of Sociology* 52 (March): 432–437.

———. [1949] 1995. *Human Society,* New York: Macmillan.

———, and Wilbert E. Moore. 1945. "Some Principles of Stratification." *American Sociological Review* 10 (April): 242–249.

Davis, Nanette J. 1975. *Sociological Constructions of Deviance: Perspectives and Issues in the Field.* Dubuque, IA: Wm. C Brown.

Death Penalty Information Center. 2006. "Number of Executions by State and Region Since 1976." Accessed February 19 (www. deathpenalty info.org).

———. 2008. "Facts About the Death Penalty." Accessed January 12 (www.deathpenaltyinfo.org).

Deegan,Mary Jo, ed. 1991.*Women in Sociology: A Bio-Biographical Sourcebook.* Westport, CT: Greenwood.

Deflem, Mathieu. 2005. "'Wild Beasts Without Nationality': The Uncertain Origins of Interpol, 1898–1910." Pp. 275–285 in *Handbook of Transnational Crime and Justice,* ed. Philip Rerchel. Thousand Oaks, CA: Sage.

Delawala, Imtyaz. 2002. "What Is Coltran?" January 21 (www .abcnews.com).

DeMott, Benjamin. 1990. *The Imperial Middle: Why Americans Can't Think Straight About Class.* New York: William Morrow.

DeNavas-Walt, Carmen, Bernadette D. Proctor, and Cheryl Miller. 2005. "Income, Poverty and Health Insurance Coverage in the United States: 2004." *Current Population Reports,* Ser. P-60, No. 229. Washington, DC: U.S. Government Printing Office.

DeNavas-Walt, Carmen, Bernadette D. Proctor, and Cheryl Hill Lee. 2006. "Income, Poverty, and Health Insurance Coverage in the United States: 2005." *Current Population Reports,* Ser. P-60, No. 231. Washington, DC: U.S. Government Printing Office.

DeNavas-Walt, Carmen, Bernadette D. Proctor, and Jessica Smith. 2007. "Income, Poverty, and Health Insurance Coverage in the United States: 2006." *Current Population Reports,* Ser. P-60, No. 233. Washington, DC: U.S. Government Printing Office.

DePalma, Anthony. 1995. "Racism? Mexico's in Denial." *New York Times,* June 11, p. E4.

DeParle, Jason. 2005. "Hispanic Group Thrives on Federal Aid." *New York Times,* May 3, pp. A1, A16.

———. 2007. "In a World on the Move, a Tiny Land Strains to Cope." *New York Times,* June, p. A1.

———. 2007. "Migrant Money Flow: A $300 Billion Current." *New York Times,* November 18, work section p. 3.

Department of Homeland Security. 2006. *The Federal Response to Hurricane Katrina: Lessons Learned.* Washington, DC: U.S. Government Printing Office.

Department of Justice. 2000. *The Civil Liberties Act of 1988: Redress for Japanese Americans.* Accessed June 29 (http://www.usdoj.gov/ crt/ora/main. html).

———. 2005. *Crime in the United States, 2004.* Washington, DC: U.S. Government Printing Office.

———. 2007. "Hate Crime Statistics, 2006" (www.fbi.gov/ucr/ucr. htm).

———. 2007a. *Crime in the United States, 2006.* Washington, DC: U.S. Government Printing Office.

Department of Labor. 1995a. *Good for Business: Making Full Use of the Nation's Capital.* Washington, DC: U.S. Government Printing Office.

———. 1995b. *A Solid Investment: Making Full Use of the Nation's Human Capital.* Washington, DC: U.S. Government Printing Office.

Devitt, James. 1999. *Framing Gender on the Campaign Trail: Women's Executive Leadership and the Press.* New York: Women's Leadership Conference.

Dickens, Charles. 1843. *A Christmas Carol.* London: Chapman and Hall. Accessed July 7, 2008 (www.gutenberg.org/dirs/4/46/46-h/ 46-h.htm).

Dillon, Sam. 1998. "Sex Bias at Border Plants in Mexico Reported by U.S." *New York Times,* January 13, p. A6.

———. 2004. "Education Can Be Long, Hard Haul for Nation's Rural Kids." *Chicago Tribune,* May 28, p. 13.

Doeringer, Peter B., ed. 1990. *Bridges to Retirement: Older Workers in a Changing Labor Market.* Ithaca, NY: ILR Press.

Domhoff, G. William. 1978. *Who Really Rules? New Haven and Community Power Reexamined.* New Brunswick, NJ: Transaction.

———. 2006. *Who Rules America?* 5th ed. New York: McGraw-Hill.

Doress, Irwin, and Jack Nusan Porter. 1977. *Kids in Cults: Why They Join. Why They Join, Why They Stay, Why They Leave.* Brookline, MA: Reconciliation Associates.

Dorn, Stan. 2008. *Uninsured and Dying Because of It.* Washington, DC: Urban Institute.

Dougherty, John, and David Holthouse. 1999. "Bordering on Exploitation." Accessed March 5 (www.phoenixnewtime.com/ issies/1998-07-09/ feature.html).

Dougherty, Kevin, and Floyd M. Hammack. 1992. "Education Organization." Pp. 535–541 in *Encyclopedia of Sociology,* vol. 2, ed. Edgar F. Borgatta and Marie L. Borgatta. New York: Macmillan.

Dowd, James J. 1980. *Stratification Among the Aged.* Monterey, CA: Brooks/Cole.

Dressler, William W., Kathryn S. Oths, and Clarence C. Gravlee. 2005. "Racial and Ethnicity in Public Health Research: Models to Explain Health Disparities." Pp. 231–252 in *Annual Review of Anthropology 2005,* ed. William H. Durham. Palo Alto, CA: Annual Reviews.

Dubner, Stephen J. 2007. "Everything You Always Wanted to Know About Street Gangs (But Didn't Know Whom to Ask)." Freakanomics blog, *New York Times,* August 6. Accessed June 10, 2008 (http://freakonomics.blogs.nytimes.com/2007/08/06/everything-you-always-wanted-to-know-about-street-gangs-but-didnt-know-whom-to-ask/).

Du Bois, W.E.B. [1903] 1994. *The Souls of Black Folk.* New York: Dover.

———. [1909] 1970. *The Negro American Family.* Cambridge, MA: M.I.T. Press.

———. [1940] 1968. *Dusk of Dawn.* New York: Schocken Books.

Dugger, Celia. 2006. "Peace Prize to Pioneer of Loans for Those Too Poor to Borrow." *New York Times,* October 14, pp. A1, A6.

Dukes, Richard L., Tara M. Bisel, Karoline N. Burega, Eligio A. Lobato, and Matthew D. Owens. 2003. "Expression of Love, Sex, and Hurt in Popular Songs: A Content Analysis of All-Time Greatest Hits." *Social Science Journal:* 643–650.

Duneier, Mitchell. 1994a. "On the Job, but Behind the Scenes." *Chicago Tribune,* December 26, pp. 1, 24.

———. 1994b. "Battling for Control." *Chicago Tribune,* December 28, pp. 1, 8.

———. 1999. *Sidewalk.* New York: Farrar, Straus and Giroux.

Durden, T. Elizabeth, and Robert A. Hummer. 2006. "Access to Healthcare Among Working-Age Hispanic Adults in the United States." *Social Science Quarterly* 87 (December): 1319–1343.

Durkheim, Émile. [1887] 1972. "Religion and Ritual." Pp. 219-238 in *Émile Durkheim: Selected Writings,* ed. A. Giddens. Cambridge: Cambridge University Press.

———. [1893] 1933. *Division of Labor in Society,* trans. George Simpson. New York: Free Press.

———. [1897] 1951. *Suicide,* trans. John A. Spaulding and George Simpson. New York: Free Press.

———. [1895] 1964. *The Rules of Sociological Method,* trans. Sarah A. Solovay and John H. Mueller. New York: Free Press.

———. [1912] 2001. *The Elementary Forms of Religious Life,* trans. Carol Cosman. New York: Oxford University Press.

Dykman, Jason. 2006. "America by the Numbers." *Time,* vol. 168, October, pp. 41–54.

## E

Ebaugh, Helen Rose Fuchs. 1988. *Becoming an Ex: The Process of Role Exit.* Chicago: University of Chicago Press.

Eckenwiler, Mark. 1995. "In the Eyes of the Law." *Internet World* (August): 74, 76–77.

Economic Mobility Project. 2007. *Economic Mobility of Immigrants in the United States.* Washington, DC: Pew Charitable Trust.

*The Economist.* 2004a. "Veil of Tears." (January 15).

———. 2004b. "Battle on the Home Front." (February 21): 8–10.

———. 2005a. "Back to the Beach?" (January 8): 54–55.

———. 2005b. "We Are Tous Québécois." (January 8): 39.

———. 2005c. "Behind the Digital Divide." (March 2): 22–25.

———. 2005d. "Chasing the Dream." (August 6): 53–55.

———. 2005e. "The Mountain Man and the Surgeon." (December 24): 24–26.

———. 2005f. "The Hidden Wealth of the Poor." (November 5): 1–14.

———. 2005g. "Not Here, Surely?" (December 10): 31–32.

———. 2006. "The World's Largest Economies." (April 1): 84.

———. 2006a. "The World's Largest Economies." (April 1): 84.

———. 2007a. "Giving to Charity: Bring Back the Victorians." (February 17): 56–57.

———. 2007b. "Africa and the Internet: The Digital Gap." (October 12): 64.

———. 2008a. "Maharishi Mahesh Yogi." (February 16): 95.

———. 2008b. "A Ravenous Dragon: A Special Report on China's Quest for Resources." (March 15): 1–22.

Edwards, Harry. 1973. *Sociology of Sport.* Homewood, IL: Dorsey Press.

EEOC. 2008. "Age Discrimination in Employment Act (ADEA) Charges FY 1997– FY 2007." Washington, DC: U.S Equal Employment Opportunity Commission. Accessed June 27 (http://www.eeoc.gov/stats/adea.html).

Ehrenreich, Barbara. 2001. *Nickel and Dimed: On (Not) Getting By in America.* New York: Metropolitan.

Herenreich, Barbara, and Arlie Russell Hochschild. 2003. *Global Woman: Nannies, Maids, and Sex Workers in the New Economy.* New York: Metropolitan Books.

Ehrlich, Paul R. 1968. *The Population Bomb.* New York: Ballantine Books.

Ehrlich, Paul R., and Anne H. Ehrlich. 1990. *The Population Explosion.* New York: Simon and Schuster.

Herlich, Paul R., and Katherine Ellison. 2002. "A Looming Threat We Won't Face." *Los Angeles Times,* January 20, p. M6.

Eitzen, D. Stanley. 2003. *Fair and Foul: Beyond the Myths and Paradoxes of Sport,* 2d ed. Lanham, MD: Rowman and Littlefield.

Elliott, Michael. 2005. "Hopelessly Divided: Being a Fan Is Like Having Your Own Personal Time Machine." *Time Magazine,* June 20, p. 76.

Ellison, Brandy. 2008. "Tracking." Pp. 301–304 in *Encyclopedia of Race, Ethnicity, and Society,* vol. 2, ed. Richard T. Schaefer. Thousand Oaks, CA: Sage.

Ellison, Ralph. 1952. *Invisible Man.* New York: Random House.

Ellul, Jacques. 1964. *The Technological Society.* New York: Knopf.

Eltman, Frank. 2007. "Wealthy Couple Charged with Slavery." Associated Press, May 24.

Ely, Robin J. 1995. "The Power of Demography: Women's Social Construction of Gender Identity at Work." *Academy of Management Journal* 38 (3): 589–634.

Engels, Friedrich [1884] 1959. "The Origin of the Family, Private Property, and the State." Pp. 392–394 in *Marx and Engels: Basic Writings on Politics and Philosophy,* ed. Lewis Feuer. Garden City, NY: Anchor Books.

Entine, Jon, and Martha Nichols. 1996. "Blowing the Whistle on Meaningless 'Good Intentions.'" *Chicago Tribune,* June 20, p. A21.

Erksine, William, and Roberta Spatter-Roth. 2006. *ASA Research Brief: Profile of 2005 ASA Membership.* Washington, DC: American Sociological Association.

Escárcega, Sylvia. 2008. "Mexico." Pp. 898–902 in *Encyclopedia of Race, Ethnicity, and Society,* vol. 2, ed. Richard T. Schaefer. Thousand Oaks, CA: Sage.

Etaugh, Claire. 2003. "Witches, Mothers and Others: Females in Children's Books." *Hilltopics* (Winter): 10–13.

Etcoff, Nancy, Susie Orbach, Jennifer Scott, and Heidi D'Agostino. 2004. "The Real Truth About Beauty: A Global Repor— Findings of the Global Study on Women, Beauty and Well-Being." Commissioned by Dove, a Unilever Beauty Brand. Accessed June 28, 2008 (http://www.campaignforrealbeauty.com/uploadedfiles/DOVE_white_paper_final.pdf).

Etzioni, Amitai. 1964. *Modern Organization.* Englewood Cliffs, NJ: Prentice Hall.

———. 1965. *Political Unification.* New York: Holt, Rinehart and Winston.

Eureka County. 2006. "EPA Hears Testimony on Proposed Radiation Rule." *Nuclear Waste Office Newsletter* (Eureka County Yucca Mountain Information Office) 11 (Winter).

## F

Faith, Nazila. 2005. "Iranian Cleric Turns Blogger in Campaign for Reform." *New York Times,* January 16, p. 4.

Farr, Grant M. 1999. *Modern Iran.* New York: McGraw-Hill.

Fausto-Sterling, A. 2000. "The Five Sexes, Revisited." *The Sciences* (July/August): 18–23.

Feagin, Joe R. 1983. *The Urban Real Estate Game: Playing Monopoly with Real Money.* Englewood Cliffs, NJ: Prentice Hall.

———. 1989. *Minority Group Issues in Higher Education: Learning from Qualitative Research.* Norman: Center for Research on Minority Education, University of Oklahoma.

———. 2001. "Social Justice and Sociology: Agenda for the Twenty-First Century." *American Sociological Review* 66 (February): 1–20.

———, Harnán Vera, and Nikitah Imani. 1996. *The Agony of Education: Black Students at White Colleges and Universities.* New York: Routledge.

Featherman, David L., and Robert M. Hauser. 1978. *Opportunity and Change.* New York: Aeodus.

Felson, David, and Akis Kalaitzidis. 2005. "A Historical Overview of Transnational Crime." Pp. 3–19 in *Handbook of Transnational Crime and Justice,* ed. Philip Reichel. Thousand Oaks, CA: Sage.

Feminist Majority Foundation. 2007. "Feminists Are the Majority." Accessed February 25 (www.feminist.org).

Ferree, Myra Marx. 2005. "It's Time to Mainstream Research on Gender." *Chronicle of Higher Education* 51 (August 21): B10.

Ferree, Myra Marx, and David A. Merrill. 2000. "Hot Movements, Cold Cognition: Thinking about Social Movements in Gendered Frames." *Contemporary Society* 29 (May): 454–462.

Feuer, Alan. 2002. "Haven for Workers in Bronx Evolves for Their Retirement." *New York Times,* August 5. Accessed June 27, 2008 (http://query.nytimes.com/gst/fullpage.html?res=9D07E7D9133BF936A3575BC0A9649C8B63).

Feuer, Lewis S. 1989. *Marx and Engels: Basic Writings on Politics and Philosophy.* New York: Anchor Books.

Fields, Jason. 2001. "America's Families and Living Arrangements." *Current Population Reports,* Ser. P-20, No. 537. Washington, DC: U.S. Government Printing Office.

———. 2003. "Children's Living Arrangements and Characteristics: March 2002." *Current Population Reports,* Ser. P-20, No. 547. Washington, DC: U.S. Government Printing Office.

———. 2004. "America's Families and Living Arrangements: 2003." *Current Population Reports,* Ser. P-20, No. 553. Washington, DC: U.S. Government Printing Office.

Finder, Alan. 1995. "Despite Tough Laws, Sweatshops Flourish." *New York Times,* January 6, pp. A1, B4.

Fine, Gary Alan. 1987. *With the Boys: Little League Baseball and Preadolescent Culture.* Chicago: University of Chicago Press.

Fine, Gary C. 2008. " Robbers Cave." Pp. 1163–1164 in *Encyclopedia of Race, Ethnicity, and Society,* vol. 3, ed. Richard T. Schaefer. Thousand Oaks, CA: Sage.

Finkel, Steven E., and James B. Rule. 1987. "Relative Deprivation and Related Psychological Theories of Civil Violence: A Critical Review." *Research in Social Movements* 9: 47–69.

Fishman, Charles. 2006. *The Wal-Mart Effect: How the World's Most Powerful Company Really Works—and How It's Transforming the American Economy.* New York: Penguin Books.

Fitzgerald, Kathleen J., and Diane M. Rodgers. 2000. "Radical Social Movement Organization: A Theoretical Model." *The Sociological Quarterly* 41 (4): 573–592.

Flacks, Richard. 1971. *Youth and Social Change.* Chicago: Markham.

Fletcher, Connie. 1995. "On the Line: Women Cops Speak Out." *Chicago Tribune Magazine,* February 19, pp. 14–19.

Flynn, Patrice. 2007. "Microfinance: The Newest Finance Technology of the Washington Consensus." *Challenge* 50 (March/April): 110–121.

Förster, Michael, and Marco Mira d'Ercole. 2005. *Income Distribution and Poverty in OECD Countries in the Second Half of the 1990s.* Paris: OECD.

Forsythe, David P. 1990. "Human Rights in U.S. Foreign Policy: Retrospect and Prospect." *Political Science Quarterly* 105 (3): 435–454.

*Fortune.* 2007. "Global 500." July 14.

Fouchè, Gladys. 2008. "Norway's Gender Deadline Passes."*The Guardian Weekly,* April 1, p.15.

Foy, Paul. 2006. "Interior Rejects Goshute Nuclear Waste Stockpile." *Indian Country Today* 20 (September 18): 1.

Franklin, John Hope, and Alfred A. Moss. 2000. *From Slavery to Freedom: A History of African Americans,* 8th ed. Upper Saddle River, NJ: Prentice Hall.

Freeman, Jo. 1973. "The Origins of the Women's Liberation Movement." *American Journal of Sociology* 78 (January): 792–811.

———. 1975. *The Politics of Women's Liberation.* New York: McKay.

Freidson, Eliot. 1970. *Profession of Medicine.* New York: Dodd, Mead.

French, Howard W. 2000. "The Pretenders." *New York Times Magazine,* December 3, pp. 86–88.

———. 2004b. "China's Textbooks Twist and Omit History." *New York Times* (December 6), p. A10.

———. 2008. "Lines of Grinding Poverty, Untouched by China's Boom." *New York Times,* January 13, p. 4.

Freudenburg,William R. 2005. "Seeing Science, Courting Conclusions: Reexamining the Intersection of Science, Corporate Cash, and the Law." *Sociological Forum* 20 (March): 3–33.

Freudenheim, Milt. 2005. "Help Wanted: Oldest Workers Please Apply." *New York Times,* March 23, pp. A1, C3.

Fridlund, Alan. J., Paul Erkman, and Harriet Oster. 1987. "Facial Expressions of Emotion; Review of Literature 1970–1983." Pp. 143–224 in *Nonverbal Behavior and Communication,* 2d ed., ed. Aron W. Seigman and Stanley Feldstein. Hillsdale, NJ: Lawrence Erlbaum.

Friedan, Betty. 1963. *The Feminine Mystique.* New York: Dell.

———. 1993. *The Fountain of Age.* New York: Simon and Schuster.

Friedman, Thomas L. 2005. *The World Is Flat: A Brief History of the Twenty-first Century.* New York: Farrar, Straus and Giroux.

Fullerton, Jr., Howard N. 1995. "The 2005 Labor Force: Growing, but Slowly." *Monthly Labor Review* (November): 29–44.

Furman, Jason. 2007. "The Effect of the 2001–06 Tax Cuts on After-Tax Incomes." Testimony before the U.S. House Committee on Ways and Means, September 6.

Furstenberg, Frank F. 2007. "The Making of the Black Family: Race and Class in Qualitative Studies in the Twentieth Century." *Annual Review of Sociology* 33: 429–348.

Furstenberg, Sheela Kennedy, Jr., Vonnie C. McCloyd, Rubén G. Rumbaut, and Richard A. Setterstein, Jr. 2004. "Growing Up Is Harder to Do." *Contexts* 3: 33–41.

Fuson, Ken. 2008. "Raid Mars Future for 3 Graduating Today from Postville." *Des Moines Register,* May 25. Accessed June 29, 2008 http://www.desmoinesregister.com/apps/pbcs.dll/article?AID=/20080525/NEWS/805250327/1001&theme=POSTVILLE_ICE_RAID).

Fuwa, Makiko. 2004. "Macro-Level Gender Inequality and the Division of Household Labor in 22 Countries." *American Sociological Review* 69 (December): 751–767.

## G

Gallup. 2007a. "Death Penalty." Accessed February 17 (www.gallup .com).

———. 2008a. "Abortion." Accessed March 6 (www.gallup.com).

———. 2008b. "Homosexual Relations." Accessed March 6 (www .gallup.com).

———. 2008c. "Religion." Accessed March 14 (www.gallup.com).

———. 2008d. "Environment." Accessed March 18 (www.gallup .com).

Gallup Opinion Index. 1978. "Religion in America, 1977–1978." (January).

Gamson, Joshua. 1989. "Silence, Death, and the Invisible Enemy: AIDS Activism and Social Movement 'Newness.'" *Social Problems* 36 (October): 351–367.

Gans, Herbert. 1971. "The Uses of Poverty: The Poor Pay All." *Social Policy* (July/August): 20–24.

Garcia-Moreno, Claudia, Henrica A. F. M. Jansen, Mary Ellsberg, Lori Heise, and Charlotte Watts. 2005. *WHO Multi-Country Study on Women's Health and Domestic Violence Against Women.* Geneva, Switzerland: WHO.

Gardner, Gary, Erik Assadourian, and Radhika Sarin. 2004. "The State of Consumption Today." Pp. 3–21 in *State of the World 2004,* ed. Brian Halweil and Lisa Mastny. New York: Norton.

Garfinkel, Harold. 1956. "Conditions of Successful Degradation Ceremonies." *American Journal of Sociology* 61 (March): 420–424.

Garner, Roberta. 1996. *Contemporary Movements and Ideologies.* New York: McGraw-Hill.

———. 1999. "Virtual Social Movements." Paper presented at Zaldfest: A Conference in Honor of Mayer Zald, September 17, Ann Arbor, MI.

Gay, Lesbian and Straight Education Network. 2008. "About GLSEN." Accessed March 14 (www.glsen.org).

Gecas, Viktor. 1992. "Socialization." Pp. 1863–1872 in *Encyclopedia of Sociology,* vol. 4, ed. Edgar F. Borgatta and Marie L. Borgatta. New York: Macmillan.

Geist, Eric L., Vasily V. Titov, and Costas E. Synolakis. 2006. "Tsunami: Wave of Change." *Scientific American* 294 (January): 56–63.

Gendell, Murray. 2008. "Older Workers: Increasing Their Labor Force Participation and Hours of Work." *Monthly Labor Review* (January): 41–54.

Gentleman, Amelia. 2007. "Police Ignore Serial Killings in Delhi Slum, Exposing Unequal Justice for India's Poor." *New York Times,* January 7, p. 8.

Gerencher, Kristen. 2007. "New Online Consumer Health Site Aims Big." Accessed May 20 (www.marketwatch.com).

Gerth, H. H., and C. Wright Mills. 1958. *From Max Weber: Essays in Sociology.* New York: Galaxy.

Giddens, Anthony. 1991. *Modernity and Self- Identity: Self and Society in the Late Modern Age.* Cambridge, UK: Polity.

Giordano, Peggy C. 2003. "Relationships in Adolescence." Pp. 257–281 in *Annual Review of Sociology, 2003,* ed. Karen S. Cook and John Hagan. Palo Alto, CA: Annual Reviews.

Giroux, Henry A. 1988. *Schooling and the Struggle for Public Life: Critical Pedagogy in the Modern Age.* Minneapolis: University of Minnesota Press.

Glaze, Lauren E., and Seri Palla. 2005. "Probation and Parole in the United States, 2004." *Bureau of Justice Statistics Bulletin* (November).

Glenn, David. 2007. "Anthropologists in a War Zone: Scholars Debate Their Role." *Chronicle of Higher Education* 54 (September 30): A1, A10–A12.

Glionna, John M. 2004. "Finding a Voice in Politics." *Los Angeles Times,* May 22, pp. A1, A22.

Global Alliance for Workers and Communities. 2003. *About Us.* Accessed April 28 (www.theglobalalliance.org).

Goering, Laurie. 2007. "The First Refugees of Global Warming." *Chicago Tribune,* May 2, pp. 1, 25.

———. 2008. "Women Urge Larger Role in Easing World's Ills." *Chicago Tribune,* March 11, p. 11.

Goffman, Erving. 1959. *The Presentation of Self in Everyday Life.* New York: Doubleday.

———. 1961. *Asylums: Essays on the Social Situation of Mental Patients and Other Inmates.* Garden City, NY: Doubleday.

———. 1963. *Stigma: Notes on Management of Spoiled Identity.* Englewood Cliffs, NJ: Prentice Hall.

———. 1979. *Gender Advertisements.* Cambridge, MA: Harvard University Press.

Golden, Frederic. 1999. "Who's Afraid of Frankenfood?" *Time,* November 29, pp. 49–50.

Goldstein, Melvyn C., and Cynthia M. Beall. 1981. "Modernization and Aging in the Third and Fourth World: Views from the Rural Hinterland in Nepal." *Human Organization* 40 (Spring): 48–55.

Gole, Nilofer. 1997. "Lifting the Veil—Reform vs. Tradition in Turkey—An Interview."*Manushi,* May 1.

Gonnut, Jean Pierre. 2001. Interview. June 18, 2001.

Gonzalez, David. 2003. "Latin Sweatshops Pressed by U.S. Campus Power." *New York Times,* April 4, p. A3.

Gottfredson, Michael, and Travis Hirschi. 1990. *A General Theory of Crime.* Palo Alto, CA: Stanford University Press.

Gottlieb, Lori. 2006. "How Do I Love Thee?" *Atlantic Monthly,* March, pp. 58, 60, 62–68, 70.

Gould, Elise. 2006. *Health Insurance Erodes for Working Families: Employer-Presided Coverage Declines for Fifth Consecutive Year.* Washington, DC: Economic Policy Institute.

———. 2007. "The Health-Finance Debate Reaches a Fever Pitch." *Chronicle of Higher Education* (April 13): B14, B15.

Gould, Larry A. 2002. "Indigenous People Policing Indigenous People: The Potential Psychological and Cultural Costs." *Social Science Journal* 39: 171–188.

Gouldner, Alvin. 1960. "The Norm of Reciprocity." *American Sociological Review* 25 (April): 161–177.

———. 1970. *The Coming Crisis of Western Sociology.* New York: Basic Books.

Government Accountability Office. 2003. *Women's Earnings: Work Patterns Partially Explain Difference Between Men's and Women's Earnings.* Washington, DC: U.S. Government Printing Office.

Gramsci, Antonio. 1929. *Selections from the Prison Notebooks,* ed. and trans. Quintin Hoare and Geoffrey Nowell Smith. London: Lawrence and Wishort.

Green, Alexander R., Dana R. Carney, Daniel J. Pallin, Long H. Ng´o, Kristal L. Raymond, Lisa I. Iezzoni, and Mahzarin R. Ban´aji. 2007. "Implicit Bias Among Physicians and Its Prediction of Thrombolysis Decisions for Black and White Patients." *Journal of General Internal Medicine* 9 (September): 1231–1238.

Greenblatt, Alan. 2005. "Upward Mobility." *CQ Researcher* 15 (April 29).

Greenhouse, Steven. 2007. "Low Pay and Broken Promises Greet Guest Workers in U.S." *New York Times,* February 28, pp. A, A14.

Grieco, Elizabeth M., and Rachel C. Cassidy. 2001. "Overview of Race and Hispanic Origin." *Current Population Reports,* Ser. CENBR/01–1. Washington, DC: U.S. Government Printing Office.

Grier, Peter. 2005. "Rich-Poor Gap Gaining Attention." *Christian Science Monitor,* June 14.

Gross, Jane. 2005. "Forget the Career. My Parents Need Me at Home." *New York Times,* November 24, pp. A1, A20.

———. 2007. "U.S. Joins Overseas Adoption Overhaul Plan." *New York Times,* December 11, p. A25.

Groza, Victor, Daniela F. Ileana, and Ivor Irwin. 1999. *A Peacock or a Crow: Stories, Interviews, and Commentaries on Romanian Adoptions.* Euclid, OH: Williams Custom Publishing.

Guerrera, Francesco, and Andrew Ward. 2007. "Women on March to Top of U.S. Companies." *Financial Times,* March 28, p.17.

Gutiérrez, Gustavo. 1990. "Theology and the Social Sciences," Pp. 214–225 in *Liberation Theology at the Crossroads: Democracy or Revolution?* ed. Paul E. Sigmund. New York: Oxford University Press.

## H

Hacker, Andrew. 1964. "Power to Do What?" Pp. 134–146 in *The New Sociology,* ed. Irving Louis Horowitz. New York: Oxford University Press.

Halle, David. 1993. *Inside Culture: Art and Class in the American Home.* Chicago: University of Chicago Press.

Hamilton, Anita. 2007. "Is Facebook Overrated?" *Time* 170 (December 3), pp. 46–48.

Harlow, Harry F. 1971. *Learning to Love.* New York: Ballantine Books.

Harrington, Michael. 1962. *The Other America: Poverty in the United States.* Baltimore: Penguin Books.

———. 1980. "The New Class and the Left." Pp. 123–138 in *The New Class,* ed. B. Bruce Briggs. Brunswick, NJ: Transaction.

Harris, Judith Rich. 1998. *The Nurture Assumption: Why Children Turn Out the Way They Do.* New York: Free Press.

Haskins, Ron. 2008. "Wealth and Economic Mobility." Chap. 4 in *Getting Ahead or Losing Ground: Economic Mobility in America.* Washington, DC: Pew Charitable Trusts. Accessed June 20 (http://economicmobility.org/assets/pdfs/EMP_WealthandEconomic Mobility_ChapterIV.pdf).

Haub, Carl. 2004.*World Population Data Sheet, 2004.* Washington, DC: Population Reference Bureau.

———. 2005. *2005 World Population Data Sheet.* Washington, DC: Population Reference Bureau.

———. 2007. *2007 World Population Data Sheet.* Washington, DC: Population Reference Bureau.

Haviland, William A. 2002. *Cultural Anthropology,* 10th ed. Belmont, CA: Wadsworth.

Harland, William A., Harald E. L. Prins, Dana Walrath, and Bunny McBride. 2005. *Cultural Anthropology: The Human Challenge,* 11th ed. Belmont, CA: Wadsworth.

Hayden, H. Thomas. 2004. "What Happened at Abu Ghraib." Accessed August 7 (www.military.com).

Hayward, Mark D., William R. Grady, and Steven D. McLaughlin. 1987. "Changes in the Retirement Process." *Demography* 25 (August): 371–386.

He, Wan, Manisha Sengupta, Victoria A. Velkoff, and Kimberly A. DeBarros. 2005. "65+ in the United States: 2005." *Current Population Reports,* Ser. P-23, No. 209. Washington, DC: U.S. Government Printing Office.

Heckert, Druann, and Amy Best. 1997. "Ugly Duckling to Swan: Labeling Theory and the Stigmatization of Red Hair." *Symbolic Interaction* 20 (4): 365–384.

Heilman, Madeline E. 2001. "Description and Prescription: How Gender Stereotypes Prevent Women's Ascent up the Organizational Ladder." *Journal of Social Issues* 57 (4): 657–674.

Henly, Julia R. 1999. "Challenges to Finding and Keeping Jobs in the Low-Skilled Labor Market." *Poverty Research News* 3 (1): 3–5.

Herman, Tom. 2008. "There's Rich, and There's the 'Fortunate 400'." The Wall Street Journal, March 5. Accessed July 16 (http://s.wsj.net/article/SB120468366051012473.html?mod=fpa_editors_picks).

Herring, Hubert B. 2006. "A Teacher's Year, a C.E.O.'s Day: The Pay's Similar." *New York Times,* September 5, p. 2.

Hertz, Rosanna. 2006. *Single by Chance. Mothers by Choice.* New York: Oxford University Press.

Hewlett, Sylvia Ann, and Carolyn Buck Luce. 2005. "Off-Ramps and On-Ramps: Keeping Talented Women on the Road to Success." *Harvard Business Review* (March): 43–53.

Hickman, Jonathan. 2002. "America's 50 Best Corporations for Minorities." *Fortune* 146 (July 8): 110–120.

Higher Education Research Institute. 2004. *Trends in Political Attitudes and Voting Behavior Among College Freshmen and Early Career College Graduates: What Issues Could Drive This Election?* Los Angeles: HERI, University of California, Los Angeles.

———. 2005. *The Spiritual Life of College Students.* Los Angeles: HERI.

Himes, Vristine L. 2001. "Elderly Americans." *Population Bulletin* 56 (December).

Hirschi, Travis. 1969. *Causes of Delinquency.* Berkeley: University of California Press.

Hitlin, Steven, and Jane Allyn Piliavin. 2004. "Values: Reviving a Dormant Concept." Pp. 359–393 in *Annual Review of Sociology, 2004,* ed. Karen S. Cook and John Hagan. Palo Alto, CA: Annual Review of Sociology.

Hochschild, Arlie Russell. 1989. *The Second Shift: Working Parents and the Revolution at Home.* New York: Viking Press.

———. 1990. "The Second Shift: Employed Women Are Putting in Another Day of Work at Home." *Utne Reader* 38 (March/April): 66–73.

———. 2000. "The Nanny Chain." *The American Prospect,* January 3, pp. 32–36. Accessed December 13, 2005 (http://www.prospect.org/print/v11/4/hochschild-a.html).

———. 2005. *The Commercialization of Intimate Life: Notes from Home and Work.* Berkeley: University of California Press.

———, with Anne Machung. 1989. *The Second Shift: Working Parents and the Revolution at Home.* New York: Viking Penguin.

Hodge, Robert W., and Peter H. Rossi. 1964. "Occupational Prestige in the United States, 1925–1963." *American Journal of Sociology* 70 (November): 286–302.

Hoefer, Michael, Nancy Rytina, and Christopher Campbell. 2006. *Estimates of the Unauthorized Immigrant Population Residing in the United States: January 2005.* Rev. No. 2006. Washington, DC: Policy Directorate Office of Immigration Statistics.

Holden, Constance. 1980. "Identical Twins Reared Apart." *Science* 207 (March 21): 1323–1328.

———. 1987. "The Genetics of Personality." *Science* 257 (August 7): 598–601.

Holder, Kelly. 2006. "Voting and Registration in the Election of November 2004." *Current Population Reports,* Ser. P-20, No. 556. Washington, DC: U.S. Government Printing Office.

Hollingshead, August B. 1975. *Elmtown's Youth and Elmtown Revisited.* New York: Wiley.

Holmes, Mary. 2006. "Love Lives at a Distance: Distance Relationships over the Lifecourse." *Sociological Research Online* 11 (3).

Homans, George C. 1979. "Nature Versus Nurture: A False Dichotomy." *Contemporary Sociology* 8 (May): 345–348.

Home School Legal Defense Association. 2005. "State Laws" and "Academic Statistics on Homeschooling." Accessed May 12 (www.hslda.org).

Hondagneu-Sotelo, Pierrette, ed. 2003. *Gender and U.S. Immigration: Contemporary Trends.* Berkeley: University of California Press.

Horowitz, Helen Lefkowitz. 1987. *Campus Life.* Chicago: University of Chicago Press.

Horrigan, John B. 2007. *A Typology of Information and Communication Technology Users.* Washington, DC: Pew Internet and American Life Project.

Hosokawa, William K. 1969. *Nisei: The Quiet Americans.* New York: William Morrow.

Hout, Michael, and Claude S. Fischer. 2002. "Why More Americans Have No Religious Preference: Politics and Generations." *American Sociological Review* 67 (April): 165–190.

Howard, Michael C. 1989. *Contemporary Cultural Anthropology,* 3d ed. Glenview, IL: Scott, Foresman.

Howard, Russell D., and Reid L. Sawyer. 2003. *Terrorism and Counterterrorism: Understanding the New Security Environment.* Guilford, CT: McGraw-Hill/Dushkin.

Huang, Gary. 1988. "Daily Addressing Ritual: A Cross-Cultural Study." Paper presented at the annual meeting of the American Sociological Association, Atlanta.

Hughes, Everett. 1945. "Dilemmas and Contradictions of Status." *American Journal of Sociology* 50 (March): 353–359.

Human Rights Campaign. 2007. "State Prohibitions on Marriage for Same-Sex Couples and Statewide Anti-Discrimination Laws and Policies." Accessed March 8, 2008 (www.hrc.org).

Hunter, Herbert M., ed. 2000. *The Sociology of Oliver C. Cox: New Perspectives: Research in Race and Ethnic Relations,* vol. 2. Stamford, CT: JAI Press.

Hurn, Christopher J. 1985. *The Limits and Possibilities of Schooling,* 2d ed. Boston: Allyn and Bacon.

## I

Ignatiev, Noel. 1995. *How the Irish Became White.* New York: Routledge.

Igo, Sarah E. 2007. *The Average American: Surveys, Citizens, and the Making of a Mass Public.* Cambridge, MA: Harvard University Press.

Innocence Project. 2008. "Facts on Post-Conviction DNA Exonerations." Accessed January 12 (www.innocenceproject.org).

———. 2008. "Innocence Project Case Profiles." Accessed January 12 (www.innocenceproject.org/know/).

International Crime Victim Survey. 2004. *Nationwide Surveys in the Industrialized Countries.* Accessed February 20 (www.ruljis.leidenuniv.nl/ group/jfcr/www/icvs).

International Institute for Democracy and Electoral Assistance. 2005. "Turnout in the World—Country by Country Performance." Modified March 7, 2005. Accessed March 15, 2008 (www.idea.int).

International Monetary Fund. 2000. *World Economic Outlook: Asset Prices and the Business Cycle.* Washington, DC: IMF.

———. 2008. "IMF Helping Countries Respond to Food Price Crisis." *IMF Survey Magazine: In the News,* June 3. Washington, DC: IMF. Accessed August 12 (http://www.imf.org/external/pubs/ft/survey/so/2008/NEW060308A.htm).

Internet Crime Complaint Center. 2007. "The Internet Crime Complaint Center Hits 1 Million!" Accessed January 12, 2008 (www.ic3.gov/media/2007/070613.htm).

Internet World Stats. 2008. "Usage and Population Statistics." Accessed March 20 (www.internetworldstats.com).

Inter-Parliamentary Union. 2007. *Women in National Parliaments.* February 29. Accessed April 1 (www.ipu.org).

Iraq Analysis Group. 2007. "About Iraq Analysis Group." Accessed January 19 (Iraqanalysis.org).

IRIN. 2008. "Burkina Faso: Food Riots Shut Down Main Towns." UN Office for the Coordination of Humanitarian Affairs. Accessed August 12 (http://www.irinnews.org/report.aspx?ReportID=76905).

Isaacs, Julia B. 2007a. *Economic Mobility of Families Across Generations.* Washington, DC: Economic Mobility Project, Pew Charitable Trusts.

———. Julia B. 2007b. *Economic Mobility of Men and Women.* Washington, DC: Economic Mobility Project.

Isaacs, Julia B., Isabel V. Sawhill, and Ron Haskins. 2008. *Getting Ahead or Losing Ground: Economic Mobility in America.* Washington, DC: Pew Charitable Trust.

ITOPF. 2006. "Statistics: International Tanker Owners Pollution Federation Limited." Accessed May 2 (www.itopf.com/stats.html).

## J

Jackson, Elton F., Charles R. Tittle, and Mary Jean Burke. 1986. "Offense-Specific Models of the Differential Association Process." 33 (April) :335–356.

Jackson, Philip W. 1968. *Life in Classrooms.* New York: Holt.

Jacobe, Dennis. 2008. "Half of Public Favors the Environment over Growth." Accessed April 9 (www.gallup.com).

Jacobs, David, Zhenchao Qian, Jason T. Carmichael, and Stephanie L. Kent. 2007. "Who Survives on Death Row? An Individual and Contextual Analysis." *American Sociological Review* 72 (August): 610–632.

Jacobs, Jerry. 2003. "Detours on the Road to Equality: Women, Work and Higher Education." *Contexts* (Winter): 32-41.

Jacobson, Jodi. 1993. "Closing the Gender Gap in Development." Pp. 61–79 in *State of the World*, ed. Lester R. Brown. New York: Norton.

James, Susan Donaldson. 2008. "Students Use Civil Rights Tactics to Combat Global Warming." ABC News, January 19. Accessed August 12 (http://abcnews.go.com/Technology/GlobalWarming/story?id=2805553&page=1).

Jargowsky, Paul A., and Rebecca Yang. 2006. "The 'Underclass' Revisited: A Social Problem in Decline." *Journal of Urban Affairs* 28 (1): 55–70.

Jasper, James M. 1997. *The Art of Moral Protest: Culture, Biography, and Creativity in Social Movements.* Chicago: University of Chicago Press.

Jenkins, J. Craig. 2004. "Social Movements: Resource Mobilization Theory." Pp. 14368–14371 in *International Encyclopedia of the Social and Behavioral Sciences,* ed. Neil J. Smelser and Paul B. Baltes. New York: Elsevier.

Jenkins, Matt. 2008. "A Really Inconvenient Truth." *Miller-McCure* 1 (March–April): 38–41.

Jewison, Norman. 1971. *The Fiddler on the Roof.* Videorecording. Directed by Norman Jewison. 179 minutes. Santa Monica, CA: Metro-Goldwyn-Mayer.

Johnson, Allan G. 1997. *The Forest and the Trees: Sociology as Life, Practice, and Promise.* Philadelphia: Temple University Press.

Johnson, Benton. 1975. *Functionalism in Modern Sociology: Understanding Talcott Parsons.* Morristown, NJ: General Learning.

Johnson, Julia Overturf. 2005. "Who's Minding the Kids? Child Care Arrangements: Winter 2002." *Current Population Reports,* ser. P-70, no. 101. Washington, DC: U.S. Government Printing Office.

Johnston, David Cay. 1994. "Ruling Backs Homosexuals on Asylum." *New York Times,* June 12, pp. D1, D6.

Jones, Nicholas A. 2005. *We the People of More Than One Race in the United States.* Census 2000 Special Reports, CENSR-22.Washington, DC: U.S. Government Printing Office.

Jones, Stephen R. G. 1992. "Was There a Hawthorne Effect?" *American Journal of Sociology* 98 (November): 451–568.

Joseph, Jay. 2004. *The Gene Illusion: Genetic Research in Psychiatry and Psychology Under the Microscope.* New York: Algora Books.

Josephson Institute of Ethics. 2006. "2006 Report Card on the Ethics of American Youth." Los Angeles: Josephson Institute. Accessed August 12, 2008 (http://charactercounts.org/pdf/reportcard/reportcard-all.pdf).

Jost, Kenneth. 2008. "Women in Politics."*CQ Researcher* 18 (March 21).

———. 2006b. "Where's Mao? Chinese Revise History Books." *New York Times,* September 1, pp. A1, A6.

Juergensmeyer, Mark. 2003. *Terror in the Mind of God: The Global Rise of Religious Violence,* 3d ed. Berkeley: University of California Press.

## K

Kaiser Family Foundation. 2001. *Few Parents Use V-Chip to Block TV Sex and Violence.* Menlo Park, CA: Kaiser Family Foundation.

———. 2005. *Sex on TV: 2005.* Santa Barbara, CA: Kaiser Family Foundation.

———. 2007. "Parents Say They're Getting Control of Their Children's Exposure to Sex and Violence in the Media—Even Online." Accessed January 2, 2008 (www.kff.org/entmedia/entmedia061907nr.cfm).

Kalish, Richard A. 1985. *Death, Grief, and Caring Relationships.* 2d ed. Monterey, CA: Brooks/Cole.

Kalita, S. Mitra. 2006. "On the Other End of the Line."*Washington Post National Week Edition,* January 9, pp. 20–21.

Kanter, Rosabeth Moss. 1993. *Men and Women of the Corporation.* New York: Basic Books.

Kapos, Shia. 2005. "Bloom Falls off the Rose for Internet Matchups." *Chicago Tribune,* February 14, sect. 4, pp. 1, 7.

Kapstein, Ethan B. 2006. "The New Global Slave Trade." *Foreign Affairs* 85 (November/December): 103–115.

Karney, Benjamin R., and John S. Crown. 2007. "Families Under Stress: An Assessment of Data, Theory, and Research on Marriage and Divorce in the Military." Santa Monica, CA: RAND Corporation.

Kasavin, Greg. 2003. "Real Life: The Full Review." GameSpot, July 11. Accessed June 3, 2008 (http://www.gamespot.com/gamespot/features/all/gamespotting/071103minusworld/1.html).

Katovich, Michael A. 1987. Correspondence, June 1.

Katz, Jason. 1999. *Tough Guise: Violence, Media, and the Crisis in Masculinity.* Videorecording. Directed by Sut Jhally. Northampton, MA : Media Education Foundation.

Katz, Michael. 1971. *Class, Bureaucracy, and the Schools: The Illusion of Educational Change in America.* New York: Praeger.

Kaufman, Gayle and Frances Goldscheider. 2007. "Do Men 'Need' a Spouse More than Women?:Perceptions of the Importance of Marriage for Men and Women." *Sociological Quarterly* 48: 29–46.

Kavada, Anastasia 2005. "Exploring the Role of the Interest in the 'Movement for Alternative Globalization': The case of the Paris 2003 European Social Forum." *Westminster Papers in Communication and Culture* 2 (1): 72–95.

Kempadoo, Kamala, and Jo Doezema, eds. 1998. *Global Sex Workers: Rights, Resistance, and Redefinition.* New York: Routledge.

Kennickell, Arthur B. 2006. "Currents and Undercurrents: Changes in the Distribution of Wealth, 1989–2004." FEDS Working Paper No. 2006-13 Acessed June 20, 2008 (http://ssrn.com/abstract=909206).

Kentor, Jeffrey, and Yong Suk Jang. 2004. "Yes, There Is a (Growing) Transnational Business Community:" *International Sociology* 19 (September): 355–368.

Kerbo, Harold R. 2009. *Social Stratification and Inequality: Class Conflict in Historical, Comparative, and Global Perspective,* 7th ed. New York: McGraw-Hill.

Kim, Kwang Chung. 1999. *Koreans in the Hood: Conflict with African Americans.* Baltimore: Johns Hopkins University Press.

Kimmel, Michael. 2004. *The Gendered Society,* 2d ed. New York: Oxford University Press.

———. 2006. "A War Against Boys?" *Dissent* (Fall): 65–70.

Kinsella, Kevin, and David R. Phillips. 2005. "Global Aging: The Challenge of Success." *Population Bulletin* 60 (March).

Kiper, Dmitry. 2008. "GodTube.com Puts Christian Worship Online." *Christian Science Monitor,* February 6.

Kiser, Edgar. 1992. "War." Pp. 2243–2247 in *Encyclopedia of Sociology,* ed. Edgar F. Borgatta and Marie L. Borgatta. New York: Macmillan.

Kitchener, Richard F. 1991. "Jean Piaget: The Unknown Sociologist." *British Journal of Sociology* 42 (September): 421–442.

Klein, Stefan. 2006. *The Science of Happiness: How Our Brains Make Us Happy—And What We Can Do to Get Happier.* New York: Marlowe.

Klinenberg, Eric. 2002. *Heat Wave: A Social Autopsy of Disaster in Chicago.* Chicago: University of Chicago Press.

Koch, Wendy. 2006. "Relatives Open Hearts and Homes." *USA Today,* March 20, p. A3.

Kochhar, Rakesh. 2004. *The Wealth of Hispanic Households: 1996 to 2002.* Washington, DC: Pew Hispanic Center.

Kohut, Andrew. 2007a. "How Young People View Their Lives, Futures, and Politics: A Portrait of 'Generation Next.'" Survey conducted in association with the Generation Next Initiative and documentary produced by MacNeil/Lehrer Productions. Washington, DC: Pew

Research Center for the People & the Press. Acessed June 1, 2008 (http://people-press.org/reports/pdf/300.pdf).

———. 2007b. "Rising Environmental Concern in 47-Nation Survey: Global Unease with Major World Powers." The Pew Global Attitudes Project. Washington, DC: Pew Research Center. Accessed June 3, 2008 (http://pewglobal.org/reports/pdf/256.pdf).

Kokmen, Leyla. 2008. "Environmental Justice for All." *Utne Reader* (March–April): 42–46.

Kolata, Gina. 1999. *Clone: The Road to Dolly and the Path Beyond.* New York: William Morrow.

Kopinak, Kathryn. 1995. "Gender as a Vehicle for the Subordination of Women *Maquiladora* Workers in Mexico." *Latin American Perspectives* 22 (Winter): 30–48.

Korczyk, Sophie M. 2002. *Back to Which Future: The U.S. Aging Crisis Revisited.* Washington, DC: AARP.

Kottak, Conrad. 2004. *Anthropology: The Explanation of Human Diversity.* New York: McGraw-Hill.

Kozol, Jonathan. 2005. *The Shame of the Nation: The Restoration of Apartheid Schooling in America.* New York: Crown.

Kreider, Rose M. 2005. "Number, Timing, and Duration of Marriages and Divorces: 2001." *Current Population Reports,* 70–97. Washington, DC: U.S. Government Printing Office.

———. 2008. "Living Arrangements of Children: 2004." *Current Population Reports,* No. 114. Washington, DC: U.S. Government. Printing Office.

Kriesberg, Louis. 1992. "Peace." Pp. 1432–1436 in *Encyclopedia of Sociology,* ed. Edgar F. Borgatta and Marie L. Borgatta. New York: Macmillan.

Kristof, Nicholas D. 1998. "As Asian Economies Shrink, Women Are Squeezed Out." *New York Times,* June 11, pp. A1, A12.

Kroll, Luisa, and Allison Fass. 2006. "The World's Billionaires." *Forbes* (March 9).

Kronstadt, Jessica, and Melissa Favreault. 2008. "Families and Economic Mobility." Washington, DC: Economic Mobility Project. Accessed August 13 (www.economicmobility.org/reports_and_research/literature_reviews?id=0004).

Kübler-Ross, Elisabeth. 1969. *On Death and Dying.* New York: Macmillan.

Kung H.C., D.L. Hoyert, J.Q. Xu, and S.L. Murphy. 2008. "Deaths: Final Data for 2005." *National Vital Statistics Reports* 56 (10). Hyattsville, MD: National Center for Health Statistics.

Kwong, Jo. 2005. "Globalization's Effects on the Environment." *Society* 42 (January/February): 21–28.

# L

Labaton, Stephan. 2003. "10 Wall St. Firms Settle with U.S. in Analyst Inquiry." *New York Times,* April 29, pp. A1, C4.

Lacey, Marc. 2008. "Hunger in Haiti Increasing Rapidly." *International Herald Tribune,* April 17. Accessed August 12 (http://www.iht.com/articles/2008/04/17/news/Haiti.php).

Ladner, Joyce. 1973. *The Death of White Sociology.* New York: Random Books.

La Ganga, Maria L. 1999. "Trying to Figure the Beginning of the End." *Los Angeles Times,* October 15, pp. A1, A28, A29.

Landale, Nancy S., and R. S. Orapesa. 2007. "Hispanic Families: Stability and Change." *Annual Review of Sociology* 33: 381–405.

Landler, Mark. 2005. "Mixed Feelings as Kyoto Pact Takes Effect." *New York Times,* February 16, pp. C1, C3.

Lang, Eric. 1992. "Hawthorne Effect." Pp. 793–794 in *Encyclopedia of Sociology,* vol. 2, ed. Edgar F. Borgatta and Marie L. Borgatta. New York: Macmillan.

Lansprey, Susan. 1995. "AAAs and 'Naturally Occurring Retirement Communities' (NORCs)." Accessed August 4, 2003 (www.aoa.gov/housing/ norcs.html).

Lareau, Annette. 2003. *Unequal Childhoods: Class, Race, and Family Life.* Berkeley: University of California Press.

Lasswell, Harold D. 1936. *Politics: Who Gets What, When, How.* New York: McGraw-Hill.

Lauer, Robert H. 1982. *Perspectives on Social Change,* 3d ed. Boston: Allyn and Bacon.

Laumann, Edward O., John H. Gagnon, and Robert T. Michael. 1994a. "A Political History of the National Sex Survey of Adults." *Family Planning Perspectives* 26 (February): 34–38.

Laumann, Edward O., John H. Gagnon, Robert T. Michael, and Stuart Michaels. 1994b. *The Social Organization of Sexuality: Sexual Practices in the United States.* Chicago: University of Chicago Press.

Leavell, Hugh R., and E. Gurney Clark. 1965. *Preventive Medicine for the Doctor in His Community: An Epidemiologic Approach,* 3d ed. New York: McGraw-Hill.

Le Bon, Gustav. 1895. *The Crowd: A Study of the Popular Mind.* New York: Macmillan.

Lee, Alfred McClung. 1983. *Terrorism in Northern Ireland.* Bayside, NY: General Hall.

Lehne, Gregory K. 1995. "Homophobia Among Men: Supporting and Defining the Male Role." Pp. 325–336 in *Men's Lives,* ed. Michael S. Kimmel and Michael S. Messner. Boston: Allyn and Bacon.

Lengermann, Patricia Madoo, and Jill Niebrugge-Brantley. 1998. *The Women Founders: Sociology and Social Theory, 1830–1930.* Boston: McGraw-Hill.

Lenski, Gerhard. 1966. *Power and Privilege: A Theory of Social Stratification.* New York: McGraw-Hill.

Leonhardt, David. 2007. "Middle-Class Squeeze Comes with Nuances." *New York Times,* April 25, pp. C1, C12.

Levinson, Daniel J., with Charlotte N. Darrow et al. 1978. *The Seasons of a Man's Life.* New York: Knopf.

Levinson, Daniel J., with Judy D. Levinson. 1996. *The Season of a Woman's Life.* New York: Knopf.

Levitt, Steven D., and Stephen J. Dubner. 2005. *Freakonomics: A Rogue Economist Explores the Hidden Side of Everything.* New York: William Morrow.

Lewis Mumford Center. 2001. *Ethnic Diversity Grows, Neighborhood Integration Is at a Standstill.* Albany, NY: Lewis Mumford Center.

Leys, Tony. 2008. "New Faces Endure Same Struggle." *Des Moines Register,* May 18, pp. 1, 11.

Lieberson, Stanley. 2000. *A Matter of Taste: How Names, Fashions, and Culture Change.* New Haven, CT: Yale University Press.

Light, Donald W. 2004. "From Migrant Enclaves to Mainstream: Reconceptualizing Informal Economic Behavior." *Theory and Society* 33: 705–737.

Linn, Susan, and Alvin F. Poussaint. 1999. "Watching Television: What Are Children Learning About Race and Ethnicity?" *Child Care Information Exchange* 128 (July): 50–52.

Lino, Mark. 2005. *Expenditures on Children by Families, 2004.* Washington, DC: U.S. Department of Agriculture, Center for Nutrition Policy and Promotion.

Liptak, Adam. 2006. "The Ads Discriminate, but Does the Web?" *New York Times,* March 5, p. 16.

Livernash, Robert, and Eric Rodenburg. 1998. "Population Change, Resources, and the Environment." *Population Bulletin* 53 (March).

Lofland, Lyn H. 1975. "The 'Thereness' of Women: A Selective Review of Urban Sociology." Pp. 144–170 in *Another Voice,* ed. M. Millman and R. M. Kanter. New York: Anchor/Doubleday.

Lopata, Helena Znaniecki. 1971. *Occupation: Housewife.* New York: Oxford University Press.

Lorber, Judith. 1994. *Paradoxes of Gender.* New Haven, CT: Yale University Press.

Louie, Miriam Ching Yoon. 2001. *Sweatshop Warriors: Immigrant Women Workers Take on the Global Factory.* Cambridge, MA: South End Press.

Lukacs, Georg. 1923. *History and Class Consciousness.* London: Merlin.

Lum, Joann, and Peter Kwong. 1989. "Surviving in America: The Trials of a Chinese Immigrant Woman." *Village Voice* 34 (October 31): 39–41.

Lumpe, Lora. 2003. "Taking Aim at the Global Gun Trade." *Amnesty Now* (Winter): 10–13.

**References**

Lundquist, Jennifer Hickes. 2006. "Choosing Single Motherhood." *Contexts* 5 (Fall): 64–67.

Luster, Tom, Kelly Rhoades, and Bruce Haas. 1989. "The Relation Between Parental Values and Parenting Behavior: A Test of the Kohn Hypothesis." *Journal of Marriage and the Family* 51 (February): 139–147.

Lyall, Sarah. 2002. "For Europeans, Love, Yes; Marriage, Maybe." *New York Times,* March 24, pp. 1–8.

Lymas, Mark. 2008. *Six Degrees: Our Future on a Hotter Planet.* Washington, DC: National Geographic.

Lynn, Barry C. 2003. "Trading with a Low-Wage Tiger." *The American Prospect* 14 (February): 10–12.

## M

MacDorman, Marian, et al. 2005. "Explaining the 2001–2002 Infant Mortality Increase: Data from the Linked Death/Infant Death Data Set." *National Vital Statistic Reports* 53 (January 24).

MacEachern, Scott. 2003. "The Concept of Race in Anthropology." Pp. 10–35 in *Race and Ethnicity: An Anthropological Focus on the United States and the World,* ed. R. Scupin. Upper Saddle River, NJ: Prentice Hall.

MacFarquhar, Neil. 2008. "Resolute or Fearful, Many Muslims Turn to Home Schooling." *New York Times,* March 26, p. A1.

Mack, Raymond W., and Calvin P. Bradford. 1979. *Transforming America: Patterns of Social Change,* 2d ed. New York: Random House.

Magnier, Mark. 2004. "China Clamps Down on Web News Discussion." *Los Angeles Times,* February 26, p. A4.

Malcolm X, with Alex Haley. 1964. *The Autobiography of Malcolm X.* New York: Grove.

Mangan, Katherine. 2006. "Survey Finds Widespread Cheating in M.B.A. Programs." *The Chronicle of Higher Education* (September 19). Accessed June 6 ( http://chronicle.com/ daily/2006/09/2006091902n.htm).

Mangum, Garth L., Stephen L. Magnum, and Andrew M. Sum. 2003. *The Persistence of Poverty in the United States.* Baltimore: Johns Hopkins University Press.

Mann, Horace. [1848] 1957. "Report No. 12 of the Massachusetts School Board." Pp. 79–97 in *The Republic and the School: Horace Mann on the Education of Free Men,* ed. L. A. Cremin. New York: Teachers College.

Marijuana Policy Project. 2007. *State-By-State Medical Marijuana Laws 2007.* Washington, DC: Marijuana Policy Project (www .mpp.org/legislation/stateby-state-medical-marijauna-laws.html).

Marosi, Richard. 2007. "The Nation: A Once-Porous Border is a Turning-Back Point." *Los Angeles Times,* March 21, pp. A1, A20.

Martelo, Emma Zapata. 1996. "Modernization, Adjustment, and Peasant Production." *Latin American Perspectives* 23 (Winter): 118–130.

Martin J.A., B. E. Hamilton, P. D. Sutton, S. J. Ventura, F. Menacker, S. Kirmeyer, and M. L. Munson. 2007. *Births: Final Data for 2005.* National Vital Statistics Reports vol. 56, no 6. Hyattsville, MD: National Center for Health Statistics.

Martin, Marvin. 1996. "Sociology Adapting to Changes." *Chicago Tribune,* July 21, sec. 18, p. 20.

Martin, Susan E. 1994. "Outsider Within the Station House: The Impact of Race and Gender on Black Women Politics." *Social Problems* 41 (August): 383–400.

Martineau, Harriet. [1837] 1962. *Society in America.* Edited, abridged, with an introductory essay by Seymour Martin Lipset. Garden City, NY: Doubleday.

———. [1838] 1989. *How to Observe Morals and Manners.* Philadelphia: Leal and Blanchard. Sesquentennial edition, ed. M. R. Hill. New York: Transaction.

Marx, Karl, and Friedrich Engels. [1847] 1955. *Selected Work in Two Volumes.* Moscow: Foreign Languages Publishing House.

Massey, Douglas S. 1998. "March of Folly: U.S. Immigration Policy After NAFTA." *The American Prospect* (March/April): 22–23.

———. 2007. *Categorically Unequal: The American Stratification System.* New York: Russell Sage Foundation.

Massey, Douglas S., and Nancy A. Denton. 1993. *American Apartheid: Segregation and the Making of the Underclass.* Cambridge, MA: Harvard University Press.

McAdam, Doug. 1988. *Freedom Summer.* New York: Oxford University Press.

McFalls, Joseph A., Jr. 2003. "Population: A Lively Introduction." *Population Bulletin* 58 (December).

McGue, Matt, and Thomas J. Bouchard, Jr. 1998. "Genetic and Environmental Influence on Human Behavioral Differences." Pp. 1–24 in *Annual Review of Neurosciences.* Palo Alto, CA: Annual Reviews.

McGurty, Eileen Maura. 2000. "Warren County, NC, and the Emergence of the Environmental Justice Movement: Unlikely Coalitions and Shared Meanings in Local Collective Action." *Society and Natural Resources* 13: 373–387.

McIntosh, Peggy. 1988. "White Privilege and Male Privilege: A Personal Account of Coming to See Correspondence Through Work and Women's Studies." Working Paper No. 189, Wellesley College Center for Research on Women, Wellesley, MA.

McKinlay, John B., and Sonja M.McKinlay. 1977. "The Questionable Contribution of Medical Measures to the Decline of Mortality in the United States in the Twentieth Century." *Milbank Memorial Fund Quarterly* 55 (Summer): 405–428.

McLaughlin, Emma, and Nicola Kraus. 2002. *The Nanny Diaries: A Novel.* New York: St. Martin's Press.

McNeil, Donald G., Jr. 2002. "W.H.O. Moves to Make AIDS Drugs More Accessible to Poor Worldwide." *New York Times,* August 23, p. D7.

Mead, George H. 1934. *Mind, Self and Society,* ed. Charles W. Morris. Chicago: University of Chicago Press.

———. 1964a. *On Social Psychology,* ed. Anselm Strauss. Chicago: University of Chicago Press.

———. 1964b. "The Genesis of the Self and Social Control." Pp. 267–293 in *Selected Writings: George Herbert Mead,* ed. Andrew J. Reck. Indianapolis, IN: Bobbs-Merrill.

Mead, Margaret. 1973. "Does the World Belong to Men—Or to Women?" *Redbook* 141 (October): pp. 46–52.

———. [1935] 2001. *Sex and Temperament in Three Primitive Societies.* New York: Perennial, Harper-Collins.

Meier, Robert F., and Gilbert Geis. 1997. *Victimless Crime? Prostitution, Drugs, Homosexuality, Abortion.* Los Angeles: Roxbury Books.

Melby, Todd. 2007. "Exploring Why We Have Sex." *Contemporary Sexuality* 41 (October): 1, 4–6.

Melia, Marilyn Kennedy. 2000. "Changing Times." *Chicago Tribune,* January 2, sec. 17, pp. 12–15.

Mendez, Jennifer Bickman. 1998. "Of Mops and Maids: Contradictions and Continuities in Bureaucratized Domestic Work." *Social Problems* 45 (February): 114–135.

Merton, Robert. 1948. "The Bearing of Empirical Research upon the Development of Social Theory." *American Sociological Review* 13 (October): 505–515.

———. 1968. *Social Theory and Social Structure.* New York: Free Press.

———, and Alice S. Kitt. 1950. "Contributions to the Theory of Reference Group Behavior." Pp. 40–105 in *Continuities in Social Research: Studies in the Scope and Methods of the American Soldier,* ed. Robert K. Merton and Paul L. Lazarsfeld. New York: Free Press.

Meston, Cindy M., and David M. Buss. 2007. "Why Humans Have Sex." *Archives of Sexual Behavior* 36: 477–507.

Meyers, Thomas J. 1992. "Factors Affecting the Decision to Leave the Old Order Amish." Paper presented at the annual meeting of the American Sociological Association, Pittsburgh.

Michels, Robert. [1915] 1949. *Political Parties.* Glencoe, IL: Free Press.

*Migration News*. 2002. "Mexico: Bush, IDs, Remittances." (December). (http:// migration.ucdavis.edu).

———. 2004. "NAFTA at 10." (January). (http://migration. ucdavis .edu).

———. 2005a. "Mexico: Migrants, Mexicans in U.S. Economy." (April). (http://migration. ucdavis.edu).

———. 2005b. "Offshoring." (January). (http://migration.ucdavis. edu).

———. 2005c. "Maquiladoras" (July). (http://migration.ucdavis.edu).

———. 2008a. "Mexico: Remittances, NAFTA, Taxes." (January). (http://migration.ucdavis.edu.mn).

———. 2008b. "Japan, Korea." (January). (http://migration.ucdavis .edu.mn).

Milgram, Stanley. 1963. "Behavioral Study of Obedience." *Journal of Abnormal and Social Psychology* 67 (October): 371–378.

———. 1975. *Obedience to Authority: An Experimental View.* New York: Harper and Row.

Miller, David L. 2000. *Introduction to Collective Behavior and Collective Action,* 2d ed. Prospect Heights, IL: Waveland Press.

Miller, David L., and JoAnne DeRoven Darlington. 2002. *Fearing for the Safety of Others: Disasters and the Small World Problem.* Paper presented at the annual meeting of the Midwest Sociological Society, Milwaukee, WI.

Miller, Reuben. 1988. "The Literature of Terrorism." *Terrorism* 11 (1): 63–87.

Mills, C. Wright. 1959. *The Sociological Imagination.* New York: Oxford University Press.

———. [1956] 2000. *The Power Elite.* New edition with afterword by Alan Wolfe. New York: Oxford University Press.

Minnesota Center for Twin and Family Research. 2008. "Minnesota Center for Twins and Family Research." Accessed January 7 (http:mctfr.psych.umn.edu/research).

Mirapaul, Matthew. 2001. "How the Net Is Documenting a Watershed Moment." *New York Times,* October 15, p. E2.

Mishel, Lawrence, Jared Bernstein, and Sylvia Allegretto. 2007. *The State of Working America, 2006/2007.* Ithaca, NY: Cornell University Press.

Mizruchi, Mark S. 1996. "What Do Interlocks Do? An Analysis, Critique, and Assessment of Research on Interlocking Directorates." Pp. 271–298 in *Annual Review of Sociology,* 1996, ed. John Hagan and Karen Cook. Palo Alto, CA: Annual Reviews.

Moaddel, Mansoor. 2007. "What the Iraqi Study Group Missed: The Iraqi People." *Footnotes* 35 (January): 1, 4.

Moen, Phyllis, and Patricia Roehling. 2005. *The Career Mystique: Cracks in the American Dream.* Lanham, MD: Rowman and Littlefield.

Mogelonsky, Marcia. 1996. "The Rocky Road to Adulthood." *American Demographics* 18 (May): 26–29, 32–35, 56.

Mohai, Paul, and Robin Saha. 2007. "Racial Inequality in the Distribution of Hazardous Waste: A National-Level Reassessment." *Social Problems* 54 (3): 343–370.

Monahan, Mary T. 2007. *2007 Identity Fraud Survey Report: Identity Fraud Is Dropping, Continued Vigilance Necessary.* Pleasanton, CA: Javelin Strategy and Research.

Monaghan, Peter. 1993. "Sociologist Jailed Because He 'Wouldn't Snitch' Ponders the Way Research Ought to Be Done." *Chronicle of Higher Education* 40 (September 1): A8, A9.

Montagu, Ashley, 1997. *Man's Most Dangerous Myth: The Fallacy of Race,* 6th ed. abridged student ed. Walnut Creek, CA: AltaMira Press.

Moore, David W. 2002. "Americans' View of Influence of Religion Settling Back to Pre–September 11 Levels." *Gallup Poll Tuesday Briefing* (December 31).

Moore, Molly. 2006. "Romance, but not Marriage." *Washington Post National Weekly Edition,* November 27, p. 18.

Moore, Wilbert E. 1967. *Order and Change: Essays in Comparative Sociology.* New York: Wiley.

———. 1968. "Occupational Socialization." Pp. 861–883 in *Handbook of Socialization Theory and Research,* ed. David A. Goslin. Chicago: Rand McNally.

Morehouse Medical Treatment and Effectiveness Center. 1999. *A Synthesis of the Literature: Racial and Ethnic Differences in Access to Medical Care.* Menlo Park, CA: Henry J. Kaiser Family Foundation.

Morris, Aldon. 2000. "Reflections on Social Movement Theory: Criticisms and Proposals." *Contemporary Sociology* 29 (May): 445–454.

Morris, Bonnie Rothman. 1999. "You've Got Romance! Seeking Love on Line." *New York Times,* August 26, p. D1.

Morrison, Denton E. 1971. "Some Notes Toward a Theory on Relative Deprivation, Social Movements, and Social Change." *American Behavioral Scientist* 14 (May/June): 675–690.

Morse, Arthur D. 1967. *While Six Million Died: A Chronicle of American Apathy.* New York: Ace.

Morselli, Carlo, Pierre Tremblay, and Bill McCarthy. 2006. "Mentors and Criminal Achievement." *Criminology* 44 (1): 17–43.

Moss, Michael, and Ford Fessenden. 2002. "New Tools for Domestic Spying, and Qualms." *New York Times,* December 10, pp. A1, A18.

Murdock, George P. 1945. "The Common Denominator of Cultures." Pp. 123–142 in *The Science of Man in the World Crisis,* ed. Ralph Linton. New York: Columbia University Press.

———. 1949. *Social Structure.* New York: Macmillan.

———. 1957. "World Ethnographic Sample." *American Anthropologist* 59 (August): 664–687.

Murphy, Caryle. 1993. "Putting Aside the Veil." *Washington Post National Weekly Edition,* April 12–18, pp. 10–11.

# N

NAACP Legal Defense and Educational Fund. 2007. *Death Row U.S.A. Winter 2007.* Washington, DC: NAACP Legal Defense and Educational Fund.

Nakao, Keiko, and Judith Treas. 1994. "Updating Occupational Prestige and Socioeconomic Scores: How the New Measures Measure Up." *Sociological Methodology* 24 (1994): 1–72.

National Advisory Commission on Criminal Justice. 1976. *Organized Crime.* Washington, DC: U.S. Government Printing Office.

National Center for Education Statistics. 2007. *Digest of Education Statistics: 2006.* Washington, DC: U.S. Government Printing Office.

National Center for Health Statistics. 2007. *Health, United States, 2007, with Chartbook on Trends in the Health of Americans.* Hyattsville, MD: National Center for Health Statistics. Accessed May 28, 2008 (http://www.cdc.gov/nchs/data/hus/hus07.pdf).

*National Geographic.* 2002. "A World Transformed." (September).

———. 2005. *Atlas of the World,* 8th ed. Washington, DC: Author.

National Institute on Aging. 1999. *Early Retirement in the United States.* Washington, DC: U.S. Government Printing Office.

*National Vital Statistics Reports.* 2008. "Births, Marriages, Divorces, and Deaths: Provisional Data for June 2007." (January 28).

Neuman, W. Lawrence. 2000. *Social Research Methods: Qualitative and Quantitative Approaches.* Boston: Allyn and Bacon.

Newman, William M. 1973. *American Pluralism: A Study of Minority Groups and Social Theory.* New York: Harper and Row.

Neumark, David. 2008. "Reassessing the Age Discrimination in Employment Act." Washington DC: AARP Public Policy Institute. Accessed June 27 (http://www.aarp.org/research/work/agediscrim/2008_09_adea.html).

Nielsen, Joyce McCarl, Glenda Walden, and Charlotte A. Kunkel. 2000. "Gendered Heteronormativity: Empirical Illustrations in Everyday Life." *Sociological Quarterly* 41 (2): 283–296.

Niezen, Ronald. 2005. "Digital Identity: The Construction of Virtual Selfhood in the Indigenous Peoples' Movement." *Comparative Studies in Society and History* 47 (3): 532–551.

Nobles, Melissa. 2000. "History Counts: A Comparative Analysis of Racial/Color Categorization in U.S. and Brazilian Censuses." *American Journal of Public Health* 90: 1738–1745.

Nolan, Patrick, and Gerhard Lenski. 2006. *Human Societies: An Introduction to Macrosociology,* 10th ed. Boulder, CO: Paradigm.

Norris, Poppa, and Ronald Inglehart. 2004. *Sacred and Secular: Religion and Politics Worldwide.* Cambridge: Cambridge University Press.

North Carolina Department of Environmental and Natural Resources. 2008. "Warren County PCB Landfill Fact Sheet." Accessed April 9 (www.wastenotnc.org/WarrenCo_Fact_Sheet.htm).

## O

Oberschall, Anthony. 1973. *Social Conflict and Social Movements.* Englewood Cliffs, NJ: Prentice Hall.

O'Connor, Anne-Marie. 2004. "Time of Blogs and Bombs." *Los Angeles Times,* December 27, pp. E1, E14–E15.

O'Donnell, Jayne, and Richard Willing. 2003. "Prison Time Gets Harder for White-Collar Crooks." *USA Today,* May 12, pp. A1, A2.

Office of Immigration Statistics. 2007. "2006 Yearbook of Immigration Statistics." Washington, DC: U.S. Department of Homeland Security.

Office of Justice Programs. 1999. "Transnational Organized Crime." *NCJRS Catalog* 49 (November/ December): 21.

Ogburn, William F. 1922. *Social Change with Respect to Culture and Original Nature.* New York: Huebsch (reprinted 1966, New York: Dell).

Ogburn, William F., and Clark Tibbits. 1934. "The Family and Its Functions." Pp. 661–708 in *Recent Social Trends in the United States,* ed. Research Committee on Social Trends. New York: McGraw-Hill.

O'Hare, William P., and Brenda Curry White. 1992. "Is There a Rural Underclass?" *Population Today* 20 (March): 6–8.

Oliver, Melvin L., and Thomas M. Shapiro. 1995. *Black Wealth/White Wealth: New Perspectives on Racial Inequality.* New York: Routledge.

Omi, Michael, and Howard Winant. 1994. *Racial Formation in the United States: From the 1960s to the 1990s,* 2d ed. New York: Routledge.

Onishi, Norimitso. 2003. "Divorce in South Korea: Striking a New Attitude." *New York Times,* September 21, p. 19.

Orfield, Gary, and Chungmei Lee. 2007. *Historic Reversals, Accelerating Resegregation, and the Need for New Integration Strategies.* Los Angeles: Civil Rights Project, UCLA.

Orum, Anthony M. 1989. *Introduction to Political Sociology: The Social Anatomy of the Body Politic,* 3d ed. Englewood Cliffs, NJ: Prentice Hall.

———. 2001. *Introduction to Political Sociology,* 4th ed. Upper Saddle River, NJ: Prentice Hall.

Osberg, Lars, and Timothy Smeeding. 2006. "'Fair' Inequality? Attitudes Toward Pay Differentials: The United States in Comparative Perspective." *American Sociological Review* 71 (June): 450–473.

## P

Pager, Devah. 2003. "The Mark of a Criminal Record." *American Journal of Sociology* 108 (March): 937–975.

Pager, Devah, and Lincoln Quillian. 2005. "Walking the Talk? What Employers Say Versus What They Do." *American Sociological Review* 70 (June): 355–380.

Pamuk, E., D. Makui, K. Heck, C. Reuban, and K. Lochren. 1998. *Health, United States 1998 with Socioeconomic Status and Health Chartbook.* Hyattsville, MD: National Center for Health Statistics.

Park, Hwa-Ok. 2005. "Grandmothers Raising Grandchildren: Family Well-Being and Economic Assistance." *Focus* 24 (Fall): 19–27.

Park, Kristin. 2005. "Choosing Childlessness Weher's Typology of Action and Motives of the Voluntarily Childless." *Sociological Inquiry* (August): 372–402.

Park, Robert E. 1922. *The Immigrant Press and Its Control.* New York: Harper.

Parker, Alison. 2004. "Inalienable Rights: Can Human-Rights Law Help to End U.S. Mistreatment of Noncitizens?" *American Prospect* (October): A11–A13.

Parsons, Talcott. 1951. *The Social System.* New York: Free Press.

———. 1966. *Societies: Evolutionary and Comparative Perspectives.* Englewood Cliffs, NJ: Prentice Hall.

———. 1975. "The Sick Role and the Role of the Physician Reconsidered." *Milbank Medical Fund Quarterly Health and Society* 53 (Summer): 257–278.

Parsons, Talcott, and Robert Bales. 1955. *Family: Socialization, and Interaction Process.* Glencoe, IL: Free Press.

Passero, Kathy. 2002. "Global Travel Expert Roger Axtell Explains Why." *Biography,* July, pp. 70–73, 97–98.

Patterson, Thomas E. 2003. *We the People,* 5th ed. New York: McGraw-Hill.

———. 2005. "Young Voters and the 2004 Election." Cambridge, MA: Vanishing Voter Project, Harvard University.

Pattillo-McCoy, Mary. 1999. *Black Picket Fences: Privilege and Peril Among the Black Middle Class.* Chicago: University of Chicago Press.

Paxton, Pamela, Sheri Kunovich, and Melanie M. Hughes. 2007. "Gender in Politics." Pp. 263–285 in *Annual Review of Sociology* 2007. Palo Alto, CA: Annual Reviews.

Pear, Robert. 1997. "Now, the Archenemies Need Each Other." *New York Times,* June 22, sec. 4, pp. 1, 4.

Pelton, Tom. 1994. "Hawthorne Works' Glory Now Just So Much Rubble." *Chicago Tribune,* April 18, pp. 1, 6.

Perrow, Charles. 1986. *Complex Organizations,* 3d ed. New York: Random House.

Perry, Joellen. 2001. "For Most, There's No Place like Home." *U.S. News & World Report* 130 (June 4): 66.

Peter, Laurence J., and Raymond Hull. 1969. *The Peter Principle.* New York: William Morrow.

Petersen, William. 1979. *Malthus.* Cambridge, MA: Harvard University Press.

Peterson, Karen. S. 2003. "Unmarried with Children: For Better or Worse." *USA Today,* August 18, pp. 1A, 8A.

Petrásová, Alexandra. 2006. *Social Protection in the European Union.* Brussels: European Union.

Petrovic, Drazen. 1994. "Ethnic Cleansing—An Attempt at Methodology." *EJIL* 5: 1–19.

Pew Internet Project. 2007. "Demographics of Internet Users." Accessed January 11 (http://www.pewinternet.org/trends/User _Demo_6.15.07.htm).

———. 2008. "Demographics of Internet Users." Accessed April 18 (www.pewinternet.org/trends/User_Demo_2.15.08.htm).

Pew Research Center. 2007. "Optimism about Black Progress Declines: Blacks See Growing Values Gap Between Poor and Middle Class." Washington, DC: Pew Research Center. Accessed July 1, 2008 (http://pewsocialtrends.org/assets/pdf/Race.pdf).

———. 2007b. "Global Unease with Major World Powers: Rising Environmental Concern in 47-Nation Survey." Pew Global Attitudes Project. Washington, DC: Pew Research Center. Accessed July 4, 2008 (http://pewglobal.org/reports/display.php?ReportID=256).

———. 2008. "U.S. Religious Landscape Survey." Pew Forum on Religion in Public Life. Washington, DC: Pew Research Center. Accessed June 14, 2008 (http://religions.pewforum.org/pdf/report-religious-landscape-study-full.pdf).

———. 2008b. "Election-Year Economic Ratings Lowest Since '92: An Even More Partisan Agenda for 2008." Pew Research Center for People and the Press. Washington, DC: Pew Research Center. Accessed July 4 (http://people-press.org/reports/display .php3?ReportID=388).

Pfeifer, Mark. 2008. "Vietnamese Americans" Pp. 1365–1368 in *Encyclopedia of Race, Ethnicity, and Society,* vol. 3, ed. Richard T. Schaefer. Thousand Oaks, CA: Sage.

Piaget, Jean. 1954. *The Construction of Reality in the Child,* trans. Margaret Cook. New York: Basic Books.

Pinderhughes, Dianne. 1987. *Race and Ethnicity in Chicago Politics: A Reexamination of Pluralist Theory.* Urbana: University of Illinois Press.

Pinkerton, James P. 2003. "Education: A Grand Compromise." *Atlantic Monthly* 291, January/ February, pp. 115–116.

Planty, M., W. Hussar, T. Snyder, S. Provasnik, G. Kena, R. Dinkes, A. Kewal-Ramani, and J. Kemp. 2008. *The Condition of Education 2008.* NCES 2008-031. Washington, DC: National Center for Education Statistics, Institute of Education Sciences, U.S. Department of Education. Accessed June 14 (http://nces.ed.gov/pubs2008/2008031.pdf).

Polletta, Francesca, and James M. Jasper. 2001. "Collective Identity and Social Movements." Pp. 283–305 in *Annual Review of Sociology, 2001,* ed. Karen S. Cook and Leslie Hogan. Palo Alto, CA: Annual Review of Sociology.

Popenoe, David, and Barbara Dafoe Whitehead. 1999. *Should We Live Together? What Young Adults Need to Know About Cohabitation Before Marriage.* Rutgers, NJ: National Marriage Project.

Population Reference Bureau. 1996. "Speaking Graphically." *Population Today* 24 (June/July): b.

———. 2004. "Transitions in World Population." *Population Bulletin* 59 (March).

Postman, Neil. 1988. "Questioning the Media." Videorecording. The January Series, January 12. Grand Rapids, MI: Calvin College.

Princiotta, D., and S. Bielick. 2006. *Homeschooling in the United States: 2003.* NCES 2006-042. Washington, DC: U.S. Department of Education, National Center for Education Statistics.

Progressive Student Labor Movement. 2008. "A Brief History of the Living Wage Debate at Harvard." Accessed July 7 (http://www.hcs.harvard.edu/~pslm/livingwage/timeline.html).

Prus, Steven G. 2007. "Age, SES, and Health: A Population Level Analysis of Health Irregularities over the Lifecourse." *Sociology of Health and Illness* 29 (March): 275–296.

Pryor, John H., Sylvia Hurtado, Victor B. Saenz, Jessica S. Korn, José Luis Santos, and William Korn. 2006. *The American Freshman: National Norms for Fall 2006.* Los Angeles: Higher Education Research Institute, UCLA.

Pryor, John H., Sylvia Hurtado, Victor B. Saenz, José Luis Santos, and William S. Korn. 2007a. *The American Freshman: Forty Year Trends.* Los Angeles: Higher Education Research Institute, UCLA.

Pryor, John H., Sylvia Hurtado, Jessica Sharkness, and William S. Korn. 2007b. *The American Freshman: National Norms for Fall 2007.* Los Angeles: Higher Education Research Institute, UCLA.

## Q

Quadagno, Jill. 2005. *Aging and the Life Course: An Introduction to Social Gerontology,* 3d ed. New York: McGraw-Hill.

Quart, Alissa. 2003. *Branded: The Buying and Selling of Teenagers.* New York: Perseus.

Quinney, Richard. 1970. *The Social Reality of Crime.* Boston: Little, Brown.

———. 1974. *Criminal Justice in America.* Boston: Little, Brown.

———. 1979. *Criminology,* 2d ed. Boston: Little, Brown.

———. 1980. *Class, State and Crime,* 2d ed. New York: Longman.

## R

Rainie, Lee. 2001. *The Commons of the Tragedy.* Washington, DC: Pew Internet and American Life Project.

Ramet, Sabrina. 1991. *Social Currents in Eastern Europe: The Source and Meaning of the Great Transformation.* Durham, NC: Duke University Press.

Rand, Michael, and Shannan Catalano. 2007. "Crime Victimization, 2006." *Bureau of Justice Statistics Bulletin* (December).

Ray, Brian D. 2006. "Research Facts on Homeschooling." Accessed April 11, 2007 (www. Nheri.org).

Reid, Luc. 2006. *Talk the Talk: The Slang of 65 American Subcultures.* Cincinnati, OH: Writer's Digest Books.

Reinharz, Shulamit. 1992. *Feminist Methods in Social Research.* New York: Oxford University Press.

Religious Tolerance. 2008. "Female Genital Mutilation (FGM): Informational Materials." Accessed March 1 (www.religioustolerance.org).

Ribando, Clare M. 2008. *CRS Report for Congress: Trafficking in Persons.* Washington, DC: Congressional Research Service.

Ridgeway, Greg. 2007. "Analysis of Racial Disparities in the New York Police Department's Stop, Question, and Frisk Practices." Santa Monica, CA: RAND Corporation.

Rideout, Victoria, Donald F. Roberts, and Ulla G. Foehr. 2005. *Generation M: Media in the Lives of 8–18-Year-Olds.* Menlo Park, CA: Kaiser Family Foundation.

Riding, Alan. 1998. "Why 'Titanic' Conquered the World." *New York Times,* April 26, sec. 2, pp. 1, 28, 29.

Rieker, Patricia R., and Chloe E. Bird. 2000. "Sociological Explanations of Gender Differences in Mental and Physical Health." Pp. 98–113 in *Handbook of Medical Sociology,* ed. Chloe Bird, Peter Conrad, and Allan Fremont. New York: Prentice Hall.

Rifkin, Jeremy. 1995. "Afterwork." *Utne Reader* (May/June): 52–62.

Riley, John W., Jr. 1992. "Death and Dying." Pp. 413–418 in *Encyclopedia of Sociology,* vol. 1, ed. Edgar F. Borgatta and Marie L. Borgatta. New York: Macmillan.

Riley, Matilda White, Robert L. Kahn, and Anne Foner. 1994a. *Age and Structural Lag.* New York: Wiley InterScience.

Riley, Matilda White, Robert L. Kahn, and Anne Foner, in association with Karin A.Mock. 1994b. "Introduction: The Mismatch between People and Structures." Pp. 1–36 in *Age and Structural Lag,* ed. Matilda White Riley, Robert L. Kahn, and Anne Foner. New York: Wiley InterScience.

Rimer, Sara. 1998. "As Centenarians Thrive, 'Old' Is Redefined." *New York Times,* June 22, pp. A1, A14.

Ritzer, George. 2002. *McDonaldization: The Reader.* Thousand Oaks, CA: Pine Forge Press.

———. 2004a. *The McDonaldization of Society,* rev. new century ed. Thousand Oaks, CA: Pine Forge Press.

———. 2004b. *The Globalization of Nothing.* Thousand Oaks, CA: Pine Forge Press.

———. 2008. *The McDonaldization of Society 5.* Thousand Oaks, CA: Sage.

Robelon, Erik W. 2007. "Moment-of-Silence' Generates Loud Debate in Illinois." *Education Week* (October 24).

Roberson, Debi, Ian Davies, and Jules Davidoff. 2000. "Color Categories Are Not Universal: Replications and New Evidence from Stone Age Culture." *Journal of Experimental Psychology* 129 (3): 369–398.

Roberts, J. Timmons, Peter E. Grines, and Jodie L. Ma´nale. 2003. "Social Roots of Global Environmental Change: A World-Systems Analysis of Carbon Dioxide Emissions." *Journal of World-Systems Research* 9 (Summer): 277–315.

Robison, Jennifer. 2002. "Feminism—What's in a Name?" Accessed February 25, 2007 (www.galluppoll.com).

Rodriguez, Richard. 2002. *Brown: The Last Discovery of America.* New York: Penguin Books.

Romano, Andrew, and Jessica Ramirez. 2007. "The Immigration Mess." *Newsweek,* June 18, p. 37.

Rose, Arnold. 1951. *The Roots of Prejudice.* Paris: UNESCO.

Rose, Peter I., Myron Glazer, and Penina Migdal Glazer. 1979. "In Controlled Environments: Four Cases of Intense Resocialization." Pp. 320–338 in *Socialization and the Life Cycle,* ed. Peter I. Rose. New York: St. Martin's Press.

Rosenberg, Douglas H. 1991. "Capitalism." Pp. 33–34 in *Encyclopedic Dictionary of Sociology,* 4th ed., ed. Dushkin Publishing Group. Guilford, CT: Dushkin.

Rosenthal, Robert, and Lenore Jacobson. 1968. *Pygmalion in the Classroom.* New York: Holt.

Rosin, Hanna. 2007. *God's Harvard: A Christian College on a Mission to Save America.* New York: Harcourt.

Rossi, Alice S. 1968. "Transition to Parenthood." *Journal of Marriage and the Family* 30 (February): 26–39.

———. 1984. "Gender and Parenthood." *American Sociological Review* 49 (February): 1–19.

Rossides, Daniel W. 1997. *Social Stratification: The Interplay of Class, Race, and Gender.* 2d ed. Upper Saddle River, NJ: Prentice Hall.

Roszak, Theodore. 1969. *The Making of a Counterculture.* Garden City, NY: Doubleday.

Rotolo, Thomas, and John Wilson. 2007. "Sex Segregation in Volunteer Work." *The Sociological Quarterly* 48: 559–585.

Rubin, Alissa J. 2003. "Pat-Down on the Way to Prayer." *Los Angeles Times,* November 25, pp. A1, A5.

Ryan, William. 1976. *Blaming the Victim,* rev. ed. New York: Random House.

Rymer, Russ. 1993. *Genie: An Abused Child's Flight from Science.* New York: HarperCollins.


# S

Saad, Lydia. 2003. "What Form of Government for Iraq?" Accessed September 26 (www.gallup.com).

———. 2004. "Divorce Doesn't Last." *Gallup Poll Tuesday Briefing,* March 30 (www.gallup.com).

———. 2005. "Gay Rights Attitudes a Mixed Bag." Accessed May 20 (www.gallup.com).

Sachs, Jeffrey D. 2005a. *The End of Poverty: Economic Possibilities for Our Time.* New York: Penguin Books.

———. 2005b. "Can Extreme Poverty Be Eliminated?" *Scientific American* 293 (September): 56–65.

Sacks, Peter. 2007. *Tearing Down the Gates: Confronting the Class Divide in American Education.* Berkeley: University of California Press.

Safire, William. 2006. "Netroots." *New York Times,* November 19. Accessed July 7, 2008 (http://www.nytimes.com/2006/11/19/magazine/19wwln_safire.html).

Sale, Kirkpatrick. 1996. *Rebels Against the Future: The Luddites and Their War on the Industrial Revolution* (with new preface by author). Reading, MA: Addison-Wesley.

Salem, Richard, and Stanislaus Grabarek. 1986. "Sociology B.A.s in a Corporate Setting: How Can They Get There and of What Value Are They?" *Teaching Sociology* 14 (October): 273–275.

Samuelson, Paul A., and William D. Nordhaus. 2005. *Economics,* 18th ed. New York: McGraw-Hill.

Sanday, Peggy Reeves. 2002. *Women at the Center: Life in a Modern Matriarchy.* Ithaca, NY: Cornell University Press.

———. 2008. Homepage. Accessed March 15 (www.sas.upenn.edu/~psanday/).

Sassen, Saskia. 2005. "New Global Classes: Implications for Politics." Pp. 143–170 in *The New Egalitarianism,* ed. Anthony Giddens and Patrick Diamond. Cambridge: Policy.

Sayer, Liana C., Suzanne M. Bianchi, and John P. Robinson. 2004. "Are Parents Investing Less in Children? Trends in Mothers' and Fathers' Time with Children." *American Journal of Sociology* 110 (July): 1–43.

Scanlan, Stephen J, and Seth L. Feinberg. 2000. "The Cartoon Society: Using *The Simpsons* to Teach and Learn Sociology." *Teaching Sociology* 28: 127–139.

Scarce, Rik. 1994. "(No) Trial (But) Tribulations: When Courts and Ethnography Conflict." *Journal of Contemporary Ethnography* 23 (July): 123–149.

———. 1995. "Scholarly Ethics and Courtroom Antics: Where Researchers Stand in the Eyes of the Law." *American Sociologist* 26 (Spring): 87–112.

———. 2005. "A Law to Protect Scholars." *Chronicle of Higher Education* (August 12): 324.

Schachtman, Tom. 2006. *Rumspringa: To Be or Not to Be Amish.* New York: North Pointe Press.

Schaefer, Richard T. 1998a. "Differential Racial Mortality and the 1995 Chicago Heat Wave." Paper presented at the annual meeting of the American Sociological Association, August, San Francisco.

———. 1998b. *Alumni Survey.* Chicago, IL: Department of Sociology, DePaul University.

———. 2006. *Racial and Ethnic Relations,* 10th ed. Upper Saddle River, NJ: Prentice-Hall.

———. 2008a. *Race and Ethnicity in the United States,* 11th ed. Upper Saddle River, NJ: Prentice Hall.

———. 2008b. "'Power' and 'Power Elite.'" In *Encyclopedia of Social Problems,* ed. Vincent Parrillo. Thousand Oaks, CA: Sage.

———. 2009. *Sociology: A Brief Introduction,* 8th edition. New York: McGraw-Hill.

Schaefer, Richard T., and William W. Zellner. 2007. *Extraordinary Groups,* 8th ed. New York: Worth.

Schaffer, Scott. 2004. *Resisting Ethics.* New York: Palgrave Macmillan.

Scharnberg, Kirsten. 2002. "Tattoo Unites WTC's Laborers." *Chicago Tribune,* July 22, pp. 1, 18.

———. 2007. "Black Market for Midwives Defies Bans." *Chicago Tribune,* November 25, pp. 1, 10.

Schmeeckle, Maria. 2007. "Gender Dynamics in Stepfamilies: Adult Stepchildren's Views." *Journal of Marriage and Family* 69 (February): 174–189.

Schmeckle, Maria, Roseann Giarrusso, Du Feng, and Vern L. Bengtson. 2006. "What Makes Someone Family? Adult Children's Perceptions of Current and Former Stepparents." *Journal of Marriage and Family* 68 (August): 595–610.

Schmidley, A. Dianne, and J. Gregory Robinson. 2003. *Measuring the Foreign-Born Population in the United States with the Current Population Survey: 1994–2002.* Washington, DC: Population Division, U. S. Bureau of the Census.

Schnaiberg, Allan. 1994. *Environment and Society: The Enduring Conflict.* New York: St. Martin's Press.

Schur, Edwin M. 1965. *Crimes Without Victims: Deviant Behavior and Public Policy.* Englewood Cliffs, NJ: Prentice Hall.

———. 1968. *Law and Society: A Sociological View.* New York: Random House.

———. 1985. "'Crimes Without Victims: A 20 Year Reassessment." Paper presented at the annual meeting of the Society for the Study of Social Problems.

Schurman, Rachel. 2004. "Fighting 'Frankenfoods': Industry Opportunity Structures and the Efficacy of the Anti-Biotech Movement in Western Europe." *Social Problems* 51 (2): 243–268.

Schwartz, Shalom H., and Anat Bardi. 2001. "Value Hierarchies Across Cultures: Taking a Similarities Perspective." *Journal of Cross-Cultural Perspective* 32 (May): 268–290.

Scott, Alan. 1990. *Ideology and the New Social Movements.* London: Unwin Hyman.

Scott, Greg. 2005. "Public Symposium: HIV/AIDS, Injection Drug Use and Men Who Have Sex with Men." Pp. 38–39 in *Scholarship with a Mission,* ed. Susanna Pagliaro. Chicago: DePaul University.

Second Life. 2008. "Economic Statistics." Accessed January 8 (http://secondlife.com/whatis/economy_stats.php).

Seidman, Steven. 1994. "Heterosexism in America: Prejudice against Gay Men and Lesbians." Pp. 578–593 in *Introduction to Social Problems,* ed. Craig Calhoun and George Ritzer. New York: McGraw-Hill.

Sernau, Scott. 2001. *Worlds Apart: Social Inequalities in a New Century.* Thousand Oaks, CA: Pine Forge Press.

Sharma, Hari M., and Gerard C. Bodeker. 1998. "Alternative Medicine." Pp. 228–229 in *Britannica Book of the Year 1998.* Chicago: Encyclopedia Britannica.

Shepherd, Jean. 2003. *Japan Performs First Transplants from Brain-Dead Donor.* Accessed June 14 (www.pntb.org/ff-rndwrld.html).

Sheskin, Ira M., and Arnold Dashefsky. 2006. "Jewish Population of the United States, 2006." In *American Jewish Year Book 2006,* ed. David Singer and Lawrence Grossman. New York: American Jewish Committee.

Shipler, David K. 2004. *The Working Poor: Invisible in America.* New York: Alfred A. Knopf.

Shirky, Clay. 2008. Here Comes Everybody: The Power of Organizing Without Organizations. New York: Penguin Books.

Shorrocks, Anthony, James Davies, Susanna Sandström, and Edward Wolff. 2006. *The World Distribution of Household Wealth.* Helsinki, Finland: United Nations University and World Institute for Development Economics Research.

Shostak, Arthur B. 2002. "Clinical Sociology and the Art of Peace Promotion: Earning a World Without War." Pp. 325–345 in *Using Sociology: An Introduction from the Applied and Clinical Perspectives,* ed. Roger A. Straus. Lanham, MD: Rowman and Littlefield.

Shupe, Anson D., and David G. Bromley. 1980. "Walking a Tightrope." *Qualitative Sociology* 2: 8–21.

Silicon Valley Cultures Project. 2004. The Silicon Valley Cultures Project website. Accessed February 3, 2005 (www2.sjsu.edu/depts/anthropology/svcp).

Silver, Ira. 1996. "Role Transitions, Objects, and Identity." *Symbolic Interaction* 10 (1): 1–20.

Simmons, Tavia, and Martin O'Connell. 2003. "Married-Couple and Unmarried-Partner Households: 2000." *Census 2000 Special Reports,* CENBR-5. Washington, DC: U.S. Government Printing Office.

Simon, Stephanie. 2007. "It's Easter; Shall We Gather at the Desktops?" *Los Angeles Times,* April 8, p. A13.

Sisson, Carmen K. 2007. "The Virtual War Family." *Christian Science Monitor,* May 29.

Smelser, Neil. 1963. *The Sociology of Economic Life.* Englewood Cliffs, NJ: Prentice Hall.

Smith, Christian. 1991. *The Emergence of Liberation Theology: Radical Religion and Social Movement Theory.* Chicago: University of Chicago Press.

Smith, Craig. 2006. "Romania's Orphans Face Widespread Abuse, Group Says." *New York Times,* May 10, p. A3.

Smith, Dan. 1999. *The State of the World Atlas,* 6th ed. London: Penguin Books.

Smith, David M., and Gary J. Gates. 2001. *Gay and Lesbian Families in the United States: Same-Sex Unmarried Partner Households.* Washington, DC: Human Rights Campaign.

Smith, Denise, and Hava Tillipman. 2000. "The Older Population in the United States." *Current Population Reports,* Ser. P-20, No. 532. Washington, DC: U.S. Government Printing Office.

Smith, Tom W. 2001. *Estimating the Muslim Population in the United States.* New York: American Jewish Committee.

———. 2003. *Coming of Age in 21st Century America: Public Attitudes Toward the Importance and Timing of Transition to Adulthood.* Chicago: National Opinion Research Center.

Snyder, Thomas D. 1996. *Digest of Education Statistics, 1996.* Washington, DC: U.S. Government Printing Office.

Sorokin, Pitirim A. [1927] 1959. *Social and Cultural Mobility.* New York: Free Press.

Spielmann, Peter James. 1992. "11 Population Groups on 'Endangered' List." *Chicago Sun-Times,* November 23, p. 12.

Sprague, Joey. 2005. *Feminist Methodologies for Critical Research: Bridging Differences.* Lanham, MD: AltaMira Press.

Squire, Peverill. 1988. "Why the 1937 *Literary Digest* Poll Failed." *Public Opinion Quarterly* 52: 125–133.

Stalker, Peter. 2000. *Workers Without Frontiers.* Boulder, CO: Lynne Reinner.

Stark, Rodney, and William Sims Bainbridge. 1979. "Of Churches, Sects, and Cults: Preliminary Concepts for a Theory of Religious Movements." *Journal for the Scientific Study of Religion* 18 (June): 117–131.

———. 1985. *The Future of Religion.* Berkeley: University of California Press.

Starr, Paul. 1982. *The Social Transformation of American Medicine.* New York: Basic Books.

Stavenhagen, Rodolfo. 1994. "The Indian Resurgence in Mexico." *Cultural Survival Quarterly* (Summer/Fall): 77–80.

Steele, Jonathan. 2005. "Annan Attacks Britain and U.S. over Erosion of Human Rights." *Guardian Weekly,* March 16, p. 1.

Stenning, Derrick J. 1958. "Household Viability Among the Pastoral Fulani." Pp. 92–119 in *The Developmental Cycle in Domestic Groups,* ed. John R. Goody. Cambridge, UK: Cambridge University Press.

Steward, Samuel M. 1990. *Bad Boys and Tough Tattoos: A Social History of the Tattoo with Gangs, Sailors, and Street-Corner Punks.* Binghamton, NY: Harrington Park Press.

Strauss, Gary. 2002. "'Good Old Boys' Network Still Rules Corporate Boards." *USA Today,* November 1, pp. B1, B2.

Stretesky, Paul B. 2006. "Corporate Self-Policing and the Environment." *Criminology* 44 (3): 671.

Sudan Tribune. 2008. "Darfur's Poorest Squeezed by Ration Cuts." (June 22). Accessed August 12 (http://www.sudantribune.com/spip.php?article27608).

Suitor, J. Jill, Staci A. Minyard, and Rebecca S. Carter. 2001. "'Did You See What I Saw?' Gender Differences in Perceptions of Avenues to Prestige Among Adolescents." *Sociological Inquiry* 71 (Fall): 437–454.

Sullivan, Harry Stack. [1953] 1968. *The Interpersonal Theory of Psychiatry.* ed. Helen Swick Perry and Mary Ladd Gawel. New York: Norton.

Sullivan, Kevin. 2006. "Bridging the Digital Divide." *Washington Post National Weekly Edition,* July 17, pp. 11–12.

Sumner, William G. 1906. *Folkways.* New York: Ginn.

Sutcliffe, Bob. 2002. *100 Ways of Seeing an Unequal World.* London: Zed Books.

Sutherland, Edwin H. 1937. *The Professional Thief.* Chicago: University of Chicago Press.

———. 1940. "White-Collar Criminality." *American Sociological Review* 5 (February): 1–11.

———. 1949. *White Collar Crime.* New York: Dryden.

———. 1983. *White Collar Crime: The Uncut Version.* New Haven, CT: Yale University Press.

Sutherland, Edwin H., Donald R. Cressey, and David F. Luckenbill. 1992. *Principles of Criminology,* 11th ed. New York: Rowman and Littlefield.

Swatos, William H., Jr., ed. 1998. *Encyclopedia of Religion and Society.* Lanham, MD: AltaMira.

Swidler, Ann. 1986. "Culture in Action: Symbols and Strategies." *American Sociological Review* 51 (April): 273–286.

Szasz, Thomas S. 1971. "The Same Slave: An Historical Note on the Use of Medical Diagnosis as Justificatory Rhetoric." *American Journal of Psychotherapy* 25 (April): 228–239.

———. 1974. *The Myth of Mental Illness,* rev. ed. New York: Harper and Row.

## T

Tannen, Deborah. 1990. *You Just Don't Understand: Women and Men in Conversation.* New York: Ballantine Books.

———. 1994a. *Talking from 9 to 5.* New York: William Morris.

———. 1994b. *Gender and Discourse.* New York: Oxford University Press.

Taylor, Dorceta E. 2000. "The Rise of the Environmental Justice Paradigm."*American Behavioral Scientist* 43 (January): 508–580.

Taylor, Jonathan B., and Joseph P. Kalt. 2005. *American Indians on Reservations: A Data Book of Socioeconomic Change Between the 1990 and 2000 Censuses.* Cambridge, MA: Harvard Project on American Indian Development.

Taylor, Verta. 1995. "Watching for Vibes: Bringing Emotions into the Study of Feminist Organizations." Pp. 223–233 in *Feminist Organizations: Harvest of the New Women's Movement,* ed. Myra Marx Ferree and Patricia Yancy Martin. Philadelphia: Temple University Press.

———. 1999. "Gender and Social Movements: Gender Processes in Women's Self-Help Movements." *Gender and Society* 13: 8–33.

———. 2004. "Social Movements and Gender." Pp. 14348–14352 in *International Encyclopedia of the Social and Behavioral Sciences,* ed. Neil J. Smelser and Paul B. Baltes. New York: Elsevier.

Telsch, Kathleen. 1991. "New Study of Older Workers Finds They Can Become Good Investments." *New York Times,* May 21, p. A16.

Terkel, Studs. 2003. *Hope Dies Last: Keeping the Faith in Difficult Times.* New York: New Press.

Terry, Sara. 2000. "Whose Family? The Revolt of the Child-Free." *Christian Science Monitor,* August 29, pp. 1, 4.

Thomas, Gordon, and Max Morgan Witts. 1974. *Voyage of the Damned.* Greenwich, CT: Fawcett Crest.

Thomas, William I. 1923. *The Unadjusted Girl.* Boston: Little, Brown.

Thomas, William I., and Dorothy Swain. 1928. *The Child in America: Behavior Problems and Programs.* New York: Knopf.

Thompson, Ginger. 2001a. "Chasing Mexico's Dream into Squalor." *New York Times,* February 11, pp. 1, 6.

———. 2001b. "Why Peace Eludes Mexico's Indians." *New York Times,* March 11, sec. WK, p. 16.

Tienda, Marta, and Faith Mitchell, ed. 2006. *Hispanics and the Future of America.* Washington, DC: National Academics Press.

Tierney, John. 1990. "Betting the Planet." *New York Times Magazine,* December 2, pp. 52–53, 71, 74, 76, 78, 80–81.

———. 2003. "Iraqi Family Ties Complicate American Efforts for Change." *New York Times,* September 28, pp. A1, A22.

Tierney, William G., and Karri A. Holley. 2008. "Intelligent Design and the Attack on Scientific Inquiry." *Cultural Studies Critical Methodologies* 8 (February): 39–49.

Tilly, Charles. 1993. *Popular Contention in Great Britain 1758–1834.* Cambridge, MA: Harvard University Press.

———. 2004. *Social Movements, 1768–2004.* Boulder, CO: Paradigm.

Tolbert, Kathryn. 2000. "In Japan, Traveling Alone Begins at Age 6. "*Washington Post National Weekly Edition* 17, May 15, p. 17.

Tonkinson, Robert. 1978. *The Mardudjara Aborigines.* New York: Holt.

Tönnies, Ferdinand. [1887] 1988. *Community and Society.* Rutgers, NJ: Transaction.

Toosi, Mitra. 2005. "Labor Force Projections to 2014: Returning Boomers." *Monthly Labor Review* (November): 25–44.

———. 2007. "Labor Force Projections to 2016: More Workers in their Golden Years." *Monthly Labor Review* (November): 33–52.

Touraine, Alain. 1974. *The Academic System in American Society.* New York: McGraw-Hill.

Traugott, Michael W. 2005. "The Accuracy of the National Preelection Polls in the 2004 Presidential Election." *Public Opinion Quarterly* 69 (5): 642–654.

Trotter III, Robert T., and Juan Antonio Chavira. 1997. *Curanderismo: Mexican American Folk Healing.* Athens: University of Georgia Press.

Ture, Kwame, and Charles Hamilton. 1992. *Black Power: The Politics of Liberation,* rev. ed. New York: Vintage Books.

Turkle, Sherry. 2004. "How Computers Change the Way We Think." *Chronicle of Higher Education* 50 (January 30): B26–B28.

Turner, Bryan S., ed. 1990. *Theories of Modernity and Postmodernity.* Newbury Park, CA: Sage.

Twitchell, James B. 2000. "The Stone Age." Pp. 44–48 in *Do Americans Shop Too Much?* ed. Juliet Schor. Boston: Beacon Press.

## U

United Jewish Communities. 2003. *The National Jewish Population Survey 2000–2001.* New York: UJC.

United Nations Development Programme. 1995. *Human Development Report 1995.* New York: Oxford University Press.

———. 2000. *Poverty Report 2000: Overcoming Human Poverty.* Washington, DC: UNDP.

———. 2006. *Human Development Report 2006. Beyond Scarcity: Power, Poverty and the Global Water Crisis.* New York: UNDP.

———. 2007. *Fighting Climate Change: Human Solidarity in a Divided World. Human Development Report 2007/2008.* New York: UNDP.

United Nations Population Division. 2005. *World Fertility Report 2003.* New York: UNPD.

United States Department of Justice, Federal Bureau of Investigation. 2007. *Crime in the United States, 2006.* Accessed June 6, 2008 (http://www.fbi.gov/ucr/cius2006/).

Urbina, Ian. 2002. "Al Jazeera: Hits, Misses and Ricochets." *Asia Times,* December 25.

———. 2004. "Disco Rice, and Other Trash Talk." *New York Times,* July 31, p. A11.

U.S. Census Bureau. 2004. *Current Population Survey (CPS)—Definitions and Explanations.* Washington, DC: U.S. Census Bureau. Accessed June 8, 2008 (http://www.census.gov/population/www/cps/cpsdef.html).

———. 2007. "Valentine's Day 2008: Feb. 14." Facts for Features, CB08-FF.02. Acessed June 9, 2008 (http://www.census.gov/Press-Release/www/releases/archives/facts_for_features_special_editions/010968.html).

———. 2007b. "Table 6— Median Duration of Marriages for People 15 Years and Over by Sex, Race, and Hispanic Origin: 2004." Accessed June 9, 2008 (http://www.census.gov/population/www/socdemo/marr-div/2004detailed_tables.html).

———. 2007c. "Table H-2: Share of Aggregate Income Received by Each Fifth and Top 5 Percent. All Races: 1967 to 2006." Accessed June 20, 2008 (http://www.census.gov/hhes/www/income/histinc/inchhtoc.html).

———. 2007d. "Table H-3: Mean Household Income Received by Each Fifth and Top 5 Percent. All Races: 1967 to 2006." Accessed June 20, 2008 (http://www.census.gov/hhes/www/income/histinc/inchhtoc.html).

———. 2007e. "Table H-6: Regions—All Races by Median and Mean Income: 1975 to 2006." Accessed June 20, 2008 (http://www.census.gov/hhes/www/income/histinc/inchhtoc.html).

———. 2007f. "PINC-03. Educational Attainment—People 25 Years Old and Over, by Total Money Earnings in 2006, Work Experience in 2006, Age, Race, Hispanic Origin, and Sex." Accessed June 21, 2008 (http://pubdb3.census.gov/macro/032007/perinc/new03_028.htm).

———.2007g. "Age and Sex of All People, Family Members and Unrelated Individuals Iterated by Income-to-Poverty Ratio and Race." Table POV01. Accessed June 27, 2008 (http://pubdb3.census.gov/macro/032007/pov/new01_100_01.htm).

———.2007h. "Table 2: Percent Reaching Stated Anniversary, by Marriage Cohort and Sex, for First and Second Marriages: 2007." Accessed August 12, 2008 (http://www.census.gov/population/socdemo/marital-hist/2004/Table2.2004.xls)

U.S. Department of Education, National Center for Education Statistics. 2007. *The Condition of Education 2007.* NCES 2007-064. Washington, DC: U.S. Government Printing Office. Accessed August 12, 2008 (http://eric.ed.gov/ERICWebPortal/contentdelivery/servlet/ERICServlet?accno=ED497043).

U.S. Patent and Trademark Office. 2008. "All Technologies (Utility Patents) Report." Accessed August 12 (http://www.uspto.gov/go/taf/all_tech.htm).

U.S. Surgeon General. 1999b. "Overview of Cultural Diversity and Mental Health Services." In Chap. 2, *Surgeon General's Report on Mental Health.* Washington, DC: U.S. Government Printing Office.

U.S. Trade Representative. 2003. *2002 Annual Report.* Washington, DC: U.S. Government Printing Office.

Utne, Leif. 2003. "We Are All Zapatistas." *Utne Reader* (November–December): 36–37.

## V

Vasagar, Jeeran. 2005. "'At Last Rwanda Is Known for Something Positive.'" *Guardian Weekly,* July 22, p. 18.

Veblen, Thorstein. [1899] 1964. *Theory of the Leisure Class.* New York: Macmillan.

———. 1919. *The Vested Interests and the State of the Industrial Arts.* New York: Huebsch.

Veenhoven, R. 2006. *Average Happiness in 95 Nations 1995–2005.* World Database of Happiness, Rank Report 2006-1d. Accessed August 12, 2008 (worlddatabaseofhappiness.eur.nl).

Venkatesh, Sudhir. 2008. *Gang Leader for a Day: A Rogue Sociologist Takes to the Street.* New York: Penguin Books.

Venter, Craig. 2000. "Remarks at the Human Genome Announcement, at the Whitehouse." Accessed June 30, 2008 (http://www.celera.com/celera/pr_1056647999).

Vidal, John. 2004. "One in Three People Will Be Elderly by 2050." *Guardian Weekly,* April 1, p. 5.

Villarreal, Andrés. 2004. "The Social Ecology of Rural Violence: Land Scarcity, the Organization of Agricultural Production, and the Presence of the State." *American Journal of Sociology* 110 (September): 313–348.

# W

Wages for Housework Campaign. 1999. "Wages for Housework Campaign." Circular. Los Angeles: Author.

Waldman, Amy. 2004a. "India Takes Economic Spotlight, and Critics Are Unkind." *New York Times,* March 7, p. 3.

———. 2004b. "Low-Tech or High, Jobs Are Scarce in India's Boon." *New York Times,* May 6, p. A3.

———. 2004c. "What India's Upset Vote Reveals: The High Tech Is Skin Deep." *New York Times,* May 15, p. A5.

Wallace, Ruth A., and Alison Wolf. 1980. *Contemporary Sociological Theory.* Englewood Cliffs, NJ: Prentice Hall.

Wallerstein, Immanuel. 1974. *The Modern World System.* New York: Academic Press.

———. 1979a. *Capitalist World Economy.* Cambridge, UK: Cambridge University Press.

———. 1979b. *The End of the World as We Know It: Social Science for the Twenty-First Century.* Minneapolis: University of Minnesota Press.

———. 2000. *The Essential Wallerstein.* New York: New Press.

Wallis, Claudia. 2008. "How to Make Great Teachers." *Time,* February 25, pp. 28–34.

Wang, Meiyan, and Fand Cai. 2006. *Gender Wage Differentials in China's Urban Labor Market.* Research Paper No. 2006/141. United Nations University World Institute for Development Economics Research.

Watts, Duncan J. 2004. "The 'New' Science of Networks." Pp. 243–270 in *Annual Review of Sociology 2004,* ed. Karen S. Cook and John Hagan. Palo Alto, CA: Annual Reviews.

Weber, Max. [1913–1922] 1947. *The Theory of Social and Economic Organization,* trans. A. Henderson and T. Parsons. New York: Free Press.

———. [1904] 1949. *Methodology of the Social Sciences,* trans. Edward A. Shils and Henry A. Finch. Glencoe, IL: Free Press.

———. [1904] 2009. *The Protestant Ethic and the Spirit of Capitalism,* trans. Talcott Parsons. New York: Scribner.

———. [1916] 1958a. "Class, Status, Party," Pp. 180–195 in *From Max Weber: Essays in Sociology,* ed. H. H. Gerth and C. Wright Mills. New York: Oxford University Press.

———. [1916] 1958b. *The Religion of India: The Sociology of Hinduism and Buddhism.* New York: Free Press.

Wechsler, Henry, J. E. Lee, M. Kuo, M. Seibring, T. F. Nelson, and H. Lee. 2002. "Trends in College Binge Drinking During a Period of Increased Prevention Efforts: Findings from Four Harvard School of Public Health College Alcohol Surveys: 1993–2001." *Journal of American College Health* 50 (5): 203–217.

Weinberg, Daniel H. 2004. "Evidence from Census 2000 About Earnings by Detailed Occupation for Men and Women." Census 2000 Special Reports, CENSR-15. Washington, DC: U.S. Census Bureau. Accessed June 26, 2008 (http://www.census.gov/prod/2004pubs/censr-15.pdf).

———, 2007. "Earnings by Gender: Evidence from Census 2000." *Monthly Labor Review* (July/August): 26–34.

Weinstein, Deena, and Michael A. Weinstein. 1999. "McDonaldization Enframed." Pp. 57–69 in *Resisting McDonaldization,* ed. Barry Smart. London: Sage.

Weinstein, Henry. 2002. "Airport Screener Curb Is Regretful." *Los Angeles Times,* November 16, pp. B1, B14.

Wells-Barnett, Ida B. 1970. *Crusade for Justice: The Autobiography of Ida B. Wells,* ed. Alfreda M. Duster. Chicago: University of Chicago Press.

West, Candace, and Don H. Zimmerman. 1983. "Small Insults: A Study of Interruptions in Cross Sex Conversations Between Unacquainted Persons." Pp. 86–111 in *Language, Gender, and Society,* ed. Barrie Thorne, Chris Kramarae, and Nancy Henley. Rowley, MA: Newbury House.

———. 1987. "Doing Gender." *Gender and Society* 1 (June): 125–151.

Western Interstate Commission for Higher Education. 2003. *Knocking at the College Door—2003.* Boulder, CO: WICHE.

———. 2008. "Knocking at the College Door 2008." Accessed July 24 (http://wiche.edu/agendabook/May_08/presentations/MizePrescott.pdf).

Whyte, William Foote. 1981. *Street Corner Society: Social Structure of an Italian Slum,* 3d ed. Chicago: University of Chicago Press.

Wickman, Peter M. 1991. "Deviance." Pp. 85–87 in *Encyclopedic Dictionary of Sociology,* 4th ed., ed. Dushkin Publishing Group. Guilford, CT: Dushkin.

Wiggins, Steve, and Stephanie Levy. 2008. "Rising Food Prices: A Global Crisis." Briefing Paper, April. London: Overseas Development Institute. Accessed August 12 (http://www.odi.org.uk/publications/briefing/bp37-april08-rising-food-prices.pdf).

Wilford, John Noble. 1997. "New Clues Show Where People Made the Great Leap to Agriculture." *New York Times,* November 18, pp. B9, B12.

Williams, Carol J. 1995. "Taking an Eager Step Back." *Los Angeles Times,* June 3, pp. A1, A14.

Williams, Christine L. 1992. "The Glass Escalator: Hidden Advantages for Men in the 'Female' Professions." *Social Problems* 39 (3): 253–267.

———. 1995. *Still a Man's World: Men Who Do Women's Work.* Berkeley: University of California Press.

Williams, David R., and Chiquita Collins. 2004. "Reparations." *American Behavioral Scientist* 47 (March): 977–1000.

Williams, Mike. 2008. "Rising Cost of Food Devastates Haiti." *Atlanta Journal Constitution,* June 17. Accessed August 12 (http://www.ajc.com/news/content/news/stories/2008/06/16/haiti_food_crisis.html).

Williams, Robin M., Jr. 1970. *American Society,* 3d ed. New York: Knopf.

Williams, Wendy M. 1998. "Do Parents Matter? Scholars Need to Explain What Research Really Shows." *Chronicle of Higher Education* 45 (December 11): B6–B7.

Wills, Jeremiah B., and Barbara J. Risman. 2006. "The Visibility of Feminist Thought in Family Studies." *Journal of Marriage and Family* 68 (August): 690–700.

Wilson, John. 1973. *Introduction to Social Movements.* New York: Basic Books.

Wilson, Robin. 2007. "The New Gender Divide." *Chronicle of Higher Education* 53 (January 26): A36–A39.

Wilson, William Julius. 1980. *The Declining Significance of Race: Blacks and Changing American Institutions,* 2d ed. Chicago: University of Chicago Press.

———. 1987. *The Truly Disadvantaged: The Inner City, the Underclass and Public Policy.* Chicago: University of Chicago Press.

———, ed. 1989. *The Ghetto Underclass: Social Science Perspectives.* Newbury Park, CA: Sage.

——. 1996. *When Work Disappears: The World of the New Urban Poor.* New York: Knopf.

——. 1999. *The Bridge over the Racial Divide: Rising Inequality and Coalition Politics.* Berkeley: University of California Press.

Wilson, William Julius, J. M. Quane, and B. H. Rankin. 2004. "Underclass." *International Encyclopedia of Social and Behavioral Sciences.* New York: Elsevier.

Winseman, Albert L. 2005. "Religion in America: Who Has None?" (December 6). Accessed March 4, 2007 (www.gallup.com).

Winter, J. Allen. 2008. "Symbolic Ethnicity." Pp. 1288–1290 in *Encyclopedia of Race, Ethnicity, and Society,* vol. 3, ed. Richard T. Schaefer. Thousand Oaks, CA: Sage.

Wirth, Louis. 1928. *The Ghetto.* Chicago: University of Chicago Press.

——. 1931. "Clinical Sociology." *American Journal of Sociology* 37 (July): 49–60.

——. 1938. "Urbanism as a Way of Life." *American Journal of Sociology* 44 (July): 1–24.

Withrow, Brian L. 2006. *Racial Profiling: From Rhetoric to Reason.* Upper Saddle River, NJ: Prentice Hall.

Witte, Griff. 2005. "The Vanishing Middle Class." *Washington Post National Weekly Edition,* September 27, pp. 6–9.

Wolf, Naomi. 1992. *The Beauty Myth: How Images of Beauty Are Used Against Women.* New York: Anchor.

Wolf, Richard. 2006. "How Welfare Reform Changed America." *USA Today,* July 18, pp. 1A, 6A.

Word, David L., Charles D. Coleman, Robert Nunziator, and Robert Kominski. 2007. "Demographic Aspects of Surnames from Census 2000." Accessed January 2, 2008 (www.census.gov/genealogy/www/surnames.pdf).

World Bank. 2000. *World Development Report 2000/2001.* Washington, DC: World Bank.

——. 2001. *World Development Report 2002. Building Instructions for Markets.* New York: Oxford University Press.

——. 2003a. *World Development Report 2003: Sustainable Development in a Dynamic World.* Washington, DC: World Bank.

——. 2003b. *Development Indicators 2003.* Washington, DC: World Bank.

——. 2004. *World Development Report 2005. A Better Investment Climate for Everyone.* Washington, DC: World Bank.

——. 2005. *World Development Indicators 2005.* Washington, DC: World Bank.

——. 2006. *Repositioning Nutrition as Central to Development: A Strategy for Large-Scale Action.* Washington, DC: World Bank.

——. 2006a. *World Development Indicators 2006.* New York: World Bank.

——. 2006b. *Global Economic Prospects 2006.* Washington, DC: World Bank.

——. 2006c. "Microfinance Comes of Age." December 7. Accessed April 24, 2007 (www.Worldbank.org).

——. 2007a. *World Development Indicators 2007.* New York: World Bank.

——. 2008. "Total GNI 2006 (Atlas Method)." Quick Reference Tables. Accessed June 16 (http://siteresources.worldbank.org/DATASTATISTICS/Resources/GNI.pdf).

World Development Forum. 1990. "The Danger of Television." (July 15): 4.

World Resources Institute. 1998. *1998–1999 World Resources: A Guide to the Global Environment.* New York: Oxford University Press.

Wright, Erik Olin, David Hachen, Cynthia Costello, and Joy Sprague. 1982. "The American Class Structure." *American Sociological Review* 47 (December): 709–726.

## Y

Yinger, J. Milton. 1970. *The Scientific Study of Religion.* New York: Macmillan.

Young, Gay. 1993. "Gender Inequality and Industrial Development: The Household Connection." *Journal of Comparative Family Studies* 124 (Spring): 3–20.

## Z

Zarembo, Alan. 2003. "Funding Studies to Suit Need." December 7, pp. A1, A20.

——. 2004. "A Theater of Inquiry and Evil." *Los Angeles Times,* July 15, pp. A1, A24, A25.

Zellner, William M. 1995. *Counter Cultures: A Sociological Analysis.* New York: St. Martin's Press.

Zellner, William M., and Richard T. Schaefer. 2006. *Extraordinary Groups,* 8th ed. New York: Worth.

Zimbardo, Philip G. 1972. "Pathology of Imprisonment." *Society* 9 (April): 4, 6, 8.

——. 2004. "Power Turns Good Soldiers into 'Bad Apples.'" *Boston Globe,* May 9 (www.prisonexp.org).

——. 2007. *The Lucifer Effect: Understanding How Good People Turn Evil.* New York: Random House.

Zola, Irving K. 1972. "Medicine as an Institution of Social Control." *Sociological Review* 20 (November): 487–504.

——. 1983. *Socio-Medical Inquiries.* Philadelphia: Temple University Press.

Zweigenhaft, Richard L., and G. William Domhoff. 2006. *Diversity in the Power Elite: How It Happened, Why It Matters,* 2d ed. New York: Rowman and Littlefield.

## Photos

**Front Matter p. iBL:** © PhotoDisc/PunchStock; **p. iBR:** Courtesy of Apple; **p. iiiT:** © Paul Miles/Axiom Photographic Agency/Getty Images; **p. iiiTM:** © Judith Wagner/zefa/Corbis; **p. iiiBM:** © Asia Images Group/Getty Images; **p. iiiB:** © iStockphoto.com/Lise Gagnep. **vT:** © iStockphoto.com/Jacob Wackerhause; **p. vB:** © iStockphoto.com/Pamela Moore; **p. viT:** © Elizabeth Dalziel/AP Wide World Photos; **p. viB:** © iStockphoto.com/David H. Lewis. **p. viiT:** © Peter Menzel/From the book "Hungry Planet, What the World Eats" by Peter Menzel and Faith D'Aluisio/www.menzelphoto. com; **p. viiB:** © iStockphoto.com/Ekaterina Monakhov; **p. viii:** © iStockphoto.com/Carrie Bottomley; **p. ixT:** © iStockphoto.com/Grigory Bibikov; **p. ixB:** © iStockphoto.com/Rich Legg; **p. x;** © Pavel Filatov/Alamy; **p. xiL:** © iStockphoto.com/Victor Maffe; **p. xiR:** © image100/Corbis; **p. xiiT:** © iStockphoto.com/Yanik Chauvin; **p. xiiB:** © Frans Lanting/Corbis; **p. xiii:** © iStockphoto.com/Jan Bryson; **p. xiv:** © iStockphoto.com/Faut Kose; **p. xv:** © iStockphoto.com/Jani Bryson. **Chapter 1 p. 0:** © Guenter Vahlkampf/Getty Images; **p. 3B:** © PhotoDisc/Getty Images; **p. 5:** © Orlando Sierra/AFP/Getty Images; **p. 6:** © Mario Tama/Getty Images; **p. 7:** Ryan McVay/Getty Images, Background: © iStockphoto.com/morganl; **p. 8:** © Mark Downey/Masterfile; **p. 10T:** © Robert Walker/Hulton Archive/Getty Images; **p. 10B:** © Rebecca Cook/Reuters/Corbis; **p. 11:** © Leon Neal/AFP/Getty Images; **p. 12T:** © Bettmann/Corbis, Frame: © iStockphoto.com/Pomortzeff; **p. 12BL:** Library of Congress Prints and Photographs Division. LC-USZ62-16530, Frame: © iStockphoto.com/Peter Zele; **p. 12BR:** © Hulton Archive/Getty Images, Frame: © iStockphoto.com/Lou Oates; **p. 13T:** © Ryan McVay/Riser/Getty Images; **p. 13B:** © Popperfoto/Getty Images; **p. 14:** © Masterfile (Royalty-Free Division); **p. 15:** © Hulton Archive/Getty Images, Frame: © iStockphoto.com/Andrea Gingerich; **p. 16T:** © iStockphoto.com/vofpalabra; **p. 16B:** © iStockphoto.com/Ashwin Kharidehal Abhirama, **p. 17T:** Medioimages/PictureQuest, Background effect: © iStockphoto.com/Hans Doddema; **p. 17B:** © Comstock Images/Alamy; **p. 18:** © PhotoDisc/SuperStock. **Chapter 2 p. 20:** © Fox Searchlight Photographer: Ken Regan. Courtesy Photofest. **p. 23:** PhotoDisc/Getty Images; **p. 24:** © Peter Dazeley/The Image Bank/Getty Images; **p. 25:** ©iStockphoto.com/Stefano Maccari; **p. 26T:** © Veer; **p. 26B:** Janis Christie/Getty Images; **p. 27:** © iStockphoto.com/Jerry Koch; **p. 28:** © Hill Street Studios/Blend Images/Getty Images; **p. 29:** © Bettmann/Corbis; **p. 30:** © iStockphoto.com/Georgina Palmer; **p. 31:** © Sally and Richard Greenhill/Alamy; **p. 33T:** © The McGraw-Hill Companies, Inc./Jill Braaten, photographer; **p. 33B:** © Masterfile (Royalty-Free Division); **p. 34:** © Penny Gentieu/JupiterImages; **p. 35T:** © Scott Barbour/Getty Images; **p. 35M:** © iStockphoto.com/Grafissimo; **p. 35B:** © Ingram Publishing/Alamy; **p. 36T:** © Weinstein Company/courtesy Everett Collection; **p. 36ML:** Fox/Photofest; **p. 36MR,** © Frank Trapper/Corbis; **p. 36B:** Doug Menuez/Getty Images; **p. 37:** © Siqui Sanchez/The Image Bank/Getty Images; **p. 39:** © Digital Vision Ltd./SuperStock. **Chapter 3 p. 54:** © Ami Vitale/Getty Images; **p. 56:** © The Granger Collection, New York; **p. 57:** © AP/Wide World Photos; **pp. 58, 59:** © Peter Menzel/From the book "Hungry Planet, What the World Eats" by Peter Menzel and Faith D'Aluisio/www.menzelphoto.com; **p. 60:** © AP/Wide World Photos; **p. 61:** Courtesy Apple; **p. 62T:** © Paramount/Courtesy Everett Collection; **p. 62B:** © Royalty-Free/Corbis; **p. 63:** © Pete Ryan/National Geographic/Getty Images; **p. 64T:** © AP/Wide World Photos; **p. 64B:** © JupiterImages/BananaStock/Alamy; **p. 65L:** © dbimages/Alamy; **p. 65R:** © ballyscanion/PhotoDisc/Getty Images; **p. 66:** © iStockphoto.com/Mustafa Deliormanli; **p. 67L:** © Paul Hartnett/PYMCA/JupiterImages; **p. 67R:** Dress: © iStockphoto.com/Igor Terekhov, Jeans: © iStockphoto.com/Andrey Armyagov; **p. 68:** © Karim Sahib/AFP/Getty Images; **p. 69:** © Rob Crandall/The Image Works; **p. 70:** © Underwood & Underwood/Corbis; **p. 71:** RubberBall Productions; **p. 72T:** © Marvy!/Corbis; **p. 72B:** © Frans Lemmens/Iconica/Getty Images; **p. 73:** © moodboard/Corbis. **Chapter 4 p. 64:** © Daniel Bosler/Photographer's Choice/Getty Images; **p. 66:** Creatas Images; **p. 67T:** © Inti St. Clair/Digital Vision/Getty Images; **p. 67B:** © Mary Evans Picture Library/The Image Works, Album: © iStockphoto.com/Mike Bentley; **p. 68T:** © Nina Leen/Time & Life Pictures/Getty Images; **p. 68B:** Barbara Penoyar/Getty Images; **p. 69:** © Digital

Vision/Alamy; **p. 70:** © Ken Wramton/Riser/Getty Images; **p. 71:** © AP/Wide World Photos; **p. 72T:** Everett Collection; **p. 72B:** © Stockbyte/Getty Images; **p. 73:** Ryan McVay/Getty Images; **p. 74:** © Mark Wilson/Getty Images; **p. 75:** © Bill Pugliano/Getty Images; **p. 76T:** © blue jean images/Getty Images; **p. 76B:** © The McGraw-Hill Companies, Inc./Jill Braaten, photographer; **p. 78T:** © iStockphoto.com/Andrea Gingerich; **p. 78B:** © iStockphoto.com/Dan Wilton; **p. 79:** © Chris Jackson/Getty Images; **p. 80T:** © iStockphoto.com/Tatiana Popova; **p. 80B:** Laptop. © iStockphoto.com/Andres Peiro Palme, Woman: © iStockphoto.com/Anna Bryukhanova; **p. 81T:** © IT Stock Free; **p. 81B:** Jack Star/PhotoLink/Getty Images; **p. 82T:** © Mike Mergen/Bloomberg News/Landov; **p. 82B:** © Thomas S. England/Photo Researchers, Inc.; **p. 83:** iStockphoto.com/Alex Mathers; **p. 84:** © Justin Sullivan/Getty Images; **p. 86L:** © Masterfile (Royalty-Free Division); **p. 86R:** PhotoDisc/Getty Images. **Chapter 5 p. 90:** © China Photo/Getty Images; **p. 92:** © AP/Wide World Photos; **p. 93:** PhotoDisc/Getty Images; **p. 94L:** © Jim West/The Image Works; **p. 94R:** Brand X Pictures; **p. 95:** © ImageDJ/Alamy; **p. 96:** © China Photos/Getty Images; **p. 97:** © Tom G. Lynn/Time & Life Pictures/Getty Images; **p. 98:** © Mario Tama/Getty Images; **p. 99:** © The McGraw-Hill Companies, Inc./John Flournoy, photographer; **p. 100:** © Stockbyte/Getty Images; **p. 101:** © Reza Estakhrian/Reportage/Getty Images; **p. 102T:** Ryan McVay/Getty Images; **p. 102B:** iStockphoto.com/Dean Turner; **p. 103:** © Daniel Barry/Getty Images; **p. 104:** © James Nielsen/Getty Images; **p. 105T:** © Gary S. Chapman/Getty Images; **p. 105B:** © iStockphoto.com/Mark Evans; **p. 106T:** © David S. Holloway/Getty Images; **p. 106M:** Polaroids on clothes line: © iStockphoto.com/David Franklin; **p. 106BL:** © Custom Medical Stock Photo/Alamy; **p. 106BM:** Adam Crowley/Getty Images; **p. 106BR:** © Muntz/Taxi/Getty Images; **p. 107:** © Kazuhiro Tanda/Taxi Japan/Getty Images; **p. 108:** Manchan/Getty Images; **p. 111:** PhotoDisc/Getty Images; **p. 112:** © Frederick M. Brown/Getty Images; **p. 114:** © Digital Vision Ltd./SuperStock. **Chapter 6 p. 114:** © Comstock/JupiterImages; **p. 116:** Comedy Central/Courtesy: Everett Collection; **p. 117T:** © Dave Robertson/Masterfile; **p. 117B:** © AP/Wide World Photos; **p. 118:** From the film OBEDIANCE ©1968 by Stanley Milgram, © renewed 1993 by Alexandra Milgram, distributed by Penn State Media Sales.; **p. 119:** Bottle cap. © iStockphoto.com/Luis Carlos, bottle: © iStockphoto.com/Dmitry Bomshtein; **p. 121:** Burke/Triolo/Brand X Pictures/JupiterImages; **p. 122T:** © Leonard McLane/Digital Vision/Getty Images; **p. 122B:** © Jose Luis Roca/AFP/Getty Images; **p. 123T:** © AP/Wide World Photos; **p. 123M:** Comstock Images/Alamy; **p. 123B:** © Masterfile (Royalty-Free Division); **p. 124:** © iStockphoto.com/Floortje; **p. 125T:** © iStockphoto.com/Tamás Dernovics; **pp. 125B, 127:** Brand X Pictures; **p. 128:** © Trista Weibell/iStockphoto.com; **p. 130:** © Image Source/Getty Images; **p. 131:** Getty Images/Digital Vision; **p. 132:** © Yasuhide Fumoto/PhotoDisc/Getty Images; **p. 133:** © SCPhotos/Alamy; **p. 135:** Amos Morgan/Getty Images. **Chapter 7 p. 138:** Dex Image/Getty Images; **p. 140T:** © David Noble Photography/Alamy; **p. 140B:** © iStockphoto.com/Jeremy Edwards; **p. 141:** © CBS/Courtesy Everett Collection; **p. 142:** © Royalty-Free/Corbis; **p. 144:** Brand X Pictures/JupiterImages; **p. 146:** © Comstock/PunchStock; **p. 147L:** © Erica Simone Leeds; **p. 147R:** Don Tremain/Getty Images; **p. 150:** TM & © Fox Searchlight. All rights reserved/Courtesy Everett Collection; **p. 151T:** © James Devaney/WireImage/Getty Images; **p. 151B:** ©Brand X Pictures/JupiterImages; **p. 152:** © Universal/Courtesy Everett Collection; **p. 154T:** Wedding picture: © iStockphoto.com/bitter, Frame: ©iStockphoto.com/sxasher; **p. 154BL:** © Mirek Towski/FilmMagic/Getty Images; **p. 155:** © iStockphoto.com/Jennifer Trenchard; **p. 156:** © Royalty-Free/Corbis; **p. 157BR:** © Erin Patrice O'Brien/Digital Vision/Getty Images; **p. 158T:** © Angela Wyant/Stone/Getty Images; **p. 158B:** CMCD/Getty Images; **p. 159:** © Justin Sullivan/Getty Images. **Chapter 8 p. 162:** © Mark Downey/Getty Images; **p. 164:** ©iStockphoto.com/Borut Trdina; **p. 165T:** © iStockphoto.com/Forest Woodward; **p. 165B:** © Comstock/PunchStock; **p. 166:** © Oliver Hoffmann/iStockphoto; **p. 167:** © Getty Images; **p. 168:** PhotoDisc/Getty Images; **p. 169:** © PhotoAlto/PunchStock; **p. 170:** PhotoDisc/Getty Images; **p. 172:** © iStockphoto.com/Robert Hunt; **p. 173:** © CinemaPhoto/Corbis; **p. 174:** ©iStockphoto.com/Michael Ciranni; **p. 175:** © Javier Pierini/Getty Images; **p. 176T:** PhotoDisc/Getty Images; **p. 176B:** © GOODSHOOT/Alamy; **p. 178:** DAJ/Getty Images; **p. 179:** © Jeff Greenberg/The Image Works; **p. 181T:** © Robert Davis; **p. 181B:** © Brand X Pictures/PunchStock; **p. 182:** © Stockdisc/PunchStock; **p. 183:** © Pavel Filatov/Alamy;

p. 187T: M. Freeman/PhotoLink/Getty Images; p. 187B: © Syracuse Newspapers/The Image Works; p. 188: © Brand X/SuperStock. Chapter 9 p. 190: © Justin Sullivan/Getty Images; p. 192T: © Jeff J. Mitchell/Getty Images; p. 192B: © Steve Granitz/WireImage/Getty Images; p. 193: © Elliott & Fry/Hulton Archive/Getty Images; p. 194: © Comstock Images/Alamy; p. 195T: © The McGraw-Hill Companies, Inc./John Flournoy, photographer; p. 195B: © Rob Wilkinson/Alamy; p. 196T: © Jorge Rey/Getty Images; p. 196B: © iStockphoto.com/Amanda Rohde; p. 198: © iStockphoto.com/René Mansi; p. 199: © Brendan McDermid/Reuters /Landov; p. 201L: PhotoLink/Getty Images; p. 201R: © Peter Macdiarmid/Getty Images; p. 202L: © AFP/Getty Images; p. 202R: National Archives and Records Administration; p. 203T: © iStockphoto.com/Ugur Evirgen; p. 203B: © Frank Micelotta/Getty Images; p. 204T: Brand X Pictures/PunchStock; p. 204B: Ryan McVay/Getty Images; p. 205: Library of Congress, Prints and Photographs Division [LC-USZ62-53202]; p. 208: © Last Resort/PhotoDisc/Getty Images; p. 209: ©iStockphoto.com/Valerie Loiseleux; p. 210T: Courtesy Everett Collection; p. 210B: © Wathiq Khuzale/Getty Images; p. 212: Amos Morgan/Getty Images. Chapter 10 p. 214: © Mario Tama/Getty Images; p. 216: © Bettmann/Corbis; p. 217T: © Per-Anders Pettersson/Getty Images; p. 217B: © Dr. Parvinder Sethi; p. 218T: © Arnaldo Magnani/Getty Images; p. 218B: © Jacobs Stock Photography/Photographer's Choice/Getty Images; p. 219: © Gabriel Bouys/AFP/Getty Images; p. 221: ©iStockphoto.com/James Reilly Wilson; p. 222: © Peter Turnley/Corbis; p. 223: Photo: ABC/Alex Mehl, © ABC/Courtesy Everett Collection; p. 225: © Brand X Pictures/PunchStock; p. 226: © iStockphoto.com/Michael Krinke; p. 227T: © Bananastock/Alamy; p. 227B: ©iStockphoto.com/Ivan Bajic; p. 228: © Tana Lee Alves/WireImage/Getty Images; p. 229: © Brand X Pictures/PunchStock; p. 230T: © iStockphoto.com/Jason R Warren; p. 230B: © Robyn Beck/AFP/Getty Images; p. 231: © Royalty-Free/Corbis; p. 232: African-American woman (TR): © iStockphoto.com/James Pauls, Asian woman with head in hand (TL): © iStockphoto.com/Eduardo Jose Bernardino, White girl sitting on stairs (BL): © iStockphoto.com/Stockphoto4u, Man with beard standing in street (BM): © iStockphoto.com/Ivar Teunissen, Children eating lunch (BR): David Buffington/Getty Images; p. 234T: TRBfoto/Getty Images; p. 234B: © Gary S. Chapman/Photographer's Choice/Getty Images; p. 235: Mark Scott/Getty Images; p. 236T: © iStockphoto.com/Alex Potemkin; p. 236B: © Michele Westmorland/PhotoDisc/Getty Images; p. 237L: © Brand X Pictures/PunchStock; p. 237R: © SuperStock. Chapter 11 p. 240: © Graeme Robertson/Getty Images; p. 242: © Getty Images; p. 243L: © Photofusion Picture Library/Alamy; p. 243R: © Henning Kaiser/DDP/Getty Images; p. 244T: © iStockphoto.com/Rafael Laguillo; p. 244B: © Chien-min Chung/Getty Images; p. 245T: Library of Congress; p. 245B: © Teh Eng Koon/AFP/Getty Images; p. 246: © Warner Brothers/Courtesy Everett Collection; p. 247: © iStockphoto.com/Alex Mathers; p. 249: © AP/Wide World Photos; p. 250: © Siqui Sanchez/The Image Bank/Getty Images; p. 251: © AP/Wide World Photos; p. 253: © iStockphoto.com/Leon Bonaventura; p. 254T: © iStockphoto.com/Frank van den Bergh; p. 254B: © iStockphoto.com/Randolf Jay Braun; p. 255T: © Photos.com Select/Index Stock; p. 255B: Pixtal/age footstock; p. 258: © Marco Di Lauro/Getty Images; p. 259: © Paula Bronstein/Getty Images; p. 262: Amos Morgan/PhotoDisc/Getty Images. Chapter 12 p. 264, Brand X Pictures/Getty Images; p. 266: © 1998 Image Ideas, Inc.; p. 267T: © Rosanne Olson/The Image Bank/Getty Images; p. 267B: © Peter Cade/Iconica/Getty Images; p. 268: © iStockphoto.com/Art Montes De Oca/Taxi/Getty Images; p. 269T: © Art Montes De Oca/Taxi/Getty Images; p. 269B: ©iStockphoto.com/Christine Balderas; p. 272: © iStockphoto.com/Jason Lugo; p. 273T: © Royalty-Free/Corbis; p. 273B: C Squared Studios/Getty Images; p. 274: © iStockphoto.com/Anton Seleznev; p. 275T: © Tetra Images/Getty Images; p. 275B: © Elisabetta Villa/Getty Images; pp. 276TL, 276TR: Bucket: © iStockphoto.com/Jack Jelly, Briefcase: © iStockphoto.com/Anna Bryukhanova; p. 276B: © Thomas Northcut/Digital Vision/Getty Images; p. 277: © Brand X Pictures/PunchStock; p. 278T: © AP/Wide World Photos; p. 278B: © Scott J. Ferrell/Getty Images; p. 279T: © Paula Bronstein/Getty Images; p. 279M: © Frank Siteman/Doctor Stock/Science Faction/Getty Images; p. 279B: ©iStockphoto.com/Justin Sneddon; p. 280: © Luedke and Sparrow/Digital Vision/Getty Images; p. 281: © Harold Eisenberger/LOOK/Getty Images; p. 282: © Royalty-Free/Corbis; p. 283: Ryan McVay/Getty Images; p. 284: © iStockphoto.com/Lise Gagne; p. 285: ©iStockphoto.com/Lisa F. Young; p. 286T: © SuperStock; p. 286B:

© Stockbyte/Getty Images. Chapter 13 p. 288: © Shaun Botterill/Getty Images; p. 290L: © AP/Wide World Photos; p. 290R: © Andersen Ross/Blend Images/Getty Images; p. 291: © Jeff Greenberg/Alamy; p. 292: © Andrew Redington/Getty Images; p. 293: Ryan McVay/Getty Images; p. 294T: © Stephen Chernin/Getty Images; p. 294B: © AP/Wide World Photos; p. 295T: © Bruce Roberts/Photo Researchers, Inc.; p. 295B: ©iStockphoto.com/Duncan Walker; p. 296T: © William Campbell/Sygma/Corbis; p. 296B: © Bettmann/Corbis; p. 297T: ©iStockphoto.com/Skip ODonnell; p. 297B: © Kathleen Finlay/Masterfile; p. 298, Don Farrall/Getty Images; p. 299: © Francis Miller/Time Life Pictures/Getty Images; p. 300: © Jim West/The Image Works; p. 301: © AP/Wide World Photos; p. 302: © The CW Network/Courtesy Everett Collection; p. 303: © Daniel Berehulak/Getty Images; p. 304T: © Digital Vision/Getty Images; p. 304B: © David McNew/Getty Images; pp. 306TL, 306TM: © Copyright 1997 IMS Communications Ltd/Capstone Design. All Rights Reserved.; p. 306TR: © liquidlibrary/PictureQuest; p. 305: American Indians: Library of Congress, Crowd shot: Ryan McVay/Getty Images; p. 306B: © iStockphoto.com/Jaroslaw Wojcik; p. 307: Brand X Pictures/PunchStock; p. 312: PhotoDisc/Getty Images; p. 315: © iStockphoto.com/Steve Dibblee; p. 316: © Comstock/PictureQuest. Chapter 14 p. 318: © Brand X Pictures/PunchStock; p. 320: Photo by Rex Features/Courtesy Everett Collection; p. 321: Ryan McVay/Getty Images; p. 323: Blend Images/Getty Images; p. 324: © The McGraw-Hill Companies, Inc./Christopher Kerrigan, photographer; p. 326T: © Spencer Grant/PhotoEdit; p. 326B: RubberBall Productions; p. 329T: © PhotoAlto/PunchStock; p. 329B: ©iStockphoto.com/Don Bayley; p. 330: Comstock Images/Alamy; p. 331T: Jules Frazier/Getty Images; p. 331B: © NBC/Courtesy Everett Collection; p. 332: © iStockphoto.com/Grigory Bibikov; p. 333T: ©iStockphoto.com/Duncan Walker; p. 333B: Anthony Saint James/Getty Images; p. 334T: © Paul Miles/Axiom Photographic Agency/Getty Images; p. 334B: © Royalty-Free/Corbis; p. 335T: © Digital Vision Ltd.; p. 335B: © Digital Vision/PunchStock; p. 338T: Steve Cole/Getty Images; p. 338B: © China Photos/Getty Images; p. 339: © Bruce Dale/National Geographic/Getty Images; p. 340B: Ryan McVay/Getty Images; p. 341TL: © Brand X Pictures/JupiterImages; p. 341TR: Wind farm: © iStockphoto.com/Mark Trost, Smokestacks: Stockbyte/PunchStock; p. 341B: © Royalty-Free/Corbis; p. 342: © Stockbyte/PunchStock. Chapter 15 p. 344: © Mandel Ngan/AFP/Getty Images; p. 346: © Digital Vision/Getty Images; p. 347: ©iStockphoto.com/Lara Seregni; p. 350: © AP/Wide World Photos; p. 351T: Ryan McVay/Getty Images; p. 351B: © The McGraw-Hill Companies/Lars Niki, photographer; p. 353: © Bettmann/Corbis; p. 354B: © PhotoDisc/PunchStock; p. 355T: Calf: © iStockphoto.com/Eric Isselée, goat: ©iStockphoto.com/Eric Isselée, pig: Ryan McVay/Getty Images, cat: ©iStockphoto.com/Blackbeck, rat: © iStockphoto.com/Butinova Elena; p. 355B: © Getty Images; p. 356: © iStockphoto.com/Clint Hild; p. 357: Library of Congress; p. 359T: © JP Laffont/Sygma/Corbis; p. 359B: © Bettmann/Corbis; p. 360T: © Mario Tama/Getty Images; p. 360B: Digital Vision/PunchStock; p. 361: © Alex Wong/Getty Images; p. 363: © Kerry-Edwards 2004, Inc./Sharon Farmer, photographer; p. 364L: The Palma Collection/Getty Images; p. 364R: PhotoDisc Collection.

## Figures/Text

Chapter 1 p. 16B: Figure adapted from ASA Research & Development Department 2006, What Can I Do with a Bachelor's Degree in Sociology," A National Survey of Seniors Majoring in Sociology: First Glances: What Do They Know and Where are They Going? American Sociological Association, January 2006, Table 5, p. 29. Chapter 2 p. 27: Figure—analysis of General Social Survey 2004 in James A. Davis et al. 2005. Used by permission of National Opinion Research Center; p. 29B: Figure copyright © 2001–2008 by Stuart Eugene Thiel. All rights reserved. p. 33: Figure adapted from Devah Pager, "The Mark of a Criminal Record," American Journal of Sociology. Copyright © 2003 by the University of Chicago Press, used by permission; p. 34T: Figure from Laura Wattenberg. 2006. The Baby Name Wizard; p. 35: Figure from Henry J. Kaiser Family Foundation. November 2005. Executive Summary of Sex on TV 4:4; a Biennial Report of the Kaiser Family Foundation (#7399). This information was reprinted with permission from the Henry J. Kaiser Family Foundation. The Kaiser Family Foundation, based in Menlo Park, CA, is a nonprofit, private operating foundation focusing on the

Credits